lonely planet

Prague & the Czech Republic

"All you've got to do is decide to go and the hardest part is over.

So go!"

TONY WHEELER, COFOUNDER – LONELY PLANET

THIS EDITION WRITTEN AND RESEARCHED BY

Neil Wilson

Mark Baker

Contents

Plan Your Trip 4

Explore Prague 56

Understand Prague 267

Survival Guide 295

Prague Maps 325

WITOLD SKRYPCZAK / GETTY IMAGES ©

CHRISTOPHER GROENHOUT / GETTY IMAGES ©

(left) **St Vitus Cathedral (p69)**

(above) **Astronomical Clock (p98)**

(right) **Beer – part of Prague's culture (p36)**

CHRISTOPHER GROENHOUT / GETTY IMAGES ©

Holešovice, Bubeneč & Dejvice p149

Prague Castle & Hradčany p60

Malá Strana p77

Staré Město p91

Žižkov & Karlín p142

Nové Město p116

Vinohrady & Vršovice p132

Smíchov & Vyšehrad p164

Welcome to Prague

Prague is the equal of Paris in terms of beauty. The history goes back a millennium. And the beer? The best in Europe.

European Hotspot

The 1989 Velvet Revolution that freed the Czechs from communism bequeathed to Europe a gem of a city to stand beside stalwarts like Rome, Amsterdam and London. Not surprisingly, visitors from around the world have come in droves, and on a hot summer's day it can feel like you're sharing Charles Bridge with half of humanity. But even the crowds can't take away from the spectacle of a 14th-century stone bridge, a hilltop castle and a lovely, lazy river – the Vltava – that inspired one of the most hauntingly beautiful pieces of 19th-century classical music, Smetana's 'Moldau'.

Art All Around

Prague's art galleries may not have the allure of the Louvre, but Bohemian art offers much to admire, from the glowing Gothic altarpieces in the Convent of St Agnes, to the luscious art nouveau works of Alfons Mucha and the magnificent collection of 20th-century surrealists, cubists and constructivists in the Veletržní Palác. The weird and witty sculpture of David Černý punctuates Prague's public spaces, and the city itself offers a smorgasbord of stunning architecture, from the soaring verticals of Gothic and the exuberance of baroque to the sensual elegance of art nouveau and the chiselled cheekbones of cubist facades.

Where Beer is God

The best beer in the world just got better. Since the invention of Pilsner Urquell in 1842, the Czechs have been famous for producing some of the world's finest brews. But the internationally famous brand names – Urquell, Staropramen and Budvar – have been equalled, and even surpassed, by a bunch of regional Czech beers and microbreweries that are catering to a renewed interest in traditional brewing. Never before have Prague's pubs offered such a wide range of ales – names you'll now have to get your head around include Kout na Šumavě, Svijanský Rytíř and Velkopopovický Kozel (try ordering that after a few pints).

Urban Explorations

Prague's maze of cobbled lanes and hidden courtyards is paradise for the aimless wanderer, always beckoning you to explore a little further. Just a few blocks from the Old Town Square you can stumble across ancient chapels, unexpected gardens, cute cafes and old-fashioned bars with hardly a tourist in sight. One of the joys of the city is its potential for exploration – neighbourhoods like Vinohrady and Bubeneč can reward the urban adventurer with countless memorable cameos, from the setting sun glinting off church domes, to the strains of Dvořák being played on an out-of-tune piano.

Why I Love Prague

By Neil Wilson, Author

How can you not love a city that has a pub with vinyl cushions on the wall above the gents urinal, so you can rest your head while you 'go'? Where you can order a beer without speaking, simply by placing a beer mat on the table? And where that beer is probably the best in the world? But it's not just exquisite ale and a wonderfully relaxed drinking culture that keep bringing me back to Prague. There's wit and weirdness in equal measures – a public fountain where two figures pee in a puddle, spelling out literary quotations; an 'industrial music' club in a 1950s nuclear bunker; and a cubist lamp post. Quirky doesn't even begin to describe it.

For more about our authors, see p352.

Church of Our Lady Before Týn (p101)

Prague's Top 10

Charles Bridge *(p79)*

1 Whether you visit alone in the morning mist or shoulder your way through the afternoon crowds, crossing Charles Bridge is the quintessential Prague experience. Built in 1357, it withstood wheeled traffic for 500-odd years – thanks, legend claims, to eggs mixed into the mortar – until it was made pedestrian-only after WWII. By day, the baroque statues stare with indifference at a fascinating parade of buskers, jazz bands and postcard sellers; at dawn, they regain some of the mystery and magic their creators sought to capture.

Malá Strana

Prague Castle *(p62)*

2 A thousand years of history is cradled within the walls of Prague's hilltop castle, a complex of churches, towers, halls and palaces that is almost a village in its own right. This is the cultural and historical heart of the Czech Republic, comprising not only collections of physical treasures, such as the golden reliquaries of St Vitus Treasury and the Bohemian crown jewels, but also the sites of great historic events such as the murder of St Wenceslas and the Second Defenestration of Prague.

Prague Castle & Hradčany

1

2

3
5
BOHU KU CHVÁLE
VLASTI K SLÁVĚ
UMĚNÍ KE CTI-VĚNUJE

Prague, Queen of Music *(p40)*

3 The city that nurtured Smetana, Dvořák and Janáček, and saw performances in his prime by Wolfgang Amadeus Mozart, has a place in musical history alongside that of Vienna. Two major festivals of classical music – Prague Spring and Strings of Autumn – grace the calendar, but the city is famous for more than just the classics. Prague has been a hotbed of European jazz since the late 1940s, and now there's a thriving live music scene that spans genres from hard rock to electronica. THE CZECH PHILHARMONIC ORCHESTRA PERFORMING AT THE RUDOLFINUM (P102)

☆ ***Entertainment***

Old Town Square *(p100)*

4 Despite the swarms of tourists, crowded pavement cafes and over-the-top commercialism, it's impossible not to enjoy the spectacle of Prague's premier public space: tour leaders, with umbrellas borne aloft like battle standards, thrusting through the crowds gathered to watch the town hall's amazing Astronomical Clock; students dressed as frogs and chickens handing out flyers for a drama production; middle-aged couples in matching cagoules and sensible shoes, frowning at pink-haired, leather-clad punks; and a bored-looking guy with a placard advertising a museum of torture instruments. Verily, all of human life is here.

Staré Město

St Vitus Cathedral *(p69)*

5 Occupying the site of a 10th-century Romanesque rotunda built by the Good King Wenceslas of Christmas carol fame, St Vitus Cathedral is the heart of Czech Catholicism, and its spires and belltower are the focus of the city skyline. Commenced in 1344 but not completed till 1929, its soaring Gothic nave is lit by gorgeous stained glass, and is home to the cultural jewels of St Wenceslas Chapel, the priceless medieval mosaics of the Golden Gate and the magnificent silver tomb of St John of Nepomuk.

Prague Castle & Hradčany

Czech Beer *(p36)*

6 'Where beer is brewed, life is good', according to an old Czech proverb. Which means that life in Prague must be very good indeed, as the city is awash in breweries both large and small. Czech beer has been famous for its quality and flavour since the invention of Pilsner Urquell in 1842, but in recent years there has been a renaissance of microbreweries and craft beers, and you can now enjoy everything from classic *ležák* (pale lager) to *kvasnicové* (yeast beer) and *kávové pivo* (coffee-flavoured beer). U ZLATÉHO TYGRA (P111)

Drinking & Nightlife

Amazing Architecture *(p46)*

7 One of Prague's prime attractions is its physical appearance. Prague Castle and the city centre are a textbook display of around 900 years of architectural evolution – bluff Romanesque, sublime Gothic, elegant Renaissance and dazzling baroque, plus 19th-century revivals of all of these – all amazingly undisturbed by the modern world and folded into a compact network of lanes, passages and culs-de-sac. And that's before you get started on the 20th century's sleek and sensual art nouveau, and Prague's uniquely Czech cubist and rondo-cubist buildings. SMETANA HALL (P96)

Architecture

Wenceslas Square *(p118)*

8 Watched over by its iconic equestrian statue of St Wenceslas, Prague's biggest square has been a gathering place during many of the great events of modern Czech history, including the Warsaw Pact invasion of 1968 and the Velvet Revolution of 1989. Today it is the throbbing commercial heart of the city, where McDonalds and Marks & Spencer rub shoulders with art-nouveau architecture, and mirrored art-deco arcades lead to stylish cafes and hidden gardens.

Nové Město

6

8

Prague Jewish Museum *(p93)*

9 The slice of Staré Město bounded by Kaprova, Dlouhá and Kozí sts is home to the remains of the once-thriving minitown of Josefov, Prague's former Jewish ghetto. The museum encompasses half a dozen ancient synagogues, a ceremonial hall and former mortuary, and the powerful melancholy of the Old Jewish Cemetery. These exhibits tell the often tragic and moving story of Prague's Jewish community, from the 16th-century creator of the Golem, Rabbi Loew, to the horrors of Nazi persecution. KLAUS SYNAGOGUE

Staré Město

Veletržní Palác *(p151)*

10 In 1996 the huge, grimly functionalist Veletržní Palác, built in 1928 to house international trade fairs, became the new home of the National Gallery's museum of 20th- and 21st-century art. This vast, ocean-liner-like building can now lay claim to being one of Prague's best (and biggest) galleries, including works by Van Gogh, Picasso, Klimt, Mucha and the Impressionists, as well as masterpieces by Czech expressionist, cubist and surrealist artists.

Holešovice, Bubeneč & Dejvice

What's New

Craft Beers

The march of the multinational brewing giants has seen the Czech love affair with beer go back to basics, with a flowering of 'fourth pipe' pubs, microbreweries and craft beers. Fourth pipe – *čtvrtá pípa* in Czech – refers to traditional brewery-owned pubs having three beers on tap. The 'fourth pipe' offers 'guest beers' from independent brewers. Several new bars have opened to cater to this trend, including Prague Beer Museum with 31 varieties of *pivo* on tap. (p110)

St Vitus Treasury

Hidden away since the 1960s, the gem-encrusted gold and silver treasures of St Vitus Treasury are once again on display in a new permanent exhibition at Prague Castle. (p63)

Farmers Markets

Praguers have finally succumbed to foodie fever, and a rash of new delis and designer restaurants has been followed by an outbreak of weekly farmers markets (www.farmarske-trziste.cz).

Sansho

The most talked-about restaurant to emerge in recent years, Sansho opened in 2011 to huge acclaim, with a formula based on championing the use of local produce. (p127)

Fusion Hotel

The trend towards boutique accommodation reaches its zenith in the explosion of designer decadence that is Fusion Hotel, aimed at both mainstream and backpacker markets. (p190)

Bílek Villa

Bílek Villa, the art-nouveau studio and family home of renowned Czech sculptor František Bílek, has been *rekonstrukce* (undergoing renovations) for 10 years – the final outcome is worth the wait. (p74)

Artbanka: Museum of Young Art

Prague's reputation for provocative art, spearheaded by *enfant terrible* David Černý, gets a boost at Artbanka: Museum of Young Art – a collection devoted to promoting the works of young Czech artists. (p104)

Veletržní Palác

The city's main gallery of 20th-century art, Veletržní Palác, has been given a major makeover, with a prettier lobby and a cool new cafe called Nové Syntéza. (p151)

KGB Museum

Indulge your fascination for the Cold War era at the KGB Museum, a new collation of spy gadgets, weapons and uniforms amassed by a Russian-born enthusiast. (p84)

For more recommendations and reviews, see **lonelyplanet.com/czech-republic/prague**

Need to Know

Currency

Czech crown (koruna česká; Kč)

Language

Czech

Visas

Generally not needed for stays of up to 90 days. Some nationalities require a Schengen visa.

Money

ATMs widely available. Credit cards accepted in most hotels and restaurants. Non-European credit cards are sometimes rejected.

Mobile Phones

GSM 900/1800 system is used. Czech SIM cards can be used in European and Australian mobile phones. Standard North American GSM1900 phones will not work, though dual-band GSM 1900/900 phones will.

Time

Central European Time (GMT/UTC plus one hour).

Tourist Information

Prague Welcome (☎221 714 444; www.praguewelcome.cz; Old Town Hall, Staroměstské náměstí 5; ⏰9am-7pm; Ⓜ Staroměstská) Has good free maps and brochures (including accommodation options). Also sells public transport tickets.

Your Daily Budget

The following are average costs per day:

Budget less than €80

➡ Dorm bed €15

➡ Self-catering and lunch specials €15

➡ Admission to major tourist attractions €10

Midrange €80–€200

➡ Double room €120–€160

➡ Three-course dinner in casual restaurant €30

➡ Concert ticket €10–€30

Top end more than €200

➡ Double room in luxury hotel €260

➡ Seven-course tasting menu in top restaurant €90

➡ Private guided tour of city with driver €200

Advance Planning

Three months before Book accommodation if visiting in high season. Check Prague Spring or Strings of Autumn programs and book tickets.

One month before Reserve tables at top-end restaurants and buy tickets online for weekend visit to Karlštejn Castle.

One week before Make Friday- or Saturday-night reservations for any restaurants you don't want to miss. Check website programs for art galleries, jazz clubs and music venues.

A few days before Reserve places on guided tours and day trips.

Useful Websites

➡ **Living Prague** (www.livingprague.com) Insider guide to the city by a British expat.

➡ **Lonely Planet** (www.lonelyplanet.com/prague) Destination information, hotel bookings, traveller forum and more.

➡ **Prague Daily Monitor** (www.praguemonitor.com) News site with English translations.

➡ **Prague Events Calendar** (www.pragueeventscalendar.com) Covers music, entertainment, culture, sport etc.

➡ **Prague Welcome** (www.praguewelcome.cz) Official tourist information website.

WHEN TO GO

May and June are peak tourist season, with fine weather and major festivals. July and August can be hot; April and October have decent weather and smaller crowds.

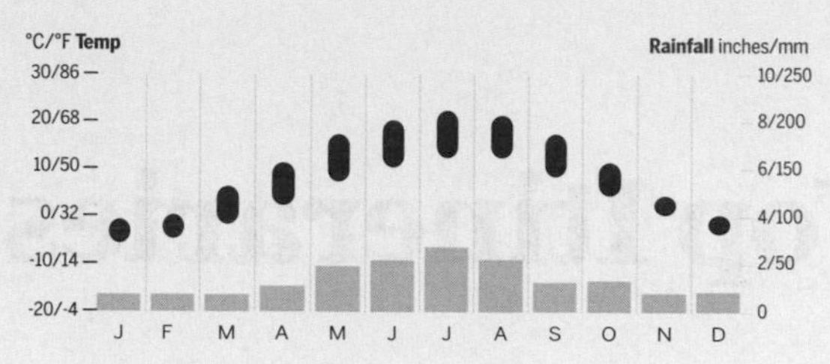

Arriving in Prague

Prague Airport Buses to Dejvice metro station depart every 10 minutes from 4am to midnight (32Kč, plus 16Kč per large piece of luggage). A taxi to the city centre costs 560Kč.

Main train station (Praha hlavní nádraží) In the city centre, with good metro and tram links.

Florenc bus station International buses arrive at Florenc bus station, just east of the city centre, with metro and tram links to the rest of the city. Some domestic bus services leave from Florenc; others depart from Holešovice bus station in the north (eg to Mělník) and Smíchov in the southwest.

For much more on **arrival** see p296

Getting Around

Prague has an integrated metro, tram and bus network – tickets are valid on all types of transport, and for transfers between them. A basic ticket (32Kč) is valid for 90 minutes – validate tickets once in yellow machines on trams and buses, and at entrances to metro stations.

➡ **Walking** Central Prague is fairly compact, and individual neighbourhoods are easily explored on foot.

➡ **Tram** Extensive network of routes, and the best way for getting around shorter distances between neighbourhoods.

➡ **Metro** Fast and frequent, good for visiting outlying areas or covering longer distances.

➡ **Bus** Not much use in city centre, except for airport and part of Žižkov; operates in areas not covered by tram or metro.

➡ **Bicycle** Increasingly popular, especially among the younger generation. New cycle routes are being opened up all the time.

➡ **Taxi** Relatively expensive, and prone to rip-off drivers in tourist areas, especially late at night.

For much more on **getting around** see p299

Sleeping

Gone are the days when Prague was a cheap holiday destination. The Czech capital now ranks alongside most western European cities when it comes to the quality and range – and price – of hotels. Book as far in advance as possible (especially during festival season in spring and autumn, at weekends, and at Easter and Christmas/New Year). Many central hotels are set in charming historic buildings, and there is a new generation of funky design hotels and hostels. There are also dozens of backpacker hostels, most of them geared to youthful party animals.

Useful Websites

➡ **AVE Travel** (www.praguehotellocator.com) Offers a huge range of hotels and apartments.

➡ **Mary's Travel & Tourist Services** (www.marys.cz) Offers private rooms, hostels, pensions, apartments and hotels in all price ranges.

➡ **Hostel.cz** (www.hostel.cz) Database of hostels and budget hotels, with online booking.

For much more on **sleeping** see p185

Top Itineraries

Day One

Prague Castle & Hradčany (p60)

Take a wander through **Prague Castle's** courtyards before the main sights open, then spend the morning visiting **St Vitus Cathedral**, the **Old Royal Palace** and the **Lobkowicz Palace**; try and time things to catch the **changing of the guard** at noon.

Lunch Lobkowicz Palace Café (p74) serves good food with a view.

Malá Strana (p77)

Descend from the castle to Malá Strana along **Nerudova** street, and stop to admire the baroque beauty of **St Nicholas Church**. From here, head to the **Wallenstein Garden** for some peace and quiet, then exit on the far side and follow the backstreets south to **Kampa**. If it's sunny, hang out in the park, and grab a drink at **Mlýnská Kavárna**, or pay a visit to the **Kampa Museum**. As day fades, stroll across **Charles Bridge** in the evening light.

Dinner Lichfield (p87) is a sophisticated place for a special dinner.

Malá Strana (p77)

Malá Strana is full of buzzy bars – **U Malého Glena** is a classic Prague bar and jazz club, with live music every night.

Day Two

Staré Město (p91)

Start the day in the **Old Town Square**; after watching the **Astronomical Clock** do its thing, climb to the top of the **Old Town Hall Tower** for a great view of the square. Head along Celetná to the **Municipal House** and have a coffee while you admire the art-nouveau decor. Buy a ticket for a concert; if you have time before lunch, take a guided tour.

Lunch Try Lokál (p109) for an authentically Czech lunch. And great beer.

Staré Město (p91)

Dedicate the afternoon to visiting the half-dozen monuments that comprise the **Prague Jewish Museum**; if you don't have the time or energy for all of them, concentrate on the **Old-New Synagogue**, the **Old Jewish Cemetery** and the **Spanish Synagogue**.

Dinner Vino di Vino (p109) is good for Italian food and wine.

Staré Město (p91)

Attend a concert in the Municipal House's **Smetana Hall** or the Klementinum's **Chapel of Mirrors**, or spend a night at the opera at the **Estates Theatre**; afterwards, explore Old Town cocktail joints such as **Hemingway Bar** and **Čili Bar**.

Day Three

Nové Město (p116)

Explore the passages and arcades around **Wenceslas Square** by following our walking tour (p126), and (as time and inclination allows) take in the historical and artistic treasures of the **National Museum**, the **Prague City Museum** and the **Mucha Museum**.

Lunch Le Patio (p127) is a favourite local lunch spot.

Smíchov & Vyšehrad (p164)

In the afternoon, take a metro ride out to Vyšehrad and explore Prague's other castle, the **Vyšehrad Citadel**, with its gorgeous views along the Vltava River. Don't miss the impressive tombs of composers Dvořák and Smetana and other famous Czechs in the **Vyšehrad Cemetery**. Walk back to the city centre along the embankment.

Dinner Head to Sansho (p127) for a memorable meal (book in advance).

Nové Město (p116)

The New Town is home to the city's most prestigious classical-music venues – try to catch a performance at the **National Theatre** (ballet), the **Prague State Opera** or the **Dvořák Museum** (concerts of Dvořák's music).

Day Four

Holešovice, Bubeneč & Dejvice (p149)

Time to escape the city for a while: take a boat trip to the rural suburb of Troja (or hire a bike and ride there) and visit **Prague Zoo** and **Troja Chateau**. Walk back into the city centre through Stromovka park (the reverse of our walking tour on p155).

Lunch Enjoy a picnic lunch in leafy Stromovka park (p153).

Holešovice, Bubeneč & Dejvice (p149)

You could spend an entire afternoon admiring modern art in the **Veletržní Palác**, but if the outdoor bug has bitten keep walking (or take a tram) to Letná Gardens for some afternoon drinking at **Letná Beer Garden**, the city's premier open-air chill-out spot.

Dinner Sasazu (p154) captures the trendy vibe of this district.

Žižkov & Karlín (p142)

Take the metro across town to Jiřího z Poděbrad station, and go up the **TV Tower** for a night-time city panorama (open till 10pm). From here, the legendary bars of Žižkov await – **Bukowski's** cocktail dive is just two blocks downhill.

If You Like...

Art & Literature

Veletržní Palác This magnificent Functionalist building harbours four floors of 20th-century and contemporary art. (p151)

Franz Kafka Museum Offers a comprehensive exploration of the claustrophobic and paranoid world of Kafka's novels, and their relation to Prague. (p84)

David Černý (p288) The witty and provocative works of Prague's most famous living artist pop up all over the city.

U Kalicha A place of pilgrimage for fans of Jaroslav Hašek's novel *The Good Soldier Svejk* – this pub is where the novel's opening scene is set. (p125)

Convent of St Agnes This branch of the National Gallery houses a precious collection of glowing Gothic altarpieces and religious sculpture. (p103)

Beer

Prague Beer Museum Not a museum but a hugely popular pub, with 31 varieties of beer on tap. (p110)

Pivovarský Dům One of the city's best microbreweries, offering classic lagers and fruit-flavoured beers produced on the premises. (p128)

U Zlatého Tygra THE classic Prague drinking den, where Václav Havel took Bill Clinton in 1994 to show him a real Czech pub. (p112)

Pivní Galerie If the idea of shopping leaves you cold, how about shopping for beer? This booze boutique stocks nearly 150

RICHARD NEBESKY / LONELY PLANET IMAGES ©

David Černý's 2004 sculpture *Proudy* (Streams; p84)

varieties from around the world. (p162)

Pivovarský Klub Six guest beers on tap and more than 200 international brands in bottles make this welcoming pub a great place to drink your way around the world. (p147)

Parks & Gardens

Wallenstein Garden Hidden away behind high walls, this gorgeous 17th-century Italianate garden is a haven of peace and tranquillity. (p83)

Letná Gardens This huge open space, once used for military parades, is now home to skateboarders, inline skaters, and glorious city panoramas. (p153)

Riegrovy Sady A 19th-century park with a grandstand view of Prague Castle, and home to one of the city's most popular beer gardens. (p134)

Vrtbov Garden Perhaps Prague's least-known garden: an 18th-century retreat peopled by stone figures from Roman mythology. (p86)

Kampa This leafy Malá Strana island, bounded by the Devil's Stream, is one of the city's most popular chill-out spots. (p84)

Classical Music

Prague Spring The Czech Republic's biggest annual cultural event, and one of Europe's most important festivals of classical music. (p42)

Rudolfinum Home to the Czech Philharmonic Orchestra, this complex of concert halls is decorated with statues of famous composers. (p102)

Municipal House Prague's most beautiful art-nouveau building houses Smetana Hall, the city's largest concert venue. (p96)

Prague State Opera The State Opera is a glorious neo-rococo setting for an annual summer festival devoted to the works of Verdi. (p130)

Original Music Theatre of Prague This ensemble performs the works of Antonín Dvořák in the baroque setting of the 18th-century Vila Amerika. (p130)

History

Prague Castle A thousand years of Bohemian history clustered on a hilltop. (p62)

Prague Jewish Museum An ancient cemetery and exhibits spread across half-a-dozen synagogues, telling the story of Prague's Jewish community. (p93)

National Monument A brutalist building and monumental statue, bearing witness to the turbulent 20th-century history of Czechoslovakia. (p144)

National Memorial to the Heroes of the Heydrich Terror A moving memorial to those who died in one of the key events of WWII. (p123)

Prague City Museum Recounts the story of the Czech capital from prehistoric times to the 20th century. (p120)

For more top Prague spots, see

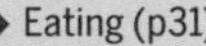

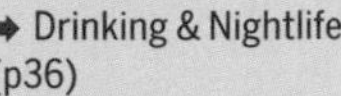

➡ Eating (p31)

➡ Drinking & Nightlife (p36)

➡ Entertainment (p40)

➡ Shopping (p43)

Offbeat Attractions

TV Tower Prague's futuristic three-legged TV Tower looks unconventional enough from a distance, but when you get up close and see the giant crawling babies… (p146)

KGB Museum The enthusastic Russian owner of this quirky little museum will talk you through his collection of spy cameras, torture kits and gruesome garrottes. (p84)

Bunkr Parukářka This is one of those 'only in Prague' places – a crowded club set in a 1950s underground nuclear bunker. (p148)

Miniature Museum If the preserved whale penises in the Strahov Library aren't weird enough for you, how about a flea wearing microscopic golden horseshoes? (p72)

Cubist Lamp Post How many cities can boast a humble lamp post designed in the Cubist style? (p126)

Month by Month

TOP EVENTS

Easter Monday, March or April

Prague Spring, May

Prague Fringe Festival, June

Strings of Autumn, October

Christmas–New Year, December

January

Days are short – the sun sets around 4.30pm in mid-January – but post–New Year accommodation prices are the cheapest you'll find, ideal for that romantic getaway in a cosy hotel with an open fireplace.

Three Kings' Day (Svátek Tří králů)

On 6 January, Three Kings' Day (also known as Twelfth Night) marks the formal end of the Christmas season. The Czechs celebrate with carol-singing, bell-ringing and gifts to the poor.

Anniversary of Jan Palach's Death

A gathering in Wenceslas Square on 19 January commemorates the Charles University student Jan Palach (www.janpalach.cz) who burned himself to death in 1969 in protest against the Soviet occupation.

February

The frost can be cruel in February, with temperatures below 10°C, so wrap up well. But the city looks mighty pretty in the snow.

Masopust

Once banned by the communists, street parties, fireworks, concerts and revelry mark the Czech version of carnival (www.carnevale.cz). Celebrations start on the Friday before Shrove Tuesday (aka Mardi Gras), and end with a masked parade.

March

The first buds of spring begin to green the city's parks and gardens, and the Easter holidays bring Easter markets, hand-painted Easter eggs, and the first tourist influx of the year.

St Matthew Fair (Matějská pout')

From the Feast of St Matthew (24 February) up to and including Easter weekend, the Výstaviště exhibition grounds fill with roller coasters, shooting galleries and stalls selling traditional heart-shaped cookies. Open 2pm to 10pm Tuesday to Friday; 10am to 10pm Saturday and Sunday.

Easter Monday (Pondělí velikonoční)

Mirthful spring! Czech boys chase girls and swat them on the legs with willow switches decked with ribbons; the girls respond with gifts of hand-painted eggs, then everyone parties. The culmination of several days of spring-cleaning, cooking and visiting family and friends.

One World (Jeden Svět)

This week-long film festival (www.oneworld.cz) is dedicated to documentaries on the subject of human rights. Screenings are held at some of the smaller cinemas around town, including Kino Světozor (p130).

Febiofest

This festival (www.febiofest.cz) of film, video and TV features new works by international film-makers. It continues throughout the Czech Republic after the Prague festival.

April

The weather transforms from shivers to sunshine. By the end of the month the sidewalks and squares are covered with outdoor cafe tables, and peak tourist season begins.

Burning of the Witches (Pálení čarodějnic)

This Czech pre-Christian (pagan) festival for warding off evil features the burning of brooms at Výstaviště and all-night, end-of-winter bonfire parties on Kampa island and in suburban backyards. It's held on 30 April.

May

May is Prague's busiest and most beautiful month, with trees and gardens in full blossom, and a string of major festivals. Book accommodation well in advance, and expect to pay top dollar.

Labour Day (Svátek práce)

Once sacred to the communists, the 1 May holiday is now mostly a picnic opportunity. To celebrate the arrival of spring, couples lay flowers at the statue of the 19th-century romantic poet Karel Hynek Mácha, author of *Máj* (May), a poem about unrequited love.

Prague Spring (Pražské jaro)

Held from 12 May to 3 June, this international music festival (www.festival.cz) is Prague's most prestigious event, with classical music concerts held in theatres, churches and historic buildings.

Prague Food Festival

A Friday-to-Sunday festival (www.praguefoodfestival.com) spread throughout the gardens on the south side of Prague Castle. It celebrates the best of Czech and international cuisine, with food stalls, cooking demonstrations, beer- and wine-tastings and children's events.

Czech Beer Festival (Český pivní festival)

During the second half of May, part of the Výstaviště exhibition grounds are consumed by the country's largest beer tent. The festival (www.ceskypivnifestival.cz) celebrates the nation's most famous product. Hog roasts, live music and 70 brands of beer.

Khamoro

This festival (www.khamoro.cz) of Roma culture, with performances of traditional music and dance, exhibitions of art and photography, and a parade through Staré Město, is usually held in late May.

June

Something of a shoulder season, June promises great weather for beer gardens and river cruises without the May festival crowds or the hordes of students who descend on the city in July and August.

Prague Fringe Festival

This nine-day binge of international theatre, dance, comedy and music (www.praguefringe.com), inspired by the innovative Edinburgh Fringe, takes place in late May/early June. Hugely popular with visitors, it's now pulling in more and more locals.

Prague Writers' Festival

A meeting of writers from around the world (www.pwf.cz), with public readings, lectures, discussions and bookshop events.

Dance Prague (Tanec Praha)

International festival of modern dance (www.tanecpraha.cz) held at theatres around Prague throughout June.

August

August weather is typically hot and humid with occasional thunderstorms. Many locals go away on holiday, while the city is overrun with visiting backpackers, students and school groups – avoid if possible.

Festival of Italian Opera

Beginning sometime in late August and extending into September, this festival (www.opera.cz) features the works of Verdi and other Italian composers performed at the Prague State Opera – your chance to see quality productions outside of the main opera season.

October

Autumn is a great time to visit – the tourist crowds start to thin out, it's pleasantly warm, and the Autumn Strings festival is less frenetic than the Prague Spring.

☆ Strings of Autumn (Struny podzimu)

Strings (www.strunypodzimu.cz) is an eclectic program of musical performances, from classical and baroque to avant-garde jazz, Sardinian vocal polyphony and contemporary Swiss yodelling. The program runs for eight weeks from mid-September to mid-November.

December

Cold and dark it may be, but a warming glass of *svařák* (mulled wine) will set you up to enjoy the city's Christmas markets and New Year celebrations. Expect peak season hotel prices.

Christmas–New Year (Vánoce–Nový Rok)

From 24 December to 1 January, tourists engulf Prague and many Czechs take an extended holiday. A Christmas market is held in the Old Town Square beneath a huge Christmas tree: also here on New Year's Eve, massive crowds gather for a huge midnight fireworks display.

Top: Masopust parade

Bottom: Twilight Christmas market, Old Town Square (p100)

With Kids

Czechs are very family oriented, and there are plenty of activities around the city for children. An increasing number of Prague restaurants cater specifically for children, with play areas and so on, and many offer a children's menu (dětský jídelníček).

RICHARD NEBESKY / LONELY PLANET IMAGES ©

Mirror Maze (p87)

Outdoor Fun

Petřín

The classic outdoor play area in central Prague, Petřín (p86) has a whole range of diversions, from the lookout tower and observatory to the mirror maze.

Children's Island

At the southern end of Malá Strana, traffic-free Children's Island (p86) is equipped with playground equipment, rope swings, a mini football pitch, a skateboarding area and a cafe-bar where parents can sip a coffee or beer.

Skateboarding & Skating

The area around the metronome monument in Letná (p153), the huge park to the east of the castle, is a favourite with local skateboarders, while the park's paths provide a perfect surface for inline skating. You can hire skates from Půjčovna bruslí Miami (p163).

If you're visiting in winter, an outdoor ice rink (10am to 9.30pm December to February) gets set up at Ovocný Trh (behind the Estates Theatre) in Staré Město. Skate hire is available.

Parks & Playgrounds

There are safe, well-designed playgrounds all over the city, with convenient city-centre ones at the north end of Kampa (p84) island (at the Malá Strana end of Charles Bridge) and on Slav Island (p124). There's an extensive list of play areas at www.livingprague.com/kids.htm.

Messing about on the River

In summer (generally April to October) you can hire rowing boats and pedalos from several jetties dotted around Slav Island, and splash around on the Vltava. If that sounds too energetic, there are lots of organised boat trips on offer (see p29).

Child-Friendly Restaurants

Hergetova Cihelna

Long famed among Prague parents for its family-friendly Sunday brunch, riverside Hergetova Cihelna (p89) now actively encourages you to bring the kids any day

NEED TO KNOW

- The maximum age for child discounts on admission fees varies from 12 to 18; children under six often get in for free.
- **Kids in Prague** (www.kidsinprague.com) has loads of useful information on places to go and things to do.
- Most top-end hotels provide a babysitting service. **Prague Family** (☎737 749 019; www.praguefamily.cz) is an agency that provides English-speaking babysitters.

of the week. The upper lounge is equipped with high chairs, a breastfeeding area, a nappy-changing station and a play area with lots of toys.

Kogo

An upmarket but relaxed Italian restaurant with outdoor tables in summer, Kogo (p127) welcomes families and provides high chairs and a separate children's menu.

Sakura

Sakura (p158) is an unpretentious Japanese sushi restaurant that has a children's play area.

Rainy-Day Fun

Puppets & Plays

Children's theatre is a long-standing Czech tradition, and there are several places in town that stage regular children's entertainment. The Spejbl & Hurvínek Theatre (p162) puts on puppet shows, while Minor Theatre (p130) stages live children's theatre.

Mořský Svět

Shark tanks and touch pools are among the attractions at Mořský Svět (p152), Prague's only aquarium.

Prague Planetarium

Regular tours of the heavens (in Czech, but a summary text in English is available) at the Prague Planetarium (p153).

Child-Friendly Museums & Galleries

Art Gallery for Children

The clue is in the name: at the Art Gallery for Children (Galerie umění pro děti; ☎732 513 559; www.galeriegud.cz; Náměstí Franze Kafky 3, Staré Město; adult/child/family 120/80/250Kč; ⏲10am-6pm Tue-Sun; Ⓜ Staroměstská) the kids not only get to look at art, but make it, add to it and alter it. There are paints and materials to play with, and even workshops for five- to 12-year-olds (only in Czech at present, though staff speak English).

Lego Museum

The Lego Museum (Muzeum Lega; 775 44 66 77; www.muzeumlega.cz; Národní 31, Staré Město; adult/child/family 200/40/450Kč; ⏲10am-8pm; 🚋 6, 9, 18, 21, 22) is Europe's largest private collection of Lego models, with a play area at the end where kids can build stuff from Lego themselves.

National Technical Museum

Sadly, all those vintage trains, planes, cars and buses are off-limits at the National Technical Museum (p152), but there are interactive exhibits in the photography and printing-industry sections.

Like a Local

Central Prague can often feel like it's populated entirely by tourists. Where are all the locals? If it's the weekend, they're probably either picking wild mushrooms or at a football or ice hockey match.

YADID LEVY / ALAMY ©

Letná Gardens (p153)

Eat Like a Local

Picnic in the Park

Get a taste for local produce by browsing the weekend farmers market (p141) in Vinohrady and putting together the makings of a picnic. Then join the crowds at Riegrovy sady (p134) for an alfresco lunch (there's a beer garden here, too), or head down to Havlíčkovy sady where you can sample Czech wine at Viniční Altán (p138).

Foraging for Fun

It has been estimated that Czechs pick more than 20 million kilograms of wild mushrooms each year. From May to October, foraging for fungi and wild berries is one of the nation's most popular pastimes, when Prague's Divoká Šárka (p161) and Michelský Les woodlands (southeast of the city centre) are thronged with locals clutching wicker baskets. Czechs learn young how to identify edible fungi, so unless you've mastered the art of mushroom identification you'd better tag along with a local expert; otherwise you can sample the fruits of the forest at a farmers market, or at restaurants advertising *hřiby* or *lesní houby*.

Celebration Days

Easter

Come Easter, the country celebrates with a joyful rite of spring. Czech boys swat their favourite girls on the legs with braided willow switches (you'll see them on sale in street markets) or splash them with water; the girls give them hand-painted eggs. Afterwards, the whole family parties – it's the end of several days of serious spring-cleaning, lots of cooking and paying visits to relatives and friends.

May Day

The May Day holiday *(Svátek práce)* on May 1 – once the communist 'holy' day, marked by huge parades – is now just a chance for a picnic or a day in the country. To celebrate the arrival of spring, many couples lay flowers at the statue of the 19th-century poet Karel Hynek Mácha (author of *Máj*, a poem about unrequited love) on Petřín.

Majáles

Prague students celebrate the first weekend of May as Majáles, a festival dating back to at least the early 19th century, which was banned under communism but revived in 1997. It starts with a midday parade – with bands, students in fancy dress, and a float bearing the Kral Majáles (King of Majáles) and Miss Majáles – from Wenceslas Square to Stromovka park, and there is an open-air party including live bands, student theatre and non-stop sausages and beer. For dates and details, check www.majales.cz (Czech only).

Sporting Obsessions

Ice Hockey

It's a toss-up whether football or ice hockey inspires more passion in the hearts of Prague sports fans, but hockey probably wins. Games are fast and furious, and the atmosphere can be electrifying – it's well worth making the effort to see a game, and take part in a genuinely Czech experience.

The Czech national team has been rampant in the last decade or so, winning the World Championship three years running (1999 to 2001) and taking the title again in 2005 and 2010. It also won Olympic gold in 1998 – a feat still celebrated for defeating the mighty Russians in the final – and bronze in 2006.

Prague's two big hockey teams are HC Sparta Praha (www.hcsparta.cz) and HC Slavia Praha (www.hc-slavia.cz), both of which compete in the 14-team national league (known as the Extraliga). Gifted young players are often lured away by the promise of big money in North America's National Hockey League, and there is a sizeable Czech contingent in the NHL.

Sparta plays at the huge, slightly run-down Tipsport Aréna (p163) at the Výstaviště exhibition grounds in Holešovice, and Slavia Praha at **O2 Arena** (☎266 212 111; www.sazkaarena.com; Ocelářská 460, Prague; 🚇3); the season runs from September to early April. Buy tickets online at www.sazkaticket.cz or www.ticketportal.cz, or at the stadium box office before matches.

Football

Prague's two big football clubs, SK Slavia Praha (www.slavia.cz) and AC Sparta Praha (www.sparta.cz), are both leading contenders in the national *fotbal* (football) league, with fiercely partisan supporters all over the country. Two other Prague-based teams – FC Bohemians (www.bohemians1905.cz) and FK Viktoria Žižkov (www.fkvz.cz) – attract fervent local support.

The season runs from August to December and February to June, and matches are mostly played on Wednesday, Saturday and Sunday afternoons. You can buy tickets (100Kč to 400Kč) at stadium box offices on match days.

The Czech national team performs well in international competitions, having won the European Championship in 1976 (as Czechoslovakia), and reached the final in 1996 and the semifinal in 2004. The team was ranked sixth in the world by FIFA in the run-up to Euro 2008, a ranking that seemed over-optimistic when it failed to qualify for the 2010 World Cup. The team qualified for the Euro 2012 championship but lost to Portugal in the quarter-final.

Home international matches are played at Slavia Praha's 21,000-seat Eden stadium (aka Synot Tip Aréna, p141) in eastern Prague.

are free, as is the beautiful Wallenstein Garden (p83) and imposing Vyšehrad Citadel (p167).

For Free

Once a famously inexpensive destination, Prague is no longer cheap; there's not much on offer without a price attached. Parks and gardens, some museums and galleries, and gazing at the glorious architecture are all free, as is the street entertainment on Charles Bridge.

Prague Without a Ticket

Without having to buy a ticket, you can wander through the courtyards and gardens of Prague Castle (p62), watch the changing of the guard ceremony and visit the western end of the nave of St Vitus Cathedral (p69), while Charles Bridge (p79), with its array of jazz bands, buskers, caricature artists and postcard sellers, is a smorgasbord of free entertainment.

Over in the Old Town Square, the hourly performance by the Astronomical Clock (p98) is a classic tick without a ticket, as is the baroque glory of the nearby Church of St Nicholas (p100). Although you'll have to pay for a guided tour of the Municipal House (p96), you can wander through the glorious art-nouveau cafe, the lobby and to the downstairs American Bar without a ticket.

Visits to most churches in Prague (except St Nicholas Church in Malá Strana) are free, as is the beautiful Wallenstein Garden (p83) and imposing Vyšehrad Citadel (p167).

Public Art

Prague has a fine collection of public art on show, all viewable for free, including the provocative and often humorous modern works of David Černý (see the boxed text, p288) and the magnificent art-nouveau monuments to Jan Hus (p100; Old Town Square) and Josef Palácký (Palackého náměstí).

Free Museums & Galleries

Museums, art galleries and other attractions with free admission include the following:

- Museum of the Infant Jesus of Prague (p85)
- Museum Montanelli (p82)
- Wallenstein Palace (p84)
- Mánes Gallery (p123)
- Futura Gallery (p169)
- Meet Factory (p169)
- Karlín Studios (p146)
- Army Museum (p146)

On the first Thursday of each month, entrance to the **Prague City Museum** (p120) is free for students, and reduced to 10Kč (from 120Kč) for everyone else.

Free Tours

A number of outfits, including the recommended **Prague Extravaganza** (www.extravaganzafreetour.com), offer guided walking tours 'for free' (ie on a no-fee, tips-only basis). The guides are local volunteers, and tours depart twice daily from outside the Cartier store on the corner of the Old Town Square and Pařížská.

Prague by Bike

Prague has a long way to go before it's a cycling town comparable with big cities in Germany. Nevertheless, there's a group of hard-core cyclists promoting commuter cycling, extending bike paths and raising driver awareness. Their efforts are starting to bear fruit.

Recommended Routes

Prague has a relatively complete, if disjointed, network of bike paths, signposted in yellow, that criss-cross the city centre and fan out in all directions. Recreational cyclists will probably be content just to putz around on one of the tours offered by the bike-rental companies, but more serious cyclists should consider buying a good map, hiring a bike and hitting the outlying trails for a day or two.

Arguably the best cycling trails lead off to the north following the Vltava River in the direction of Germany. Someday, the Prague–Dresden run will be the stuff of cycling legend, but for now there are still significant gaps in the route. That said, the path northward along the river is nearly complete as far as the town of Kralupy nad Vltavou (20km from Prague; it's possible to return by rail), from where you can continue on back roads to Mělník (p181). There are plenty of bridges and ferries to take you back and forth across the river, and some really great trails leading inland along the way. From the centre of Prague, start off at Čechův most (the bridge over the Vltava by the InterContinental Hotel), ride across the bridge and up the hill to Letná. From there, follow the signs to Stromovka and on to Prague Zoo. The riverside trail (waymarked A2) continues northward from here.

Remember to pack water and sunscreen and always watch out for cars. Czech drivers, inexplicably, are rabidly anticyclist.

Maps

Most large bookstores stock cycling maps *(cykloturisticka mapa)*. One of the best maps to look out for is the latest Freytag & Berndt *Praha a Okoli* (Prague & Surroundings; 1:75,000), which costs about 149Kč. Another good choice for the northwestern section of the city is *Z prahy na kole, Severozapad* (Around Prague by Bike, Northwest; 1:65,000) for about 75Kč.

Websites

➡ **City Bike** (www.citybike-prague.com) Bike rental including helmet, padlock and map.

➡ **Grant's Prague Bike Blog** (http://praguebikeblog.blogspot.com) An American expat's cycling exploits, with great ride ideas, maps and photos.

➡ **Greenways** (www.pragueviennagreenways.org) Details of a 402km cycle trail linking Prague and Vienna.

➡ **Prague City Hall** (http://doprava.praha mesto.cz) Click 'Praha cyklistická' then 'English version' for info on bike trails and rules for cyclists.

➡ **Praha Bike** (www.prahabike.cz) Hires out good, new bikes with lock, helmet and map, plus free luggage storage.

Prague Tours

Prague offers so much intriguing history and culture that it's easy to feel overwhelmed. A guided tour can ease you into an aspect of the city that reflects your interests, and let you get some exercise, too. The Prague Welcome (p301) office in the Old Town Hall provides details of tours.

ORIEN HARVEY / LONELY PLANET IMAGES ©

eing the sights from a boat on the Vltava River

Walking Tours

The corner of the Old Town Square outside the Old Town Hall is usually clogged with dozens of people touting for business as walking guides; the quality varies, but some of the better ones are listed here. Most operators don't have an office – you can join a walk by just turning up at the starting point and paying your money.

Amazing Walks of Prague (☎777 069 685; www.amazingwalks.com; per person 300-500Kč) Guide Roman Bílý is especially strong on WWII, the Communist era and the Jewish Quarter.

Prague Walks (☎222 322 309; www.praguewalks.com; per person 220-990Kč) Runs interesting jaunts with themes such as Prague's history and architecture, Žižkov pubs and the Velvet Revolution.

World War II in Prague (☎605 918 596; www.ww2inprague.com; per person 600Kč) Highly recommended for anyone interested in military history, with a chance to visit the underground HQ of the Prague resistance, and compare archive photos of WWII Prague with their present-day locations.

Prague Special Tours (☎777 172 177; www.prague-special-tours.com; per person 600Kč) Its communism tour visits a genuine 1950s underground nuclear bunker (the same one that houses the nightclub Bunkr Parukářka (p148)).

Boat Tours

Evropská Vodní Doprava (EVD; ☎224 810 030; www.evd.cz; Čechův most, Staré Město; 🚋17) Offers a one-hour cruise departing hourly from 10am to 6pm (adult/child 220/110Kč) and a two-hour cruise to Vyšehrad (420/350Kč), departing at 3.30pm.

Prague Passenger Shipping (Pražská Paroplavební Společnost / PPS; ☎224 930 017; www.paroplavba.cz; Rašínovo nábřeží 2, Nové Město; ⏰Apr-Oct; Ⓜ Karlovo Náměstí) Runs a photogenic one-hour cruise taking in the National Theatre, Střelecký island and Vyšehrad, departing at 11am, 2pm, 4pm, 5pm and 6pm April to September (adult/child 190/90Kč). Also offers a 1¼-hour boat trip to Troja (near the zoo; 150/80Kč one-way) departing at 8.30am on weekdays in May and June only; at 9.30am, 12.30pm and

3.30pm daily May to mid-September, and at weekends and holidays in April and from mid-September to the end of October. Returning boats depart from Troja at 11am, 2pm and 5pm.

Prague Venice (☎776 776 779; www.prague-venice.cz; Platnéřská 4, Staré Město; ⏰10.30am-11pm Jul & Aug, to 8pm Mar-Jun, Sep & Oct, to 6pm Nov-Feb; 🚋17) Runs entertaining 45-minute cruises in small boats under the hidden arches of Charles Bridge and along the Čertovka millstream in Kampa.

Bike Tours

City Bike (p300) Has 2½-hour guided tours, departing at 11am, 2pm and 5pm May to September, and 11am and 2pm April and October. Tours take in the Old Town, the Vltava River and Letná park, and include a stop at a riverside pub.

Praha Bike (p300) Offers a 2½-hour guided cycling tour through the city or an easy evening pedal through the parks. Tours depart at 2.30pm mid-March to October and also at 11.30am and 5.30pm May to September. Trips outside the city can also be arranged, including a full day's tour to Karlštejn Castle (1290Kč).

AVE Bicycle Tours (☎251 551 011; www.bicycle-tours.cz; guided tour 1190Kč, self-guided tour 600Kč; ⏰Apr-Oct) Operates a full-day guided bicycle tour from Prague to Karlštejn Castle (one-way), including hotel pick-up, bike hire, lunch at Karlštejn and a train ticket back to the city. It also offers bike trips to Konopiště and one-week tours through the Czech countryside.

Segway Tours

A Segway – an electrically powered, two-wheeled 'personal transportation system' – allows you to cover more ground in less time than on foot.

Prague Segway Tours (☎724 280 838; www.prague-segway-tours.com; Maltézské náměstí 7, Malá Strana; per person 1490Kč; 🚋12, 20, 22) Three-hour guided tours of the Old Town and Malá Strana depart daily at 9am and 2pm.

Prague on Segway (☎775 588 588; www.pragueonsegway.com; Vlašská 2, Malá Strana; per person 1990Kč; 🚋12, 20, 22) Offers three-hour private, customised guided tours by Segway for one or two people.

Tram Tours

Nostalgic Tram No 91 (☎233 343 349; www.dpp.cz; Patočkova 4, Public Transport Museum; adult/child 35/20Kč; ⏰departs hourly noon-5.30pm Sat, Sun & holidays Mar–mid-Nov) Vintage tram cars dating from 1908 to 1924 trundle along a special route, starting at the Public Transport Museum and going via stops at Prague Castle, Malostranské náměstí, the National Theatre, Wenceslas Square, náměstí Republiky and Štefánikův most to finish at Výstaviště. You can get on and off at any stop, and buy tickets on board (ordinary public transport tickets and passes are not valid).

Jewish-Interest Tours

Precious Legacy Tours (☎222 321 954; www.legacytours.net; Kaprova 13, Staré Město; per person 880Kč; ⏰tours 10.30am & 2pm Sun-Fri) Offers a three-hour walking tour of Prague's Josefov district (the fee includes admission to four synagogues, but not the Staronová Synagogue – this is 200Kč extra). There's also a daily six-hour excursion to Terezín (1160Kč per person; departs 10am); for more information on Terezín, see p182.

Wittmann Tours (☎222 252 472; www.wittmann-tours.com; per person 880Kč; ⏰Josefov tours at 10.30am & 2pm Sun-Fri mid-Mar–Dec) Offers a three-hour walking tour of Josefov, and seven-hour day trips to Terezín (1250Kč per person), daily May to October, four times a week in April, November and December.

Beef *guláš* and dumplings

Eating

Traditional Czech cuisine is a cardiologist's nightmare, a cholesterol-laden menu of meat accompanied by high-calorie dumplings washed down with copious quantities of beer. When it comes to food, the ultimate Czech put-down is to describe it as neslaný *or* nemaslý *('not salty' or 'not fatty'). But if you put aside your notions of healthy eating for a few days, you'll find traditional Czech food to be very tasty.*

Breakfast, Lunch & Dinner

A typical Czech breakfast *(snídaně)* is a light affair consisting of *chléb* (bread) or *rohlík* (bread roll) with butter, cheese, jam or yoghurt, washed down with tea or coffee. A hotel breakfast buffet will normally also include cereals, eggs, ham or sausage. Some Czechs eat breakfast at self-service *bufety,* which are open between 6am and 8am – these serve up soup or hot dogs, which are washed down with coffee or even beer. Some eateries serve Western-style breakfasts.

You can also go to a *pekárna* or *pekařství* (bakery), or to one of the French or Viennese bakeries, for *loupáčky* (like croissants but smaller and heavier). Czech bread, especially rye, is excellent and varied.

Oběd (lunch) is traditionally the main meal of the day and, except for on Sundays, it's often a hurried affair. Czechs are usually early risers, and so they may sit down to lunch as early as 11.30am, though late-comers can still find leftovers for lunch in many restaurants as late as 3pm.

NEED TO KNOW

Price Ranges

In our listings we have used the following price ranges to indicate the cost of a main course at dinner:

€ less than 200Kč

€€ 200Kč to 450Kč

€€€ more than 450Kč

Opening Hours

Lunch is generally noon to 3pm, and dinner 6pm to 9pm. Most Prague restaurants, however, are open all day, from 11am or noon to 10pm or 11pm.

Reservations

It's always a good idea to reserve a table at upmarket restaurants, especially during the high season; almost without fail the phone will be answered by someone who speaks English.

Tipping

In most tourist-area places the helpful message 'Tips Not Included', in English (hint, hint), is printed on the bill. The usual rate is 10% of the total. Usual practice in pubs, cafes and midrange restaurants is to round up the bill to the next 10Kč (or the next 20Kč if it's over 200Kč).

Smoking

In 2010, pubs and restaurants in the Czech Republic had to choose one of the following three labels to be displayed at the entrance to the premises: smoking allowed, smoking prohibited, or mixed. The latter is used for places that have separate (ie physically isolated) spaces for smokers and nonsmokers.

Having stuffed themselves at lunchtime, for many Czechs *večeře* (dinner) is a light meal, perhaps only a platter of cold meats, cheese and pickles with bread.

Czech Specialities

The first course of a meal is usually a hearty *polévka* (soup) – often *bramboračka* (potato soup), *houbová polévka* (mushroom soup) or *hovězí vývar* (beef broth). Ones worth looking out for are *cibulačka* (onion soup), a delicious, creamy concoction of caramelised onions and herbs, and *česnečka* (garlic soup), a powerfully pungent broth that is curiously addictive.

Other common appetisers include *Pražská šunka* (Prague ham), for which the capital is famous. It is cured in brine and smoked; the best stuff is *šunka od kosti* (ham off the bone).

What roast beef and Yorkshire pudding is to the English, *vepřová pečeně s knedlíky a kyselé zelí* (roast pork with dumplings and sauerkraut) is to the Czechs; it's a dish so ubiquitous that it is often abbreviated to *vepřo-knedlo-zelo*. The pork is rubbed with salt and caraway seeds, and roasted long and slow – good roast pork should fall apart, meltingly tender, at the first touch of a fork or finger.

The dumplings should be light and fluffy. *Houskové knedlíky* (bread dumplings) are made from flour, yeast, egg yolk and milk, and are left to rise like bread before being cooked in boiling water and then sliced. The best *knedlíky* are homemade, but the ones you'll find in most pubs and restaurants will be factory-produced. Alternatively, you may be served *bramborové knedlíky* (potato dumplings); if you thought bread dumplings were filling, just wait until you try these stodge-bombs.

Other staples of Czech restaurant menus include *svíčková na smetaně* (slices of marinated roast beef served with a sour-cream sauce garnished with lemon and cranberries); *guláš* (a casserole of beef or pork in a tomato, onion and paprika gravy); and *vepřový řízek* (Wiener schnitzel; a thin fillet of pork coated in breadcrumbs and fried, served with potato salad or *hranolky* – French fries).

Poultry is another popular main course, either roasted or served as *kuře na paprice* (chicken in spicy paprika-cream sauce). *Kachna* (duck), *husa* (goose) and *krůta* (turkey) usually come roasted, with gravy, dumplings and sauerkraut. A few restaurants specialise in game; the most common are *jelení* (venison), *bažant* (pheasant), *zajíc* (hare) and *kanec* (boar) – fried or roasted and served in a mushroom sauce or as *guláš*.

Seafood is found only in a handful of expensive restaurants, but freshwater fish – usually *kapr* (carp) or *pstruh* (trout) – are plentiful. *Štika* (pike) and *úhoř* (eel) are found on more specialised menus. Note that the price of fish on the menu is sometimes not for the whole fish but per 100g. Ask how much the trout weighs before you order it!

The classic Czech dessert is *ovocné knedlíky* (fruit dumplings), but once again the best are to be found at domestic dinner tables rather than in restaurants. Large, round dumplings made with sweetened, flour-based dough are stuffed with berries, plums or apricots, and served drizzled with melted butter and a sprinkle of sugar.

Desserts on offer in traditional pubs and restaurants consist of *kompot* (canned/preserved fruit), either on its own or *pohár* – in a cup with *zmrzlina* (ice cream) and whipped cream. *Palačinky* or *lívance* (pancakes) are also very common. Other desserts include *jablkový závin* (apple strudel), *makový koláč* (poppy-seed cake) and *ovocné koláče* (fruit slices). For cakes and pastries it is better to go to a *kavárna* (cafe) or *cukrárna* (cake shop).

Celebrating with Food

Christmas is the most important celebration on the Czech domestic calendar, and food and drink play an important part. Christmas Eve (Š*tědrý den*, or 'generous day') is a day of abstinence from meat, with people saving their appetite for the evening meal, which is traditionally *smažený kapr* (crispy, fried carp) served with *bramborový salát* (potato salad). The carp are farmed in medieval *rybníky* (fish ponds) in the countryside, mostly in South Bohemia, and in December they are brought to city markets where they are sold, live, from water-filled barrels. In many homes, the Christmas carp then gets to swim around in the bathtub until it's time for the frying pan.

There is no national tradition as to what is served on Christmas Day *(vánoce)*, but meat is definitely back on the menu; *pečená kachna* (roast duck), served with gravy and dumplings, is a widespread favourite. There are also *vánoční cukrovi* (Christmas cookies), baked according to traditional family recipes, and *vánočka,* Bohemia's answer to Christmas cake, though it's actually made with bread dough, sweetened with sugar, flavoured with lemon, nutmeg, raisins and almonds, and plaited; it is usually served after the Christmas Eve dinner.

New Year's Eve *(Silvestr)* is also a big celebration. These days few people still prepare the traditional New Year's Eve dinner of *vepřový ovar* (boiled pig's head) served with grated horseradish and apple, but the day is still a big party day, with plates of *chlebičký* (small, open sandwiches), *bramborky* (potato pancakes) and other snacks, and bottles of *šampaňské* or other sparkling wine on hand to toast the bells at midnight.

Etiquette

Although the vast majority of Prague's tourist-oriented restaurants have long since adopted international manners, a dinner in a Czech home or a traditional eatery still demands traditional local etiquette.

To the Czech way of thinking, only barbarians would begin a meal without first saying *dobrou chuť* (the Czech equivalent of *bon appetit* – the correct response is to repeat the phrase); even the waiters in tourist restaurants will murmur *dobrou*

FUNNY, I DON'T REMEMBER ORDERING THAT!

Keep in mind that nothing comes for free in Prague restaurants – if the waiter offers you fries with that, and you accept, you'll be charged for them. Bread, mayonnaise, mustard, vegetables… almost everything has a price tag. Many restaurants also have a *couvert* (cover charge), which every diner must pay regardless of what they eat and even if they eat nothing. It's not a scam; it's just the way things are done. If the menu has no prices, ask for them. Don't be intimidated by the language barrier; know exactly what you're ordering. If something's not available and the waiter suggests an alternative, ask for the price. Immediately return anything you didn't order and don't want, such as bread, butter or side dishes; don't just leave it to one side or chances are they'll appear on your bill. Most importantly, though, don't let paranoia ruin your meal. The majority of overcharging happens at tourist-oriented restaurants in the city centre. If you're not eating in the Old Town Square or Wenceslas Square, or if you're at a new place run by young Czechs, you're unlikely to have any problems.

SPANISH BIRDS & MORAVIAN SPARROWS

Many Czech dishes have names that don't offer a clue as to what's in them, but certain words will give you a hint: *šavle* (sabre; something on a skewer); *tajemství* (secret; cheese inside rolled meat); *překvapení* (surprise; meat, capsicum and tomato paste rolled into a potato pancake); *kapsa* (pocket; a filling inside rolled meat); and *bašta* (bastion; meat in spicy sauce with a potato pancake).

Two strangely named dishes that are familiar to all Czechs are *Španělský ptáčky* (Spanish birds; sausage and gherkin wrapped in a slice of veal, served with rice and sauce) and *Moravský vrabec* (Moravian sparrow; a fist-sized piece of roast pork). But even Czechs may have to ask about *Tajemství Petra Voka* (Peter Voka's mystery; carp with sauce) and *Dech kopáče Ondřeje* (the breath of grave-digger Andrew; fillet of pork filled with extremely smelly Olomouc cheese).

chuť as they place the plates on your table. And the first drink of the evening is always accompanied by a toast – usually *na zdraví* (nahz-drah-*vee;* literally, 'to health') – as you clink first the tops and then the bottoms of your glasses, and finally touch the glass to the table before drinking.

It's considered bad manners to talk while eating, and especially to distract a guest while they are enjoying their food, so conversation is usually kept to a minimum while food is being consumed; the time for talk is between courses and after the meal.

Eating by Neighbourhood

- **Prague Castle & Hradčany** (p74)Surprisingly few places to eat, with one or two hidden gems.
- **Malá Strana** (p87) Lots of quality restaurants, and more touristy spots with great riverside settings.
- **Staré Město** (p107) Tourist central around the Old Town Square, but plenty of good Czech eateries to be found in the backstreets.
- **Nové Město** (p125) Lots of fast food and street kiosks, but also many good restaurants.
- **Vinohrady & Vršovice** (p134) Upmarket area that is home to some of the city's best restaurants.
- **Žižkov & Karlin** (p146) Rough and ready – mostly pub grub and pizza plus some good Indian and Pakistani restaurants.
- **Holešovice, Bubeneč & Dejvice** (p154) Up-and-coming area with some excellent but thinly spread dining options.
- **Smíchov & Vyšehrad** (p154) Not much choice in Vysehrad, but Smichov has a decent range of restaurants.

Lonely Planet's Top Choices

Sansho (p127) Local produce with Asian flavours and shared, informal dining.

Lichfield (p87) Classy and sophisticated hotel restaurant with an international menu.

Lokal (p109) Classic Czech dishes and great beer in a bright, modern beer hall.

Maitrea (p109) Vegetarian and vegan cuisine with unexpected designer decor.

Mozaika (p134) Vinohrady locals can't get enough of this French-inspired bistro.

Oliva (p128) A little touch of the Mediterranean in Nové Město.

Sasazu (p154) The best Asian cuisine north of the river, with a great nightclub attached.

Da Emanuel (p156) Snug and quiet Italian place, ideal for a romantic dinner.

Best by Budget

$

Café Lounge (p87)

Cukrkávalimonáda (p87)

Las Adelitas (p134)

Mistral Café (p109)

Kabul (p110)

$$

Café Savoy (p89)

Ambiente Pasta Fresca (p110)

Kofein (p134)

U Malé Velryby (p87)

Argument (p156)

$$$

Aromi (p134)

V zátiší (p109)

U Modré Kachničky (p89)

U Zlaté Hrušky (p76)

Hergetova Cihelna (p89)

Best by Cuisine

Czech

Kolkovna (p109)

Zelená Zahrada (p136)

Restaurace Chudoba (p137)

Perpetuum (p157)

Zlatý Klas (p170)

Indian & Pakistani

The Pind (p136)

Indian Jewel (p109)

Masala (p136)

Mailsi (p147)

Manni (p147)

Italian

Vino di Vino (p109)

Ristorante Sapori (p134)

Ambiente Pasta Fresca (p110)

Kogo (p127)

Osteria da Clara (p134)

Southeast Asian

Bangkok (p89)

Sakura (p158)

Hanil (p147)

Noi (p89)

Modrý Zub (p127)

Best for Breakfast

Le Patio (p127)

Café Lounge (p87)

Café Pavlač (p146)

Globe Bookstore & Café (p128)

Fraktal (p159)

Best for Vegetarians

Beas Vegetarian Dhaba (p110)

Café FX (p137)

Country Life (p110)

Lehká Hlava (p110)

Maitrea (p109)

Outdoor restaurant overlooking the Vltava River

Drinking & Nightlife

Bars in Prague go in and out of fashion with alarming speed, and trend spotters are forever flocking to the latest 'in' place only to desert it as soon as it becomes mainstream. The best areas to go looking for good drinking dens include Vinohrady, Žižkov, Holešovice, the area south of Národní třída in Nové Město and the lanes around the Old Town Square in Staré Město.

Drinking

Even in these times of encroaching coffee culture, *pivo* (beer) remains the lifeblood of Prague. Many people drink at least one glass of beer every day – local nicknames for beer include *tekutý chleb* (liquid bread) and *živá voda* (life-giving water) – and it's still possible to see people stopping off for a small glass of beer on their way to work in the morning. And come the evening, beer reigns supreme. There's nothing Praguers enjoy more than getting together in a local bar and swapping stories over a *pivo* or two. Or three...

BEER

There are two main varieties of beer: *světlé* (light) and *tmavy* or *černé* (dark). The *světlé* is a pale amber or golden lager-style beer with a crisp, refreshing, hoppy flavour. Dark beers are sweeter and more full-bodied, with a rich, malty or fruity flavour.

Czechs like their beer served at cellar temperature (around 6°C to 10°C) with a tall, creamy head (known as *pěna,* meaning foam). Americans and Australians may find it a bit warm, but this improves the flavour. Most draught beer is sold in *půllitr* (0.5L) glasses; if you prefer a small beer, ask for a *malé pivo* (0.3L). Some bars confuse the issue by using 0.4L glasses, while others offer a German-style 1L mug known as a *tuplák*.

A recent trend has seen the emergence of the 'fourth pipe' (*čtvrtá pípa*) pub. Prague pubs traditionally offered just three beers on tap, all from one large brewery such as Pilsner Urquell; some pioneering bar owners added a 'fourth pipe' to allow them to offer a rotating range of guest beers from various independent regional breweries. Many now have five, six or even more pipes.

For more on Czech beer, see p292.

PUB ETIQUETTE

There's an etiquette to be observed if you want to sample the atmosphere in a traditional *hospoda* (pub) without drawing disapproving stares from the regulars. First off, don't barge in and start rearranging chairs – if you want to share a table or take a spare seat, first ask *'je tu volno?'* (is this free?). It's normal practice in crowded Czech pubs to share tables with strangers.

Take a beer mat from the rack and place it in front of you, and wait for the bar staff to come to you; waving for service is guaranteed to get you ignored. When the waiter approaches, just raise your thumb for one beer, thumb and index finger for two, etc – it's automatically assumed that you're here for the beer. Even just a nod will do. The waiter will keep track of your order by marking a slip of paper that stays on your table; whatever you do, don't write on it or lose it (you'll have to pay a fine if you do).

As soon as the level of beer in your glass falls to within an inch of the bottom, the eagle-eyed waiter will be on his/her way with another. But never, as people often do in Britain, pour the dregs of the old glass into the new – this is considered to be deeply uncivilised behaviour.

If you don't want any more beer brought to your table, place a beer mat on top of your glass. When you want to pay up and go, get the waiter's attention and say *'zaplatím'* (I'll pay). He or she will total up the marks on your slip of paper, and you pay there, at the table.

NEED TO KNOW

Opening Hours

Most bars are open from 11am till midnight, though many stay open till 1am or later, especially on Friday and Saturday nights.

How Much?

The price of a half-litre of draught beer varies enormously, from around 25Kč to 40Kč in pubs catering mainly to local drinkers, to 90Kč and up at outdoor tables in the tourist-thronged Old Town Square. Most tourist-oriented bars in the city centre charge 40Kč to 80Kč.

Cocktails in the city centre range from 150Kč to 300Kč, depending on the quality of the ingredients and the fanciness of the surroundings, while good-quality Czech wine in a specialist wine bar will cost from 300Kč to 400Kč a bottle.

Tipping

Normal practice is to round up the bill to the next 10Kč (or the next 20Kč if it's over 200Kč). Change is usually counted out starting with the big notes, then on down to the smallest coins. If you say *děkuji* (thank you) during this process, the bartender will stop and assume that the rest is a tip.

WINE

Grapes have been grown in the Czech lands since the 14th century, when Charles IV imported vines from Burgundy; their descendants are still thriving on the slopes beneath Mělník Chateau.

The standard of Czech wine has soared since the fall of communism, as small producers have concentrated on the quality end of the market. Although Czech red wines – such as the South Moravian speciality Svatovavřinecké (St Lawrence) – are mostly pretty average, Czech whites can be very good indeed. The varieties to look out for are Veltinské zelené (Grüner Veltlin), Rýnský ryzlink (riesling) and Müller-Thurgau. Tanzberg and Sonberk are both excellent winemakers.

For about three weeks each year from the end of September to mid-October, you will see shops and street stalls selling *burčak*. This is 'young wine', freshly extracted grape juice in the early stages of

TANKOVÉ PIVO

One recent innovation that you will come across in many Prague pubs is the phenomenon of *tankové pivo* (tanked beer). Ordinarily beer goes stale through contact with oxygen in the air. Tanked beer is delivered in sterile plastic bags that are stored in chilled stainless steel tanks (often in plain view in the pub). Compressed air forced between the tank and the bag forces the beer through the tap without it having to come into contact with oxygen, a system that allows pubs to serve fresh, unpasteurised beer (vastly superior in flavour to the more common, heat-treated keg beer).

fermentation. It is cloudy yellow in appearance and innocently sweet in flavour, more like a soft drink than a wine. But beware – it contains 5% to 8% alcohol.

Later in the year, as winter sets in, you'll notice the *svařák* stalls appearing in the streets. Short for *svařené vino* (mulled wine), *svařák* is red wine heated and flavoured with sugar and spices.

SPIRITS

Probably the most distinctive of Czech *lihoviny* (spirits) is Becherovka. Produced in the West Bohemian spa town of Karlovy Vary, famous for its 12 sulphurous, thermal springs, the bitter, herbal liqueur is often served as an aperitif, and is increasingly used as an ingredient in cocktails.

The fiery and potent *slivovice* (plum brandy) is said to have originated in Moravia, where the best brands still come from. The best commercially produced *slivovice* is R Jelínek from Vizovice. Other regional spirits include *meruňkovice* (apricot brandy) and juniper-flavoured *borovička*.

The deadliest locally produced spirit is absinthe. While it's banned in many countries, in part because of its high alcohol content, absinthe is legal in the Czech Republic. Unfortunately, connoisseurs of absinthe consider Hill's absinthe – the biggest-selling brand of Czech-made absinthe – little better than highly alcoholic mouthwash. However, it does form the basis of an evil cocktail that was popular among clubbers a few years ago – the H-Bomb (Hill's mixed with Semtex, a Czech brand of energy drink).

Clubbing

Prague's club scene is nothing to rave about. With few exceptions, the city's dance clubs cater to crowds of partying teenagers and tourists weaned on MTV Europe – if you want to dance to anything other than '80s hits or happy house, you'll have to look long and hard. Prague's main strengths are its alternative music clubs, DJ bars, 'experimental' venues such as Palác Akropolis (p148) and the Roxy (p112), and places that are just plain weird, such as Bunkr Parukářka (p148).

Refreshingly, dress codes don't seem to have reached Prague yet, and it's unlikely you'll be knocked back anywhere unless you're stark naked. And there are even a few places that would probably be OK with that…

Check out www.prague.tv, www.techno.cz/party or www.hip-hop.cz for up-to-date club listings (the latter two are in Czech, but you can work out what's going on).

Drinking & Nightlife by Neighbourhood

➡ **Prague Castle & Hradčany** (p76)The area has a couple of interesting cafes and pubs, but goes very quiet in the evenings.

➡ **Malá Strana** (p89) A lively drinking scene with smart modern bars and plenty of live music.

➡ **Staré Město** (p110) Outdoor tables around the Old Town Square, and snug atmospheric bars and jazz joints in the backstreets.

➡ **Nové Město** (p128) A hotbed of sports bars, Irish pubs and girlie bars much frequented by visiting stag parties.

➡ **Vinohrady & Vršovice** (p137) Trendy neighbourhoods where you can seek out the latest cocktail bars and cool cafes.

➡ **Žižkov & Karlin** (p147) The best areas for down-to-earth pubs packed with locals downing glasses of the city's cheapest beer.

➡ **Holešovice, Bubeneč & Dejvice** (p158) Up-and-coming suburbs with a range of working-class pubs, newer cafes and student hangouts.

Lonely Planet's Top Choices

Pivovarský Klub (p147) A dream come true for fans of real ale.

U Vystřeleného oka (p148) The quintessential Žižkov neighbourhood pub.

Sasazu (p161) Prague's classiest and most popular dance club.

Fraktal (p159) A classic expat hangout on the far side of the river.

Best Grand Cafes

Kavárna Obecní dům (p112)

Café Imperial (p128)

Café Savoy (p89)

Grand Cafe Orient (p112)

Kavárna Slavia (p122)

Kavárna Lucerna (p129)

Best Traditional Pubs

U Zlatého Tygra (p111)

U Slovanské Lípy (p148)

Pivnice U Černého Vola (p76)

Svijanský Rytíř (p160)

Hospůdka Obyčejný svět (p138)

Klášterní Pivnice (p160)

Best Cocktail Bars

Hemingway Bar (p110)

Bukowski's (p147)

Čili Bar (p111)

Bar & Books Mánesova (p139)

Andaluský Pes (p160)

Best for Regional Beers

Prague Beer Museum (p110)

Klášterní pivnice (p160)

Jáma (p128)

Pivovarský Klub (p147)

U Slovanské Lípy (p148)

Best Cool Cafes

Café Kaaba (p138)

Krásný ztráty (p111)

Literární Kavárna Řetězová (p111)

Blatouch (p138)

Galerie Kavárna Róza K (p138)

Ryba Na Ruby (p139)

Best Alternative Clubs

Palác Akropolis (p148)

Roxy (p112)

Bunkr Parukářka (p148)

XT3 (p148)

Radost FX (p140)

Best Microbreweries

Pivovarský Dům (p128)

Klášterní pivovar Strahov (p76)

U Medvídků (p111)

Novoměstský pivovar (p129)

U Fleků (p129)

Best Wine Bars

Bokovka (p128)

Monarch Vinný Sklep (p112)

Viniční Altán (p138)

Best Beer Gardens

Letná Beer Garden (p159)

Riegrovy Sady (p137)

Parukářka (p148)

Entertainment

Across the spectrum, from ballet to blues, jazz to rock and theatre to film, there's a bewildering range of entertainment on offer in this eclectic city. Prague is now as much a European centre for jazz, rock and hip hop as it is for classical music. The biggest draw, however, is still the Prague Spring festival of classical music and opera.

Music

CLASSICAL MUSIC

There are half a dozen concerts of one kind or another almost every day during the summer, making a fine soundtrack to accompany the city's visual delights. Many of these are chamber concerts performed by aspiring musicians in the city's churches – gorgeous but chilly (take an extra layer, even on a summer day) and not always with the finest of acoustics. However, a good number of concerts, especially those promoted by people handing out flyers in the street, are second-rate, despite the premium prices that foreigners pay. If you want to be sure of quality, go for a performance by one of the city's professional orchestras.

Box offices are open from 30 minutes to one hour before the start of a performance. For classical music, opera and ballet listings, check out www.heartofeurope.cz and www.czechopera.cz.

LIVE MUSIC

Prague has a high-energy live-music scene, with rock, metal, punk, electro, industrial, hip hop and newer sounds at a score of DJ and live-music venues; most have a cover charge of around 50Kč to 200Kč. Most clubs stay open till at least 2am or 3am, and some keep going till 6am. As well as the venues listed here, clubs such as Palác Akropolis and Roxy also host local and international live rock bands. Keep an eye open for flyers that are posted around town.

JAZZ

Prague has lots of good jazz clubs to choose from, many of which have been around for decades. Most have a cover charge of around 100Kč to 300Kč.

Film

Prague has more than 30 cinemas, some showing first-run Western films, some showing Czech films, and including several excellent art-house cinemas. For cinema listings check the 'Night & Day' section of the *Prague Post* or www.prague.tv.

Most films are screened in their original language with Czech subtitles *(české titulky)*, but Hollywood blockbusters are often dubbed into Czech *(dabing)*; look for the labels 'tit' or 'dab' on cinema listings. Czech-language films with English subtitles are listed as having *anglický titulky*.

Movies are normally screened twice in the evening, around 7pm and 9pm, though multiplexes show films all day long. Most cinemas screen matinees on weekends.

Theatre

Most Czech drama is, not surprisingly, performed in Czech, which rather diminishes its appeal to non-Czech speakers. However, there are some English-language productions and many predominantly visual shows at which language is not a barrier. There's also the Prague Fringe Festival (www.praguefringe.com), which takes place in early June and offers plenty of English-language theatre.

Prague is famous for its black-light theatre – occasionally called just 'black theatre' – a hybrid of mime, drama, dance and special effects in which actors wearing fluorescent costumes do their thing in front of a black backdrop lit only by ultraviolet light (it's a growth industry in Prague, with at least half a dozen venues). An even older Czech tradition is puppetry, and the city has several marionette shows on offer.

Entertainment by Neighbourhood

➡ **Prague Castle & Hradčany** (p70) Very little happens in this neighbourhood after dark – best head elsewhere!

➡ **Malá Strana** (p89) Good selection of small, intimate live-music venues.

➡ **Staré Město** (p112) Home to many classical music venues and old-school jazz clubs.

➡ **Nové Město** (p129) Prague State Opera and the National Theatre rub shoulders with sports bars and stag parties.

➡ **Vinohrady & Vršovice** (p140) The heart of Prague's gay scene; also lots of trendy clubs and bars.

➡ **Žižkov & Karlin** (p148) The place for classic, sticky-floored, down-and-dirty rock joints.

➡ **Holešovice, Bubeneč & Dejvice** (p161) Up-and-coming clubs and experimental venues.

➡ **Smíchov & Vyšehrad** (p172) Some good experimental venues in Smíchov; open-air classical concerts in Vyšehrad.

NEED TO KNOW

Listings

For reviews, day-by-day listings and a directory of venues, consult the 'Night & Day' section of the weekly *Prague Post* (www.praguepost.com). Monthly listings booklets include *Culture in Prague* and the Czech-language *Přehled*, available from Prague Information Service tourist offices.

For web-based entertainment listings, check out:

➡ www.praguewelcome.cz/en/todo

➡ www.heartofeurope.cz

➡ pragueeventscalendar.com/en

Buying Tickets

The 'wholesalers' with the largest agency networks are Bohemia Ticket International (BTI), FOK and Ticketpro; the others probably get their tickets from them.

➡ **Bohemia Ticket International** (BTI; ☎224 227 832; www.ticketsbti.cz; Malé náměstí 13, Staré Město; ⏰9am-5pm Mon-Fri) Provides tickets for all kinds of events. There's another **branch** (☎224 215 031; Na příkopě 16, Nové Město; ⏰10am-7pm Mon-Fri, to 5pm Sat, to 3pm Sun) near the Municipal House.

➡ **FOK Box Office** (☎222 002 336; www.fok.cz; U Obecního Domu 2, Staré Město; ⏰10am-6pm Mon-Fri) Prague Symphony Orchestra box office, for classical concert tickets; also open for one hour before performances begin.

➡ **Ticketcentrum** (☎296 333 333; Rytířská 31, Staré Město; ⏰9am-12.30pm & 1-5pm Mon-Fri) Walk-in centre for all kinds of tickets; branch of Ticketpro.

➡ **Ticketpro** (www.ticketpro.cz; Vodičkova 36, Pasáž Lucerna, Nové Město; ⏰noon-4pm & 4.30-8.30pm Mon-Fri) Tickets are available here for all kinds of events. There are Ticketpro branches in PIS offices and many other places.

➡ **Ticketstream** (www.ticketstream.cz) Internet-based booking agency that covers events in Prague and all over the Czech Republic.

PRAGUE SPRING

First held in 1946, the Prague Spring (Pražské jaro) international music festival is the Czech Republic's best-known annual cultural event. It begins on 12 May, the anniversary of composer Bedřich Smetana's death, with a procession from his grave at Vyšehrad to the Municipal House (p96), and a performance there of his patriotic song cycle *Má vlast* (My Homeland). The festival runs until 3 June, and the beautiful concert venues are as big a drawcard as the music.

Tickets can be obtained through the official **Prague Spring Box Office** (Map p332; ☎227 059 234; www.prague-spring.net; náměstí Jana Palacha, Staré Město; ⏰10am-6pm Mon-Fri; 🚋17, 18) in the Rudolfinum, or from any branch of Ticketpro.

If you want a guaranteed seat at a Prague Spring concert try to book it by mid-March at the latest, though a few seats may still be available as late as the end of May.

Lonely Planet's Top Choices

Cross Club (p161) The ultimate in Prague's 'industrial' nightclubs, packed with mechanical gadgets.

Palác Akropolis (p148) A long-standing Prague institution, host to all kinds of live music.

Roxy (p112) The queen of the city's experimental scene, mixing art, music and live performance.

Smetana Hall (p113) An art-nouveau setting to match the splendour of Smetana's music.

JazzDock (p172) Evening jazz gigs with a view over the Vltava River.

Best Jazz & Blues

Reduta Jazz Club (p129)

AghaRTA Jazz Centrum (p112)

Blues Sklep (p112)

Jazz Club U Staré Paní (p112)

U malého Glena (p90)

Best Live Music

Malostranská Beseda (p90)

Lucerna Music Bar (p129)

Rock Café (p129)

XT3 (p148)

Vagon (p112)

Best Classical & Opera

National Theatre (p130)

Prague State Opera (p130)

Estates Theatre (p113)

Dvořák Hall (p113)

Chapel of Mirrors (p104)

Best Theatre

Archa Theatre (p130)

Theatre on the Balustrade (p113)

Švandovo Divadlo Na Smíchově (p172)

La Fabrika (p162)

Best Clubbing

SaSaZu (p154)

Bunkr Parukářka (p148)

Sedm Vlků (p148)

Futurum (p171)

Radost FX (p140)

Best for Kids

Minor Theatre (p130)

National Marionette Theatre (p113)

Spejbl & Hurvínek Theatre (p162)

Best Gay & Lesbian

Friends (p112)

ON Club (p140)

Café Celebrity (p139)

Termix (p140)

Shopping

In the past decade or so, Prague's shopping scene has changed beyond recognition. An influx of global brand names and glitzy new malls has left the city's main shopping streets looking very much like those of any other European capital. Imported goods often carry Western European prices, but Czech products remain affordable for Czechs and cheap for Westerners.

Specialities

GLASS & CRYSTAL

One of Prague's best buys is Bohemian crystal (*sklo*) – anything from simple glassware to stupendous works of art, sold at some three-dozen upmarket places in the shopping zone. Prices aren't radically different from shop to shop, though they are highest in the city centre.

HANDICRAFTS

In the tourist areas of Prague, many shops – notably Manufaktura (p115) – stock quality craft items made of wood, ceramic, straw, textiles and other materials, handmade in traditional styles. Things to look for include painted Easter eggs, wooden utensils, ceramics with traditional designs, linen with traditional stitching, and Bohemian lacework. Notably popular are figures of Krtek (Little Mole), a Czech cartoon character dating from the 1950s.

Traditional wooden marionettes (and more delicate and lifelike ones made of plaster) are also available in many shops.

JEWELLERY

Amber (*jantar*) and gemstones mined in the Czech Republic are good value, and popular as souvenirs or gifts. Amber is better value here than over the border in Germany. This fossilised tree resin is usually honey-yellow in colour, although it can be white, orange, red or brown. Czech garnets (*český granát*) – sometimes called 'Czech rubies' – are usually red but can be many other colours, or even colourless.

MUSIC

Good buys include CDs and sheet music of the works of famous Czech composers (such as Smetana, Dvořák, Janáček and Martinů) as well as Bohemian folk music – even *dechovka* (brass-band 'polka' music). There are almost as many music shops in Prague as bookshops.

Shopping Areas

WENCESLAS SQUARE (SEE MAP P338)

The city centre's single biggest – and most exhausting – retail zone is around Wenceslas Square (Václavské náměstí), its pavements jammed with browsing visitors and locals making beelines for their favourite stores. You can find pretty much everything here, from high fashion boutiques and music megastores to run-of-the-mill department stores and gigantic book emporia. Many of the more interesting shops are hidden away in arcades and passages, such as the Lucerna Palace (p121).

The other main shopping drag intersects with the lower end of Wenceslas Square, comprising Na Příkopě, 28.října and Národní Třída. Most of the big stores and malls are concentrated on Na Příkopě, with the biggest of them all – the **Palladium Praha Shopping Centre** (Map p336; Náměstí

NEED TO KNOW

Opening Hours

Prague shops usually open anywhere between 8am and 10am, and close between 5pm and 7pm Monday to Friday. They open from 8.30am to noon or 1pm on Saturday. Major shops, department stores and tourist businesses also open on weekends (usually from 9am to 6pm), but local shops may be closed on Saturday afternoon and Sunday.

Consumer Taxes

Value-added tax (VAT, or DPH in Czech) is applied at 10% on food (including restaurant meals), books and periodicals, and 20% on the sale of most goods and services. This tax is included in the marked price and not added at the cash register.

It is possible to claim VAT refunds of up to 14% of the purchase price for purchases totalling more than 2000Kč that are made in shops displaying the 'Tax Free Shopping' sticker. They will give you a Tax Free Shopping voucher, which you then need to present to customs for validation when you leave the country (which must be within three months of the date of purchase). You can then claim your refund either at a duty-free shop in the airport (after passing through passport control) or from a cash-refund office back home (within six weeks of the purchase date). For more information, see www.globalrefund.com.

Republiky) – at its northeast end, opposite Municipal House.

STARÉ MĚSTO (SEE MAP P332)

In Staré Město, the elegant avenue of Pařížská is lined with international designer houses including Dior, Boss, Armani and Louis Vuitton. In contrast, the winding lanes between the Old Town Square and Charles Bridge are full of tacky souvenir shops flaunting puppets, Russian dolls and 'Czech This Out' T-shirts. However, other parts of Staré Město – notably Dlouhá, Dušní and Karoliny Světlé – are becoming known for a concentration of designer fashion boutiques, art galleries and quirky independent shops.

VINOHRADY (SEE MAP P344)

As Prague's ritziest residential district, it is not very surprising that Vinohrady is also home to the greatest number of furniture and home-decor shops in the city. If you are a fan of design or decoration, you should definitely hike the miracle mile along Vinohradská between the Muzeum and Jiřího z Poděbrad metro stops to see the latest in couches, kitchens and carpets.

Shopping by Neighbourhood

➡ **Prague Castle & Hradčany** (p76) There's not much in the way of shopping here.

➡ **Malá Strana** (p90) Mostly tourist-oriented shopping, with a few designer boutiques and bookshops tucked away in back alleys.

➡ **Staré Město** (p113) The best area in the city for Czech designer fashion.

➡ **Nové Město** (p130) This is the main shopping area, with all the big European high-street names from Marks & Spencer to Mothercare.

➡ **Vinohrady & Vršovice** (p140) Upmarket neighbourhoods with chic arty-crafty shops and designer furniture.

➡ **Holešovice, Bubeneč & Dejvice** (p162) Some interesting specialist shops, plus the city's best farmers market.

➡ **Smíchov & Vyšehrad** (p173) Home to Nový Smíchov, one of Prague's biggest and busiest shopping malls.

Lonely Planet's Top Choices

Art Deco Galerie (p114) Antique and reproduction items from the 1920s and '30s.

Modernista (p114) Beautiful reproduction furniture in classic styles from art deco and cubist to functionalist and Bauhaus.

Globe Bookstore & Café (p131) A great selection of new and secondhand books in English, and a cafe to read them in.

Klara Nademlýnská (p114) High fashion from one of the Czech Republic's best known and most respected designers.

Obchod s uměním (p140) Original paintings, prints and sculpture from 1900 to 1940, when Czech artists were at the forefront of the European avant-garde.

Pivní Galerie (p162) A beer-drinker's heaven, with 150 varieties from all over the Czech Republic.

Best for Fashion

Bohème (p114)

Leeda (p113)

Pavla & Olga (p90)

TEG (p114)

Best for Books

Big Ben (p114)

Palác Knih Neo Luxor (p131)

Kiwi (p131)

Best for Arts & Crafts

Manufaktura (p115)

Hunt-Kastner Artworks (p162)

Galerie České Plastiky (p130)

Kubista (p114)

Qubus (p115)

Best for Music

Bazar (p131)

Bontonland (p131)

Maximum Underground (p115)

Talacko (p115)

Best for Antiques

Antikvita (p162)

Bric A Brac (p115)

Antique Music Instruments (p76)

Icons Gallery (p76)

Vetešnictvi (p90)

Best for Jewellery

Belda Jewellery (p131)

Granát Turnov (p115)

Frey Wille (p115)

Art Décoratif (p114)

Best Markets

Dejvice Farmers Market (p157)

Vinohrady Farmers Market (p141)

Pražská Tržnice (p162)

Havelská Market (p115)

Best for Glass & Crystal

Moser (p131)

Bořek Šípek (p114)

Dům Porcelánu (p141)

Le Patio Lifestyle (p115)

Architecture

Historic Prague

Prague's historic architecture, stretching back more than 1000 years, is a major drawcard. The backstreets of Staré Město and Malá Strana are living textbooks of the steady march of European architecture over the years. Thankfully, the city's historic core escaped significant damage in WWII, so it records a millennium of urban development, with baroque facades encasing Gothic houses perched on top of Romanesque cellars – all following a street plan that emerged in the 11th century.

Romanesque

Romanesque architecture, characterised by rounded facades, arched doorways and massive walls, was all the rage in Europe from the 10th to the 12th centuries, and was the reigning style during the rise of the early Bohemian kings. The oldest buildings in Prague date from this period, but not many of the original structures have survived intact. Prague's finest Romanesque building is the Basilica of St George (pictured below right) at Prague Castle, but the style is perhaps best preserved in the handful of rotundas (circular churches) that are, amazingly, still standing. The finest examples include the early 12th-century Rotunda of St Longinus (Map p338) in Nové Město and the late-11th century Rotunda of St Martin (p167) in Vyšehrad.

Gothic

Romanesque evolved into Gothic architecture in the 13th and 14th centuries. This is Prague's signature style, and is characterised by tall, pointed arches, ribbed vaults, external flying buttresses, and tall, narrow windows with intricate tracery supporting massive stained glass.

Czech Gothic architecture flourished in the 14th century during the rule of Charles IV, especially in the hands of architect Peter Parler (Petr Parléř), who was best known for the eastern part of St Vitus Cathedral (pictured above right) at Prague Castle. Parler was also responsible for the Gothic design of Charles Bridge and the Old Town Bridge Tower (p108). Another master builder was Benedikt Rejt, whose finest legacy is the petal-shaped vaulting of Vladislav Hall (1487–1500) in the Old Royal Palace (p65) at Prague Castle. The Old Town Hall (p97), with its Astronomical Clock, dates from this period as well. Curiously, the golden tops that crown the many Gothic steeples around town were not part of the original design, but were added in the 19th century, when the craze of neo-Gothic swept the city and much of the rest of Europe.

Opposite page
1. St Vitus Cathedral (p69) **2.** Basilica of St George (p66)

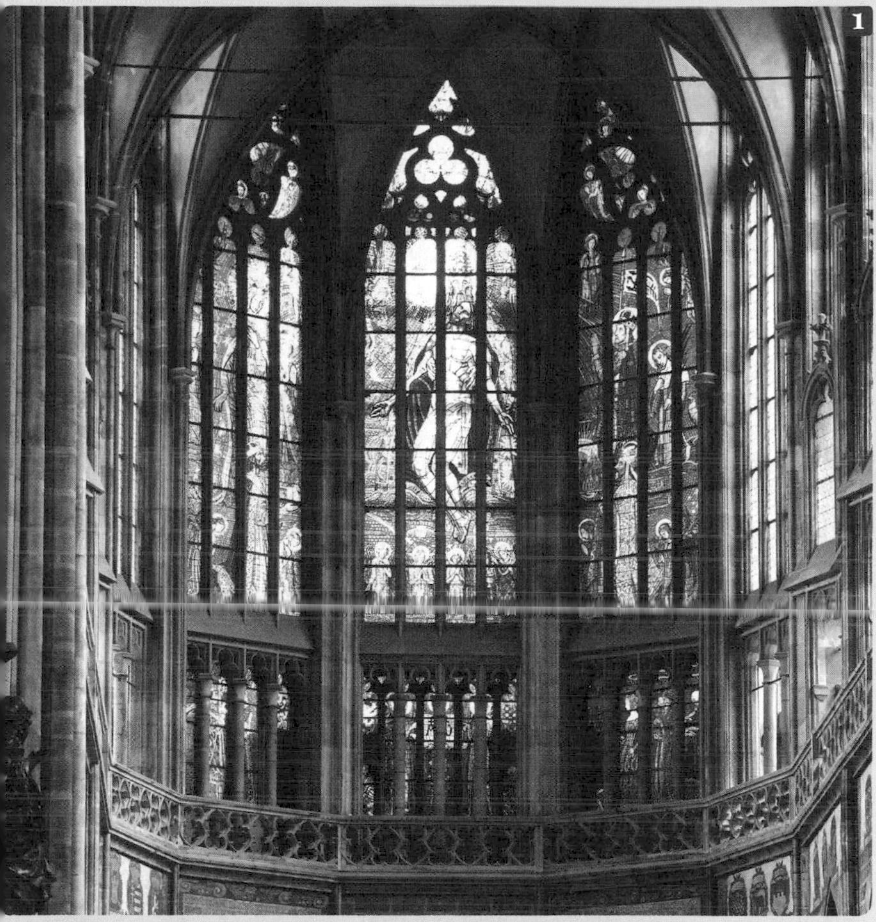

CHRISTER FREDRIKSSON / LONELY PLANET IMAGES ©

RICHARD NEBESKÝ / LONELY PLANET IMAGES ©

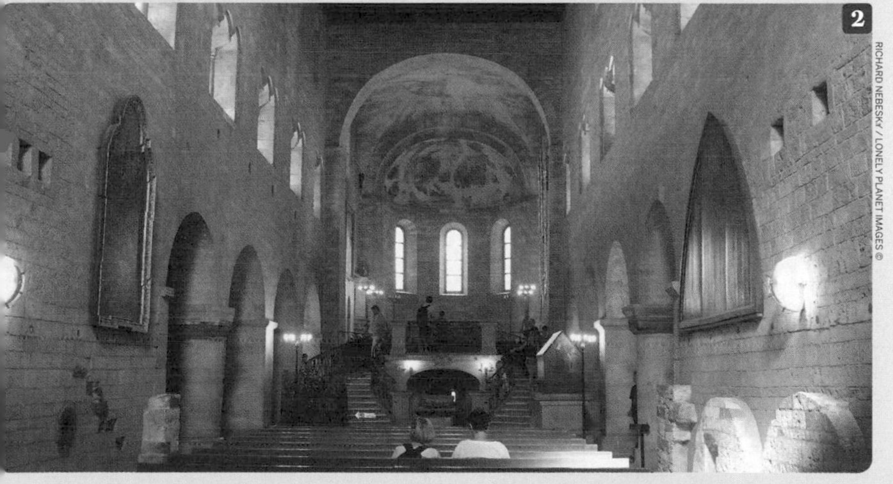

Renaissance

When the Habsburgs assumed the Bohemian throne in the early 16th century, they invited Italian architects to Prague to help create a royal city worthy of their status. The Italians brought a new enthusiasm for classical forms, an obsession with symmetry and a taste for exuberant decoration.

The mix of styles gave rise to a 'Bohemian Renaissance', featuring the technique of sgraffito – from the Italian word 'to scrape' – literally creating design patterns by scraping through an outer layer of pale plaster to reveal a darker surface underneath.

The Summer Palace (1538–60; p63), in the gardens north of Prague Castle, was built for Queen Anna, the consort of Prague's first Habsburg ruler Ferdinand I. It is almost pure Italian Renaissance. The Schwarzenberg Palace (1546–67; p74) in Hradčany and the House at the Minute (1546–1610) in Staré Město, to the left of the Astronomical Clock (p98), are good examples of sgraffito.

Baroque

In the aftermath of the Thirty Years' War (1618–48), the Habsburg empire embarked on a campaign to rebuild and re-Catholicise the Czech lands. The ornate baroque style, with its marble columns, frescoed ceilings and rich ornamentation, was used by the church as an instrument of persuasion.

The most impressive example of baroque style is St Nicholas Church (1704–55) in Malá Strana, the work of Bavarian father and son Kristof and Kilian Ignatz Dientzenhofer. Its massive green dome dominates the area in a fitting symbol of the Catholic Church's dominance over 18th-century Prague. The final flourish of late baroque was rococo, featuring even more-elaborate decoration. The Kinský Palace (1755–65; p100) has a gleaming rococo facade.

Clockwise from top left

1. Schwarzenberg Palace (p74) **2.** Summer Palace (p63) fountain **3.** Kinský Palace (p100) **4.** House at the Minute, Old Town Square, Staré Město

1

4

BEST HISTORICAL ARCHITECTURE IN PRAGUE

- **Basilica of St George** (p66)
- **St Vitus Cathedral** (p69)
- **Charles Bridge** (p79)
- **St Nicholas Church** (p82)
- **Municipal House** (p96)

JONATHAN SMITH / LONELY PLANET IMAGES ©

2

EYE UBIQUITOUS / ALAMY ©

3

WESLEY ROEEFTS / ALAMY ©

Neoclassical

After the exuberance of the 17th and 18th centuries, 19th- century architecture was comparatively dull. Architects felt that baroque and rococo had taken pure decoration as far as it could go and there was a need to simplify styles. They looked to classical Greece and Rome for inspiration.

Neoclassical and other 'historicist' styles are closely associated with the 19th-century Czech National Revival. The Estates Theatre (1783; p103) is a good example of neoclassical design. The National Theatre (1881; p122) and National Museum (1891; p121) were built in neo-Renaissance style, and are noteworthy not so much for the architecture but for what they represented: the chance for Czechs to show they were the equals of their Viennese overlords.

The flamboyant Spanish Synagogue (1868; p95; pictured right) in Josefov is another good example of neoclassicism, but here the style being aped is not Roman or Greek, but Moorish, recalling Jewish roots in Spain.

Art Nouveau

As the 19th century drew to a close, Czech architects began to tire of linear neoclassical facades and the pompous style of imperial Vienna. They were looking for something new and found inspiration in Paris with art nouveau and its emphasis on beauty.

The city's finest expression of art nouveau is the magnificent Municipal House (1906–12; pictured above far right). Every aspect of the building's decoration was designed by leading Czech artists of the time, most famously Alfons Mucha, who decorated the Lord Mayor's Hall.

Art nouveau was frequently applied to upmarket hotels, including Hotel Central (1899–1901) on Hybernská in Nové Město, and Grand Hotel Evropa (1906; p118; pictured far right) on Wenceslas Square.

1

Cubist

In just one decade (1910–20), barely half a dozen architects bequeathed to Prague a unique legacy of buildings that were influenced by the Cubist art movement. The Cubist style spurned the regular lines of traditional architecture and the sinuous forms of art nouveau in favour of triangular and pyramidal forms, emphasising diagonals rather than horizontals and verticals and achieving a jagged, almost crystalline effect.

Some of Prague's finest Cubist houses can be seen in the neighbourhood below the Vyšehrad fortress. Another appealing example is the House of the Black Madonna (1912) in Staré Město, which houses the Museum of Czech Cubism (p103). Prague also boasts a Cubist lamp post (1915; p126; pictured right).

Clockwise from top left
1. Spanish Synagogue (p95) **2.** Municipal House (p96)
3. Grand Hotel Evropa (p118) **4.** Cubist lamp post (p126)

WESLEY ROBERTS / ALAMY / LONELY PLANET IMAGES ©

RICHARD NEBESKY / LONELY PLANET IMAGES ©

RICHARD NEBESKY / LONELY PLANET IMAGES ©

JOHN ELK III / LONELY PLANET IMAGES ©

Modern Prague

The early-modern mantra that 'form follows function' found a receptive audience among architects who came of age in the 1920s and '30s. **Functionalism** – similar to Germany's Bauhaus school – appealed to architects for its conscious rejection of superfluous ornamentation, such as with art nouveau, coupled with the use of high-quality building materials to add texture and color. Notable functionalist works in Prague include the Bat'a shoe store (1929; p131; pictured below right) on Wenceslas Square, Veletržní Palác (1928;) in Holešovice and Adolf Loos's Villa Müller (1930) in the suburb of Střešovice.

The **communist** style, which flourished from the 1950s through the 1980s, is typically derided these days for resulting in ugly, nondescript buildings, but some critics are starting to soften their views. It's not that the buildings are good, but at least they're bad in an interesting way. In the 1950s, architects were forced to design in the bombastic Stalinist, socialist realist style, such as the former Hotel International (now the Hotel Crowne Plaza; 1954) in Dejvice. The 1970s saw a communist version of Brutalism emerge, such as Prague's Kotva (p115) department store. The TV Tower (1987, pictured above right) in Žižkov dates from the end of the communist period. Its sheer scale dwarfs everything around.

Arguably the most interesting structure of the **post–Velvet Revolution period** is the so-called Dancing Building (1992–96; pictured far right) in Nové Město, designed by Czech-based Croatian architect Vlado Milunič and American Frank Gehry. The building's resemblance to a pair of dancers spurred the nickname 'Fred and Ginger', after the legendary dancing duo of Astaire and Rogers. Some of the best new architecture is going up in former industrial districts, such as Smíchov, Karlín and Holešovice, including the refurbishment of a former factory to create a space for the DOX Centre for Contemporary Art (p152), which opened in 2008.

Clockwise from top left
1. TV tower (p146) **2.** Dancing Building (p123)
3. Bat'a shoe store (p131)

1

3

BEST MODERN ARCHITECTURE IN PRAGUE

➡ **Villa Müller** (☎224 312 012; www.mullerovavila.cz; Nad Hradním Vodojemem 14, Střešovice; 🚊1, 2, 18 to Ořechovka)
➡ **Veletržní Palác** (p151)
➡ **Hotel Crowne Plaza** (p195)
➡ **TV Tower** (p146)
➡ **Dancing Building** (p123)

17
8306

Highlights of the Czech Republic

Many architectural movements that swept through Prague were felt in the countryside as well. Architectural splendours include the Gothic Karlštejn Castle, the breathtaking Renaissance castle at Český Krumlov and the wacky bone church in Kutná Hora.

Spa Architecture

1 The spa craze that enthralled Europe in the 19th and early 20th centuries gave the Czech Republic two of the continent's most beautiful spa resorts in Karlovy Vary (p222) and Mariánské Lázně (p229).

The bone church (p178) at Kutná Hora

2 The eerie 19th-century ossuary at Sedlec monastery, near Kutná Hora, defies easy architectural description – or any other type of description, for that matter.

Karlštejn Castle (p175)

3 Emperor Charles IV had this Gothic castle built in the mid-14th century to house the crown jewels. The spires were added in the 19th century. These days, it's the most popular destination for day-trippers outside of Prague.

Český Krumlov Castle (p205)

4 Arguably the country's number two castle after Prague, the soaring Renaissance tower, remodelled in the 16th century, dominates the charming riverside town below and is visible for miles around

Hluboka Castle (p203)

5 The 19th century was all about imitation in architecture. This folly, in neo-Gothic style, evolved from the vision of the Schwarzenberg family, who modelled their creation after Windsor Castle in the UK. .

Clockwise from top left
1. Colonnade, Mariánské Lázně **2.** Sedlec Ossuary, Kutná Hora **3.** Karlštejn Castle **4.** Český Krumlov Castle

RICHARD NEBESKY / LONELY PLANET IMAGES ©

2

JOHN ELK III / LONELY PLANET IMAGES ©

3

JOHN ELK III / LONELY PLANET IMAGES ©

Explore Prague & the Czech Republic

PRAGUE'S TOP SIGHTS

Neighbourhoods at a Glance

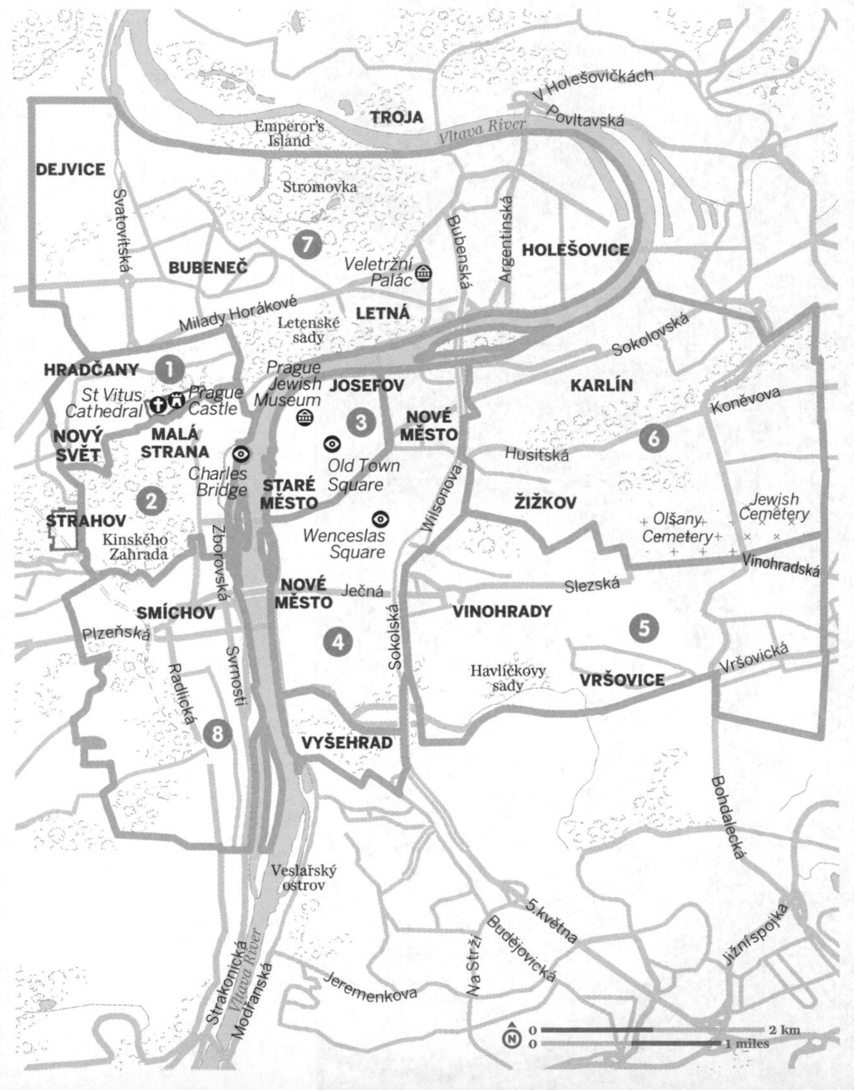

1 Prague Castle & Hradčany (p60)

The tourist hotspot of Prague Castle is perched on a hilltop above the Vltava River, with the attractive and peaceful residential area of Hradčany stretching westward to the Loreta and Strahov Monastery. Hradčany became a borough of Prague in 1598, after which the Habsburg nobility built many palaces here in the hope of cementing their influence with the rulers in the castle.

2 Malá Strana (p77)

Malá Strana (the 'Little Quarter') is a charming district of Renaissance palaces and gardens, with an idyllic riverside setting. It is home to the beautiful baroque Church of St Nicholas, the elegant Wallenstein Garden and museums of music and modern art, as well as many excellent restaurants and bars. Prague's scenic centrepiece, Charles Bridge, links Malá Strana to Staré Město on the far side of the river.

3 Staré Město (p91)

Staré Město – meaning 'Old Town' – is the historic heart of medieval Prague, centred on one of Europe's most spectacular town squares (Old Town Square, or Staroměstské náměstí). It is home to some of the city's most iconic sights, including the Old Town Hall Tower, the Astronomical Clock, the Municipal House and the Prague Jewish Museum. The maze of cobbled streets and narrow alleys leading away from Old Town Square is perfect for exploring.

4 Nové Město (p116)

The 'New Town' – new in the 14th century, that is – wraps around the Old Town, and finds a focus in the broad, historic boulevard of Wenceslas Square. Its sprawl of mostly 19th- and early 20th-century buildings encompasses important museums and galleries, impressive architecture and the city centre's main shopping streets.

5 Vinohrady & Vršovice (p132)

The name Vinohrady means 'vineyards' and refers to the vines that were cultivated here in centuries past. These days, the area is one of the city's most desirable residential neighbourhoods, known for its excellent restaurants and fashionable bars and cafes. Adjacent Vršovice, to the south, is not quite as sophisticated, though parts are slowly gentrifying.

6 Žižkov & Karlín (p142)

Žižkov has long had a reputation as a rough-and-ready, working-class neighbourhood full of left-wing revolutionary fervour. Today it is one of the city's liveliest districts, with more bars per capita than any other part of Prague, and home to two prominent, communist-vintage hilltop landmarks: the TV Tower and the National Monument. Karlín lies to the north of Žižkov, between Žižkov Hill and the Vltava River. It is undergoing massive redevelopment, but the older part of the district, along Křižíkova, is an up-and-coming area with lots of lovely old art-nouveau buildings.

7 Holešovice, Bubeneč & Dejvice (p149)

Holešovice, Bubeneč and Dejvice are contiguous neighbourhoods, running east to west, north of the Old Town across the Vltava River. They're mainly residential districts, but have their share of decent hotels and restaurants and two beautiful parks, Letná Gardens (Letenské sady) and Stromovka.

8 Smíchov & Vyšehrad (p164)

Smíchov, south of Malá Strana, is a former industrial area that has seen a recent boom in office and luxury hotel construction. The area has few sights but lots of pubs. Vyšehrad, south of Nové Město, is a leafy residential area, dominated by an ancient castle said to be where Prague was founded.

Prague Castle & Hradčany

Neighbourhood Top Five

1. Explore the historic palaces, churches and glorious gardens of **Prague Castle** (p62).
2. Soak up the stunning view from the summit of the **Great South Tower of St Vitus Cathedral** (p70).
3. Absorb the atmosphere of ancient wisdom at the **Strahov Library** (p71).
4. Admire the baroque beauty of the **Loreta** (p73).
5. Wander through the peaceful medieval backstreets of the **Nový Svět** (p74) district.

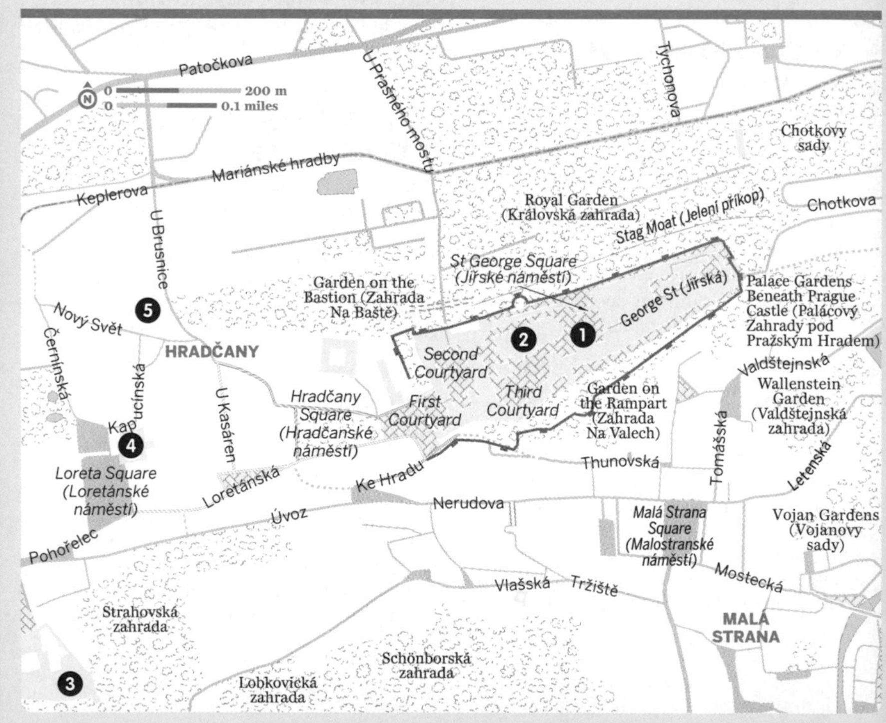

For more detail of this area, see Map p330

Explore: Prague Castle & Hradčany

Weirdly, this can be both the most crowded and the least crowded neighbourhood in the city. While Prague Castle is thronging with tourists, just a few blocks away you can find yourself alone in the cobbled backstreets of Nový Svět.

The castle is the big attraction, of course, but overcrowding can spoil the experience. To avoid the worst of the crowds, try to visit the castle early or late – before 10.30am or after 3.30pm – on a weekday if possible. Remember your ticket is valid for two consecutive days – better two quiet mornings than cramming it all into one crowded day.

We've organised this section starting with the castle's main entrance at the western end, then moving through the various courtyards and sights before exiting at the eastern end. You'll need at least two hours to see the main sights, and a full day if you want to visit everything.

Note that you can wander through the castle grounds and gardens without a ticket – this can be a magical experience on a summer evening, when the courtyards are almost deserted – but you'll need a ticket for all of the main historic buildings.

Local Life

➡ **Drinking Dens** This may be the most tourist-heavy district in Prague, but there are still some drinking dens that are favoured by locals, notably the cool cafe-bar U Zavěšenýho Kafe (p76), and the traditional beer hall called Pivnice U Černého Vola (p76).

➡ **Walking the Dog** Hradčany residents out for a stroll avoid the crowds by taking to the Stag Moat on the north side of the castle – you can walk in peace from the Powder Bridge east to Pod Bruskou, near Malostranská metro station.

Getting There & Away

➡ **Metro** The nearest metro station is Malostranská, but from here it's a stiff climb up the Old Castle Steps to the eastern end of the castle. Hradčanská station is about 10 minutes' walk north of the castle, but it's an easy, level walk to Hradčany and the castle.

➡ **Tram** Take line 22 from Národní třída on the southern edge of Staré Město, Malostranská náměstí in Malá Strana, or Malostranská metro station to the Pražský hrad stop. If you want to explore Hradčany first, stay on the tram until Pohořelec, the second stop after this one.

Lonely Planet's Top Tip

Prague Castle is perched on top of a steep hill – a sweaty climb in warm weather. To explore the neighbourhood without having to walk uphill, begin at the Pohořelec tram stop and wander via Strahov Monastery and the Loreta to the castle – all downhill. From the castle it's downhill through Malá Strana to Charles Bridge.

Best Places to Eat

➡ Lobkowicz Palace Café (p74)

➡ Villa Richter (p76)

➡ Malý Buddha (p76)

For reviews, see p74 ➡

Best Places to Drink

➡ U Zavěšenýho Kafe (p76)

➡ Klášterní pivovar Strahov (p76)

➡ Pivnice U Černého Vola (p76)

For reviews, see p76 

WITOLD SKRYPCZAK / LONELY PLANET IMAGES ©

TOP SIGHTS
PRAGUE CASTLE

Prague Castle – Pražský hrad, or just *hrad* to Czechs – is Prague's most popular attraction. Looming above the Vltava's left bank, its serried ranks of spires, palaces and towers dominate the city centre like a fairy-tale fortress. Within its walls lies a varied and fascinating collection of historic buildings, museums and galleries that are home to some of the Czech Republic's greatest artistic and cultural treasures.

The castle has always been the seat of Czech rulers as well as the official residence of the head of state. Its history begins in the 9th century, when Prince Bořivoj founded a fortified settlement here. It grew haphazardly as rulers made their own additions – there have been four major reconstructions, from that of Prince Soběslav in the 12th century to a classical facelift under Empress Maria Theresa (r 1740–80) – creating an eclectic mixture of architectural styles.

First Courtyard

The First Courtyard lies within the castle's **main gate** (Map p330) on Hradčany Square (Hradčanské náměstí), flanked by huge, baroque statues of battling Titans (1767–70) that dwarf the castle guards standing beneath them. After the fall of communism in 1989, then-president Václav Havel hired his old pal Theodor Pistek, the costume designer on the film *Amadeus* (1984), to replace their communist-era khaki uniforms with the stylish pale-blue kit they now wear, which harks back to the army of the first Czechoslovak Republic of 1918 to 1938.

DON'T MISS...

- Story of Prague Castle
- Lobkowicz Palace
- St Vitus Treasury
- Basilica of St George
- Golden Lane

PRACTICALITIES

- Pražský hrad
- Map p330
- ☎224 372 423
- www.hrad.cz
- Hradčanské náměstí
- ⏲grounds 5am-midnight Apr-Oct, 6am-11pm Nov-Mar; gardens 10am-6pm Apr & Oct, to 7pm May & Sep, to 9pm Jul & Aug, closed Nov-Mar; historic buildings 9am-6pm Apr-Oct, to 4pm Nov-Mar
- 🚋22, 23 to Pražský hrad

The **changing of the guard** takes place every hour on the hour, but the longest and most impressive display is at noon, when banners are exchanged while a brass band plays a fanfare from the windows of the **Plečnik Hall** (Plečnikova síň; Map p330), which overlooks the First Courtyard.

Second Courtyard

You pass through the Matthias Gate into the Second Courtyard, centred on a baroque fountain and a 17th-century well with lovely Renaissance latticework. On the right, the **Chapel of the Holy Cross** (kaple sv Kříže; 1763) houses the treasury of St Vitus Cathedral.

St Vitus Treasury

The 18th-century Chapel of the Holy Cross houses the **St Vitus Treasury** (Svatovítský poklad; Map p330; ☎224 372 442; www.kulturanahrade.cz; II. nádvoří, Pražský hrad; adult/concession/family 300/150/600Kč; ⏲10am-6pm; 🚊22), a spectacular collection of ecclesiastical bling that was founded by Charles IV in the 14th century. Gold and silver reliquaries crusted in diamonds, emeralds and rubies contain saintly relics ranging from fragments of the True Cross to the withered hand of a Holy Innocent. The oldest items include a reliquary arm of St Vitus dating from the early 10th century, while the most impressive treasures range from a gold coronation cross of Charles IV (1370) to a diamond-studded baroque monstrance of 1708.

Royal Garden

A gate on the northern side of Prague Castle leads to the **Powder Bridge** (Prašný most; 1540), which spans the Stag Moat and leads to the **Royal Garden** (Královská zahrada; ⏲10am-dusk Apr-Oct; 🚊22, 23), which started life as a Renaissance garden built by Ferdinand I in 1534. It is graced by several gorgeous Renaissance structures.

The most beautiful of the garden's buildings is the 1569 **Ball-Game House** (Míčovna; Map p330), a masterpiece of Renaissance sgraffito where the Habsburgs once played a primitive version of badminton. To the east is the **Summer Palace** (Letohrádek; Map p330), or Belvedere (1538–60), the most authentic Italian Renaissance building outside Italy, and to the west the 1695 former **Riding School** (Jízdárna; Map p330). All three are used as venues for temporary exhibitions of modern art.

Prague Castle Picture Gallery

The same Swedish army that looted the famous bronzes in the Wallenstein Garden (p83) in 1648 also nicked Rudolf II's art treasures. This **gallery**

THE STAG MOAT

A footpath on the west side of the Powder Bridge leads down into the Stag Moat (Jelení příkop), and doubles back through a modern (and rather Freudian) red-brick tunnel beneath the bridge. If you follow the path east along the moat you'll end up at a busy road that leads down to Malostranská metro station. A gate on the outer wall of the castle, overlooking the moat, leads to a nuclear shelter started by the communists in the 1950s but never completed; its tunnels run beneath most of the castle.

In the 1920s President Masaryk hired a Slovene architect, Jože Plečnik, to renovate the castle; his changes created some of its most memorable features and made the complex more tourist-friendly.

A WORLD RECORD

According to the *Guinness World Records*, Prague Castle is the largest ancient castle in the world – 570m long, an average of 128m wide and occupying 7.28 hectares.

PRAGUE CASTLE

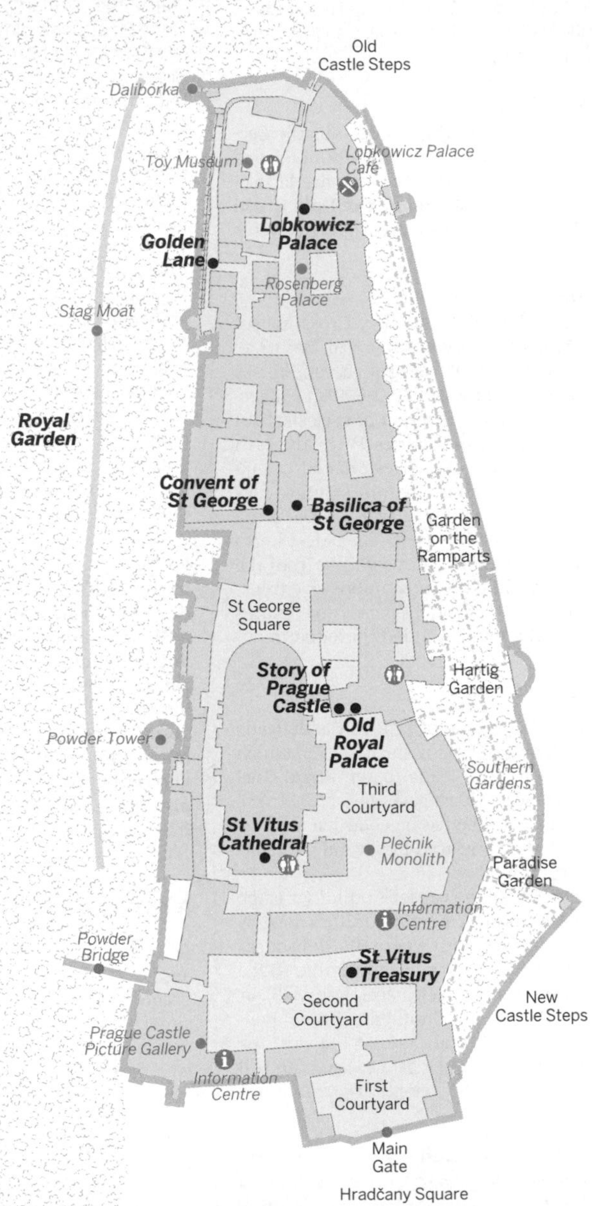

Changing of the guard, main gate, Prague Castle

(Map p330; adult/child 150/80Kč, 4-6pm Mon Apr-Oct admission free; ⌚9am-6pm Apr-Oct, to 4pm Nov-Mar) in the castle's beautiful Renaissance stables houses an exhibition of 16th- to 18th-century European art, based on the Habsburg collection that was begun in 1650 to replace the lost paintings; it includes works by Cranach, Holbein, Rubens, Tintoretto and Titian.

Third Courtyard

As you pass through the passage on the eastern side of the Second Courtyard, the huge western facade of St Vitus Cathedral soars directly above you; to its south (to the right as you enter) lies the Third Courtyard. At its entrance you'll see a 16m-tall **granite monolith** dedicated to the victims of WWI, designed by Jože Plečnik in 1928, and a copy of a 14th-century bronze figure of **St George** slaying the dragon; the original is on display in the Story of Prague Castle exhibition.

The courtyard is dominated by the southern facade of St Vitus Cathedral, with its grand centrepiece the Golden Gate (see p70).

Old Royal Palace

The **Old Royal Palace** (Starý královský Palác; Map p330; admission with Prague Castle tour ticket; ⌚9am-6pm Apr-Oct, to 4pm Nov-Mar) at the courtyard's eastern end is one of the oldest parts of the castle, dating from 1135. It was originally used only by Czech princesses, but from the 13th to the 16th centuries it was the king's own palace.

ROYAL CROWN OF BOHEMIA

The royal crown of Bohemia was created for Charles IV in 1346 using gold from the ducal coronet once worn by St Wenceslas. It is studded with 18 sapphires, 15 rubies, 25 emeralds and 20 pearls; some of the stones are 7cm to 10cm across and weigh 60 to 80 carats. The cross on top is said to contain a thorn from Christ's crown of thorns – it bears the inscription 'Hic est spina de corona Domini' (Here is a thorn from the Lord's crown). The crown, along with the rest of the crown jewels, is kept locked away in the Coronation Chamber above the Chapel of St Wenceslas in St Vitus Cathedral.

St George may be most familiar as the patron saint of England, but he was also an important royal saint in Bohemia. George's legendary slaying of the dragon came to represent the triumph of Christianity over paganism, a symbol eagerly adopted by devout monarchs, including Vratislav I, the founder of the Basilica of St George.

The **Vladislav Hall** (Vladislavský sál) is famous for its beautiful, late-Gothic vaulted ceiling (1493–1502) designed by Benedikt Rejt. Though over 500 years old, the flowing, interwoven lines of the vaults have an almost art-nouveau feel, in contrast to the rectilinear form of the Renaissance windows. The vast hall was used for banquets, councils and coronations, and for indoor jousting tournaments – hence the **Riders' Staircase** (Jezdecké schody) on the northern side, designed to admit a knight on horseback. All the presidents of the republic have been sworn in here.

A door in the hall's southwestern corner leads to the former offices of the **Bohemian Chancellery** (České kanceláře). On 23 May 1618, in the second room, Protestant nobles rebelling against the Bohemian Estates and the Habsburg emperor threw two of his councillors and their secretary out of the window. They survived, as their fall was broken by the dung-filled moat, but this Second Defenestration of Prague sparked off the Thirty Years' War.

At the eastern end of the Vladislav Hall, steps lead up to a balcony that overlooks **All Saints' Chapel** (kaple Všech svatých; Map p330); a door to the right leads to a terrace with great views of the city. To the right of the Riders' Staircase you'll spot an unusual Renaissance doorway framed by twisted columns, which leads to the **Diet** (Sněmovna), or Assembly Hall, which displays another beautifully vaulted ceiling and a case containing replicas of the **Bohemian crown jewels**.

Story of Prague Castle

Housed in the Gothic vaults beneath the Old Royal Palace, this huge and impressive **museum** (www.story-castle.cz; adult/child 140/70Kč, with tour tickets free; ⌚9am-6pm Apr-Oct, 9am-4pm Nov-Mar) ranks alongside the Lobkowicz Palace as one of the most interesting collections of artefacts in the castle. It traces 1000 years of the castle's history, from the building of the first wooden palisade to the present day, illustrated by models of the site at various stages in its development.

The exhibits include the grave of a 9th-century warrior discovered in the castle grounds, the helmet and chain mail worn by St Wenceslas, and a replica of the gold crown of St Wenceslas, which was made for Charles IV in 1346. Anyone with a serious interest in Prague Castle should visit here first as orientation.

St George Square

St George Square (Jiřské náměstí), the plaza to the east of St Vitus Cathedral, lies at the heart of the castle complex.

Basilica of St George

The striking, brick-red, early baroque facade that dominates the square conceals the Czech Republic's best-preserved Romanesque **basilica** (Bazilika Sv Jiří; Map p330; Jiřské náměstí; admission with Prague Castle tour ticket; ⌚9am-6pm Apr-Oct, to 4pm Nov-Mar), established in the 10th century by Vratislav I (the father of St Wenceslas). What you see today is mostly the result of restorations made between 1887 and 1908.

The austerity of the Romanesque nave is relieved by a baroque double staircase leading to the apse, where fragments of 12th-century frescoes survive. In front of the stairs lie the tombs of Prince Boleslav II (d 997; on the left) and Prince Vratislav I (d 921). The arch beneath the stairs allows a glimpse of the 12th-century crypt; Přemysl kings are buried here and in the nave.

Convent of St George

The very ordinary-looking building to the left of the basilica was Bohemia's first convent, established in 973 by Boleslav II. Closed and converted to an army barracks in 1782, it now houses a branch of the **National Gallery** (Klášter Sv Jiří; www.ngprague.cz; Jiřské náměstí 33; admission with Prague Castle long-tour ticket or adult/concession 150/80Kč; ⌚10am-6pm Tue-Sun), featuring a collection of 19th-century Bohemian art. Highlights include the art-nouveau sculpture of Josef Myslbek, Stanislav Sucharda and Bohumil Kafka; the glowing portraits by Josef Mánes; and the atmospheric forest landscapes by Július Mařák.

Powder Tower

A passage to the north of St Vitus Cathedral leads to the **Powder Tower** (Prašná Věž; Map p330; admission with Prague Castle long-tour ticket; ⌚9am-6pm Apr-Oct, to 4pm Nov-Mar), also called Mihulka, which was built in the 15th century as part of the castle's defences. Later it became the workshop of cannon- and bellmaker Tomáš Jaroš, who cast the bells for St Vitus Cathedral. Today it houses an exhibition on the history of the Castle Guard.

George Street & Around

George St (Jiřská) runs from the Basilica of St George to the castle's eastern gate.

Golden Lane

The picturesque alley known as **Golden Lane** (Zlatá ulička; admission with Prague Castle tour ticket; ⌚9am-6pm Apr-Oct, to 4pm Nov-Mar) runs along the northern wall of the castle. Its tiny, colourful cottages were built in the 16th century for the sharpshooters of the castle guard, but were later used by goldsmiths. In the 19th and early 20th centuries they were occupied by artists, including the writer Franz Kafka (who frequently visited his sister's house at No 22 from 1916 to 1917).

The cottages have been restored to show a variety of former uses. One is a goldsmith's workshop, another a tavern, and one the home of celebrated Prague fortune-teller Matylda Průšová, who died at the hands of the Gestapo during WWII; Kafka's sister's cottage is now a bookshop. The most evocative is No 12 at the far eastern end, the cosy former home of an amateur film historian who seems to have just popped out for lunch – archive footage of the castle is projected on the living-room wall.

Daliborka

This **tower** (Zlatá ulička; admission with Prague Castle tour ticket; ⌚9am-6pm Apr-Oct, to 4pm Nov-Mar) is named after the knight Dalibor of Kozojedy, imprisoned here in 1498 for supporting a peasant rebellion, and later executed. According to legend, he played a violin that could be heard throughout the castle; composer Bedřich Smetana based his 1868 opera *Dalibor* on the tale. You can peer into the bottle dungeon, and see a small display of torture instruments.

GARDEN ON THE RAMPARTS

At the castle's eastern gate, you can either descend the Old Castle Steps to Malostranská metro station or take a sharp right and wander back to Hradčany Square through the **Garden on the Ramparts** (Zahrada na valech; ⌚10am-6pm Apr & Oct, to 7pm May & Sep, to 9pm Jun & Jul, to 8pm Aug, closed Nov-Mar). The terrace garden offers superb views across the rooftops of Malá Strana and permits a peek into the back garden of the British embassy. Alternatively, you can descend to Malá Strana through the terraced Palace Gardens Beneath Prague Castle (p83).

Standing outside the Daliborka tower is the modern bronze sculpture *Parable with a Skull*, by Jaroslav Róna (who also created the Franz Kafka Monument in Josefov). Supposedly inspired by one of Kafka's characters, it shows a prostrate human figure bearing a giant skull on its back. (You may see homeless people in Prague begging in this traditional but submissive and rather despairing pose.)

Lobkowicz Palace

This 16th-century **palace** (Lobkovický Palác; www.lobkowicz.cz; Jiřská 3; adult/concession/family 275/200/690Kč; ⌚10.30am-6pm) houses a private museum known as the Princely Collections, which includes priceless paintings, furniture and musical memorabilia. You tour with an audio guide dictated by owner William Lobkowicz and his family – this personal connection really brings the displays to life, and makes the palace one of the castle's most interesting attractions.

Built in the 16th century, the palace has been home to the aristocratic Lobkowicz family for around 400 years. Confiscated by the Nazis in WWII, and again by the communists in 1948, the palace was finally returned in 2002 to William Lobkowicz, an American property developer and grandson of Maximilian, the 10th Prince Lobkowicz, who fled to the USA in 1939.

Highlights of the museum include paintings by Cranach, Breughel the Elder, Canaletto and Piranesi, original musical scores annotated by Mozart, Beethoven and Haydn (the 7th prince was a great patron of music – Beethoven dedicated three symphonies to him), and an impressive collection of musical instruments. But it's the personal touches that make an impression, such as the 16th-century portrait of a Lobkowicz ancestor wearing a ring that William's mother still wears today, and an old photo album with a picture of a favourite family dog smoking a pipe.

The palace has an excellent cafe (p74), and stages concerts of classical music at 1pm each day.

Rosenberg Palace

This Renaissance **palace** (Rožmberský palác; Jiřská 1; admission included with Prague Castle long-tour ticket; ⌚9am-6pm Apr-Oct, to 4pm Nov-Mar; 🚋22) once served as the 'Institute of Noblewomen' – effectively a home for aristocratic ladies fallen on hard times, founded by Empress Maria Theresa in 1755. The palace chapel soars three storeys high, decorated with trompe l'œil paintings and frescoes, and there's a recreation of a lady's bedchamber, complete with commode and elaborate period mousetrap!

Toy Museum

The second-largest **toy museum** (Muzeum Hraček; Jiřská 6; adult/concession/family 60/30/120Kč; ⌚9.30am-5.30pm; 🚋22) in the world houses an amazing collection, with some artefacts dating back to ancient Greece, but it can be a bit frustrating for the kids as most displays are hands-off. Toys range from model trains and teddy bears to Victorian dolls, Action Men and the definitive Barbie collection.

PRAGUE CASTLE TICKETS

There are two kinds of ticket (each valid for two days), which allow entry to different combinations of sights:

Long Tour (adult/child/family 350/175/700Kč) – includes St Vitus Cathedral, Old Royal Palace, Story of Prague Castle, Basilica of St George, Convent of St George, Powder Tower, Golden Lane and Daliborka, Prague Castle Picture Gallery, Powder Tower and Rosenberg Palace.

Short Tour (adult/child/family 250/125/500Kč) – includes St Vitus Cathedral, Old Royal Palace, Basilica of St George, Golden Lane and Daliborka.

You can buy tickets at either of two information centres in the **Second** and **Third Courtyards** (☎224 372 423, 224 372 419; www.hrad.cz; ⌚9am-6pm Apr-Oct, to 4pm Nov-Mar), or from ticket offices at the entrances to Golden Lane, the Old Royal Palace and the Story of Prague Castle exhibition.

TOP SIGHTS
ST VITUS CATHEDRAL

Built over a timespan of almost 600 years, St Vitus is one of the most impressive and richly endowed cathedrals in central Europe. It is pivotal to the religious and cultural life of Prague and the Czech Republic, housing treasures that range from the 14th-century Bohemian crown jewels to glowing art-nouveau stained glass, and the tombs of Bohemian saints and rulers from St Wenceslas and St John of Nepomuk to emperors Charles IV and Rudolf II.

The Nave

The foundation stone of the cathedral was laid in 1344 by Emperor Charles IV, on the site of a 10th-century Romanesque rotunda dedicated to St Wenceslas. The architect, Matthias of Arras, began work on the choir in the French Gothic style, but died eight years later. His German successor, Peter Parler – a veteran of Cologne's cathedral – built most of the eastern part, but it was only in 1861 that a concerted effort was made to complete the project – everything between the western door and the crossing was built during the late 19th and early 20th centuries. It was finally consecrated in 1929.

Inside, the **nave** is flooded with colour from **stained-glass windows** created by eminent Czech artists of the early 20th century – note the one by art-nouveau artist Alfons Mucha in the third chapel on the northern side (to the left as you enter), which depicts the lives of Sts Cyril and Methodius (1909). Nearby is a **wooden sculpture of the crucifixion** (1899) by František Bílek.

Walk up to the crossing, where the nave and transept meet, which is dominated by the huge and colourful **south**

DON'T MISS...

- Stained glass by Alfons Mucha
- South window
- Tomb of St John of Nepomuk
- Chapel of St Wenceslas
- Golden Gate

PRACTICALITIES

- Katedrála Sv Víta
- Map p330
- 257 531 622
- www.katedrala svatehovita.cz
- III. nádvoří, Pražský hrad
- admission incl in Prague Castle ticket
- 9am-6pm Mon-Sat & noon-5pm Sun Apr-Oct, 9am-4pm Mon-Sat & noon-4pm Sun Nov-Mar
- Malostranská

THE GOLDEN GATE

The cathedral's south entrance is known as the Golden Gate (Zlatá brána), an elegant, triple-arched Gothic porch designed by Peter Parler (best seen from the castle's Third Courtyard). Above it is a **mosaic of the Last Judgment** (1370–71) – on the left, the godly are raised into Heaven by angels; on the right, sinners are cast down into Hell by demons; and in the centre, Christ reigns in glory with saints Procopius, Sigismund, Vitus, Wenceslas, Ludmila and Adalbert below. Beneath them, on either side of the central arch, Charles IV and his wife kneel in prayer.

The cathedral crypt (no longer open to the public) contains marble sarcophagi with the remains of Czech rulers including Charles IV, Wenceslas IV, George of Poděbrady and Rudolf II.

CROWN JEWELS

On the southern side of the Chapel of St Wenceslas, a small door, sealed with seven locks, hides a staircase leading up to the Crown Chamber, where the Bohemian crown jewels are kept (not open to the public, but you can see replicas in the Old Royal Palace).

window (1938) by Max Švabinský, depicting the Last Judgment – note the fires of Hell burning brightly in the lower right-hand corner. In the north transept, beneath the baroque organ, are three carved wooden doors decorated with **reliefs of Bohemian saints**, with smaller panels beneath each saint depicting their martyrdom – look on the left-hand door for St Vitus being tortured in a cauldron of boiling oil. Next to him is the martyrdom of St Wenceslas; he is down on one knee, clinging to a lion's-head door handle, while his treacherous brother Boleslav drives a spear into his back. You can see that very door handle on the other side of the church, on the door to the Chapel of St Wenceslas.

The Ambulatory

The eastern end of the cathedral is capped with graceful late-Gothic vaulting dating from the 14th century. In the centre lies the ornate **Royal Mausoleum** (1571–89) with its cold marble effigies of Ferdinand I, his wife Anna Jagellonská and their son Maximilián II.

As you round the far end of the ambulatory you pass the **tomb of St Vitus** – as well as being a patron saint of Bohemia, Vitus is a patron of actors, entertainers and dancers. Further round is the spectacular, baroque silver **tomb of St John of Nepomuk**, its draped canopy supported by a squadron of silver angels (the tomb contains two tons of silver in all).

The nearby **Chapel of St Mary Magdalene** contains the grave slabs of cathedral architects Matthias of Arras and Peter Parler. Beyond is the ornate, late-Gothic **Royal Oratory**, a fancy balcony with ribbed vaulting carved to look like tree branches. The biggest and most beautiful of the cathedral's numerous side chapels is Parler's **Chapel of St Wenceslas**. Its walls are adorned with gilded panels containing polished slabs of semiprecious stones. Wall paintings from the early 16th century depict scenes from the life of the Czechs' patron saint, while even older frescoes show scenes from the life of Christ.

Great South Tower

The cathedral's **bell tower** (III. nádvoří, Pražský hrad; admission 100Kč; ⏲10am-7pm Apr-Oct, 10am-5pm Nov-Mar; 🚊22) was left unfinished in the 15th century; its soaring Gothic lines are capped by a Renaissance gallery added in the late 16th century, and a bulging spire that dates from the 1770s. You can climb the 297 steps to the top for excellent views; the entrance is in the castle's Third Courtyard (admission not included in castle tour ticket). You also get a close look at the clockworks, dating from 1597. The tower's **Sigismund Bell**, cast in 1549, is the largest bell in the Czech Republic.

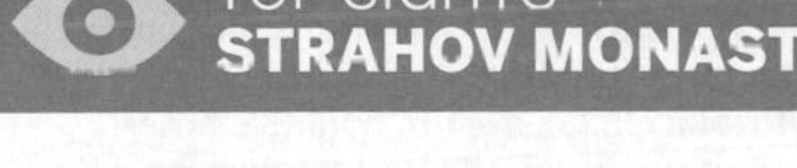

TOP SIGHTS
STRAHOV MONASTERY

In 1140 Vladislav II founded Strahov Monastery for the Premonstratensian order. The present monastery buildings, completed in the 17th and 18th centuries, functioned until the communist government closed them down and imprisoned most of the monks; they returned in 1990.

Inside the main gate is the **Church of St Roch** (Kostel sv Rocha), which was built in 1612 and is now an art gallery, and the **Church of the Assumption of Our Lady** (Kostel Nanebevzetí Panny Marie; Map p330), built in 1143 and heavily decorated in the 18th century in the baroque style; Mozart is said to have played the organ here.

Strahov Library

Strahov Library (Strahovská knihovna; Map p330; www.strahovskyklaster.cz; Strahovské nádvoří 1; adult/concession 80/50Kč; ⌚9am-noon & 1-5pm; 🚋22, 25) (pictured) is the largest monastic library in the country, with two magnificent baroque halls dating from the 17th and 18th centuries. You can peek through the doors but, sadly, you can't go into the halls themselves – it was found that fluctuations in humidity caused by visitors' breath was endangering the frescoes. There's also a display of historical curiosities.

The stunning interior of the two-storey-high **Philosophy Hall** (Filozofický sál; 1780–97) was built to fit around the carved and gilded floor-to-ceiling walnut shelving that was rescued from another monastery in South Bohemia (access to the upper gallery is via spiral staircases concealed in the corners). The feeling of height here is accentuated by a grandiose ceiling fresco, *Mankind's Quest for True Wisdom* – the figure of Divine Providence is enthroned in the centre amid a burst of golden light, while around the edges are figures ranging from Adam and Eve to the Greek philosophers.

DON'T MISS...

- Strahov Library
- Miniature Museum

PRACTICALITIES

- Strahovský klášter
- Map p330
- ☎224 511 137, 233 107 718
- www.strahovskyklaster.cz
- Strahovské nádvoří 1
- 🚋22, 25

EXIT TO PETŘÍN

The doorway at the eastern end of Strahov Monastery's main courtyard leads into the terraced orchards and parkland of Petřín, which enjoys some of the finest panoramas in Prague. A pleasant stroll leads southeast to the Petřín Lookout Tower (p86), with grand views over Malá Strana and the Vltava River to the spires of the Old Town, the TV Tower and the National Monument on Vítkov Hill.

Lying on a table in the corridor connecting Strahov Library's two baroque halls, beside the model ship and narwhal tusk, are two long, brown, leathery things. If you ask, the prudish attendant will tell you they're elephants' trunks, but they're actually preserved whales' penises.

TIME FOR A PINT...

The monks of Strahov were known not only for their academic prowess, but also for their ale – a brewery was built here in 1628. It closed in 1907 but was reopened in 2000, and now the Klášterní pivovar Strahov (p76) serves some of Prague's best beers to thirsty visitors.

The lobby outside the hall contains an 18th-century **Cabinet of Curiosities**, displaying the grotesquely shrivelled remains of sharks, skates, turtles and other sea creatures; these flayed and splayed corpses were prepared by sailors, who passed them off to credulous landlubbers as 'sea monsters'. Another case (beside the door to the corridor) contains historical items, including a miniature coffee service made for the Habsburg empress Marie Louise in 1813, which fits into four false books.

The corridor leads to the older but even more beautiful **Theology Hall** (Teologiský sál; 1679). The low, curved ceiling is thickly encrusted in ornate baroque stuccowork, and decorated with painted cartouches depicting the theme of 'True Wisdom', which was acquired, of course, through piety; one of the mottoes that adorns the ceiling is 'initio sapientiae timor domini' ('the beginning of wisdom is the fear of God').

On a stand outside the hall door is a facsimile of the library's most prized possession, the **Strahov Evangeliary**, a 9th-century codex in a gem-studded, 12th-century binding. A nearby bookcase houses the **Xyloteka** (1825), a set of booklike boxes, each one bound in the wood and bark of the tree it describes, with samples of leaves, roots, flowers and fruits inside.

Strahov Picture Gallery

In Strahov Monastery's second courtyard is the **Strahov Picture Gallery** (Strahovská Obrazárna; Map p330; www.strahovskyklaster.cz; Strahovské II.nádvoří; adult/child 60/30Kč; ⌚9am-noon & 12.30-5pm; 🚊22, 25), with a valuable collection of Gothic, baroque, rococo and romantic art on the 1st floor and temporary exhibits on the ground floor. Some of the medieval works are extraordinary – don't miss the very modern-looking 14th-century Jihlava Crucifix. You can also wander around the monastery's cloister, refectory and chapter house.

Miniature Museum

Siberian technician Anatoly Konyenko used to manufacture tools for microsurgery, but these days he prefers to spend 7½ years crafting a pair of golden horseshoes for a flea. This **museum** (Muzeum Miniatur; Map p330; Strahovské II.nádvoří; adult/child 70/50Kč; ⌚9am-5pm; 🚊22) displays his handiwork, which includes the Lord's Prayer inscribed on a single human hair, a grasshopper clutching a violin, and a camel caravan silhouetted in the eye of a needle. Weird but fascinating.

TOP SIGHTS
LORETA

The Loreta is a place of pilgrimage founded by Benigna Kateřina Lobkowicz in 1626, designed as a replica of the supposed Santa Casa (Sacred House; the home of the Virgin Mary) in the Holy Land. Legend says the original Santa Casa was carried by angels to the Italian town of Loreto as the Turks advanced on Nazareth.

Santa Casa

The duplicate Santa Casa is in a courtyard surrounded by cloistered arcades, churches and chapels. The interior is adorned with 17th-century frescoes and reliefs depicting the Virgin Mary's life, and an ornate silver altar with a wooden effigy of Our Lady of Loreto. Above the courtyard's entrance 27 bells play 'We Greet Thee a Thousand Times' on the hour.

Churches

Behind the Santa Casa is the **Church of the Nativity of Our Lord** (kostel Narození Páně), built in 1737. The interior includes skeletons of the Spanish saints Felicissima and Marcia.

At the corner of the courtyard is the unusual **Chapel of Our Lady of Sorrows** (kaple Panny Marie Bolestné), featuring a crucified bearded lady. She was St Starosta, pious daughter of a Portuguese king who promised her to the king of Sicily against her wishes. After a night of tearful prayers she awoke with a beard, the wedding was called off, and her father had her crucified. She was later made patron saint of the needy and the godforsaken.

Treasury

The church's treasury (1st floor) remains a bastion of religious bling centred on the 90cm-tall Prague Sun (Pražské slunce), made of solid silver and gold and studded with 6222 diamonds. Photography is not allowed unless you pay an extra 100Kč.

DON'T MISS...

- Santa Casa
- Treasury

PRACTICALITIES

- Map p330
- 220 516 740
- www.loreta.cz
- Loretánské náměstí 7
- adult/concession/family 130/100/270Kč
- 9am-12.15pm & 1-5pm Apr-Oct, to 4pm Nov-Mar
- 22

SIGHTS

PRAGUE CASTLE — CASTLE

See p62.

ST VITUS CATHEDRAL — CHURCH

See p69.

STRAHOV MONASTERY — MONASTERY

See p71.

LORETA — CHURCH

See p73.

BÍLEK VILLA — GALLERY

Map p330 (Bílkova Vila; ☎224 322 021; www.citygalleryprague.cz; Mickiewiczova 1; adult/child 120/60Kč; ⏰10am-6pm Tue-Sun; 🚋18, 22) This striking art-nouveau villa, designed by sculptor František Bílek in 1911, now houses a museum of his unconventional works. Bílek's distinctive sculptures, mostly in wood, take inspiration from his religious beliefs. Dramatic compositions such as *The Fall* show Adam and Eve cowering in fear of God's wrath, while *Wonderment* expresses the feeling of awe at God's presence.

Bílek's most famous work is a wooden relief of *The Crucifixion*, on display in St Vitus Cathedral – you can see a charcoal preliminary sketch of it among the artist's drawings in the 1st-floor gallery. The villa served not only as a studio but also as the artist's home, and there are several rooms with handmade art-nouveau furniture designed by Bílek, all rich in symbolism. Be sure to ask for an English text at the ticket desk – it will provide some much needed context.

NOVÝ SVĚT QUARTER — NEIGHBOURHOOD

Map p330 (🚋22, 23 to Brusnice) In the 16th century, houses were built for castle staff in an enclave of curving cobblestone streets down the slope north of the Loreta. Today, these diminutive cottages have been restored and painted in pastel shades, making the 'New World' quarter a perfect alternative to the castle's crowded Golden Lane. Danish astronomer Tycho Brahe once lived at Nový Svět 1.

ŠTERNBERG PALACE — GALLERY

Map p330 (Šternberský palác; ☎233 090 570; www.ngprague.cz; Hradčanské náměstí 15; adult/child 150/80Kč; ⏰10am-6pm Tue-Sun; 🚋22) The baroque Šternberg Palace is home to the National Gallery's collection of 14th- to 18th-century European art, including works by Goya and Rembrandt. Fans of medieval altarpieces will be in heaven; there are also several Rubens, some Rembrandts and Breughels, and a large collection of Bohemian miniatures.

Pride of the gallery is the glowing *Feast of the Rosary* by Albrecht Dürer, an artist better known for his engravings. Painted in Venice in 1505 as an altarpiece for the church of San Bartolomeo, it was brought to Prague by Rudolf II; in the background, beneath the tree on the right, is the figure of the artist himself. For a bit of grotesque, snot-nosed realism, it's worth a trip to the back of the 1st floor to see the 16th-century Dutch painting *The Tearful Bride*.

SCHWARZENBERG PALACE — GALLERY

Map p330 (Schwarzenberský palác; ☎224 810 758; www.ngprague.cz; Hradčanské náměstí 2; adult/child 150/80Kč; ⏰10am-6pm Tue-Sun; 🚋22) Sporting a beautifully preserved facade of black-and-white Renaissance sgraffito, the Schwarzenberg Palace houses the National Gallery's collection of baroque art. Sadly, a lot of the paintings are poorly lit and suffer from reflections from windows – a shame, as the inside of the palace is less impressive than the outside, and the collection is really only of interest to aficionados.

The ground floor is given over to two masters of baroque sculpture, Matthias Braun and Maximilian Brokof, whose overwrought figures appear to have been caught in a hurricane, such is the liveliness of their billowing robes. The highlights of the 1st floor are the moody 16th-century portraits by Petr Brandl and Jan Kupecký, while the top floor boasts a display of engravings by Albrecht Dürer.

EATING

Most of the restaurants in the castle district are aimed squarely at the tourist crowds, and the whole area becomes pretty quiet in the evenings after the castle closes. The following places, which are a cut above the usual tourist eateries regarding character and cuisine, are worth seeking out.

LOBKOWICZ PALACE CAFÉ — CAFE $$

Map p330 (☎233 312 925; Jiřská 3; mains 200-300Kč; ⏰10am-6pm; 📶👪; 🚋22) This cafe, housed in the 16th-century Lobkowicz Pal-

START **HRADČANSKÁ METRO STATION**

END **PETŘÍN**

DISTANCE **2.5KM**

DURATION **ONE HOUR**

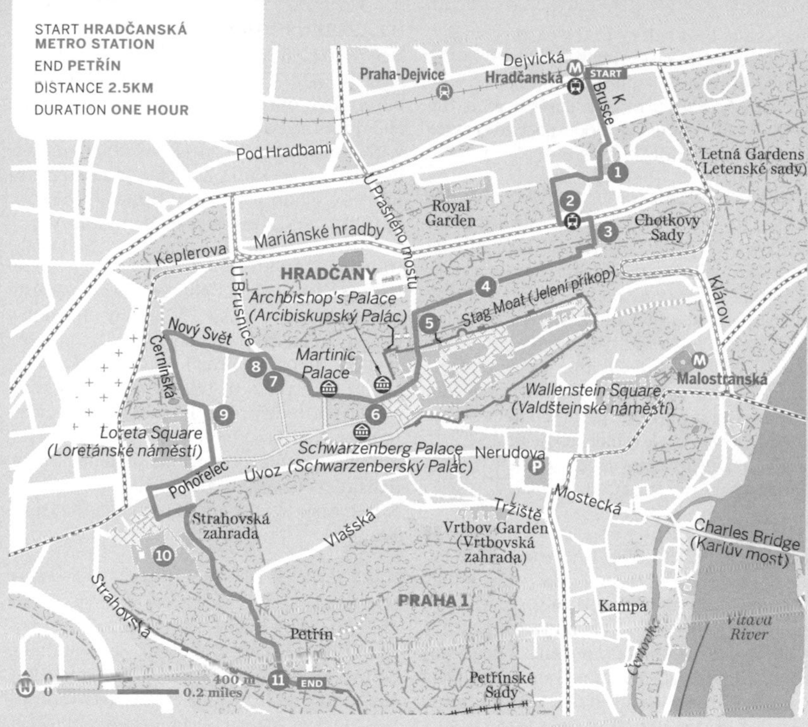

Neighbourhood Walk

Hradčany

From the metro station follow K Brusce towards the stone portal of the **1 Písek Gate**. This baroque gateway, decorated with carved military emblems, was built in 1721 as part of Prague's new fortifications; the streets on either side still follow the outlines of the bastions.

Turn right on U Písecké Brány, and then left onto Tychonova. Here you will pass two **2 Cubist houses** designed by Josef Gočár. Cross Mariánské Hradby and enter the Royal Garden (open April to October only) beside the beautiful, Renaissance **3 Summer Palace**.

Turn right, continue past the equally stunning **4 Ball-Game House**, and follow the upper rim of the Stag Moat to the western end of the gardens. Go through the gate and turn left to enter the Second Courtyard of Prague Castle via **5 Powder Bridge**.

Leave the courtyard via the first gate on the right, which leads into **6 Hradčany Square**, once the heart of the aristocratic quarter of Hradčany, and now watched over by a statue of Tomáš Garrigue Masaryk, the first president of Czechoslovakia. At the far end bear right on Kanovnická, past the pretty **7 Church of St John Nepomuk**, built in 1729 by the king of Prague baroque, Kilian Dientzenhofer.

Turn left into Nový Svět, a picturesque cluster of cottages once inhabited by court artisans. **8 No 1 Nový Svět** was the home of astronomer Tycho Brahe and, after 1600, his successor Johannes Kepler. Turn left on Černínská to the pretty square in front of the extravagantly baroque **9 Loreta**; opposite is the imposing facade of the Černín Palace, dating from 1692.

Turn right into Pohořelec – a little alley at No 9 leads into the courtyard of **10 Strahov Monastery**, where you can visit the library before going through the gate at the eastern end of the courtyard into the gardens above Malá Strana. Turn right on the footpath here (signposted 'Rozhledna & Bludiště') and finish with a pleasant stroll along to the **11 Petřín Lookout Tower**.

ace, is the best eatery in the castle complex by an imperial mile. Try to grab one of the tables on the balconies at the back – the view over Malá Strana is superb, as is the goulash. The coffee is good, too, and service is fast and friendly.

U ZLATÉ HRUŠKY CZECH $$$

Map p330 (☎220 941 244; www.restaurantuzlatehrusky.cz; Nový Svět 3; mains 450-700Kč; ⏰11am-1am; 🚊22, 25) 'At the Golden Pear' is a cosy, wood-panelled gourmets' corner, serving Bohemian fish, fowl and game dishes (tripe fricassee is a speciality) and frequented by locals and visiting dignitaries as well as tourists (the Czech foreign ministry is just up the road, and Margaret Thatcher once dined here). In summer get a table in its leafy *zahradní restaurace* (garden restaurant) across the street.

VILLA RICHTER CZECH, FRENCH $$

Map p330 (☎257 219 079; www.villarichter.cz; Staré zamecké schody 6; mains 150-300Kč, 3-course dinner 945Kč; ⏰11am-11pm; Ⓜ Malostranská) Housed in a restored 18th-century villa in the middle of a replanted medieval vineyard, this place is aimed squarely at the hordes of tourists thronging up and down the Old Castle Steps. But the setting is special – outdoor tables on terraces with one of the finest views in the city – and the menu of classic Czech dishes doesn't disappoint.

If you want something fancier, the Piano Nobile restaurant within the villa itself offers a French-influenced fine-dining menu.

MALÝ BUDDHA ASIAN $

Map p330 (☎220 513 894; www.malybuddha.cz; Úvoz 46; mains 140-250Kč; ⏰noon-10.30pm Tue-Sun; 🌱; 🚊22, 25) Candlelight, incense and a Buddhist shrine characterise this intimate, vaulted restaurant that tries to capture the atmosphere of an oriental tearoom. The menu is a mix of Asian influences, with authentic Thai, Chinese and Vietnamese dishes, many of them vegetarian, and a drinks list that includes ginseng wine, Chinese rose liqueur and all kinds of tea. Credit cards are not accepted.

DRINKING

This is a fairly quiet district, with drinking venues limited to laid-back cafes and a couple of traditional pubs.

U ZAVĚŠENÝHO KAFE BAR

Map p330 (☎605 294 595; Úvoz 6; ⏰11am-midnight; 📶; 🚊12, 20, 22) A superb drinking den barely five minutes' walk from the castle. Head for the back room, quirkily decorated with weird art and mechanical curiosities by local artist Kuba Krejci, and an ancient jukebox. Foaming Pilsner Urquell is 38Kč a half-litre, and the coffee is damn fine, too.

PIVNICE U ČERNÉHO VOLA PUB

Map p330 (☎220 513 481; Loretánské náměstí 1; ⏰10am-10pm; 🚊22, 25) Many religious people make a pilgrimage to the Loreta, but just across the road, the 'Black Ox' is a shrine that pulls in pilgrims of a different kind. This surprisingly inexpensive beer hall is visited by real-ale aficionados for its authentic atmosphere and lip-smackingly delicious draught beer, Velkopopovický Kozel, brewed in a small town southeast of Prague.

KLÁŠTERNÍ PIVOVAR STRAHOV BREWERY

Map p330 (Strahov Monastery Brewery; ☎233 353 155; www.klasterni-pivovar.cz; Strahovské nádvoří 301; ⏰10am-10pm; 🚊22, 25) Dominated by two polished copper brewing kettles, this convivial little pub serves up two varieties of its St Norbert beer – *tmavý* (dark), a rich, tarry brew with a creamy head, and *polotmavý* (amber), a full-bodied, hoppy lager, both 59Kč per 0.4L. There's also a strong (6.3% abv) IPA-style beer.

SHOPPING

ANTIQUE MUSIC INSTRUMENTS ANTIQUES

Map p330 (☎220 514 287; www.antiques.cz; Pohořelec 9; ⏰9am-6pm; 🚊22, 25) It may not get the prize for most inventive shop name, but this place is a real treasure-trove of vintage stringed instruments. You'll find an interesting stock of antique violins, violas and cellos dating from the 18th century to the mid-20th century, as well as bows, cases and other musical accessories.

In the same premises you'll find **Icons Gallery** (Map p330; ☎233 353 777; Pohořelec 9; ⏰9am-6pm; 🚊22, 25), a luminous collection of Russian and Eastern European religious icons, as well as lots of other decorative objets d'art, watches, porcelain and art-nouveau glassware.

Malá Strana

PRAGUE CASTLE TO CHARLES BRIDGE | NORTHERN MALÁ STRANA | SOUTHERN MALÁ STRANA | PETŘÍN

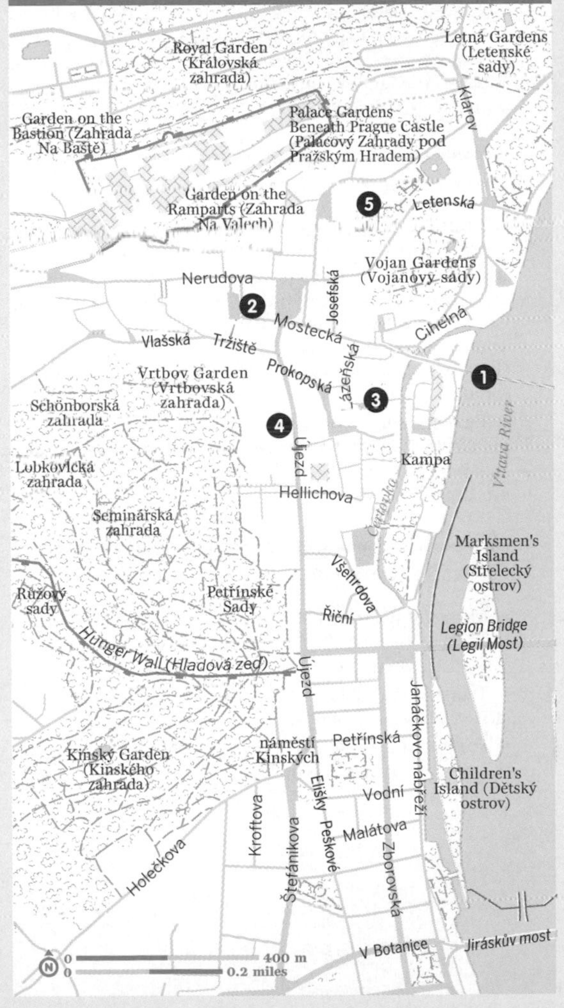

For more detail of this area, see Map p328

Neighbourhood Top Five

1 Experience the bustle and throng of **Charles Bridge** (p79), a crowded half-kilometre of baroque statues, busking jazz musicians, postcard sellers, caricature artists, snapshotting tourists and stunning views. Better still, experience the bridge at its most romantic, at dawn.

2 Gaze in wonder at the florid frescoes and *trompe l'oeuil* trickery that adorn the soaring vaults and domes of **St Nicholas Church** (p82).

3 Remember the repression of communist-era Prague with a visit to the **John Lennon Wall** (p83), where local youths once gathered in a spirit of rebellion.

4 Admire the faith and passion that has gone into creating the countless costumes that adorn the **Infant Jesus of Prague** (p85).

5 Escape from the crowds with a stroll among the aristocratic fripperies of the impressive – and unexpected – **Wallenstein Garden** (p83).

Lonely Planet's Top Tip

Charles Bridge is a victim of its own popularity – too often your experience of Prague's most beautiful location will be of squeezing through the crowds, trying to catch a glimpse of the view. If you want to experience the bridge at its most atmospheric, set your alarm clock for an early start. Try to arrive around dawn (check http://timeanddate.com for sunrise times), and enjoy a leisurely stroll across the bridge in perfect peace before returning to your hotel for breakfast.

Best Places to Eat

- Café Lounge (p87)
- Lichfield (p87)
- Cukrkávalimonáda (p87)
- U Malé Velryby (p87)
- Café de Paris (p89)

For reviews, see p87 ➡

Best Places to Drink

- Mlýnská Kavárna (p89)
- Klub Újezd (p89)
- Malostranská beseda (p90)
- U Malého Glena (p90)

For reviews, see p89 ➡

Explore: Malá Strana

Almost too picturesque for its own good, the baroque district of Malá Strana (Little Quarter) tumbles down the hillside between Prague Castle and the river. The focal point of the neighbourhood is Nerudova street, which links the castle to Malostranské náměstí, Malá Strana's main square, dominated by the soaring green dome of St Nicholas Church. To its north is a maze of palaces and gardens, home to government offices and foreign embassies; to the south are more parks and gardens straggling along the banks of the Vltava before merging into the more commercialised streets of Smíchov.

Once you get away from the crowded pavements of Nerudova and Mostecká – the main tourist route between the castle and Charles Bridge – there are cobbled backstreets to explore, with hidden historic gardens, quaint and colourful house signs perched above doorways, and countless little bars and cafes where you can while away an afternoon.

Local Life

- **Popular Hangouts** Picturesque it may be, but Malá Strana is also a place of work for many Praguers, filled as it is with government offices, embassies and consulates. Favourite hangouts for locals include Vojan Gardens (p88) and Kampa Park (p84), which are filled with lunch-hour loafers on sunny days, while Kafíčko (p90) and Mlýnská Kavárna (p89) are popular venues for after-work drinks.
- **Petřín** Summer or winter, Petřín (p86) is every bit as popular with local families as it is with tourists. Come the weekend, the hill's lookout tower and mirror maze are thronging with excited kids.

Getting There & Away

- **Metro** Malostranská metro station is in northern Malá Strana, about five minutes' walk from Malostranské náměstí.
- **Tram** Lines 12, 20 and 22 run along Újezd with stops at Hellichová and Malostranské náměstí.
- **Funicular** A funicular railway links Malá Strana with the summit of Petřín Hill.

TOP SIGHTS
CHARLES BRIDGE

Strolling across Charles Bridge is everybody's favourite Prague activity. However, by 9am it can be a 500m-long fairground, with an army of tourists squeezing through a gauntlet of hawkers and buskers beneath the impassive gaze of the baroque statues that line the parapets – try to visit early or late. In the crush, don't forget to look at the bridge itself (the bridge towers have great views) and the grand vistas up and down the river.

DON'T MISS...

- The view from the Old Town Bridge Tower
- St John of Nepomuk Statue
- Busking jazz musicians

PRACTICALITIES

- Karlův most
- Malostranské náměstí
- 🚋17, 18 to Karlovy lázně

History

In 1357 Charles IV commissioned Peter Parler (the architect of St Vitus Cathedral) to replace the 12th-century Judith Bridge, which had been washed away by floods in 1342. (You can see the only surviving arch of the Judith Bridge by taking a boat trip with Prague Venice (p30)).

The new bridge was completed in 1390, and took Charles' name only in the 19th century – before that it was known simply as Kamenný most (Stone Bridge). Despite occasional flood damage, it withstood wheeled traffic for 500-odd years – thanks, legend says, to eggs mixed into the mortar (though recent investigations have disproved this myth) – until it was made pedestrian-only after WWII.

The Bridge Towers

Perched at the eastern end of Charles Bridge, the elegant late-14th-century **Old Town Bridge Tower** (Staroměstská mostecká věž; Map p332; www.prazskeveze.cz; Charles Bridge; adult/child 75/55Kč; ⏲10am-11pm Apr-Sep, to 10pm Mar & Oct, to 8pm Nov-Feb; 🚋17, 18) was built not only as a fortification but also as a triumphal arch marking the entrance to the Old Town. Like the bridge itself, it was designed by Peter Parler and incorporates many symbolic elements. Here, at the end of the Thirty Years' War, an invading Swedish army was finally

CHARLES BRIDGE STATUES

Starting from the western (Malá Strana) end, with odd numbers on your left and even ones on your right, the statues that line the bridge are as follows:

➡ **1 Sts Cosmas & Damian** (1709) Third-century physician brothers.

➡ **2 St Wenceslas** (sv Václav; 1858) Patron saint of Bohemia.

➡ **3 St Vitus** (sv Víta; 1714) Patron saint of Prague.

➡ **4 Sts John of Matha & Félix de Valois** (1714) The 12th-century French founders of the Trinitarian order.

➡ **5 St Philip Benizi** (sv Benicius; 1714) Miracle worker and healer.

➡ **6 St Adalbert** (sv Vojtěch; 1709) Prague's first Czech bishop, canonised in the 10th century. Replica.

➡ **7 St Cajetan** (1709) Italian founder of the Theatine order.

➡ **8 The Vision of St Luitgard** (1710) In which Christ appears to the blind saint and allows her to kiss his wounds.

➡ **9 St Augustine** (1708) Reformed hedonist, theological fountainhead of the Reformation, and patron saint of brewers. Replica.

➡ **10 St Nicholas of Tolentino** (1706) Patron of Holy Souls. Replica.

➡ **11 St Jude Thaddaeus** (1708) Patron saint of hopeless causes.

➡ **12 St Vincent Ferrer** (1712) A 14th-century Spanish priest, shown with **St Procopius**, Hussite warrior-priest.

➡ **13 St Anthony of Padua** (1707) A disciple of St Francis of Assisi.

➡ **14 St Francis Seraphinus** (1855) Patron of the poor and abandoned.

➡ **15 St John of Nepomuk** (1683) Bronze. Patron saint of Czechs.

➡ **16 St Wenceslas as a boy** (c 1730) With his grandmother and guardian St Ludmilla, patroness of Bohemia.

➡ **17 St Wenceslas** (1853) With **St Sigismund**, son of Charles IV, and **St Norbert**, 12th-century German founder of the Premonstratensian order.

➡ **18 St Francis Borgia** (1710) A 16th-century Spanish priest.

➡ **19 St John the Baptist** (1857) By Josef Max.

➡ **20 St Christopher** (1857) Patron saint of travellers.

➡ **21 Sts Cyril & Methodius** (1938) These two introduced Christianity and a written script (Cyrillic) to the Slavs in the 9th century.

➡ **22 St Francis Xavier** (1711) A 16th-century Spanish missionary celebrated for his work in the Orient. Replica.

➡ **23 St Anne with Madonna & Child** (1707) St Anne is the mother of the Virgin Mary.

➡ **24 St Joseph** (1854) Husband of the Virgin Mary.

➡ **25 Crucifix** (1657) With an invocation in Hebrew saying 'holy, holy, holy Lord' (funded by the fine of a Jew who had mocked it in 1696).

➡ **26 Pietá** (1859) Mary holding the body of Christ following crucifixion.

➡ **27 Madonna with St Dominic** (1709) Spanish founder of the Dominicans, with **St Thomas Aquinas**. Replica.

➡ **28 Sts Barbara, Margaret & Elizabeth** (1707) St Barbara, patron saint of miners; St Margaret, patron saint of expectant mothers; and St Elizabeth, a Slovak princess who renounced the good life to serve the poor.

➡ **29 Madonna with St Bernard** (1709) Founder of the Cistercian order in the 12th century. Replica.

➡ **30 St Ivo of Kermartin** (1711) Patron saint of lawyers and orphans. Replica.

repulsed by a band of students and Jewish ghetto residents.

On the 1st floor there's a small exhibition and a video explaining the astronomical and astrological symbolism of Charles Bridge and the bridge tower, while the 2nd floor has a rather dull exhibit about Charles IV. The main justification for paying the admission fee, however, is the amazing view from the top of the tower.

There are actually two towers at the Malá Strana end of Charles Bridge. The lower one was originally part of the long-gone 12th-century Judith Bridge, while the taller one was built in the mid-15th century in imitation of the Staré Město tower. The taller **Malá Strana Bridge Tower** (Map p328; adult/child 50/30Kč; ⌚10am-6pm Apr-Nov) is open to the public and houses an exhibit on alchemists during the reign of Rudlof II, though like its Staré Město counterpart, the main attraction is the view from the top.

The Statues

The first monument erected on Charles Bridge was the crucifix near the eastern end, in 1657. The first statue – the Jesuits' 1683 tribute to St John of Nepomuk – inspired other Catholic orders, and over the next 30 years a score more went up, like ecclesiastical billboards. New ones were added in the mid-19th century, and one (plus replacements for some lost to floods) in the 20th. As most of the statues were carved from soft sandstone, several weathered originals have been replaced with copies. Some originals are housed in the Casements at Vyšehrad; others are in the Lapidárium in Holešovice.

The most famous figure is the monument to **St John of Nepomuk**. According to the legend on the base of the statue, Wenceslas IV had him trussed up in armour and thrown off the bridge in 1393 for refusing to divulge the queen's confessions (he was her priest), though the real reason had to do with the bitter conflict between church and state; the stars in his halo allegedly followed his corpse down the river. Tradition says that if you rub the bronze plaque, you will one day return to Prague. A bronze cross set in the parapet between statues 17 and 19 marks the point where he was thrown off.

BRADÁČ

At the Staré Město end of the bridge, look over the downstream parapet at the retaining wall on the right and you'll see a carved stone head known as Bradáč (Bearded Man). When the river level rose above this medieval marker, Praguers knew it was time to head for the hills. A blue line on the modern flood gauge nearby shows the level of the 2002 flood, no less than 2m above Bradáč!

Pickpocket gangs work the bridge day and night, so keep your purse or wallet safe.

FLOOD DAMAGE

Although the bridge has survived for more than 600 years, it was badly damaged in the floods of 1890 when three of the arches collapsed. You can see photographs of the damage and repair work in the Charles Bridge Museum (p107).

SIGHTS

Prague Castle to Charles Bridge

CHARLES BRIDGE BRIDGE
See p79.

NERUDOVA STREET
Map p328 (🚋12, 20, 22) Following the tourist crowds downhill from the castle via Ke Hradu, you soon arrive at Nerudova, architecturally the most important street in Malá Strana; most of its old Renaissance facades were 'baroquefied' in the 18th century. It's named after the Czech poet Jan Neruda (famous for his short stories, *Tales of Malá Strana*), who lived at the **House of the Two Suns** (dům U dvou slunců; Map p328; Nerudova 47) from 1845 to 1857.

The **House of the Golden Horseshoe** (dům U zlaté podkovy; Map p328; Nerudova 34) is named after the relief of St Wenceslas above the doorway – his horse was said to be shod with gold. From 1765 Josef of Bretfeld made his **Bretfeld Palace** (Map p328; Nerudova 33) a social hot spot, entertaining Mozart and Casanova. The baroque **Church of Our Lady of Unceasing Succour** (kostel Panny Marie ustavičné pomoci; Map p328; Nerudova 24) was a theatre from 1834 to 1837, and staged Czech plays during the Czech National Revival.

Most of the buildings bear house signs. Built in 1566, **St John of Nepomuk House** (Map p328; Nerudova 18) is adorned with the image of one of Bohemia's patron saints, while the **House at the Three Fiddles** (dům U tří houslíček; Map p328; Nerudova 12), a Gothic building rebuilt in Renaissance-style during the 17th century, once belonged to a family of violin makers.

FREE **MUSEUM MONTANELLI** GALLERY
Map p328 (☎257 531 220; www.muzeummontanelli.com; Nerudova 13; ⏲noon-6pm Tue-Sat, noon-4pm Sun; 🚋12, 20, 22) Tourists, drawn in by an attractive cafe, rub shoulders with connoisseurs of the Czech art world in this private gallery. Having rapidly become a focus for contemporary art in Prague, it provides a showcase for up-and-coming artists from Central and Eastern Europe, as well as staging exhibitions by more established international names.

TOP SIGHTS
ST NICHOLAS CHURCH

Malá Strana is dominated by the huge green cupola of St Nicholas Church, one of Central Europe's finest baroque buildings. It was begun by baroque architects Kristof and Kilian Dientzenhofer; Anselmo Lurago finished it in 1755.

On the ceiling, Johann Kracker's 1770 *Apotheosis of St Nicholas* is Europe's largest fresco (clever *trompe l'oeil* technique has made the painting merge almost seamlessly with the architecture). In the first chapel on the left is a mural by Karel Škréta, which includes the church official who kept track of the artist as he worked; he is looking out through a window in the upper corner.

Mozart himself tickled the ivories on the 2500-pipe organ in 1787, and was honoured with a requiem Mass here (14 December 1791). Take the stairs up to the gallery to see Škréta's gloomy 17th-century Passion Cycle paintings and the scratchings of bored 1820s tourists.

You can climb the church's **bell tower** (Map p328; adult/child 70/50Kč; ⏲10am-10pm Apr-Sep, to 8pm Mar & Oct, to 6pm Nov-Feb) via a separate entrance on the corner of Malostranské náměstí and Mostecká. During the communist era, the tower was used to spy on the nearby American embassy – on the way up you can still see a cast-iron urinal that was installed for the use of the watchers.

DON'T MISS...

- Ceiling frescoes
- 2500-pipe organ
- Gallery
- Bell Tower

PRACTICALITIES

- Kostel sv Mikuláše
- Map p328
- ☎257 534 215
- Malostranské náměstí 38
- adult/child 70/35Kč
- ⏲9am-5pm Mar-Oct, to 4pm Nov-Feb
- 🚋12, 20, 22

TOP SIGHTS
JOHN LENNON WALL

After his murder on 8 December 1980, John Lennon became a pacifist hero for many young Czechs. An **image of Lennon** was painted on a wall in a secluded square opposite the French Embassy (there is a niche on the wall that looks like a tombstone), along with political graffiti and Beatles lyrics. Despite repeated coats of whitewash, the secret police never managed to keep it clean for long, and the Lennon Wall became a political focus for Prague youth (most Western pop music was banned by the communists, and some Czech musicians were even jailed for playing it).

Post-1989 weathering and lightweight graffiti ate away at the political messages and images, until little remained of Lennon but his eyes, but visiting tourists began making their own contributions. The wall is the property of the Knights of Malta, and they have repainted it several times, but it soon gets covered with more Lennon images, peace messages and inconsequential tourist graffiti. In recent years the Knights have bowed to the inevitable and now don't bother to whitewash it any more.

DON'T MISS...

- Try to spot the image of Lennon among the myriad graffiti

PRACTICALITIES

- Map p328
- Velkopřevorské náměstí
- 🚋12, 20, 22

MALOSTRANSKÉ NÁMĚSTÍ SQUARE

Map p328 (🚋12, 20, 22) Malostranské náměstí, Malá Strana's main square, is divided into an upper and lower part by St Nicholas Church, the district's most distinctive landmark. The square has been the hub of Malá Strana since the 10th century, though it lost some of its character when Karmelitská street was widened early in the 20th century, and a little more when Prague's first Starbucks opened here in 2008.

Today, it's a mixture of official buildings and touristy restaurants, with a tram line through the middle of the lower square. The nightclub and bar at No 21, Malostranská beseda (p90), was once the old town hall. Here in 1575 non-Catholic nobles wrote the so-called České Konfese (Czech Confession), a pioneering demand for religious tolerance addressed to the Habsburg emperor that was eventually passed into Czech law by Rudolf II in 1609. On 22 May 1618 Czech nobles gathered at the **Smiřický Palace** (Map p328; Malostranské náměstí 18) to plot a rebellion against the Habsburg rulers – the next day they flung two Habsburg councillors out of a window in Prague Castle.

Northern Malá Strana

PALACE GARDENS BENEATH PRAGUE CASTLE GARDENS

Map p330 (Palácové zahrady pod Pražským hradem; ☎257 010 401; www.palacove zahrady.cz; Valdštejnská 12-14; adult/child 80/50Kč; ⏰10am-9pm Jun & Jul, to 8pm Aug, to 7pm May & Sep, to 6pm Apr & Oct; 🚋12, 20, 22) These beautiful, terraced gardens on the steep southern slopes below the castle date from the 17th and 18th centuries, when they were created for the owners of the adjoining palaces. They were restored in the 1990s and contain a Renaissance loggia with frescoes of Pompeii and a baroque portal with sundial that cleverly catches the sunlight reflected off the water in a triton fountain.

There are two entrances: one on Valdštejnská street next to the Palffy Palace Restaurant, and one at the top of the hill in the Garden on the Ramparts at Prague Castle.

FREE **WALLENSTEIN GARDEN** GARDENS

Map p328 (Valdštejnská zahrada; Letenská 10; ⏰7.30am-6pm Mon-Fri, 10am-6pm Sat & Sun Mar-Oct; Ⓜ Malostranská) This huge, walled garden is an oasis of peace amid the bustle of Malá Strana's streets. Its finest feature is the huge **loggia** decorated with scenes from the Trojan Wars, flanked to one side by an aviary with a pair of Eagle Owls, and an enormous fake **stalactite grotto** – see how many hidden animals and grotesque faces you can spot.

The **bronze statues** of Greek gods lining the avenue opposite the loggia are copies – the originals were carted away by marauding Swedes in 1648 and now stand outside the royal palace of Drottningholm near Stockholm. At the eastern end of the garden is an **ornamental pond**, home to some seriously large carp, and the **Wallenstein Riding School** (Valdštejnská jízdárna; Map p328; ☎257 073 136; www.ngprague.cz; Valdštejnská 3; adult/child 150/70Kč; ⊙10am-6pm Tue-Sun), which hosts changing exhibitions of modern art. Enter the garden on Letenská (beside Malostranská metro station) or via the Wallenstein Palace.

FREE WALLENSTEIN PALACE — PALACE

Map p328 (Valdštejnský palác; ☎257 071 111; Valdštejnské náměstí 4; ⊙10am-5pm Sat & Sun Apr-Oct, to 4pm Sat & Sun Nov-Mar; 🚋12, 20, 22) Valdštejnské náměstí, a small square northeast of Malostranské náměstí, is dominated by the monumental 1630 palace of **Albrecht of Wallenstein**, general of the Habsburg armies, who financed its construction with properties confiscated from Protestant nobles he defeated at the Battle of Bílá Hora in 1620. It now houses the Senate of the Czech Republic, but you can visit some rooms on weekends.

The ceiling fresco in the **Baroque Hall** shows Wallenstein as a warrior at the reins of a chariot, while the unusual oval **Audience Hall** has a fresco of Vulcan at work in his forge.

FRANZ KAFKA MUSEUM — MUSEUM

Map p328 (Muzeum Franzy Kafky; ☎257 535 373; www.kafkamuseum.cz; Cihelná 2b; adult/child 180/120Kč; ⊙10am-6pm Apr-Oct, to 5pm Mon-Thu & to 6pm Fri-Sun Nov-Mar; 🚋12, 20, 22) This much-hyped exhibition on the life and work of Prague's most famous literary son, entitled 'City of K', explores the intimate relationship between the writer and the city that shaped him, through the use of original letters, photographs, quotations, period newspapers and publications, and video and sound installations.

Does it vividly portray the claustrophobic bureaucracy and atmosphere of brooding menace that characterised Kafka's world? Or is it a load of pretentious bollocks? You decide.

PROUDY (DAVID ČERNÝ SCULPTURE) — ART

Map p328 (Streams; Hergetova Cihelná; Ⓜ Malostranská) Cries of disbelief, laughter and raised cameras greet *Proudy* (Streams; 2004) by David Černý, a saucy animatronic sculpture of two guys pissing in a puddle shaped like the Czech Republic. The microchip-controlled sculptures are writing out famous quotations from Czech literature with their 'pee'.

KGB MUSEUM — MUSEUM

Map p328 (☎272 048 047; Vlašska 13; admission 180Kč; ⊙9am-8pm; 🚋12, 20, 22) The enthusiastic Russian collector of KGB memorabilia who established this small museum will show you around his treasure trove of genuine spy cameras, concealed pistols, weapons (including an original garotte, known as 'Stalin's scarf') and sinister electrical 'interrogation equipment' (read: torture). There are also rare photographs of Prague taken in 1968 by a KGB officer, with ordinary citizens strangely absent from the street scenes.

MALTESE SQUARE — SQUARE

Map p328 (Maltézské náměstí; 🚋12, 20, 22, 23 to Malostranské náměstí) References to the Knights of Malta around Malá Strana hark back to 1169, when that military order established a monastery in the Church of Our Lady Beneath the Chain on this square. Disbanded by the communists, the Knights have regained much property under post-1989 restitution laws, including the Lennon Wall.

Southern Malá Strana

KAMPA — PARK

Map p328 (🚋12, 20, 22) Kampa – an 'island' created by Čertovka (the Devil's Stream) – is the most peaceful and picturesque part of Malá Strana. It was once farmland (the name Kampa comes from *campus,* Latin for 'field'), but in the 13th century Prague's first mill, the **Sovovský mlýn** (now Kampa Museum), was built here, and other mills followed.

The north part of the island was settled in the 16th century after being raised above flood level. (In 1939 the river was so low that it was again joined to the mainland, and coins and jewellery were found in the dry channel.) The houses are clustered around a picturesque little square called **Na Kampě**; at its northern end, at about waist height on the wall to the left of the little gallery under the stairs leading up to Charles Bridge, is a small **memorial plaque** that reads *Výska vody 4.žáří 1890* (height of waters, 4 September 1890), marking the level reached by the floodwaters of 1890. Directly above it – above head height – is another marking the height of the 2002 floods.

The area where the Čertovka passes under Charles Bridge is sometimes called **Prague's Venice** – the channel is often crowded with dinky tour boats.

KAMPA MUSEUM GALLERY

Map p328 (Muzeum Kampa; ☎257 286 147; www.museumkampa.cz; U Sovových Mlýnů 2; adult/concession 220/110Kč; ⊙10am-6pm; 🚋12, 20, 22) Housed in a renovated mill building, this gallery is devoted to 20th-century and contemporary art from Central Europe. The highlights of the permanent exhibition are extensive collections of bronzes by Cubist sculptor Otto Gutfreund and paintings by František Kupka, a pioneer of abstract art.

The most impressive canvas is Kupka's *Cathedral,* a pleated mass of blue and red diagonals suggesting a curtain with a glimpse of darkness beyond. Outside the museum you can get a close-up look at one of David Černý's famous crawling babies (the ones that swarm over the TV Tower in Žižkov).

CZECH MUSEUM OF MUSIC MUSEUM

Map p328 (České muzeum hudby; ☎257 257 777; www.nm.cz; Karmelitská 2/4; adult/concession 120/60Kč; ⊙1-6pm Mon, 10am-8pm Wed, 9am-6pm Fri, 10am-6pm Thu, Sat & Sun; 🚋12, 20, 22) A 17th-century baroque monastery building with an impressive central atrium makes a beautiful setting for Prague's Museum of Music. The museum's permanent exhibition, entitled 'Man-Instrument-Music', explores the relationship between human beings and musical instruments through the ages, and showcases an incredible collection of violins, guitars, lutes, trumpets, flutes and harmonicas.

TOP SIGHTS
MUSEUM OF THE INFANT JESUS

The **Church of Our Lady Victorious** (kostel Panny Marie Vítězné), built in 1613, has on its central altar a 47cm-tall waxwork figure of the baby Jesus, brought from Spain in 1628. Known as the **Infant Jesus of Prague** (Pražské Jezulátko), it is said to have protected Prague from the plague and from the destruction of the Thirty Years' War. An 18th-century German prior, ES Stephano, wrote about the miracles, kicking off what eventually became a worldwide cult; today the statue is visited by a steady stream of pilgrims, especially from Italy, Spain and Latin America. It was traditional to dress the figure in beautiful robes, and over the years various benefactors donated richly embroidered dresses. Today the Infant's wardrobe consists of more than 70 costumes donated from all over the world; these are changed regularly in accordance with a religious calendar.

At the back of the church is the **museum**, displaying a selection of the frocks used to dress the Infant; shops in the street nearby sell copies of the wax figure. Looking at all this, you can't help thinking about the Second Commandment ('Thou shalt not make unto thee any graven image...') and the objectives of the Reformation. Jan Hus must be spinning in his grave.

DON'T MISS...

- Wax figure of the Infant Jesus of Prague
- Clothing worn by the Infant Jesus

PRACTICALITIES

- Muzeum Pražského Jezulátka
- Map p328
- ☎257 533 646
- www.pragjesu.info
- Karmelitská 9
- ⊙church 8.30am-7pm Mon-Sat, to 8pm Sun; museum 9.30am-5.30pm Mon-Sat & 1-6pm Sun, closed 1 Jan, 25 & 26 Dec & Easter Mon
- 🚋12, 20, 22

Highlights include a grand piano once played by Mozart in 1787, and the Rožmberk Court Ensemble of 16th-century woodwind instruments. The exhibits are brought to life by recordings of music played using the actual instruments on display.

VRTBOV GARDEN GARDENS

Map p328 (Vrtbovská zahrada; ☎257 531 480; www.vrtbovska.cz; Karmelitská 25; adult/concession 60/50Kč; ⏲10am-6pm Apr-Oct; 🚋12, 20, 22) This 'secret garden', hidden along an alley at the corner of Tržiště and Karmelitská, was built in 1720 for the Earl of Vrtba, the senior chancellor of Prague Castle. It's a formal baroque garden, climbing steeply up the hillside to a terrace graced with baroque statues of Roman mythological figures by Matthias Braun – see if you can spot Vulcan, Diana and Mars.

Below the terrace (on the right, looking down) is a tiny studio once used by Czech painter Mikuláš Aleš, and above is a little lookout with good views of Prague Castle and Malá Strana.

QUO VADIS (DAVID ČERNÝ SCULPTURE) MONUMENT

Map p328 (Where Are You Going; Vlašská 19; 🚋12, 20, 22) Not strictly a public monument, this golden Trabant car on four legs is a David Černý tribute to 4000 East Germans who occupied the garden of the then West German embassy in 1989, before being granted political asylum and leaving their Trabants behind. Today's German embassy is happy for you to peer through its back fence at the sculpture.

Head uphill along Vlašská, turn left into a children's park, and left again to find it.

FREE **CHILDREN'S ISLAND** PARK

Map p328 (Dětský ostrov; access from Nábřežní; ⏲24hr; 👪; Ⓜ Anděl) Prague's smallest island offers a leafy respite from the hustle and bustle of the city, with a selection of swings, slides, climbing frames and sandpits to keep the kids busy, as well as a rope swing, skateboard ramp, mini football pitch, netball court, and lots of open space for older siblings to run wild.

There are plenty of benches to take the strain off weary parental legs, and a decent bar and restaurant at the southern end.

Petřín

This 318m-high hill is one of Prague's largest green spaces. It's great for quiet, tree-shaded walks and fine views over the 'City of a Hundred Spires'. There were once vineyards here, and a quarry that provided the stone for most of Prague's Romanesque and Gothic buildings.

Petřín is easily accessible on foot from Strahov Monastery, or you can ride the **funicular railway** *(lanová draha)* from Újezd up to the top. You can also get off two-thirds of the way up at Nebozízek.

In the peaceful **Kinský Garden** (Kinského zahrada), on the southern side of Petřín, is the 18th-century wooden **Church of St Michael** (kostel sv Michala), transferred here, log by log, from the village of Medveďov in Ukraine. Such structures are rare in Bohemia, though still common in Ukraine and northeastern Slovakia.

PETŘÍN LOOKOUT TOWER VIEWPOINT

Map p328 (Petřínská rozhledna; ☎257 320 112; adult/child 105/55Kč; ⏲10am-10pm Apr-Sep, to 8pm Mar & Oct, to 6pm Nov-Feb; 🚋funicular railway) The summit of Petřín is topped off with a 62m-tall Eiffel Tower lookalike built in 1891 for the Prague Exposition. You can climb its 299 steps for some of the best views in Prague – on clear days you can see the forests of Central Bohemia to the southwest. (There's also a lift.) On the way to the tower you cross the **Hunger Wall** (Hladová zeď), running from Újezd to Strahov. These fortifications were built in 1362 under Charles IV, and are so named because they were built by the poor of the city in return for food – an early job-creation scheme.

PETŘÍN FUNICULAR RAILWAY RAILWAY

Map p328 (Lanová draha na Petřín; ☎800 19 18 17; www.dpp.cz; Újezd; adult/child 24/12Kč; ⏲9am-11.30pm Apr-Oct, 9am-11.20pm Nov-Mar; 🚋12, 20, 22) First opened in 1891, Prague's little funicular railway now uses modern coaches that trundle back and forth on 510m of track, saving visitors a climb up Petřín hill. It runs every 10 minutes (every 15 minutes November to March) from Újezd to the Petřín Lookout Tower, with a stop at Nebozízek. Ordinary public transport tickets, valid on tram and metro, are valid on the funicular, too.

MIRROR MAZE HISTORIC BUILDING

Map p328 (Zrcadlové bludiště; adult/child 75/55Kč; ⏲10am-10pm Apr-Sep, 10am-8pm Mar & Oct, 10am-6pm Nov-Feb; funicular railway) Below the Petřín Lookout Tower is the Mirror Maze, also built for the 1891 Prague Exposition. As well as the maze of distorting mirrors, which was based on the Prater in Vienna, there's a diorama of the 1648 battle between Praguers and Swedes on Charles Bridge.

Opposite is the **Church of St Lawrence** (kostel sv Vavřince), which contains a ceiling fresco depicting the founding of the church in 991 at a pagan site with a sacred flame.

MUSAION MUSEUM

Map p328 (Ethnographical Museum; ☎257 214 806; Kinského zahrada 98; adult/child 70/40Kč; ⏲10am-6pm Tue-Sun; 6, 9, 12, 20) This renovated summer palace houses the National Museum's ethnographic collection, with exhibits covering traditional Czech folk culture and art, including music, costume, farming methods and handicrafts. There are regular folk concerts and workshops demonstrating traditional crafts such as blacksmithing and woodcarving; in the summer months there's a garden cafe.

MEMORIAL TO THE VICTIMS OF COMMUNISM MONUMENT

Map p328 (Památník obětem komunismu; cnr Újezd & Vítězná; 6, 9, 12, 20, 22) This striking sculptural group consists of several ragged human figures (controversially, all are male) in progressive stages of disintegration, descending a staggered slope. A bronze strip in the ground in front of them records the terrible human toll of the communist era – 205,486 arrested; 170,938 driven into exile; 248 executed; 4500 who died in prison; and 327 shot while trying to escape across the border.

EATING

You'll be spoilt for choice looking for somewhere to eat in Malá Strana. The tourist crowds are swelled by hungry office workers from the district's many embassies and government offices, and this well-heeled clientele ensures that there are lots of quality restaurants offering a wide range of cuisines. Many of the best restaurants take advantage of a riverside location, or are perched on a hillside with a view over the city.

CAFÉ LOUNGE CAFE €

Map p328 (☎257 404 020; www.cafe-lounge.cz; Plaská 8; mains 100-300Kč; ⏲7.30am-10pm Mon-Fri, 9am-1pm Sat, 9am-5pm Sun; 6, 9, 12, 20, 22) Cosy and welcoming, Café Lounge sports an art-deco atmosphere, superb coffee, exquisite pastries, and an extensive wine list. The all-day cafe menu offers freshly made salads and corn-bread sandwiches, while lunch and dinner extends to dishes such as venison goulash or roast pike-perch with caraway seeds. Great breaksfasts too (served till 11am weekdays, till noon weekends).

LICHFIELD INTERNATIONAL €€

Map p328 (☎266 112 284; www.theaugustine.com; Letenská 12; mains 270-460Kč; ⏲11am-11pm; 12, 20, 22) Named after society photographer Lord Lichfield, whose images of celebrities adorn the walls, this stylish yet relaxed restaurant is worth seeking (it's hidden away in the Augustine Hotel). The menu ranges from down-to-earth but delicious dishes such as ox cheeks braised in the restaurant's own St Thomas beer, to top-end favourites such as grilled lobster, fresh oysters and caviar.

CUKRKÁVALIMONÁDA INTERNATIONAL €

Map p328 (☎257 225 396; www.cukrkavalimonada.com; Lázeňská 7; mains 100-180Kč; ⏲9am-7pm; 12, 20, 22) A cute little cafe-cum-restaurant that combines minimalist modern styling with Renaissance-era painted timber roof-beams, CKL offers fresh, home-made pastas, frittatas, ciabattas, salads and pancakes (sweet and savoury) by day and a slightly more sophisticated bistro menu in the early evening. There's also a good breakfast menu offering ham and eggs, croissants, and yoghurt, and the hot chocolate is to die for.

Since you ask, the name means 'sugar, coffee, lemonade' – the phrase is the Czech equivalent of 'eeny-meeny-miny-moe'.

U MALÉ VELRYBY SEAFOOD €€

Map p328 (☎257 214 703; www.umalevelryby.cz; Maltézské náměstí 15; mains 300-400Kč; ⏲noon-3pm & 6-11pm; 12, 20, 22) 'The Little Whale' is a tiny place – only eight tables – run by chef-proprietor Jason from Cork, Ireland, who gets fresh seafood flown in daily from French markets. The seafood chowder is tasty and filling, the honey-glazed lamb shank with lemon and thyme is meltingly tender, and the tapas exceedingly more-ish. Make sure Jason himself is in the kitchen to be sure of a top-quality dinner.

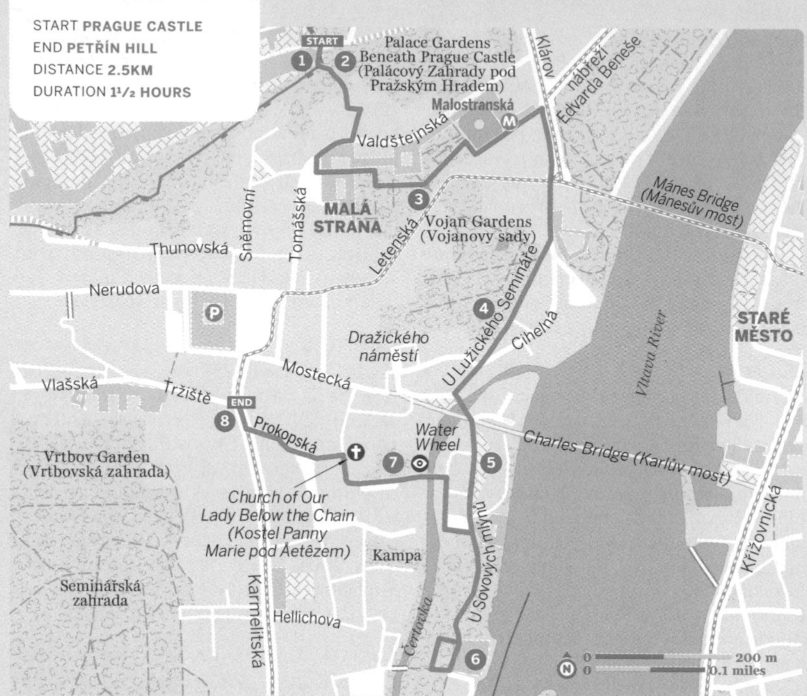

Neighbourhood Walk

Malá Strana Gardens

From the ❶ **Lookout** at the eastern entrance to Prague Castle, go into the Garden on the Ramparts and find the entrance to the ❷ **Palace Gardens** Beneath Prague Castle. (Open from April to October; in winter, begin from Malostranská metro station and walk along Valdštejnská to the Wallenstein Palace.)

Exit the Palace Gardens on Valdštejnská and turn right, then left into the Wallenstein Palace and through the courtyard to the ❸ **Wallenstein Garden**. Head for the northeastern corner and leave through the gate beside Malostranská metro station. Turn right on Klárov and continue along U Lužického Semináře. A gate on the right leads to the ❹ **Vojan Gardens**, a peaceful corner where local folk sit in the sun on the park benches.

Continue along U Lužického Semináře and bear left across the little bridge over the Čertovka (Devil's Stream). Pass under Charles Bridge and through the picturesque square of ❺ **Na Kampě** into the leafy riverside park known as Kampa (from the Latin campus, meaning 'field'), one of the city's favourite chill-out zones and home to the modern art collections of the ❻ **Kampa Museum**.

Retrace your steps and bear left along Hroznová, a backstreet that leads to a bridge over the Čertovka beside a water wheel. The bridge is covered in padlocks placed there by young couples as a sign of enduring love (a fad inspired by Italian novelist Federico Moccia).

The bridge leads to a tiny cobbled square with the ❼ **John Lennon Wall** on one side and the baroque palace that houses the French embassy on the other. The far end of the square curves right, past the severe Gothic towers of the Church of Our Lady Below the Chain. Turn left opposite the church and bear right along Prokopská; cross busy Karmelitská and turn right.

Just past the bar called U malého Glena is an alley on your left that leads to the ❽ **Vrtbov Garden**, one of Malá Strana's least visited but most beautiful gardens.

CAFÉ DE PARIS FRENCH €€

Map p328 (☎603 160 718; www.cafedeparis.cz; Maltézské náměstí 4; mains 230-290Kč; ⏰noon-midnight; 🚋12, 20, 22) A little corner of France tucked away on a quiet square, the Café de Paris is straightforward and unpretentious. So is the menu – just a couple of choices, onion soup or foie gras terrine to start, followed by entrecôte steak with chips, salad and a choice of sauces (they're very proud of the Café de Paris sauce, made to a 75-year-old recipe with 35 ingredients).

There are also one or two daily specials, including a vegetarian alternative. The wine list offers a decent range of French wines, including a Muscadet that's good value at 399Kč a bottle.

CAFÉ SAVOY INTERNATIONAL €€

Map p328 (☎257 311 562; www.ambi.cz; Vítězná 5; mains 120-350Kč; ⏰8am-10.30pm Mon-Fri, 9am-10.30pm Sat & Sun; 📶; 🚋6, 9, 22) The Savoy is a beautifully restored belle époque cafe, with haughty black-and-white-suited waiting staff and a Viennese-style menu of hearty soups, salads and roast meals. There's also a good breakfast menu with plenty of healthy choices, including a 'Full English', an American breakfast, and eggs cooked half-a-dozen ways.

U MODRÉ KACHNIČKY CZECH €€€

Map p328 (☎257 320 308; www.umodrekachnicky.cz; Nebovidská 6; mains 450-600Kč; ⏰noon-4pm & 6.30pm-midnight; 🚋12, 20, 22) A plush and chintzy 1930s-style hunting lodge hidden away on a quiet side street, 'At the Blue Duckling' is a pleasantly old-fashioned place with quiet, candlelit nooks perfect for a romantic dinner. The menu is heavy on traditional Bohemian duck and game dishes, such as roast duck with *slivovice* (plum brandy), plum sauce and potato pancakes.

HERGETOVA CIHELNA INTERNATIONAL €€€

Map p328 (☎296 826 103; www.kampagroup.com; Cihelná 2b; mains 300-600Kč; ⏰11.30am-1am; 📶👪; Ⓜ Malostranská) Housed in a converted 18th-century *cihelná* (brickworks), this place enjoys one of Prague's hottest locations, with a riverside terrace offering sweeping views of Charles Bridge and the Old Town waterfront. The menu is as sweeping as the view, ranging from seafood and upmarket burgers to Asian dishes such as stir-fried beef and lamb curry. There's also a decent kids' menu and play area.

BANGKOK THAI, JAPANESE €€

Map p328 (☎722 943 933; www.bangkokrestaurant.cz; Josefská 1; mains 120-300Kč; ⏰11am-11pm; 📶🌶; 🚋12, 20, 22) Easily missed, this backstreet Asian restaurant is set in a maze of gaudily decorated Gothic vaults only a few yards from Malá Strana's main square. The Japanese half of the menu is nothing special, but the Thai dishes – including red and green curries, spicy beef salad, and pad thai noodles – are authentically hot, and fragrant with lemongrass and coriander.

NOI THAI €€

Map p328 (☎257 311 411; www.noirestaurant.cz; Újezd 19; mains 180-290Kč; ⏰11am-1am; 📶👪; 🚋12, 20, 22) A restaurant that feels a bit like a club, Noi is super stylish but with a chilled-out, Far Eastern atmosphere. The decor is based around lotus blossoms, lanterns and soft lighting, and the menu follows the Asian theme with competent Thai dishes such as chicken in red curry, and pad thai noodles, which – unusually for a Prague restaurant – actually have a hefty chilli kick.

DRINKING & NIGHTLIFE

Malá Strana is the place to go for pavement table people-watching, with lots of cafes and bars spilling out onto the streets – especially on Malostranské náměstí and on Nerudova, which leads up to the castle. Places here range from cute teahouses and cafes to traditional cellar-pubs and funky bars.

MLÝNSKÁ KAVÁRNA BAR

Map p328 (☎222 329 060; Kampa Park; ⏰4pm-1am Mon-Tue, noon-midnight Wed-Fri, 9am-2am Sat, noon-4pm & 9pm-midnight Sun; 📶; 🚋6, 9, 12, 20, 22) This cafe-bar in Kampa Park has existed in various guises since the communist era, and you might still hear it called Tato Kejkej, its previous incarnation, or just Mlýn (the mill). A wooden footbridge leads to the smoky, dimly lit interior which is peopled with local artists (David Černý is a regular), writers and politicians (look out for foreign minister Karel Schwarzenberg).

KLUB ÚJEZD BAR

Map p328 (☎251 510 873; www.klubujezd.cz; Újezd 18; ⏰2pm-4am; 🚋6, 9, 12, 20, 22) Klub Újezd is one of Prague's many 'alternative' bars, spread over three floors (DJs in the cellar, and a cafe upstairs) and filled with a fascinating collection of original art and weird wrought-iron sculptures. Clamber onto a two-tonne bar stool in the agreeably grungy street-level bar, and sip on a beer beneath a scaly, fire-breathing sea-monster.

MALOSTRANSKÁ BESEDA BAR, CLUB

Map p328 (257 409 123; www.malostranskabeseda.cz; Malostranské náměstí 21, Malá Strana; box office 5-9pm Mon-Sat, to 8pm Sun, bar 4pm-1am; 12, 20, 22) Malá Strana's four-storey pleasure palace reopened in 2010 after a five-year reconstruction. The fabled music club on the 2nd floor is back and better than ever, with a lively roster of cabaret acts, jazz and old Czech rockers (shows 150-250Kč). There's also an art gallery on the top floor and a big beer hall in the basement, with a bar and restaurant on the ground floor.

U MALÉHO GLENA BAR, JAZZ

Map p328 (257 531 717; www.malyglen.cz; Karmelitská 23; 10am-2am, till 3am Fri & Sat, music from 9.30pm; ; 12, 20, 22) 'Little Glen's' is a lively American-owned bar and restaurant where hard-swinging local jazz or blues bands play every night in the cramped and steamy stone-vaulted cellar. There are Sunday-night jam sessions where amateurs are welcome (as long as you're good!) – it's a small venue, so get here early if you want to see, as well as hear, the band.

KAFÍČKO CAFE

Map p328 (724 151 795; Míšenská 10; 10am-10pm; ; 12, 20, 22) This little cafe, with cream walls, bentwood chairs and arty photographs, is an unexpected setting for some of Prague's finest tea and coffee. Choose from a wide range of quality roasted beans from all over the world, and have them freshly ground and made into espresso, cappuccino or latte (40Kč to 55Kč); the espresso is served, as it should be, with a glass of water.

U ZELENÉHO ČAJE CAFE

Map p328 (257 530 027; Nerudova 19; 11am-10pm; 12, 20, 22) 'At the Green Tea' is a charming little olde-worlde teahouse on the way up to the castle. The menu offers around a hundred different kinds of tea (45Kč to 80Kč a pot) from all over the world, ranging from classic green and black teas from China and India to fruit-flavoured teas and herbal infusions, as well as tempting cakes and tasty sandwiches.

BLUE LIGHT COCKTAIL BAR

Map p328 (257 533 126; www.bluelightbar.cz; Josefská 1; 6pm-3am; 12, 20, 22) The Blue Light is a dark and atmospheric hangout, as popular with locals as with tourists, where you can sip a caipirinha or cranberry colada as you cast an eye over the vintage jazz posters, records, old photographs and decades-worth of scratched graffiti that adorn the walls. The background jazz is recorded rather than live, and never overpowers your conversation. Often heaving on weekend nights.

HOSTINEC U KOCOURA PUB

Map p328 (257 530 107; Nerudova 2; 12, 20, 22) 'The Tomcat' is a long-established traditional pub, still enjoying its reputation as a former favourite of former president Havel, and still managing to pull in a mostly Czech crowd despite being in the heart of touristville (maybe it's the ever-present pall of cigarette smoke). It has relatively inexpensive beer for this part of town – 34Kč for 0.5L of draught Pilsner Urquell or Bernard.

SHOPPING

VETEŠNICTVI ANTIQUES

Map p328 (257 530 624; Vítezná 16; 10am-5pm Mon-Fri, to noon Sat; 6, 9, 12, 20, 22) This is an Aladdin's cave of secondhand goods, bric-a-brac and junk with, in all likelihood, some genuine antiques for those who know what they're looking for. There's affordable stuff for all, from communist-era lapel pins, medals, postcards, old beer mugs and toys to crystal, shot glasses, porcelain, china, pipes and spa cups, all presided over by a bust of Lenin.

SHAKESPEARE & SONS BOOKS

Map p328 (257 531 894; www.shakes.cz; U Lužického Semináře 10; 11am-7pm; 12, 20, 22) An English-language bookshop.

PAVLA & OLGA FASHION

Map p328 (728 939 872; Vlašská 13; 2-6pm Mon-Fri; 12, 20, 22) Sisters Pavla and Olga Michalková originally worked in the film and TV industry before setting up their own fashion label, creating a unique collection of quirky and cute hats, clothes and accessories. Past customers have included Czech supermodel Tereza Maxová, Britpop band Blur and photographer Helmut Newton.

Staré Město

OLD TOWN SQUARE & AROUND | JOSEFOV | ALONG THE ROYAL WAY | SOUTHWESTERN STARÉ MĚSTO

Neighbourhood Top Five

❶ Tour the half-dozen monuments that comprise the **Prague Jewish Museum** (p93), a moving memorial to the Czech capital's once-thriving Jewish community.

❷ Check out Prague's **Municipal House** (p96) – a tour de force of art-nouveau extravagance.

❸ Join the crowds in the Old Town Square to witness the **Astronomical Clock** (p98) do its thing.

❹ Admire the skill of master craftspeople at the **Museum of Decorative Arts** (p99).

❺ **Shop** (p113) for art, antiques and designer fashion in the atmospheric Staré Město backstreets.

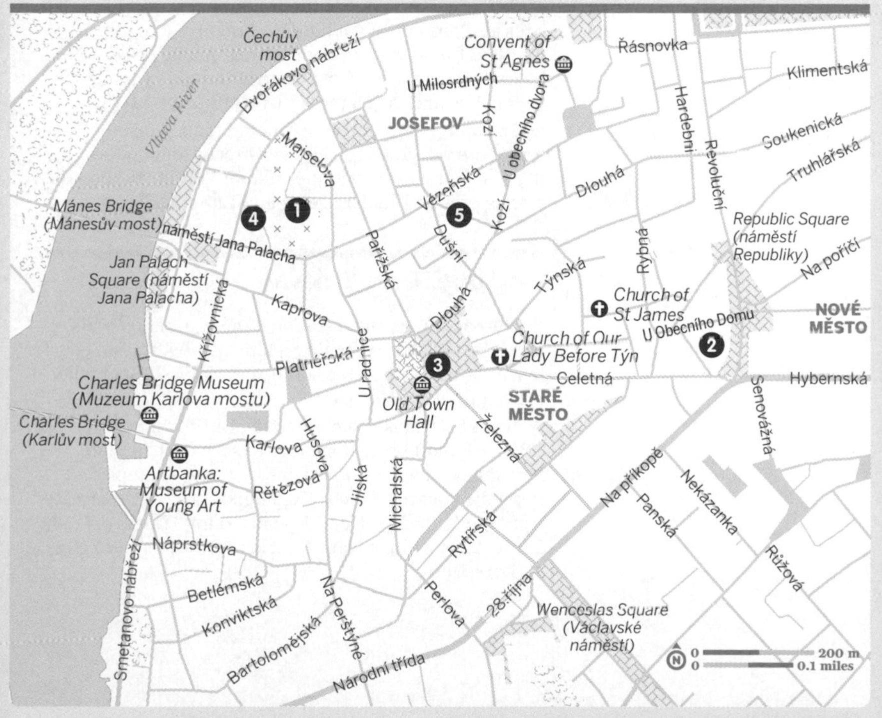

For more detail of this area see Map p332

Lonely Planet's Top Tip

Get away from the Old Town Square and Karlova! Huge crowds throng the square and the narrow street that links it to Charles Bridge, but just a few blocks away – try wandering along Anenská – you can find yourself exploring backstreets almost on your own.

Best Places to Eat

- Mistral Café (p109)
- Lokál (p109)
- Maitrea (p109)
- Indian Jewel (p109)
- Vino di Vino (p109)

For reviews, see p107

Best Places to Drink

- Prague Beer Museum (p110)
- Hemingway Bar (p110)
- Krásný ztráty (p111)
- Čili Bar (p111)
- Kozička (p111)

For reviews, see p110

Explore: Staré Město

If the labyrinth of narrow streets around the Old Town Square can be said to have a 'main drag', it's the so-called Royal Way, the ancient coronation route to Prague Castle, running from the Powder Gate along Celetná to the Old Town Square and Little Square (Malé náměstí), then along Karlova and across Charles Bridge.

To the north of the Old Town Square, half-a-dozen historic synagogues, a town hall and the Old Jewish Cemetery are all that survive of the once-thriving Jewish quarter of Josefov – the slice of Staré Město bounded by Kaprova, Dlouhá and Kozí. Most of the district's buildings were demolished around the turn of the 20th century, when massive redevelopment saw the old slums replaced with expensive new apartments.

To the south, the meandering lanes and passageways between Karlova and Národní třída are Prague's best territory for aimless wandering. When the crowds thin out late in the day, this area can cast such a spell that it's quite a surprise to emerge from its peaceful backstreets into the bustle of the 21st century.

Local Life

- **Popular Hangouts** The clue is in the name: Lokál (p109), a modern take on the traditional *pivnice* (small beer hall), has proved a hit with Praguers looking for good Czech food and beer at reasonable prices. Meanwhile, students from Charles University hang out over coffee and magazines at Krásný ztráty (p111).
- **Shopping** Staré Město is where Prague's fashionistas come to track down the hottest threads among the dozens of designer boutiques that proliferate in the streets around Dlouhá, Dušní and Karolíny Světlé.

Getting There & Away

- **Metro** Staroměstská station is a few minutes' walk northwest of the Old Town Square, Můstek station is five minutes' walk to the south, and Náměstí Republiky is five minutes to the east.
- **Tram** No trams run close to the Old Town Square. Trams 17 and 18 run along the western edge of Staré Město near the river, while lines 5, 8 and 14 stop at Republic Square (Náměstí Republiky), across the street from the Municipal House (Obecní dům). Trams 6, 9, 18, 21 and 22 run along Národní třída on the southern edge of Staré Město.

TOP SIGHTS
PRAGUE JEWISH MUSEUM

In one of the most grotesquely ironic acts of WWII, the Nazis took over the management of the Prague Jewish Museum – first established in 1906 to preserve artefacts from synagogues that were demolished during the slum clearances in Josefov around the turn of the 20th century – with the intention of creating a 'museum of an extinct race'. They shipped in materials and objects from destroyed Jewish communities throughout Bohemia and Moravia, helping to amass what is probably the world's biggest collection of sacred Jewish artefacts and a moving memorial to seven centuries of oppression.

Old-New Synagogue

Completed around 1270, the **Old-New Synagogue** (Staronová synagóga; Map p332; www.jewishmuseum.cz; Červená 2; 🚋17) is Europe's oldest working synagogue and one of Prague's earliest Gothic buildings. You step down into it because it pre-dates the raising of Staré Město's street level in medieval times to guard against floods. Men must cover their heads (a hat or bandanna will do; paper yarmulkes are handed out at the entrance). Note that entry is not included with a Prague Jewish Museum ordinary ticket.

Around the central chamber are an entry hall, a winter prayer hall and the room from which women watch the men-only services. The interior, with a pulpit surrounded by a 15th-century wrought-iron grill, looks much as it would have 500 years ago. The 17th-century scriptures on the walls were recovered from beneath a later 'restoration'. On the eastern wall is the Holy Ark that holds the Torah scrolls. In a

DON'T MISS...

- Old-New Synagogue
- Old Jewish Cemetery
- Spanish Synagogue

PRACTICALITIES

- Židovské muzeum Praha
- Map p332
- ☎222 317 191
- www.jewishmuseum.cz
- Reservation Centre, U starého hřbitova 3a
- ordinary ticket adult/child 300/200Kč, combined ticket 480/320Kč
- ⏲9am-6pm Sun-Fri Apr-Oct, to 4.30pm Nov-Mar
- Ⓜ Staroměstská

TICKETS

An ordinary ticket (adult/ child 300/200Kč) gives admission to all six main monuments; a combined ticket (adult/child 480/320Kč) includes the Old-New Synagogue as well. Admission to the Old-New Synagogue alone costs 200/140Kč. You can buy tickets at the Reservation Centre, the Pinkas Synagogue, the Spanish Synagogue and the shop opposite the entrance to the Old-New Synagogue.

In the Old Jewish Cemetery is the gravestone of Rabbi Judah Loew ben Bezalel, chief rabbi of Prague in the late 16th century. He is associated with the legend of the Golem, a supernatural being created from the mud of the Vltava River. He breathed life into the creature using secret incantations, and bid it to protect Prague's Jews.

MAISEL'S GIFT

Mordechai Maisel (1528–1601) was known for his philanthropy, paying for the paving of the ghetto streets, providing for Jewish widows and orphans, and building and bequeathing the Maisel Synagogue (rebuilt in neo-gothic style in 1905).

glass case at the rear, little light bulbs beside the names of the prominent deceased are lit on their death days.

With its steep roof and Gothic gables, this looks like a place with secrets, and at least one version of the Golem legend ends here. Left alone on the Sabbath, the creature runs amok; Rabbi Loew rushes out in the middle of a service, removes its magic talisman and carries the lifeless body into the synagogue's attic, where some insist it still lies.

Across the narrow street is the elegant 16th-century **High Synagogue** (Vysoká synagóga; Map p332; Červená 2), so-called because its prayer hall (closed to the public) is upstairs. Around the corner is the **Jewish Town Hall** (Židovská radnice; Map p332; Maiselova 18; ⏲closed to the public; Ⓜ Staroměstská), built by Mordechai Maisel in 1586 and given its rococo facade in the 18th century. It has a clock tower with one Hebrew face where the hands, like the Hebrew script, run 'backwards'.

Pinkas Synagogue

The handsome **Pinkas Synagogue** (Pinkasova synagóga; Map p332; www.jewishmuseum.cz; Široká 3; ⏲9am-6pm Sun-Fri Apr-Oct, to 4.30pm Nov-Mar; Ⓜ Staroměstská) was built in 1535 and used for worship until 1941. After WWII it was converted into a memorial, with wall after wall inscribed with the names, birth dates, and dates of disappearance of the 77,297 Czech victims of the Nazis. It also has a collection of paintings and drawings by children held in the Terezín concentration camp during WWII.

Old Jewish Cemetery

The Pinkas Synagogue contains the entrance to the **Old Jewish Cemetery** (Starý židovský hřbitov; Map p332; Pinkas Synagogue, Široká 3; Ⓜ Staroměstská), Europe's oldest surviving Jewish graveyard (pictured p93). Founded in the early 15th century, it has a palpable atmosphere of mourning even after two centuries of disuse (it was closed in 1787); however, remember that this is one of Prague's most popular sights, so if you're hoping to have a moment of quiet contemplation you'll probably be disappointed. Around 12,000 crumbling stones (some brought from other, long-gone cemeteries) are heaped together, but beneath them are perhaps 100,000 graves, piled in layers because of the lack of space.

The most prominent graves, marked by pairs of marble tablets with a 'roof' between them, are near the main gate; they include those of Mordechai Maisel and Rabbi Loew. The oldest stone (now replaced by a replica) is that of Avigdor Karo, a chief rabbi and court poet to Wenceslas IV, who died in 1439.

Most stones bear the name of the deceased and his or her father, the date of death (and sometimes of burial), and poetic texts. Elaborate markers from the 17th and 18th centuries are carved with bas-reliefs, some of them indicating the deceased's occupation – look out for a pair of hands marking the grave of a pianist.

Since the cemetery was closed, Jewish burials have taken place at the Jewish Cemetery in Žižkov. There are remnants of another old Jewish burial ground at the foot of the TV Tower in Žižkov.

You exit the cemetery through a gate between the Klaus Synagogue and the Ceremonial Hall.

Ceremonial Hall & Klaus Synagogue

Built in 1912, the **Ceremonial Hall** (Obřadní síň; Map p332; 9am-6pm Sun-Fri Apr-Oct, to 4.30pm Nov-Mar; 17) was formerly the mortuary for the Old Jewish Cemetery, and is the site of an interesting exhibition on Jewish traditions relating to illness and death. The neighbouring baroque **Klaus Synagogue** (Klauzová synagóga; Map p332; www.jewishmuseum.cz; U starého hřbitova 1; 9am-6pm Sun-Fri Apr-Oct, to 4.30pm Nov-Mar; 17, 18) houses a good exhibit on Jewish ceremonies of birth and death, worship and special holy days.

Maisel Synagogue

A block to the southeast of the Ceremonial Hall and Klaus Synagogue lies the neo-Gothic **Maisel Synagogue** (Maiselova synagóga; Map p332; Maiselova 10; 9am-6pm Sun-Fri Apr-Oct, to 4.30pm Nov-Mar; M Staroměstská), which replaced a Renaissance original built by Mordechai Maisel, mayor of the Jewish community, in 1592. It houses an exhibit on the history of the Jews in Bohemia and Moravia from the 10th to the 18th centuries, with displays of ceremonial silver, textiles, prints and books.

Spanish Synagogue

About two blocks east of the Maisel Synagogue is the **Spanish Synagogue** (Španělská synagóga; Map p332; www.jewishmuseum.cz; Vězeňská 1; 9am-6pm Sun-Fri Apr-Oct, to 4.30pm Nov-Mar; M Staroměstská). Named after its striking Moorish interior and dating from 1868, its exhibit continues the story of the Jews in the Czech Republic from emancipation to the present day.

MENDELSSOHN IS ON THE ROOF

The roof of the Rudolfinum (p102), on the western edge of Josefov, is decorated with statues of famous composers. It housed the German administration during WWII, when the Nazi authorities ordered that the statue of Felix Mendelssohn – who was Jewish – must be removed.

In *Mendelssohn is on the Roof*, a darkly comic novella about life in wartime Prague, the Jewish writer Jiří Weil weaves a wryly amusing story around this true-life event. The two Czech labourers given the task of removing the statue can't tell which of the two dozen or so figures is Mendelssohn – they all look the same, as far as they can tell. Their Czech boss, remembering his lectures in 'racial science', tells them that Jews have big noses. 'Whichever one has the biggest conk, that's the Jew.'

So the workmen single out the statue with the biggest nose – 'Look! That one over there with the beret. None of the others has a nose like his' – then sling a noose around its neck and start to haul it over. As their boss walks across to check on their progress, he gapes in horror as they start to topple the figure of the only composer on the roof that he does recognise – Richard Wagner.

TOP SIGHTS
MUNICIPAL HOUSE

Restored in the 1990s after decades of neglect, Prague's most exuberant and sensual building is a labour of love, every detail of its design and decoration carefully considered, every painting and sculpture loaded with symbolism. The restaurant and cafe flanking the entrance are like walk-in museums of art-nouveau design; upstairs are half-a-dozen sumptuously decorated halls that you can visit by guided tour (three to four tours per day).

History

The Municipal House stands on the site of the Royal Court, seat of Bohemia's kings from 1383 to 1483 (when Vladislav II moved to Prague Castle), which was demolished at the end of the 19th century. Between 1906 and 1912 this magnificent art-nouveau palace was built in its place – a lavish joint effort by around 30 leading artists of the day, creating a cultural centre that was the architectural climax of the Czech National Revival.

Entrance & Lobby

The mosaic above the entrance, **Homage to Prague**, is set between sculptures representing the oppression and rebirth of the Czech people; other sculptures along the top of the facade represent history, literature, painting, architecture and music. You pass beneath a wrought-iron and stained-glass canopy into an interior that's art nouveau down to the doorknobs (you can look around the lobby and the downstairs bar for free, or book a guided tour in the information centre).

Smetana Hall

First stop on the guided tour is Smetana Hall, Prague's biggest concert hall, with seating for 1200 ranged beneath an art-nouveau glass dome. The stage is framed by sculptures representing the Vyšehrad legend (to the right) and Slavonic dances (to the left). On 28 October 1918 an independent Czechoslovak Republic was declared in Smetana Hall, and in November 1989 meetings took place here between the Civic Forum and the Jakeš regime.

The Prague Spring (Pražské jaro) music festival always opens on 12 May, the anniversary of Smetana's death, with a procession from Vyšehrad to the Municipal House followed by a gala performance of Smetana's symphonic cycle *Má vlast* (My Homeland) in Smetana Hall.

Lord Mayor's Hall

Several impressive official apartments follow Smetana Hall, but the highlight of the tour is the octagonal Lord Mayor's Hall (Primatorský sál), whose windows overlook the main entrance. Every aspect of its decoration was designed by Alfons Mucha, who also painted the superbly moody murals that adorn the walls and ceiling. Above you is an allegory of Slavic Concord, with intertwined figures representing the various Slavic peoples watched over by the Czech eagle. Figures from Czech history and mythology, representing the civic virtues, occupy the spaces between the eight arches, including Jan Hus as Spravedlnost (justice), Jan Žižka as Bojovnost (military prowess) and the Chodové (medieval Bohemian border guards) as beady-eyed Ostražitost (vigilance).

DON'T MISS...

- Art-nouveau mosaics
- Smetana Hall
- Lord Mayor's Hall

PRACTICALITIES

- Obecní dům
- Map p332
- 222 002 101
- www.obecnidum.cz
- náměstí Republiky 5
- guided tours adult/child 290/240Kč
- public areas 7.30am-11pm, information centre 10am-8pm
- Náměstí Republiky

TOP SIGHTS
OLD TOWN HALL

Prague's Old Town Hall, founded in 1338, is a hotchpotch of medieval buildings presided over by a tall Gothic tower with a splendid Astronomical Clock (p98). The town hall has several historic attractions, and hosts art exhibitions on the ground floor and the 2nd floor.

Guided Tour

The guided tour takes you through the council chamber and assembly room, with beautiful mosaics dating from the 1930s, before visiting the Gothic chapel and taking a look at the inner workings of the 12 Apostles who parade above the Astronomical Clock every hour. The tour is rounded off with a trip through the Romanesque and Gothic cellars beneath the building.

Tower

The town hall's best feature is the view from the 60m-tall **tower** (Věž radnice; Map p332; ☎12444; www.prazskeveze.cz; Staroměstské náměstí 1; adult/child 105/55Kč; ⏲10am-10pm Mon, 9am-10pm Tue-Sun; Ⓜ Staroměstská), which is well worth the climb (there's also a lift).

Exterior

A plaque on the building's eastern face lists the 27 Protestant nobles who were beheaded here in 1621 after the Battle of Bílá Hora; white crosses on the ground mark where the deed was done. If you look at the neo-Gothic eastern gable, you can see that its right-hand edge is ragged – the wing that once extended north from here was blown up by the Nazis in 1945, on the day before the Soviet army marched into the city.

DON'T MISS...

- The view from the top of the tower
- The guided tour, where you can see the inner workings of the 12 Apostles

PRACTICALITIES

- Staroměstská radnice
- Map p332
- ☎12444
- www.prazskeveze.cz
- Staroměstské náměstí 1
- guided tour adult/child 105/85Kč
- ⏲11am-6pm Mon, 9am-6pm Tue-Sun
- Ⓜ Staroměstská

TOP SIGHTS
ASTRONOMICAL CLOCK

Every hour, on the hour, crowds gather beneath the Old Town Hall Tower to watch the Astronomical Clock in action. Despite a slightly underwhelming performance that takes only 45 seconds, the clock is one of Europe's best-known tourist attractions, and a 'must-see' for visitors to Prague. After all, it's historic, photogenic and – if you take time to study it – rich in intriguing symbolism.

DON'T MISS...

- The parade of Apostles during the hourly chimes
- The carved figures of Vanity, Greed, Death and Pagan Invasion
- The beautifully painted 19th-century calendar wheel

PRACTICALITIES

- Map p332
- Old Town Hall, Staroměstské náměstí
- chimes on the hour 9am-9pm
- M Staroměstská

The Chimes

The Old Town Hall's original clock of 1410 was improved in 1490 by Master Hanuš, producing the mechanical marvel you see today. Legend has it that Hanuš was blinded afterwards so he could not duplicate his work elsewhere.

Four figures beside the clock represent the deepest civic anxieties of 15th-century Praguers: **Vanity** (with a mirror), **Greed** (with his money bag; originally a Jewish moneylender, but cosmetically altered after WWII), **Death** (the skeleton) and **Pagan Invasion** (represented by a Turk). The four figures below these are the Chronicler, Angel, Astronomer and Philosopher.

On the hour, Death rings a bell and inverts his hourglass, and the 12 Apostles parade past the windows above the clock, nodding to the crowd. On the left side are Paul (with a sword and a book), Thomas (lance), Jude (book), Simon (saw), Bartholomew (book) and Barnabas (parchment); on the right side are Peter (with a key), Matthew (axe), John (snake), Andrew (cross), Philip (cross) and James (mallet). At the end, a cock crows and the hour is rung.

The Clock Face

On the upper face, the disk in the middle of the fixed part depicts the world known at the time – with Prague at the centre, of course. The gold sun traces a circle through the blue zone of day, the brown zone of dusk (Crepusculum in Latin) in the west (Occasus), the black disc of night, and dawn (Aurora) in the east (Ortus). From this the hours of sunrise and sunset can be read. The curved lines with black Arabic numerals are part of an astrological 'star clock'.

The **sun arm** points to the hour (without any daylight-saving time adjustment) on the Roman-numeral ring; the top XII is noon and the bottom XII is midnight. The outer ring, with Gothic numerals, reads traditional 24-hour Bohemian time, counted from sunset; the number 24 is always opposite the sunset hour on the fixed (inner) face.

The **moon**, with its phases shown, also traces a path through the zones of day and night, riding on the offset moving ring. On the ring you can also read which houses of the zodiac the sun and moon are in. The hand with a little star at the end of it indicates sidereal (stellar) time.

The Calendar Wheel

The calendar wheel beneath the clock's astronomical wizardry, with 12 seasonal scenes celebrating rural Bohemian life, is a duplicate of one painted in 1866 by the Czech Revivalist Josef Mánes. You can have a close look at the beautiful original in the Prague City Museum. Most of the dates around the calendar wheel are marked with the names of their associated saints; 6 July honours Jan Hus.

R C-ARD NEBESKY / LONELY PLANET IMAGES ©

TOP SIGHTS
MUSEUM OF DECORATIVE ARTS

This museum opened in 1900 as part of a European movement to encourage a return to the aesthetic values sacrificed to the Industrial Revolution. Its four halls are a feast for the eyes, full of 16th- to 19th-century artefacts such as furniture, tapestries, porcelain and a fabulous collection of glasswork.

Exhibition

The neo-Renaissance building is itself a work of art, the facade decorated with reliefs representing the various decorative arts and the Bohemian towns famous for them. The staircase leading up from the entrance hall to the main exhibition on the 2nd floor is decorated with colourful ceramics, stained-glass windows and frescoes representing graphic arts, metalworking, ceramics, glassmaking and goldsmithing. It leads to the ornate Votive Hall, which houses the **Karlštejn Treasure**, a hoard of 14th-century silver found hidden in the walls of Karlštejn Castle in the 19th century.

To the right is a textiles exhibit and a fascinating collection of clocks, watches, sundials and astronomical devices. To the left is the **glass and ceramics hall**, with exquisite baroque glassware, a collection of Meissen porcelain and Czech glass, ceramics, and furniture in cubist, art-nouveau and art-deco styles. The best pieces are by Josef Gočár and Pavel Janák.

The **graphic arts section** has some fine art-nouveau posters, and the **gold and jewellery exhibit** contains some real curiosities – amid the Bohemian garnet brooches, 14th-century chalices, diamond-studded monstrances and art-nouveau silverware you will find a Chinese rhino-horn vase in a silver mount, a delicate nautilus shell engraved with battle scenes, and a silver watchcase in the shape of a skull.

DON'T MISS...

- Karlštejn Treasure
- Cubist ceramics
- Art-nouveau posters

PRACTICALITIES

- Umělecko-průmyslové muzeum
- Map p332
- ☎251 093 111
- www.upm.cz
- 17.listopadu 2
- permanent collection adult/child 80/40Kč, temporary exhibitions 80/40Kč, combined 120/70Kč, combined admission with Galerie Rudolfinum 180/100Kč
- ⏲10am-7pm Tue, to 6pm Wed-Sun
- 🚊17

SIGHTS

Old Town Square & Around

OLD TOWN HALL — HISTORIC BUILDING

See p97.

ASTRONOMICAL CLOCK — HISTORIC SITE

See p98.

OLD TOWN SQUARE — SQUARE

Map p332 (Staroměstské náměstí; Ⓜ Staroměstská) One of Europe's biggest and most beautiful urban spaces, the Old Town Square (Staroměstské náměstí, or Staromák for short) has been Prague's principal public square since the 10th century, and was its main marketplace until the beginning of the 20th century.

There are busking jazz bands and alfresco concerts, political meetings and fashion shows, plus Christmas and Easter markets, all watched over by Ladislav Šaloun's brooding art-nouveau **statue of Jan Hus**. It was unveiled on 6 July 1915, which was the 500th anniversary of Hus' death at the stake.

The brass strip on the ground nearby is the so-called **Prague Meridian**. Until 1915 the square's main feature was a 17th-century plague column, whose shadow used to cross the meridian at high noon.

KINSKÝ PALACE — GALLERY

Map p332 (Palác Kinských; ☎224 810 758; www.ngprague.cz; Staroměstské náměstí 12; adult/child 150/80Kč; ⏰10am-6pm Tue-Sun; Ⓟ; Ⓜ Staroměstská) The late-baroque Kinský Palace sports Prague's finest rococo facade, completed in 1765 by the redoubtable Kilian Dientzenhofer. Today, the palace is home to a branch of the National Gallery, housing its collection of ancient and oriental art, ranging from ancient Egyptian tomb treasures and Greek Apulian pottery (4th century BC) to Chinese and Japanese decorative art and calligraphy.

Alfred Nobel, the Swedish inventor of dynamite, once stayed in the palace; his crush on pacifist Bertha von Suttner (née Kinský) may have influenced him to establish the Nobel Peace Prize (she was the first woman laureate in 1905). Many older Praguers have a darker memory of the place, for it was from its balcony in February 1948 that Klement Gottwald proclaimed communist rule in Czechoslovakia. There are Kafka connections here, too – young Franz once attended a school around the back of the building, and his father ran a shop in the premises next to the House at the Stone Bell, now occupied by the Kafka Bookshop.

HOUSE AT THE STONE BELL — GALLERY

Map p332 (Dům U kamenného zvonu; ☎224 828 245; www.ghmp.cz; Staroměstské náměstí 13; adult/child 120/60Kč; ⏰10am-8pm Tue-Sun; Ⓜ Staroměstská) During restoration in the 1980s the baroque stucco facade was stripped away from this elegant medieval building to reveal the original 14th-century Gothic stonework; the eponymous stone bell is on the building's corner. Inside, two restored Gothic chapels now serve as branches of the Prague City Gallery (with changing exhibits of modern art) and as chamber-concert venues.

CHURCH OF ST NICHOLAS — CHURCH

Map p332 (Kostel sv Mikuláše; Staroměstské náměstí; ⏰noon-4pm Mon, 10am-4pm Tue-Sat, noon-3pm Sun; Ⓜ Staroměstská) The baroque wedding cake in the northwestern corner of the Old Town Square is the Church of St Nicholas, built in the 1730s by Kilian Dientzenhofer (not to be confused with the Dientzenhofers' masterwork in Malá Strana). Considerable grandeur has been worked into a very tight space; originally the church was wedged behind the Old

OLD TOWN ORIGINS

The origins of Staré Město (Old Town) date back to the 10th century, when a marketplace and settlement grew up on the east bank of the river. In the 12th century this was linked to the castle district by Judith Bridge, the forerunner of Charles Bridge, and in 1231 Wenceslas I honoured it with a town charter and the beginnings of a fortification.

The town walls are long gone, but their line can still be traced along the streets of Národní třída, Na příkopě (which means 'on the moat') and Revoluční, and the Old Town's main gate – the Powder Gate – still survives.

TOP SIGHTS
CHURCH OF OUR LADY BEFORE TÝN

Its distinctive twin Gothic spires make the Church of Our Lady Before Týn an unmistakable Old Town landmark. Like something out of a 15th-century fairytale, they loom over the Old Town Square, decorated with a golden image of the Virigin Mary made in the 1620s from the melted-down Hussite chalice that previously adorned the church.

The church's name originates from the Týn Courtyard behind the church. Though impressively Gothic on the outside, the church's interior is smothered in heavy baroque. Two of the most interesting features are the huge rococo **altar** on the northern wall and the **tomb of Tycho Brahe**, the Danish astronomer who was one of Rudolf II's most illustrious court scientists (he died in 1601 of a burst bladder following a royal piss-up – he was too polite to leave the table to relieve himself).

As for the church's exterior, the north portal overlooking Týnská ulička is topped by a remarkable **14th-century tympanum** that shows the Crucifixion. It was carved by the workshop of Charles IV's favourite architect, Peter Parler. (This is a copy; the original is in the Lapidárium.)

The church is an occasional concert venue and has a very grand-sounding pipe organ.

DON'T MISS...

- View of the floodlit spires at night
- Tympanum depicting the Crucifixion
- Tycho Brahe's tomb

PRACTICALITIES

- Kostel Panny Marie před Týnem
- Map p332
- ☎222 318 186
- www.tyn.cz
- Staroměstské náměstí
- ⌚10am-1pm & 3-5pm Tue-Sat, 10.30am-noon Sun Mar-Oct
- Ⓜ Staroměstská

Town Hall's northern wing (destroyed in 1945).

Chamber concerts are often held beneath its stucco decorations, a visually splendid (though acoustically mediocre) setting.

TÝN COURTYARD SQUARE

Map p332 (Týnský dvůr; entrances on Malá Štupartská & Týnská ulička; ⌚24hr; Ⓜ Náměstí Republiky) This picturesque courtyard tucked behind the Church of Our Lady Before Týn was originally a sort of medieval caravanserai – a fortified hotel, trading centre and customs office for visiting foreign merchants. Established as long ago as the 11th century, it was busiest and most prosperous during the reign of Charles IV. Now attractively renovated, the courtyard houses shops, restaurants and hotels. The courtyard is still often referred to by its German name, Ungelt (meaning 'customs duty').

In the northwest corner is the 16th-century **Granovsky Palace** (Map p332), with an elegant Renaissance loggia, and sgraffito and painted decoration depicting biblical and mythological scenes. Across the yard, to the right of the V Ungeltu shop, is the **House at the Black Bear** (dům U černého medvěda; Map p332), whose baroque facade is adorned with a statue of St John of Nepomuk above the door and a bear in chains on the corner, a reminder of the kind of 'entertainment' that once took place here.

Josefov

PRAGUE JEWISH MUSEUM MUSEUM

See p93.

MUSEUM OF DECORATIVE ARTS MUSEUM

See p99.

PAŘÍŽSKÁ STREET

Map p332 (Ⓜ Staroměstská) When the Josefov ghetto was cleared at the turn of the 20th century, the broad boulevard of Pařížská třída (Paris Ave) was driven in a straight line through the heart of the old slums. This was a time of widespread infatuation with the French art-nouveau style, and the avenue and its side streets were lined with elegant apartment buildings adorned with stained glass and sculptural flourishes. In the last decade Pařížská has become a

TOP SIGHTS
CHURCH OF ST JAMES

The great Gothic mass of the Church of St James began in the 14th century as a Minorite monastery church, and was given a beautiful baroque facelift in the early 18th century. But in the midst of the gilt and stucco is a grisly memento: on the inside of the western wall (look up to the right as you enter) hangs a **shrivelled human arm**. Legend claims that when a thief tried to steal the jewels from the statue of the Virgin around the year 1400, the Virgin grabbed his wrist in such an iron grip that his arm had to be lopped off. (The truth may not be far behind: the church was a favourite of the guild of butchers, who may have administered their own justice.)

Pride of place inside goes to the over-the-top **tomb**, found in the northern aisle, of Count Jan Vratislav of Mitrovice, an 18th-century lord chancellor of Bohemia. It's well worth a visit to enjoy St James' splendid **pipe organ** and famous acoustics. Recitals – free ones at 10.30am or 11am after Sunday Mass – and occasional concerts are not always advertised by ticket agencies, so check the noticeboard outside.

DON'T MISS...

- The thief's arm
- The tomb of Count Jan Vratislav of Mitrovice
- An organ recital

PRACTICALITIES

- Kostel sv Jakuba
- Map p332
- Malá Štupartská 6
- 9.30am-noon & 2-4pm
- M Náměstí Republiky

glitzy shopping strand, studded with expensive brand names such as Dior, Louis Vuitton and Fabergé.

FRANZ KAFKA MONUMENT MONUMENT

Map p332 (cnr Vězeňská & Dušní; M Staroměstská) Jaroslav Róna's unusual sculpture of a mini-Franz sitting piggyback on his own headless body was unveiled in 2003. Commissioned by Prague's Franz Kafka Society, it stands beside the Spanish Synagogue.

JAN PALACH SQUARE SQUARE

Map p332 (náměstí Jana Palacha; 17, 18) Jan Palach Square is named after the young Charles University student who in January 1969 set himself alight in Wenceslas Square in protest against the Soviet invasion. On the eastern side of the square, beside the entrance to the philosophy faculty building where Palach was a student, is a bronze memorial plaque with a ghostly death mask.

RUDOLFINUM HISTORIC BUILDING

Map p332 (227 059 270; www.ceskafilharmonie.cz; Alšovo nábřeží 12; 17, 18) Presiding over Jan Palach Square is the Rudolfinum, home to the Czech Philharmonic Orchestra. This and the National Theatre, both designed by architects Josef Schulz and Josef Zítek, are considered Prague's finest neo-Renaissance buildings. Completed in 1884, the Rudolfinum served between the wars as the seat of the Czechoslovak parliament, and during WWII as the administrative offices of the occupying Nazis.

The impressive **Dvořák Hall**, its stage dominated by a vast organ, is one of the main concert venues for the Prague Spring festival (p42). The northern part of the complex (entrance facing the river) houses the Galerie Rudolfinum. There's also a sumptuous **cafe** with tables ranged amid the Corinthian splendour of the Column Hall.

GALERIE RUDOLFINUM GALLERY

Map p332 (227 059 205; www.galerierudolfinum.cz; Alšovo nábřeží 12; adult/child 150/90Kč, combined admission with Museum of Decorative Arts 180/100Kč; 10am-6pm Tue, Wed & Fri-Sun, to 8pm Thu; 17,18) Housed in the Rudolfinum complex of concert halls, this gallery specialises in changing exhibitions of contemporary art.

Along the Royal Way

MUNICIPAL HOUSE HISTORIC BUILDING
See p96.

POWDER GATE TOWER
Map p332 (Prašná brána; www.prazskeveze.cz; Na příkopě; adult/child 75/55Kč; ⏲10am-10pm Apr-Sep, to 8pm Oct & Mar, to 6pm Nov-Feb; Ⓜ Náměstí Republiky) The 65m-tall Powder Gate was begun in 1475 on the site of one of Staré Město's original 13 gates. The tower houses exhibitions of medieval weapons and instruments, many of which were used in films shot in Prague, including *Van Helsing*, *Chronicles of Narnia* and *Blade II*, but the main attraction is the view from the top.

The gate was built during the reign of King Vladislav II Jagiello as a ceremonial entrance to the city, but was left unfinished after the king moved from the neighbouring Royal Court to Prague Castle in 1483. The name comes from its use as a gun powder magazine in the 18th century. Josef Mocker rebuilt and decorated it and put up a steeple between 1875 and 1886, giving it its neo-Gothic icing.

MUSEUM OF CZECH CUBISM GALLERY
Map p332 (Muzeum Českého Kubismu; ☎224 211 746; www.ngprague.cz; Ovocný trh 19; adult/child 100/50Kč; ⏲10am-6pm Tue-Sun; Ⓜ Náměstí Republiky) Though dating from 1912, Josef Gočár's House of the Black Madonna (dům U černé Matky Boží) – Prague's first and finest example of cubist architecture – still looks modern and dynamic. It now houses three floors of remarkable cubist paintings and sculpture, as well as furniture, ceramics and glassware in cubist designs.

ESTATES THEATRE HISTORIC BUILDING
Map p332 (Stavovské divadlo; ☎224 902 231; www.narodni-divadlo.cz; Ovocný trh 1; Ⓜ Můstek) Prague's oldest theatre and finest neoclassical building, the Estates Theatre is where the premiere of Mozart's *Don Giovanni* was performed on 29 October 1787, with the maestro himself conducting. Opened in 1783 as the Nostitz Theatre (after its founder, Count Anton von Nostitz-Rieneck), it was patronised by upper-class German citizens and thus came to be called the Estates Theatre – the Estates being the traditional nobility.

TOP SIGHTS
CONVENT OF ST AGNES

In the northeastern corner of Staré Město is the former Convent of St Agnes, Prague's oldest surviving Gothic building. The 1st-floor rooms hold the National Gallery's permanent collection of medieval and early Renaissance art (1200–1550) from Bohemia and Central Europe, a treasure house of glowing Gothic altar paintings and polychrome religious sculptures.

In 1234 the Franciscan Order of the Poor Clares was founded by Přemysl king Wenceslas I, who made his sister Anežka (Agnes) the first abbess of the convent. Agnes was beatified in the 19th century; Pope John Paul II canonised her as St Agnes of Bohemia just weeks before the revolutionary events of November 1989.

In the 16th century the convent was handed over to the Dominicans, and after Joseph II dissolved the monasteries it became a squatters' paradise. The complex was restored in the 1980s. In addition to the art gallery and the 13th-century cloister, you can visit the French Gothic **Church of the Holy Saviour** (Map p332), which contains the tombs of St Agnes and of Wenceslas I's Queen Cunegund. Alongside this is the **Church of St Francis** (Map p332), where Wenceslas I is buried; part of its ruined nave now serves as a chilly concert hall.

DON'T MISS...

- Gothic altarpieces painted by medieval masters
- Church of the Holy Saviour

PRACTICALITIES

- Klášter sv Anežky
- Map p332
- ☎224 810 628
- www.ngprague.cz
- U Milosrdných 17
- adult/child 150/80Kč
- ⏲10am-6pm Tue-Sun
- 🚋5, 8, 14

After WWII it was renamed the Tylovo divadlo (Tyl Theatre) in honour of the 19th-century Czech playwright Josef Kajetán Tyl. One of his claims to fame is the Czech national anthem, *Kde domov můj?* (Where is My Home?), which came from one of his plays. In the early 1990s the theatre's name reverted to Estates Theatre. To see the grand interior you'll need to attend a performance – the program is on the website.

KLEMENTINUM HISTORIC BUILDING

Map p332 (☎222 220 879; www.klementinum.cz; entrances on Křížovnická, Karlova & Mariánské náměstí; guided tour adult/child 220/140Kč; ⊙10am-5pm Apr-Oct, to 4pm Nov, Dec & Mar; Ⓜ Staroměstská) The Klementinum is a vast complex of beautiful baroque and rococo halls, now mostly occupied by the Czech National Library. Most of the buildings are closed to the public, but you can walk freely through the courtyards, or take a 50-minute guided tour of the baroque Library Hall, the Astronomical Tower and the Chapel of Mirrors.

When the Habsburg emperor Ferdinand I invited the Jesuits to Prague in 1556 to boost the power of the Roman Catholic Church in Bohemia, they selected one of the city's choicest pieces of real estate and in 1587 set to work on the **Church of the Holy Saviour** (kostel Nejsvětějšího Spasitele; Map p332), Prague's flagship of the Counter-Reformation. Its western facade faces Charles Bridge, its sooty stone saints glaring down at the traffic jam of trams and tourists on Křížovnické náměstí.

After gradually buying up most of the adjacent neighbourhood, the Jesuits started building their college, the Klementinum, in 1653. By the time of its completion a century later it was the largest building in the city after Prague Castle. When the Jesuits fell out with the pope in 1773, it became part of Charles University.

The baroque **Library Hall** (1727), magnificently decorated with ornate gilded carvings and a ceiling fresco depicting the Temple of Wisdom, houses thousands of theological volumes dating back to 1600. Also dating from the 1720s, the **Astronomical Tower** (Map p332) is capped with a huge bronze of Atlas and was used as an observatory until the 1930s; it houses a display of 18th-century astronomical instruments.

The **Chapel of Mirrors** (Zrcadlová kaple; Map p332; ☎222 220 879; www.klementinum.

TOP SIGHTS
ARTBANKA: MUSEUM OF YOUNG ART

The shabby halls of a decaying 18th-century aristocratic palace make the perfect setting for this gallery dedicated to promoting the work of contemporary Czech and international artists. The entire collection is splendidly provocative, from the vending machine in the lobby that dispenses graffiti-making supplies to the huge branded can on the top floor labelled as being full of 'Artist's Shit'.

The gallery supports young Czech and Slovak artists by buying the best of their work, exhibiting it in the gallery, and also renting it out to prestigious private and public organisations. There are a few big names, too, including David Černý, whose imposing installation *Gun* – four huge handguns pointing at each other – is suspended in the palace courtyard. Some exhibits are genuinely shocking, including 'fireside rugs' made with the skins of dogs and cats, 'sexy' underwear fashioned from real rat fur, and naked images of gay Nazis.

The palace was used as office space during the communist era, and the clumsily installed 1950s wiring and heating have been left in place as a symbol of the contempt the authorities had for artistic achievement.

DON'T MISS...

- ➡ David Černý's *Gun* installation
- ➡ Graffiti-supplies vending machine
- ➡ Huge can of 'Artist's Shit'

PRACTICALITIES

- ➡ Map p332
- ➡ ☎240 200 207
- ➡ www.amoya.cz
- ➡ Karlova 2
- ➡ adult/concession 160/80Kč
- ➡ ⊙10am-7pm
- ➡ 🚋17, 18

THE ROYAL WAY

The Royal Way (Královská cesta) was the ancient processional route followed by Czech kings on their way to St Vitus Cathedral for coronation. The route leads from the **Powder Gate** (Prašná brána) along Celetná, through the Old Town Square and Little Square (Malé náměstí), along Karlova (Charles St) and across **Charles Bridge** to Malá Strana Square (Malostranské náměstí), before climbing up Nerudova to the castle. The only procession that makes its way along these streets today is the daily crush of tourists shouldering their way past a gauntlet of gaudy souvenir shops and bored-looking leaflet touts.

Celetná, leading from the Powder Gate to the Old Town Square, is an open-air museum of pastel-painted baroque facades covering Gothic frames resting on Romanesque foundations, deliberately buried to raise Staré Město above the floods of the Vltava River. But the most interesting building – Josef Gočár's delightful **House of the Black Madonna** (dům U černé Matky Boží), now the Museum of Czech Cubism (p103) – dates only from 1912.

Little Square, the southwestern extension of the Old Town Square, has a Renaissance fountain with a 16th-century wrought-iron grill. Here, several fine baroque and neo-Renaissance exteriors adorn some of Staré Město's oldest structures. The most colourful is the 1890 **VJ Rott Building** (Map p332), decorated with wall paintings by Mikuláš Aleš, which now houses the Prague incarnation of the Hard Rock Café.

A dog-leg from the southwestern corner of the square leads to narrow, cobbled Karlova, which continues as far as Charles Bridge – this section is often choked with tourist crowds. On the corner of Liliová is the house called **At the Golden Snake** (U zlatého hada; Map p332), the site of Prague's first coffee house, opened in 1708 by an Armenian named Deomatus Damajan.

Karlova sidles along the massive southern wall of the Klementinum before emerging at the riverside on Křížovnické náměstí. On the north side of the square is the 17th-century **Church of St Francis Seraphinus** (kostel sv Františka Serafinského; Map p332), its dome decorated with a fresco of the Last Judgment. It belongs to the Order of the Knights of the Cross with the Red Star, the only Bohemian order of Crusaders still in existence.

Just south of Charles Bridge, at the site of the former Old Town mill, is **Novotného lávka** (Map p332; Novotného lávka, Staré Město), a riverside terrace full of sunny, overpriced *vinárny* (wine bars) with great views of the bridge and castle, its far end dominated by a statue of composer Bedřich Smetana.

Our walking tour, Not Quite the Royal Way (p108), follows roughly the same route but avoids most of the crowds.

com; adult/child incl Astronomical Tower & Baroque Library 220/140Kč ; ⏲10am-7pm, tours hourly Mon-Thu, every 30min Fri-Sun) dates from the 1720s and is an ornate confection of gilded stucco, marbled columns, fancy frescoes and ceiling mirrors – think baroque on steroids. Concerts of classical music are held here daily (tickets are available at most ticket agencies).

There are two other interesting churches in the Klementinum. The **Church of St Clement** (kostel sv Klimenta; Map p332; ⏲services 8.30am & 10am Sun), lavishly redecorated in the baroque style from 1711 to 1715 to plans by Kilian Dientzenhofer, is now a Greek Catholic chapel. Conservatively dressed visitors are welcome to attend the services. And then there's the elliptical **Chapel of the Assumption of the Virgin Mary** (Vlašská kaple Nanebevzetí Panny Marie; Map p332), built in 1600 for the Italian artisans who worked on the Klementinum (it's still technically the property of the Italian government).

MARIONETTE MUSEUM — MUSEUM

Map p332 (Muzeum loutek; ☎222 228 511; www.puppetart.com; Karlova 12; adult/child 100/50Kč; ⏲10am-8pm May-Oct, noon-6pm Nov-Apr; 🚋17, 18) Rooms peopled with a multitude of authentic, colourful marionettes illustrate the evolution of this wonderful Czech tradition from the late 17th to early 19th centuries. The star attractions are the Czech children's favourites, Spejbl and

THE MISSING MONUMENTS

Prague witnessed several profound changes of political regime during the 20th century: from Habsburg empire to independent Czechoslovak Republic in 1918; to Nazi Protectorate from 1938 to 1945; to communist state in 1948; and back to democratic republic in 1989.

Each change was accompanied by widespread renaming of city streets and squares to reflect the heroes of the new regime. The square in front of the Rudolfinum, for example, has been known variously as Smetanovo náměstí (Smetana Square; 1919–42 and 1945–52); Mozartplatz (Mozart Square; 1942–45); náměstí Krasnoarmějců (Red Army Square; 1952–90); and náměstí Jana Palacha (Jan Palach Square; 1990–present).

This renaming was often followed by the removal of monuments erected by the previous regime. Here are three of Prague's most prominent 'missing monuments'.

The Missing Virgin

If you look at the ground in the Old Town Square (Staroměstské náměstí) about 50m south of the Jan Hus statue, you'll see a circular stone slab set among the cobblestones at the far end of the brass strip marking the Prague Meridian. This was the site of a Marian column (a pillar bearing a statue of the Virgin Mary), erected in 1650 in celebration of the Habsburg victory over the Swedes in 1648. It was surrounded by figures of angels crushing and beating down demons – a rather unsubtle symbol of a resurgent Catholic Church defeating the Protestant Reformation.

The column was toppled by a mob – who saw it as a symbol of Habsburg repression – on 3 November 1918, five days after the declaration of Czechoslovak independence. Its remains can be seen in the Lapidárium (p152).

The Missing Dictator

If you stand in the Old Town Square and look north along the arrow-straight avenue of Pařížská you will see, on a huge terrace at the far side of Čechův most, a giant metronome. If the monumental setting seems out of scale that's because the terrace was designed to accommodate the world's biggest statue of Stalin. Unveiled in 1955 – two years after Stalin's death – the 30m-high, 14,000-tonne colossus showed Uncle Joe at the head of two lines of communist heroes, Czech on one side, Soviet on the other. Cynical Praguers accustomed to constant food shortages quickly nicknamed it *fronta na maso* (the meat queue).

The monument was dynamited in 1962, in deference to Khrushchev's attempt to airbrush Stalin out of history. The demolition crew was instructed, 'it must go quickly, there mustn't be much of a bang, and it should be seen by as few people as possible'. The Museum of Communism (p121) has a superb photo of the monument – and of its destruction.

The Missing Tank

Náměstí Kinských, at the southern edge of Malá Strana, was until 1989 known as náměstí Sovětských tankistů (Soviet Tank Crews Square), named in memory of the Soviet soldiers who 'liberated' Prague on 9 May 1945. For many years a Soviet T-34 tank – allegedly the first to enter the city (in fact it was a later Soviet 'gift') – squatted menacingly atop a pedestal here.

In 1991 artist David Černý decided that the tank was an inappropriate monument to the Soviet soldiers and painted it bright pink. The authorities had it painted green again, and charged Černý with a crime against the state. This infuriated many parliamentarians, 12 of whom repainted the tank pink. Their parliamentary immunity saved them from arrest and secured Černý's release.

After complaints from the Soviet Union the tank was removed. Its former setting is now occupied by a circular fountain surrounded by park benches; the vast granite slab in the centre is split by a jagged fracture, perhaps symbolic of a break with the past. The tank still exists, and is still pink – it's at the Military Museum in Lešany, near Týnec nad Sázavou, 30km south of Prague.

Hurvínek – kids and adults alike can enjoy the Czech equivalent of Punch and Judy at the Spejbl & Hurvínek Theatre.

CHARLES BRIDGE MUSEUM MUSEUM

Map p332 (Muzeum Karlova Mostu; ☎776 776 779; www.charlesbridgemuseum.com; Křížovnické náměstí 3; adult/concession 150/70Kč; ⊙10am-8pm May-Sep, to 6pm Oct-Apr; 17, 18) Founded in the 13th century, the Order of the Knights of the Cross with the Red Star were the guardians of Judith Bridge (and its successor Charles Bridge), with their 'mother house' at the Church of St Francis Seraphinus on Křížovnické náměstí. This museum, housed in the order's headquarters, covers the history of Prague's most famous landmark.

There are displays on ancient bridge-building techniques, masonry and carpentry, and models of both the Judith and Charles Bridges. In Room 16 you can descend into the foundations of the building to see some of the original stonework of Judith Bridge (dating from 1172), but perhaps the most impressive exhibits are the old photographs of flood damage to Charles Bridge in 1890, when three arches collapsed and were swept away.

SMETANA MUSEUM MUSEUM

Map p332 (Muzeum Bedřicha Smetany; ☎222 220 082; www.nm.cz; Novotného lávka 1; adult/child 50/25Kč; ⊙10am-noon & 12.30-5pm Wed-Mon; 17, 18) This small museum is devoted to Bedřich Smetana, Bohemia's favourite composer. It isn't that interesting unless you're a Smetana fan, and has only limited labelling in English, but there's a good exhibit on popular-culture's feverish response to Smetana's opera *The Bartered Bride* – it seems Smetana was the Andrew Lloyd Webber of his day.

Southwestern Staré Město

BETHLEHEM CHAPEL CHURCH

Map p332 (Betlémská kaple; ☎224 248 595; Betlémské náměstí 3; adult/child 60/30Kč; ⊙10am-6.30pm Tue-Sun Apr-Oct, to 5.30pm Nov-Mar; 6, 9, 18, 21, 22) The Bethlehem Chapel is one of Prague's most important churches, being the true birthplace of the Hussite cause. In 1391, Reformist Praguers won permission to build a church where services could be held in Czech instead of Latin, and proceeded to construct the biggest chapel Bohemia had ever seen, able to hold 3000 worshippers.

Jan Hus preached here from 1402 to 1412, marking the emergence of the Reform movement from the sanctuary of the Karolinum (where he was rector). It's now a national cultural monument. In the 18th century the chapel was torn down. Remnants were discovered around 1920, and from 1948 to 1954 – because Hussitism had official blessing as an ancient form of communism – the whole thing was painstakingly reconstructed in its original form, based on old drawings, descriptions, and traces of the original work. Architecturally it was a radical departure, with a simple square hall focused on the pulpit rather than the altar.

Only the southern wall of the chapel is brand new. You can still see some original parts in the eastern wall: the pulpit door, several windows and the door to the preacher's quarters. These quarters, including the rooms used by Hus and others, are also original; they are now used for exhibits. The wall paintings are modern, and are based on old Hussite tracts. The indoor well pre-dates the chapel.

The chapel has an English text available at the door. Every year on the night of 5 July, the eve of Hus' burning at the stake in 1415, a commemorative celebration is held here, with speeches and bell-ringing.

NÁPRSTEK MUSEUM MUSEUM

Map p332 (Náprstkovo muzeum; ☎224 497 500; www.nm.cz; Betlémské náměstí 1; adult/child 80/50Kč; ⊙10am-6pm Tue-Sun; 6, 9, 18, 21, 22) The small Náprstek Museum houses an ethnographical collection of Asian, African and American cultures, founded by Vojta Náprstek, a 19th-century industrialist with a passion for both anthropology and modern technology (his technology exhibits are now part of the National Technical Museum in Holešovice).

The Old Town is littered with tourist traps, especially around the Old Town Square, but there are also plenty of excellent restaurants to discover. The maze of streets leading away from the Old Town Square contains many hidden gems, while the swanky strip of Pařížská boasts a more obvious string

START **REPUBLIC SQUARE (NÁMĚSTÍ REPUBLIKY)**

END **CHARLES BRIDGE**

DISTANCE **1.5KM**

DURATION **45 MINUTES**

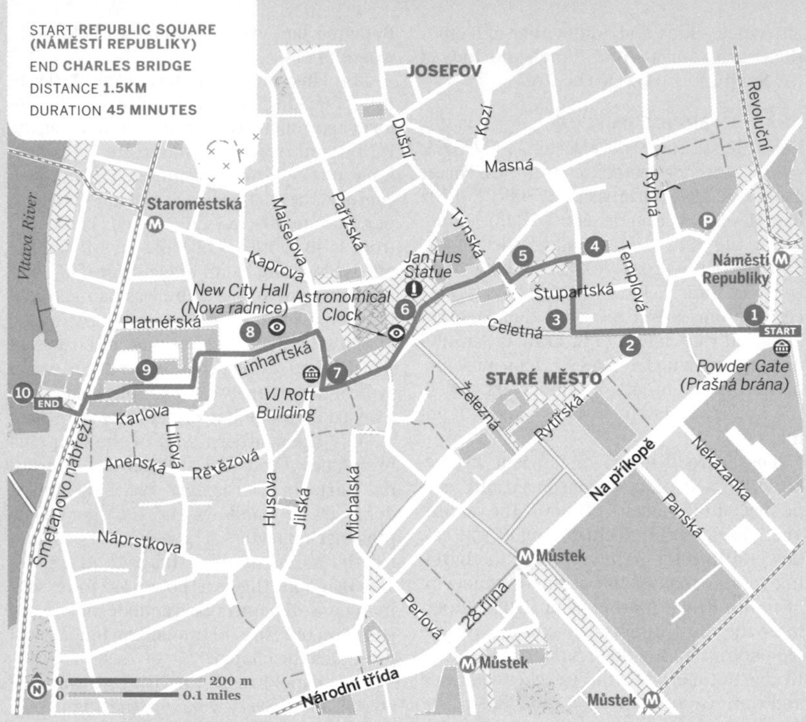

Neighbourhood Walk

Not Quite the Royal Way

From **1** **Republic Square** head towards the Powder Gate and set off along Celetná, which is lined with interesting buildings including the **2** **House of the Black Madonna**, a fine example of cubist architecture, and home to the Museum of Czech Cubism.

Turn right into the passage at Celetná 17, which leads past the **3** **Celetna Theatre**, and then go straight ahead along Malá Štupartská for a look at the baroque sculptures of the **4** **Church of St James**. The cobbled passage near Big Ben Bookshop leads to the **5** **Týn Courtyard**, a lovely square with a Renaissance loggia. Exit at the far end and go along the alley to the right of the Church of Our Lady Before Týn.

You emerge into the **6** **Old Town Square**, dominated by the brooding statue of Jan Hus and the Gothic tower of the Old Town Hall. If you've timed it right, join the crowd to watch a performance by the Astronomical Clock. Continue past the clock to reach **7** **Little Square** (Malé náměstí); ahead is the VJ Rott Building, decorated with murals by Mikuláš Aleš (now home to the Hard Rock Café). Bear right and then left into Linhartská.

This leads to the quieter **8** **Mariánské náměstí** (Virgin Mary Square) and New City Hall (Nova radnice), seat of Prague's city council. The facade is framed by brooding art-nouveau statues by Ladislav Šaloun (the same chap who created the Jan Hus statue in the Old Town Square).

Facing New City Hall is the main gate of the **9** **Klementinum**. Go through the gate and turn left; on the right is the Chapel of Mirrors, where classical concerts are held daily. Continue through the triple arch, then turn right to pass through quiet courtyards (look up to the right to see a sculpture of a child with a paper plane perched on a ledge).

At the far end of the Klementinum you emerge into the bustling crowds of Křížovnické náměstí. End your walk by climbing up the **10** **Old Town Bridge Tower** for a view over Charles Bridge.

of stylish, upmarket eateries. The classic Staré Město dining room is in a brick-lined cellar – you'll soon become a connoisseur of subterranean decor.

MISTRAL CAFÉ BISTRO €

Map p332 (☎222 317 737; www.mistralcafe.cz; Valentinská 11; mains 130-250Kč; ⏰9am-11pm Mon-Fri, 10am-11pm Sat & Sun; 📶; Ⓜ Staroměstská) Is this the coolest bistro in the Old Town? Pale stone, bleached birchwood and potted shrubs make for a clean, crisp, modern look, and the clientele of local students and office workers clearly appreciate the competitively priced, well-prepared food. Fish and chips in crumpled brown paper with lemon and black-pepper mayo – yum!

LOKÁL CZECH €

Map p332 (☎222 316 265; lokal-dlouha.ambi.cz; Dlouhá 33; mains 100-200Kč; ⏰11am-1am Mon-Fri, noon-1am Sat, noon-10pm Sun; 🚋5, 8, 14) Who'd have thought it possible? A classic Czech beer hall (albeit with slick modern decor); excellent *tankové pivo* (tanked Pilsner Urquell); a daily-changing menu of traditional Bohemian dishes; smiling, efficient, friendly service; and a no-smoking area! Top restaurant chain Ambiente has turned its hand to Czech cuisine, and the result has been so successful that the place is always busy, mostly with locals.

MAITREA VEGETARIAN €

Map p332 (☎221 711 631; www.restaurace-maitrea.cz; Týnská ulička 6; mains 130-160Kč; ⏰11.30am-11.30pm Mon-Fri, noon-11.30pm Sat & Sun; 🚭; Ⓜ Staroměstská) Maitrea (a Buddhist term meaning 'the future Buddha') is a beautifully designed space full of flowing curves and organic shapes, from the sensuous polished-oak furniture and fittings to the blossom-like lampshades. The menu is inventive and wholly vegetarian, with dishes such as red bean chilli tortillas, beetroot cakes with sauerkraut and polenta, and pasta with smoked tofu, spinach and parmesan.

INDIAN JEWEL INDIAN €€

Map p332 (☎222 310 156; www.indianjewel.cz; Týn 6; mains 235-275Kč; ⏰11am-11pm; Ⓜ Staroměstská) A long, vaulted room in a medieval building makes an elegant setting for one of Prague's best Indian restaurants, with marble floors, chunky wooden chairs, copper tableware and restrained oriental decor; tables spill into the courtyard in summer. The food impresses, too, with light and flaky parathas, richly spiced sauces, and plenty of fire in the hotter curries.

VINO DI VINO ITALIAN €€

Map p332 (☎222 311 791; www.vinodivinopraha.cz; Štupartská 18; mains 250-300Kč; ⏰noon-10pm; Ⓜ Náměstí Republiky) This Italian wine shop and delicatessen doubles as a restaurant, with a menu that makes the most of all those imported goodies – bresaola with smoked mozzarella, *spaghetti alla chitarra* (with squid and pecorino), and *saltimbocca alla Romana* (beef fillet with prosciutto and sage). Good list of Italian wines, too, including excellent Montepulciano d'Abbruzzo at 590Kč a bottle.

V ZÁTIŠÍ INTERNATIONAL, MODERN CZECH €€€

Map p332 (☎222 221 155; Liliová 1; 2-/3-course meal 890/990Kč; ⏰noon-3pm & 5.30-11pm; 🚋17, 18) 'Still Life' is one of Prague's top restaurants, famed for the quality of its cuisine. The decor is bold and modern, with quirky glassware, boldly patterned wallpapers and cappuccino-coloured crushed-velvet chairs. Of the 10 or so main courses on offer, four are seafood and the rest are meat – nothing vegetarian. There are also gourmet versions of traditional Czech dishes – the crispy roast duckling with red cabbage and herb dumplings is superb. If the three-course dinner is not enough, you can lash out on the five-course *dégustation* menu (1170Kč; plus 770Kč extra for wines to match the dishes).

AMBIENTE PIZZA NUOVA ITALIAN €€

Map p332 (☎221 803 308; Revoluční 1; mains 165-400Kč; ⏰11.30am-11.30pm; Ⓜ Náměstí Republiky) A good idea from the Ambiente team is this cool 1st-floor space next to the Kotva shopping centre, filled with big tables and banquettes with picture windows overlooking náměstí Republiky. For a fixed price (298Kč per person before 6pm, 365Kč after) you get an all-you-can-eat pasta and pizza deal (salad and antipasti buffet and pizza-pasta combined costs 475/555Kč). Wine by the glass is around 75Kč.

KOLKOVNA CZECH €€

Map p332 (☎224 819 701; www.kolkovna-restaurant.cz; V Kolkovně 8; mains 170-350Kč; ⏰11am-midnight; Ⓜ Staroměstská) Owned and operated by the Pilsner Urquell brewery, Kolkovna is a stylish, modern take on the traditional Prague pub, with decor by top Czech designers, and posh (but hearty) versions of classic Czech dishes such as goulash, roast duck and Moravian sparrow, as well as the Czech favourite, pork and dumplings. All washed down with exquisite Urquell beer, of course.

KABUL AFGHAN €

Map p332 (☎224 235 452; www.kabulrestaurant.cz; Karolíny Světlé 14; mains 160-260Kč; ⊙noon-11pm; ✎; 🚋6, 9, 18, 22) Cosy rather than cramped, the Kabul has a welcoming, old-world atmosphere with worn wooden furniture and oriental rugs draped on the walls. It serves a range of unusual Afghani dishes, including *ashak* (a sort of ravioli stuffed with chopped leeks and mint, served with a rich sauce of minced beef and tomato), various lamb and chicken kebabs, and tasty vegetarian specialities.

AMBIENTE PASTA FRESCA ITALIAN €€

Map p332 (☎224 230 244; Celetná 11; mains 190-250Kč; ⊙11am-midnight; ✎; Ⓜ Náměstí Republiky) Slick styling and service with a smile complement an extensive menu at this busy Italian restaurant. Choose from dishes such as melt-in-the-mouth carpaccio of beef, piquant spaghetti *aglio-olio* with chilli and crisp pancetta, and rich creamy risotto with asparagus and white wine, plus there is a wide range of Italian and Czech wines. There's a long, narrow cafe at street level, and a cellar restaurant down below.

LEHKÁ HLAVA VEGETARIAN €

Map p332 (☎222 220 665; www.lehkahlava.cz; Boršov 2; mains 120-220Kč; ⊙11.30am-11.30pm Mon-Fri, noon-11.30pm Sat & Sun; ✎; 🚋17, 18) Tucked away down a narrow cul-de-sac, Lehká Hlava (the name means 'clear head') exists in a little world of its own. There are two unusually decorated dining rooms, both with a vaguely psychedelic vibe – tables lit from within, studded with glowing glass spheres or with a radiant wood-grain effect. In the kitchen the emphasis is on healthy, freshly prepared vegetarian and vegan dishes, ranging from hummus and roast vegies to spicy Asian stir-fry.

COUNTRY LIFE VEGETARIAN €

Map p332 (☎224 213 366; www.countrylife.cz; Melantrichova 15; mains 90-180Kč; ⊙10.30am-7.30pm Mon-Thu, 10.30am-3pm Fri, noon-6pm Sun; ✎; Ⓜ Můstek) Prague's first-ever health-food shop opened in 1991, and is an all-vegan cafeteria and sandwich bar offering inexpensive salads, sandwiches, pizzas, vegetarian goulash, sunflower-seed burgers and soy drinks (food is sold by weight, around 30Kč per 100g). There is plenty of seating in the rear courtyard but it can still get crowded at lunchtime, so go early or buy sandwiches to go.

BEAS VEGETARIAN DHABA VEGETARIAN, INDIAN €

Map p332 (☎608 035 727; Týnská 19; mains 90-130Kč; ⊙11am-8pm Mon-Sat, to 6pm Sun; ✎; Ⓜ Náměstí Republiky) Tucked away in a courtyard off Týnská, this friendly, informal little restaurant offers vegetarian curries (cooked by chefs from North India), which are served with rice, salad, chutneys and raita. Unusually for Prague, there's some genuine chilli heat in the food, which is tasty and good value (food sold by weight, around 16Kč per 100g).

BAKESHOP PRAHA BAKERY, SANDWICHES €

Map p332 (☎222 316 823; www.bakeshop.cz; Kozí 1; sandwiches 75-200Kč; ⊙7am-9pm; Ⓜ Staroměstská) This fantastic bakery sells some of the best bread in the city, along with pastries, cakes and takeaway sandwiches, wraps, salads and quiche.

DRINKING & NIGHTLIFE

The Old Town is tourist central, with crowded pubs and prices to match. But all you have to do is explore the maze of narrow backstreets that radiate from the Old Town Square to find hidden gems such as Čili Bar, Duende and Literární Kavárna Řetězová.

PRAGUE BEER MUSEUM PUB

Map p332 (☎732 330 912; www.praguebeermuseum.com; Dlouhá 46; ⊙noon-3am; 🚋5, 8, 14) Although the name seems aimed at the tourist market, this lively and always heaving pub is very popular with Praguers. There are no fewer than 31 beers on tap (plus an extensive beer menu with tasting notes to guide you). Try a sample board – a wooden platter with five 0.15L glasses containing five beers of your choice.

HEMINGWAY BAR COCKTAIL BAR

Map p332 (☎773 974 764; www.hemingwaybar.eu; Karolíny Světlé 26; ⊙5pm-1am Mon-Fri, 7pm-

1am Sat & Sun; 📶; 🚋17, 21) The Hemingway is a snug and sophisticated hideaway with dark leather benches and a library-like backroom, flickering candlelight and polite and professional bartenders. There's a huge range of quality spirits (especially rum), first-class cocktails, champagne and cigars.

KRÁSNÝ ZTRÁTY CAFE

Map p332 (☎775 755 143; www.krasnyztraty.cz; Náprstkova 10; ⏰9am-1am Mon-Fri, noon-1am Sat & Sun; 📶; 🚋17, 18) This cool cafe – the name translates as something like 'beautiful destruction' – doubles as an art gallery and occasional music venue, and is hugely popular with students from nearby Charles University. There are Czech newspapers and books to leaf through, chilled tunes on the sound system, and a menu of gourmet teas and coffees to choose from.

ČILI BAR COCKTAIL BAR

Map p332 (☎777 945 848; www.cilibar.cz; Kožná 8; ⏰5pm-2am; Ⓜ Můstek) This tiny cocktail bar could not be further removed in atmosphere from your typical Old Town drinking place. Cramped and smoky – there are Cuban cigars for sale – with battered leather armchairs competing for space with a handful of tables, it's friendly, relaxed and lively. Don't miss the speciality of the house – a shot of rum mixed with finely chopped red chillis (minimum three shots).

U MEDVÍDKŮ BEER HALL

Map p332 (At the Little Bear; ☎224 211 916; www.umedvidku.cz; Na Perštýně 7; ⏰beer hall 11.30am-11pm, museum noon-10pm; 📶; Ⓜ Národní Třída) The most micro of Prague's microbreweries, with a capacity of only 250L, U Medvídků started producing its own beer only in 2005, though its beer hall has been around for many years. What it lacks in size, it makes up for in strength – the dark lager produced here, marketed as X-Beer, is the strongest in the country, with an alcohol content of 11.8% (as strong as many wines).

Available in bottles only (122Kč for 0.33L), it's a malty, bitter-sweet brew with a powerful punch; handle with caution! There's also Budvar on tap at 32Kč for 0.4L.

KOZIČKA BAR

Map p332 (☎224 818 308; www.kozicka.cz; Kozí 1; ⏰noon-4am Mon-Fri, 6pm-4am Sat, 7pm-3am Sun; Ⓜ Staroměstská) The 'Little Goat' is a buzzing, red-brick basement bar decorated with cute steel goat sculptures, serving Krušovice on tap at 45Kč for 0.5L (though watch out – the bartenders will occasionally sling you a 1L *tuplák* if they think you're a tourist). It fills up later in the evening with a mostly Czech crowd, and makes a civilised setting for a late-night session.

DUENDE BAR

Map p332 (☎775 186 077; www.barduende.cz; Karolíny Světlé 30; ⏰1pm-midnight Mon-Fri, 3pm-midnight Sat, 4pm-midnight Sun; 🚋17, 18) Barely five minutes' walk from Charles Bridge but half a world away in atmosphere, this cute little bar is the opposite of touristy – a bohemian drinking den that pulls in an arty, mixed-age crowd of locals. Here you can enjoy a drink while casting an eye over the fascinating photos and quirky art that cover the wall, or listen to live guitar or violin.

JAMES JOYCE PUB

Map p332 (☎224 818 851; www.jamesjoyceprague.cz; U obecního dvora 4; ⏰11am-midnight, to 1am Fri & Sat; 📶; 🚋5,8,14) You probably don't go to Prague to visit an Irish bar, but if you're here in winter this friendly pub offers something rarely seen in Prague bars: an open fire. Toast your toes while sipping a Guinness, or downing the all-day Irish breakfast fry, including Clonakilty black pudding.

KÁVA KÁVA KÁVA CAFE

Map p332 (☎224 228 862; Platýz pasáž, Národní třída 37; ⏰7am-10pm Mon-Fri, 9am-10pm Sat & Sun; 📶; Ⓜ Národní Třída) Serves some of the best coffee in town – the large cappuccino is almost big enough to bathe in – accompanied by toasted bagels, croissants, cakes and pastries.

LITERÁRNÍ KAVÁRNA ŘETĚZOVÁ CAFE

Map p332 (☎222 220 681; Řetězová 10; ⏰noon-11pm Mon-Fri, 5-11pm Sat & Sun; 🚋17, 21) This cafe is the kind of place where you can imagine yourself tapping out the Great Prague Novel on your laptop with a half-finished coffee on the table beside you. It's a plain, vaulted room with battered wooden furniture, a scatter of rugs on the floor, old black-and-white photos on the wall, and a relaxed atmosphere where you can read a book without feeling self-conscious.

U ZLATÉHO TYGRA PUB

Map p332 (☎222 221 111; www.uzlatehotygra.cz; Husova 17; ⏰3-11pm; Ⓜ Staroměstská) The 'Golden Tiger' is one of the few Old Town drinking holes that has hung on to its soul – and its low prices (38Kč per 0.5L of Pilsner Urquell), considering its location. It was novelist Bohumil Hrabal's favourite hostelry – there are photos of him on the walls – and the place that Václav Havel took Bill Clinton in 1994 to show him a real Czech pub.

MONARCH VINNÝ SKLEP WINE BAR

Map p332 (224 239 602; www.monarch.cz; Na Perštýně 15; 3pm-midnight Mon-Sat; M Národní Třída) The Monarch wine cellar is one of the best places in town to get to know Czech wines. Despite its knowledgeable staff and vast selection of vintages, it manages to avoid any air of pretentiousness, and has a tempting menu of nibbles – cheeses, olives, prosciutto, salami and smoked duck – to accompany your wine, which is not as expensive as you might expect.

FRIENDS CLUB

Map p332 (226 211 920; www.friendsclub.cz; Bartolomějská 11; 7pm-6am; ; M Národní Třída) Friends is a welcoming gay bar and club serving excellent coffee, cocktails and wine. It's a good spot to sit back with a drink and check out the crowd, or join in the party spirit on assorted theme nights, which range from Czech pop music and movies to beach parties and comedy nights (see website for listings).

KAVÁRNA OBECNÍ DŮM CAFE

Map p332 (222 002 763; www.kavarnaod.cz; náměstí Republiky 5; 7.30am-11pm; ; M Náměstí Republiky) The spectacular cafe in Prague's opulent Municipal House (p96) (Obecní dům) offers the opportunity to sip your cappuccino amid an orgy of art-nouveau splendour. Also worth a look is the neat little American Bar in the basement of the building, all polished wood, stained glass and gleaming copper.

GRAND CAFE ORIENT CAFE

Map p332 (Ovocný trh 19, Nové Město; M Náměstí Republiky) Prague's only Cubist cafe, the Orient was designed by Josef Gočár and is Cubist down to the smallest detail, including the lampshades and coat hooks. It was restored and reopened in 2005, having been closed since 1920. Decent coffee and inexpensive cocktails.

ENTERTAINMENT

ROXY CLUB, PERFORMING ARTS

Map p332 (224 826 296; www.roxy.cz; Dlouhá 33; admission free-300Kč Fri & Sat; 7pm-midnight Mon-Thu, to 6am Fri & Sat; 5, 8, 14) Set in the ramshackle shell of an art-deco cinema, the legendary Roxy has nurtured the more independent and innovative end of Prague's club spectrum since 1987 – this is the place to see the Czech Republic's top DJs. On the 1st floor is NoD, an 'experimental space' that stages drama, dance, performance art, cinema and live music. Best nightspot in Staré Město.

JAZZ CLUB U STARÉ PANÍ JAZZ

Map p332 (602 148 377; www.jazzstarapani.cz; Michalská 9; admission 250Kč; 7pm-1am Wed-Sun, music from 9pm; M Můstek) Located in the basement of the Hotel U Staré Paní, this long-established but recently revamped jazz club caters to all levels of musical appreciation. There's a varied program of modern jazz, soul, blues and Latin rhythms, and a dinner menu if you want to make a full evening of it.

AGHARTA JAZZ CENTRUM JAZZ

Map p332 (222 211 275; www.agharta.cz; Železná 16; admission 250Kč; 7pm-1am, music 9pm-midnight; M Můstek) AghaRTA has been staging top-notch modern jazz, blues, funk and fusion since 1991, but moved into this central Old Town venue only in 2004. A typical jazz cellar with red-brick vaults, the centre also has a music shop (open 7pm to midnight), which sells CDs, T-shirts and coffee mugs. As well as hosting local musicians, the centre occasionally stages gigs by leading international artists.

BLUES SKLEP JAZZ

Map p332 (221 466 138; www.bluessklep.cz; Liliová 10; admission 100-150Kč; bar 7pm-2.30am, music 9pm-midnight; 17, 18) One of the city's newer jazz clubs, the Blues Sklep (*sklep* means 'cellar') is a typical Old Town basement with dark, Gothic-vaulted rooms that provide an atmospheric setting for regular nightly jazz sessions. Bands play anything from trad New Orleans jazz to bebop, blues, funk and soul.

VAGON LIVE MUSIC

Map p332 (733 737 301; www.vagon.cz; Palác Metro, Národní třída 25; gigs 100Kč, admission after midnight free; 7pm-5am Mon-Thu, to 6am

Fri & Sat, to 1am Sun; 📶; 🚋6, 9, 18, 22, Ⓜ Národní Třída) With its entrance tucked away in a shopping arcade, Vagon is more like a student-union bar than a club as such, but it always has a friendly, chilled-out atmosphere. There's live music pretty much every night, from local blues artists, through Pink Floyd and Led Zep tribute bands, to classic Czech rock bands. From midnight into the small hours the dancing continues as a DJ-hosted 'rockothèque'.

DVOŘÁK HALL CONCERT VENUE

Map p332 (Dvořákova síň; ☎227 059 227; www.ceskafilharmonie.cz; náměstí Jana Palacha 1; tickets 200-600Kč; ⏲box office 10am-12.30pm & 1.30-6pm Mon-Fri; Ⓜ Staroměstská) The Dvořák Hall in the neo-Renaissance Rudolfinum is home to the world-renowned Czech Philharmonic Orchestra (Česká filharmonie). Sit back and be impressed by some of the best classical musicians in Prague.

ESTATES THEATRE OPERA, BALLET

Map p332 (Stavovské divadlo; ☎224 902 322; www.narodni-divadlo.cz; Ovocný trh 1; tickets 30-1260Kč; ⏲box office 10am-6pm; Ⓜ Můstek) The Estates Theatre is the oldest theatre in Prague, famed as the place where Mozart conducted the premiere of *Don Giovanni* on 29 October 1787. Mozartissimo – a medley of highlights from several of Mozart's operas, including *Don Giovanni* – is performed here several times a week from May to August (see www.bmart.cz); the rest of the year sees various opera, ballet and drama productions.

SMETANA HALL CLASSICAL MUSIC

Map p332 (Smetanova síň; ☎222 002 101; www.obecnidum.cz; náměstí Republiky 5; tickets 250-600Kč; ⏲box office 10am-6pm; Ⓜ Náměstí Republiky) Smetana Hall, centrepiece of the stunning Municipal House (p96) (Obecní dům), is the city's largest concert hall, with seating for 1200. This is the home venue of the Prague Symphony Orchestra (Symfonický orchestr hlavního města Prahy), and also stages performances of folk dance and music.

IMAGE THEATRE PERFORMING ARTS

Map p332 (Divadlo Image; ☎222 314 448; www.imagetheatre.cz; Pařížská 4; tickets 480Kč; ⏲box office 9am-8pm; Ⓜ Staroměstská) Founded in 1989, this company uses creative black-light theatre along with pantomime, modern dance and video – not to mention liberal doses of slapstick – to tell its stories. The staging can be very effective, but the atmosphere is often dictated by the audience's reaction.

NATIONAL MARIONETTE THEATRE PERFORMING ARTS

Map p332 (Národní divadlo marionet; ☎224 819 323; www.mozart.cz; Žatecká 1; adult/child 590/490Kč; ⏲box office 10am-8pm; Ⓜ Staroměstská) Loudly touted as the longest-running classical marionette show in the city – it has been performed almost continuously since 1991 (a fact, some say, that is reflected in the enthusiasm of the performances) – *Don Giovanni* is a life-sized puppet version of the Mozart opera that has spawned several imitations around town. Younger kids' attention might begin to wander fairly early on during this two-hour show.

TA FANTASTIKA PERFORMING ARTS

Map p332 (☎222 221 366; www.tafantastika.cz; Karlova 8; tickets 720Kč; ⏲box office 11am-9.30pm; Ⓜ Staroměstská) Established in New York in 1981 by Czech émigré Petr Kratochvil, Ta Fantastika moved to Prague in 1989. The theatre produces black-light theatre based on classic literature and legends such as *Excalibur*, *The Picture of Dorian Gray* and *Joan of Arc*. The most popular show is *Aspects of Alice,* based on *Alice in Wonderland*.

THEATRE ON THE BALUSTRADE THEATRE

Map p332 (Divadlo Na Zábradlí; ☎222 868 868; www.nazabradli.cz; Anenské náměstí 5; tickets 100-325Kč; ⏲box office 2-8pm Mon-Fri, 2hr before show starts Sat & Sun; 🚋17, 18) The theatre where Václav Havel honed his skills as a playwright four decades ago is now the city's main venue for serious Czech-language drama, including works by a range of foreign playwrights translated into Czech. There are also regular performances in English with Czech subtitles.

SHOPPING

LEEDA FASHION

Map p332 (☎224 234 056; www.leeda.cz; Bartolomějská 1; ⏲11am-7pm Mon-Sat; 🚋6, 9, 18, 22) This original Czech label, created by two young Prague designers, Lucie Kutálková and Lucie Trnkov, has established a well-earned reputation for turning out colourful, hip and stylish clothes, from T-shirts to designer dresses – and all at very reasonable prices.

ART DECO GALERIE ANTIQUES

Map p332 (224 223 076; www.artdecogalerie-mili.com; Michalská 21; 2-7pm Mon-Fri; Můstek) Specialising in early-20th-century items, this shop has a wide range of 1920s and '30s stuff, including clothes, handbags, jewellery, glassware and ceramics, along with knick-knacks such as the kind of cigarette case you might imagine Dorothy Parker pulling from her purse.

MODERNISTA HOMEWARES

Map p332 (224 241 300; www.modernista.cz; Celetná 12; 11am-7pm; Náměstí Republiky) Modernista is an elegant gallery specialising in reproduction 20th-century furniture in classic styles ranging from art deco and Cubist to functionalist and Bauhaus, including sensuously curved chairs that are a feature of the Icon Hotel, and an unusual chaise lounge by Adolf Loos (a copy of the one in the Villa Müller (p52)). The shop is inside the arcade at Celetná 12 (not visible from the street).

ART DÉCORATIF ARTS & CRAFTS

Map p332 (222 002 350; www.artdecoratif.cz; U Obecního Domu 2; 10am-8pm; Náměstí Republiky) This is a beautiful shop dealing in Czech-made reproductions of art-nouveau and art-deco glassware, jewellery and fabrics, including some stunning vases and bowls. It's also an outlet for the gorgeously delicate creations of Jarmila Plockova, granddaughter of Alfons Mucha, who uses elements of his paintings in her work.

KUBISTA HOMEWARES

Map p332 (224 236 378; www.kubista.cz; Ovocný trh 19; 10am-6pm Tue-Sun; Náměstí Republiky) Appropriately located in the Museum of Czech Cubism in Prague's finest cubist building, this shop specialises in limited-edition reproductions of distinctive cubist furniture and ceramics, and designs by masters of the form such as Josef Gočár and Pavel Janák. It also has a few original pieces for serious collectors with serious cash to spend.

BOŘEK ŠÍPEK GLASSWARE

Map p332 (224 814 099; www.boreksipek.com; Valentinská 11; 10am-6pm Mon-Fri, 11am-5pm Sun; Staroměstská) This is the showroom for the striking and colourful glassware of Bořek Šípek, one of the Czech Republic's leading architects and designers. His work may not be to everyone's taste, but his eccentric creations are certainly eye-catching.

BIG BEN BOOKS

Map p332 (224 826 565; www.bigbenbookshop.com; Malá Štupartská 5; 9am-8pm Mon-Fri, 10am-8pm Sat, 11am-6pm Sun; Náměstí Republiky) Big Ben is a small but well-stocked English-language bookshop, with shelves devoted to Czech and European history, books on Prague, travel (including Lonely Planet guides), science fiction, children's books, poetry and the latest fiction best sellers. There are also English-language newspapers and magazines at the counter.

KLARA NADEMLÝNSKÁ FASHION

Map p332 (224 818 769; www.klaranademlynska.cz; Dlouhá 3; 10am-7pm Mon-Fri, to 6pm Sat; Staroměstská) Klara Nademlýnská is one of the Czech Republic's top fashion designers, having trained in Prague and worked for almost a decade in Paris. Her clothes are characterised by clean lines, simple styling and quality materials, making for a very wearable range that covers the spectrum from swimwear to evening wear via jeans, halter tops, colourful blouses and sharply styled suits.

TEG FASHION

Map p332 (222 327 358; www.timoure.cz; V Kolkovně 6; 10am-7pm Mon-Fri, 11am-5pm Sat; Staroměstská) TEG (Timoure et Group) is the design team created by Alexandra Pavalová and Ivana Šafránková, two of Prague's most respected fashion designers. This boutique showcases their quarterly collections, which feature a sharp, imaginative look that adds zest and sophistication to everyday, wearable clothes. There's a second **branch** (Map p332; 224 240 737; Martinská 4; 10am-7pm Mon-Fri, to 5pm Sat; Národní Třída) near Národní třída.

BOHÈME FASHION

Map p332 (224 813 840; www.boheme.cz; Dušní 8; 11am-7pm Mon-Fri, to 5pm Sat; Staroměstská) This boutique showcases the designs of Hana Stocklassa and her associates, with collections of knitwear, leather and suede clothes for women. Sweaters, turtlenecks, suede skirts, linen blouses, knit dresses and stretch denim suits seem to be the stock in trade, and there's a range of jewellery to choose from as well.

LE PATIO LIFESTYLE HOMEWARES

Map p332 (☎222 310 310; www.lepatiolifestyle.com; Dušní 8; ⏲10am-7pm Mon-Sat, 11am-7pm Sun; Ⓜ Staroměstská) There are lots of high-quality household accessories here, from wrought-iron chairs and lamps forged by Bohemian blacksmiths to scented wooden chests made by Indian carpenters. Plus you'll find funky earthenware plant pots, chunky crystal wine glasses in contemporary designs, and many more tempting items that you just *know* will fit into your already crammed suitcase...

MANUFAKTURA ARTS & CRAFTS

Map p332 (☎257 533 678; www.manufaktura.cz; Melantrichova 17; ⏲10am-8pm; Ⓜ Můstek) There are several Manufaktura outlets across town, but this small branch near the Old Town Square seems to keep its inventory especially enticing. You'll find great Czech wooden toys, beautiful-looking (if extremely chewy) honey gingerbread made from elaborate medieval moulds, and seasonal gifts such as hand-painted Easter eggs.

QUBUS ARTS & CRAFTS

Map p332 (☎222 313 151; www.qubus.cz; Rámová 3; ⏲10am-6pm Mon-Fri; Ⓜ Staroměstská) This small design studio looks more impressive online than in the flesh, but Qubus – run by leading Czech designers Maxim Velčoský and Jakon Berdych – is worth a visit if you're interested in cutting-edge household accessories ranging from 'liquid lights' (lamps in the form of teardrops) to crystal wine glasses in the shape of disposable plastic cups. Whatever floats your avant-garde boat...

FREY WILLE JEWELLERY

Map p332 (☎272 142 228; www.frey-wille.com; Havířská 3; ⏲10am-7pm Mon-Sat, noon-6pm Sun; Ⓜ Můstek) An Austrian jewellery maker famed for its enamel work, Frey Wille produces a distinctive range of highly decorative pieces. Its traditional paisley and Egyptian designs are complemented by a range of art-nouveau designs based on the works of Alfons Mucha.

GRANÁT TURNOV JEWELLERY

Map p332 (☎222 315 612; www.granat.eu; Dlouhá 28-30; ⏲10am-6pm Mon-Fri, to 1pm Sat; Ⓜ Náměstí Republiky) Part of the country's biggest jewellery chain, Granát Turnov specialises in Bohemian garnet, and has a huge range of gold and silver rings, necklaces, brooches and cufflinks featuring the small, dark blood-red stones. There's also pearl and diamond jewellery, and less expensive pieces set with the dark green semi-precious stone known in Czech as *vltavín* (moldavite).

MAXIMUM UNDERGROUND MUSIC

Map p332 (☎724 307 198; www.maximum.cz; Jílská 22; ⏲11am-7pm Mon-Sat; Ⓜ Můstek) On the 1st floor in an arcade just off Jílská, this place is stocked with CDs and LPs of indie, punk, hip hop, techno and other genres. It also has a selection of new and second-hand street and club wear for those seeking that Central European grunge look.

TALACKO MUSIC

Map p332 (☎224 813 039; www.talacko.cz; Rybná 29; ⏲10am-6pm Mon-Fri, to 4pm Sat; Ⓜ Náměstí Republiky) Pick up the score for Mozart's *Don Giovanni* or Dvořák's *New World Symphony* at this eclectic sheet-music shop. Or you might enjoy some popular music favourites – how about '101 Beatles Songs for Buskers'?

BRIC A BRAC ANTIQUES

Map p332 (☎224 815 763; Týnská 7; ⏲10am-6pm; Ⓜ Náměstí Republiky) This is a wonderfully cluttered cave of old household items and glassware and toys and apothecary jars and 1940s leather jackets and cigar boxes and typewriters and stringed instruments and... Despite the junky look of the place, the knick-knacks are surprisingly expensive, but the affable Serbian owner can give you a guided tour around every piece in his extensive collection.

HAVELSKÁ MARKET MARKET

Map p332 (Havelská; ⏲7.30am-6pm Mon-Fri, 8.30am-6pm Sat & Sun; Ⓜ Můstek) Souvenirs have insinuated themselves among the fruit and veg of this formerly produce-only market. While the shops on either side of the street are selling entirely resistible tat, the market stalls are worth a quick browse for fresh honey or sweets, as well as colourfully painted eggs sold in the run-up to Easter.

KOTVA SUPERMARKET

Map p332 (www.od-kotva.cz; Revoluční 1; ⏲9am-8pm Mon-Fri, 9am-6pm Sat, 10am-6pm Sun; Ⓜ Náměstí Republiky) For self-catering, head to this basement supermarket.

Nové Město

NORTHERN NOVÉ MĚSTO | WENCESLAS SQUARE & AROUND | ALONG THE RIVER | CHARLES SQUARE & AROUND

Neighbourhood Top Five

❶ Admire some of the city's finest 20th-century architecture in and around **Wenceslas Square** (p118), from the art-nouveau extravagance of the Hotel Evropa to the sleekly functionalist **Mánes Gallery** (p123) and the exuberant **Dancing Building** (p123).

❷ Attend a performace of Dvořák's music in the Víla Amerika by the **Original Music Theatre of Prague** (p130).

❸ Learn about a dramatic WWII assassination in the **National Memorial to the Heroes of the Heydrich Terror** (p123).

❹ Discover the beautiful art-nouveau masterpieces of Prague's most famous artist at the **Mucha Museum** (p122).

❺ Explore the magnificent arcades, such as those in **Lucerna Palace** (p121), and hidden gardens of Nové Město on foot (p126).

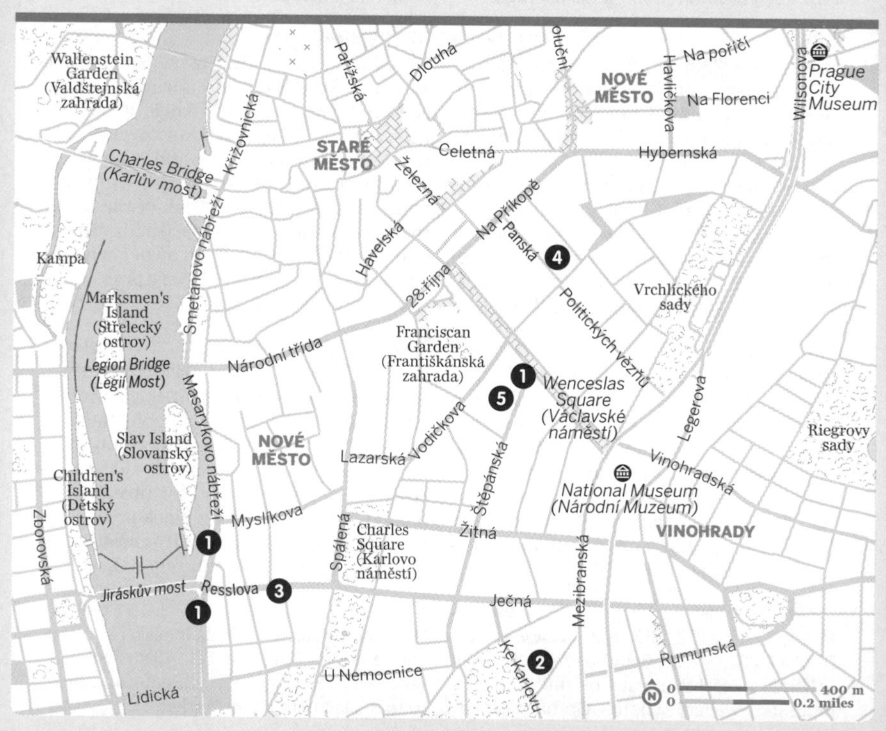

For more detail of this area, see Maps p336 and p338

Explore: Nové Město

Nové Město means 'New Town', although this crescent-shaped district to the east and south of Staré Město was new only when it was founded by Charles IV in 1348. It extends eastwards from Revoluční and Na Příkopě to Wilsonova and the main railway line, and south from Národní třída to Vyšehrad.

Most of Nové Město's outer fortifications were demolished in 1875 – a section of wall still survives in the south, facing Vyšehrad – but the original street plan of the area has been essentially preserved, with three large market squares that once provided the district's commercial focus: Senovážné náměstí (Hay Market Square), Wenceslas Square (Václavské náměstí; originally called Koňský trh, or Horse Market) and Charles Square (Karlovo náměstí; originally called Dobytčí trh, or Cattle Market).

Though originally a medieval neighbourhood, most of the surviving buildings in this area are from the 19th and early 20th centuries, many of them among the city's finest examples of art-nouveau, neo-Renaissance, Czech National Revival and functionalist architecture. Many blocks are honeycombed with pedestrian-only arcades – Prague's famous *pasážy* (passages) – lined with shops, cafes, cinemas and theatres.

Local Life

➡ **A Night at the Opera** Get dressed up to the nines and join the crowds of similarly spruced-up Praguers attending a performance at the Prague State Opera (p130) – only tourists dress down.

➡ **Popular Hangouts** The Bokovka (p128) wine bar is owned by a couple of Czech film directors, and is a popular meeting place for local arty types. Kávovarna (p128) is another place where locals outnumber tourists by a long way, despite being a few steps from Wenceslas Square.

Getting There & Away

➡ **Metro** The city's three metro lines all intersect in Nové Město, at Muzeum and Můstek stations at the eastern and western ends (respectively) of Wenceslas Square, and at Florenc station in northern Nové Město, while Karlovo náměstí station on line B serves southern Nové Město.

➡ **Tram** Cutting across the middle of Wenceslas Square, trams 3, 9, 14 and 24 run along Vodičkova and Jindřišská. Lines 17 and 21 run along the river embankment in the west.

Lonely Planet's Top Tip

If you want to get away from the crowds and constant traffic of Wenceslas Square, find your way to the **Franciscan Garden** (p123) – an oasis of peace just a short stroll away from the urban madness.

Best Places to Eat

➡ Sansho (p127)
➡ Le Patio (p127)
➡ Oliva (p128)
➡ Suterén (p127)
➡ Kogo (p127)

For reviews, see p125 ➡

Best Places to Drink

➡ Bokovka (p128)
➡ Pivovarský Dům (p128)
➡ Kávovarna (p128)
➡ Café Imperial (p128)
➡ Jáma (p128)

For reviews, see p128 ➡

TOP SIGHTS
WENCESLAS SQUARE

More a broad boulevard than a typical city square, Wenceslas Square has witnessed a great deal of Czech history – a giant Mass was held here during the revolutionary upheavals of 1848; in 1918 the creation of the new Czechoslovak Republic was celebrated here; and in 1989 the fall of communism was announced here. Originally a medieval horse market, the square was named after Bohemia's patron saint during the nationalist revival of the mid-19th century.

Velvet Revolution

Following a police attack on a student demonstration on 17 November 1989, angry citizens gathered in Wenceslas Square by the thousands night after night. A week later, in a stunning mirror image of Klement Gottwald's 1948 proclamation of communist rule in Old Town Square, Alexander Dubček and Václav Havel stepped onto the balcony of the Melantrich Building to a thunderous and tearful ovation, and proclaimed the end of communism in Czechoslovakia.

St Wenceslas Statue

At the southern end of the square is Josef Myslbek's muscular equestrian statue of St Wenceslas (sv Václav), the 10th-century pacifist Duke of Bohemia and the 'Good King Wenceslas' of Christmas carol fame. Flanked by other patron saints of Bohemia – Prokop, Adalbert, Agnes and Ludmila – he has been plastered with posters and bunting at every one of the square's historical moments.

Memorial to the Victims of Communism

Near the statue, a memorial to the victims of communism bears photographs and epitaphs to Jan Palach and other anticommunist rebels. In contrast, the square around the shrine has become a monument to capitalism, a gaudy gallery of fast-food outlets and expensive shops.

Architecture

➡ **Grand Hotel Evropa** (Map p338; ☎224 228 117; www.hotelevropa.cz; Ⓜ Můstek) (No 25; 1906) Perhaps the most beautiful building on the square, art-nouveau inside and out; look at the French restaurant at the rear of the ground floor, and at the 2nd-floor atrium.

➡ **Melantrich Building** (Map p338) (No 36; 1914) Now a Marks & Spencer; the balcony overlooking Tramvaj Café is where Havel and Dubček announced the end of communist rule.

➡ **Wiehl House** (Wiehlův dům; Map p338) (No 34; 1896) Has a gorgeous facade decorated with neo-Renaissance murals by top Czech artist Mikuláš Aleš and others; it's named after its designer, Antonín Wiehl.

➡ **Baťa shoe store** (Map p338) (No 6; 1929) A functionalist masterpiece designed by Ludvík Kysela for Tomáš Baťa, art patron and founder of the worldwide shoe empire.

➡ **Lindt Building** (Map p338) (No 4; 1927) Also designed by Ludvík Kysela, and one of the republic's earliest functionalist buildings.

➡ **Koruna Palace** (Palác Koruna; Map p338; ⏲ 7am-10pm mid Apr-mid Sep, 7am-8pm mid Sep-mid Oct, 8am-7pm mid Oct-mid-Apr) (No 1; 1914) This art nouveau design by Antonín Pfeiffer has a tower topped with a crown of pearls; note its tiny but charming facade around the corner on Na Příkopě.

DON'T MISS...

- ➡ St Wenceslas Statue
- ➡ Memorial to the Victims of Communism
- ➡ Grand Hotel Evropa
- ➡ Bat'a Shoe Store

PRACTICALITIES

- ➡ Václavské náměstí
- ➡ Map p338
- ➡ Ⓜ Můstek, Muzeum

TOP SIGHTS
NATIONAL MUSEUM

Looming above Wenceslas Square is the neo-Renaissance bulk of the National Museum, designed in the 1880s by Josef Schulz as an architectural symbol of the Czech National Revival. Its magnificent interior is a shrine to the cultural, intellectual and scientific history of the Czech Republic.

History

Completed in 1891, the imposing facade of the National Museum dominates the southern end of Wenceslas Square, and has played a part in many of the historical events that happened here. The building was occupied by the Nazis during WWII, and was damaged by a bomb on 7 May 1945, allegedly dropped by the last enemy plane to fly over the city during the German withdrawal. In 1968, invading Warsaw Pact troops apparently mistook the museum for the former National Assembly or the radio station, and raked it with gunfire; the light-coloured areas on the facade are patched up bullet holes. And in January 1969 the student Jan Palach set himself on fire here in protest at the Warsaw Pact invasion – you'll find a cross-shaped **memorial** set into the pavement, to the left of the fountain in front of the museum, that marks the spot where he fell.

Main Building

The museum's main building is closed until 2015 for a major overhaul that will create extended exhibition spaces, covered courtyards and a museum shop and cafe. The marbled splendour of the interior, which has appeared in several Hollywood films including *Mission Impossible* with Tom Cruise, *From Hell* starring Johnny Depp, and *Casino Royale* with Daniel Craig, will remain unchanged. The opulent **main staircase** is an extravaganza of polished limestone and serpentine, lined with paintings of Bohemian castles and medallions of kings and emperors. The domed **pantheon**, with four huge lunette paintings of (strangely womanless) Czech legend and history by František Ženíšek and Václav Brožík, houses bronze busts and statues of the great and the good of Czech art and science.

New Building

In 2009 the museum expanded into the old Radio Free Europe/Radio Liberty building next door. The so-called New Building now hosts changing exhibitions on various historical, scientific and technological themes. These range from subjects such as the gold treasure of Košice (a hoard of gold coins and jewellery discovered in Slovakia in 1935), famous Czech and Slovak inventors, and 100 years of the Olympic games, to an exhibition on Czechoslovakia under communist rule, which provided some grimly fascinating insights into this dark period of recent history. Between 1948 and 1989 at least 280 civilians died trying to cross the border to the west. During the same period 584 of the 19,000-strong border guard died, including 185 suicides, 39 shot, and 243 through injury and accident; only 11 were killed by escapees.

DON'T MISS...

- Main staircase
- Pantheon
- Exhibition on communist rule

PRACTICALITIES

- Národní muzeum
- Map p338
- ☎224 497 111
- www.nm.cz
- Václavské náměstí 68
- admission to new building only, adult/child 80/40Kč
- 10am-6pm, to 8pm 1st Wed of the month, closed 1st Tue of the month
- Muzeum

SIGHTS

Northern Nové Město

PRAGUE MAIN TRAIN STATION ARCHITECTURE

Map p336 (Praha Hlavní Nádraží; Wilsonova; closed 12.40-3.15am; M Hlavní Nádraží) What? The railway station is a tourist attraction? Perhaps not all of it, but it's certainly worth heading to the top floor for a look at the grimy, soot-blackened splendour of the original art-nouveau entrance hall that was designed by Josef Fanta and built between 1901 and 1909.

The dilapidated, domed interior is adorned with a mosaic of two nubile ladies, the Latin inscription *Praga: mater urbium* (Prague, Mother of Cities) and the date '28. října r:1918' (28 October 1918, Czechoslovakia's Independence Day). The hall is currently home to the Fantová Kavárna (Fanta Cafe), but there are plans to use the space for displaying the *Slav Epic,* a series of 20 historical paintings on a grand scale by art-nouveau artist Alfons Mucha. The paintings are currently displayed at Veletržní Palác (p151).

JINDŘIŠSKÁ TOWER TOWER

Map p336 (Jindřišská věž; 224 232 429; www.jindrisskavez.cz; Jindřišská 1; adult/child 80/35Kč; 10am-7pm; 3, 9, 14, 24) This bell tower, dating from the 15th century but rebuilt in Gothic style in the 1870s, dominates the end of Jindřišská, a busy street running northeast from Wenceslas Square. Having stood idle for decades, the tower was renovated and reopened in 2002 as a tourist attraction, complete with exhibition space, whisky bar, cafe and restaurant, and a lookout gallery on the 10th floor.

JUBILEE SYNAGOGUE SYNAGOGUE

Map p338 (Jubilejní synagóga; 222 319 002; Jeruzalémská 7; adult/child 80/50Kč; 11am-5pm Sun-Fri Apr-Oct, closed on Jewish holidays; M Hlavní Nádraží) You don't have to be an architecture buff to appreciate the rather striking and colourful Moorish facade of the Jubilee Synagogue. This grand building, also called the Velká synagóga (Great Synagogue), dates from 1906. Note the names of the donors on the stained-glass windows, and the grand organ above the entrance.

TOP SIGHTS
PRAGUE CITY MUSEUM

This excellent museum, opened in 1898, is devoted to the history of Prague from prehistoric times to the 20th century. Among the many intriguing exhibits are the **Astronomical Clock's original 1866 calendar wheel** with Josef Mánes' beautiful painted panels representing the months – that's January at the top, toasting his toes by the fire, and August near the bottom, sickle in hand, harvesting the corn.

The medieval and renaissance galleries display lots of fascinating household artefacts, including a reliquary made of carved bone, plus more valuable items such as a 16th-century bronze figure of Hercules which was perhaps created for the Wallenstein Palace (it was found in a private house in the Old Town in 1905).

But what everybody comes to see is Antonín Langweil's astonishing **1:480 scale model of Prague** as it looked between 1826 and 1834. The display is most rewarding after you get to know Prague a bit, as you can spot the changes – look at St Vitus Cathedral, for example, still only half-finished. Labels are in English as well as Czech.

DON'T MISS...

- Antonín Langweil's impressively detailed scale model of Prague
- Manes' beautiful calendar wheel

PRACTICALITIES

- Muzeum hlavního města Prahy
- Map p336
- 224 816 773
- www.muzeumpraha.cz
- Na Poříčí 52, Karlin
- adult/child 120/50Kč
- 9am-6pm Tue-Sun
- M Florenc

Wenceslas Square & Around

WENCESLAS SQUARE SQUARE

See p118.

NATIONAL MUSEUM MUSEUM

See p119.

LUCERNA PALACE ARCHITECTURE

Map p338 (Palác Lucerna; www.lucerna.cz; Vodičkova 36; 🚋3, 9, 14, 24) The most elegant of Nové Město's many shopping arcades runs through the art-nouveau Lucerna Palace (1920), between Štěpánská and Vodičkova streets. The complex was designed by Václav Havel (grandfather of the ex-president), and is still partially owned by the family. It includes theatres, a cinema, shops, a rock club and several cafes and restaurants.

In the marbled atrium hangs artist David Černý's sculpture **Kun** (Horse), a wryly amusing counterpart to the equestrian statue of St Wenceslas in Wenceslas Square. Here St Wenceslas sits astride a horse that is decidedly dead; Černý never comments on the meaning of his works, but it's safe to assume that this Wenceslas (Václav in Czech) is a reference to Václav Klaus, former prime minister and now president of the Czech Republic.

The neighbouring Novák Arcade, connected to the Lucerna and riddled by a maze of passages, has one of Prague's finest art nouveau facades (overlooking Vodičkova), complete with mosaics of country life.

MUSEUM OF COMMUNISM MUSEUM

Map p338 (Muzeum Komunismu; ☎224 212 966; www.muzeumkomunismu.cz; Na Příkopě 10; adult/concession/child under 10yr 190/150Kč/free; ⏲9am-9pm; Můstek) It's difficult to think of a more ironic site for a museum of communism – in an 18th-century aristocrat's palace, between a casino on one side and a McDonald's on the other. Put together by an American expat and his Czech partner, the museum tells the story of Czechoslovakia's years behind the Iron Curtain in photos, words and a fascinating and varied collection of…well, stuff.

The empty shops, corruption, fear and double-speak of life in socialist Czechoslovakia are well conveyed, and there are rare photos of the Stalin monument that once stood on Letná terrace – and its spectacular destruction. Be sure to watch the video about protests leading up to the Velvet Revolution: you'll never think of it as a pushover again.

NA PŘÍKOPĚ STREET

Map p338 (Ⓜ Můstek) Na Příkopě (On the Moat), along with Revoluční (Revolution), 28.října (28 October 1918; Czechoslovak Independence Day) and Národní třída (National Ave), follows the line of the moat that once ran along the foot of Staré Město's city walls (the moat was filled in at the end of the 18th century).

Na Příkopě meets Wenceslas Square at Na Můstku (On the Little Bridge). A small stone bridge once crossed the moat here – you can still see a remaining arch in the underground entrance to Můstek metro station, on the left just past the ticket machines.

In the 19th century this fashionable street was the haunt of Prague's German cafe society. Today it is (along with Wenceslas Square and Pařížská) the city's main upmarket shopping precinct, lined with banks, shopping malls and tourist cafes.

NÁRODNÍ TŘÍDA

(Map p338) Národní třída (National Ave) is central Prague's 'high street', a stately row of midrange shops and grand public buildings, notably the National Theatre at the Vltava River end.

Fronting Jungmannovo náměstí, at the eastern end, is an imitation Venetian palace known as the **Adria Palace** (Map p338; Národní třída 36, Nové Město). Its distinctive, chunky architectural style, dating from the 1920s, is known as 'rondocubism'. Note how the alternating angular and rounded window pediments echo similar features in neoclassical baroque buildings such as the Černín Palace.

Beneath it is the **Adria Theatre**, birthplace of Laterna Magika and meeting place of Civic Forum in the heady days of the Velvet Revolution. From here, Dubček and Havel walked to the Lucerna Palace and their 24 November 1989 appearance on the balcony of the Melantrich Building. Wander through the arcade for a look at the lovely marble, glass and brass decoration; the main atrium has a 24-hour clock from the 1920s, flanked by sculptures depicting the signs of the zodiac. It was once the entrance to the offices of the Adriatica

TOP SIGHTS
MUCHA MUSEUM

This fascinating (and busy) museum features the sensuous art-nouveau posters, paintings and decorative panels of Alfons Mucha (1860–1939), as well as many sketches, photographs and other memorabilia. The exhibits include countless artworks showing Mucha's trademark Slavic maidens with flowing hair and piercing blue eyes, bearing symbolic garlands and linden boughs.

There are also photos of the artist's Paris studio, one of which shows a trouserless **Gaugin** playing the harmonium; a powerful canvas entitled *Old Woman in Winter*; and the original 1894 poster of actress **Sarah Bernhardt** as Giselda, which shot him to international fame.

Mucha was commissioned by Parisian jeweller George Fouquet to create a collection of art-nouveau jewellery – and Fouquet's entire jewellery shop (the original interior is preserved in the Musée Carnavalet in Paris). In 1910 he was invited to design the Lord Mayor's Hall in Prague's Municipal House and, following the creation of Czechoslovakia in 1918, he designed the new nation's banknotes and postage stamps. But his crowning achievement was the *Slav Epic*, a series of huge, historical paintings npw on display at the Veletržní Palác (p151).

The 30-minute **documentary** about Mucha is worth watching, and puts his achievements into perspective.

DON'T MISS...

- The classic 1894 poster of Sarah Bernhardt that made Mucha famous.
- The photograph of a trouserless Gaugin in Mucha's studio.
- The documentary about Mucha's life.

PRACTICALITIES

- Muchovo muzeum
- Map p336
- ☎221 451 333
- www.mucha.cz
- Panská 7
- adult/child 180/120Kč
- ⌚10am-6pm
- Ⓜ Můstek

insurance company (hence the building's name).

Along the street, inside the arcade near No 16, is a bronze plaque on the wall with a cluster of hands making the peace sign and the date '17.11.89', in memory of students beaten up by police on that date.

West of Voršilská, the lemon-yellow walls of the **Convent of St Ursula** (klášter sv Voršila; Map p338; Národní třída 10) frame a pink church, which has a lush baroque interior that includes a battalion of Apostle statues. Out the front is a figure of St John of Nepomuk, and in the facade's lower-right niche is a statue of St Agatha holding her severed breasts – one of the more gruesome images in Catholic hagiography.

Across the road at No 7 is the art-nouveau facade (by Osvald Polívka) of the **Viola Building** (Národní třída 7), former home of the Prague Insurance Co, with the huge letters 'PRAHA' entwined around five circular windows, and mosaics spelling out *život, kapitál, důchod, věno* and *pojišťuje* (life, capital, income, dowry and insurance). The building next door, a former publishing house, is also a Polívka design.

On the southern side at No 4, looking like it has been built out of old TV screens, is the **Nová Scéna** (1983), the 'New National Theatre' building, now home of Laterna Magika (p130).

Finally, facing the Vltava near Smetanovo nábřeží is the magnificent National Theatre (Národní divadlo). Across from the theatre is the **Kavárna Slavia**, known for its art-deco interior and river views, and once the place to be seen or to grab an after-theatre meal. Now renovated, it's once again the place to be seen – though mainly by other tourists.

NATIONAL THEATRE THEATRE

Map p338 (Národní divadlo; www.narodni-divadlo.cz; Ostrovní 1, main entrance on Národní třída; 🚋6, 9, 18, 21, 22) The National Theatre is the neo-Renaissance architectural flagship of the Czech National Revival, and one of Prague's most impressive buildings. Funded entirely by private donations and decorated inside and out by a roll-call of prominent Czech artists, architect Josef Zítek's masterpiece burned down within weeks of its 1881 opening but, incredibly, was funded again and restored in less than two years.

CHURCH OF OUR LADY OF THE SNOWS — CHURCH

Map p338 (Kostel Panny Marie Sněžné; www.pms.ofm.cz; Jungmannovo náměstí 18; MMůstek) This Gothic church at the northern end of Wenceslas Square was begun in the 14th century by Charles IV, but only the chancel was ever completed, which accounts for its proportions – seemingly taller than it is long. Charles had intended it to be the grandest church in Prague; the nave is higher than that of St Vitus Cathedral, and the altar is the city's tallest.

It was a Hussite stronghold, ringing with the sermons of Jan Želivský, who led the 1419 defenestration that touched off the Hussite Wars. The church is approached through an arch in the Austrian Cultural Institute on Jungmannovo náměstí, but you can get a good view of the exterior from the neighbouring **Franciscan Garden** (Map p338; entrances on Jungmannovo náměstí, pasáž Vodičkova ulice & pasáž Václavské náměstí). Beside the church is the Chapel of the Pasov Virgin, now a venue for temporary art exhibitions.

Along The River

DANCING BUILDING — ARCHITECTURE

Map p338 (Tančící dům; www.tancici-dum.cz; Rašínovo nábřeží 80; 17, 21) The Dancing Building was built in 1996 by architects Vlado Milunić and Frank Gehry. The curved lines of the narrow-waisted glass tower clutched against its more upright and formal partner led to it being christened the 'Fred & Ginger' building, after legendary dancing duo Fred Astaire and Ginger Rogers. It's surprising how well it fits in with its ageing neighbours.

FREE MÁNES GALLERY — GALLERY

Map p338 (Výstavní síň Mánes; 224 932 938; www.ncvu.cz/manes; Masarykovo nábřeží 1; 10am-8pm Tue-Sun; 17, 21) Spanning a branch of the river beneath a 15th-century water tower is the Mánes Building (1927–30), a masterpiece of functionalist architecture designed by Otakar Novotný. It houses an art gallery founded in the 1920s by a group of artists, headed by painter Josef Mánes, as an alternative to the Czech Academy of Arts.

TOP SIGHTS NATIONAL MEMORIAL TO THE HEROES OF THE HEYDRICH TERROR

The Church of Sts Cyril & Methodius houses a moving memorial to the seven Czech paratroopers who were involved in the assassination of Reichsprotektor Reinhard Heydrich in 1942 (see the boxed text, p125), with an exhibit and video about Nazi persecution of the Czechs.

The paratroopers hid in the church's crypt for three weeks after the killing, until their hiding place was betrayed by the Czech traitor Karel Čurda. The Germans besieged the church, first attempting to smoke the paratroopers out and then flooding the crypt with fire hoses. Three paratroopers were killed in the ensuing fight; the other four took their own lives rather than surrender to the Germans.

In the **crypt** itself you can still see the bullet marks and shrapnel scars on the walls, and signs of the paratroopers' last desperate efforts to dig an escape tunnel to the sewer under the street. On the Resslova side of the church, the narrow gap in the wall of the crypt where the Germans inserted their fire hoses is still pitted with **bullet marks**.

DON'T MISS...

- The bullet-scarred exterior wall of the church.
- The moving exhibit in the crypt.

PRACTICALITIES

- Národní památník hrdinů Heydrichiády
- Map p338
- 224 916 100
- www.pamatnik-heydrichiady.cz
- Resslova 9
- adult/concession 75/35Kč
- 9am-5pm Tue-Sun Mar-Oct, 9am-5pm Tue-Sat Nov-Feb
- MKarlovo Náměstí

THE RIVERFRONT

The Nové Město riverfront, stretching south from the National Theatre to Vyšehrad, is lined with some of Prague's grandest 19th- and early-20th-century architecture. It's a great place for an evening stroll, when the setting sun gilds the facades with a beautiful golden light.

Masarykovo nábřeží (Masaryk Embankment) sports a series of stunning art-nouveau buildings. At No 32 is the duck-egg green **Goethe Institute** (Map p338; Masarykovo nábřeží 32), once the East German embassy, while No 26 is a beautiful apartment building with owls perched in the decorative foliage that twines around the door, dogs peeking from the balconies on the 5th floor, and birds perched atop the balustrade.

No 16 is the **House of the Hlahol Choir** (Map p338; Masarykovo nábřeží 16), built in 1906 by Josef Fanta for a patriotic choral society associated with the Czech National Revival. It's decorated with elaborate musical motifs and topped by a giant mosaic depicting Music – the motto beneath translates as 'Let the song reach the heart; let the heart reach the homeland'.

At the next bridge is **Jirásek Square** (Jiráskovo náměstí), dedicated to writer Alois Jirásek (1851–1930), author of *Old Czech Legends* (studied by all Czech schoolchildren) and an influential figure in the drive towards Czechoslovak independence. His statue is overlooked by the famous Dancing Building (p123).

A little further along the riverbank is **Rašínovo nábřeží 78**, an apartment building designed by the grandfather of ex-president Václav Havel – this was where Havel first chose to live (in preference to Prague Castle) after being elected as president in December 1989, surely the world's least pompous presidential residence.

Two blocks south, on Palackého náměstí, is Stanislav Sucharda's extraordinary art-nouveau **František Palacký Memorial** (Map p338; Palackého náměstí); a swarm of haunted bronze figures (allegories of the writer's imagination) swirling around a stodgy statue of the 19th-century historian and giant of the Czech National Revival.

It is still one of Prague's best venues for viewing contemporary art, with a lively program of changing exhibitions. However, will be closed for renovation works until September 2013.

SLAV ISLAND — ISLAND

Map p338 (Slovanský ostrov; Masarykovo nábřeží; 🚊17, 21) This island is a sleepy, dog-eared sandbank with pleasant gardens, river views and several jetties where you can hire rowing boats. In the middle stands **Žofín**, a 19th-century cultural centre that has been restored and opened as a restaurant and social venue. In 1925 the island was named after the Slav conventions that had taken place here since 1848.

The island's banks were reinforced with stone in 1784, and a spa and dye works were built in the early part of the following century. Bohemia's first train had a demonstration run here in 1841, roaring down the island at a rattling 11km/h. At the southern end is **Šitovská věž** (Map p338), a 15th-century water tower (once part of a mill) with an 18th-century onion-dome roof.

Charles Square & Around

CHARLES SQUARE — SQUARE

Map p338 (Karolovo náměstí; Ⓜ Karlovo náměstí) With an area of more than seven hectares, Charles Square is the city's biggest square; it's more like a small park, really, and was originally the city's cattle market. Presiding over it is the **Church of St Ignatius** (kostel sv Ignáce; Map p338; Ječná 2), a 1660s baroque tour de force designed for the Jesuits by Carlo Lurago.

The baroque palace at the southern end of the square belongs to Charles University. It's known as **Faust House** (Faustův dům; Map p338; Karlovo náměstí 40) because, according to a popular story, this house was where Mephisto took Dr Faust away to hell through a hole in the ceiling, and because of associations with Rudolf II's English court alchemist, Edward Kelley, who toiled here in the 16th century trying to convert lead into gold.

NEW TOWN HALL HISTORIC BUILDING

Map p338 (Novoměstská radnice; ☎224 948 229; www.nrpraha.cz; Karlovo náměstí 23; adult/child 50/30Kč; ⏰10am-6pm Tue-Sun May-Sep; Ⓜ Karlovo Náměstí) The New Town Hall was built in the late 14th century, when the New Town was still new. From the window of the main hall (the tower was not built until 1456), two of Wenceslas IV's Catholic councillors were flung to their deaths in 1419 by followers of the Hussite preacher Jan Želivský, sparking off the Hussite Wars.

This event gave 'defenestration' (throwing out of a window) a lasting political meaning, and a similar scenario was repeated at Prague Castle in 1618. You can visit the Gothic Hall of Justice, which was the site of the defenestration, and climb the 221 steps to the top of the tower.

DVOŘÁK MUSEUM MUSEUM

Map p338 (Muzeum Antonína Dvořáka; ☎224 923 363; www.nm.cz; Ke Karlovu 20; adult/child 50/25Kč, combined ticket with Czech Museum of Music 150/75Kč; ⏰10am-1.30pm & 2-5pm Tue, Wed & Fri-Sun, 11am-3.30pm & 4-7pm Thu Apr-Sep, 9.30am-1.30pm & 2-5pm Tue-Sun Oct-Mar; Ⓜ IP Pavlova) The most striking building in the drab neighbourhood south of Ječná is the energetically baroque Vila Amerika, a 1720s, French-style summer house designed by (you guessed it) Kilian Dientzenhofer. It's one of the city's finest baroque buildings and now houses a museum dedicated to the composer Antonín Dvořák. Special **concerts** (p130) of Dvořák's music are staged here from May to October.

CHARLES UNIVERSITY BOTANICAL GARDEN GARDEN

Map p338 (Botanická zahrada Univerzity Karlovy; ☎221 951 879; www.bz-uk.cz; Viničná 7; garden free, glasshouses adult/child 50/25Kč; ⏰10am-7.30pm Apr-Aug, to 6pm Aug & Sep, to 5pm Feb & Mar, to 4pm Nov-Jan; 🚋18, 24) Just south of Karlovo náměstí (main entrance on Na Slupi) is Charles University's botanical garden. Founded in 1775 and moved from Smíchov to its present site in 1898, it's the country's oldest botanical garden. The steep, hillside garden concentrates on Central European flora and is especially pretty in spring.

U KALICHA HISTORIC BUILDING

Map p338 (At the Chalice; ☎224 912 557; www.ukalicha.cz; Na Bojišti 12; ⏰11am-11pm; Ⓜ IP Pavlova) This is where the eponymous antihero was arrested at the beginning of Jaroslav Hašek's comic novel of WWI, *The Good Soldier Švejk* (which Hašek cranked out in instalments from his own local pub). The pub is milking the connection for all it's worth – it's an essential port of call for Švejk fans, but the rest of us can find cheaper beer and dumplings elsewhere.

EATING

The New Town has an eclectic collection of eating places, with cafes and traditional Czech pubs as well as a range of international restaurants. The main eating areas are Wenceslas Square and Na Příkopě, lined with restaurants offering cuisines from across the world,

THE HEYDRICH ASSASSINATION

In 1941, in response to a series of crippling strikes and sabotage operations by the Czech resistance movement, the German government appointed SS general Reinhard Heydrich, an antisubversion specialist, as Reichsprotektor of Bohemia and Moravia. Heydrich immediately cracked down on resistance activities with a vengeance.

In a move designed to support the resistance and boost Czech morale, Britain secretly trained a team of Czechoslovak paratroopers to assassinate Heydrich. It was code-named Operation Anthropoid and, astonishingly, it succeeded. On 27 May 1942, two paratroopers, Jan Kubiš and Jozef Gabčík, attacked Heydrich as he rode in his official car through the city's Libeň district – he died from the wounds. The assassins and five co-conspirators fled but were betrayed in their hiding place in the Church of Sts Cyril & Methodius; all seven died in the ensuing siege.

The Nazis reacted with a frenzied wave of terror, which included the annihilation of two entire Czech villages, Ležáky and Lidice, and the shattering of the underground movement.

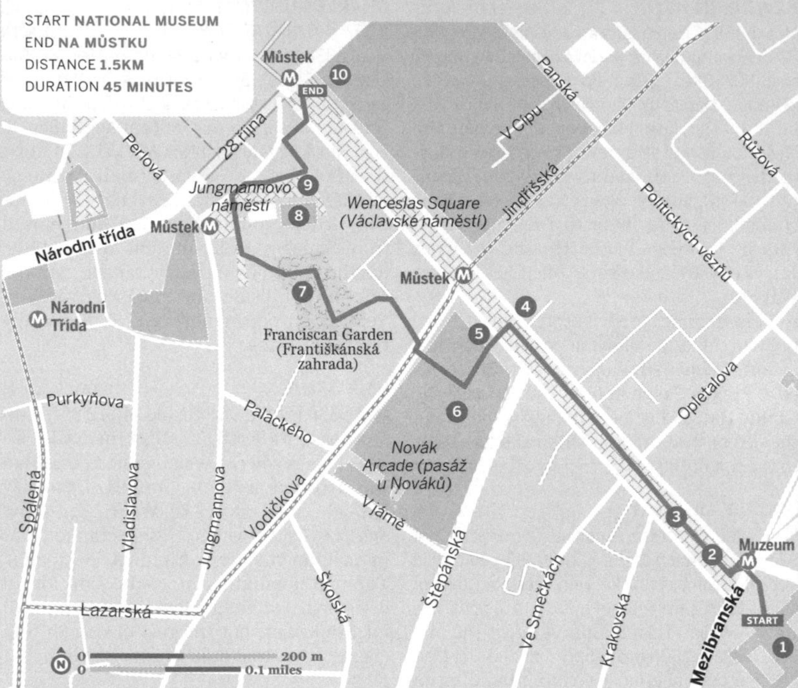

Neighbourhood Walk

Around Wenceslas Square

Begin at the 1 National Museum, at the upper end of Wenceslas Square. At the foot of the steps is a pavement **memorial to student Jan Palach**.

Cross Mezibranská to the equestrian 2 **statue of St Wenceslas**, the 10th-century 'Good King Wenceslas' of Christmas-carol fame. A flower bed downhill from the statue contains a 3 **Memorial to the Victims of Communism**. Around the anniversary of Jan Palach's death (19 January) the memorial is surrounded by votive candles.

Wander down the middle of the square, admiring the grand buildings on either side, including the 4 **Grand Hotel Evropa** at No 25. Opposite at No 36 is the 5 **Melantrich Building**, where the death of Czech communism was pronounced by Alexander Dubček and Václav Havel in 1989.

Turn left into **Pasáž Rokoko**, a mirror-lined art-deco arcade. It leads to the central atrium of the 6 Lucerna Palace arcade, dominated by David Černý's **Kun** (Horse), an ironic twist on the St Wenceslas statue outside. Turn right and exit onto Vodičkova, and bear right across the street to enter the **Světozor arcade**, with a beautiful **stained-glass window** dating from the late 1940s – an advertisement for Tesla Radio, an old Czech electronics company.

At the far end of the arcade, turn left into the 7 **Franciscan Garden**, a hidden oasis of peace and greenery. Exit diagonally opposite into Jungmannovo náměstí, go past the arch leading to the 8 Church of Our Lady of the Snows and turn right.

Keep to the right of the Lancôme shop, and you will find what must be the only 9 **Cubist lamp post** in the world, dating from 1915. Turn left here and then right through the **Lindt arcade** to emerge at the foot of Wenceslas Square.

Across the street, on the corner with Na Příkopě, is the art-nouveau 10 **Koruna Palác** (Crown Palace) – look up and you will see the corner tower with the crown of pearls that gives the building its name.

from Italy to India and Argentina to Japan; there are also lots of less obvious and more appealing eateries hidden in the backstreets between Wenceslas Square and the river.

SANSHO ASIAN, FUSION €€

Map p336 (222 317 425; www.sansho.cz; Petrská 25; mains 120-300Kč, 6-course dinner 750Kč; 11.30am-10.30pm Tue-Thu, 11.30am-11.30pm Fri, 6-11.30pm Sat; 3, 8, 24) Friendly and informal best describes the atmosphere at this ground-breaking new restaurant where British chef Paul Day champions Czech farmers by sourcing all his meat and vegetables locally. There is no menu – the waiter will explain what dishes are available, depending on market produce. Typical dishes include salmon sashimi, pork belly with Asian spices, and 12-hour beef rendang.

LE PATIO INTERNATIONAL €€

Map p338 (224 934 375; www.lepatio.cz; Národní třída 22; mains 200-420Kč; 8am-11pm Mon-Fri, 9am-11pm Sat & Sun; Národní Třída) It's easy to walk past this place on bustling Národní třída without noticing it, but it's well worth dropping in to sample its accomplished menu of local and international dishes in a relaxed atmosphere that hints of oriental travel – a ship's prow, lots of Asian-style lamps, paintings and textiles. There's a good breakfast menu too (served till 11am) with French, American and healthy options.

SUTERÉN INTERNATIONAL €€

Map p338 (224 933 657; Masarykovo nábřeží 26; mains 300-450Kč; 11.30am-4pm & 5pm-midnight Mon-Fri, 6pm-midnight Sat; 17, 21) 'The Basement' is a beautiful cellar space, where modern detailing complements the old red-brick and wooden beams perfectly. Cream linen chairs, set at gleaming black tables surround a circular glass bar with a colourful aquarium along one wall. The menu leans towards seafood, beef and game, ranging from Thai fishcakes to beef Madagascar (with brandy and cracked pepper sauce).

KARAVANSERÁJ LEBANESE €

Map p338 (224 930 390; www.klubcestovatelu.cz; Masarykovo nábřeží 22; mains 130-230Kč; 11am-11pm Mon-Thu, to midnight Fri, noon-midnight Sat, noon-10pm Sun; 17, 21) This restaurant and tearoom cultivates a ramshackle, relaxed and welcoming atmosphere, with its batik tablecloths, wicker chairs, oriental knick-knacks and library of travel guidebooks. The menu is mostly Lebanese – baba ganoush, falafel, hummus and lamb kebabs – with a couple of Indian dishes thrown in, and there's a huge range of speciality teas to choose from.

KOGO ITALIAN €€€

Map p336 (221 451 259; www.kogo.cz; Na Příkopě 22, Slovanský dům; mains 250-680Kč; 11am-11pm; Náměstí Republiky) Chic and businesslike, but also relaxed and family-friendly (highchairs provided), Kogo is a stylish restaurant serving top-notch pizza, pasta, and Italian meat and seafood dishes – the rich, tomatoey *zuppa di pesce* (fish soup) is delicious, as is the *risotto alla pescatora* (made with squid, mussels, shrimp and octopus). On summer evenings, candlelit tables filled with conversation spill over into the leafy courtyard.

MODRÝ ZUB ASIAN €

Map p338 (222 212 622; www.modryzub.com; Jindřišská 5; mains 155-275Kč; 11am-11pm Mon-Fri, noon-11pm Sat, to 10pm Sun; 3, 9, 14, 24) This slick, stylish and deservedly popular noodle bar is ideal for a quick hit of chilli and ginger, just a few paces away from Wenceslas Square. Sit on the high bench along the back wall and peruse a menu that includes dim sum, warm Thai salads, red, green and yellow Thai curries, stir-fries with fresh Asian flavours, and noodles served all ways.

SIAM ORCHID THAI €€

Map p336 (222 319 410; Na Poříčí 21; mains 150-210Kč; 10am-10pm; 3, 8, 24, 26) The setting – a scatter of plastic tables and chairs on a 1st-floor balcony hidden up a passage beside a department store – looks none too promising, but this tiny restaurant, tucked away beside a Thai massage studio, offers some of the city's most authentic Thai cuisine. From the crisp, grease-free *po-pia thot* (spring rolls with pork and black mushrooms) and succulent *kai sa-te* (chicken satay) to the fiery *kaeng khiao wan kai* (chicken in green curry with basil), pretty much everything on the menu is a delight.

PIZZERIA KMOTRA PIZZA €

Map p338 (224 934 100; V Jirchářích 12; pizza 110-160Kč; 11am-midnight; Národní Třída) One of Prague's oldest and best pizzerias, 'the Godmother' can rustle up more than two dozen varieties of pizza, from margherita to marinara, cooked in a genuine wood-fired pizza oven. Sit beside the bar upstairs, or head down to the basement where you can watch the chef slinging pizza dough in the open kitchen.

OLIVA MEDITERRANEAN €€

Off Map p338 (☎222 520 288; www.olivarestaurant.cz; Plavecká 4; mains 235-465Kč; ⊙11.30am-3pm & 6pm-midnight Mon-Fri, 6pm-midnight Sat; 🚊3, 7, 16, 17, 21) A small, friendly, family-run restaurant focusing on fresh Mediterranean cuisine, Oliva offers a menu of carefully prepared dishes that include linguine with mussels, white wine and herbs; and confit lamb with with cous-cous and pomegranate salad. It's also famous for its all-you-can-eat tiger prawn buffet, served with a choice of accompaniments including garlic and herbs, and coconut and coriander sauce (690Kč per person).

GLOBE BOOKSTORE & CAFÉ CAFE €

Map p338 (☎224 934 203; www.globebookstore.cz; Pštrossova 6; mains 110-225Kč; ⊙9.30am-midnight; 📶; Ⓜ Karlovo Náměstí) This appealing bookshop-cafe serves nachos, burgers, chicken wings and salads till 11pm nightly, and also offers an excellent brunch menu (9.30am to 4pm Saturday and Sunday) that includes an American classic (bacon, egg and hash browns), blueberry pancakes, full English fry, and freshly squeezed juices. Lighter breakfasts are served 9.30am to 11.30am weekdays.

DRINKING & NIGHTLIFE

Nové Město, particularly the area around Wenceslas Square, is still a bit of a magnet for stag parties and groups of young lads on the piss – best avoided if you're looking for a quiet drink. But there are plenty of good drinking holes, too. Check out the streets south of Národní třída near the river, where you'll find lots of studenty cafes and quirky wine bars.

PIVOVARSKÝ DŮM BREWERY

Map p338 (☎296 216 666; www.gastroinfo.cz/pivodum; cnr Ječná & Lipová; ⊙11am-11pm; 🚊4, 6, 10, 16, 22) While the tourists flock to U Fleků, locals gather here to sample the classic Czech lager (40Kč per 0.5L) that is produced on the premises, as well as wheat beer and a range of flavoured beers (including coffee, banana and cherry, 40Kč per 0.3L). The pub itself is a pleasant place to linger, decked out with polished copper vats and brewing implements and smelling faintly of malt and hops.

KÁVOVARNA CAFE

Map p338 (☎296 236 233; Štěpánská 61, Pasáž Lucerna; ⊙8am-midnight; Ⓜ Můstek) This retro-styled place has bentwood chairs and curved wooden benches in the smoky, dimly lit front room (there's a nonsmoking room beyond the bar), with exhibitions of arty black-and-white photography on the walls. The coffee is good and reasonably priced, and there's delicious Kout na Šumavě beer on tap at a very reasonable 37Kč per half litre.

JÁMA BAR

Map p338 (☎224 222 383; www.jamapub.cz; V Jámě 7; ⊙11am-1am; 📶; Ⓜ Muzeum) Jáma ('the Hollow') is a popular American expat bar plastered with old rock gig posters ranging from Led Zep and REM to Kiss and Shania Twain. There's a little beer garden out the back shaded by lime and walnut trees, smiling staff serving up a rotating selection of regional beers and microbrews, and a menu that includes good burgers, steaks, ribs and chicken wings.

BOKOVKA WINE BAR

Map p338 (☎721 262 503; www.bokovka.com; Pštrossova 8; ⊙4pm-1am; Ⓜ Karlovo Náměstí) Owned by a syndicate of oenophiles including film directors Jan Hřebejk and David Ondříček, this quaint little bar is named after the movie *Sideways* (*bokovka* in Czech), which was set in the California vineyards. The main attraction (other than the chance of being served by a film director) is the extensive menu of top-notch Moravian wines.

CAFÉ IMPERIAL CAFE

Map p336 (☎246 011 440; www.cafeimperial.cz/; Na Poříčí 15; ⊙7am-11pm; Ⓜ Náměstí Republiky) First opened in 1914, and given a complete facelift in 2007, the Imperial is a tour de force of art-nouveau tiling – the walls and ceiling are covered in original ceramic tiles, mosaics, sculptured panels and bas-reliefs, with period light fittings and bronzes scattered about. The coffee is good, there are cocktails in the evening, and the cafe menu offers all-day English and American breakfasts.

FRIENDS COFFEE HOUSE CAFE

Map p338 (☎272 049 665; www.milujikavu.cz; Palackého 7; ⏲9am-9pm Mon-Fri, noon-8pm Sat & Sun; 📶; 🚋3, 9, 14, 24) It's easy to walk past this place, but it is worth seeking out – head through the back to find a couple of relaxing rooms, one fitted out as a library, with well-spaced tables and comfy chairs. They take their coffee seriously here, using only freshly roasted and ground coffee beans (counter service only). Excellent, freshly prepared sandwiches are also available.

KAVÁRNA LUCERNA CAFE

Map p338 (☎224 215 495; Palác Lucerna, Štěpánská 61; ⏲10am-midnight; 📶; 🚋3, 9, 14, 24) The least touristy of Prague's grand cafes, the Lucerna is part of an art-nouveau shopping arcade designed by the grandfather of ex-president Václav Havel. Filled with faux marble, ornamental metalwork and glittering crystal lanterns (*lucerna* is Czech for lantern), this 1920s gem has arched windows overlooking David Černý's famous *Kůň* (Horse) sculpture hanging beneath the glass-domed atrium.

NOVOMĚSTSKÝ PIVOVAR BREWERY

Map p338 (New Town Brewery; ☎224 232 448; www.npivovar.cz; Vodičkova 20; ⏲10am-11.30pm Mon-Fri, 11.30am-11.30pm Sat, noon-10pm Sun; 🚋3, 9, 14, 24) Like U Fleků, the 'New Town Brewery' (established in 1993) has largely been taken over by coach-party tour groups, but it's considerably cheaper (38Kč for 0.5L, available in both light and dark varieties), and the food is not only edible but actually rather good. If you haven't booked, though, you'll be lucky to get a table.

U FLEKŮ BREWERY

Map p338 (☎224 934 019; www.ufleku.cz; Křemencová 11; ⏲10am-11pm; Ⓜ Karlovo Náměstí) A festive warren of drinking and dining rooms, U Fleků is a Prague institution, though usually clogged with tour groups high on oompah music and the tavern's home-brewed, 13° black beer (59Kč for 0.4L), known as Flek. Purists grumble but go along anyway because the beer is good, though tourist prices have nudged out many locals.

Beware the waiter asking if you want to try a Becherovka (Czech liqueur) – it's not a great accompaniment to beer, and it'll add 80Kč to the bill.

KAVÁRNA EVROPA CAFE

Map p338 (☎224 228 117; Václavské náměstí 25; ⏲9.30am-11pm; Ⓜ Můstek) The Grand Hotel Evropa sports the most atmospheric cafe on Wenceslas Square, a fading museum of over-the-top art nouveau. Sadly, it has long since become a tourist trap, with second-rate cakes and coffee and rip-off prices, but it's still worth a look inside just for the architecture and decor.

☆ ENTERTAINMENT

REDUTA JAZZ CLUB JAZZ

Map p338 (☎224 933 487; www.redutajazzclub.cz; Národní třída 20; admission 300Kč; ⏲9pm-3am; 📶; Ⓜ Národní Třída) The Reduta is Prague's oldest jazz club, founded in 1958 during the communist era – it was here in 1994 that former US president Bill Clinton famously jammed on a new saxophone presented to him by Václav Havel. It has an intimate setting, with smartly dressed patrons squeezing into tiered seats and lounges to soak up the big-band, swing and Dixieland atmosphere.

ROCK CAFÉ LIVE MUSIC

Map p338 (☎224 933 947; www.rockcafe.cz; Národní třída 20; admission free-150Kč; ⏲10am-3am Mon-Fri, 5pm-3am Sat, 5pm-1am Sun; Ⓜ Národní Třída) Not to be confused with the Hard Rock Café, this multifunction club is the offspring of the influential Nový Horizont art movement of the 1990s. It sports a stage for DJs and live rock bands, a funkily decorated 'rock cafe', a cinema, a theatre, an art gallery and a CD shop.

Live bands are mostly local, ranging from nu-metal to folk rock to Doors and Sex Pistols tribute bands. Music from 7.30pm.

LUCERNA MUSIC BAR LIVE MUSIC

Map p338 (☎224 217 108; www.musicbar.cz; Palác Lucerna, Vodičkova 36; admission 100-500Kč; ⏲8pm-4am; 🚋3, 9, 14, 24) Nostalgia reigns supreme at this atmospheric old theatre, now looking a little dog-eared, with anything from Beatles tribute bands to mainly Czech artists playing jazz, blues, pop, rock and more on midweek nights. But the most popular event is the regular 1980s and '90s video party held every Friday and Saturday night, which pulls in huge crowds of young locals bopping along to Duran Duran and Gary Numan.

ORIGINAL MUSIC THEATRE OF PRAGUE CLASSICAL MUSIC

Map p338 (Originální hudební divadlo Praha; ☎281 932 662; www.musictheatre.cz; Ke Karlovu 20, Vila Amerika; tickets 595Kč; ⏲concerts 8pm Wed & Sat May-Oct; MIP Pavlova) The pretty little Vila Amerika was built in 1717 as an aristocrat's immodest summer retreat. These days it's home to the Dvořák Museum (p125) and stages performances of Dvořák's works by the Original Music Theatre of Prague, complete with period costume. Tickets are available through BTI.

NATIONAL THEATRE OPERA, BALLET

Map p338 (Národní divadlo; ☎224 901 377; www.narodni-divadlo.cz; Národní třída 2; tickets 30-1000Kč; ⏲box offices 10am-6pm; 🚋6, 9, 18, 21, 22) The much-loved National Theatre provides a stage for traditional opera, drama and ballet by the likes of Smetana, Shakespeare and Tchaikovsky, sharing the program alongside more modern works by composers and playwrights such as Philip Glass and John Osborne. The box offices are in the Nový síň building next door, and in the Kolowrat Palace (opposite the Estates Theatre).

PRAGUE STATE OPERA OPERA, BALLET

Map p338 (Státní opera Praha; ☎224 901 886; www.opera.cz; Wilsonova 4; opera tickets 100-1150Kč, ballet tickets 100-800Kč; ⏲box office 10am-5.30pm Mon-Fri, 10am-noon & 1-5.30pm Sat & Sun; MMuzeum) The impressive neo-rococo home of the Prague State Opera provides a glorious setting for performances of opera and ballet. An annual Verdi festival takes place here in August and September, and less conventional shows, such as Leoncavallo's rarely staged version of *La Bohème*, are also performed here.

KINO SVĚTOZOR CINEMA

Map p338 (☎608 330 088; www.kinosvetozor.cz; Vodičkova 41; tickets 90-120Kč; 📶; MMůstek) The Světozor is under the same management as Žižkov's famous Kino Aero, but is more central, and has the same emphasis on classic cinema and art-house films screened in their original language – everything from *Battleship Potemkin* and *Casablanca* to *Annie Hall* and *The Motorcycle Diaries*.

ARCHA THEATRE THEATRE

Map p336 (Divadlo Archa; ☎221 716 111; www.archatheatre.cz; Na poříčí 26; tickets 150-880Kč; ⏲box office 10am-6pm Mon-Fri; 🚋5, 8, 14) The Archa (Ark) has been described as Prague's alternative National Theatre, a multi-functional venue for the avant garde and the experimental. As well as contemporary drama (occasionally in English) – Václav Havel's *Leaving* has been performed here – dance and performance art, the theatre also stages live music, from Indian classical to industrial noise.

LATERNA MAGIKA PERFORMING ARTS

Map p338 (☎224 931 482; www.laterna.cz; Národní třída 4, Nova Scéna; tickets 210-680Kč; ⏲box office 9am-6pm Mon-Fri, 10am-6pm Sat & Sun; 🚋6, 9, 18, 21, 22) Laterna Magika has been wowing audiences since its first cutting-edge multimedia show caused a stir at the 1958 Brussels World Fair. Its imaginative blend of dance, music and projected images continues to pull in the crowds. Nová Scena, the futuristic building next to the National Theatre, has been home to Laterna Magika since it moved from its birthplace in the Adria Palace in the mid-1970s.

MINOR THEATRE THEATRE

Map p338 (Divadlo Minor; ☎222 231 351; www.minor.cz; Vodičkova 6; adult/child 150/100Kč; ⏲box office 10am-1.30pm & 2.30-8pm Mon-Fri, 11am-6pm Sat & Sun; MKarlovo Náměstí) Divadlo Minor is a wheelchair-accessible children's theatre that offers a fun mix of puppets, clown shows and pantomime. There are performances (in Czech) at 3pm Saturday and Sunday and at 6pm Thursday and Friday, and you can usually get a ticket at the door.

SHOPPING

GALERIE ČESKÉ PLASTIKY ARTS & CRAFTS

Map p336 (Czech Sculpture Gallery; ☎222 310 684; www.art-pro.cz; Revoluční 20; ⏲10am-6pm Mon-Fri; 🚋5, 8, 14) This commercial gallery is a treasure house of 20th-century and contemporary Czech sculpture, paintings, prints and photography. There are regular themed exhibitions, and all items are for sale, at prices ranging from 2000Kč to 2 million Kč.

GLOBE BOOKSTORE & CAFÉ
BOOKS

Map p338 (☎224 934 203; www.globebookstore.cz; Pštrossova 6; ⏰9.30am-midnight Sun-Wed, 9.30am-1am Thu-Sat; 📶; Ⓜ Karlovo Náměstí) A popular hang out for book-loving expats, the Globe is a cosy English-language bookshop with an excellent cafe-bar (p128) in which to peruse your purchases. There's a good range of new fiction and nonfiction, a big selection of secondhand books, and newspapers and magazines in English, French, Spanish, Italian, German and Russian. Plus art exhibitions and film screenings.

PALÁC KNIH NEO LUXOR
BOOKS

Map p338 (☎296 110 368; www.neoluxor.cz; Václavské náměstí 41; ⏰8am-8pm Mon-Fri, 9am-7pm Sat, 10am-7pm Sun; Ⓜ Muzeum) Palác Knih Neo Luxor is Prague's biggest bookshop – head for the basement to find a wide selection of fiction and nonfiction in English, German, French and Russian, including Czech authors in translation. You'll also find internet access, a cafe and a good selection of international newspapers and magazines.

KIWI
BOOKS, MAPS

Map p338 (☎224 948 455; www.kiwick.cz; Jungmannova 23; ⏰9am-6.30pm Mon-Fri, 10am-2pm Sat; 🚋3, 9, 14, 24) This small specialist travel bookshop stocks a huge range of maps covering not only the Czech Republic but also many other countries. It also has an extensive selection of Lonely Planet guidebooks.

MOSER
GLASS

Map p336 (☎224 211 293; www.moser-glass.com; Na Příkopě 12; ⏰10am-8pm; Ⓜ Můstek) One of the most exclusive and respected of Bohemian glassmakers, Moser was founded in Karlovy Vary in 1857 and is famous for its rich and flamboyant designs. The shop on Na Příkopě is worth a browse as much for the decor as for the goods – it's in a magnificently decorated, originally Gothic building called the House of the Black Rose (dům U černé růže).

BELDA JEWELLERY
JEWELLERY

Map p338 (☎224 931 052; www.belda.cz; Mikulandská 10; ⏰11am-6pm Mon-Fri; Ⓜ Národní Třída) Belda & Co is a long-established Czech firm dating from 1922. Nationalised in 1948, it was revived by the founder's son and grandson, and continues to create gold and silver jewellery of a very high standard. Its range includes its own angular, contemporary designs, as well as reproductions based on art-nouveau designs by Alfons Mucha.

BAZAR
MUSIC

Map p338 (☎602 313 730; www.cdkrakovska.cz; Krakovská 4; ⏰11am-7pm Mon-Fri, 10am-3pm Sat; Ⓜ Muzeum) There's a vast selection of secondhand CDs, LPs and videos to browse through here, representing a wide range of genres. Czech and Western pop jostle with jazz, blues, heavy metal, country and world music, though with most LPs costing around 300Kč to 450Kč this place is not exactly what you'd call a bargain basement.

BONTONLAND
MUSIC

Map p338 (☎224 473 080; www.bontonland.cz; Václavské náměstí 1-3; ⏰9am-8pm Mon-Fri, 10am-8pm Sat, 10am-7pm Sun; 📶; Ⓜ Můstek) Supposedly the biggest music megastore in the Czech Republic, with pretty much everything including Western chart music, classical, jazz, dance and heavy metal, as well as an extensive collection of Czech pop. It also sells Blu-ray discs and DVDs, iPods and accessories, and has a large PlayStation arena and internet cafe.

JAN PAZDERA
PHOTOGRAPHY

Map p338 (☎224 216 197; www.fotopazdera.cz; Vodičkova 28; ⏰10am-6pm Mon-Fri, to 1pm Sat; 🚋3, 9, 14, 24) The friendly and knowledgeable staff members at this long-standing shop are happy to show you around their impressive stock of secondhand cameras, darkroom gear, lenses, binoculars and telescopes. Models range from the basic but unbreakable Russian-made Zenit to expensive Leicas.

BAT'A
SHOES

Map p338 (☎221 088 478; www.bata.cz; Václavské náměstí 6; ⏰9am-9pm Mon-Fri, 9am-8pm Sat, 10am-8pm Sun; Ⓜ Můstek) Established by Tomáš Baťa in 1894, the Baťa footwear empire is still in family hands and is one of the Czech Republic's most successful companies. The flagship store on Wenceslas Square, built in the 1920s, is considered a masterpiece of modern architecture, and houses six floors of shoes (including international brands as well as Baťa's own), handbags, luggage and leather goods.

Vinohrady & Vršovice

Neighbourhood Top Five

❶ Stroll lovely **Riegrovy sady** (p134), with photo-op-worthy vistas out over to Prague Castle in the distance and to the Old Town and the main train station below. Follow your walk with a beer at the beer garden in the park.

❷ Sip some wine in the open air at Vinohrady's **Viniční Altán** (p138).

❸ Have a meal to remember at a great restaurant such as **Aromi** (p134).

❹ Sneak a peek inside the modern masterpiece that is the **Church of the Most Sacred Heart of Our Lord** (p134).

❺ Enjoy a coffee and take in the hustle and bustle of Peace Square (náměstí Míru) at **Sahara Café** (p138).

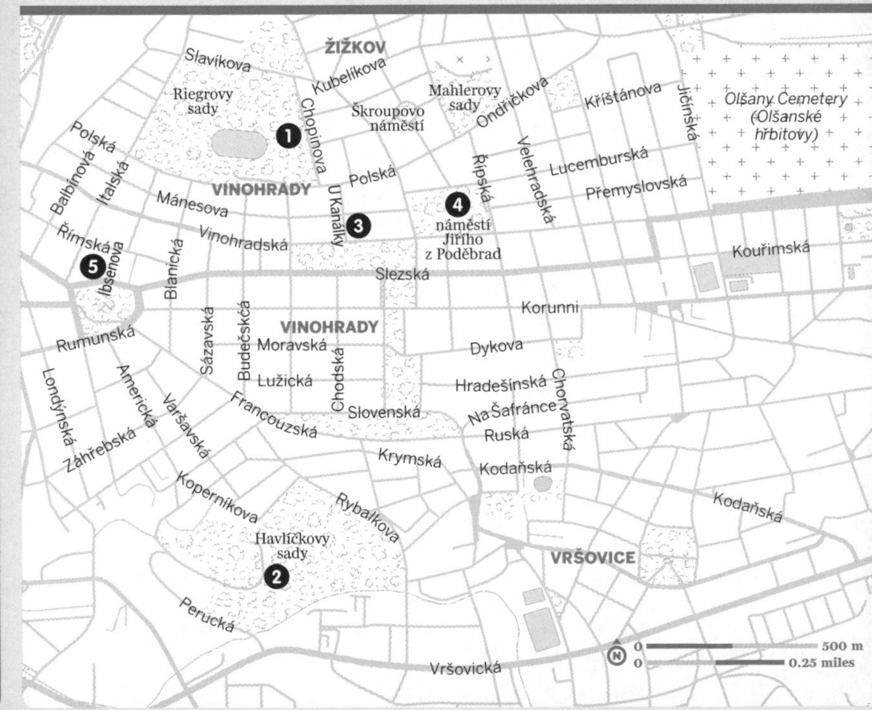

For more detail of this area, see Map p344 ➡

Explore: Vinohrady & Vršovice

Vinohrady and Vršovice are largely residential, and mostly off the tourist trail. Vinohrady, in particular, has a well-earned rep as the stomping ground for upwardly mobile singles and young couples. For visitors, the money and success have a big upside: Vinohrady has some of the city's best restaurants and cafes. After you've seen the sights in the centre, you'll want to head here for that perfect meal. Most of the places are clustered within walking distance of the main metro stops: Náměstí Míru and Jiřího z Poděbrad. After dinner, there are several pubs and clubs around. Žižkov, where much of the serious drinking in Prague takes place, is just a short walk or cab ride away.

Local Life

➡ **Popular Hangouts** If you get a warm evening, head to the beer garden in Riegrovy sady (p137). Great neighbourhood cafes include Café Kaaba (p138), Blatouch (p138) and Kavárna Róza K (p138), all of which attract a younger clientele and offer good coffee and free wi-fi.

➡ **Markets** The grassy area above the Jiřího z Poděbrad metro station is home to a popular farmers market (p141) every Wednesday and Saturday morning. Come for homegrown food and lots of fun.

➡ **Shopping** Vinohrady's main street, Vinohradská, is the centre of home design in Prague, and even if you're not in the position to buy anything, it's fun to poke around the various shops and see the latest in interior fashion. One of our favourites is Stockist (p140).

Getting There & Away

➡ **Metro** Vinohrady is easily reached from around the city by metro line A (green), which stops at at Náměstí Míru, Jiřího z Poděbrad and Flora. Trams are better for getting to Vršovice.

➡ **Tram** Several tram lines service Vinohrady. The popular tram 22 runs all the way from Prague Castle to Náměstí Míru and continues into Vršovice. Tram 11 links Muzeum with several points in Vinohrady, including Jiřího z Poděbrad and Flora. Other trams that go to Vinohrady include 4, 10 and 16. Tram 4 also services Vršovice.

Lonely Planet's Top Tip

There aren't many traditional sights in Vinohrady, so the best way to enjoy this part of Prague is simply to put the map away and amble at will, admiring the fine townhouses and lovely quality of life here in one of Prague's nicest residential areas.

Best Places to Eat

➡ Mozaika (p134)
➡ Kofein (p134)
➡ Aromi (p134)
➡ Osteria Da Clara (p134)
➡ The Pind (p136)

For reviews, see p134 ➡

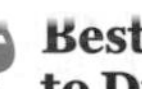

Best Places to Drink

➡ Riegrovy Sady Beer Garden (p137)
➡ Viniční Altán (p138)
➡ Café Kaaba (p138)
➡ Blatouch (p138)
➡ Sokolovna (p138)

For reviews, see p137 ➡

Best Places to Dance

➡ Techtle Mechtle (p140)
➡ Radost FX (p140)
➡ ON Club (p140)
➡ Termix (p140)
➡ Le Clan (p140)

For reviews, see p140 ➡

SIGHTS

CHURCH OF THE MOST SACRED HEART OF OUR LORD — CHURCH

Map p344 (Kostel Nejsvětějšího Srdce Páně; www.srdcepane.cz; náměstí Jiřího z Poděbrad 19, Vinohrady; services 8am & 6pm Mon-Sat, 9am, 11am & 6pm Sun; Jiřího z Poděbrad) This church, from 1932, is one of Prague's most original pieces of 20th-century architecture. It's the work of Jože Plečnik, a Slovenian architect who also worked on Prague Castle. The church is inspired by Egyptian temples and early Christian basilicas. It's usually only open to the public during masses.

RIEGROVY SADY — GARDENS, PARK

Map p344 (Rieger Gardens; Vinohrady; Jiřího z Poděbra) Vinohrady's largest and prettiest park was designed as a classic English garden in the 19th century, and it's still a good place to put down a blanket and chill out. The bluff towards the back of the park affords photo-op-worthy shots of Prague Castle. In summer, the park's open-air beer garden (p137) is the place to be. The park's entrance is on Chopinova, across from Na Švíhance.

EATING

Outside the centre, Vinohrady has Prague's largest concentration of good restaurants, and the choice is only getting better as the area continues to move upmarket. Most restaurants are clustered around náměstí Míru and the residential street Mánesova that parallels Vinohradská from the Muzeum to the Jiřího z Poděbrad metro stops.

MOZAIKA — INTERNATIONAL €€

Map p344 (224 253 011; www.restaurantmozaika.cz; Nitranská 13, Vinohrady; mains 180-450Kč; Jiřího z Poděbrad) One of the most dependably good restaurants in the neighbourhood. The theme is an updated French bistro, with beef tournedos and *boeuf bourguignon* sharing the spotlight with international entrees such as stir-fries, BBQ pork ribs and our personal favourite: salmon wrapped in seaweed and served with wasabi mashed potatoes. Advance booking essential.

AROMI — ITALIAN €€€

Map p344 (222 713 222; www.aromi.cz; Mánesova 78, Vinohrady; mains 400-600Kč; noon-11pm Mon-Sat, to 10pm Sun; 11, Jiřího z Poděbrad) Red brick, polished wood and country-style furniture create a rustic atmosphere in this gourmet Italian restaurant. Brisk and businesslike at lunchtime, romantic in the evening, Aromi has a reputation for authentic, excellent Italian cuisine. Advance booking essential.

OSTERIA DA CLARA — ITALIAN €€

Map p344 (271 726 548; www.daclara.com; Mexická 7, Vršovice; mains 200-400Kč; 11am-3pm & 6-11pm Mon-Fri, noon-3.30pm & 6-11pm Sat; 4, 22, Náměstí Míru) This minuscule Tuscan-style trattoria offers some of the most authentic and best-value Italian cooking in the city, though it will take a good map to find the place. The menu varies, but expect a handful of creative pasta dishes and main courses built around duck, beef, pork and seafood. Reserve in advance – there are only a few tables.

KOFEIN — SPANISH €€

Map p344 (273 132 145; www.ikofein.cz; Nitranská 9, Vinohrady; tapas plates 55-75Kč; 11am-midnight Mon-Fri, 5pm-midnight Sat & Sun; 11, Jiřího z Poděbrad) One of the hottest restaurants in town is this Spanish-style tapas place not far from the Jiřího z Poděbrad metro station. Descend into a lively space to see a red-faced chef minding the busy grill. Our faves include marinated trout with horseradish and pork belly confit with celeriac. Service is prompt and friendly. Book ahead.

RISTORANTE SAPORI — ITALIAN €€

Map p344 (www.ristorante-praha.cz; Americká 20, Vinohrady; mains 185-395Kč; Náměstí Míru) This elegant Italian restaurant is the best in the immediate vicinity for a proper tablecloth dinner with all the trimmings. We like the calamari with arugula garlic and cherry tomatoes. Offers daily lunch specials with mains priced under 150Kč. Handsome light decor with hardwood floors; excellent wine list.

LAS ADELITAS — MEXICAN €

Map p344 (222 542 031; www.lasadelitas.cz; Americká 8, Vinohrady; mains 150-210Kč; Náměstí Míru) This small, informal Mexican restaurant run by a group of friends from Mexico offers the closest thing to

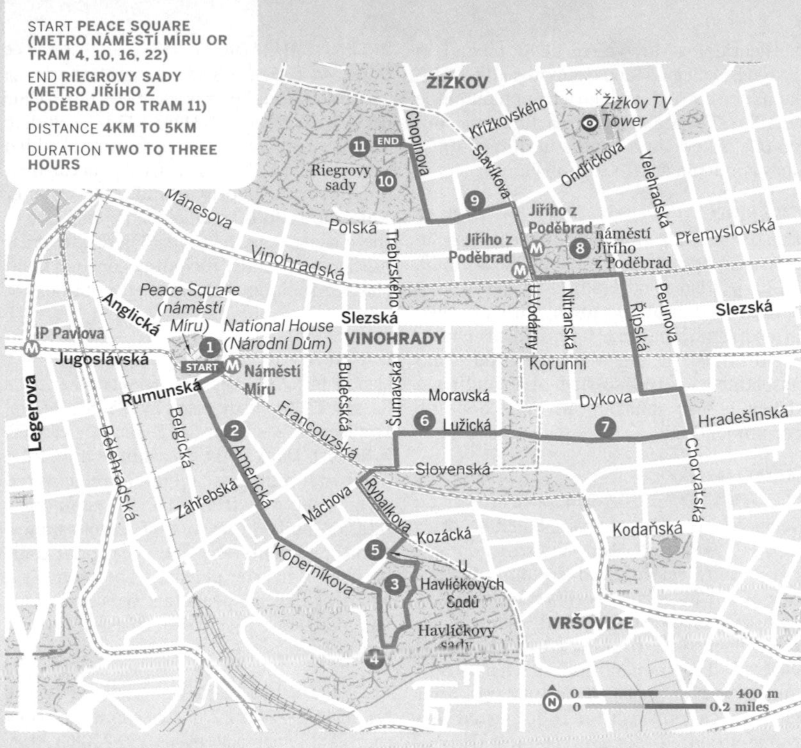

Neighbourhood Walk

Handsome Vinohrady

This walk covers a lot of ground but has few hills. It meanders along some of Prague's nicest residential streets.

Known affectionately to Czechs as 'Mirák' – a diminutive form of 'Míru' – leafy ❶ **Peace Square** (náměstí Míru) is the lively heart of Vinohrady. Leave the square via ❷ **Americká**, a quiet residential street leading south.

At the end of the street, the rocky hillside park ❸ **Havlíčkovy sady** marks the border between Vinohrady and Vršovice and is popular with lovers (since it's secluded). There's no prescribed walk for exploring the park – just choose the most inviting path leading downhill. Look for signs to the Viniční Altán wine garden.

Open-air wine gardens are a rarity in Prague and none is as attractive as ❹ **Viniční Altán**, with its wooden gazebo overlooking a terraced hillside lined with grapevines.

Retrace your steps through the park, back to the street ❺ **U Havlíčkových Sadů**. Follow this to the right, then make a left onto Rybalkova. Follow Rybalkova to Máchova. At Máchova turn right, crossing Francouzská onto Šumavská, and then make a right at ❻ **Lužická**. Lužická empties out into a small park. Cut through the park and onto the street Hradešínská.

This street has some of the most beautiful villas in the city. The most famous is at ❼ **Hradešínská 6**, built by early-modern architect Jan Kotěra in 1908. Turn left at Chorvatská and left again onto Dykova, then right onto Řípská, with a view of Žižkov's TV Tower.

Řípská takes you to Vinohradská and the ❽ **Church of the Most Sacred Heart of Our Lord** (náměstí Jiřího z Poděbrad). Find the street Slavíkova that runs past the church's entrance and follow it to Polská.

Walk left onto ❾ **Polská** for another row of handsome townhouses. Take a right onto Chopinova and walk uphill to Na Švíhance. The entrance to ❿ **Riegrovy sady** is opposite Na Švíhance. The ⓫ **Riegrovy sady beer garden** is 30m from the entrance.

authentic Tex-Mex you're likely to find in Prague. Delicious tacos, burritos and enchiladas are crafted with love from handmade tortillas. The ambience is a little sterile, but no one is here for a candle-lit dinner – just very good and good-value nosh.

THE PIND INDIAN €€

Map p344 (222 516 085; www.thepind.cz; Korunní 67, Vinohrady; mains 190-300Kč; ; 10, 11, 16, Jiřího z Poděbrad) One of the best Indian restaurants in town, with a refined atmosphere, making it a decent choice for dinner. The menu features the usual assortment of Indian dishes, including a delicious fish masala. Advance booking recommended.

HAMTAM MIDDLE EASTERN €

Map p344 (267 312 944; www.hamtam.cz; Voroněžská 19, Vršovice; mains 80-120Kč; ; 4, 22, Náměstí Míru) Vršovice doesn't have many really good restaurants, but one of our favourites is this relatively new spot that mixes Turkish and Middle Eastern influences to winning effect. The menu changes daily depending on what's fresh and in season, so you'll have to take your chances. On our visit the beef roasted in a coffee-flavoured sauce served on wide noodles was a big hit.

THE TAVERN AMERICAN €

Off Map p344 (www.eng.thetavern.cz; Chopinova 26, Vinohrady; mains 95-150Kč; 6-10pm Thu-Sun; 11, Jiřího z Poděbrad) This cosy sit-down burger joint is the creation of a husband-and-wife team of American expats who wanted to create the perfect burger using organic products and free-range, grass-fed beef. It's packed most nights, so reservations are a must; they ask that reservation requests be sent in by email. Great fries and bourbon-based cocktails too. Dinner only.

U BILÉ KRÁVY STEAKHOUSE €€

Map p344 (224 239 570; www.bilakrava.cz; Rubešova 10, Vinohrady; mains 170-400Kč; Náměstí Míru, Muzeum) This French-run, Lyonnais-styled bistro has some of the best steaks, at the best prices, in town. The name 'White Cow' refers to the Charollais breed of white cows from Burgundy, the source of the restaurant's signature steaks. Added charms include an authentic bistro feel and excellent wine selection.

ZELENÁ ZAHRADA CZECH €€

Map p344 (222 518 159; www.zelena-zahrada.eu; Šmilovského 12, Vinohrady; mains 130-300Kč; ; 4, 22, Náměstí Míru) This secluded, upscale restaurant draws a star-studded crowd, including on at least one occasion – judging by the photos on the wall – crooner Karel Gott. Book in advance to snag one of the coveted garden seats. There are great luncheon specials, including (on our visit) chicken roulade with mashed potatoes for 85Kč.

U DĚDKA INTERNATIONAL €

Map p344 (222 522 784; www.udedka.cz; Na Kozačce 12, Vinohrady; mains 130-280Kč; 11am-1am Mon-Fri, 4pm-1am Sat & Sun; ; 4, 22, Náměstí Míru) This pleasantly upmarket pub-restaurant has a quiet, tree-covered terrace out the front. The contemporary interior pulls in a mix of Czech professionals, students and the occasional tourist from a nearby pension. The menu is a blend of Czech specialties plus well-done bar food, such as chicken quesadillas and cheeseburgers.

PIZZERIA GROSSETO ITALIAN €

Map p344 (224 252 778; www.grosseto.cz; Francouzská 2, Vinohrady; mains 130-200Kč; ; Náměstí Míru) This bustling Vinohrady pizzeria serves very good pizzas, with inventive toppings such as asparagus and ricotta cheese, as well as homemade pastas and original desserts. The garden terrace at the back is a secluded gem and something of a local secret.

MASALA INDIAN €

Map p344 (222 251 601; www.masala.cz; Mánesova 13, Vinohrady; mains 150-250Kč; noon-11pm Mon-Fri, 5-11pm Sat & Sun; ; 11) An unpretentious Indian restaurant, with all of the good food and none of the stultifying atmosphere and stiff service you normally find at Indian places here. The owners aim for what they call home-style service, meaning relaxed presentation and good home cooking. One minor quibble: the food could use more spice. Advance booking essential.

LOVING HUT VEGETARIAN €

Map p344 (222 515 006; www.lovinghut.cz; Londýnská 35, Vinohrady; 11am-9pm Mon-Sat; ; Náměstí Míru, IP Pavlova) Part of a citywide chain of nonsmoking, no-alcohol vegan/vegetarian restaurants. The menu includes items such as vegetarian sushi, curry soup, and other Asian-inspired vegetarian dishes. There's a great-value self-service buffet weekdays from 11am to 4pm.

PASTIČKA CZECH €€

Map p344 (☎222 253 228; www.pasticka.cz; Blanická 25, Vinohrady; mains 149-429Kč; ⏰11am-10pm Mon-Fri, 5-11pm Sat & Sun; 📶; 🚋11, Ⓜ Jiřího z Poděbrad) A warm, inviting ground-floor pub with a little garden out the back, Pastička is great for a beer or a meal. The interior design is part 1920s Prague and part Irish pub. Most come for the beer, but the mix of international and traditional Czech dishes is very good.

PHO VIETNAM VIETNAMESE €

Map p344 (Slavikova 1, Vinohrady; mains 79-100Kč; 🖉; 🚋11, Ⓜ Jiřího z Poděbrad) This stand-up and takeaway Vietnamese joint gets jammed at lunchtime for arguably the best Vietnamese-style noodle soup *(pho)* in town, at very reasonable prices. Snippets from the menu include spicy beef with green beans, and beef with *pho bo* rice noodles. There are also plenty of items for vegetarians.

CAFÉ FX VEGETARIAN €

Map p344 (☎603 193 711; www.radostfx.cz; Bělehradská 120, Vinohrady; mains 120-240Kč; 📶🖉; Ⓜ IP Pavlova) For more than two decades Café FX has been a vegetarian beacon in the gritty neighbourhood surrounding the IP Pavlova metro stop. The food – mostly salads, stir-fries and veggie burgers – is reliably good, though the menu has changed little since opening day and it's hard not to get the feeling the place is coasting.

MIRELLIE ITALIAN €€

Map p344 (www.mirellie.cz; Korunní 23, Vinohrady; mains 135-390Kč; 📶🖉; Ⓜ Náměstí Míru) This pleasingly upscale Italian restaurant is a good lunch or dinner choice. The specialties here include grilled fish and meats and very good pasta. While the cuisine is Italian, many of the servers hail from the former Yugoslavia, so expect a lot of good-natured waiter bravado – welcome or not.

RESTAURACE CHUDOBA CZECH €

Map p344 (☎222 250 624; www.restaurace chudoba.cz; Vinohradská 67, Vinohrady; mains 130-280Kč; ⏰11am-1am Mon-Sat, 11am-midnight Sun; 🚋11) This upmarket Czech tavern-restaurant occupies a choice corner on a leafy section of Vinohradská. The patrons are mostly young professionals and couples out for an after-work beer or a good and reasonably priced Czech meal. The decor plays with the 'Ye Olde Vinohrady' theme, with sepia-toned photos on the wall and polished wooden floors.

HA NOI VIETNAMESE €

Map p344 (☎222 521 430; Slezská 57, Vinohrady; mains 80-120Kč; ⏰10am-10pm Mon-Fri, 2-11pm Sat; Ⓜ Jiřího z Poděbrad, Flora) Ha Noi remains arguably the best of a handful of mostly mediocre Vietnamese restaurants around Prague. Decent spring rolls, both fresh and fried, and two types of seasoned *pho* are on offer. The unremarkable set-up – just a few wooden tables and the standard oriental kitsch – make it better suited to a hearty lunch than that special night out.

MASSIMO ITALIAN €

Map p344 (☎606 633 992; Donska 11, Vršovice; mains 175-220Kč; 🚋4, 22, Ⓜ Náměstí Míru) Vršovice seems to have a knack for good Italian restaurants. This place opened in March 2012 and has already established itself as a solid neighbourhood option. Expect the usual round of pasta first courses and a good range of meat and fish dishes. There are good-value lunch specials under 100Kč per dish.

DRINKING & NIGHTLIFE

It may lack some of Žižkov's authentic grit, but Vinohrady is a great area for bar- and cafe-hopping. Check out the streets surrounding Peace Square (náměstí Míru), particularly along Americká, as well as Mánesova and those around the big park, Riegrovy sady, which has either Prague's best or second-best open-air beer garden (depending on whom you ask and where they live). Vinohrady is also the centre of Prague's gay life, and you'll find many gay-friendly cafes and clubs here.

RIEGROVY SADY BEER GARDEN BEER GARDEN

Map p344 (Riegrovy sady, Vinohrady; ⏰noon-1am summer only; 🚋11, Ⓜ Jiřího z Poděbrad) There's a good-natured rivalry between this beer garden and the one across the river at Letná as to which one is best. We're not sure, but this one is pretty good. Order beers at the

VINOHRADY'S VINEYARDS

Prague is generally known for beer, not wine. And that's probably for good reason. It may come as a surprise, then, that several centuries ago vineyards in Prague produced a substantial amount of wine, and the centre of this activity was in Vinohrady (which means literally 'vineyards'). Vinohrady, so the story goes, got its start in winemaking all the way back in the 14th century, when Emperor Charles IV ordered the first grapes to be planted. The vineyards lasted around 400 years before the area was given over mostly to farms and eventually luxury townhouses. A small section of the vineyards survives to this day around the area of the Viniční Altán (p138) open-air wine garden.

bar and carry them to your table. To find it, go to Polská, turn up Chopínova, and enter the park across from Na Švíhance.

VINIČNÍ ALTÁN WINE BAR

Map p344 (www.vinicni-altan.cz; Havlíčkovy sady 1369, Vršovice; ⌚11am-10pm, summer only; 🚊4, 6, 7, 22, 24) Prague's nicest open-air wine garden claims to be its oldest as well – apparently established by Emperor Charles IV himself. Enjoy a glass of locally made white or red on a refurbished wooden gazebo overlooking the vineyards and the Nusle valley. There's no easy way to get here; try cutting through Vinohrady, following Americká and then continuing through Havlíčkovy sady. On trams 6, 7 and 24, stop at Otakarova then walk (uphill); for 4 and 22 stop at Jana Masaryka then walk.

BLATOUCH CAFE

Map p344 (☎222 328 643; www.blatouch.cz; Americká 17, Vinohrady; 📶; Ⓜ Náměstí Míru) This popular cafe is an excellent choice to relax, surf the net on free wi-fi and enjoy a good coffee or glass of wine. The vibe is student-friendly and relaxed. There are also some light food items available, such as salads and sandwiches.

HOSPŮDKA OBYČEJNÝ SVĚT PUB

Map p344 (☎224 257 161; www.obycejnysvet.com; Korunní 96, Vinohrady; ⌚11am-12.30am Mon-Fri, noon-12.30am Sat, 1pm-midnight Sun; 🚊10, 16, Ⓜ Náměstí Jiřího z Poděbrad) This traditional pub has something of a British gentlemen's club feel about it. There's an excellent range of beers on hand, including harder-to-find varieties from Ježek and Lobkowicz, plus decent food and a friendly, welcoming atmosphere.

CAFÉ KAABA CAFE

Map p344 (www.kaaba.cz; Mánesova 20, Vinohrady; ⌚8am-10pm Mon-Fri, 9am-10pm Sat, 10am-10pm Sun; 📶; 🚊11) Café Kaaba is a stylish little cafe-bar with retro furniture and pastel-coloured decor that comes straight out of the 1959 Ideal Homes Exhibition. It serves up excellent coffee (made with freshly ground imported beans). Note that the wi-fi is only free for customers from opening until 6pm.

SOKOLOVNA PUB

Map p344 (www.restaurantsokolovna.cz; Slezská 22, Vinohrady; Ⓜ Náměstí Míru) It might be a little unfair to consign Sokolovna to the 'pub' category. After all, it's also a pretty good restaurant, serving excellent traditional Czech food, including a good-value luncheon special. But it's a great beer joint too, with unpasteurised Pilsner Urquell (tankové pivo) on tap served in a dignified 1930s interior.

SAHARA CAFÉ CAFE

Map p344 (www.saharacafe.com; Náměstí Míru 6, Vinohrady; 📶; Ⓜ Náměstí Míru) The beautifully minimalist, Morocco-inspired interior here sets a design standard that few places can match; unfortunately, the food doesn't always live up to the decor. Still, if it's just a cup of coffee or a glass of wine you're after, then you can hardly do flashier in this neighbourhood.

GALERIE KAVÁRNA RÓZA K CAFE

Map p344 (☎222 544 696; www.rozak.webnode.cz; Belgická 17, Vinohrady; ⌚8.30am-1am Mon-Fri, noon-1am Sat & Sun; 📶; Ⓜ Náměstí Míru) We liked this place so much better when it was called Medúza, but it's still one of the best cafes in Vinohrady. The clientele is mostly students who come for coffee and conversation. Serves light food as well.

ŽLUTÁ PUMPA BAR

Map p344 (www.zluta-pumpa.info; Belgická 11, Vinohrady; 📶; Ⓜ Náměstí Míru, IP Pavlova) There aren't many student watering holes left in trendy Vinohrady, but the 'Yellow Pump' has been a neighbourhood fixture for over a decade. There's a tiny bar area and several adjacent small rooms, and normally every seat in the house is filled. There's a complete range beers, wines and cocktails, plus average but edible Mexican food.

VINÁRNA VÍNEČKO WINE BAR

Map p344 (www.vineckopraha.cz; Londýnská 29, Vinohrady; ⌚1pm-1am Mon-Sat, 3-11pm Sun; 📶; Ⓜ Náměstí Míru) This delightful wine bar has a popular front terrace and a wide selection of local wines, available by the bottle or glass. There's also a back garden with picnic tables. While the menu is short on serious food, there are some smaller items such as sausages, ham and cheese to nibble on between sips.

MOTOR CAFE CAFE

Map p344 (☎602 653 055; Korunní 98, Vinohrady; 📶; 🚋10, 16, Ⓜ Náměstí Jiřího z Poděbrad) Fun 1950s- and '60s-era throwback cafe, with old-time motorcycles, TV sets and radios tossed around as furnishings. People come mostly for coffee or beer, but you can also get a traditional Czech breakfast of bread rolls, ham and cheese (99Kč). There's a computer in the corner to check email (per hr 50Kč).

DOBRÁ TRAFIKA CAFE

Map p344 (☎737 907 635; www.dobratrafika.cz; Korunní 42, Vinohrady; ⌚7.30am-11pm Mon-Fri, 8am-11pm Sat, 9am-11pm Sun; 📶; 🚋10, 16, Ⓜ Náměstí Míru) From the outside, you'd never know there was a cute little coffee shop tucked behind this tobacconist on busy Korunní. The shop is a great place to buy teas, sweets and gifts. At the back there's a small room for drinking coffee and a larger garden for just hanging out. Popular with students.

KAVÁRNA ZANZIBAR CAFE

Map p344 (☎222 520 315; www.kavarnazanzibar.cz; Americká 15, Vinohrady; ⌚8am-11pm Mon-Fri, 10am-11pm Sat & Sun; 📶; Ⓜ Náměstí Míru) Zanzibar started out years ago as a place to buy newspapers and tobacco products. Over the years it's evolved into a homey space that serves as either a cafe, bar or informal restaurant, depending on your mood. The terrace out the front is pleasant in nice weather.

AL CAFETERO CAFE, WINE BAR

Map p344 (www.alcafetero.cz; Blanická 24, Vinohrady; ⌚8.30am-9.30pm Mon-Thu, 8.30am-6pm Fri; 📶; 🚋11, Ⓜ Náměstí Míru, Muzeum) This quirky little cafe and wine bar, just between Vinohradská and náměstí Míru, has several things going for it, including arguably the best coffee drinks in Prague. There's also an excellent wine selection and a rigorously enforced nonsmoking policy, which makes it comfortable for lingering over the newspaper.

CAFÉ CELEBRITY CAFE

Map p344 (☎222 511 343; www.celebritycafe.cz; Vinohradská 40, Vinohrady; ⌚8am-1am Mon-Fri, 10am-2am Sat, 10am-midnight Sun; Ⓜ Náměstí Míru) This gay-friendly cafe is part of the cluster of gay-friendly places that make up the old Radio Palác building. The Celebrity offers early-morning breakfasts weekdays and a more relaxed brunch on weekends. At other times, it's great coffee and people-watching.

RYBA NA RUBY CAFE, CLUB

Map p344 (☎731 570 704; www.rybanaruby.net; Mánesova 87, Vinohrady; ⌚2pm-midnight Mon-Sat; 📶; Ⓜ Jiřího z Poděbrad) Ryba Na Ruby is something different for Vinohrady: an eco-friendly teashop on the ground floor with a laid-back bar/club downstairs. This is a great place to stock up on things like fair trade teas and coffees, plus organic foodstuffs such as nuts, spices, cocoa, jams and oils. The below-ground club is a relaxed space for a beer or a coffee.

BAR & BOOKS MÁNESOVA COCKTAIL BAR

Map p344 (☎222 724 581; www.barandbooks.cz; Mánesova 64, Vinohrady; ⌚5pm-3am; 🚋11) This upmarket New York–style cocktail and cigar bar occupies a former rugby pub and couldn't be more different in terms of atmosphere. It's been given a bad rap for its cocktail prices, but the truth is if you stick to the basics, the prices aren't much higher here than elsewhere. Try to book a table in advance.

MAMA COFFEE CAFE

Map p344 (☎773 263 333; www.mamacoffee.cz; Londýnská 49, Vinohrady; ⌚8.30am-8pm Mon-Fri, 10.30am-8pm Sat & Sun; 📶👶; Ⓜ Náměstí Míru) One of several Mama Coffee branches around town that specialise in home-roasted fair-trade coffees imported from around the world. Mama Coffees are famously laid-back as well as being stroller- and kid-friendly.

ENTERTAINMENT

RADOST FX CLUB

Map p344 (224 254 776; www.radostfx.cz; Bělehradská 120, Vinohrady; admission 100-250Kč; 10pm-6am; ; IP Pavlova) Though not quite as trendy as it once was, slick and shiny Radost is still capable of pulling in the crowds, especially for its Thursday hip hop and R & B night, FXbounce (www.fxbounce.com; women enter free). The place has a chilled-out, bohemian atmosphere, with an excellent lounge and vegetarian restaurant that keeps serving into the small hours.

TECHTLE MECHTLE CLUB

Map p344 (www.techtle-mechtle.cz; Vinohradská 47, Vinohrady; 5pm-4am Mon-Sat; ; 11, Muzeum, Jiřího z Poděbrad) A popular cellar dance bar on Vinohrady's main drag. The name translates to 'hanky panky' in Czech and that's what most of the swanky people who come here are after. In addition to a well-tended cocktail bar, you'll find a decent restaurant and dance floor and occasional special events. Arrive early to get a good table.

ON CLUB CLUB, LIVE MUSIC

Map p344 (www.onclub.cz; Vinohradská 40, Vinohrady; 10pm-5am; 11, Muzeum) The ON Club is the latest incarnation of a series of gay and gay-friendly clubs to occupy the cavernous Radio Palác building. The crowd is mostly men, but there are some women, and everyone is welcome. Most nights there's a disco, but weekends usually bring big-name DJs and occasional live music.

GAY-FRIENDLY VINOHRADY

Over the years Vinohrady has evolved into the unofficial centre of gay Prague, and you'll find most of the city's better gay-friendly cafes and clubs in this area. While the scene changes with the season and venues come and go, as we researched this guide some of the more popular places included the following:

- ON Club (p140)
- Radost FX (p140)
- Termix (p140)
- Café Celebrity (p139)
- Le Clan (p140)

FREE **TERMIX** CLUB

Map p344 (222 710 462; www.club-termix.cz; Třebízckého 4a, Vinohrady; 8pm-5am Wed-Sun; Jiřího z Poděbrad) Termix is one of Prague's most popular gay dance clubs, with an industrial hi-tech vibe (lots of shiny steel and glass and plush sofas) and a young crowd that contains as many tourists as locals. The smallish dance floor fills up fast and you may have to queue to get in.

LE CLAN CLUB

Map p344 (www.leclan.cz; Balbínova 23, Vinohrady; admission 80-200Kč; 2am-10am Tue-Fri, 2am-noon Sat & Sun; Muzeum) A French-accented after-party club, with DJs on two floors, lots of bars, cosy armchairs and myriad rooms stuffed with people who want to party until dawn. It's usually got a good, decadent vibe, and tends to get more (not less) crowded as the night wears on.

SHOPPING

OBCHOD S UMĚNÍM ARTS & CRAFTS

Map p344 (224 252 779; Korunní 34, Vinohrady; 11am-5pm Mon-Fri; 10, 16, Náměstí Míru) The 'Shop with Art' specialises in original paintings, prints and sculpture from 1900 to 1940, when Czech artists were at the forefront in movements such as Constructivism, Surrealism and Cubism. Naturally, these artworks fetch astronomical prices these days, but it's still fun to drop by and browse.

STOCKIST INTERIOR DESIGN, HOMEWARES

Map p344 (286 017 560; www.stockist.cz; Vinohradská 41, Vinohrady; 10am-7.30pm Mon-Fri, 10am-2pm Sat; Muzeum) This is our favourite of the dozen or so high-end furniture and interior-design stores that line this end of Vinohradská and several adjoining streets. Offers some of the biggest names in contemporary design from Italy, Germany and the UK.

KAREL VÁVRA MUSIC

Map p344 (Lublaňská 65, Vinohrady; 9am-5pm Mon-Fri; IP Pavlova) Handmade fiddles decorate the interior of this old-fashioned violin workshop where Karel and his assistants beaver away making and repairing these instruments in time-honoured fashion. Even if you are not in search of a

CHECK OUT A SPARTA SLAVIA FOOTBALL MATCH

Prague's 'second' first-division football (soccer) club, SK Slavia Praha, plays its home matches at Vršovice's **Synot Tip Aréna** (SK Slavia or Eden Stadium; ☎731 126 104; www.synottiparena.cz; Vladivostocká, Vršovice; match tickets 150-400Kč; 🚋6, 7, 22, 24). While Slavia often plays second fiddle to Prague's other big team, Sparta Praha, Slavia actually has the longer lineage of the two, dating back to 1892. It's even an honorary member of England's Football Association.

Slavia has won the national championship on several occasions, mostly recently in the 2009 season. Perhaps its most unusual record is the design of its distinctive red-and-white striped uniforms, which have remained unchanged for more than 100 years. The football season runs from August to May.

Synot Tip Aréna also plays host to some big-name rock acts during the summer open-air music season. Past shows have included REM, Depeche Mode and Iron Maiden. The 2012 season was expected to bring Bruce Springsteen and the Red Hot Chili Peppers to Prague, among others. Purchase tickets for games and concerts online through Ticketpro (www.ticketpro.cz) or at the stadium ticket office.

custom-made violin, it's worth a look just for the time-warp atmosphere.

VINOHRADY FARMERS MARKET — MARKET

Map p344 (Farmářské tržiště; www.farmarsketrziste.cz; náměstí Jiřího z Poděbrad, Vinohrady; ⏲8am-2pm Wed & Sat; 👪; Ⓜ Jiřího z Poděbrad) Every Wednesday and Saturday, farmers descend onto the grassy square above the Jiřího z Poděbrad metro station to sell their fresh fruits and vegetables, as well as baked goods, meats and cheeses. It's fun for the whole family.

DŮM PORCELÁNU — GLASS

Map p344 (☎221 505 320; www.dumporcelanu.cz; Jugoslávská 16, Vinohrady; ⏲9am-7pm Mon-Fri, 9am-5pm Sat, 2-5pm Sun; Ⓜ IP Pavlova) The 'House of Porcelain' is a kind of factory outlet for the best Czech porcelain makers, including Haas & Czjzek and Thun, both based in western Bohemia. The flatware, china, blue onion pattern porcelain and other items are all priced to draw in local buyers – not tourists.

ATRIUM FLÓRA — SHOPPING CENTRE

Map p346 (☎255 741 712; www.atrium-flora.cz; Vinohradská 151, Vinohrady; ⏲9am-9pm Mon-Sat, 10am-9pm Sun; 📶; Ⓜ Flóra) You could be anywhere in the world in this shiny, glittering shrine to consumerism. Slick cafes share floor space with girly emporia selling tiny T-shirts, sparkly make-up and globalised brand names (Sergio Tacchini, Hilfiger, Nokia, Puma, Lacoste, Guess, Diesel, Apple...). There's also a food court upstairs, an eight-screen multiplex cinema and an IMAX cinema.

Žižkov & Karlín

Neighbourhood Top Five

❶ Pay a visit to one of Prague's most prominent landmarks, the **National Monument** (p144), where you can learn about 20th-century Czech history, and visit the laboratory where communist president Klement Gottwald was enbalmed.

❷ Ascend to the top of Žižkov's other noteworthy landmark, the **TV Tower** (p146), for outstanding city views.

❸ Enjoy the ultimate Žižkov experience – a crawl of its classic, crowded pubs, including **U Vystřeleného oka** (p148).

❹ Rock up to a live gig at the **Palác Akropolis** (p148), a stalwart of Prague's alternative music scene.

❺ Descend into the earth at the unique **Bunkr Parukářka** (p148), a club located in a 1950s nuclear bunker.

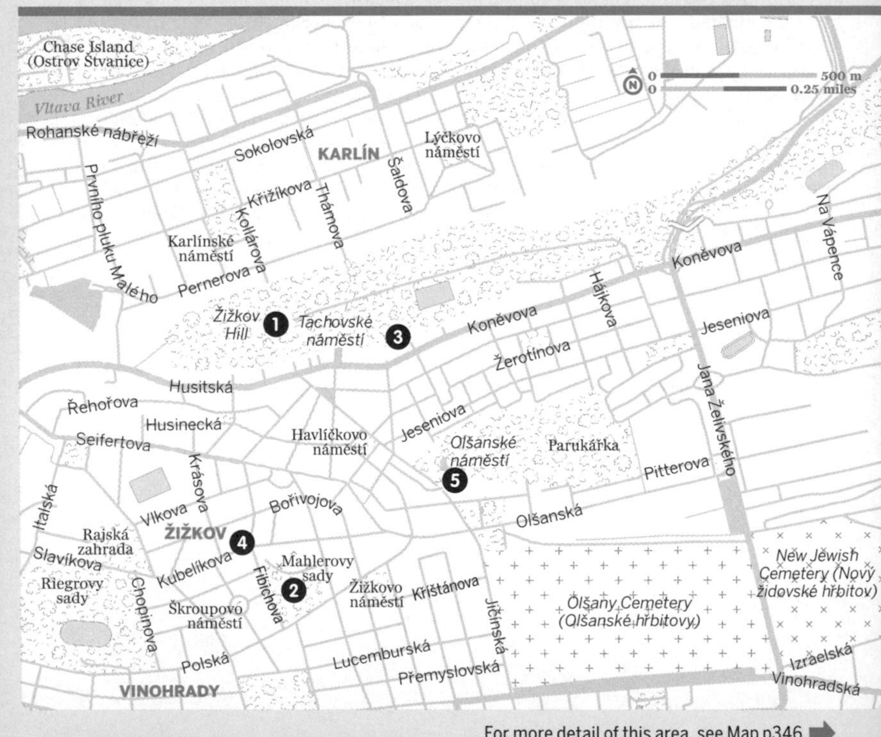

For more detail of this area, see Map p346 ➡

Explore: Žižkov & Karlín

Named after the one-eyed Hussite hero Jan Žižka, Žižkov was one of Prague's earliest industrial suburbs. It has long had a reputation as a rough-and-ready, working-class neighbourhood, and was full of left-wing revolutionary fervour well before the communist takeover of 1948 – in fact, it was an independent municipality from 1881 till 1922 and was known as the 'people's republic of Žižkov'.

Today it is one of Prague's liveliest districts, with more bars per capita than any other part of Prague. It's still pretty rough around the edges, which puts off a lot of visitors, though the streets are as safe as the rest of the city. There are a couple of major sights (the National Monument and the TV Tower) which could be covered in an afternoon, but the main attraction here is the bars – devote at least one night to exploring Žižkov's pub scene.

The mostly residential suburb of Karlín is squeezed between Žižkov Hill and the Vltava River. It was devastated by the floods of 2002, and since then has been undergoing massive redevelopment, with office complexes rising along the river banks. The older part of the district, along Křižíkova, has lots of lovely old art-nouveau buildings and is great for some aimless wandering – Lýčkovo náměstí is one of the prettiest squares in the city.

Local Life

➡ **Popular Hangouts** Tourists are notable by their absence in Žižkov and Karlín, so most places are 'local'. Café Pavlač (p146) is a popular place for weekend brunch, while Kuře V Hodinkách (p147) pulls in local crowds with live music as well as good food.

➡ **Park Life** Sunny days see crowds of locals out for a stroll in the park. The most popular spots are Žižkov Hill (locals often refer to it by its old name, Vítkov Hill) and Parukářka – the latter has a great beer garden.

➡ **Football** Supporters of local club FK Viktoria Žižkov (p26) are even more passionate than fans of Sparta and Slavia – see a home match for a real Žižkov experience.

Getting There & Away

➡ **Bus** Buses 133 and 175 run from outside Florenc metro station along Husitská at the foot of Žižkov Hill, useful for the Army Museum and National Monument.

➡ **Metro** There are no metro stations in Žižkov itself – the nearest is Jiřího z Poděbrad on line A, a five-minute walk south from the TV Tower. Line B runs through Karlín.

➡ **Tram** Lines 5, 9 and 26 run along Seifertova, in the centre of Žižkov, while lines 8 and 24 run along Sokolovská in Karlín.

Lonely Planet's Top Tip

The viewing platforms in Žižkov's TV Tower stay open till 10pm – skip the daytime crowds and turn up just in time for sunset to enjoy a really special view of the city.

Best Places to Eat

➡ Café Pavlač (p146)
➡ Kuře V Hodinkách (p147)
➡ Manni (p147)
➡ Hanil (p147)

For reviews, see p146 ➡

Best Places to Drink

➡ U Vystřeleného oka (p148)
➡ Pivovarský Klub (p147)
➡ Bukowski's (p147)
➡ U Slovanské Lípy (p148)

For reviews, see p147 

TOP SIGHTS
NATIONAL MONUMENT

The huge monument atop Žižkov Hill is not, strictly speaking, a legacy of the communist era – construction began in the 1930s. But in the minds of most Praguers over a certain age it is inextricably linked with the Communist Party of Czechoslovakia, and in particular with Klement Gottwald, the country's first 'worker-president'. Although the massive functionalist structure has all the elegance of a nuclear power station, the interior is a spectacular extravaganza of polished art-deco marble, gilt and mosaics, and home to a fascinating museum of 20th-century Czechoslovak history.

History

The famous Battle of Vítkov Hill took place in July 1420 on the long, narrow ridge that separates the Žižkov and Karlín districts, when the Hussite forces of Jan Žižka defeated the Holy Roman Emperor Sigismund.

Designed in the 1920s as a memorial to Žižka, and to the soldiers who had fought for Czechoslovak independence in WWI, the National Monument was still under construction in 1939 when the occupation of Czechoslovakia by Nazi Germany made the 'Monument to National Liberation', as it was then called, seem like a sick joke.

After 1948 the Communist Party appropriated the story of Jan Žižka and the Hussites for propaganda purposes, extolling them as shining examples of Czech peasant power. The communists completed the National Monument with the installation of the **Tomb of the Unknown Soldier**

DON'T MISS...

- Klement Gottwald's enbalming laboratory
- War memorial
- View from the rooftop lookout point
- Giant statue of Jan Žižka

PRACTICALITIES

- Národní Památník na Vítkově
- Map p346
- ☎222 781 676
- www.nm.cz
- U Památníku 1900, Žižkov
- exhibition only adult/child 60/30Kč, roof terrace 80/40Kč, combined ticket 110/60Kč
- ⏲10am-6pm Wed-Sun Apr-Oct & Thu-Sun Nov-Mar
- 🚌133, 207

and Bohumil Kafka's gargantuan bronze statue of Žižka. But they didn't stop there.

In 1953 the monument's mausoleum – originally intended to hold the remains of Tomáš Garrigue Masaryk, Czechoslovakia's founding father – received the embalmed body of the recently deceased Klement Gottwald, displayed to the public in a refrigerated glass chamber, just like his more illustrious comrade Lenin in Moscow's Red Square.

After 1989, the remains of Gottwald and other communist dignitaries were removed, and the building lay closed for 20 years. However, after a two-year renovation project it reopened to the public in 2009 as a museum of Czechoslovak history from 1918 to 1992.

Museum

The monument's central hall – once home to a dozen marble sarcophagi bearing the remains of communist luminaries – houses a moving **war memorial** with sculptures by Jan Sturša. There are exhibits recording the founding of the Czechoslovak Republic in 1918, WWII, the 1948 coup, the Soviet invasion of 1968 – poignant newsreel footage and a handful of personal possessions record the tragic story of Jan Palach, who set himself alight to protest the Soviet invasion – and the Velvet Revolution of 1989. Steps lead down to the columbarium, where the ashes of prominent Czechs were once stored.

But the most grimly fascinating part of the museum is the Frankenstein-like **laboratory** beneath the Liberation Hall, where scientists once battled to prevent Klement Gottwald's corpse from decomposing. On display in a glass-walled sarcophagus by day, his body was lowered into this white-tiled crypt every night for another frantic round of maintenance and repair. In the corner is the refrigerated chamber where Gottwald spent his nights (now occupied by the shattered remains of his sarcophagus), and in the adjoining room is a phalanx of 1950s control panels, switches and instruments that once monitored the great leader's temperature and humidity.

Žižkov Hill

Next to the monument, dominating the western end of Žižkov Hill (formerly called Vítkov Hill), is a giant statue of Jan Žižka on horseback (pictured left). It was commissioned in 1931 from the Prague sculptor Bohumil Kafka (no relation to Franz), who had a huge studio specially constructed for the project and worked on the statue until his death in 1941, by which time he had succeeded only in creating a full-size plaster version. The statue was eventually cast in bronze – 16.5 tonnes of it – in 1950 and unveiled on 14 July of that year, the anniversary of the Battle of Vítkov Hill.

TAKE A TRAM

Rather than climb steeply up from Husitská immediately below the monument, a much more enjoyable approach is to take tram 1, 9 or 16 to the Ohrada stop on Koněvova at the eastern end of Žižkov Hill, and enjoy an easy walk along the crest of the hill, with great views to either side – south across the rooftops of Žižkov to the TV Tower, and north over Karlín to the Vltava River and the hills above Troja.

In the 1950s a visit to Klement Gottwald's tomb was a compulsory outing for school groups and busloads of visiting tourists from Warsaw Pact countries. Gottwald's morticians, however, were not as adept as Lenin's – by 1962 the body had decayed so badly that it had to be cremated.

ROOFTOP VIEWS

The lookout point on the museum's roof offers a superb view over the city, and there's an appealing cafe on the 1st floor with an outdoor terrace.

SIGHTS

NATIONAL MONUMENT MUSEUM

See p144.

FREE ARMY MUSEUM MUSEUM

Map p346 (Armádní muzeum Žižkov; ☎973 204 924; www.vhu.cz; U památníku 2, Žižkov; 9.30am-6pm Tue-Sun; 133, 207) On the way up Žižkov Hill you will find this grim-looking barracks of a museum, with a rusting T34 tank parked outside. It's for military enthusiasts only, with exhibits on the history of the Czechoslovak Army and resistance movement from 1918 to 1945, including a small display of personal effects of one of the paratroopers who took part in the 1942 assasination of Reichsprotektor Reinhard Heydrich.

NEW JEWISH CEMETERY CEMETERY

Map p346 (Nový židovské hřbitov; ☎226 235 248; www.kehilaprag.cz; Izraelská 1, Žižkov; 9am-5pm Sun-Thu & to 2pm Fri Apr-Oct, 9am-4pm Sun-Thu & to 2pm Fri Nov-Mar, closed on Jewish holidays; MŽelivského) Franz Kafka is buried in this cemetery, which opened around 1890 when the older Jewish cemetery – now at the foot of the TV Tower – was closed. To find **Kafka's grave** (Map p346), follow the main avenue east (signposted), turn right at row 21, then left at the wall; it's at the end of the 'block'. Fans make a pilgrimage on 3 June, the anniversary of his death.

The entrance is beside Želivského metro station; men should cover their heads (yarmulkes are available at the gate). Last admission is 30 minutes before closing.

FREE KARLÍN STUDIOS GALLERY

Map p346 (☎734 244 581; www.karlinstudios.cz; Křižíkova 34, Karlín; noon-6pm Wed-Sun; MKřižíkova) Housed in a converted factory building, this complex of artists' studios includes a public art gallery that showcases the best of Czech contemporary art, plus two small commercial galleries. This is the place to come and see what's happening at the cutting edge of art in the city.

OLŠANY CEMETERY CEMETERY

Map p346 (Olšanské Hřbitovy; Vinohradská 153, Žižkov; free admission; 8am-7pm May-Sep, to 6pm Mar, Apr & Oct, to 5pm Nov-Feb; 5, 10, 11, 16) Huge and atmospheric, Prague's main burial ground was founded in 1680 to handle the increased deaths during a plague epidemic. **Jan Palach**, the student who set himself on fire in January 1969 to protest the Soviet invasion, is buried here. To find his **grave** (Map p346), enter the main gate (flanked by flower shops) on Vinohradská and turn right – it's about 50m along on the left of the path.

The oldest gravestones can be found in the northwestern corner of the cemetery, near the 17th-century **Chapel of St Roch** (kaple sv Rocha; Map p346). There are several entrances to the cemetery running along Vinohradská, east of Flora metro station, and also beside the chapel on Olšanská.

TV TOWER TOWER

Map p346 (Televizní Vysílač; ☎724 251 286; www.praguerocket.com; Mahlerovy sady 1, Žižkov; adult/child 120/60Kč; 10am-10pm; MJiřího z Poděbrad) Prague's tallest landmark – and, depending on your tastes, either its ugliest or its most futuristic feature – is the 216m-tall TV Tower, erected between 1985 and 1992. But more bizarre than its architecture are the 10 giant crawling babies that appear to be exploring the outside of the tower – an installation called **Miminka** (Mummy; Map p346) by artist David Černý.

The viewing platforms, reached by high-speed lifts, have comprehensive information boards in English and French explaining what you can see; there's also a restaurant at 66m up (closed for renovation at the time of research, but due to reopen in summer 2012).

EATING

Žižkov is more famous for its pubs than its restaurants, but there are new places springing up every year to add to the stalwarts that have been around for ages. We haven't been able to recommend any restaurants in Karlín yet, but if you're in the area check out Pivovarský Klub, a drinking venue that serves good traditional pub grub.

CAFÉ PAVLAČ CAFE €

Map p346 (☎222 721 731; www.cafepavlac.cz; Víta Nejedlého 23, Žižkov; mains 90-190Kč; 10am-11pm Mon-Fri, noon-midnight Sat, noon-11pm Sun; 5, 9, 26) This smart and stylish cafe-bar is a sign of the new Žižkov, forsaking spit-and-sawdust earthiness for designer metalwork, edgy art and architectural magazines. It does excellent coffee and hot chocolate, and the food menu runs from breakfast (ham and eggs, croissants or muesli with yoghurt), to lunch specials, to dinner dishes of pasta, salads and steaks.

HANIL JAPANESE, KOREAN €€

Map p346 (☎222 715 867; Slavíkova 24, Žižkov; mains 350-500Kč; ⌚11am-2.30pm & 5.30-11pm Mon-Sat, 5.30-11pm Sun; Ⓜ Jiřího z Poděbrad) White walls, lattice screens, paper lanterns and polished granite tables create a relaxed and informal setting where a mixed crowd of businesspeople, locals and expats enjoys authentic Japanese and Korean cuisine. Tuck into a bowl of *bibimbap* (rice topped with meat and pickled vegetables spiced with hot pepper paste), or order a sashimi platter – the sushi here is probably the best in town (70Kč to 150Kč per piece).

MANNI PAKISTANI, INDIAN €

Map p346 (☎222 511 660; www.mannirestaurant.cz; Seifertova 11, Žižkov; mains 100-200Kč; ⌚11am-11pm Mon-Fri, noon-11pm Sat & Sun; ; 5, 9, 26) This plain but welcoming restaurant, with its bright red-and-white decor, photos of Kashmiri mountains, and smiling, English-speaking staff, feels more like Bradford than Žižkov. And the food is just as authentic as you'd get in the UK's curry capital, with halal meat, richly spiced sauces, and plenty of chilli heat. The weekday lunch special costs just 89Kč.

KUŘE V HODINKÁCH CZECH, INTERNATIONAL €

Map p346 (☎222 734 212; www.kurevhodinkach.eu; Seifertova 26, Žižkov; mains 140-240Kč; ⌚11am-1am Mon-Fri, noon-1am Sat & Sun; 5, 9, 26) This music-themed pub is decked out in rock memorabilia, and with a choice of buzzing street-level bar or more intimate brick-vaulted basement it's more upmarket than most Žižkov pubs and has a classy kitchen to match. The menu includes chicken Caesar salad, barbecued steak with Dijon mustard sauce, and a rich, dark and tasty goulash with bacon dumplings.

The pub is named after a 1972 album by Czech jazz-rock band Flamengo, which was banned by the communist authorities (it means 'Chicken in the Watch' – hey, it was the '70s, psychedelic drugs and all that...).

RESTAURACE AKROPOLIS INTERNATIONAL €

Map p346 (☎296 330 913; www.palacakropolis.com; Kubelíkova 27, Žižkov; mains 90-250Kč; ⌚11am-12.30am Mon-Thu, 11am-1.30am Fri, 3pm-12.30am Sat & Sun; ; 5, 9, 26) The cafe in the famous Palác Akropolis club is a Žižkov institution, with its eccentric combination of marble panels, quirky metalwork light fittings and weird fishtank installations designed by local artist František Skála. The menu has a good selection of vegetarian dishes, from nachos to gnocchi, plus great garlic soup, searingly hot buffalo wings and steak tartare.

MAILSI PAKISTANI €€

Map p346 (☎222 717 783; www.pakistani-restaurant-mailsi.eu; Lipanská 1, Žižkov; mains 200-400Kč; ⌚noon-3pm & 6-11.30pm; ; 5, 9, 26) Mailsi was Prague's first Pakistani restaurant, and is still one of the city's best for authentic, home-style curry cuisine. Service is courteous and the food delicious. The *bhaji* is rather plain – just onion and potato thinly sliced, dipped in spiced flour and fried, but very light and crisp – while the *murgh dal* consists of tender chicken in a cumin-spiced lentil sauce.

DRINKING & NIGHTLIFE

Žižkov is famous for having more pubs per head of population than any other city district in Europe, and – depending on your tastes – offers the most authentic or the most terrifying pub-crawling experience in Prague. Be prepared for smoke, sticky floors, wall-to-wall noise and some heroically drunk companions.

BUKOWSKI'S COCKTAIL BAR

Map p346 (☎222 212 676; Bořivojova 86, Žižkov; ⌚6pm-2am; 5, 9, 26) Like many of the drinking dens that are popular among expats, Bukowski's is more a cocktail dive than a cocktail bar. Named after hard-drinking American writer Charles Bukowski, it cultivates a dark and slightly debauched atmosphere – the decor is self-consciously 'interesting' (when you can see it through the smoke-befogged candlelight) – but it peddles quality cocktails and cigars, and has friendly bartenders and cool tunes.

TOP CHOICE **PIVOVARSKÝ KLUB** BEER HALL

Map p346 (☎222 315 777; www.gastroinfo.cz/pivoklub/; Křižíkova 17, Karlín; ⌚11am-11.30pm;

Ⓜ Florenc) This bar is to beer what the Bodleian Library is to books – wall-to-wall shelves lined with myriad varieties of bottled beer from all over the world, and six guest beers on tap. Perch on a bar stool or head downstairs to the snug cellar and order some of the pub's excellent grub (such as authentic *guláš* with bacon dumplings for 235Kč) to soak up the beer.

U SLOVANSKÉ LÍPY PUB

Map p346 (☎222 780 563; Tachovské náměstí 6, Žižkov; ⊙4-11pm Mon-Sat; 🚌133, 207) A classic Žižkov pub, plain and unassuming outside and in, 'At the Linden Trees' (the linden is a Czech and Slovak national emblem) has become something of a place of pilgrimage for beer lovers. The reason is its range of beers from the Kout na Šumavě brewery, including a superb *světlý ležák*, and the dark and powerful *tmavý speciál*, which weighs in at a head-spinning 18° (see p292).

TOP CHOICE **U VYSTŘELENÉHO OKA** PUB

Map p346 (☎222 540 465; www.uvoka.cz; U Božích Bojovníků 3, Žižkov; ⊙4.30pm-1am Mon-Sat; 🚌133, 207) You've got to love a pub that has vinyl pads on the wall above the gents' urinals to rest your forehead on. 'The Shot-Out Eye' – the name pays homage to the one-eyed Hussite hero atop the hill behind the pub – is a bohemian (with a small 'b') hostelry with a raucous Friday-night atmosphere where the cheap Pilsner Urquell pulls in a typically heterogeneous Žižkov crowd.

BUNKR PARUKÁŘKA CLUB

Map p346 (☎603 423 140; www.parukarka.eu; Na Kříže, Olšanské náměstí, Žižkov; admission free-50Kč; 🚋5, 9, 26) Only in Prague… A graffiti-covered steel door in the hillside at the west end of Parukářka park leads to a vast circular staircase that descends into a 1950s nuclear bunker where a makeshift bar serves cheap beer in plastic glasses. This is the unlikely setting for one of Prague's most unusual clubs, a claustrophobic shrine to all the weird and wonderful avant-garde electronic music genres you can think of. The opening hours vary – check listings on the website.

SEDM VLKŮ CLUB

Map p346 (☎222 711 725; www.sedmvlku.cz; Vlkova 7, Žižkov ; ⊙5pm-3am Mon-Sat; 🚋5, 9, 26) 'Seven Wolves' is a two-level, art-studenty cafe/bar and club. At street level there's candlelight, friendly staff, weird wrought-iron work and funky murals, and music low enough to have a conversation; down in the darkened cellar, DJs pump out techno, breakbeat, drum 'n' bass, jungle and reggae from 9pm on Friday and Saturday nights.

XT3 LIVE MUSIC

Map p346 (☎222 783 463; www.xt3.cz; Rokycanova 29, Žižkov ; admission free-100Kč; ⊙bar 11am-2am Mon-Thu, 11am-5am Fri, 2pm-5am Sat, 2pm-2am Sun, club from 6pm; 🚋5, 9, 26) This is the essential Žižkov club – scruffy, laid-back, eclectic and great fun. There's a lively bar at street level, all red-brick arches and wood-and-leather booths, plus a cavern-like club venue that hosts local DJs and live music (from hardcore rock to acoustic singer-songwriters).

PARUKÁŘKA BAR

Map p346 (Olšanská; 🚋5, 9, 26) Little more than a ramshackle wooden hut in a park overlooking Žižkov, with plenty of outdoor tables and lots of sweet-smelling smoke wafting about in the evenings. Has Gambrinus on tap.

☆ ENTERTAINMENT

PALÁC AKROPOLIS LIVE MUSIC, CLUB

Map p346 (☎296 330 911; www.palacakropolis.cz; Kubelikova 27, Žižkov; admission free-50Kč; ⊙club 7pm-5am; 🚋5, 9, 26 to Lipanska) The Akropolis is a Prague institution, a labyrinthine, sticky-floored shrine to alternative music and drama. Its various performance spaces host a smorgasbord of musical and cultural events, from DJs to string quartets to Macedonian Roma bands to local rock gods to visiting talent – Marianne Faithfull, the Flaming Lips and the Strokes have all played here.

KINO AERO CINEMA

Map p346 (☎271 771 349; www.kinoaero.cz; Biskupcova 31, Žižkov; tickets 60-100Kč; 🚋5, 9, 10, 16, 19) The Aero is Prague's best-loved art-house cinema, with themed programs, retrospectives and unusual films, often in English or with English subtitles. This is the place to catch reruns of classics from *Smrt v Benátkách* (Death in Venice) to *Život Briana* (The Life of Brian). The same managers run a similar venue in the city centre, Kino Světozor (p130).

Holešovice, Bubeneč & Dejvice

Neighbourhood Top Five

❶ Spend at least part of a day touring the excellent modern art museum at **Veletržní Palác** (p151). This often-overlooked branch of the National Gallery has fine examples of early-modern Czech Surrealist and Cubist art. Oh, and you might want to see the stuff from Schiele, Klimt, Picasso and Van Gogh too.

❷ Admire the view over the Old Town and Charles Bridge from the bluff overlooking the Vltava River at **Letná Gardens** (p153).

❸ Enjoy a traditional pub meal at a classic joint such as **Restaurace U Veverky** (p157).

❹ Splurge on some fancy Asian cooking at **Sasazu** (p154), then dance at the energetic Sasazu club next door.

❺ Get out of town (well, briefly) with a short excursion to the **Prague Zoo** (p152).

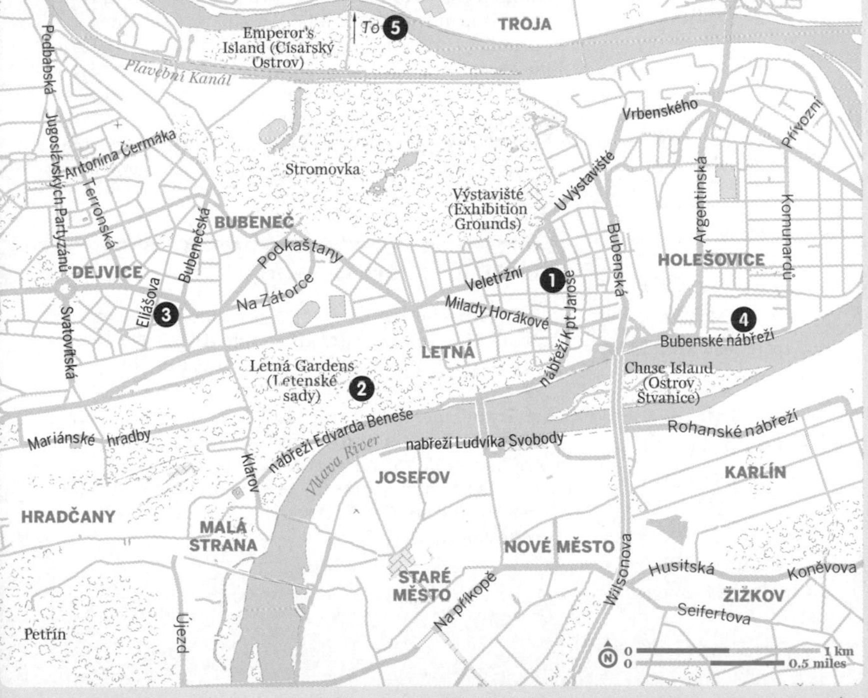

For more detail of this area, see Maps p348 and p350 ➡

Lonely Planet's Top Tip

The area of Holešovice, Bubeneč and Dejvice has two of Prague's finest pieces of green, **Letná Gardens** (p153) and **Stromovka** (p153), so once you've tired of the crowds and cobblestones, head here to walk the paths and get some fresh air. Letná is the more accessible of the two, with beautiful hilltop vistas over the city's 14th-century skyline. Stromovka is larger and more remote and the perfect place to relax with a blanket and a book.

Best Places to Eat

- Da Emanuel (p156)
- Restaurace U Veverky (p157)
- Argument (p156)
- Sasazu (p154)
- Peperoncino (p156)

For reviews, see p154 ➡

Best Places to Drink

- Letná beer garden (p159)
- Fraktal (p159)
- Kabinet (p161)
- Na Slamníku (p159)
- Na Staré Kovárně (p158)

For reviews, see p158 ➡

Best Places to Party

- Cross Club (p161)
- Sasazu (p161)
- Mecca (p162)
- Club Club (p158)
- La Bodega Flamenca (p160)

For reviews, see p161 ➡

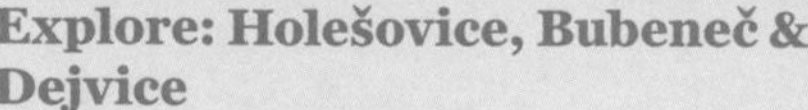

Explore: Holešovice, Bubeneč & Dejvice

The contiguous neighbourhoods of Holešovice, Bubeneč and Dejvice cut across a huge swath of land to the north of the Old Town across the Vltava. It's nearly impossible to explore the area in one go: instead, focus on specific destinations, such as restaurants, clubs or museums. Main hubs include Strossmayerovo náměstí in Holešovice, Letenské náměstí in Bubeneč and the area around the Dejvická metro station in Dejvice. Each of these has interesting pockets of pubs and little holes-in-the-wall to give a flavour of Prague life away from the central tourist throng. You won't want to miss the modern art museum at the Veletržní Palác, which you can easily combine with a visit to one of the pretty parks at Letná or Stromovka. Further afield, Prague Zoo and the Troja Chateau occupy bucolic settings amid rolling hills.

Local Life

➡ **Popular Hangouts** Spend a warm evening in summer at the Letná beer garden (p159). Get your beer in a plastic cup from the kiosk and head for a picnic table.

➡ **Shopping** The grassy knoll above the Dejvická metro station comes to life every Saturday from 9am to 2pm with a farmers market (p157). Farmers bring their products to town and local residents turn out in droves.

➡ **Spectator Sports** 'Go local' with a colourful 'Sparta Praha' scarf and head to Generali Aréna (p163; Sparta Stadium) to check out a football (soccer) match. Go to the website to see if there's a match scheduled during your visit. You can usually snag tickets on match day at the stadium's visitor centre.

Getting There & Away

➡ **Metro** To reach Holešovice, use the Vltavská or Nádraží Holešovice stations on line C (red). For Dejvice, use the Hradčanská or Dejvická stations on line A (green).

➡ **Tram** Lines 5, 12, 14, 15 and 17 run along Dukelských Hrdinů, the main north–south street in Holešovice; trams 1, 8, 15, 25 and 26 run east–west on Milady Horákové, serving both Holešovice and Bubeneč. Lines 2, 8, 20 and 26 all pass through Vítězné náměstí in the centre of Dejvice.

TOP SIGHTS
VELETRŽNÍ PALÁC

The National Gallery's vast Museum of Art of the 20th and 21st Centuries (Trade Fair Palace) is often overlooked by visitors, more bedazzled by Prague's Gothic and baroque heritage. A short tram ride from the centre, the entire building is stuffed with works by Van Gogh, Picasso, Schiele, Munch and Klimt, as well as many Czech masterpieces.

The main holdings are arranged on four floors, in rough chronological order top-to-bottom. Take the elevator to the 4th floor and work your way down.

Highlights on the 4th floor (Czech art to 1930) include paintings by Alfons Mucha, Max Švabinský and the early master of abstraction, František Kupka (tracing his shift from representational art to abstraction post-WWI).

On the 3rd floor (the Interwar Period and French Masters), look for Czech Cubists Bohumil Kubišta and Josef Čapek. Impressive French holdings include works by Rodin, Cézanne, Gauguin, Van Gogh, Monet and Picasso. Don't miss the functionalist architecture exhibition.

On the 2nd floor (Czech art from 1930 to 1980) our favourite is Surrealist Josef Šima and his beautifully spare and subtly sexualized landscapes.

The 1st floor (International Masters) features greatest hits from Klimt, Schiele, Munch and Oskar Kokoschka, whose expressionist paintings of Prague in the 1930s are simply mind-blowing.

DON'T MISS...

- *Green Corn*, Vincent Van Gogh, 3rd floor
- *Self Portrait*, Pablo Picasso, 3rd floor
- *Dead Town*, Egon Schiele, 1stfloor
- *Charles Bridge*, Oskar Kokoschka, 1st floor

PRACTICALITIES

- Museum of Art of the 20th and 21st Centuries
- Map p348
- ☎224 301 122
- www.ngprague.cz
- Dukelských hrdinů 47, Holešovice
- adult/concession 180/90Kč
- ⏱10am-6pm Tue-Sun
- 🚋12, 14, 17

SIGHTS

The districts of Holešovice, Bubeneč and Dejvice are spread out over a wide geographic area. Most of the important sights are near Holešovice's Výstaviště Exhibition grounds, and within walking distance of the Veletržní Palác. The National Technical Museum is situated just behind Letná Gardens.

Holešovice

VELETRŽNÍ PALÁC MUSEUM

See p151.

NATIONAL TECHNICAL MUSEUM MUSEUM

Map p348 (Národní Technické Muzeum; ☎220 399 111; www.ntm.cz; Kostelní 42, Holešovice; adult/concession 170/90Kč; ⊙10am-6pm Tue-Sun; ♿; 🚊1, 8, 15, 25) Prague's most family-friendly museum finally reopened its doors in 2011 after a multi-year renovation that added several interactive displays to its already immense and impressive holdings of historic planes, trains and automobiles. The renovation also added new exhibits on astronomy, photography, printing and architecture.

DOX CENTRE FOR CONTEMPORARY ART GALLERY

Map p348 (☎295 568 123; www.doxprague.org; Poupětova 1, Holešovice; adult/concession 180/90Kč; ⊙10am-6pm Wed-Mon; 🚊5, 12) This edgy, noncommercial art gallery and exhibition space forms the nucleus of Holešovice's expanding rep as one of the city's more hip districts. The exhibitions highlight a wide range of media, including video, sculpture, photography and painting. You'll find a cafe and an excellent bookstore (heavy on art and architecture) on the upper level. Closed Tuesday.

KŘIŽÍK'S FOUNTAIN FOUNTAIN

Map p348 (Křižíkova fontána; www.krizikova fontana.cz; U Výstaviště 1, Holešovice; admission around 200Kč; ⊙performances hourly 8-11pm Mar-Oct; 🚊5, 12, 14, 15, 17) Each evening from spring to autumn the musical Křižík's Fountain performs its computer-controlled light-and-water dance. Performances range from classical music such as Dvořák's New World Symphony to rousing works performed by Andrea Bocelli, Queen or the Scorpions. Check the website for what's on. The show is best after sunset – from May to July go for later shows.

MOŘSKÝ SVĚT AQUARIUM

Map p348 (☎220 103 275; www.morskysvet.cz; U Výstaviště 1, Holešovice; adult/concession 280/180Kč; ⊙10am-7pm; 🚊5, 12, 14, 15, 17) The Czech 'Sea World' has the largest water tank in the country, with a capacity of around 100,000L. Some 4500 living species of fish and sea creatures are on display, with a good (and suitably scary) set of sharks. The cramped interior will be disappointing if you're used to larger 'Sea World'-type amusement parks around the world.

LAPIDÁRIUM MUSEUM

Map p348 (☎233 375 636; www.nm.cz; U Výstaviště 1, Holešovice; adult/concession 50/30Kč; ⊙noon-6pm Wed-Sun; 🚊5, 12, 14, 15, 17) An outlying branch of the National Museum and an often-overlooked gem, the Lapidárium is a repository for some 400 sculptures from the 11th to the 19th centuries. The exhibits include Bohemia's oldest surviving stone sculpture, parts of the Renaissance Krocín Fountain that once stood on the Old

WORTH A DETOUR

WORTH A DETOUR: PRAGUE ZOO

Prague's family-friendly **zoo** (Zoo Praha; ☎296 112 111; www.zoopraha.cz; U Trojského zámku 120, Troja; adult/concession/family 150/100/450Kč; ⊙9am-7pm Jun-Aug, to 6pm Apr, May, Sep & Oct, to 5pm Mar, to 4pm Nov-Feb; ♿; Ⓜ Nádraží Holešovice, 🚌112) is north of Holešovice, reachable by bus 112 from Nádraží Holešovice metro station, or a 15-minute walk from Stromovka park. Visit on a weekday if possible – weekends get ridiculously crowded.

The 60-hectare wooded grounds are on the northern banks of the Vltava. Pride of place, atop the hill, goes to a herd of Przewalski's horses (the zoo played an important part in saving them from extinction) and the Komodo dragons. Other attractions include a miniature cable car and kids' play area.

THE PRAGUE FLOOD, 10 YEARS ON

More than a decade has passed since Prague was struck by one of the worst floods in its thousand-plus years of existence. Following heavy rains in the summer of 2002, the Vltava overflowed its banks on August 13–14 that year. The worst-affected areas were low-lying parts of Malá Strana and Smíchov, but the river district of Holešovice was also hit hard, sustaining damages amounting to hundreds of millions of crowns, but thankfully little loss of life.

While much of the flood damage has since been repaired, and the flood even spurred some much-needed new investment, there are still places where you can see the extent of the disaster. In Holešovice, the hardest-hit areas were along Bubenské nábřeží, which borders the river, and further to the east along the streets of Jateční and Plynární, in low-lying eastern Holešovice. The gleaming new construction you see in this area has largely arisen since the flooding and in many cases to replace buildings that were lost in the deluge.

Prague Zoo, which borders the Vltava's far northern banks, is another survivor. The floods struck the zoo particularly hard and a number of animals, including an elephant, a hippopotamus and a gorilla, were tragically lost. One of the saddest stories to arise from those days concerns a sea lion from the zoo named Gaston. In the early days of the flooding, it was reported that Gaston had managed to make it to the river and was swimming to Germany. Indeed, he made it all the way to Dresden, only to die of exhaustion once he got there.

Town Square, and several original statues from Charles Bridge.

PRAGUE PLANETARIUM PLANETARIUM

Map p348 (Planetárium Praha; ☎220 999 001; www.planetarium.cz; Královská obora 233, Holešovice; shows in Czech/English 80/200Kč; ⏰8.30am-noon & 1-8pm Mon-Thu, 9.30am-noon & 1-6pm Sat & Sun; 🚋5, 12, 14, 15, 17) The planetarium in Stromovka park, just west of Výstaviště, presents various slide and video presentations in addition to the star shows. Most shows are in Czech only, but one or two of the more popular ones provide a text summary in English (check the website for details). There's also an astronomical exhibition in the main hall.

Bubeneč

STROMOVKA PARK

Map p350 (Královská obora; entry to the park at Nad Královskou oborou 21, Bubeneč; 🚋1, 8, 15, 25, 26 to Letenské náměstí plus a 10 minute walk north) Stromovka, west of Výstaviště, is Prague's largest park. In the Middle Ages, it was a royal hunting preserve, which is why it's sometimes called the Královská obora (Royal Hunting Ground). Rudolf II had rare trees planted here and several lakes created. It's now the preserve of strollers, joggers, cyclists and in-line skaters.

LETNÁ GARDENS PARK

Map p350 (Letenské sady, Bubeneč; 🚋1, 8, 15, 25, 26 to Letenské náměstí) The lovely Letná Gardens is a large park that occupies a bluff over the Vltava river, north of the Old Town, with postcard-perfect views out over the city, the river and the bridges. It's perfect for walking, jogging, in-line skating, and beer drinking at the popular beer garden (p159) at the park's eastern end. From the tram stop it is a further five- or 10-minute walk south.

ECOTECHNICAL MUSEUM MUSEUM

Map p350 (Ekotechnické Muzeum; ☎777 170 636; www.ekotechnickemuseum.cz; Papírenská 6, Bubeneč; adult/family 120/250Kč; ⏰10.30am-4pm Tue-Sun May-Oct; Ⓜ Hradčanská, 🚌131) This museum is located in Prague's historic sewage-treatment plant, which dates from the late-19th century. Guided tours (book in advance) take you through the labyrinth of sewers beneath the building. The main attraction is the vast amount of machinery needed to service a bustling 19th-century city. The plant was originally designed to service a city of 500,000 but remained in operation until 1967, when the city's population had already exceeded a million.

Dejvice

HOTEL CROWNE PLAZA HISTORIC BUILDING
Map p350 (Hotel International; ☎296 537 111; www.ichotelsgroup.com; Koulova 15, Dejvice; 🚋8) The silhouette of this huge Stalin-era building in Dejvice will be familiar to anyone who has visited Moscow. Originally called the Hotel International, it was built in the 1950s to a design inspired by a tower of Moscow University, right down to the Soviet-style star on top of the spire. The interior is just as impressive.

EATING

Most of the better places to eat in this area are clustered along the residential streets around Dejvická metro station. You'll find another grouping within walking distance of Strossmayerovo náměstí and in the area around Letenské náměstí.

Holešovice

SASAZU ASIAN €€
Map p348 (☎284 097 455; www.sasazu.com; Bubenské nábřeží 306, Block 25, Holešovice market, Holešovice; mains 220-460Kč; ⏲noon-midnight Sun-Thu, noon-1am Fri & Sat; 🚋1, 3, 5, 25, Ⓜ Vltavská) This upmarket Asian restaurant (connected to the club of the same name) has by many accounts the best Asian cooking in Prague. While prices for individual entrees are not outrageous for what's on offer, portions are on the small side. Book in advance, especially on weekends.

KORBEL CZECH €
Map p348 (☎222 986 095; Komunardů 30, Holešovice; mains 119-230Kč; 📶; 🚋1, 3, 5, 25) This slightly below-ground restaurant is packed at lunchtime, a testament to the very good and great-value Czech cooking. The space is noisy and energetic; service is cool but polite.

LA CRÊPERIE FRENCH €
Map p348 (☎220 878 040; www.lacreperie.cz; Janovského 4, Holešovice; mains 60-140Kč; ⏲9am-11pm Mon-Sat, to 10pm Sun; 🚋1, 5, 8, 12, 14, 15, 17, 25, 26, Ⓜ Vltavská) Odd place to put an authentic French crêperie, in a forgotten corner of Holešovice. Still, if you happen to be in the area, it's worth a stop for excellent sweet and savoury open-faced crêpes called galettes. The *galette complet* (ham and cheese with an egg on top) makes an excellent and filling breakfast.

BOHEMIA BAGEL AMERICAN €
Map p348 (☎220 806 541; www.bohemiabagel.cz; Dukelských hrdinů 48, Holešovice; mains 120-240Kč; ⏲9am-11pm; 📶; 🚋5, 14, 15, 17) This hamburger, bagel and breakfast outfit remains the best all-round place to grab a light meal in this barren stretch (at least from a culinary standpoint) of Holešovice. It runs a popular brunch on weekends.

LUCKY LUCIANO PIZZERIA €
Map p348 (☎220 875 900; www.luckyluciano.cz; Dělnická 28, Holešovice; mains 100-150Kč; 📶🖉; 🚋1, 5, 12, 14, 15, 25, Ⓜ Vltavská) You're in luck if you're staying at Sir Toby's Hostel: this little pizzeria nearby serves very good pizza, as

WORTH A DETOUR

WORTH A DETOUR: TROJA CHATEAU

This **chateau** (Zámek Troja; www.ghmp.cz; U Trojského Zámku 1, Troja; adult/concession 120/60Kč; ⏲10am-6pm Tue-Sun Apr-Oct, closed Nov-Mar; Ⓜ Nádraží Holešovice, 🚌112) is a 17th-century baroque palace built for the Šternberk family, inspired by Roman country villas seen by the architect on a visit to Italy. A visit to the chateau can easily be combined with a trip to Prague Zoo, since the two are side by side. It's also a pleasant 20-minute walk from Stromovka park, including crossing a dramatic footbridge over the Vltava.

The sumptuously decorated palace now houses collections of the Prague City Gallery and exhibits explaining the sculptures and frescoes that adorn the palace itself. There's free admission to the grounds, where you can wander in the beautiful French gardens, watched over by a gang of baroque stone giants on the balustrade outside the southern door.

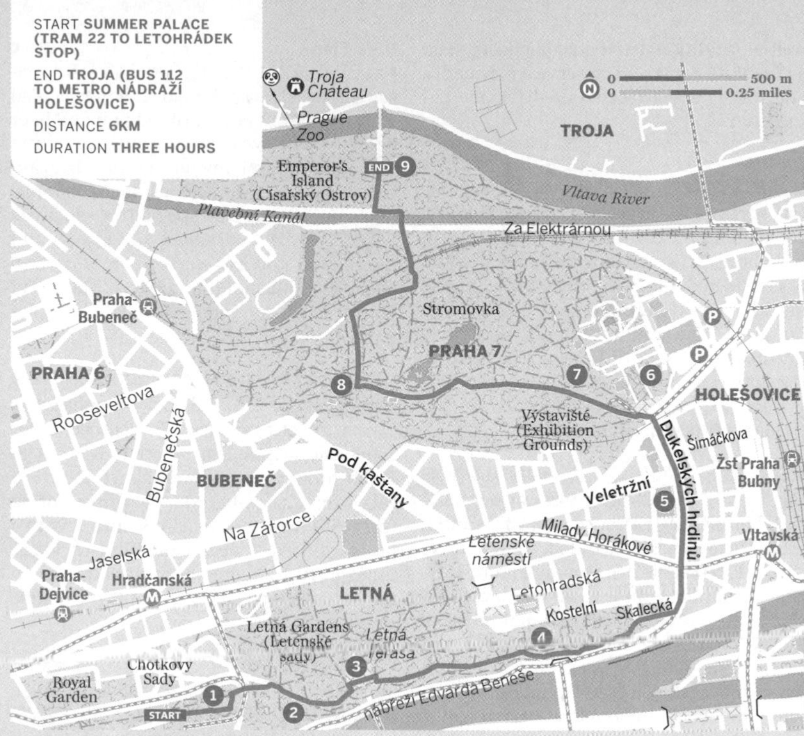

Neighbourhood Walk

Lovely Letná Gardens & Stromovka Park

This walk takes you through two of Prague's nicest parks and leaves you just a short walk from Prague Zoo.

Begin at the Summer Palace (Letohrádek) north of Prague Castle. A path leads east into Chotkovy sady; in the centre of the park you will find a ❶ **stone grotto** dedicated to novelist Josef Zeyer. A footbridge leads across Chotkova into Letná Gardens. Follow the path, which bears right and then make a further right to visit ❷ **Hanavský Pavilón** for a superb panorama.

Keep walking along the bluff above the Vltava before arriving at a monumental terrace topped by a giant, creaking ❸ **metronome** that sits on a spot once occupied by a giant statue of Stalin. Continue east and you'll eventually arrive at the ❹ **Letná beer garden**.

Beyond the beer garden, the path slopes down through pretty flower gardens. Leave the park and continue downhill on Skalecká, then turn left along busy Dukelských hrdinů. Follow this street north for 400m, stopping to visit the ❺ **Veletržní Palác** and eventually the Výstaviště exhibition grounds. If you're in the mood for more culture, stop by ❻ **Lapidárium** to wander among some of the city's finest sculptures.

Bear left at the entrance to Výstaviště and follow the path to the right of the terminal loop of tram 5, passing the ❼ **Prague Planetarium** as you enter the former royal hunting ground, Stromovka.

From here, wander through Stromovka at your leisure, heading vaguely north. In the distance on a hill toward the west you'll see the Renaissance ❽ **Mistodržitelský Summer Palace**, where Bohemian royals used to hang out on their hunting trips.

Following the signs to 'Troja' and 'Zoo', walk under a railway line. From here go up some steps to enter ❾ **Emperor's Island** (Císařský ostrov); the road eventually leads to a pedestrian bridge over the main branch of the Vltava. From here, you are a short walk to Troja Chateau or the Prague Zoo.

well as traditional Italian appetisers such as *insalata caprese*. The service is friendly, and there's a big tree-covered terrace out the front.

CAPUA PIZZERIA €

Map p348 (☎233 382 659; www.capua.cz; Milady Horákové 9, Holešovice; mains 100-150Kč; ; 1, 8, 15, 25, 26) This corner restaurant just above Strossmayerovo náměstí is widely considered the best pizza place in the neighbourhood. But in truth it's only good, not great. The inviting interior is divided into two rooms, with nonsmokers getting the larger and nicer one to the right. The pizzas are thin-crusted and follow the usual formula of Italian combinations.

MOLO 22 INTERNATIONAL €€

Map p348 (☎220 563 348; www.molo22.cz; U Průhonu 22, Holešovice; mains 150-320Kč; 8am-11pm Mon-Fri, 10am-11pm Sat & Sun; ; 5, 12, 15, MVltavská) Staropramen brewery-run restaurant with a clean, modern interior and an upscale international menu of Caesar salads, chicken wraps, pastas and steaks. Draws a lively lunch crowd on work days, and makes for a decent dinner before a night spent cubbing at Mecca (p162) across the street.

Bubeneč

PEPERONCINO ITALIAN €€

Map p348 (☎233 312 438; www.restaurant-peperoncino.cz; Letohradská 34, Bubeneč; mains 150-300Kč; ; 1, 8, 15, 25, 26) Insider's choice for good, reasonably priced Italian cooking in Bubeneč. The grilled octopus and beans starter is a neighbourhood favourite, but we're partial to the beef or tuna carpaccio. The pastas and main courses are all excellent and the wine list has lots of affordable Czech and Italian choices.

ARGUMENT INTERNATIONAL €€

Map p350 (☎220 510 427; www.argument-restaurant.cz; Bubenečská 19, Bubeneč; mains 219-379Kč; ; MHradčanská) Upscale dining in Prague 6 that perennially gets mentioned alongside the city's best restaurants, but with prices roughly half of what you would pay in the centre. There's no defining culinary theme here, more a hodge-podge of international favourites, steaks, pasta and seafood, and even a terrific burger. Reserve in advance.

U VILÉMA CZECH €

Map p350 (☎224 322 010; Československé armády 3, Bubeneč; mains 80-150Kč; MHradčanská) This popular neighbourhood pub and beer garden has a welcoming atmosphere and very good 11° Svijany on tap for a bargain 25Kč. The menu includes many simple, home-cooked Czech specialties, such as *pečené hovězí* (roast beef and gravy) and the house goulash served on a potato pancake. Nonsmoking between 11am and 2pm. The garden makes a welcome respite in summer.

HANAVSKÝ PAVILÓN CZECH, INTERNATIONAL €€€

Map p350 (☎233 323 641; www.hanavskypavilon.cz; Letenské sady 173, Bubeneč; mains 250-490Kč; 11am-1am, terrace to 11pm; 18) Perched on a terrace high above the river, this ornate, neo-baroque pavilion dating from 1891 houses a smart restaurant with a postcard-perfect view of the Vltava bridges. From April to September you can dine on the outdoor terrace. There's a three-course set menu of Czech classics.

ČÍNSKÁ ZAHRADA CHINESE €€

Map p350 (☎233 379 656; Šmeralová 11, Bubeneč; mains 150-300Kč; 1, 8, 15, 25, 26) 'Chinese Garden' is a neighbourhood joint that's just authentic enough to draw people from around the city. In fact, it's not uncommon to see lines of Asian tourists streaming here at meal times. The very hot 'dry fried chicken' (pieces of chicken cooked on the bone in red pepper flakes) is one of the local favourites.

NAD KRÁLOVSKOU OBOROU CZECH, PUB €

Map p350 (☎220 912 319; www.nadkralovskouoborou.cz; Nad Královskou oborou 31, Bubeneč; mains 140-250Kč; ; 1, 8, 15, 25, 26) This lovingly restored traditional Czech pub is an oasis for good beer (and food) along the southern (upper) border of Stromovka park. The relaxed pub vibe endures and the Czech cooking is more imaginative here than usual, with some harder-to-find-venison dishes on the menu.

Dejvice

DA EMANUEL ITALIAN €€€

Map p350 (☎224 312 934; www.daemanuel.cz; Charlese De Gaulla 4, Dejvice; mains 400-500Kč; noon-11pm; 8, MDejvická) This small, elegant Italian restaurant, on a quiet residential street, is one of Dejvice's true destination restaurants. The main dining room, perched romantically below an arched brick ceiling, holds around a dozen tables, each with a vase of fresh flowers and covered in white linens. Since it's small, you'll have to book in advance.

RESTAURACE U VEVERKY CZECH €

Map p350 (223 000 223; www.uveverky.com; Eliášova 14, Dejvice; mains 129-330Kč; MHradčanská) This highly rated traditional pub has some of the best-tasting, good-value lunches in the city and is worth a detour. The set-up is classic, with a drinking room out the front and two big dining rooms in the back. The restaurant is filled with the welcoming smell of grilled onions and beer. Reserve in advance.

PERPETUUM CZECH €€

Map p350 (233 323 429; www.restauraceperpetuum.cz; Na Hutích 9, Dejvice; mains 230-380Kč; 11.30am-11pm Mon-Sat; ; MDejvická) Having duck is one of the culinary highlights of the Czech Republic. Here, duck is the only thing on the menu and the kitchen clearly knows what it is doing. Choose the Czech standard of a roast bird, served with bread dumplings and red cabbage, or dabble in gamier wild duck or the sweetish Barbarie duck.

KULAT'ÁK CZECH €

Map p350 (773 973 037; www.kulatak.cz; Vítězné áměstí 12, Dejvice; mains 139-259Kč; ; 2, 8, 20, 26, MDejvická) The local branch of a Pilsner Urquell–run chain does not disappoint, offering decent Czech cooking in an authentic but spiffed-up atmosphere. This is a good place to try specialties such as *svíčková na smetaně* (braised beef with cranberries and dumplings) or *Moravský vrabec* (Moravian 'sparrow' – a cut of roast pork with a side of bread and bacon dumplings).

PIZZERIA GROSSETO ITALIAN €

Map p350 (233 342 694; www.grosseto.cz; Jugoslávských Partyzánů 8, Dejvice; mains 120-180Kč; ; 8, MDejvická) This is a lively, friendly pizzeria (with a genuine wood-fired pizza oven) that pulls in crowds of students from the nearby university campus. As well as a huge choice of pizza varieties, the menu offers salads, pastas, risotto, roast chicken, steak and grilled salmon. Reservations are essential.

MIRELLIE ITALIAN €€

Map p350 (222 959 999; www.mirellie.cz; VP Čkalova 14, Dejvice; mains 180-390Kč; ; MDejvická, Hradčanská) Given Da Emanuel's high prices, Dejvice was crying out for an affordable Italian option that doesn't cut corners. Mirellie delivers. The specialties here include grilled meats, fresh fish and homemade pasta, topped with inventive sauces such as spiced lamb ragout.

CAFE CALMA INTERNATIONAL €

Map p350 (602 235 660; www.calma.cz; Kyjevska 2, Dejvice; mains 80-150Kč ; 7.30am-10pm Mon-Fri, 9am-10pm Sat, 10.30am-10pm Sun; ; MDejvická) Cute neighbourhood cafe with a French bakery feel, complete with big bright windows and worn hardwood floors. The ambitions go beyond coffee and cake, and this is an excellent choice for lunch, with daily specials in the 100Kč to 150Kč range for items such as baked salmon or traditional roast sirloin with dumplings.

KAVALA GREEK €€

Map p350 (224 325 181; www.kavala-praha.cz; Charlese De Gaulla 5, Dejvice; mains 290-350Kč; ; 8, MDejvická) If you can't get in at

THE DEJVICE FARMERS MARKET

The past few years have a seen a huge growth in interest in sustainable agriculture and organic foods in the Czech Republic, and thankfully spurred the opening of farmers markets across Prague. The first and still the best of these is in **Dejvice** (Farmářský trh; www.ceskefarmarsketrhy.cz; Vítězné Náměstí, Dejvice; 9am-2pm Sat Mar-Nov; ; MDejvická), on the grassy square adjacent to Dejvická metro station.

Every Saturday morning from March to November, farmers from around the country descend on the square to sell their fruits and vegetables as well as fresh bread and other baked goods, meats and cheeses.

The market has evolved into more than just a chance to buy fresh produce. A sunny morning usually brings thousands of people onto the square and the atmosphere becomes something akin to a carnival. It's a great outing for the whole family.

Da Emanuel, try this Greek taverna across the street. There are the usual classics such as souvlaki and moussaka, plus a delicious seafood mezza that could easily be a meal in itself. The indoor dining room, with sponged walls and light woods, is a little too cute – better is the front garden.

BUDVARKÁ CZECH, PUB €

Map p350 (☎222 960 820; www.budvarkadejvice.cz; Wuchterlova 22, Dejvice; mains 119-199Kč; ; 2, 8, 20, 26, MDejvická) Handsome Czech pub owned and operated by the Budvar brewery. You'll find the complete 'Budweiser' family of beers here, including the hard-to-find yeast and dark varieties. There's also excellent Czech pub food served in a pretty accurate rendition of a 19th-century tap room. There's a smoking room out front and a large nonsmoking area in the back.

SAKURA JAPANESE €€

Map p350 (☎774 785 077; www.sushisakura.cz; Náměstí Svobody 1, Dejvice; mains 180-320Kč; ; MDejvická) This is one of the best sushi places in Prague. It occupies a smart 1930s functionalist building, and the open interior is a blend of contemporary Japanese and Czech modern. The 'volcano' roll features spicy tuna; the 'crunch' roll comes lightly fried, with gently cooked salmon tucked inside. There's a small play area for children.

NA URALE CZECH, PUB €

Map p350 (☎224 326 820; Uralská 9, Dejvice; mains 100-220Kč; 11am-1am; ; 8, MDejvická) A formerly grotty Czech pub that's greatly cleaned up its act in recent years, adding beautiful crimson walls and stone-tile floors. The kitchen has also had an upgrade, but the prices for well-done Czech dishes such as goulash and roast pork are barely higher than at a typical workers' pub.

STAROČESKÁ KRČMA CZECH €€

Map p350 (☎224 321 505; www.staroceskakrcma.cz; VP.Čkalova 15, Dejvice; mains 140-320Kč; MHradčanská, Dejvická) A very good traditional Czech tavern, Staročeská Krčma specialises in huge portions of grilled meats, such as steaks, pork and chicken. The setting is meant to evoke an old-fashioned inn or country cottage, with big wooden tables, an open fireplace and stacks of wood sitting around. The pork dishes excel, while the steaks are only good.

DRINKING & NIGHTLIFE

The neighbourhoods of Holešovice, Bubeneč and Dejvice straddle a fairly wide range of socio-economic levels. Holešovice and the area around Letenské náměstí in Bubeneč are filled with classic 'old man' pubs and student watering holes. Dejvice is a bit posher, with a slightly more upscale selection of pubs and cafes.

Holešovice

NA STARÉ KOVÁRNĚ PUB

Map p348 (☎233 371 099; www.starakovarna.cz; Kamenická 17, Holešovice; 11am-1am; 1, 8, 15, 25, 26) The motorcycle hanging from the ceiling sets a rakish tone for this pub. The food is two notches above standard bar fare – and has even garnered raves from local critics – but few people come just for the food. It's a shot-and-a-beer joint in the best sense of the term.

ERHARTOVA CUKRÁRNA CAFE

Map p348 (☎233 312 148; www.erhartovacukrarna.cz; Milady Horákové 56, Holešovice; 10am-7pm; ; 1, 8, 15, 25, 26) This stylish 1930s-era cafe and sweetshop in a refurbished functionalist building is adjacent to the local branch of the public library. It draws a mix of students, older folk and mothers with strollers, attracted mainly by the cookies, doughnuts and cinnamon rolls, as well as an ice cream in hot weather.

CLUB CLUB BAR, CLUB

Map p348 (☎776 653 646; www.clubclub.cz; Ovenecká 6, Holešovice; 5pm-4am; 1, 8, 15, 25, 26 to Letenské náměstí) This neighbourhood bar doubles as arguably the best night and music club in the immediate vicinity of Letenské náměstí. It's a good place to finish the night secure in the knowledge you aren't likely to get rousted out until the wee hours.

KUMBAL CAFE

Map p348 (☎777 559 842; www.kumbal.cz; Heřmanová 12, Holešovice; 9am-9.30pm; ; 1, 5, 8, 12, 14, 15, 17, 25, 26) Another stylish coffee bar in a 1930s functionalist building, that manages to be both hip and comfortable at the same time. There's good coffee and tea drinks, though not much on the menu aside from a few simple sandwiches and a daily soup (usually vegetarian).

LONG TALE CAFÉ CAFE

Map p348 (☎266 310 701; www.longtalecafe.cz; Osadní 25, Holešovice; ⏰9am-7pm; 📶; 🚋1, 3, 12, 14, 25) Inviting, smoke-free cafe that draws a pleasing mix of office workers, mothers with strollers and the occasional freelance writer, who come for the excellent coffee drinks, relaxed vibe and very good, reasonably priced salads and sandwiches.

OUKY DOUKY CAFE

Map p348 (☎266 711 531; www.oukydouky.cz; Janovského 14, Holešovice; ⏰8am-midnight; 📶; 🚋1, 5, 8, 12, 14, 15, 17, 25, 26) This was the original home of the Globe Bookstore & Coffeehouse in the 1990s, and a kind of eclectic, San Francisco funkiness lingers. Today it houses a used bookstore, with a worn-out selection of Czech-language books, and an inviting cafe filled with students, bored housewives and a wandering expat or two (looking for the Globe).

BIO OKO CAFE, BAR

Map p348 (☎233 382 606; www.biooko.net; Františka Křížka 15, Holešovice; ⏰3pm-2am; 📶; 🚋1, 8, 15, 25, 26) The cafe/bar in the repertory cinema Bio Oko is a gem. It's classically retro as befits a cinema that regularly shows arty faves from the 1950s and '60s. Serving good espresso-based drinks as well as beer and cocktails, it's a nice choice for before or after the show.

NOVÁ SYNTÉZA CAFE, BAR

Map p348 (☎725 822 983; www.ngprague.cz; Dukelských Hrdinů 47, Holešovice; ⏰10am-10pm Tue-Sun; 📶; 🚋1, 8, 15, 25, 26) The cafe/bar in the Veletržní Palác is billed as an 'experimental' space, meaning it occasionally holds happenings and performances. Whatever, it's a convenient spot to plop yourself down after taking in the museum's considerable holdings.

BONDY BAR BAR

Map p348 (Tusarova 29, Holešovice; ⏰5pm-3am; 🚋1, 3, 5, 25) This subterranean, smoky beer-and-darts den is not to everyone's taste; nevertheless it represents an acceptable late-hours, last-drink venue and the absolute antithesis of the posh, upscale hub-bub at nearby Sasazu (p161).

U SV ANTONÍČKA PUB

Map p348 (Podplukovníka Sochora 20, Holešovice; 🚋1, 5, 8, 12, 14, 15, 17, 25, 26) A relative rarity these days so close to the centre: a fully unreconstructed Czech pub and all that entails, including cantankerous old locals, an occasional hygiene issue with the glassware, layers of smoke, and toilets that will have to be buried in a nuclear landfill someday. Yet it has a certain retrograde charm. Not for the faint-hearted.

Bubeneč

TOP CHOICE **LETNÁ BEER GARDEN** BEER GARDEN

Map p350 (Letenský zámeček; ☎233 378 208; www.letenskyzamecek.cz; Letenské sady 341, Bubeneč; ⏰11am-11pm, summer only; 🚋1, 8, 15, 25, 26 to Letenské náměstí) No accounting of watering holes in the neighbourhood would be complete without a nod toward the city's best beer garden, situated at the eastern end of the Letná Gardens (p153). Buy a takeaway beer from a small kiosk and grab a picnic table, or sit on a small terrace where you can order beer-by-the-glass and decent pizza. From the tram stop it is a five- or 10-minute walk south.

FRAKTAL BAR

Map p350 (☎777 794 094; www.fraktalbar.cz; Šmeralová 1, Bubeneč; mains 100-300Kč; 📶; 🚋1, 8, 15, 25, 26) This subterranean space under a corner house near Letenské náměstí is easily the friendliest bar this side of the Vltava River. This is especially true for English speakers, as Fraktal serves as a kind of unofficial expat watering hole. There's also good bar fare such as burgers. The only drawback is the early closing time (last orders 11.30pm).

NA SLAMNÍKU PUB, BEER GARDEN

Map p350 (www.koncertynaslamniku.wz.cz; Wolkerova 12, Bubeneč; 🚋1, 8, 15, 25, 26) A great traditional Czech pub and beer garden dating from the 19th century, Na Slamníku is tucked away in a small valley in Bubeneč, just behind the sprawling Russian embassy. There are a couple of drinking rooms inside and a peaceful shady garden in front in summer. Check the website for occasional live music on weekends.

HELLS BELLS — PUB

Map p348 (☎733 734 918; www.hellsbells.cz; Letohradská 50, Bubeneč; ⏰11am-12.30am Mon-Thu, 11am-2am Fri & Sat, noon-10pm Sun; 📶; 🚋1, 8, 15, 25, 26 to Letenské náměstí) Raucous beer pub with a mostly student-age clientele that makes for a good place to continue-on to after the Letná beer garden closes down. There's decent Czech food as well, including good-value daily lunch specials.

POTRVÁ — CAFE

Map p350 (☎723 305 330; www.potrva.cz; Srbská 2, Bubeneč; ⏰noon-midnight Mon-Fri, 3pm-midnight Sat & Sun; 📶; Ⓜ Hradčanská) This relaxing cafe just a short walk across the railway tracks from Hradčanská metro station is a good place for quiet reflection during the day, and occasional live music and open-mic nights in the evening. Mostly coffee and drinks on the menu, but it does serve small bites such as soups and sandwiches.

LA BODEGA FLAMENCA — BAR

Map p350 (☎233 374 075; www.labodega.cz; Šmeralová 5, Bubeneč; ⏰4pm-1am Sun-Thu, to 3am Fri & Sat; 🚋1, 8, 15, 25, 26) La Bodega resides in an atmospheric, red-brick cellar. With the Latin music turned down low, the crowd seems a bit more reflective (at least compared with the crew at Fraktal next door). Most people come for a beer or sangria, but there's also a nice selection of tapas on hand. Also live music and dance some nights.

TĚSNĚ VEDLE BURUNDI — CAFE, PUB

Map p350 (www.burundi.cz; Sládkova 4, Bubeneč; ⏰10am-10pm; 🚋1, 8, 15, 25, 26) A curious pub/coffee house hybrid that draws a mix of intellectuals, students, ageing rockers and garden-variety neighbourhood drinkers. There's a vaguely old-school, dissident whiff about the place, making it a more satisfying spot to linger than the swish bars in the city centre.

ANDALUSKÝ PES — COCKTAIL BAR

Map p350 (☎777 666 137; www.andaluskypes.cz; Korunovační 4, Bubeneč; ⏰11pm-3am; 🚋1, 8, 15, 25, 26) 'Le Chien Andalou' is an after-hours cocktail bar with retro flair. The inviting front room, sporting velvet bar stools and glittery walls, attracts a kind of Edward Hopper *Nighthawks* crowd. The back rooms have a more risqué feel – dark and crowded some nights – with faces recognisable only by the glow of their cigarettes.

SVIJANSKÝ RYTÍŘ — PUB

Map p350 (☎233 378 342; www.svijansky-rytir.cz; Jirečkova 13, Bubeneč; ⏰11am-10pm Mon-Fri; 🚋1, 8, 15, 25, 26) Inviting pub that serves authentic Czech cuisine – heavy on staples such as pork and chicken schnitzels – but the real draw here is the availability of highly regarded Svijany beers, both light and dark, including the flagship 12° Rytíř and the stronger but even more fabled 13° Kníže. Closed weekends.

ALCHYMISTA — CAFE

Map p350 (☎233 383 746; www.alchymista.cz; Jana Zajívce 7, Bubeneč; ⏰10.30am-7.30pm, later in summer; 📶; 🚋1, 8, 15, 25, 26) This old-fashioned coffee house with an adjacent art gallery is an oasis in the culturally barren neighbourhood behind Sparta Stadium. Freshly ground coffees, a serious selection of teas (no Lipton in a bag here), and freshly made cakes and strudels draw a mostly local crowd.

AKÁDEMIE — BAR

Map p350 (☎233 375 236; Šmeralová 5, Bubeneč; ⏰5pm-3am; 🚋1, 8, 15, 25, 26) This cavernous bar has several pool tables and dart boards to amuse in case you tire of sitting around chewing the fat. The game of choice here is eight ball; the tables are large and well maintained. Waiters bring your beers to the table, and everything is toted up – billiards included – at the end.

ZTRACENÝ RÁJ — BAR

Map p350 (☎252 545 013; www.lunchtime.cz/ztraceny-raj; Čechova 9, Bubeneč; 🚋1, 8, 15, 25, 26) One of several mostly student-oriented cafes and bars on this leafy street just off Letenské náměstí. Not much to lure you here aside from decent Pilsner Urquell on tap at non-touristy prices, a general convivial vibe and some scruffy picnic tables out front that feel just right on a warm evening.

KLÁŠTERNÍ PIVNICE — PUB

Map p350 (☎723 026 104; Ovenecká 15, Bubeneč; ⏰9.30am-10pm; 🚋1, 8, 15, 25, 26) Not for the mild mannered, this old man's pub serves excellent, hard-to-find Klášter beer. The main drinking room gets pretty smoky and crowded with crusty regulars and, indeed, a whole day can go by without a single female visitor, but you can't argue with the beer. A perfectly preserved Prague pub undisturbed by modern life.

Dejvice

KABINET CAFE

Map p350 (☎233 326 668; Terronská 25, Dejvice; ⊙11am-11pm Mon-Fri, 3-11pm Sat & Sun; 📶; 🚋8, Ⓜ Dejvická) A retro 1920s-style coffee house, Kabinet is situated in a cool cubist building in a pleasantly residential part of Dejvice. Old cameras, posters and photographs emphasise the throwback feel. The name of the cafe, for Czechs, recalls early school days – a 'kabinet' being a teacher's office – to add to the nostalgic feel.

KAVÁRNA ALIBI CAFE

Map p350 (www.alibi.cz; Svatovítská 6, Dejvice; ⊙noon-midnight Mon-Fri, 4pm-midnight Sat & Sun; 📶; 🚋2, 8, 20, 26, Ⓜ Dejvická) Lively, smoky coffee house that is usually packed with students. It's a perfect spot to curl up with a coffee or a beer, write some postcards, consult your Lonely Planet guide or have a heart-to-heart chat with your travelling companion.

POTREFENÁ HUSA PUB

Map p350 (☎233 341 022; www.staropramen.cz; Verdunská 23, Dejvice; ⊙11am-1am Mon-Fri, noon-1am Sat & Sun; 📶; 🚋2, 8, 20, 26, Ⓜ Dejvická) The Dejvice branch of the Potrefená Husa chain is a dependable alternative if you're looking for something clean and tourist-friendly. There's a full complement of high-quality pub food, TVs on the wall, and a well-heeled crowd that keeps things hopping.

☆ ENTERTAINMENT

CROSS CLUB CLUB, LIVE MUSIC

Map p348 (☎736 535 053; www.crossclub.cz; Plynární 23, Holešovice; admission free-150Kč; ⊙cafe noon-2am, club 6pm-4am; 📶; Ⓜ Nádraží Holešovice) An industrial club in every sense of the word: the setting in an industrial zone; the thumping music (both DJs and live acts); and the interior, an absolute must-see jumble of gadgets, shafts, cranks and pipes, many of which move and pulsate with light to the music. The program includes occasional live music, theatre performances and art happenings.

TOP CHOICE **SASAZU** CLUB, LIVE MUSIC

Map p348 (☎284 097 455; www.sasazu.com; Bubenské nábřeží 306, block 25, Holešovice market, Holešovice; admission 200-1000Kč; ⊙9pm-5am; 📶; 🚋1, 3, 5, 25, Ⓜ Vltavská) One of the most popular dance clubs in the city, Sasazu attracts the fashionable elite and hangers-on in equal measure. If you're

WORTH A DETOUR

WORTH A DETOUR: DIVOKÁ ŠÁRKA

If you're in the mood to get away from it all, plan an outing here – one of the city's prettiest and most remote nature parks, **Divoká Šárka** (☎603 723 501; www.koupaliste-sarka.webnode.cz; Evropská, Dejvice; adult/concession 60/20Kč; ⊙swimming pool 9am-7pm Jun-Aug; 🚋20, 26). The park is best known for its eerie lunar landscape of barren rocks and hills at its western end, but it actually stretches for miles through forests and valleys along the Šárecký potok (Šárka Creek). The easiest way to access the park is by tram; both lines 20 and 26 terminate at the edge of the park. You can return by tram the way you came or walk a 7km trail that circles back toward the Vltava, from where you can catch another tram.

The park is named after the mythical warrior Šárka, who is said to have thrown herself off a cliff here after the death of her enemy, the handsome Ctirad – whom she either seduced and murdered (committing suicide afterwards to avoid capture), or fell in love with and failed to protect (killing herself out of grief and guilt), depending on which version of the legend you prefer.

In addition to hiking, the area is perfect for spreading out a picnic blanket. In summer, there's a swimming pool with icy cold water, and a number of pubs.

To hike back toward town, find the red-marked trail that runs all the way to the suburb of Podbaba, where the creek empties into the Vltava. Once you've hit the river, look for the tower of the unmissable Hotel Crowne Plaza (p154), with a gold star on top. Head toward the hotel, from where you can pick up tram 8, which brings you back to the Dejvická metro station, or stay aboard all the way to Náměstí Republiky.

into big dance floors and long lines (hint: go early), this is your place. Check the website for occasional big-name live acts (such as Underworld and Morcheeba in recent years).

MECCA CLUB

Map p348 (☎602 711 225; www.mecca.cz; U Průhonu 3, Holešovice; admission 100-200Kč; ⏲10pm-6am Wed-Sat; 🚋5, 12, 15) This former warehouse in Holešovice has been going strong for more than a decade and is still one of the best of the city's dance clubs, with a big DJ-dominated dance floor and pumping sound system. The club was undergoing a makeover in 2012, but was poised to reopen for 2013.

LA FABRIKA THEATRE, PERFORMING ARTS

Map p348 (☎774 417 644; www.lafabrika.cz; Komunardů 30, Holešovice; admission 100-400Kč; ⏲varies with events; 🚋1, 3, 5, 12, 25, Ⓜ Nádraží Holešovice, Vltavská) The name refers to a 'factory', but this is actually a former paint warehouse that's been converted into an experimental performance space. Depending on the night, come here to catch some live music (jazz or cabaret), theatre, dance or film. Consult the website for the latest program. The ticket office and bar open about an hour before events begin.

BIO OKO CINEMA

Map p348 (Oko Cinema; ☎608 330 088; www.biooko.net; Františka Křížka 15, Holešovice; tickets from 100Kč; 📶; 🚋1, 5, 8, 12, 14, 15, 17, 25, 26) This repertory cinema shows a varied program of underground films, selections from film festivals, documentaries, big-budget movies, and classics from around the world. Most films are shown in the original language (not necessarily English), with Czech subtitles. Check the website for the latest film showings.

ALFRED VE DVOŘE THEATRE

Map p348 (☎233 376 985; www.alfredvedvore.cz; Františka Křížka 36, Holešovice; tickets 100-150Kč; ⏲box office 5.30-11pm Mon-Fri, 1.30-11pm Sat & Sun ; 🚋1, 5, 8, 12, 14, 15, 17, 25, 26) An artistic treasure in an unlikely spot in Holešovice, the Alfred regularly stages demanding works of drama, dance, cabaret and movement theatre, including occasional performances in English. Check the website for details. The box office is at the nearby Bio Oko.

SPEJBL & HURVÍNEK THEATRE THEATRE

Map p350 (Divadlo Spejbla a Hurvínka; ☎224 316 784; www.spejbl-hurvinek.cz; Dejvická 38, Dejvice; tickets 80-120Kč; ⏲box office 10am-2pm & 3-6pm Tue-Fri, 1-5pm Sat & Sun; Ⓜ Dejvická) Created in 1930 by puppeteer Josef Skupa, Spejbl and Hurvínek are the Czech marionette equivalents of Punch and Judy, although they are father and son rather than husband and wife. The shows are in Czech, but most can be followed regardless of which language you speak.

SHOPPING

ANTIKVITA ANTIQUES

Map p350 (☎233 336 601; www.antikvita.cz; Na Hutích 9, Dejvice; ⏲10am-5pm Mon-Fri; Ⓜ Dejvická) This antique shop is a collector's delight, crammed with cases and cabinets overflowing with vintage toys, model trains, dolls, coins, medals, jewellery, clocks, watches, militaria, porcelain figures, postcards, glassware and much more. If you have something to sell, Antikvita holds buying sessions on Wednesday and Thursday.

PIVNÍ GALERIE FOOD & DRINK

Map p348 (☎220 870 613; www.pivnigalerie.cz; U Průhonu 9, Holešovice; ⏲noon-7pm Tue-Fri; 🚋1, 3, 5, 25) If you think Czech beer begins and ends with Pilsner Urquell, a visit to the tasting room at Pivní Galerie (the Beer Gallery) will lift the scales from your eyes. Here you can sample and purchase a huge range of Bohemian and Moravian beers – nearly 150 varieties from 30 different breweries – with expert advice from the owners.

HUNT-KASTNER ARTWORKS ART

Map p348 (☎222 969 887; www.huntkastner.com; Kamenická 22, Holešovice; ⏲1-6pm Tue-Fri, 2-6pm Sat; 🚋1, 8, 15, 25, 26) This small gallery behind the Letná Gardens (p153) highlights some of the best up-and-coming Czech artists working in the visual arts, including painting, photography and video. The owners are enthusiastic and happy to talk about local art with walk-ins.

PRAŽSKÁ TRŽNICE MARKET

Map p348 (Prague Market Hall; ☎220 800 945; Bubenské nábřeží 306, Holešovice; ⏲7am-6pm Mon-Fri, to 2pm Sat; 🚋1, 3, 5, 25) Almost a suburb in itself, Prague's sprawling, slightly

CATCH A SPARTA PRAHA ICE HOCKEY MATCH

The Czechs have an illustrious history in ice hockey, perennially placing at the top of the world rankings and regularly sending the cream of the crop to the North American National Hockey League. One of the top teams of the Czech Extraliga, Sparta Praha, plays its home games at Holešovice's **Tipsport Aréna** (Sportovní Hala; Map p348; ☎266 727 443; www.hcsparta.cz; Za Elektrámou 419, Holešovice; match tickets 180-300Kč; 5, 12, 14, 15, 17). Tickets are usually available for matches during the regular season, which runs from September through April. Buy tickets online at **TicketPortal** (www.ticketportal.cz) or at the stadium box office.

depressing city market includes a large open-air area selling fresh fruit, vegetables and flowers, and dozens of stalls selling everything from cheap clothes to garden gnomes.

SPORTS & ACTIVITIES

GENERALI ARÉNA SPECTATOR SPORT
Map p350 (Sparta Stadium; ☎296 111 400; www.sparta.cz; Milady Horákové 98, Bubeneč; tickets 100-400Kč; box office 9am-noon Mon-Fri & 1-5.30pm Mon-Thu, to 4pm Fri; 1, 8, 15, 25, 26) Generali Aréna, with a capacity of more than 20,000, is the home ground of Sparta Praha – winner of the Czech football (soccer) league in 2001, 2003, 2005 and 2007. Tickets are available at the box office (entrance No 1) during the week or two hours before match time. The season runs from mid-summer to the following spring.

PŮJČOVNA BRUSLÍ MIAMI OUTDOOR EQUIPMENT
Map p350 (Miami Skate Rental; ☎731 281 571; www.pujcovna-brusli.cz; Nad Štolou 1, Holešovice; skate rental per hour 90Kč plus deposit; 9am-9pm May-Sep; 1, 8, 15, 25, 26) A great way to spend a summer day: you can rent in-line skates from this place (staff speak a bit of English), which is close to the National Technical Museum (p152), then head off to explore the extensive skating trails in Letná Gardens before enjoying a cold one at the Letná beer garden (p159).

Smíchov & Vyšehrad

Neighbourhood Top Five

❶ Spend a sunny afternoon at the **Vyšehrad Citadel** (p167), with views from the rampart walls over the city. Don't miss the evocative cemetery, with its pantheon to Czech arts luminaries. Pack a picnic and, with luck, catch an open-air concert.

❷ Spend an evening drinking and discussing at a rowdy Smíchov pub such as **Zlatý klas** (p170).

❸ Enjoy an evening of jazz on the river at **JazzDock** (p172).

❹ Check out some off-the-wall art or a crazy club happening at David Černý's **Meet Factory** (p169).

❺ Have a great meal in the open air at **Rio's** (p170) in Vyšehrad.

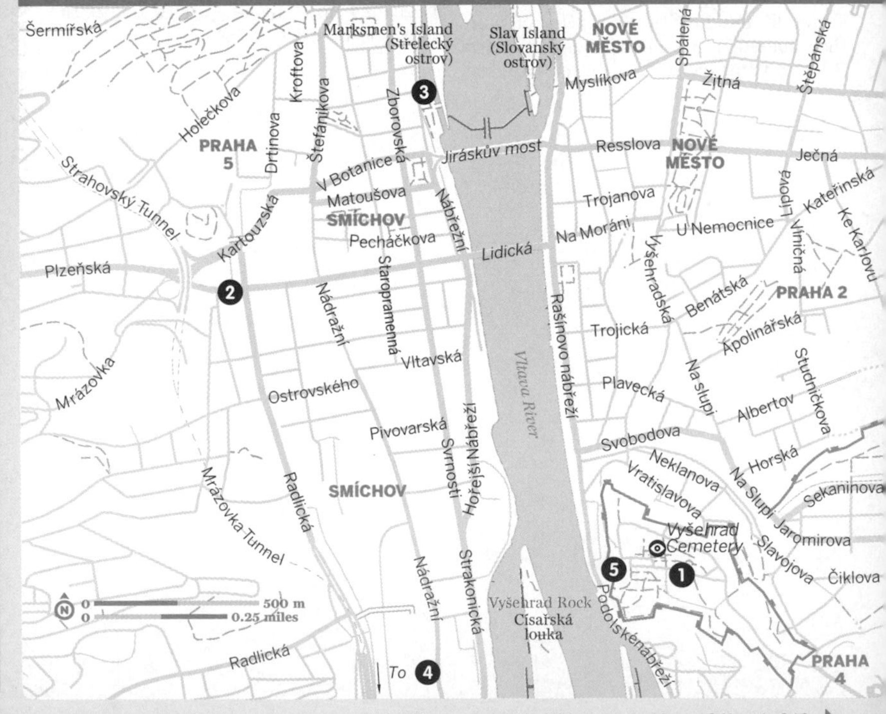

For more detail of this area see Maps p341 and p342

Explore: Smíchov & Vyšehrad

While the districts of Smíchov and Vyšehrad both lie to the south of the historic city centre, they occupy different sides of the Vltava River and could not be more different in character.

Smíchov, a former industrial area, lacks many traditional sights, but has some great pubs and classic restaurants. It's also home to many of the city's better hotels, especially around Anděl metro station, so you might find yourself spending more time in this area than you thought. Vyšehrad is relatively remote, and the only reason you'd likely find yourself here is to tour the Vyšehrad citadel and cemetery. That said, Vyšehrad is an oasis of green, with commanding views over the city and Vltava River.

Local Life

➡ **Popular hangouts** Don't let Smíchov's gleaming office towers fool you, this is a hard-drinking 'hood with some great traditional pubs. For starters, try Zlatý Klas (p170), U Bílého lva (p170) or Hlubina (p171). All of these serve decent food, too.

➡ **Strolling** The parkland of the Vyšehrad citadel is one of the city's most beloved venues for simply walking around and enjoying a fine afternoon.

➡ **Shopping** Going local in Smíchov is all about hitting the mall: Nový Smíchov (p173) to be precise. There are tons of shops, cafes, restaurants, a big supermarket in the basement and a multiplex cinema up top.

Getting There & Away

➡ **Metro** Smíchov lies on line B (yellow). The heart of the district is at Anděl station. A second metro stop, Smíchovské Nádraží, is further south. Vyšehrad lies 10 minutes on foot from Vyšehrad metro station (on line C, red).

➡ **Tram** Smíchov is easily accessible by tram. Lines 4, 7, 10 and 14 rumble across the Vltava from Charles Square (Karlovo náměstí) to Smíchov; from Malá Strana take trams 12 or 20 south. Vyšehrad is better reached by metro, but trams 17 and 21 run along the riverbank below the citadel. It's a steep climb up.

Lonely Planet's Top Tip

The hilltop fortress of Vyšehrad is an oasis of calm in a busy city. The grassy bluffs surrounding the cathedral can be a wonderful place to throw down a blanket and have a picnic, while enjoying the gorgeous views out over the river and onto Prague Castle in the distance.

Best Places to Eat

➡ Artisan (p169)
➡ Rio's (p170)
➡ Na Verandách (p170)
➡ Zlatý klas (p170)
➡ U Bílého lva (p170)

For reviews, see p169 

Best Places to Drink

➡ Hlubina (p171)
➡ Lokal Blok (p171)
➡ Kavárna Jarda Mayer (p172)
➡ V Cafe (p172)
➡ Cafe Citadela (p172)

For reviews, see p171 

Best Places to Party

➡ Futurum (p171)
➡ JazzDock (p172)
➡ Meet Factory (p169)
➡ Back Doors (p171)
➡ Hells Bells (p172)

For reviews, see p172 

TOP SIGHTS
VYŠEHRAD CEMETERY

Every capital has its 'famous' cemetery, where the heroes of the nation are buried. Think Père Lachaise in Paris or Highgate in London. In Prague, the prime piece of permanent real estate is here at Vyšehrad. Music lovers will want to see the graves of Czech greats Antonín Dvořák and Bedřich Smetana. But even if you're not familiar with the Czech pantheon, you'll enjoy the intricately designed headstones, lovely gardens and peaceful, reflective atmosphere.

A 'Who's Who' of Czech Luminaries

The cemetery got its start in the 19th century, when the parish graveyard was first made into a memorial for famous figures of Czech culture.

The 600 or so graves in the cemetery read like a 'who's who' in Czech arts and letters. In addition to the graves of composers Smetana and Dvořák, noted writers Karel Čapek, Jan Neruda and Božena Němcová are all buried here. There's a directory of famous names at the entrance.

Many of the tombs and headstones are works of art – Dvořák's is a sculpture by Ladislav Šaloun, the art-nouveau sculptor who also created the Jan Hus monument in the Old Town Square. To find it from the gate beside the church, head straight across to the colonnade on the far side and turn left; it's the fifth tomb on your right.

For the real heroes, an elaborate pantheon called the Slavín (loosely, 'Hall of Fame'; pictured), designed by Antonín Wiehl, was added at the eastern end in 1894; its 50-odd occupants include painter Alfons Mucha, sculptor Josef Myslbek and architect Josef Gočár. The haunting motto reads *'Ač Zemeřeli Ještě Mluví'* ('though dead, they still speak').

FAMOUS GRAVES

- Antonín Dvořák, composer
- Bedřich Smetana, composer
- Alfons Mucha, artist
- Karel Čapek, writer
- Max Švabinský, painter

PRACTICALITIES

- Vyšehradský hřbitov
- Map p341
- ☎249 198 815
- www.praha-vysehrad.cz
- K Rotundé 10, Vyšehrad
- ⌚8am-7pm May-Sep, to 6pm Mar, Apr & Oct, to 5pm Nov-Feb
- Ⓜ Vyšehrad

TOP SIGHTS
VYŠEHRAD CITADEL

The complex of buildings and structures that make up the Vyšehrad citadel has played an important role in Czech history for more than 1000 years. While not many of the ancient buildings have survived to the present day (indeed, most structures date from the 18th century, when the complex was used as a fortress), the citadel is still viewed as Prague's spiritual home. The main sights are spread out over a wide area. Part of the fun is simply to stroll the park-like grounds and admire the views.

DON'T MISS...

- Casements
- Brick Gate
- Gothic Cellar
- Church of Sts Peter & Paul
- Rotunda of St Martin

PRACTICALITIES

- Map p341
- ☎241 410 348
- www.praha-vysehrad.cz
- V Pevnosti 5 (information centre)
- Vyšehrad Citadel admission free, Basilica of St Lawrence admission 10Kč
- grounds 24hr, information centre 9.30am-6pm Apr-Oct, to 5pm Nov-Mar
- Ⓜ Vyšehrad

The Birthplace of Prague

Legend has it that this high hill is the very place where Prague was born. According to myth, a wise chieftain named Krok built a castle here in the 7th century, and Libuše, the cleverest of his three daughters, famously prophesied that a great city would rise someday in the valley of the Vltava.

Unfortunately, there's scant evidence for Libuše's prophecy (though it does make for a nice story). According to the legend, Libuše went on to marry a ploughman named Přemysl, who founded both the city of Prague and the Přemysl dynasty. (That last part may be true since there really was a Přemysl dynasty, but records from these days are scarce.)

Archaeological digs on Vyšehrad have turned up proof that the site was permanently settled from as early as the 9th century. Indeed, early Přemysl rulers seemed to like Vyšehrad; Boleslav II (r 972–99) may have lived here for a time. By the mid-11th century there was a fortified settlement, and Vratislav II (r 1061–92) moved his court here from Hradčany, beefing up the walls and adding a castle and the **Basilica of St Lawrence** (Map p341; admission 10Kč; 11am-5pm Mon-Fri, 11.30am-4pm Sat & Sun; Ⓜ Vyšehrad). His successors stayed until 1140, when Vladislav II returned to Hradčany.

While little physical evidence remains of Vyšehrad from the period, a hint of the area's magnificent past is seen at the 11th-century **Rotunda of St Martin** (Rotunda sv Martina; Map p341; ☎241 410 348; www.praha-vysehrad.cz; V Pevnosti, Vyšehrad; open only during mass; Ⓜ Vyšehrad), Prague's oldest surviving building. The door and frescoes date from a renovation made about 1880. The rotunda is normally closed, but the interior can be viewed during mass (times are posted at the door). In addition, the **Gothic Cellar** (Gotický sklep; Map p341; ☎241 410 348; www.praha-vysehrad.cz; Vyšehradský sady, Vyšehrad; adult/child 50/30Kč; 9.30am-6pm Apr-Oct, to 5pm Nov-Mar; Ⓜ Vyšehrad) houses a permanent exhibition called 'The Historic Faces of Vyšehrad', which focuses on both the myths and the facts concerning the origins of Vyšehrad.

Ups & Downs

After Vladislav II moved the court back to Hradčany, Vyšehrad faded into the background for around two centuries. It took the reign of Charles IV, in the 14th century, to recognise the complex's symbolic importance to the Czech nation. He repaired the walls and joined them to those of his new town, Nové Město. He built a small palace (now gone) and

ACCESSING THE CITADEL

The main entrance to Vyšehrad citadel is through the grand 17th-century **Leopold Gate** (Leopoldova Brána; Map p341) on the southeastern end. Nearby, you'll see the only surviving remnants of the 14th-century Gothic **Peak Gate** (Špička brána; Map p341), which now houses the tourist information office. From here, there's no prescribed viewing route. Be sure to check out the **battlements** on the northern side of the complex, with wonderful views out over the city and Prague Castle in the distance. Beside the southwestern bastion are the foundations of a **royal palace** that was built by Emperor Charles IV in the 14th century but dismantled in 1655.

Vyšehrad served as an Austrian fortress in the 17th and 18th centuries and was occupied for a time by both the French and the Prussians. Today it's mostly a peaceful green park with great views across the river, the haunt of old ladies walking their dogs, mothers playing with their children on the lawns, and young lovers canoodling on park benches.

decreed that the coronations of Bohemian kings should begin with a procession from here to Hradčany.

While the Gothic-spired **Church of Sts Peter & Paul** (Kostel sv Petra a Pavla; Map p341; ☎249 113 353; www.praha-vysehrad.cz; K Rotundé 10, Vyšehrad; adult/child 30/10Kč; ⊙9am-noon & 1-5pm Wed-Mon; MVyšehrad) certainly looks like it may have come from Charles IV's day, in fact the church has been built and rebuilt several times over the centuries. The arresting twin spires are visible from around the city and have become the symbol of Vyšehrad. They date from the end of the 19th century and the brief architectural craze that gripped Prague at that time known as neo-Gothic. Don't miss the church's interior: a swirling acid trip of art-nouveau frescoes painted in the 1920s by various Czech artists.

Unfortunately, nearly everything up here was wiped out during the Hussite Wars of the 15th century. The fortress remained a ruin – except for a ramshackle township of artisans and traders – until after the Thirty Years' War, which ended in 1648, when Habsburg Emperor Leopold I once again refortified it.

A Baroque Fortress

While most Praguers, these days, associate Vyšehrad with the ancient founding of the city around the first millennium, much of what you see today dates from more recent times, when the fortress was used by the Austrian Habsburgs to secure their western and northern borders from Prussian and French advances in the 17th and 18th centuries. Both the French and the Prussians did occupy Vyšehrad for brief periods in the mid-18th century and contributed to the citadel's development as a fort.

This fascinating military history is on display at the **Brick Gate & Casements** (Map p341; ☎241 410 348; www.praha-vysehrad.cz; Vratislavova, Vyšehrad; admission: Brick Gate 20Kč, Casemates adult/child 50/30Kč; ⊙9.30am-6pm Apr-Oct, to 5pm Nov-Mar; Vyšehrad), situated on the northern side of the fortress. The Brick Gate houses a fascinating exhibition explaining the military history of Vyšehrad as well as other fortresses in the city. The casements, in particular, are a real treat. A 30-minute tour takes you through a system of vaulted brick tunnels within the ramparts that were built up in the 18th century. The highlight is the barrel-vaulted **Gorlice Hall**, which was once used as a place for troops to muster in secret. Now it is home to six of the original **baroque statues** from Charles Bridge.

DAVID ČERNÝ: ARTIST-PROVOCATEUR

Czech artist David Černý (b 1967) first made international headlines in 1991 when he painted Prague's memorial to the WWII Soviet tank crews bright pink, a shocking display that managed to mock both the former communist government's overenthusiastic celebration of Soviet war prowess and its rewriting of history.

Since then, Černý has cultivated a reputation as the enfant terrible of the Prague art scene – his works often turn into major media events, occasionally with the police involved.

Černý achieved international notoriety in 2009 with his massive installation *Entropa*, exhibited in Brussels as part of the Czech Republic's holding of the EU's rotating presidency. The installation, comprised of mini sculptures dedicated to each member of the EU, was meant to poke fun at national stereotypes. Bulgaria, for example, was depicted as a Turkish-style toilet. It caused nothing short of an international scandal, made all the worse when it was discovered that Černý had lied when he claimed *Entropa* was the collective work of several European artists. In the end, *Entropa* was hastily dismantled and brought back to Prague and is now seeking a permanent home.

Černý is also heavily involved in promoting cross-cultural links with artists abroad through his sprawling Meet Factory artist-in-residency project in Smíchov.

SIGHTS

Smíchov

FUTURA GALLERY GALLERY

Map p342 (☎251 511 804; www.futuraprojekt.cz; Holečkova 49, Smíchov ; admission free; ⏰11am-6pm Wed-Sun; 🚋4, 7, 9, 10) The Futura Gallery focuses on all aspects of contemporary art, ranging from painting, photography and sculpture to video, installations and performance art. In the gallery's garden, you'll find a rather shocking and amusing permanent installation by David Černý, called **Brownnosers** (Map p342).

MEET FACTORY GALLERY

(☎251 551 796; http://meetfactory.cz; Ke Sklárně 15, Smíchov; admission free; ⏰varies by event; 🚋12, 14, 20 to Lihovar) David Černý's Meet Factory is a remarkable project that unites artists from around the world to live and create in this cavernous, abandoned factory south of Smíchovské nádraží. The space is used for exhibitions, happenings, film screenings, theatrical performances and concerts. The location is out of the way, so be sure to check the website for the opening hours and program of events before heading out.

Vyšehrad

VYŠEHRAD CEMETERY CEMETERY

See p166.

VYŠEHRAD CITADEL FORTRESS

See p167.

EATING

Of the two districts, Smíchov and Vyšehrad, the former clearly has much more variety. The area around Anděl metro station, in particular, has exploded with restaurants in recent years. Many of these are chains, but there are several good, traditional pubs to choose from too. Offerings are more limited in Vyšehrad.

Smíchov

ARTISAN INTERNATIONAL €€

Map p342 (☎257 218 277; www.artisanrestaurant.cz; Rošickýh 4, Smíchov; mains 200-400Kč; ⏰11am-midnight Mon-Thu, to 1am Fri & Sat, to 11pm Sun; 📶🌶; 🚋6, 9, 12, 20 to Švandovo divadlo) Artisan is tricky to find but worth the effort for the best meal to be had in the Smíchov area, bar none. The menu has a weekly range of fish, chicken and beef entrées, and the pasta is homemade. Check the website for weekly tapas and wine-tasting evenings. There's a small garden that's open in warm weather.

U BÍLÉHO LVA CZECH €

Map p342 (www.ubileholva.eu; Na Bělidle 30, Smíchov; mains 135-240Kč; 📶; Ⓜ Anděl) There's been a pub here since 1883, and everything at the 'White Lion' certainly feels authentic, down to the hardwood bench seating and shiny taps at the bar. The menu is a greatest hits list of traditional dishes, including local 'Smíchovský' goulash, served with fresh onions on top and big bread dumplings on the side.

ZLATÝ KLAS CZECH €

Map p342 (☎251 562 539; www.zlatyklas.cz; Plzeňská 9, Smíchov; mains 130-200Kč; ⏰11am-11pm Sun-Thu, 11.30am-1am Fri & Sat; Ⓜ Anděl) This very popular pub and restaurant offers well-done Czech grub such as roast pork, goulash and fried chicken breast in a kitsch but comfortable space. Zlatý Klas also offers fresh unpasteurised beer *(tankové pivo)* from Plzeň, a local badge of honour. The service is fast and friendly, but you'll have to book in advance in the evening.

BABIČKA RESTAURACE CZECH €

Map p342 (☎257 327 251; www.jetset.cz; Radlická 1C, Smíchov ; mains 130-195Kč; 📶; Ⓜ Andel) This bustling Czech place, which shares a space next to a bar and club called Jet Set, specialises in old-fashioned traditional cooking such as *svíčková na smetaně* (braised beef served with cream and cranberries) as well as duck and even the Slovak national dish, *halušky*, potato dumplings served with sheep's cheese and bacon bits. Access is from a plaza that runs off Stroupežnického.

NA VERANDÁCH CZECH €€

Map p342 (☎257 191 200; www.pivovary-staropramen.cz; Nádražní 84, Smíchov; mains 130-280Kč; ⏰11am-1am Mon-Fri, 4pm-1am Sat & Sun; 📶; Ⓜ Anděl) This pub and restaurant, managed by the Potrefená husa chain, is inside the Staropramen brewery, and while lots of people come here to eat, it's perfectly fine to come in just for a super-fresh beer (there are seven varieties on tap). The menu is high-end fast food: ribs, burgers and chicken breasts as well as standard Czech dishes.

PIZZERIA CORLEONE PIZZA €

Map p342 (☎251 511 244; www.corleone.cz; Na Bělidle 42, Smíchov; mains 120-250Kč; ⏰11am-11.30pm; 📶✍; Ⓜ Anděl)

This lively neighbourhood restaurant is arguably the best pizza option in Smíchov. The wood-fired pizza oven turns out all the classics, from margherita to moscardina, and the restaurant also allows you to choose your own toppings.

U MÍKULÁŠE DAČÍCKÉHO CZECH €€

Map p342 (☎257 322 334; Victora Huga, Smíchov; mains 200-300Kč; ⏰11am-midnight; Ⓜ Anděl) This is an honest-to-goodness, old-fashioned *vinárna* (wine bar) – complete with traditional atmosphere and excellent Czech cooking. The owners have gone for the 'Ye Olde Middle Ages' look, with dark woods, red tablecloths, and pictures showing the lords enjoying their wine. Reserve in advance.

Vyšehrad

RIO'S VYŠEHRAD MEDITERRANEAN €€

Map p341 (☎224 922 156; www.riorestaurant.cz; Štulcova 2, Vyšehrad; mains 250-600Kč; ⏰10am-midnight; Ⓜ Vyšehrad) Located opposite the Church of Sts Peter & Paul, this is an attractive modern restaurant set in an ancient building. There's an elegant indoor dining room, but the main drawcard is the garden, a lovely spot for an outdoor meal in summer. The international gourmet menu includes dishes such as salad of grilled octopus, veal saltimbocca and chargrilled Argentinian beef.

U NEKLANA CZECH €€

Map p341 (☎224 916 051; Neklanova 30, Vyšehrad; mains 150-270Kč; ⏰11am-midnight; 🚋7, 18, 24) U Neklana is a welcoming local pub nestled in the corner of one of Prague's coolest apartment buildings, a cubist classic dating from 1915. Decked out in cheerful colours, it dishes up hearty Czech fare such as potato and mushroom soup served in a scooped-out loaf of rye bread. The menu is in English and German as well as Czech.

SUMMA ARX GREEK €

(www.summarx.cz; Mikuláše z Husi 1, Vyšehrad; mains 120-190Kč; 📶; Ⓜ Vyšehrad) This inviting Greek-Czech place is tucked away behind a football pitch in the distant shadow of the Vyšehrad spires, not far from Vyšehrad metro station. It's gained a modest citywide following for very good grilled meats and souvlaki as well as traditional

Czech items such as goulash. Nonsmoking from 11am to 3pm daily.

DRINKING & NIGHTLIFE

Smíchov continues to surprise. Every year brings at least one or two new bar or cafe openings. Most of the action is clustered near Anděl metro station, anchored by Nový Smíchov shopping centre. Vyšehrad is a different story. There's no nightlife to speak of here, though there are a couple of cafes for relaxing as you take in the sights.

Smíchov

HLUBINA
PUB

Map p342 (257 328 184; www.restaurace-hlubina.cz; Lidická 37, Smíchov; MAnděl) This traditional neighbourhood pub serves unfiltered Pilsner Urquell from large tanks *(tankové pivo)* to ensure freshness. The pub is bigger than it looks and there's space for drinking (and eating) on several levels. Most come for the beer, but the traditional pub cooking is not bad at all.

LOKAL BLOK
PUB

Map p342 (251 511 490; http://lokalblok.cz; náměstí 14. října 10, Smíchov; noon-1am Mon-Fri, 4pm-1am Sat & Sun; ; MAnděl) The perfect Prague combination: a raucous pub and a state-of-the-art climbing wall (though presumably you're supposed to climb before you drink and not vice versa). Most nights there's a lively crowd, fuelled by Pilsner Urquell on tap and some good Mexican eats, such as quesadillas and nachos. Highly recommended.

FUTURUM
CLUB

Map p342 (257 328 571; http://futurum.musicbar.cz; Zborovská 7, Smíchov; admission 100-150Kč; 7pm-2am; 7, 9, 12, 14) Futurum is a cross-fertilisation of alternative and mainstream, with a bizarre decor that looks like an art-deco ballroom collided with Flash Gordon's spaceship. On midweek nights there's occasional live performances of jazz and soul, indie bands and record launches, but what really pulls in the crowds is the regular Friday and Saturday night '80s and '90s dance party.

BACK DOORS
BAR

Map p342 (257 315 824; www.backdoors.cz; Na Dělidle 30, Smíchov; 11am-1am; 4, 6, 7, 9, 10, 14, 20, MAnděl) This upmarket cellar-bar-restaurant-club is inspired by similar spaces in New York and Amsterdam (though the subterranean Gothic cellar look could only be Prague). It offers decent Czech DJs and a relaxed vibe most nights, though it can get stuffy on a crowded weekend night. If you're hungry, there's a full menu of well-done international dishes.

KÁVA KÁVA KÁVA
CAFE

Map p342 (257 314 277; www.kava-coffee.cz; Lidická 42, Smíchov; mains 70-120Kč; 7am-10pm; ; MAnděl) The Smíchov branch of the popular internet cafe Káva Káva Káva

THE TRUTH ABOUT SMÍCHOV

Smíchov has got to be Prague's most economically varied – even schizophrenic – district. For years it languished as a depressed industrial backwater that was home to Prague's largest Roma community. At the same time, the hills south and west of Anděl metro station, not far from the Barrandov film studios, had some of the city's swankiest villas.

These days, those jarring contrasts are seen in the area around Anděl. It's filled with gleaming office towers, the vast Nový Smíchov shopping centre, the Staropramen brewery, and some of the city's hottest boutique hotels – but just down the road, near Smíchovské nádraží train station, the poverty and neglect set in again.

As with the city's other riverside districts, Smíchov both suffered and benefited from the tragic flood that struck Prague in 2002. Low-lying areas were submerged, but in the aftermath there was a welcome infusion of development capital. One boost came a few years back, when artist David Černý decided to establish his 'Meet Factory' performance art space amid the tenements and abandoned factories south of Smíchovské nádraží.

in Staré Město is bigger than the original, with two large rooms as well as a garden out the back. There's a small menu of salads and sandwiches and you can buy local beers by the bottle. There are computers for surfing the net (60Kč per hour).

KAVÁRNA JARDA MAYER CAFE
Map p342 (www.kavarnajardamayer.cz; Staropramenná 22, Smíchov; ⌚3pm-midnight Mon-Fri, 5pm-midnight Sat & Sun; 📶; Ⓜ Anděl) This popular student cafe occupies a light airy space in a quiet corner away from the hustle of Anděl metro station. There's not much to eat, but there's decent coffee and good Černá hora beer. The atmosphere is relaxed and perfect for hanging out or just sitting around surfing the net.

DOG'S BOLLOCKS BAR
Map p342 (☎775 736 030; www.dogsbollocks.cz; Nádražní 82, Smíchov; ⌚5pm-midnight Mon, 5pm-3am Tue-Sat; Ⓜ Anděl) This run-of-the-mill bar and nightspot is not far from the Staropramen Brewery and is a decent choice if you're staying in the area and don't want to go too far for your fun. In spite of the English-friendly name, it draws mostly Czech students and young professionals letting loose.

HELLS BELLS BAR
Map p342 (☎722 302 559; www.hellsbells.cz; Na Bělidle 27, Smíchov; ⌚3pm-3am; Ⓜ Anděl) Despite the glitzy office towers, Smíchov is still a down and dirty kind of place, and this heavy metal bar is where the locals let it all hang out. Loud, crowded and fun – the late closing time makes it a perfect ticket for that last drink of the night.

WASH CAFÉ CAFE
Map p342 (☎608 703 805; Nádražní 308/66, Smíchov; ⌚10am-1am Mon-Fri, 11am-1am Sat & Sun; 📶; 🚋12, 14, 20) This wacky combination of a self-serve laundry and cafe sports '70s-era thrift-shop furniture and a laid-back vibe. Not worth making a special trip for but if you happen to be in the 'hood, it's easily the coolest spot around for coffee. Also serves beer, wine, mixed drinks and snacks. You can wash clothes (75Kč per load).

Vyšehrad

V CAFE CAFE
Map p341 (☎725 740 717; www.vcafe.cz; K rotundě 3, Vyšehrad; ⌚11am-9.30pm; 📶; Ⓜ Vyšehrad) This pretty summer terrace may be the nicest place within the Vyšehrad citadel area to relax over a coffee or beer or a light meal of grilled sausages.

CAFE CITADELA CAFE
Map p341 (Vyšehrad Citadel, Vyšehrad; ⌚9.30am-6pm; Ⓜ Vyšehrad) This relaxed beer garden and cafe is a perfect place to cool off under the trees. You'll find it just on the edge of the sculpture garden, south of the cathedral. Most come for coffee or beer, but there's also a small menu of salads, omelettes and sweets.

☆ ENTERTAINMENT

JAZZDOCK JAZZ
Map p342 (☎774 058 838; www.jazzdock.cz; Janáčkovo nábřeží 2, Smíchov; admission 90-150Kč; ⌚4pm-3am; 🚋7, 9, 12, 14, Ⓜ Anděl) Most of Prague's jazz clubs are smoky cellar affairs. This riverside club is a definite step up, with a clean, modern decor and a decidedly romantic view out over the Vltava. This place draws some of the best local talent and occasional international acts. Go early or book to get a good table. Shows normally begin at 7pm and 10pm.

ŠVANDOVO DIVADLO NA SMÍCHOVĚ THEATRE
Map p342 (Šandovo Theatre in Smíchov; ☎257 318 666; www.svandovodivadlo.cz; Stefaníkova 57, Smíchov; tickets 150-300Kč; ⌚box office 11am-2pm & 2.30-7pm Mon-Fri, 5-7pm Sat & Sun; 🚋6, 9, 12, 20) This experimental theatre space, performing Czech and international dramatic works, is admired for its commitment to staging 'English-friendly' performances. It also hosts occasional live music and dance, as well as regular 'Stage Talks', unscripted discussions with noted personalities.

SHOPPING

NOVÝ SMÍCHOV
SHOPPING CENTRE

Map p342 (☎251 511 151; www.novysmichov.eu; Plzeňská 8, Smíchov; 9am-9pm; Wi-Fi; M Anděl) Nový Smíchov is a vast shopping centre that occupies an area the size of several city blocks. It's an airy, well-designed space with plenty of fashion boutiques and niche-market stores. Besides all the big brand names, there's a large computer store, a food court, a virtual-games hall, a 12-screen multiplex cinema and a well-stocked Tesco hypermarket.

MAPIS
MAPS

Map p342 (☎257 315 459; www.mapis.cz; Štefánikova 63, Smíchov; 9am-6.30pm Mon-Fri; tram 6, 9, 12, 20) Mapis is a specialist map shop with a wide selection of local, national and international maps, including hiking maps and city plans covering not just the city but also the whole of the Czech Republic.

Day Trips from Prague

Karlštejn Castle p175

Visiting the Czech Republic's most famous castle, perched on a hilltop like a fairytale fortress, is the most popular day-trip from Prague.

Konopiště Chateau p177

The former country retreat of Archduke Franz Ferdinand (whose assassination sparked-off WWI) offers a fascinating insight into its aristocratic owner.

Kutná Hora p178

Built on the riches generated by silver mining, Kutná Hora once rivalled Prague in importance, and still boasts a treasure house of historical monuments.

Mělník p181

The Lobkowicz family chateau and its tiny but historic vineyard are the focus of Bohemia's modest wine-growing region.

Terezín p182

This grim 18th-century fortress served as a concentration camp during WWII, and is today a moving museum to the horrors of the Holocaust.

TOP SIGHTS
KARLŠTEJN CASTLE

Rising above the village of Karlštejn, 30km southwest of Prague, Karlštejn Castle is rightly one of the top attractions in the Czech Republic. This fairytale medieval fortress is in such good shape that it wouldn't look out of place on Disneyworld's Main Street. Unfortunately, the crowds that throng its courtyards come in theme-park proportions too – in summer it's mobbed with visitors, ice-cream vendors and souvenir stalls.

Thankfully, the peaceful surrounding countryside offers views of Karlštejn's stunning exterior that rival anything you'll see on the inside. If at all possible, visit midweek or out of season, and avoid the queues at the castle ticket office by purchasing your tickets in advance online at www.rezervace.npu.cz.

Karlštejn Information Centre (Informační centrum Karlštejn; ☎311 681 370; www.karlstejnsko.cz; Karlštejn 334, Pension Vinice; ⌚8am-8pm) is across the road from the main car park.

History

Perched high on a crag overlooking the Berounka River, Karlštejn was born of a grand pedigree, starting life in 1348 as a hideaway for the crown jewels and treasury of the Holy Roman Emperor Charles IV. Run by an appointed burgrave, the castle was surrounded by a network of landowning knight-vassals, who came to the castle's aid whenever enemies moved against it.

Karlštejn again sheltered the Bohemian and the Holy Roman Empire crown jewels during the Hussite Wars of

DON'T MISS...

- Chapel of the Holy Cross
- Knight's Hall
- Charles IV's Bedchamber
- Audience Hall
- Jewel House
- Views from the Great Tower

PRACTICALITIES

- Hrad Karlštejn
- ☎311 681 617
- www.hradkarlstejn.cz
- Tour 1 adult/child 270/180Kč, Tour 2 300/200Kč, Tour 3 120/60Kč
- ⌚9am-6.30pm Jul & Aug, to 5.30pm Tue-Sun May, Jun & Sep, to 4.30pm Tue-Sun Apr & Oct, reduced hours Nov-Mar

EATING & DRINKING

Get away from the hordes milling up and down the main route to the castle at **Restaurace Pod Dračí Skálou** (☎311 681 177; www.poddraciskalou.eu; Karlštejn 130; mains 110-240Kč; ⏰11am-11pm Mon-Sat, 11am-8pm Sun; 📶), an appealing country inn with outdoor tables and a barbecue grill, where a half-litre of Pilsner Urquell is only 25Kč. The menu is rustic Czech, with lots of grilled or roast pork, beef and chicken. Take the first road on the left heading up to the castle, or walk down the footpath just outside the castle gate (red markers, signposted 'Beroun').

From the train station, you can travel to the castle in a horse-drawn cart (per person 150Kč).

A SLOVAK SPECIALITY

Situated on the main road up to Karlštejn Castle, the atmospheric **Restaurant U Janů** (☎311 681 210; info@ujanu.cz; Karlštejn 28; mains 110-240Kč) has a decent dollop of authentic charm, and a menu that includes the Slovak speciality, *halušky* (bacon and cheese dumplings).

the early 15th century, but fell into disrepair as its defences became outmoded. Considerable restoration work, not least by Josef Mocker – the king of Prague's neo-Gothic architecture – in the late 19th century has returned the castle to its former glory.

Guided Tours

Admission to the castle is by guided tour only; there are three tours available in English. Tour 1 (adult/child 270/180Kč, 50 minutes) passes through the **Knight's Hall**, still daubed with the coats-of-arms and names of the knight-vassals, **Charles IV's Bedchamber**, the **Audience Hall**, and the **Jewel House**, which includes treasures from the Chapel of the Holy Cross and a replica of the St Wenceslas Crown.

Tour 2 (adult/child 300/200Kč, 70 minutes, May to October only) must be booked in advance and takes in the **Marian Tower**, with the Church of the Virgin Mary and the Chapel of St Catherine, then moves on to the Great Tower for the castle's star attraction, the exquisite **Chapel of the Holy Cross**. Designed by Charles IV for the safekeeping of the crown jewels of the Holy Roman Empire, and of sacred relics of the Crucifixion, the chapel's walls and vaulted ceiling are adorned with thousands of polished semiprecious stones set in gilt stucco in the form of crosses, and with religious and heraldic paintings. For Tour 2, book as far in advance as possible.

Tour 3 (adult/child 120/60Kč, 40 minutes, May to October only) visits the upper levels of the **Great Tower**, the highest point of the castle, which provides stunning views over the surrounding countryside.

Getting There & Away

Trains from Prague's main train station to Beroun (via Praha-Smíchov) stop at Karlštejn (95Kč return, 45 minutes, every 30 minutes). Note that trains are shown as departing from platform 1J, which means the southern (*jih* in Czech) end of platform 1. From the train station or the main car park, it's a 20- or 30-minute uphill walk to the castle. If this doesn't appeal, you can take a shared taxi (per person 100Kč).

TOP SIGHTS
KONOPIŠTĚ CHATEAU

Konopiště Chateau is not only a monument to the obsessions of early 20th-century Habsburg aristocrats, but also an insight into one of the most famous names in European history – the Archduke Franz Ferdinand d'Este, heir to the Austro-Hungarian throne, whose assassination in 1914 sparked WWI.

You'll need a full day to make the most of a visit here: the walk to the chateau passes through pleasant parkland, so try to choose a sunny day. Plan on doing one of the guided tours of the chateau (Tour 3 is the best), and leave time to explore the beautiful landscaped grounds that surround it.

The Chateau

Konopiště is a testament to the archduke's twin obsessions – hunting and St George. Having renovated the massive Gothic and Renaissance building in the 1890s and installed all the latest technology – including electricity, central heating, flush toilets, showers and a lift – Franz Ferdinand decorated his home with his hunting trophies.

His game books record that he shot about 300,000 creatures. About 100,000 animal trophies adorn the walls. The crowded **Trophy Corridor** (Tour 1 and 3), with a forest of mounted animal heads, and the antler-clad **Chamois Room** (Tour 3), with its 'chandelier' fashioned from a stuffed condor, are truly bizarre sights.

The archduke's collection of art and artefacts relating to St George is no less impressive, amounting to 3750 items, many of which are on show in the **St George Museum** (muzeum sv Jiří; adult/child 30/15Kč; ⏲10am-1pm & 1.30-5pm Sat & Sun Jun-Aug, to 4pm Sep, closed Oct-May).

Tours

There are three guided tours in English. Tour 3 (adult/ child 310/210Kč) is the most interesting, visiting the **private apartments** used by the archduke and his family, which have remained unchanged since the state took possession of the chateau in 1921. Tour 2 (adult/child 210/130Kč) takes in the **Great Armoury**, one of the most impressive collections of weapons in Europe, while Tour 1 (adult/child 210/130Kč) visits the grand apartments of the south wing.

DON'T MISS...

- Chamois Room
- Trophy Corridor
- St George Museum

PRACTICALITIES

- Zámek Konopiště
- ☎317 721 366
- www.zamek-konopiste.cz
- Tour 1 or 2 adult/child 210/130Kč, Tour 3 310/210Kč
- ⏲open 10am-noon & 1-5pm Tue-Sun Jun-Aug, to 4pm Apr, May & Sep, 10am-noon & 1-3pm Sat & Sun Oct & Nov, closed Dec-Mar

EATING & DRINKING

After visiting the chateau, head down the hill to **Stará Myslivna** (☎317 700 280; www.staramyslivna.com; Konopiště 2; mains 120-280Kč), a Czech restaurant set in a 19th-century gamekeeper's lodge.

Getting There & Away

There are **buses** from Prague's Roztyly metro station to Benešov (105Kč return, 40 minutes, twice hourly) – their final destination is usually Pelhřímov or Jihlava. There are also buses from Prague's Florenc bus station (120Kč return, 40 minutes, eight daily). There are **trains** from Prague's Hlavní nádraží to Benešov u Prahy (135Kč return, 1¼ hours, hourly).

Konopiště is 2km west of Benešov. Local bus 2 (12Kč, six minutes, hourly) runs from a stop on Dukelská, 400m north of the train station (turn left out of the station, take first right on Tyršova and then first left) to the castle car park. If you'd rather walk, turn left out of the train station, go left across the bridge over the railway, and follow the yellow markers west along Konopištská street.

Kutná Hora

Explore

Enriched by the silver ore that veined the surrounding hills, the medieval city of Kutná Hora became the seat of Wenceslas II's royal mint in 1308, producing silver groschen that were then the hard currency of Central Europe. Boom-time Kutná Hora rivalled Prague in importance, but by the 16th century the mines began to run dry, and its demise was hastened by the Thirty Years' War and the devastating fire of 1770. The town became a Unesco World Heritage Site in 1996, luring visitors with a smorgasbord of historic sights. It looks its flower-bedecked best in May and June but is worth a full day's visit at any time of year. It's a 10-minute walk from the main train station to Sedlec Ossuary, and a further 2.5km to the Old Town.

The Best...

➡ **Sight** Sedlec Ossuary (p178)

➡ **Place to Eat** Pivnice Dačický (p181)

➡ **Place to Drink** Kavárna Mokate (p181)

Top Tip

Buy a return train ticket to Kutná Hora Město station, near the centre of the Old Town, so that you don't have to walk or take a bus back to the main train station.

Getting There & Away

Bus There are only two or three direct buses a day (weekdays only) from Prague's Florenc bus station to Kutná Hora (140Kc return, 1¼ hours); the train is a better bet.

Train There are direct trains from Prague's main train station to Kutná Hora hlavní nádraží every two hours (196Kč return, 55 minutes). Five minutes after the arrival of the Prague train (and before the departure of return trains) a little railcar shuttles from platform 1 to Kutná Hora Město station (six minutes).

Need to Know

➡ **Location** 65km (1½ hours) east of Prague.

➡ **Kutná Hora Tourist Office** (Informační centrum; ☎327 512 378; www.guide.kh.cz; Palackého náměstí 377; ⏰9am-6pm Apr-Sep, 9am-5pm Mon-Fri & 10am-4pm Sat & Sun Oct-Mar) Books accommodation, rents bicycles (per day 220Kč) and offers internet access (per minute 1Kč, minimum 15Kč).

➡ **Sedlec Tourist Office** (Informační centrum Sedlec; ☎326 551 049; Zámecká 279; ⏰9am-5pm Apr-Nov, to 4pm Dec-Mar, closed 1-2pm)

SIGHTS

SEDLEC OSSUARY CHRISTIAN

(Kostnice; ☎327 561 143; www.ossuary.eu; Zámecká 127; adult/concession 60/40Kč; ⏰8am-6pm Mon-Sat Apr-Sep, 9am-5pm Mar & Oct, 9am-4pm Nov-Feb) When the Schwarzenbergs purchased Sedlec monastery in 1870 they allowed a local woodcarver to get creative with the bones piled in the crypt (the remains of around 40,000 people), resulting in the remarkable 'bone church' of Sedlec Ossuary. Garlands of skulls hang from the vaulted ceiling – around a chandelier containing at least one of each bone in the human body.

Four pyramids of stacked bones squat in each of the corner chapels, and crosses, chalices and monstrances of bone adorn the altar. From April to October a minibus runs on demand (per person 35Kč, minimum three people) between Sedlec, Kutná Hora town centre and the Cathedral of St Barbara.

CZECH SILVER MUSEUM MUSEUM

(České muzeum stříbra; ☎327 512 159; www.cms-kh.cz; Barborská 28; Tour 1 adult/concession 70/40Kč, Tour 2 120/80Kč, combined 140/90Kč;

Kutná Hora

Sights

1 Barborská ... C4
2 Czech Silver Museum ... C3
3 Gallery of Central Bohemia ... B4
4 Italian Court ... D2

Eating

5 Kavárna Mokate ... C3
6 Pivnice Dačický ... C2
7 U Sňeka Pohodáře ... E1

Sleeping

8 Hotel Zlatá Stoupa ... F2
9 Penzión Centrum ... D2
10 Penzión U Kata ... G1

Kutná Hora

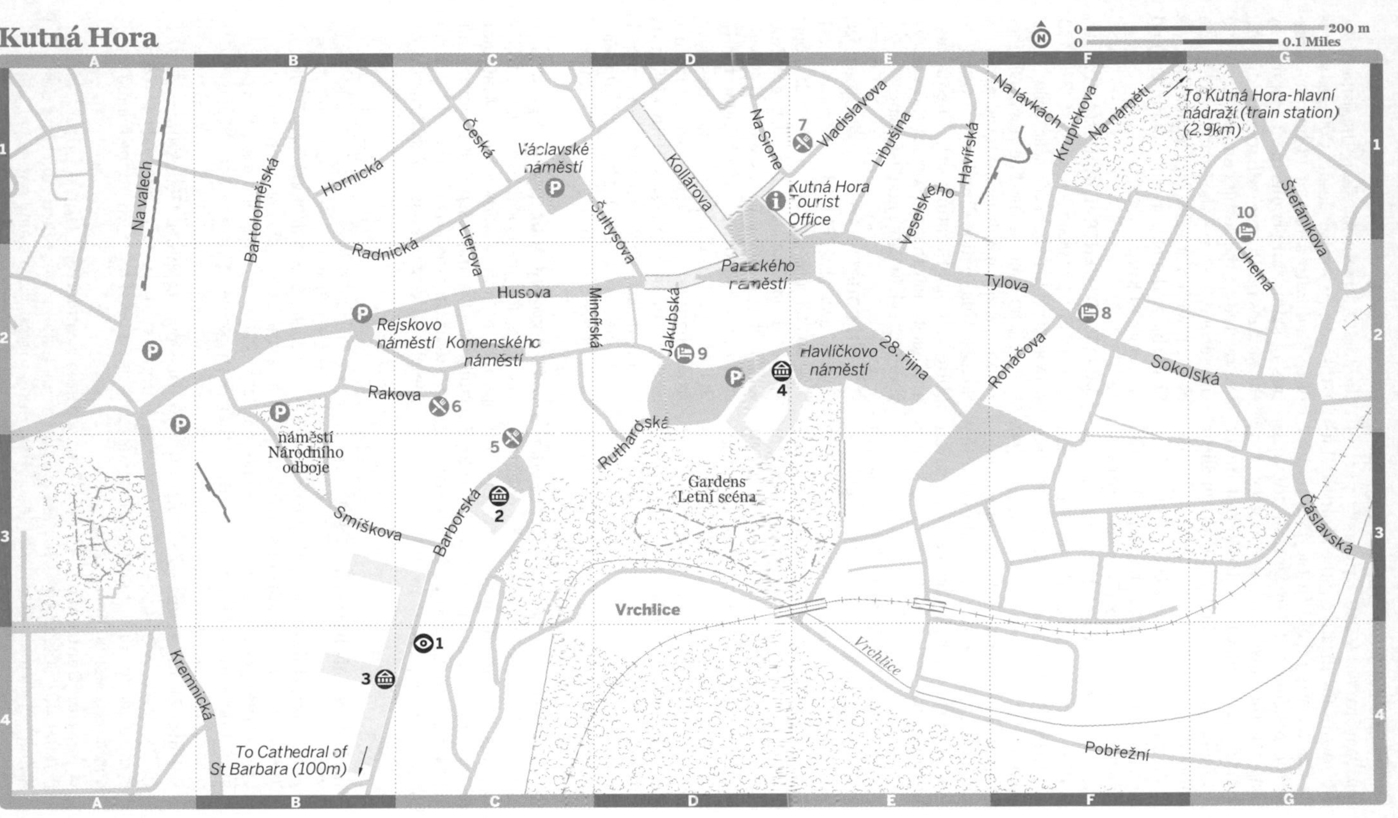

0 200 m
0 0.1 Miles
A
B
C
D
E
F
G
1
2
3
4
Na valech
Bartolomějská
Hornická
Radnická
Česká
Václavské náměstí
Lierova
Šultysova
Kollárova
Na Sione
Vladislavova
Libušina
Veselského
Havířská
Na lávkách
Krupičkova
Na náměti
To Kutná Hora-hlavní nádraží (train station) (2.9km)
Štefánikova
Uhelná
Kutná Hora Tourist Office
Palackého náměstí
Husova
Mincířská
Jakubská
Tylova
Sokolská
Roháčova
28. října
Havlíčkovo náměstí
Rejskovo náměstí
Komenského náměstí
Rakova
náměstí Národního odboje
Ruthardská
Gardens Letní scéna
Smíškova
Barborská
Vrchlice
Čáslavská
Pobřežní
Kremnická
To Cathedral of St Barbara (100m)
1
2
3
4
5
6
7
8
9
10

⌚10am-6pm Jul & Aug, 9am-6pm May, Jun & Sep, 9am-5pm Apr & Oct) Originally part of the town's fortifications, the **Hrádek** (Little Castle) was rebuilt in the 15th century as the residence of Jan Smíšek, administrator of the royal mines, who grew rich from silver he illegally mined right under the building. It now houses the Czech Silver Museum.

Visiting is by **guided tour**. Tour 1 (one hour) leads through the main part of the museum where the exhibits celebrate the mines that made Kutná Hora wealthy, including a huge wooden device once used to lift loads weighing as much as 1000kg from the 200m-deep shafts. Tour 2 (90 minutes) allows you to don a miner's helmet and explore 500m of medieval mine shafts. Kids need to be aged at least seven for this tour.

CATHEDRAL OF ST BARBARA CHURCH

(Chrám sv Barbora; ☎327 512 115; Barborská; adult/concession 60/40Kč; ⌚10am-4pm Mon, 9am-5.30pm Tue-Sun May-Sep, 10am-4pm daily Oct-Apr) Kutná Hora's greatest monument is the Gothic Cathedral of St Barbara. Rivalling Prague's St Vitus in size and magnificence, its soaring nave culminates in elegant, six-petalled ribbed vaulting, and the ambulatory chapels preserve original 15th-century frescoes, some of them showing miners at work.

Construction was begun in 1380, interrupted during the Hussite Wars and abandoned in 1558 when the silver began to run out. The cathedral was finally completed in neo-Gothic style at the end of the 19th century. Take a walk around the outside of the church, too; the terrace at the east end enjoys the finest view in town.

BARBORSKÁ STREET

Barborská street runs along the front of the 17th-century former Jesuit College, and is decorated with a row of 13 baroque **statues** of saints, an arrangement inspired by the statues on Prague's Charles Bridge. All are related to the Jesuits and/or the town; the second statue – the woman holding a chalice, with a stone tower at her side – is St Barbara, the patron saint of miners and therefore of Kutná Hora.

GALLERY OF CENTRAL BOHEMIA GALLERY

(Galerie Středočeského kraje; ☎725 377 433; www.gask.cz; Barborská 53; adult/child 120Kč/free; ⌚10am-6pm Tue-Fri) The town's former Jesuit College has been restored and now houses this regional gallery devoted to 20th- and 21st-century art. There's also a gallery shop that showcases the work of young Czech artists and designers.

ITALIAN COURT HISTORIC BUILDING

(Vlašský dvůr; ☎327 512 873; Havlíčkovo náměstí 552; adult/concession 105/65Kč; ⌚9am-6pm Apr-Sep, 10am-5pm Mar & Oct, 10am-4pm Nov-Feb) Just east of St James Church (kostel sv Jakuba; 1330) lies the Italian Court, the former Royal Mint – it got its name from the master craftsmen from Florence brought in by Wenceslas II to kick-start the business, and who began stamping silver coins here in 1300. The original treasury rooms hold an exhibit on coins and minting.

The **guided tour** (with English text) visits the few historical rooms open to the public, notably a 15th-century **Audience Hall**, with two impressive 19th-century murals depicting the 1471 election of Vladislav Jagiello as king of Bohemia, and the *Decree*

SLEEPING IN KUTNÁ HORA

➡ **Penzión U Kata** (☎327 515 096; www.ukata.cz; Uhelná 596; s/d/tr 500/760/1140Kč; P@🛜) You won't lose your head over the rates at this good-value family hotel called 'The Executioner'. Bikes can be rented for 220Kč per day, and it's a short stroll from the bus station. Downstairs there's a welcoming Czech beer hall and restaurant.

➡ **Hotel Zlatá Stoupa** (☎327 511 540; www.zlatastoupa.cz; Tylova 426; s/d from 1350/2150Kč; P🛜) If you feel like spoiling yourself, the most luxurious place in town is the elegantly furnished 'Golden Mount'. We like a hotel room where the minibar contains full-sized bottles of wine.

➡ **Penzión Centrum** (☎327 514 218; www.penzioncentrum.com; Jakubská 57; s/d/tr 700/1100/1300Kč; P@) Tucked away in a quiet, flower-bedecked courtyard off Kutná Hora's main drag, this place offers snug rooms and a sunny garden.

of Kutná Hora being proclaimed by Wenceslas IV and Jan Hus in 1409.

EATING & DRINKING

PIVNICE DAČICKÝ BEER HALL €

(☎327 512 248; www.dacicky.com; Rakova 8; mains 120-330Kč; ⊙11am-11pm) Get some froth on your moustache at this old-fashioned, wood-panelled Bohemian beer hall, where you can dine on dumplings and choose from five draught beers, including Pilsner Urquell, Budvar and Primátor yeast beer.

U SŇEKA POHODÁŘE ITALIAN €

(☎327 515 987; www.usneka.cz; Vladislavova 11; mains 100-235Kč; 📶) Kutná Hora's best Italian flavours are found at this cosy local favourite that's very popular for takeaway or dine-in pizza and pasta. And no, we don't know why it's called 'The Contented Snail'.

KAVÁRNA MOKATE CAFE

(Barborská 37; ⊙8am-10pm Mon-Fri, 10am-10pm Sat, 10am-8pm Sun) This cosy little cafe, with ancient earthenware floor tiles, timber beams, mismatched furniture and oriental rugs, dishes up a wide range of freshly ground coffees and exotic teas, as well as iced tea and coffee in summer.

Mělník

Explore

Mělník sprawls over a rocky promontory surrounded by the flat Central Bohemian plains. The bus station is 800m east of the town centre, so you begin with a gentle uphill walk along Kapitan Jaroše street. Pass below the prominent clock tower to the main square, then bear left for the chateau.

Plan on taking a chateau tour in the morning, followed by lunch, then a stroll around the other sites – they're all close together. Don't miss the **terrace** on the far side of the chateau, with superb views across the river to the Central Bohemian plains. The vines below the terrace are supposedly descendants of the first vines introduced to Bohemia, by Charles IV in the 14th century. They're now used to make the chateau's own wines.

The Best...

- **Sight** Ossuary (p182)
- **Place to Eat** Buffalo (p182)
- **Place to Drink** Galerie A Čajovná Ve Věží (p182)

Top Tip

Bring along a packed lunch, grab a bench on the terrace on the far side of the chateau, and enjoy a picnic with a view.

Getting There & Away

Bus Buses run to Mělník (48Kč, 45 minutes, every 30 minutes weekdays, hourly weekends) from stop 10 in the bus station outside Praha-Holešovice train station; buy your ticket from the driver (one-way only, no return tickets).

Need to Know

- **Location** 30km (one hour) north of Prague.
- **Mělník Tourist Office** (☎315 627 503; www.melnik.cz; Legionářů 51; ⊙9am-5pm) Sells maps and historical guides and can help with accommodation.

SIGHTS

MĚLNÍK CHATEAU PALACE

(Zámek Mělník; ☎315 622 121; www.lobkowicz-melnik.cz; Svatováclavská 19; adult/concession 100/80Kč; ⊙9.30am-5pm May-Sep) This Renaissance chateau was acquired by the Lobkowicz family in 1739; the family opened it to the public in 1990. You can wander through the former living quarters, which are crowded with a rich collection of baroque furniture and 17th- and 18th-century paintings, on a **self-guided tour** with English text.

Additional rooms have changing exhibits of modern works and a fabulous collection of 17th-century maps and engravings detailing Europe's great cities. A separate tour descends to the 14th-century **wine cellars**, where you can taste the chateau's wines; a shop in the courtyard sells the chateau's own label. Wine-tasting sessions held in the shop cost from 100Kč to 250Kč.

CHURCH OF STS PETER & PAUL CHURCH

(kostel sv Petra a Pavla; ☎315 622 337; Na Vyhlídce) Next to the chateau is this 15th-century Gothic church, with baroque furnishings and remnants of its Romanesque predecessor incorporated into the rear of the building. Climb to the top of the **church tower** (Vyhlídková věž; adult/child 40/20Kč; ⏲10am-12.30pm & 1.15-5pm Tue-Sun) for superlative views.

The church crypt is now an **ossuary** (kostnice; adult/child 30/15Kč; ⏲9.30am-12.30pm & 1.15-4pm Tue-Fri, 10am-12.30pm & 1.15-4pm Sat & Sun), packed with the bones of around 10,000 people, dug up to make room for 16th-century plague victims. The bones are arranged in the shapes of anchors, hearts and crosses (symbols of faith, love and hope). This crypt is much more visceral and claustrophobic than the Sedlec Ossuary (p178); the floor is of beaten earth, and you literally rub shoulders with the bones.

EATING & DRINKING

BUFFALO AMERICAN €

(☎722 736 867; www.buffalorestaurant.cz; Palackého 135; mains 120-210Kč; ⏲11am-10pm;) Just 150m southeast of the main square, this American-style restaurant has a laid-back atmosphere, a summer garden out the back, and a finger-lickingly authentic Tex-Mex menu (buffalo wings, burgers, steaks, quesadillas, nachos). There's a choice of Pilsner Urquell, Holba and Bernard beers.

GALERIE A ČAJOVNÁ VE VĚŽÍ CAFE

(☎315 621 954; www.vez.melnicek.cz; ulice 5 května; ⏲noon-10pm Mon-Fri, 2-10pm Sat & Sun) Inside the medieval Prague Gate tower, this atmospheric cafe/art gallery spreads across three floors and is served by an ingenious dumbwaiter: write your order on the note pad, ding the bell, and the tray goes down, returning moments later with your order. Choose from a range of freshly ground coffees, exotic teas, local wines, beer and *medovina* (mead).

Terezín

Explore

The former concentration camp of Terezín provides a sobering reminder of the horrors inflicted on the Czech people during WWII.

It's possible to visit Terezín on a guided day trip from Prague, but in our experience these tours tend to be a bit rushed. Our advice is to allow a full day, bring a picnic lunch, and begin by visiting the Ghetto Museum (where you can pick up information leaflets and maps) and Magdeburg Barracks. It's worth walking past the old railway siding to see the crematorium before crossing the river to take a self-guided tour of the Lesser Fortress.

Top Tip

Rather than eat at one of Terezín's crowded tourist restaurants, take a bus or taxi to attractive Litoměřice, 3km to the north. The town square has several good eateries.

Getting There & Away

Bus Direct buses from Prague to Litoměřice (165Kč return, one hour, hourly), stop at Terezín. They depart from the bus station outside Praha-Holešovice train station. There are buses between Litoměřice bus station and Terezín (9Kč, eight minutes, at least hourly).

Need to Know

➡ **Location** 60km (1½ hours) north of Prague.

➡ **Terezín Information Centre** (Městské infocentrum; ☎416 782 616; www.terezin.cz; náměstí Československé armády 179; ⏲8am-5pm Mon-Thu, 8am-1.30pm Fri, 9am-3pm Sun, closed Sat)

SIGHTS

MAIN FORTRESS HISTORIC SITE

(Hlavní pevnost) The sheer scale of the walls and moats surrounding the Main Fortress is impossible to fathom – mainly because the town is inside the fortifications. Initially, you may think the central square looks no different from other Old Town centres.

TEREZÍN'S HISTORY

A massive bulwark of stone and earth, the fortress of Terezín (Theresienstadt in German) was built in 1780 by Emperor Joseph II with a single purpose: to keep the enemy out. Ironically, it is more notorious for keeping people in – it served as a political prison in the later days of the Habsburg empire. **Gavrilo Princip**, the assassin who killed Archduke Franz Ferdinand in 1914, was incarcerated here during WWI, and when the Germans took control during WWII the fortress became a grim holding pen for Jews bound for extermination camps. In contrast to the colourful, baroque face of many Czech towns, Terezín is a stark but profoundly evocative monument to a darker aspect of Europe's past.

The bleakest phase of Terezín's history began in 1940 when the Gestapo established a prison in the Lesser Fortress. Evicting the inhabitants from the Main Fortress the following year, the Nazis transformed the town into a transit camp through which some 150,000 people eventually passed en route to the death camps. For most, conditions were appalling. Between April and September 1942 the ghetto's population increased from 12,968 to 58,491, leaving each prisoner with only 1.65 sq m of space and causing disease and starvation on a terrifying scale. In the same period, there was a 15-fold increase in the number of deaths within the prison walls.

Terezín later became the centrepiece of one of the Nazis' more extraordinary public relations coups. Official visitors to the fortress, including representatives of the Red Cross, saw a town that was billed as a kind of Jewish 'refuge', with a Jewish administration, banks, shops, cafes, schools and a thriving cultural life – it even had a jazz band – in a charade that twice completely fooled international observers. In reality Terezín was home to a relentlessly increasing population of prisoners, regular trains departing for the gas chambers of Auschwitz, and the death by starvation, disease or suicide of some 35,000 people.

Wander past the walls en route to the Lesser Fortress, however, and a different picture emerges.

At the heart of the Main Fortress is the neat grid of streets that makes up the town of Terezín. There's little to see except the 19th-century Church of the Resurrection, the former Commandant's office, the neoclassical administrative buildings and the surrounding grid of houses with their awful secrets. South of the square are the remains of a railway siding, built by prisoners, on which carriage-loads of further prisoners arrived – and departed.

GHETTO MUSEUM MUSEUM

(muzeum ghetta; ☎416 782 225; www.pamatnik-terezin.cz; Komenského 15 1; adult/child 170/140Kč, combined with Lesser Fortress 210/160Kč; ⏰9am-6pm Apr-Oct, to 5.30pm Nov-Mar) The Ghetto Museum explores the rise of Nazism and life in the Terezín ghetto. The building once accommodated the camp's 10- to 15-year-old boys; haunting images painted by them still decorate the walls.

The former **Magdeburg Barracks** (Magdeburská kasárna), which served as the seat of the Jewish 'town council', houses an annex to the main museum. Here you can visit a reconstructed dormitory and see exhibits on the rich cultural life that somehow flourished against this backdrop of fear.

There is also a small exhibit in the grim **Crematorium** (Krematorium; ⏰10am-6pm Sun-Fri Apr-Oct, to 4pm Sun-Fri Nov-Mar) in the **Jewish Cemetery** just off Bohušovická brána, about 750m south of the main square.

The Ghetto Museum has multilingual self-guide pamphlets and guides (some of them ghetto survivors) to offer assistance.

LESSER FORTRESS HISTORIC SITE

(Malá pevnost; ☎416 782 576; www.pamatnik-terezin.cz; Pražská; adult/child 170/140Kč, combined with Ghetto Museum 210/170Kč; ⏰8am-6pm Apr-Oct, to 4.30pm Nov-Mar) The best way to see Terezín's Lesser Fortress is to take a **self-guided tour** through the prison barracks, isolation cells, workshops and morgues, past execution grounds and former mass graves. The Nazis' mocking concentration camp slogan, *Arbeit Macht*

Frei ('Work Makes You Free'), hangs above the gate to the inner yard. It would be hard to invent a more menacing location, and it is only while wandering through the seemingly endless tunnels beneath the walls that you begin to fully appreciate the vast dimensions of the fortress.

In front of the fortress is a **National Cemetery**, established in 1945 for the victims exhumed from the Nazis' mass graves.

EATING

MEMORIAL CAFÉ & RESTAURANT CZECH €

(☎416 783 082; náměstí Československé armády; meals 130-270Kč) To be honest, there aren't any restaurants in Terezín that are genuinely recommendable. This place in the Hotel Memorial, serving hearty Czech meals and kosher wines on a sunny terrace, is the best of a mediocre bunch.

Sleeping

Prague offers a wide range of accommodation options, from cosy, romantic hotels set in historic town houses to luxurious international chain hotels, and from budget hostels and pensions to sharply styled boutique hotels. Meanwhile, more and more travellers are discovering the pleasures of renting an apartment in Prague.

Room Rates & Seasons

A double room in a midrange hotel in central Prague costs around 4000Kč (€160) in high season; outside the centre, this might fall to about 3000Kč. Top-range hotels cost from 4000Kč up, with the best luxury hotels charging 6000Kč and more. Budget options charge less than 2000Kč for a double room.

Note that some midrange and top-end hotels quote rates in euros. At these hotels you can pay cash in Czech crowns if you like, but the price will depend on the exchange rate on the day you settle the bill.

The rates quoted here are for the high season, which generally covers April to June, September and October, and the Christmas/New Year holidays. July and August are mid-season, and the rest of the year is low season, when rates can drop by 30% or 40%.

Even high-season rates can be inflated by up to 15% on certain dates, notably at New Year, Easter, during the Prague Spring festival, and at weekends (Thursday to Sunday) in May, June and September.

Apartments

The cost of a short-term stay in a self-catering apartment is comparable with a midrange hotel room, and means minimal transport costs, access to cheap local food, and the freedom to come and go as you like. Typical rates for a two-person apartment with a combined living room/bedroom, bathroom, TV and kitchenette range from around 2000Kč per night in the outer suburbs, to around 3500Kč or 4500Kč for an apartment near the Old Town Square.

Accommodation Agencies & Websites

➡ **Alfa Tourist Service** (☎224 230 037; www.alfatourist.cz; Opletalova 38, Nové Město; ⌚9am-5pm Mon-Fri) Can provide accommodation in hostels, pensions, hotels and private rooms.

➡ **AVE Travel** (☎251 551 011; www.praguehotellocator.com) A 24-hour call centre and web-based agency with a huge range of hotels and apartments on offer.

➡ **Happy House Rentals** (☎224 946 890; www.happyhouserentals.com; Jungmannova 30, Nové Město; ⌚9am-6pm Mon-Fri) Specialises in short- and long-term rental apartments.

➡ **Hostel.cz** (☎415 658 580; www.hostel.cz) Website database of hostels and budget hotels, with a secure online booking system.

➡ **Lonely Planet** (http://hotels.lonelyplanet.com) For more accommodation reviews and recommendations by Lonely Planet authors; you can also book online here.

➡ **Mary's Travel & Tourist Service** (Map p344; ☎222 254 007; www.marys.cz; Italská 31, Vinohrady; ⌚9am-7pm Mon-Fri, 10am-5pm Sat & Sun) Friendly, efficient agency offering private rooms, hostels, pensions, apartments and hotels in Prague and surrounding areas.

➡ **Prague Apartments** (☎604 168 756; www.prague-apartment.com) Web-based service with comfortable, IKEA-furnished flats. Availability of apartments shown online.

➡ **Stop City** (Map p344; ☎222 521 233; www.stopcity.com; Vinohradská 24, Vinohrady; ⌚10am-8pm) Specialises in apartments, private rooms and pensions in the city centre, Vinohrady and Žižkov areas.

NEED TO KNOW

Price Guide
The categories used in this chapter indicate the cost per night of a standard double room in high season.

- **€** less than 2000Kč (less than €80)
- **€€** 2000Kč to 4000Kč (€80 to €160)
- **€€€** more than 4000Kč (more than €160)

Reservations
Booking your accommodation in advance is strongly recommended (especially if you want to stay in or near the centre), and there are dozens of agencies that will help you find a place to stay. The more reliable agencies should be able to find you a bed even if you turn up in peak periods without a booking.

Smoking
The ban on smoking in public places that came into effect in the Czech Republic in 2010 does not apply to hotels – each establishment comes up with its own rules. In our listings we have used the no-smoking icon  for places that are entirely non-smoking (though they may have an outdoor 'designated smoking area').

Lonely Planet's Top Choices

Hotel Aria (p188) A musical theme lifts this luxurious, romantic spot into the realms of fantasy.

Fusion Hotel (p190) It's a hostel, it's a hotel, it's designer heaven...

Golden Well Hotel (p188) Historic, luxury hotel in the ultimate location – right beneath the castle walls.

Icon Hotel (p191) This cutting-edge designer hotel is a hangout for Prague's beautiful people.

Absolutum Hotel (p193) Boutique gorgeousness at reasonable prices; it's out of the centre but right on the main tram route.

Czech Inn (p192) Great value and atmosphere in an up-and-coming neighbourhood.

Best by Budget

€
ArtHarmony (p191)

Hostel Elf (p193)

Mosaic House (p190)

Pension Královský Vinohrad (p192)

Sir Toby's Hostel (p194)

€€
Domus Henrici (p188)

Lokál Inn (p188)

Hunger Wall Residence (p189)

Perla Hotel (p190)

Art Hotel (p194)

€€€
Savic Hotel (p189)

Le Palais Hotel (p191)

Anděl's Hotel Prague (p195)

Ametyst (p193)

Louren Hotel (p192)

Best for Families

Dům u velké boty (p189)

Hotel Suite Home (p191)

Hotel 16 U Sv Kateřiny (p191)

ArtHarmony (p191)

Hotel Julian (p196)

Best for Romance

Domus Henrici (p188)

Romantik Hotel U Raka (p188)

Grand Hotel Praha (p189)

Anděl's Hotel Prague (p195)

Where to Stay

Neighbourhood	For	Against
Prague Castle & Hradčany	Very convenient for the castle, and generally a quiet and peaceful neighbourhood.	Limited choice of restaurants, few bars, and a long walk uphill from the Malá Strana nightlife.
Malá Strana	In the thick of things, close to Charles Bridge; accommodation is often in beautiful historic buildings.	Accommodation is mostly quite expensive, but still gets booked out well in advance.
Staré Město	As central as it gets, in easy walking distance of most attractions; many hotels in historic properties.	Can be noisy and crowded in high season; a bit of a hike to the nearest tram stops.
Nové Město	Central, with good transport connections and a vast choice of eating places, and handy for the main train station	The prime area for visiting stag parties, so can be noisy at nights, and in parts slightly seedy.
Vinohrady & Vršovice	Classy neighbourhood with often spacious and elegant accommodation, excellent restaurants and sophisticated nightlife.	Few attractions in the immediate area, and a bit of a hike from the city centre.
Žižkov & Karlín	Competitively priced accommodation; though it feels out of the centre, it's only three or four tram stops from Wenceslas Square. Excellent local bars.	Some parts look a bit rough and run-down; can be noisy on main streets. Lots of steep hills and long staircases, many places without elevators.
Holešovice, Bubenec & Dejvice	Offers a wide range of good-value accommodation, with plenty of good restaurants in the area.	A fair distance from the centre, especially Dejvice which is about 20 minutes by tram or 10 minutes by metro.
Smíchov & Vyšehrad	Lower prices. Both neighbourhoods have metro stations just two stops from the city centre.	Not easily walkable to main sights; some parts have a rough-around-the-edges atmosphere.

Hradčany

DOMUS HENRICI HOTEL €€

Map p330 (220 511 369; www.domus-henrici.cz; Loretánská 11; d/ste from 3250/4000Kč; 22, 25) This historic building in a quiet corner of Hradčany is intentionally nondescript out front, hinting that peace and privacy are top priorities here. There are eight spacious and stylish rooms, half with private fax, scanner/copier and internet access (via an ethernet port), and all with polished wood floors, large bathrooms, comfy beds and fluffy bathrobes.

ROMANTIK HOTEL U RAKA HOTEL €€

Map p330 (220 511 100; www.romantikhoteluraka.cz; Černínská 10; s/d from 2125/2375Kč; 22) Concealed in a manicured rock garden in a quiet corner of Hradčany, the historic Romantik Hotel U Raka is an atmospheric, late-18th-century timber cottage with just six elegant, low-ceilinged doubles, complete with timber beams, wooden floors and red-brick fireplaces. With its cosy bedrooms, attentive staff, artistic decor and farmhouse-kitchen-style breakfast room, it's ideal for a romantic getaway, and the castle is less than 10 minutes' walk away. Be sure to book at least a few months ahead.

HOTEL MONASTERY HOTEL €€

Map p330 (233 090 200; www.hotelmonastery.cz; Strahovské nádvoří 13; s/d from 2500/2800Kč; 22, 25) Ancient meets modern at this small hotel in the peaceful courtyard of Strahov Monastery, where the only noise likely to disturb you is the occasional tolling of a church bell. The 12 quirkily shaped rooms in this 17th-century building have been given a bright, modern makeover with polished wood floors, plain white walls hung with photos of Prague, and a splash of colour from the bedspread and sofa.

Malá Strana

LOKÁL INN INN €€

Map p328 (257 014 800; www.lokalinn.cz; Míšeňská 12; d/ste from 3475/4475Kč; 12, 20, 22) Polished parquet floors and painted wooden ceilings abound in this 18th-century house designed by Prague's premier baroque architect, Kilian Dientzenhofer. The eight rooms and four suites are elegant and uncluttered, and the rustic, stone-vaulted cellars house a deservedly popular pub and restaurant run by the same folk as Lokál (p109), a popular Czech beer hall in Staré Město. (Best ask for a quiet room if you plan to be in bed before the pub shuts.)

HOTEL NERUDA BOUTIQUE HOTEL €€

Map p328 (257 535 557; www.hotelneruda.cz; Nerudova 44; r from 2225Kč; 12, 20, 22) Set in a tastefully renovated Gothic house dating from 1348, the Neruda has decor that is chic and minimalist in neutral tones enlivened by the odd splash of colour, with a lovely glass-roofed atrium and a sunny roof terrace. The bedrooms share the modern, minimalist decor and are mostly reasonably sized, but be aware that some of the rooms in the top of the building are a bit on the cramped side – ask for one on the 1st or 2nd floor.

HOTEL ARIA BOUTIQUE HOTEL €€€

Map p328 (225 334 111; www.ariahotel.net; Tržíště 9; d from 6625Kč; 12, 20, 22) The Aria offers five-star luxury with a musical theme – each of the four floors is dedicated to a musical genre (jazz, opera, classical and contemporary), and each room celebrates a particular artist or musician and contains a selection of their music that you can enjoy on the in-room hi-fi system. Service is professional and efficient, and the rooms are furnished with crisp bedlinen, plump continental quilts, Molton Brown toiletries and complimentary chocolates.

GOLDEN WELL HOTEL HOTEL €€€

Map p328 (257 011 213; www.goldenwell.cz; U Zlaté Studně 4; d/ste from 6250/12,500Kč; Malostranská) The Golden Well is one of Malá Strana's hidden secrets, tucked away at the end of a cobbled cul-de-sac – a Renaissance house that once belonged to Emperor Rudolf II, perched on the southern slope of the castle hill. The rooms are quiet and spacious, with polished wood floors, reproduction period furniture, and blue-and-white bathrooms with underfloor heating and whirlpool baths; many have views over the Palace Gardens below. The hotel has an excellent **restaurant** (Map p328; 257 533 322; www.terasauzlatestudne.cz; U Zlaté Studně 4; mains 720-1150Kč; noon-11pm; Malostranská) and terrace with a superb outlook over the city.

HUNGER WALL RESIDENCE APARTMENTS €€
Map p328 (257 404 040; www.hungerwall.eu; Plaská 8; 2-person apt from 2850Kč; ; 6, 9, 12, 20) The Hunger Wall offers bright, stylish, modernised apartments at very reasonable rates. From the smiling welcome at reception to the spotlessly clean rooms, the atmosphere here is resolutely 'new Prague', with facilities that include an excellent cafe (p87), a conference room and a tiny gym. Located in the quieter southern part of Malá Strana, you're only two tram stops south of Malostranské náměstí and Charles Bridge.

PENSION DIENTZENHOFER PENSION €€
Map p328 (257 311 319; www.dientzenhofer.cz; Nosticova 2; s/d/ste from 1725/2425/3750Kč; ; 12, 20, 22) Take a room in this homely pension and you're rubbing shoulders with famous figures from the past – this lovely 16th-century house was once the home of the Dientzenhofer family of architects who designed many of Prague's most famous baroque landmarks. Set in a peaceful park only five minutes' walk from Charles Bridge, the house has seven plain but comfortable rooms and a couple of good-value suites that sleep up to five.

DESIGN HOTEL SAX HOTEL €€
Map p328 (257 531 268; www.hotelsax.cz; Jánský vršek 3; s/d from 2175/2950Kč; ; 12, 20, 22) Set in a quiet corner of Malá Strana, amid embassies and monastery gardens, the Sax is refreshingly different. The building is 18th-century on the outside, but the interior has been remodelled with classic furniture and design from the 1950s, '60s and '70s. There's a dramatic glass-roofed atrium where the courtyard used to be; bold and colourful retro decor; stylish, uncluttered bedrooms and impeccable service.

DŮM U VELKÉ BOTY PENSION €€
Map p328 (257 532 088; www.dumuvelkeboty.cz; Vlašská 30; d 3150Kč; ; 12, 20, 22) Location, location, location – those three little words that mean so much. The quaint little 'House at the Big Boot' is on a quiet square opposite the German embassy, just five minutes' walk from the castle, and the same from Charles Bridge. The warren of ancient rooms is furnished in an understated and elegant way, with a period atmosphere – for families, there are two neighbouring doubles that share a bathroom – and the owners are unfailingly helpful.

Staré Město

RESIDENCE KAROLINA APARTMENTS €€
Map p332 (224 990 900; www.residencekarolina.com; Karoliny Světlé 4; 2-/4-person apt 3175/5475Kč; ; 6, 9, 19, 21, 22) We're going to have to invent a new category of accommodation – boutique apartments – to cover this array of 20 beautifully furnished flats. Offering one- or two-bedroom options, all apartments have spacious seating areas with comfy sofas and flat-screen TVs, sleek modern kitchens and dining areas. The location is good too, set back on a quiet street but close to a major tram stop, and just two blocks from a Tesco supermarket for your self-catering supplies.

SAVIC HOTEL HOTEL €€€
Map p332 (224 248 555; www.savic.eu; Jilská 7; r from 4125Kč; ; Národní Třída) From the complimentary glass of wine when you arrive to the comfy king-size beds, the Savic certainly knows how to make you feel welcome. Housed in the former monastery of St Giles, the hotel is bursting with character and full of delightful period details including old stone fireplaces, beautiful painted timber ceilings and fragments of frescoes. The bedrooms are furnished in antique style with parquet floors, dark wooden furniture, wingback armchairs and plush sofas, while the bathrooms are lined with polished marble.

GRAND HOTEL PRAHA APARTMENTS €€€
Map p332 (221 632 556; www.grandhotelpraha.cz; Staroměstské náměstí 22-25; r from 4250Kč, apt from 6225Kč; ; Staroměstská) Three lovely baroque buildings on the Old Town Square have been converted into a luxury hotel with large, well-appointed rooms filled with heavy antique furniture and rugs, paintings, wooden floors and chandeliers. Some have the additional charm of painted wooden-beamed ceilings. The most luxurious rooms are in the 'Apostolic Residence' at No 25, which also boasts a magnificent attic apartment (sleeps up to five) with spiral staircase and massive timber beams. The unique selling point, though, is its location – you can hang out your window and watch the Astronomical Clock do its thing.

HOTEL U MEDVÍDKŮ PENSION €€

Map p332 (224 211 916; www.umedvidku.cz; Na Perštýně 7; s/d/tr from 1950/2450/2950Kč; @; Národní Třída) Cosy and centrally located, 'At the Little Bear' is a traditional beer hall (p111) on the southern edge of the Old Town that also provides accommodation. The rooms have polished hardwood floors and dark wooden furniture, with good-sized bathrooms (and good water pressure in the showers). Some of the 1st-floor rooms have Renaissance painted wooden ceilings, and a few are almost big enough to be called a suite (the 'historic' rooms, which have a bit of character, cost 10% more than the ordinary ones).

HOTEL JOSEF BOUTIQUE HOTEL €€

Map p332 (221 700 111; www.hoteljosef.com; Rybná 20; s/d from 3225/3475Kč; @; Náměstí Republiky) Designed by London-based Czech architect Eva Jiřičná, the Josef is one of Prague's most stylish contemporary hotels. The minimalist theme that is evident in the stark, white lobby with its glass spiral staircase is continued in the bedrooms, where things are kept clean and simple with plenty of subtle neutral tones. The glass-walled en suites are especially attractive, boasting extra-large rainfall shower heads and glass bowl basins.

PERLA HOTEL BOUTIQUE HOTEL €€

Map p332 (221 667 707; www.perlahotel.cz; Perlová 1; s/d from 1975/2225Kč; ; Můstek) The 'Pearl' on Pearl St is typical of the slinky, appealing designer hotels that have sprung up all over central Prague. Here the designer has picked a – surprise, surprise – pearl motif that extends from the giant pearls that form the reception desk to the silky, lustrous bedspreads and huge screen prints on the bedroom walls. The rooms are on the small side, but the decor is sleek and modern with muted colours offset by bright-red lacquered chairs and glossy black-tiled bathrooms.

U ZELENÉHO VĚNCE PENSION €€

Map p332 (222 220 178; www.uzv.cz; Řetězová 10; s/d/tr 2000/2600/2900Kč; @; 17, 18) Located on a quiet side street, but only a few minutes' stroll from the Old Town Square, the 'Green Garland' is a surprisingly rustic retreat right in the heart of the city. Set in a restored 14th-century building, it takes its name from the house-sign above the door. The bedrooms vary in size – some cramped and some spacious – but all are spotlessly clean and simply but appealingly decorated, with exposed medieval roof beams in the attic rooms. The English-speaking owner is unfailingly polite and helpful.

OLD PRAGUE HOSTEL HOSTEL €

Map p332 (224 829 058; www.oldpraguehostel.com; Benediktská 2; dm from 375Kč, s/d from 1000/1200Kč; @; Náměstí Republiky) Cheerful and welcoming, with colourful homemade murals brightening the walls, this is one of Prague's most sociable hostels, with a good mix of people from backpackers to families. Facilities are good, with lockers in the dorms, luggage storage and 24-hour reception, though the mattresses on the bunks are a bit on the thin side. The staff are very helpful and the location could hardly be more central, just five minutes' walk east of the Old Town Square.

Nové Město

MOSAIC HOUSE HOTEL, HOSTEL €€

Map p338 (221 595 350; www.mosaichouse.com; Odboru 4; s/d from 1840/2520Kč, dm from 300Kč; ; Karlovo Náměstí) A blend of four-star hotel and boutique hostel, Mosaic House is a cornucopia of designer detail, from the original 1930s mosaic in the entrance hall to the silver spray-painted tree brances used as clothes-hanging racks. The backpackers dorms are kept separate from the private rooms, but have the same high-quality decor and design. The top-floor private bedrooms cost about 33% more than standard doubles but are worth it for the spacious balconies with city views, and the relative peace and quiet. All have incredibly stylish bathrooms with water-efficient raindance showers; other green technology includes the use of intelligent heating systems, solar panels and greywater recycling.

FUSION HOTEL BOUTIQUE HOTEL, HOSTEL €

Map p336 (226 222 800; www.fusionhotels.com; Panská 9; dm/d/tr 400/2000/2600Kč; @; 3, 9, 14, 24) Billing itself as an 'affordable design hotel', Fusion certainly has style in abundance. From the revolving bar and the funky sofas that litter the public areas, to the individually decorated bedrooms that resemble miniature modern-art galleries – all white walls and black trim with tiny splashes of colour – the place exudes 'cool'. You can choose between the world's most stylish backpacker dorms and private doubles, triples and family rooms, all decorated with works by young Czech artists and kitted out with hi-tech extras such as Apple TV.

HOTEL YASMIN BOUTIQUE HOTEL €€

Map p338 (234 100 100; www.hotel-yasmin.cz; Politických Vězňů 12; r from 3600Kč; P; Muzeum) This designer hotel, a block east of Wenceslas Square, is very cutting edge, a blend of space age and organic. The public areas are covered in motifs in the shape of jasmine blossoms and decorated with birch-twig arrangements and chrome balls. The spacious bedrooms have a neutral palette of white, beige and tan, the clean lines set off by plants, flowers or a curved edge; the bathrooms are in black tile and chrome.

HOTEL SUITE HOME APARTMENTS €€

Map p338 (222 230 833; www.hotelsuitehomeprague.com; Příčná 2; 2-person ste from 3850Kč; ; Karlovo Náměstí) Straddling the divide between apartments and hotels, this place offers the space and convenience of a suite with private bathroom and kitchen along with hotel facilities such as 24-hour reception, maid service and breakfast room. It's a good choice for families, with suites for up to six; the rooms are pleasantly old-fashioned, and some on the upper floors have good views towards the castle. There's a lift, though it's a bit on the small side – important, as the building has five floors. Check the website for special rates.

ICON HOTEL BOUTIQUE HOTEL €€€

Map p338 (221 634 100; www.iconhotel.eu; V Jámě 6; r from 3000Kč; ; 3, 9, 14, 24) Staff clothes by Diesel, computers by Apple, beds by Hästens – pretty much everything in this gorgeous boutique hotel has a designer stamp on it. Appearing on Europe's trendiest hotels lists, the Icon's sleekly minimalist rooms are enlivened with a splash of imperial purple from the silky bedspreads, while the curvy, reproduction art-deco armchairs are supplied by Modernista (p114). Hi-tech touches include iPod docks, Skype phones and fingerprint-activated safes.

HOTEL 16 U SV KATEŘINY HOTEL €€

Map p338 (224 920 636; www.hotel16.cz; Kateřinská 16; s/d/tr 2400/3000/3600Kč; ; Karlovo Náměstí) Near the Botanic Gardens and about five minutes' walk from Karlovo Náměstí metro station, Hotel 16 is a friendly, family-run place with just 14 rooms, tucked away in a very quiet corner of town where you're more likely to hear birdsong than traffic. The rooms vary in size and are simply but smartly furnished; the best, at the back, have views onto the peaceful terraced garden. Buffet breakfast is included in the price, and the hotel has a lift.

MISS SOPHIE'S HOSTEL €

Map p338 (296 303 530; www.miss-sophies.com; Melounova 3; dm from 410Kč, s/d/apt 1760/2000/2360Kč; ; IP Pavlova) This hostel makes a pleasant change from the usual characterless backpacker hive. There's a touch of contemporary style here, with oak-veneer floors and stark, minimalist decor – the main motif is 'distressed' concrete, along with neutral colours and black metal-framed beds. The place is famous for its 'designer' showers, with autographed glass screens and huge rainfall shower heads. There is a very cool lounge in the basement, with red-brick vaults and black leather sofas, and reception (open 24 hours) is staffed by a young, multilingual crew who are always eager to help.

ARTHARMONY PENSION €

Map p338 (222 542 931; www.artharmony.cz; Ječná 12; dm/d from 325/1800Kč; ; 4, 6, 10, 16, 22) Quirkily decorated with colourful wall paintings, rustic timber and real silver-birch trees, this pension stands out from the crowd. There's an easygoing, family-friendly, vaguely hippy-ish atmosphere; you can choose to stay in a shared room (from three to six people, doesn't really feel like a dorm), a private room with shared bathroom, or a private room with en suite. Staff are super helpful, and there's a residents' lounge and communal kitchen. Note – reception is on the 2nd floor, and there is no elevator.

Vinohrady & Vršovice

LE PALAIS HOTEL HOTEL €€€

Map p344 (234 634 111; www.vi-hotels.com; U Zvonařky 1, Vinohrady; r from €230, ste from €400; P; 6, 11) Le Palais is housed in a gorgeous belle époque building dating from the end of the 19th century that was once home to Czech artist Luděk Marold (1865–98; his former apartment is now rooms 407 to 412). It has been beautifully restored, complete with original floor mosaics, period fireplaces, marble staircases, wrought-iron balustrades, frescoes, painted ceilings and delicate stucco work.

The luxury bedrooms are decorated in warm shades of yellow and pink, while the various suites – some located in the corner tower, some with a south-facing balcony – make the most of the hotel's superb location, perched on top of a bluff with views of the Vyšehrad fortress. Within easy walking distance of bars and restaurants in Vinohrady and about 15 minutes by foot from the top of Wenceslas Square.

LOUREN HOTEL BOUTIQUE HOTEL €€€

Map p344 (☎224 250 025; www.louren.cz; Slezská 55, Vinohrady; s/d/ste 4500/4800/5500Kč; ; 11, M Jiřího z Poděbrad) Popular with business travellers, the Louren is a small luxury hotel with 13 rooms and seven suites, set in a grand 19th-century apartment building. Stylish decor and attentive service are accompanied by thoughtful little touches such as bathrobes and fresh flowers. The rooms are decorated in restful, neutral tones (lots of cream and light wood).

The building dates from 1889 and has been restored to its former grandeur. Service can't be faulted, and the staff are courteous and very helpful. Rates are frequently discounted on its website.

ARKADA BOUTIQUE HOTEL €€

Map p344 (☎242 429 111; www.arkadahotel.cz; Balbínová 8, Vinohrady; s/d from €70/90; P; 11, M Muzeum) This relatively new hotel in Vinohrady comes highly recommended for offering a great combination of style, comfort and location. The rooms are well appointed, with a retro-1930s feel that fits the style of the building. Rooms have flatscreen TVs, free internet access and minibars. Ask to see a couple before choosing, since the decor differs from room to room.

The location is about five minutes by foot to the top of Wenceslas Square and within easy walking distance of some of the best Vinohrady clubs and restaurants.

CZECH INN HOSTEL, HOTEL €

Map p344 (☎267 267 600; www.czech-inn.com; Francouzská 76, Vinohrady; dm 285-385Kč, s/d 1320/1540Kč, apt from 1650Kč; P; 4, 22) The Czech Inn calls itself a hostel, but the boutique label wouldn't be out of place. Everything seems sculpted by an industrial designer, from the iron beds to the brushed-steel flooring and minimalist square sinks. The Czech Inn offers a variety of accommodation, from standard hostel dorm rooms to good-value private doubles (with or without attached bathroom) and apartments.

A bank of internet terminals in the lobby and an excellent buffet breakfast in the adjoining bar-cafe round out the charms. The nearest metro station is 10 minutes on foot or a short tram ride away.

PENSION KRÁLOVSKÝ VINOHRAD PENSION €

Map p344 (☎222 515 093; www.kralovskyvinohrad.cz; Šmilovského 10, Vinohrady; d from 1500Kč, ste from 2100Kč; P; 4, 22) This pension occupies a lovely 1910 apartment building in a leafy backstreet. The cheaper rooms are plain but functional, while the larger rooms and 'suites' (two-room apartments) are more stylishly decorated and furnished with antiques and stripped pine furniture. The suites also have minibars and tables and chairs. Offers steep discounts on the website.

HOTEL ANNA HOTEL, PENSION €€

Map p344 (☎222 513 111; www.hotelanna.cz; Budečská 17, Vinohrady; s/d from €70/90, ste from €100; P; M Náměstí Míru) Hotel Anna is small and friendly, with helpful and knowledgeable employees. The late-19th-century building retains many of its art-nouveau features, and the bedrooms are bright and cheerful with floral bedspreads and arty black-and-white photos of Prague buildings on the walls. There are two small suites on the top floor, one of which has a great view towards the castle.

The hotel is tucked away on a quiet backstreet but close to the metro and lots of good restaurants and bars; you can walk to the top end of Wenceslas Square in 10 minutes. Check the website for special offers.

HOLIDAY HOME PENSION €

Map p344 (☎222 512 710; www.holidayhome.cz; Americká 37, Vinohrady; s/d from 1225/1450Kč; P; M Náměstí Míru) This simple pension offers good value in one of the city's nicest residential neighbourhoods. Don't expect anything fancy in spite of the elegant setting. The rooms are plain and small, with tiny beds. The location is ideal, just a short walk to the Náměstí Míru metro stop.

AMETYST BOUTIQUE HOTEL €€€

Map p344 (222 921 921; www.hotelametyst.cz; Jana Masaryka 11, Vinohrady; s/d from €160/225; P; Náměstí Míru) The polished Ametyst straddles the line between boutique and hotel, with just enough style points in the lobby (nice retro flagstone) and the rooms (hardwood floors, arty lamps and flatscreen TVs) to put it in the boutique camp. All the rooms have air-conditioning and wi-fi access, and there are tubs and hair dryers in the bathrooms.

On a negative note, rack rates have risen steeply in the past couple of years, though the hotel does offer frequent discounts on its website. There are dozens of places to relax within easy walking distance in one of the nicest parts of leafy Vinohrady.

HOTEL LUNÍK HOTEL €€

Map p344 (224 253 974; www.hotel-lunik.cz; Londýnská 50, Vinohrady; s/d from 2100/3000Kč; P; Náměstí Míru or IP Pavlova) Clean, attractive and smallish, Hotel Luník is on a quiet residential street a block from Peace Square and between the Náměstí Míru and IP Pavlova metro stations. The lobby and public areas exude a quiet sophistication. The rooms are homey and slightly old-fashioned, with attractive green-tiled bathrooms. The friendly receptionist may be willing to negotiate room rates on slow nights.

ORION APARTMENTS €€

Map p344 (222 521 706; www.okhotels.cz; Americká 9, Vinohrady; 2-/4-person apt 2100/2400Kč; P; Náměstí Míru) Good-value apartment rentals in an upmarket section of Vinohrady, within easy walking distance of Náměstí Míru and Havlíčkovy sady. All 26 apartments are equipped with a small kitchen, including a fridge and coffeemaker. Several have multiple rooms and can accommodate groups. Ask to see a couple of rooms since they are slightly different. Some come with hardwood floors, others with carpet.

Žižkov & Karlín

HOTEL ALWYN BOUTIQUE HOTEL €€

Map p346 (222 334 200; www.hotelalwyn.cz; Vítkova 26, Karlín; s/d from 2900/3400Kč; 8, 24) The Alwyn is the first designer hotel to appear in the up-and-coming district of Karlín. Set on a quiet side street only a few tram stops east of Staré Město, the hotel sports deliciously modern decor in shades of chocolate brown, beige and burnt orange, with lots of polished wood and deco-style sofas in the cocktail bar, and super-comfortable Hästens beds in the rooms. It's designed for both business and pleasure, with a conference room, gym, sauna and massage centre.

HOTEL THEATRINO HOTEL €€

Map p346 (227 031 894; www.hoteltheatrino.cz; Bořivojova 53, Žižkov; s/d from 1925/2125Kč; 5, 9, 26) The design of some hotels could be described as theatrical, but there can't be too many that were actually designed as a theatre. Dating from 1910, the art- nouveau building that houses this hotel was originally a cultural centre, Žižkov's equivalent of the Municipal House – guests here can enjoy a buffet breakfast in what was originally the theatre auditorium. The rooms are plain and modern, but the public areas are filled with beautiful period features, from wrought-iron handrails to stained-glass windows.

HOSTEL ELF HOSTEL €

Map p346 (222 540 963; www.hostelelf.com; Husitská 11, Žižkov; dm from 340Kč, s/d 1230/1960Kč; Florenc) Young, hip and sociable, Hostel Elf welcomes a steady stream of party-hearty backpackers from across the globe to its well-maintained dorms. The dorms are immaculately clean and brightly decorated with graffiti art and murals. There's a little beer-garden terrace and cosy lounge, with free tea and coffee and cheap beer, and Žižkov with its many pubs is right on the doorstep; the downside is the noisy train line that runs close by. The hostel is less than 10 minutes' walk from Florenc bus and metro stations; the area looks run-down, but is safe.

Holešovice, Bubeneč & Dejvice

ABSOLUTUM HOTEL BOUTIQUE HOTEL €€

Map p348 (222 541 406; www.absolutumhotel.cz; Jablonského 639/4, Holešovice; s/d 2500/3200Kč; P; Praha-Holešovice Nádraží Holešovice) A highly recommended, eye-catching boutique hotel, the Absolutum is located across from Nádraží Holešovice metro station. While the neighbourhood wouldn't win a beauty contest, the hotel compensates with a nice list of amenities, including beautifully designed rooms with exposed brickwork, well-appointed modern bathrooms (many rooms have a tub), air-conditioning, an excellent restaurant, a wellness centre and free parking.

The friendly receptionist is sometimes willing to cut rates if you happen to arrive on a slow night. The hotel restaurant is close enough to Praha-Holešovice train station that you could jump over for a quick meal if you have to wait for a train.

SIR TOBY'S HOSTEL HOSTEL €

Map p348 (246 032 610; www.sirtobys.com; Dělnická 24, Holešovice; dm 200-400Kč, s/d 950/1200Kč; 1, 3, 5, 25) Set in a refurbished apartment building with a spacious kitchen and common room, Sir Toby's is only 10 minutes north of the city centre by tram. The dorms have between six and 10 bunks, including all-female rooms, and the bigger dorms are some of the cheapest in Prague. All rooms are light and clean, but don't expect anything fancy.

The mattresses are a little on the thin side, but all sheets and blankets are provided at no extra cost. There's a communal kitchen for self-caterers to do their thing, a lounge and a relaxing garden where you can sit back and chat.

PLAZA ALTA HOTEL HOTEL €€

Map p348 (220 407 082; www.plazahotelalta.com; Ortenovo náměstí 22, Holešovice; s/d from €80/100; 5, 12, 15, Nádraží Holešovice) The snazziest hotel in this part of town draws mostly business clientele and travellers looking for a full-service property within easy reach (one tram stop) of the Praha-Holešovice train station and the Nádraží Holešovice metro station. The rooms have a tasteful contemporary look, with comfy mattresses and bold, striped bedspreads. All of the rooms have air-conditioning and minibars.

It's great value if you manage to snag a good deal from the hotel's website. The '7 Tacos' restaurant off the lobby (open until 11pm) serves Mexican food and is not a bad option if you're arriving late and don't have the energy to go back out.

HOTEL LEON HOSTEL, HOTEL €

Map p348 (220 941 351; www.antee.cz; Ortenovo náměstí 26, Holešovice; s/d from 940/1440Kč; 5, 12, 15, Nádraží Holešovice) The Hotel Leon advertises itself as something between a hostel and a small hotel. In truth, it's actually much nicer than a standard hostel and not much more expensive (especially if you share a three- or four-bed room). The rooms are basic, with no TV or much of anything else, but are quiet and clean, with adjoining bathrooms.

If noise is an issue, ask for a quieter room overlooking the back garden. There's a common room for TV and a shared computer for internet access. It's one tram stop (Ortenovo náměstí) from the Nádraží Holešovice train and metro station.

HOTEL DENISA PENSION, HOTEL €€

Map p350 (224 318 969; www.hotel-denisa.cz; Národní Obrany 33, Dejvice; s/d from 1620/1800Kč; Dejvická) This small, family-run hotel in a turn-of-the-century apartment building on a quiet side street has been thoroughly renovated and represents excellent value for money. Rooms have nice thick mattresses, flat-screen TVs, minibars and high-speed wi-fi connections. The location has always been a plus, just a few minutes' walk to the Dejvická metro stop, as well as convenient to the airport.

ART HOTEL BOUTIQUE HOTEL €€

Map p350 (233 101 331; www.arthotel.cz; Nad Královskou Oborou 53, Bubeneč; s/d from €90/120; 1, 8, 15, 25, 26, Sparta stop) There are lots of word-of-mouth recommendations for this small hotel hidden away in the normally quiet neighbourhood behind Sparta stadium. The hotel has sleek, modern styling, with a display of contemporary Czech art in the lobby, and art photography on the walls of the rooms.

The hotel may look out of the way on the map, but it's only a few minutes' walk from tram 8, which will take you to the city centre in about 10 minutes.

PLUS PRAGUE HOSTEL HOSTEL €

Map p348 (220 510 046; www.plusprague.com; Přívozní 1, Holešovice; dm 300Kč, r 1600Kč; Nádraží Holešovice) The cheerful Plus Prague Hostel is one tram stop from Nádraží Holešovice (take any tram heading east as you exit the station to Ortenovo náměstí). Cheap rates, clean rooms with en suite bathrooms, friendly staff and an indoor swimming pool make this a special place. It also offers four- to eight-bed female-only dorm rooms, outfitted with hair dryers and fluffier towels.

HOTEL CROWNE PLAZA HOTEL €€

Map p350 (☎296 537 111; www.ichotelsgroup.com; Koulova 15, Dejvice; d from €90; P ⊖ ❄ @ ☜; 🚋8, Zelená stop) Originally called the Hotel International, this stunning Socialist Realist palace was built in the 1950s in the style of Moscow University, complete with Soviet star atop the tower. The rooms are mostly standard chain-hotel style, with all the necessities but not many luxuries. The deluxe rooms, on the higher floors, are more spacious and have good views over the city.

The building itself is really something special, covered in polished marble, bas-reliefs and frescoes of the noble worker. The Socialist-style 'luxury' extends to the beautiful lobby. Tram 8 can take you to the city centre in about 15 minutes.

HOTEL BELVEDERE HOTEL €€

Map p348 (☎220 106 111; www.hhotels.cz; Milady Horákové 19, Holešovice; s/d from 1800/2200Kč; P ⊖ @ ☜; 🚋1, 8, 15, 25, 26) The Belvedere is an old communist-era hotel that has been completely refurbished, and now provides good-value accommodation within easy reach of the city centre. The standard rooms are nothing special, but they're comfortable and spotlessly clean. The 'executive' rooms (from 3000Kč in season) are much more spacious, with soundproofed windows, smart crimson drapes and bedspreads, and huge marble-lined bathrooms.

Check the website for occasional steep discounts, especially in mid-summer. The large breakfast room has a slightly institutional feel, but the food is good and there's plenty of it. There's a tram stop outside the front door, and it's only 10 minutes to Náměstí Republiky metro station on tram 8. There's a good Japanese restaurant on the ground floor.

A&O HOSTEL HOSTEL €

Map p348 (☎220 870 252; www.aohostels.com; U Výstaviště 1/262, Holešovice; dm €12, s/d €15/36; ⊖ @ ☜; MNádraží Holešovice) This clean, well-maintained hostel is in a converted apartment building a short walk from the Nádraží Holešovice train and metro stations. The rooms are plain with wooden floors and white walls, lending a slightly institutional feel. The rates fluctuate from day to day, depending on demand. Book well in advance to lock in a lower rate.

HOTEL EXTOL INN HOTEL €

Map p348 (☎220 802 549; www.extolinn.cz; Přístavní 2, Holešovice; s/d from 1050/1500Kč; P ⊖ @ ☜; 🚋1, 3, 5, 25) The bright, modern Extol Inn provides budget accommodation in an up-and-coming neighbourhood within easy reach of the city centre. The cheapest rooms (on the upper floors) are basic, no-frills affairs with shared bathrooms. More expensive three-star rooms (doubles from 1800Kč) have private bathrooms, TVs, minibars and free use of the hotel spa. There's a public internet terminal in the lobby. Wheelchair-accessible.

HOTEL LETNÁ PENSION, HOTEL €

Map p350 (☎233 374 763; www.prague-hotelletna.com; Na Výšinách 8, Bubeneč; s/d from €50/60; P ⊖ @ ☜; 🚋1, 8, 15, 25, 26) Small and pleasant, Hotel Letná is in a 19th-century apartment block on a quiet street not far from Sparta Stadium. Don't be put off by the musty lobby; the rooms are fresher and are quiet and clean. Most have minibars, and tubs and hair dryers in the bathroom. Ask to see several rooms since they are all slightly different.

Smíchov & Vyšehrad

ANDĚL'S HOTEL PRAGUE BOUTIQUE HOTEL €€€

Map p342 (☎296 889 688; www.vi-hotels.com; Stroupežnického 21, Smíchov; r from €150; P ⊖ ❄ @ ☜; MAnděl) This sleek designer hotel, all stark contemporary in white with black and red accents, has floor-to-ceiling windows, DVD and CD players, internet access and modern art in every room. The bathrooms are a wonderland of polished chrome and frosted glass. The website offers packages with significant discounts from the rack rate.

Superior 'club rooms' come with pleasurable perks, such as bathrobes and slippers, newspapers delivered to your room and free room-service breakfast.

ANGELO HOTEL BOUTIQUE HOTEL €€€

Map p342 (☎234 801 111; www.vi-hotels.com; Radlická 1g, Smíchov; r from €130; P ⊖ ❄ @ ☜; MAnděl) The Angelo is the brighter, more-extravagant cousin of nearby Anděl's Hotel. It has the same slick lobby presentation and hi-tech room decor, but instead of the Anděl's muted whites, the Angelo is a riot of rich colour. Both are owned by the same Austrian group, Vienna International, and there's not much difference between the two in terms of price or service.

HOTEL UNION HOTEL €€

(☎261 214 812; www.hotelunion.cz; Ostrčilovo náměstí 4, Vyšehrad; s/d 1800/3000Kč; P ⊖ ❄ @ ᯤ; 🚊7, 18, 24) A grand old hotel from 1906, the Union was nationalised by the communists in 1958 and returned to the former owner's family in 1991. Comfortably renovated, with a few period touches left intact, the hotel is at the foot of the hill below Vyšehrad fortress. Bedrooms are plain but pleasant.

Ask for one of the deluxe corner rooms, which are huge and have bay windows with a view of either Vyšehrad or distant Prague Castle.

HOTEL JULIAN HOTEL €€

Map p342 (☎257 311 150; www.hoteljulian.com; Elišky Peškové 11, Smíchov; s/d from €105/130; P ⊖ ❄ @ ᯤ; 🚊6, 9, 12, 20) A deservedly popular small hotel with helpful staff and a quiet location just south of Malá Strana. The smart, well-kept bedrooms are decorated with relaxing pastels and pine-topped furniture. The public areas include a clubby drawing room with a library and open fire. The property markets itself as a 'romantic' hotel and offers special deals over the internet for couples.

If you're travelling with kids or in a group, there are a couple of family rooms that can hold up to six people, and there's also a wheelchair-accessible room. The in-room air-conditioning can be a life-saver in hot weather.

HOTEL ARBES-MEPRO HOTEL €€

Map p342 (☎257 210 410; www.hotelarbes.cz; Viktora Huga 3, Smíchov; s/d from 1900/2400Kč; P ⊖ @; M Anděl) Clean, quiet and excellent value, the Arbes is a down-to-earth tonic to the many high-rise, flashier hotels in Smíchov. The hotel is family-run and friendly, and the rooms are basic, with modern furnishings and clean bathrooms. Ask for a courtyard room if noise is an issue. There's limited street parking, but there's paid parking near the hotel (per night 450Kč).

Viktora Huga is a quiet street, about two blocks from the Anděl metro station and the Nový Smíchov (p173) shopping centre, with excellent connections to the centre.

IBIS PRAHA MALÁ STRANA HOTEL €€

Map p342 (☎221 701 700; www.ibishotel.com; Plzeňská 14, Smíchov; s/d from €69/89; P ⊖ ❄ @ ᯤ; M Anděl) Nevermind it's nowhere near Malá Strana (but nice try by the marketing department), Smíchov's IBIS hotel is a great addition to the neighbourhood, offering a little of the splash of Anděl's Hotel (p195), but at less than half the price. The rooms are standard issue, but they have air-conditioning and free wi-fi. Breakfast not included.

The building's aggressively modern style actually looks rather good amid the futuristic boxes found around the area of the Anděl metro station. It's also an easy walk to public transport and the shopping centre.

ARPACAY HOSTEL HOSTEL €

Map p342 (☎251 552 297; www.arpacayhostel.com; Radlická 76, Smíchov; dm 320-400Kč, s/d 800/1300Kč; P ⊖ @ ᯤ; 🚊7, M Smíchovské Nádraží) This clean, colourful hostel is near the Smíchovské Nádraží train station and is the best cheap accommodation in the immediate vicinity. Though it is not within walking distance of the centre, it's not a bad trip with metro line B from the train station (access via a bridge across the tracks) or with tram 7, which leaves practically from the hostel's doorstep.

The relatively remote location keeps prices a little lower here than at competing hostels, and there's free wi-fi throughout. Accommodation is in two buildings that straddle a busy road. There's a small terrace out back of the main building for relaxing on warm evenings.

Best of Bohemia

EXPLORE BOHEMIA

The Czech Republic's western province boasts surprising variety. Český Krumlov, with its riverside setting and dramatic Renaissance castle, is in a class by itself, but lesser-known towns like Třeboň in the south and Loket in the west exude unexpected charm. Big cities like České Budějovice and Plzeň offer urban attractions like great museums and restaurants. The spa towns of western Bohemia were world famous in the 19th century and retain old-world lustre.

Bohemia in One Week

Focus your efforts: choose between the historic castle towns of the south or the spa resorts of the west. Český Krumlov deserves two nights, with your remaining time split between Třeboň and České Budějovice. If you opt for the west, spend a night in Plzeň and divide the rest of the week between Karlovy Vary and Mariánské Lázně.

Bohemia in Two Weeks

Two weeks is enough time to fully explore the province. Spend one week in the south, enjoying Český Krumlov and České Budějovice. For the second week, head west: book a long stay at a spa and treat yourself like royalty.

České Budějovice

Explore

České Budějovice (pronounced chesky *bood*-yo-vit-zah) is the provincial capital of southern Bohemia and a natural base

Bohemia

for exploring the region. Transport connections to nearby Český Krumlov are good, meaning you could easily spend the day there and evenings here. While České Budějovice lacks top sights, it does have one of Europe's largest main squares (the biggest in the Czech Republic) and a charming labyrinth of narrow lanes and winding alleyways. It's also the home of 'Budvar' beer (aka Czech 'Budweiser'), and a brewery tour usually tops the 'must-do' list.

The Best...

➡ **Sight** Budweiser Budvar Brewery (p199)

➡ **Place to Eat** Masné Kramý (p201)

➡ **Place to Drink** Mighty Bar Velbloud (p203)

Top Tip

If you're traveling during the ice-hockey season (September to April) try to catch the home team **HC Mountfield** in action at Budvar Arena (p204). Tickets can usually be bought on the spot.

Getting There & Away

Bus From Prague, **Student Agency** (☎800 100 300; www.studentagency.cz) yellow buses leave from Na Knížecí bus station (150Kč, 2½ hours) at the Anděl metro station (Line B). There are decent bus services from České Budějovice to Český Krumlov (35Kč, 45 minutes), Tábor (70Kč, one hour) and Třeboň (40Kč, 30 minutes).

Train From Prague, there's a frequent train service (222Kč, 2½ hours, hourly). Regular (slow) trains trundle to Český Krumlov (32Kč, 45 minutes).

Car From Prague, the drive takes 2½ hours following the D1 motorway toward Brno and then heading south on Hwy E55.

Need to Know

➡ **Location** 160km south of Prague.

➡ **Municipal Information Centre** (Městské Informarční Centrum; ☎386 801 413; www.c-budejovice.cz; náměstí Přemysla Otakara II 2; ⌚8.30am-6pm Mon-Fri, to 5pm Sat, 10am-4pm Sun May-Sep, 9am-5pm Mon-Fri, to 1pm Sat, closed Sun Oct-Apr) Books tickets, tours and accommodation, and has free internet.

➡ **Česká Spořitelna** (☎956 744 630; www.csas.cz; FA Gerstnera 2151/6; ⌚8.30am-4pm Mon-Fri) ATM and currency exchange.

SIGHTS

BUDWEISER BUDVAR BREWERY BREWERY

(☎387 705 347; www.visitbudvar.cz; cnr Pražská & K Světlé; adult/child 100/50Kč; ⌚9am-5pm daily Mar-Dec, Tue-Sat Jan & Feb; 2) One of the highlights of a trip to České Budějovice is a chance to see where original Budweiser beer was born. Brewery tours depart daily at 2pm from April to November. The tour highlights modern production methods, with the reward being a glass of Budvar deep in the brewery's chilly cellars. The brewery is 3km north of the main square.

In the 19th century, the founders of US brewer Anheuser-Busch chose the brand name Budweiser because it was synonymous with good beer. Since the late 19th century, both breweries have used the name, and a legal arm-wrestle over the brand continues. The legal machinations subsided slightly in 2007, with Anheuser-Busch signing a deal to distribute Budvar (as 'Czechvar') in the USA. To confuse matters, České Budějovice's second brewery, Samson, produces a beer called 'BB Budweiser'.

NÁMĚSTÍ PŘEMYSLA OTAKARA II SQUARE

Map p200 (náměstí Přemysla Otakara II) This mix of arcaded buildings centred on **Samson's Fountain** (Samsonova kašna; 1727) is the broadest plaza in the country, spanning 133m. Among the architectural treats is the 1555 Renaissance **Town Hall** (radnice), which received a baroque facelift in 1731. The figures on the balustrade – Justice, Wisdom, Courage and Prudence – are matched by an exotic quartet of bronze gargoyles.

BLACK TOWER TOWER

Map p200 (Černá věž; ☎386 801 413; U Černé věže 70/2; adult/concession 30/20Kč; ⌚10am-6pm Tue-Sun Apr-Oct) This dominating, 72m Gothic-Renaissance tower was built in 1553. Climb its 225 steps (yes, we counted them) for fine views. The tower's two **bells** – the Marta (1723) and Budvar (1995; a gift from the brewery) – are rung daily at noon.

Beside the tower is the **Cathedral of St Nicholas** (katedrála sv Mikuláše), built as a church in the 13th century, rebuilt in 1649, then made a cathedral in 1784.

MUSEUM OF SOUTH BOHEMIA MUSEUM

Map p200 (Jihočeské muzeum; ☎387 929 311; www.muzeumcb.cz; Dukelská 1; ⌚see website)

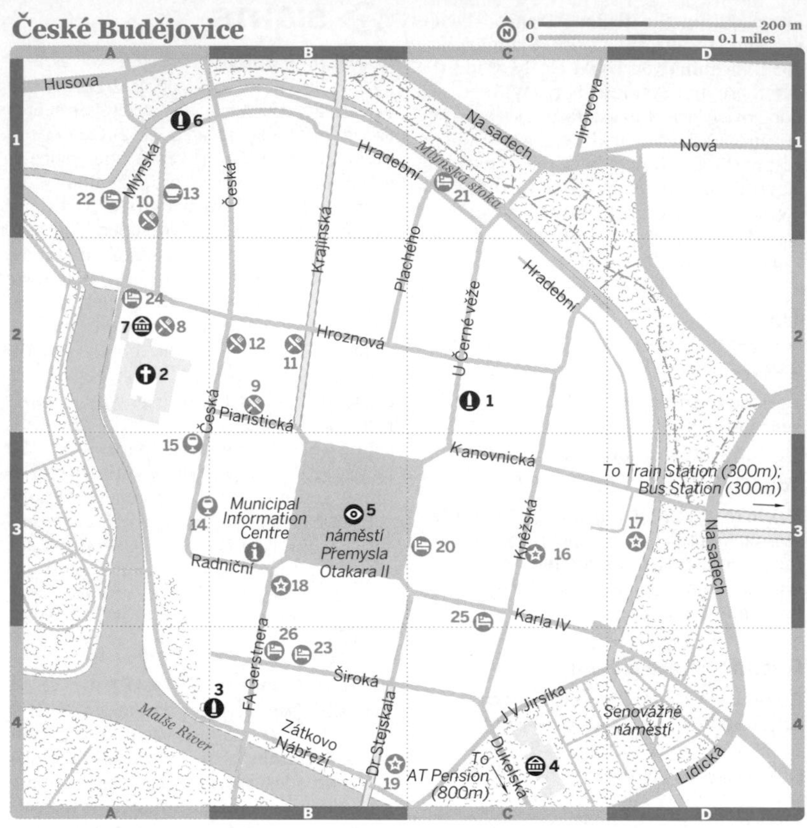

České Budějovice

Sights

1 Black Tower C2
2 Church of the Sacrifice of the Virgin A2
3 Iron Maiden Tower B4
4 Museum of South Bohemia C4
5 Náměstí Přemysla Otakara II B3
6 Rabenštejn Tower A1
7 South Bohemian Motorcycle Museum A2

Eating

8 Fresh Salad & Pizza A2
Greenhouse .... (see 26)
9 Indická B2
10 La Cabana A1
11 Masné Kramý B2
12 U Tři Sedláku B2

Drinking

13 Café Hostel A1
14 Singer Pub A3
15 Vinárna Solnice A3

Entertainment

16 Chamber Philharmonic Orchestra of South Bohemia C3
17 Conservatory D3
18 Modrý Dveře Jazz & Blues B3
19 South Bohemian Theatre B4

Sleeping

20 Grandhotel Zvon C3
21 Hotel Bohemia C1
22 Hotel Budweis A1
23 Hotel Dvořak B4
24 Hotel Klika A2
25 Hotel Malý Pivovar C3
26 Penzión Centrum B4

The Museum of South Bohemia holds an enormous collection of historic books, coins and weapons. It was closed in 2012 for reconstruction and, during research for this book, it wasn't clear when it would re-open: check the website for the latest information.

Around the Old Town

The tiny alleyways that radiate from gigantic náměstí Přemysla Otakara II invite a few hours of exploration. The Old Town is surrounded by a picturesque canal, **Mlýnská stoka**, and the **Malše River**, as well as extensive gardens where the town walls once stood. Only a few bits of the Gothic fortifications remain, including the **Rabenštejn Tower** (Rabenštejnská věž; Map p200; cnr Hradební & Panská; adult/concession 40/20Kč; ⏱10am-6pm Mon-Fri, 9am-noon Sat), and the 15th-century **Iron Maiden Tower** (Železná Pana; Map p200; Zátkovo Nábřeží), a crumbling former prison. Along Hroznová, on Piaristické náměstí, is the **Church of the Sacrifice of the Virgin** (Kostel Obětování Panny Marie; Map p200; Piaristické náměstí) and a former **Dominican Monastery** with a splendid pulpit. Enter the church from the Gothic cloister.

SOUTH BOHEMIAN MOTORCYCLE MUSEUM — MUSEUM

Map p200 (Jihočeské Motocyklové muzeum; ☎723 247 104; www.motomuseum.cz; Piaristické náměstí; adult/concession 50/20Kč; ⏱10am-6pm) There's nearly 100 historic motorcycles on display at this unlikely, ecclesiastical setting for a motorcycle museum. In addition to motorbikes, there are old-time bicycles and model airplanes on display.

EATING & DRINKING

MASNÉ KRAMÝ — CZECH €

Map p200 (☎387 201 301; www.masne-kramy.cz; Krajinská 13; mains 129-239Kč) No visit to České Budějovice would be complete without stopping at this renovated 16th-century meat market (now a popular pub) for excellent Czech food and a cold Budvar. You'll find all the Czech staples, including the house 'brewer's goulash', on the food menu. The drinks menu is equally important: try the superb unfiltered yeast beer. Advance booking essential.

U TŘI SEDLÁKU — CZECH €

Map p200 (☎387 222 303; www.utrisedlaku.cz; Hroznová 488; mains 100-170Kč) Locals celebrate that nothing much has changed at U Tři Sedláku since its opening in 1897. Tasty meaty dishes go with the Pilsner Urquell that's constantly being shuffled to busy tables.

INDICKÁ — INDIAN €€

Map p200 (Gateway of India; ☎777 326 200; www.indickarestaurace.cz; Piaristická 22; mains 120-220Kč; ⏱11am-11pm Mon-Sat; 📶🍴) From Chennai to the Czech Republic comes respite for travellers wanting something different. Request spicy because they're used to dealing with more timid local palates. Daily lunch specials (85Kč to 100Kč) are good value.

FRESH SALAD & PIZZA — PIZZERIA €

Map p200 (☎387 200 991; Hroznová 21; salads 70-100Kč, pizza 100-130Kč; 📶🍴) This lunch spot with outdoor tables lives up to its name, serving healthy salads and (slightly) less healthy pizza dished up by a fresh and funky, youthful crew.

LA CABANA — SPANISH €€

Map p200 (☎387 202 820; www.lacabana.org; Panská 14; tapas plates 100-150Kč, mains 220-400Kč; ⏱11am-1am Mon-Sat) Rustic and authentic Spanish food (the owners cooked in Spain for several years) can be enjoyed either in the Castilian style garden or in the lovely heritage interior here. After tapas or mains (including paella for 23Kč), ask to see the amazing upstairs room that was entirely hidden for many centuries.

GREENHOUSE — CAFE, VEGETARIAN €

Map p200 (☎387 311 802; www.chcijistzdrave.cz; Biskupská 130/3; meals 100Kč; ⏱7am-4pm Mon-Fri; 🍴) České Budějovice's best vegetarian flavours are at this modern self-service cafe. The healthy array of soups, salads and casseroles changes daily, with wraps and baguettes for smaller appetites. Here's your best chance to try organic Czech beer as well.

VINÁRNA SOLNICE — WINE BAR

Map p200 (☎775 579 427; www.vinarnasolnice.cz; Česká 66; ⏱11am-11pm Mon-Thu, to midnight Fri, 6pm-midnight Sat) This clean and friendly wine bar offers an amazing selection of the best Czech wines, as well as carefully selected bottles from Austria, Germany, Italy and elsewhere. They also have light appetisers, soups and salads to nibble on between sips.

SINGER PUB PUB

Map p200 (386 360 186; www.singerpub.cz; Česká 55) With Czech and Irish beers, and good cocktails, don't be surprised if you get the urge to rustle up something on the Singer sewing machines scattered around here. If not, challenge the regulars to a game of *foosball* with a soundtrack of noisy rock.

CAFÉ HOSTEL CAFE

Map p200 (387 204 203; www.cafehostel.cz; Panská 13; noon-10pm Mon-Fri, from 5pm Sat & Sun;) No, it's not a hostel, but it is a cosy cafe-bar with occasional DJ sets and live music. The scruffy rear garden could most charitably be described as a work in progress.

SLEEPING

HOTEL BUDWEIS HOTEL €€

Map p200 (389 822 111; www.hotelbudweis.cz; Mlýnská 6; s/d 2200-2800Kč;) The Hotel Budweis opened its doors in 2010, hived out of an old grain mill with a picturesque canal-side setting. The owners have opted for a smart contemporary look. All of the rooms have air-conditioning and are wheelchair accessible. There are two good restaurants in house, and the central location puts other eating and drinking options just a short walk away.

GRANDHOTEL ZVON HOTEL €€

Map p200 (381 601 611; www.hotel-zvon.cz; náměstí Přemysla Otakara II 28; r 2600-4400Kč;) 'Since 1533' says the sign, but we're pretty sure Zvon – one of the city's leading hotels – has been renovated since then. The ritzy facade across three main-square buildings is let down by standard rooms, but the executive rooms (add a whopping 80% to listed prices) would be classy in any town.

HOTEL BOHEMIA HOTEL €€

Map p200 (386 360 691; www.bohemiacb.cz; Hradební 20; s/d incl breakfast 1490/1790Kč;) Carved wooden doors open to a restful interior inside these two old burghers' houses in a quiet street. The restaurant comes recommended by the tourist information office.

PENZIÓN CENTRUM PENSION €€

Map p200 (387 311 801; www.penzioncentrum.cz; Biskupská 130/3; s/d/tr incl breakfast 1000/1400/1800Kč;) Huge rooms with satellite TV, queen-sized beds with crisp white linen, and thoroughly professional staff all make this a top reader-recommended spot near the main square.

HOTEL MALÝ PIVOVAR HOTEL €€

Map p200 (386 360 471; www.malypivovar.cz; Karla IV 8-10; s/d 2000/2800Kč;) With a cabinet of sports trophies and sculpted leather sofas, the lobby resembles a gentlemen's club. However the elegant and traditionally furnished rooms will please both the men and the ladies, and it's just a short stroll to the cosy Budvarka beer hall downstairs.

HOTEL KLIKA HOTEL €€

Map p200 (387 318 171; www.hotelklika.cz; Hroznová 25; s/d incl breakfast 1400/1800Kč;) This is an excellent, good-value option, with an attractive riverside location. The modern rooms are light and airy, and anywhere that integrates 14th-century walls into their design is OK by us.

HOTEL SAVOY HOTEL €€

(387 201 719; www.hotel-savoy-cb.cz; Bedřicha Smetany 1a; s/d/tr 1500/2000/2500Kčl;) The Savoy has spacious, modern rooms decorated with art-deco-style furniture (the combination works) and a quiet location just north of the Old Town. Look forward to České Budějovice's friendliest reception staff, too.

HOTEL DVOŘAK HOTEL €€

Map p200 (386 322 349; www.hoteldvorakcb.cz; náměstí Přemysla Otakara II 36; s/d 1600/2000Kč ;) Don't be fooled by the elegant facade: the Dvořak's rooms are modern and clean, but lacking character. The friendly staff and good-value last-minute specials (up to 40% off) still make this a worthwhile standby, and the location is excellent.

AT PENSION PENSION €

(386 351 598; www.atpension.cz; Dukelská 15; s/d 490/750Kč, breakfast 50Kč;) Don't hold your breath for stunning (or even late-20th-century) decor, but this convenient spot is mighty friendly with mighty big breakfasts (not included in the room rate).

UBYTOVNA U NÁDRAŽÍ HOSTEL €

(☎972 544 648; www.ubytovna.vors.cz; Dvořákova 161/14; s 450-490Kč, d 660-730Kč; ⊜@📶) Recently renovated, this tower block a few hundred metres from the bus and train stations has good-value accommodation with shared bathrooms (usually sharing with just one other room). Shared kitchens are also available; popular with longer-stay students.

ENTERTAINMENT

MIGHTY BAR VELBLOUD CLUB, LIVE MUSIC

(☎608 666 651; www.velbloud.info; U Tří lvů 4; ⏲from 5pm Mon-Sat) Loud and fun club with an eclectic schedule of live music, covering anything from neo-punk to Roma DJs to German rockabilly. Check the website to see what's on offer during your visit.

MODRÝ DVEŘE JAZZ & BLUES JAZZ, BLUES

Map p200 (☎386 359 958; www.modrydvere.cz; Biskupská 1; admission 50-70Kč; 📶) By day

WORTH A DETOUR: A WHIFF OF WINDSOR AT HLUBOKÁ NAD VLTAVOU

The delightful confection known as **Hluboká Chateau** (☎387 843 911; www.zamek-hluboka.eu; Zámek; Tour 1 adult/concession 250/160Kč, Tour 2 230/160Kč, Tour 3 170/80Kč; ⏲9am-5pm Tue-Sun May-Jun, to 6pm Jul & Aug, to 4.30pm Apr, Sep & Oct, 10am-4pm Nov- Feb, closed Mar) is one of the most popular day trips from České Budějovice. Buses make the journey to the main square in **Hluboká nad Vltavou** every 30 to 60 minutes (20 minutes, 20Kč).

A crow pecking the eyes from a Turk's head (the grisly Schwarzenberg family crest) is the recurrent motif of the chateau's decor, but this image is totally at odds with the building's overt romanticism.

Built by the Přemysl rulers in the latter half of the 13th century, Hluboká was taken from the Protestant Malovec family in 1662 as punishment for supporting an anti-Habsburg rebellion, and then sold to the Bavarian Schwarzenbergs. Two centuries later, they gave the chateau the English Tudor/Gothic face it wears today, modelling its exterior on Britain's Windsor Castle.

Crowned with crenellations and surrounded by a dainty garden, Hluboká is too prissy for some, but this remains the second-most visited chateau in Bohemia after Karlštejn, and for good reason.

There are three English-language **tours** available: Tour 1 (called the 'representation room' on the website) focuses on the castle's public areas; Tour 2 goes behind the scenes in the castle apartments; Tour 3 explores the kitchens. Tour 1 is all most visitors will need to get the flavour of the place. Unless the chateau is crowded, tours do not run between 12.30pm and 1pm; the last tour commences an hour before closing time. Tours in Czech are 100Kč cheaper. The surrounding park is open throughout the year (admission free).

An annual **music festival** (www.sinfonie.cz) is held in the chateau grounds in summer. Performances range from Czech folk to jazz and chamber music.

The exquisite **South Bohemian Aleš Gallery** (Alšova jihočeská galérie; ☎387 967 041; www.ajg.cz; Zámek 144; adult/concession 80/40Kč; ⏲9am-6pm Apr-Oct) is to the right of the castle gate in a former riding school (jízdárna). On display is a fabulous permanent collection of Czech religious art from the 14th to 16th centuries, plus 17th-century Dutch masters and changing exhibits of modern art.

While most visitors treat Hluboká as a day outing, it is possible to stay the night. The **Hotel Bakalář** (☎775 775 603; www.hotel-bakalar.cz; Masarykova 69; s/d 400/750Kc; 🅿⊜), in the middle of town, has functional rooms and a decent pub/restaurant on site, and rents-out bikes (per day 200Kč). Alternatively, the **Tourist Information Centre** (☎387 966 164; www.hluboka.cz; Masarykovo 35; ⏲9am-6pm), which has internet access and publishes a useful map, can recommend private rooms (also watch for 'Zimmer frei' or 'privát' signs along the main street, Masarykovo).

There are a few restaurants scattered about that cater to day-trippers. An easy in-out option is **Pizzerie Ionia** (☎728 258 160; www.pizzerieionia.cz; Masarykova 35; pizza 105-170Kč; ⏲noon-10pm Mon-Sat, noon-6pm Sun), just near the information centre.

Modrý Dveře is a welcoming bar/cafe with vintage pics of Sinatra. At dusk the lights dim for live music – blues and jazz on Thursdays (from 8pm), and DJs on most Friday nights.

SOUTH BOHEMIAN THEATRE THEATRE
Map p200 (Jihočeské divadlo; ☎386 356 925; www.jihoceskedivadlo.cz; Dr Stejskala 23) The city's main theatre presents plays (usually in Czech), operas and concerts.

CHAMBER PHILHARMONIC ORCHESTRA OF SOUTH BOHEMIA CLASSICAL MUSIC
Map p200 (☎386 353 561; www.music-cb.cz; Kněžská 6; tickets around 180Kč; ⏰box office 1pm-5pm Mon-Fri) Concerts take place in an atmospheric converted former church. The repertoire ranges from standard classical to folk music and children's specials: consult the website for current listings. Buy tickets at the box office or the concert venue an hour before the start of each performance.

CONSERVATORY CLASSICAL MUSIC
Map p200 (konzervatoř; ☎386 720 111; www.konzervatorcb.cz; Kanovnická 22) This musical academy hosts weekly performances.

CINESTAR CINEMA
(☎385 799 999; www.cinestar.cz; Milady Horákové 1498, Obchodní Centrum Čtyři Dvory) One kilometre west of the centre, this multiplex shows Hollywood's latest.

SPORTS & ACTIVITIES

BUDVAR ARENA ICE HOCKEY
(☎386 107 160; www.hokejcb.cz; FA Gerstnera; tickets 100-220Kč; ⏰box office from 1pm match days Sep-Apr) This winter arena is home ice for the city's Extraliga ice hockey team, **HC Mountfield**. You can purchase tickets on match days at the arena box office, or over the club's website. Check the website to see if there's a match scheduled during your visit.

PLAVECKÝ STADION SWIMMING
(☎387 949 411; www.c-budejovice.cz; Sokolský ostrov 4; per hour adult/child 50/35Kč; ⏰7am-9.45pm Mon-Fri, 10am-9.45pm Sat, 10am-7.45pm Sun) This sports hall has swimming pools and saunas open to the public.

Český Krumlov

Explore

Outside of Prague, Český Krumlov is arguably the Czech Republic's only other world-class sight and must-see. From a distance, the town looks like any other in the Czech countryside, but once you get closer and see the Renaissance castle towering over the undisturbed 17th-century townscape, you'll feel the appeal; this really is that fairytale town the tourist brochures promised. Český Krumlov is best approached as an overnight destination; it's too far for a comfortable day trip from Prague. Consider staying two nights, and spend one of the days hiking or biking in the surrounding woods and fields.

The Best...

- **Sight** Český Krumlov Castle (p205)
- **Place to Eat** Laibon (p206)
- **Place to Drink** Zapa Cocktail Bar (p207)

Top Tip

If you're visiting in July or August, try to book tickets for the annual **International Music Festival** (Mezinárodní hudební festival; ☎380 711 797; www.festivalkrumlov.cz; Latrán 37; ⏰concerts mid-Jul–Aug), one of the highlight's of the Czech festival season.

Getting There & Away

Train From Prague (260Kč, 3½ hours), the train journey requires a change in České Budějovice. Buses are usually quicker and cheaper. There's regular train service between České Budějovice and Český Krumlov (32Kč, 45 minutes).

Bus From Prague, **Student Agency** (www.studentagency.cz) coaches (195Kč, three hours) leave regularly from the Na Knížecí bus station at Anděl metro station (line B). Book in advance for weekends or in July and August.

Car The drive from Prague is a strenuous three hours along mostly two-lane highway. Take the D1 motorway in the direction of Brno, and turn south on Hwy E55.

Need to Know

- **Location** 180km south of Prague.
- **Infocentrum** (380 704 622; www.ckrumlov.info; náměstí Svornosti 1; 9am-7pm Jun-Aug, 9am-6pm Apr, May, Sep & Oct, 9am-5pm Nov-Mar) Provides transport and accommodation information, as well as maps and audio guides.
- **Internet Access** The Infocentrum has computers on hand for internet access (per five minutes 5Kč).

SIGHTS

TOP CHOICE **ČESKÝ KRUMLOV CASTLE** CASTLE

Map p206 (380 704 711; www.castle.ckrumlov.cz; Zámek; Tour 1 adult/concession 250/160Kč, Tour 2 240/140Kč, Theatre Tour 380/220Kč, tower 50/30Kč; 9am-6pm Tue-Sun Jun-Aug, 9am-5pm Apr, May, Sep & Oct) Český Krumlov's striking Renaissance castle, occupying a promontory high above the town, began life in the 13th century. It acquired its present appearance in the 16th to 18th centuries under the stewardship of the noble Rožmberk and Schwarzenberg families. The castle's interiors are accessible by guided tour only, though you can stroll the grounds and climb the **tower** on your own.

Three main **tours** are offered: Tour 1 (one hour) takes in the opulent Renaissance rooms; Tour 2 (one hour) visits the Schwarzenberg portrait galleries and their 19th-century apartments. The Theatre Tour (40 minutes, 10am to 4pm Tuesday to Sunday May to October) explores the chateau's remarkable rococo theatre.

Wandering through the courtyards and **gardens** is free. Scramble up the castle tower for views over the town below.

MUSEUM FOTOATELIÉR SEIDEL MUSEUM

Map p206 (380 712 354; www.seidel.cz; Linecká 272; adult/concession 100/70Kč; hourly tours 9am-4pm) Not far from the castle gardens, this photography museum presents a moving retrospective of the work of local photographers Josef Seidel and his son František. Especially poignant are the images recording early 20th-century life in nearby villages. In the high season you should be able to join an English-language tour; if not, let the pictures tell the story.

Inner Town & Around

Below the castle, the town fans out in a confusing web of backstreets and alleyways, bridges and riverbanks. The best way to get your bearings is simply to follow your nose. The centre of town is defined by náměstí Svornosti, with its 16th-century **Town Hall** (Map p206; www.ckrumlov.info; náměstí Svornosti) and **Marian Plague Column** (Mariánský sloupek; Map p206; náměstí Svornosti), dating from 1716. Several buildings feature valuable stucco and painted decorations: note the hotel at **No 13** and the house at **No 14**. Back at the square, follow Horní uphill and past Kostelní to the 14th-century **Church of St Vitus** (kostel sv Víta; Map p206; 380 711 336; www.farnostck.bcb.cz; Horní 156; 9am-6pm). Continue on Horní past the 1588 **Jesuit college** (Jesuitská kolej), now housing the plush Hotel Růže.

EGON SCHIELE ART CENTRUM MUSEUM

Map p206 (380 704 011; www.schieleartcentrum.cz; Široká 71; adult/concession 120/70Kč; 10am-6pm Tue-Sun) This excellent private gallery houses a small retrospective of the controversial Viennese painter Egon Schiele (1890–1918), who lived in Krumlov in 1911, and raised the ire of townsfolk by hiring young girls as nude models. For this and other sins he was eventually driven out. The centre also houses interesting temporary exhibitions.

REGIONAL MUSEUM MUSEUM

Map p206 (Regionální muzeum v Českém Krumlové; 380 711 674; www.museum-krumlov.eu; Horní 152; adult/concession 50/25Kč; 9am-noon & 12.30-5pm Tue-Sun) This small museum features folk art from the Šumava region, archaeology, history, fine arts, furnishings and weapons. The highlight is a room-sized model of Český Krumlov c 1800. Just next to the museum is a small grassy area with an amazing view out over the castle.

MARIONETTE MUSEUM MUSEUM

Map p206 (380 711 175; www.mozart.cz; Latrán 6; adult/concession 80/50Kč; 9am-6pm Apr-Aug, 10am-4pm Sep & Oct) This branch of the National Marionette Theatre in Prague is housed in the former Church of St Jošt, and displays a full range of Czech marionettes and puppets through the ages, including theatres and stage sets.

EATING & DRINKING

Booking ahead for dinner in July and August is recommended.

TOP CHOICE LAIBON — VEGETARIAN €€

Map p206 (☎728 676 654; www.laibon.cz; Parkán 105; mains 90-180Kč;) Candles and vaulted ceilings create a great boho ambience in the best little vegetarian teahouse in Bohemia. Just paging through the menu with seldom-seen words like guacamole and hummus can start the mouth watering. The riverside setting's pretty fine as well. Order the blueberry dumplings for dessert.

NONNA GINA — ITALIAN €

Map p206 (☎380 717 187; Klášteriní 52; pizza 90-155Kč) Authentic Italian flavours from the authentic Italian Massaro family feature in this pizzeria down a quiet lane. Grab an outdoor table and pretend you're in Naples.

KRČMA V ŠATLAVSKÉ — CZECH €€

Map p206 (☎380 713 344; www.satlava.cz; Horní 157; mains 150-260Kč) Nirvana for meat-lovers, this medieval barbecue cellar serves sizzling platters in a funky labyrinth illuminated by candles and the flickering flames of open grills. Booking ahead is essential. Be forewarned: summer months bring tour-bus crowds.

HOSPODA NA LOUŽI — CZECH €

Map p206 (☎380 711 280; www.nalouzi.cz; Kájovská 66; mains 90-170Kč) Nothing's changed in this wood-panelled *pivo* (beer) parlour for almost a century. Locals and tourists pack Na Louži for huge meals and tasty dark (and light) beer from the Eggenberg brewery.

U DWAU MARYÍ — CZECH €

Map p206 (☎380 717 228; www.2marie.cz; Parkán 104; mains 100-200Kč) The 'Two Marys' medieval tavern recreates old recipes and

Český Krumlov

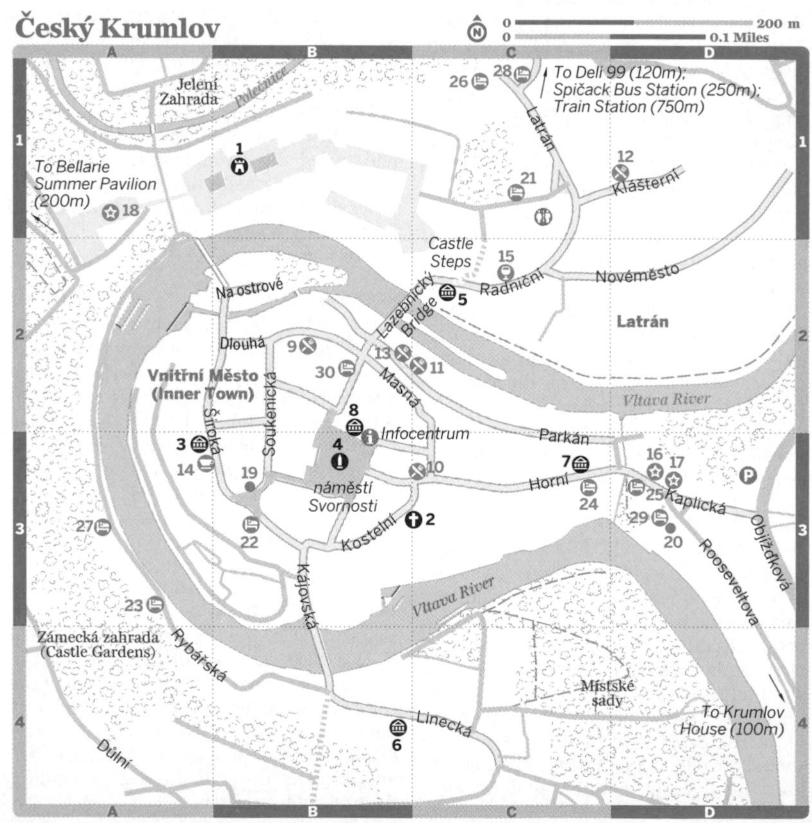

presents an opportunity to try dishes made with buckwheat and millet (all tastier than they sound). Wash the food down with a goblet of mead or choose a 21st-century Pilsner. In summer it's a tad touristy, but the stunning riverside castle views easily compensate.

CIKÁNSKÁ JIZBA CZECH €

Map p206 (☎380 717 585; Dlouhá 31; mains 120-250Kč; ⏲3pm-midnight Mon-Sat) At the 'Gypsy Room' there's often live Roma music at the weekends to go with the menu of meaty Czech favourites.

DELI 99 SANDWICHES €

(☎721 750 786; www.hostel99.cz/deli-99; Latrán 106; snacks and sandwiches 60-80Kč; ⏲7am-7pm Mon-Sat, 8am-5pm Sun; 📶✍) Bagels, sandwiches, organic juices and wi-fi all tick the box marked 'Slightly Homesick Traveller'.

ZAPA COCKTAIL BAR COCKTAIL BAR

Map p206 (☎380 712 559; www.zapabar.cz; Latrán 15; ⏲6pm-1am) Český Krumlov empties out after dinner, but Zapa keeps going most nights until after midnight. Expect great cocktails and a relaxed vibe.

CAFÉ SCHIELE CAFE

Map p206 (☎380 704 011; www.schieleart centrum.cz; Široká 71; ⏲10am-7pm; 📶) A lovely cafe housed in the art gallery, with ancient oak floorboards, mismatched furniture and a grand piano with sawn-off legs serving as a coffee table. Excellent fair-trade coffee.

SLEEPING

CASTLE APARTMENTS APARTMENT €€

Map p206 (☎380 725 110; www.zameckaapart ma.cz; Latrán 45-47; apt 1800-3800Kč; 🚭📶) Three adjoining houses near the castle district have been transformed into comfortable private apartments that offer wooden floors, and modern kitchenettes and bathrooms (no additional charge for the romantic views). Castle Apartments just may be Český Krumlov's best-value accommodation option.

U MALÉHO VÍTKA HOTEL €€

Map p206 (☎380 711 925; www.vitekhotel.cz; Radničnl 27; P🚭📶) We really like this small hotel in the heart of the Old Town. The room furnishings are of high-quality, hand-crafted wood, and each room is named after a traditional Czech fairytale character. The downstairs restaurant and cafe are very good, too.

PENSION KAPR PENSION €

Map p206 (☎602 409 360; www.penzionkapr.cz; Rybářská 28; s 1000Kč, d 1200-1800Kč; @📶) OK, it may be named after a fish (carp), but

Český Krumlov

Sights

1	Český Krumlov Castle	B1
2	Church of St Vitus	C3
3	Egon Schiele Art Centrum	A3
4	Marian Plague Column	B3
5	Marionette Museum	C2
6	Museum Fotoateliér Seidel	B4
7	Regional Museum	C3
8	Town Hall	B2

Eating

9	Cikánská Jizba	B2
	Hospoda Na Louži	(see 22)
10	Krčma v Šatlavské	C3
11	Laibon	C2
12	Nonna Gina	D1
13	U Dwau Maryí	B2

Drinking

14	Café Schiele	A3
15	Zapa Cocktail Bar	C2

Entertainment

16	Divadelní Klub Ántré	D3
17	Městské Divadlo	D3
18	Revolving Theatre	A1

Sports & Activities

19	Expedicion	B3
20	Maleček	D3

Sleeping

21	Castle Apartments	C1
22	Hospoda Na Louži	B3
23	Hostel Postel	A3
24	Hotel Růže	C3
25	Pension Barbakán	D3
26	Pension Danny	C1
27	Pension Kapr	A3
28	Pension Lobo	C1
29	Pension Myší Díra	D3
30	U Malého Vítka	B2

this riverside pension, with exposed bricks and 500 years of history, has a quiet location and wonderful views of the Old Town. The lovely rooms, with whitewashed walls and wooden floors, are all named after the owners' children.

TOP CHOICE DILETTANTE'S HANGOUT GUESTHOUSE €
(☎728 280 033; www.dilettanteshangout.com; Plesivecke náměstí 93; r 790-990Kč; ⊖) Don't be fooled by the bland exterior. Inside this intimate homestay are three romantic, arty rooms decorated with mementoes of the owner's global wanderings. Each room is unique, but they're all cosy and eclectic. There are kitchenettes for self-catering.

KRUMLOV HOUSE HOSTEL €
(☎380 711 935; www.krumlovhostel.com; Rooseveltova 68; dm/d/tr 300/750/1350Kč; ❄📶) Perched above the river, Krumlov House is friendly and comfortable, and has plenty of books, DVDs and local information to feed your inner wanderer. Lots of day trips are on offer. The owners are English-speaking and traveller-friendly.

PENSION MYŠÍ DÍRA PENSION €
Map p206 (☎380 712 853; www.ceskykrumlov-info.cz; Rooseveltova 28; s/d from 1290/1590Kč; P⊖@) This welcoming pension has a great location overlooking the river, and bright, beautiful rooms with lots of pale wood and quirky handmade furniture. Deluxe rooms and weekend accommodation (June to August) are 300Kč extra, but rates fall by 40% in winter. Breakfast is served in your room.

HOSPODA NA LOUŽI HOTEL €€
Map p206 (☎380 711 280; www.nalouzi.cz; Kájovská 66; r 1350-1700Kč; ⊖) The outside dates from 1459, with an early-20th-century interior... But in this new century, what counts are the 11 cosy rooms above a great pub. Accommodation is tight in summer; winter rates may drop by up to 40%.

HOSTEL SKIPPY HOSTEL €
(☎380 728 380; www.hostelskippy.webs.com; Plešivecká 123; dm/s/d 280/290/666Kč; ⊖) Less boisterous than some other CK hostels, Skippy is more like hanging out at a friend's place. The creative owner, 'Skippy', is an arty, muso type, so you might be surprised with an impromptu jam session in the front room. The location is absolute riverfront. It's a compact spot, so you'll need to book ahead.

HOSTEL POSTEL HOSTEL €
Map p206 (☎380 715 631; www.hostelpostel.cz; Rybářská 35; dm/d 300/650Kč; ⊖@📶) Situated near a couple of good local pubs, Hostel Postel has a sunny courtyard with shady umbrellas to help you wake up slowly after a big night. All accommodation is in superclean, two- to four-bed rooms.

HOTEL RŮŽE HOTEL €€€
Map p206 (☎380 772 100; www.hotelruze.cz; Horní 154; s/d 4000/5300Kč; P⊖❄@📶) CK's flashest hotel fills the old Jesuit college and is popular with tour groups who enjoy a bit of medieval bling. We're not sure about the mannequins in the lobby: have they escaped from the nearby wax museum? Accommodation is tight in summer; winter rates may drop by up to 40%.

PENSION SEBASTIAN PENSION €
(☎608 357 581; www.sebastianck.com; 5 Května Ul; s/d/tr incl breakfast 790/1090/1590Kč; ⊖📶) An excellent option just a 15-minute walk south of the Old Town in the suburb of Plešivec, with slightly cheaper rates than more-central pensions. Larger four-bed rooms (1780Kč) are good for families, and there's a garden gazebo for end-of-day drinks and barbecues. The well-travelled owners also run tours of the surrounding region. Breakfast is included.

PENSION DANNY PENSION €
Map p206 (☎380 712 710; www.pensiondanny.cz; Latrán 72; d incl breakfast from 990Kč; ⊖📶) Exposed beams plus restored brickwork equals simple charm. As with many other places in town, the pension tends to fill up in summer, but is much emptier and cheaper in winter.

PENSION BARBAKÁN PENSION €
Map p206 (☎380 717 017; www.barbakan.cz; Kaplická 26; s/d incl breakfast from 1300/1700Kč; @📶) Originally the town's gunpowder arsenal, Barbakán now creates fireworks of its own with super-comfy rooms featuring bright and cosy wooden decor. Sit in the grill restaurant (mains 150Kč to 210Kč) and watch the tubing and rafting action on the river below.

PENSION LOBO PENSION €
Map p206 (☎380 713 153; www.pensionlobo.cz; Latrán 73; s/d incl breakfast 1000/1200Kč; P⊖📶)

Bright, comfortable rooms and refurbished bathrooms make this Old Town pension good value. Have breakfast in your room and enjoy views of romantic CK at the same time.

ENTERTAINMENT

DIVADELNÍ KLUB ÁNTRÉ LIVE MUSIC

Map p206 (☎605 882 342; www.klubantre.cz; Horní 2;) The best up-and-coming Czech bands often include the Ántré on their national schedules. The website is not very helpful, so ask at the Infocentrum (p205) to see if anything's on during your visit.

MĚSTSKÉ DIVADLO THEATRE

Map p206 (☎380 727 370; www.divadlo.ckrumlov.cz; Horní 2) The town theatre holds regular performances. Check the website for the current program.

REVOLVING THEATRE THEATRE

Map p206 (Otáčivé hlediště Český Krumlov; ☎386 350 925; www.otacivehlediste.cz; Castle Gardens; tickets 400-800Kč; ⏲Jun-Sep) Ballet, opera, plays and puppetry are all performed at this unique outdoor theatre. Check the website or ask the Infocentrum (p205) about what's on. The Infocentrum also sells tickets to performances.

KINO J&K CINEMA

(☎380 711 892; www.ckrumlov.cz/kinojk; Špičák 134) Screens the latest Hollywood fare.

SPORTS & ACTIVITIES

MALEČEK CANOEING

Map p206 (☎380 712 508; http://en.malecek.cz; Rooseveltova 28; 2-person canoe per 30 mins 390Kč; ⏲9am-5pm) In summer, messing about on the river is a great way to keep cool. Rent a canoe and splash around locally, or take a full-day trip down the river from the town of Rožmberk (850Kč, six to eight hours).

EXPEDICION BICYCLE RENTAL, ADVENTURE TOUR

Map p206 (☎607 963 868; www.expedicion.cz; Soukenická 33; ⏲9am-7pm) Expedicion rents bikes (per day 290Kč), arranges horse riding (per hour 250Kč), and operates action-packed day trips (1680Kč including lunch) incorporating horse riding, fishing, mountain biking and rafting in the nearby Newcastle Mountains region.

SEBASTIAN TOURS GUIDED TOUR

(☎607 100 234; www.sebastianck-tours.com; 5 Května Ul, Plešivec; day trip to Hluboká nad Vltavou per person 599Kč) Sebastian Tours can get you discovering South Bohemia on guided tours including stops at Hluboká nad Vltavou and České Budějovice. Also offers shuttle bus service to destinations further afield like Linz, Vienna and Salzburg in Austria.

SLUPENEC STABLES HORSE RIDING

(☎723 832 459; www.jk-slupenec.cz; Slupenec 1; horse riding per hour/day 300/2200Kč) Slupenec Stables hires horses for trips and riding lessons. The stables are 2.5km south of town. Book through the Infocentrum (p205).

Třeboň

Explore

Třeboň is traditionally known throughout the Czech Republic for its many fish ponds, which produce much of the carp consumed around the country on Christmas Eve. The ponds are still there, but these days they're also prized for aesthetic reasons: they make a picturesque backdrop while hiking or biking through the Třeboňsko Protected Landscape. Třeboň itself is a low-key overnighter, with a handful of sights and decent hotels. It can also be visited as an easy day trip from České Budějovice.

The Best...

- **Sight** Třeboň Chateau (p211)
- **Place to Eat** Rožmberská Bašta (p212)
- **Place to Drink** Regent Brewery (p212)

Top Tip

Třeboň is a charming town, but a real highlight of a visit here is to get into the open air on the trails. The Tourist Office (p211) can advise on hiking and biking possibilities (and bike rentals).

Třeboň

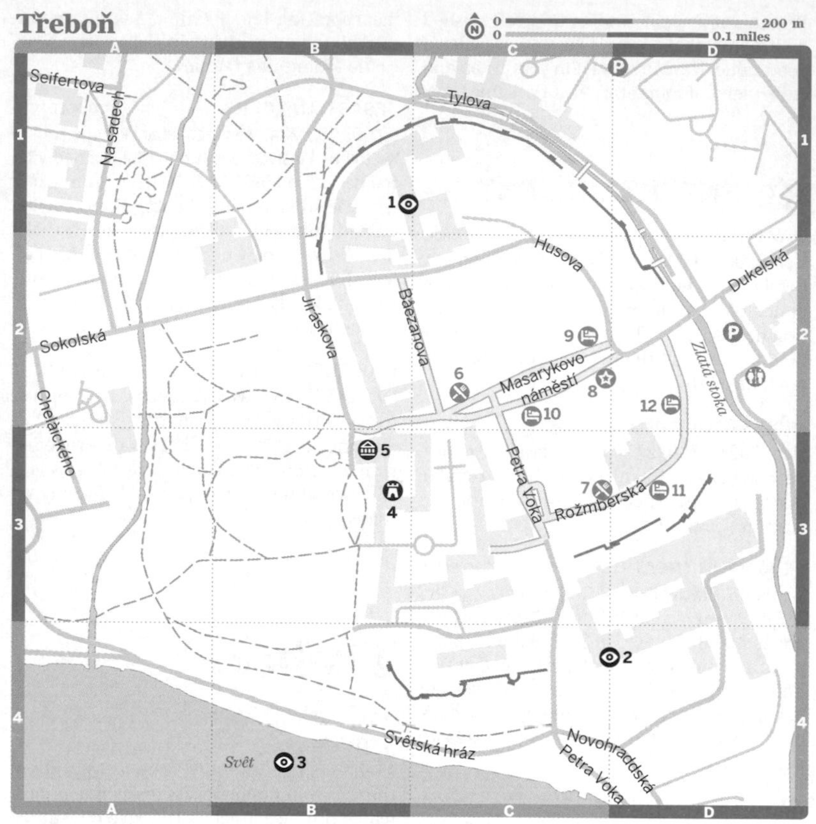

Třeboň

Sights

1 Augustine Monastery B1
2 Regent Brewery D4
3 Rybník Svět B4
4 Třeboň Chateau B3
5 Třeboň Landscape & People Exhibition B3

Eating

Bílý Koníček ..... (see 9)
6 Fish & Steak C2
7 Rožmberská Bašta C3

Drinking

Regent Brewery ..... (see 2)

Entertainment

8 Kino Světozor C2

Sleeping

9 Bílý Koníček C2
10 Hotel Zlatá Hvězda C2
11 Penzion Modrá Růže D3
12 Penzion Zlatá Stoka D2

Getting There & Away

Train There are frequent trains from Prague (200Kč, three hours), though connections require a change Veselí nad Lužnicí. You can also catch a train from Tábor (71Kč, one hour).

Bus Several daily buses leave from Florenc bus station in Prague (138Kč, three hours). Hourly buses run from České Budějovice (30Kč, 30 minutes).

Car Třeboň is a two-hour drive south of Prague, starting out south toward Brno on the D1 motorway and then turning off at the E55 Hwy and following the signs. From České Budějovice the drive takes 30 minutes on Hwy 34.

Need to Know

➡ **Location** 145km south of Prague.

➡ **Tourist Office** (Informační Středisko; ☎384 721 169; www.trebon-mesto.cz; Masarykovo náměstí 103; ⏲9am-4pm Mon-Fri) Provides maps and information on bike rental.

➡ **Internet Access** The tourist office has computers for checking the internet.

SIGHTS

TŘEBOŇ CHATEAU — CASTLE

Map p210 (Zámek ; ☎384 721 193; www.zamek-trebon.eu; Zámek 115; adult 100-150Kč, concession 50-75Kč; ⏲9am-5.15pm Tue-Sun Jun-Aug, to 4pm Apr-May & Sep-Oct; closed Nov-Mar) Třeboň's main attraction is its Renaissance chateau, which includes a **museum** displaying furniture and weapons. Entry is by one of three guided **tours**: Tour A takes you through the castle's Renaissance interiors; Tour B focusses on a 19th-century Schwarzenberg apartment; and in summer (July and August) a third tour explores the chateau's cellars.

Today's chateau dates from 1611, the replacement for a Gothic castle destroyed by fire. Originally built by the Rožmberk family, it then became one of the main residences of the Schwarzenbergs. On the western side of the castle, the **Třeboň Landscape & People Exhibition** (Expozice Třeboňslo karjina a lidé; Map p210; ☎384 274 912; adult/concession 50/30Kč; ⏲9am-5pm daily May-Sep, closed Mon Apr & Oct, closed Nov-Mar) has an interactive overview of the history of carp farming.

SCHWARZENBERG MAUSOLEUM — MAUSOLEUM

(Švarcenberská Hrobka; www.zamek-trebon.eu; Park U Hrobky; adult/concession 50/30Kč, tours with English-speaking guide (by prior arrangement) 90/50Kč; ⏲9am-5.15pm Tue-Sun Jun-Aug, to 4pm Apr-May & Sep-Oct) Many Schwarzenbergs are buried in this 1877, neo-Gothic mausoleum in Park U Hrobky, on the other side of the pond from Třeboň. The crypt lies about 15-minute walk from the centre along well-marked paths.

Around Masarykovo Náměstí

The main attractions here are the Renaissance and baroque houses on the square and within the town walls (which date from 1527). Don't miss the **Town Hall** on the square, **St Giles Church** (kostel sv Jiljí) and the **Augustine monastery**.

FREE AUGUSTINE MONASTERY — MONASTERY

Map p210 (Augustinský klášter; Husova; ⏲9am-6pm Mon-Sat) The Augustine monastery was established by the Rožmberk family in 1367. The oldest parts include the cloister in the convent and the Chapel of St Vincent, which dates from the end of the 14th century. The monastery complex includes **St Giles Church** (kostel sv Jiljí).

REGENT BREWERY — BREWERY

Map p210 (Pivovar Bohemia Regent ; ☎384 721 319; www.pivovar-regent.cz; Trocnovské náměstí 124) Třeboň's municipal brewery was founded in 1379 and still turns out excellent beers sold under the 'Bohemia Regent' label. Brewery tours need to be pre-booked

TOURING A CARP POND

The area around Třeboň is dotted with literally hundreds of fish ponds, many dating back several centuries. Eating fish is near-and-dear to the hearts of land-locked Czechs. Indeed, the most important meal of the year, at Christmas Eve, is centred around carp, and much of the nation's carp is raised right here.

One of the main fishponds, **Rybník Svět** (Svět Pond; Map p210), is an easy 10-minute walk from Třeboň's central square. There's a well-marked trail that borders the pond for several kilometres, with helpful sign-posting along the way. Part of the edge of the pond is lined with working fish foundries, where you can see how the fish are stored and harvested for that all-important Christmas meal (the carp are fried and served with potato salad, while sundry inedible bits are boiled-up to make carp soup).

by telephone or email. Prices depend on the time of day and number of people. Don't miss the brewery's open-air terrace in nice weather.

EATING & DRINKING

ROŽMBERSKÁ BAŠTA

CZECH €€

Map p210 (☎731 175 902; www.rozmberska-basta.cz; Rožmberská 59; mains 170-290Kč; ⏱11am-10pm) You'll find good fish dishes at this homespun little restaurant, on a quiet side street near the main square. The specialty here is grilled or fried pikeperch. There's a small open-air terrace out the back.

FISH & STEAK

INTERNATIONAL €

Map p210 (☎384 392 595; www.vratislavskydum.cz; cnr Masarykovo náměstí 97 & Březanova; pizza 80-130Kč, mains 120-290Kč; 📶📝) The name is 'Fish & Steak', but pizzas are really the name of the game here. You can have your slice outside in main-square splendour, or you can head inside to enjoy the vaulted ceiling and colourful decor. The fish and meat dishes are also very good.

BÍLÝ KONÍČEK

CZECH €

Map p210 (☎384 721 213; www.hotelbilykonicek.cz; Masarykovo náměstí 97; mains 110-180Kč) The house restaurant on the ground floor of the Bílý Koníček (p213) hotel is a reliable choice for standard Czech dishes, like roast pork and *wienerschnitzel,* served by friendly waitresses. There's a small terrace, and the restaurant makes a nice place to return to for a beer in the evening.

REGENT BREWERY

PUB

Map p210 (Pivovar Bohemia Regent; ☎384 721 319; www.pivovar-regent.cz; Trocnovské náměstí 124; mains 80-120Kč) Always busy, and always serving Třeboň's excellent local beers and well-priced local food. A half-litre of beer is cheaper here than in Prague; our favourite is the 11° light lager. In nice weather head for the open-air terrace at the back.

SLEEPING

HOTEL ZLATÁ HVĚZDA

HOTEL €€

Map p210 (☎384 757 111; www.zhvezda.cz; Masarykovo náměstí 107; s/d incl breakfast 1400/2400Kč; P⊖@📶) Třeboň's smartest offering has flash rooms, a spa centre and a bowling alley, all in a 430-year-old building right on the main square. The helpful reception desk serves as a second tourist information office and can suggest good hikes and cycling tours. Also has bikes for hire (per day 300Kc).

PENZION MODRÁ RŮŽE

PENSION €

Map p210 (☎384 722 167; www.modra-ruze.cz; Rožmberská 39; s 450-740Kč, d 720-1000Kč; @📶) With super-helpful owners providing loads of local information, this pension on a quiet lane is one of Třeboň's best. It's often busy, so it pays to book ahead.

WALKING THE TŘEBOŇSKO PROTECTED LANDSCAPE

Much of the area around Třeboň, with its wooded areas and fish ponds, has been designated as a protected landscape. A good walk through the region begins at Masarykovo náměstí. Follow the blue-marked trail northeast to **Na Kopečku** (1.5km, 30 minutes). From Na Kopečku, keep on the blue-marked trail to **Hodějov Pond** (7.5km, 2½ hours). A yellow trail then runs west to **Smítka** (2km, 45 minutes) where it joins a red trail heading north to **Klec** and a primitive campsite (6km, two hours).

From there, for a further 13km (four hours), the red trail runs north, past more fish ponds, forests and small villages to **Veselí nad Lužnicí**, a major railway junction. Camping is allowed only in official campsites throughout the protected landscape region. You can also ride this route on your mountain bike.

An alternative 12km leisurely route runs around the Rybník Svět (p211) fish pond on a well-marked trail (around four hours), beginning just south of the Regent Brewery (p211). The trail is flagged with 16 information boards in Czech, German and English, and also takes in the Schwarzenberg Mausoleum (p211). Ask at the Tourist Office (p211) for a map; it also has details on other walks in the area and can help with bike-hire info.

PENZION ZLATÁ STOKA PENSION €

Map p210 (☎728 031 433; www.zlatastoka.cz; Rožmberská 65; s/d/apt 700/950/1120Kč) Spacious, modern rooms with terracotta tiles, leather furniture and bright decor come as standard at the 'Golden Canal'. Breakfast isn't included, but there are a couple of cafes literally metres away.

BÍLÝ KONÍČEK HOTEL €

Map p210 (☎384 721 213; www.hotelbilykonicek.cz; Masarykovo náměstí 97; s/d 800/1000Kč; P) An attractive Renaissance facade hides what's only an ordinary hotel, but the location can't be beaten and the price is fair for what you get. The rooms are unadorned and on the small side. There's free parking at the rear and a decent restaurant downstairs, serving basic Czech fare.

ENTERTAINMENT

KINO SVĚTOZOR CINEMA

Map p210 (☎384 722 050; www.kinotrebon.cz; Masarykovo náměstí 103) Screens Hollywood movies.

Tábor

Explore

The town of Tábor, south of Prague, earned its place in Czech history in the 15th century as the home of the most radical wing of the Hussite movement. These days, there aren't many radicals left, but Tábor makes for a convenient lunch-and-a-stroll stopover on the trip south toward České Budějovice and Český Krumlov. The most interesting sights here are Hussite-related: there's an educational museum on Hussite history, and some of the town's centuries-old underground passages, used by fighters during wartime, have been opened to the public. There are also two excellent hotels and a handful of clean, reasonably priced pensions.

The Best...

- **Sight** Underground Passages (p214)
- **Place to Eat** Goldie (p215)
- **Place to Drink** MP7 (p215)

Top Tip

For a relatively large town (by Czech standards), Tábor lacks good restaurants. This is one place where eating at the hotel is usually the best option.

Getting There & Away

Train From Prague, regular trains depart from the main station (140Kč, 1½ hours), but they are generally more expensive and less convenient than the bus.

Bus There's regular bus service from Prague's Florenc station (93Kč, two hours).

Car By car from Prague, the drive takes 90 minutes. Take the D1 motorway in the direction of Brno, bearing south on Hwy E55 and follow the signs to Tábor.

Need to Know

- **Location** 90km south of Prague.
- **Infocentrum** (☎381 486 230; www.tabor.cz; Žižkovo náměstí 2; ⌚8.30am-7pm Mon-Fri, 10am-4pm Sat & Sun May-Sep, 9am-4pm Mon-Fri Oct-Apr) Books accommodation and rents audio guides.
- **Česká Spořitelna** (☎956 744 120; www.csas.cz; tř. 9 května 518; ⌚8.30am-4pm Mon-Fri) Centrally located ATM and money exchange.

SIGHTS

ŽIŽKOVO NÁMĚSTÍ SQUARE

Map p214 (Žižkovo náměstí) Žižkovo náměstí is Tabor's handsome main square. On every side it's lined with late-Gothic, Renaissance and baroque houses, and in the middle is a **fountain** (1567) with a statue of the Hussite commander Jan Žižka (see boxed text p215) after whom the square is named. The two stone tables nearby were probably used by the Hussites for religious services.

HUSSITE MUSEUM MUSEUM

Map p214 (Husitské muzeum; ☎381 254 286; www.husitskemuzeum.cz; Žižkovo náměstí; adult/concession 60/40Kč; ⌚9am-5pm daily Apr-Oct, Wed-Sat Nov-Mar) Situated in Tábor's former late-Gothic **Town Hall** (Stará radnice) this museum traces the origins and history of the Hussite movement in the

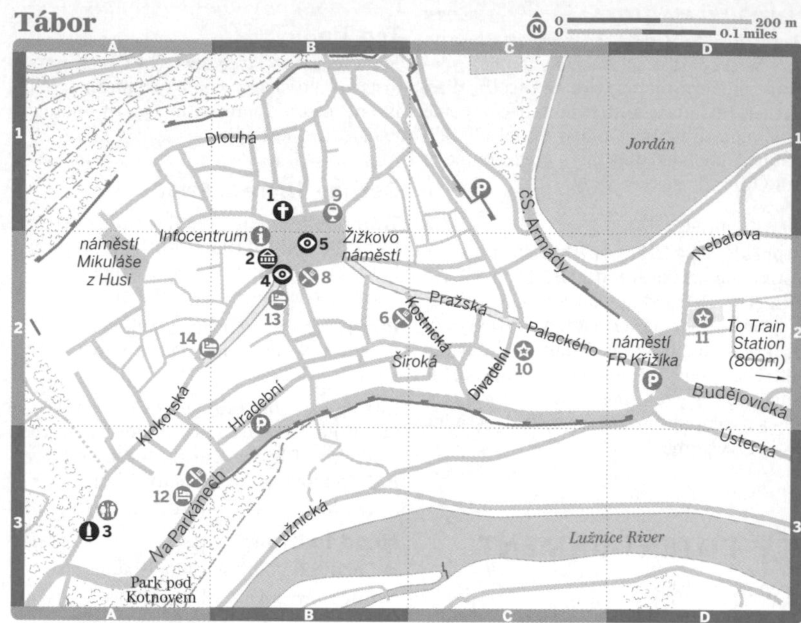

Tábor

Sights

1 Church of the Transfiguration of Our Lord on Mt Tábor B1
Historical Museum .... (see 3)
2 Hussite Museum B2
3 Kotnov Tower A3
4 Underground Passages B2
5 Žižkovo Náměstí B2

Eating

6 Café Pizzerie B2
7 Dvořák A3
Goldie .... (see 13)
8 Kafe & Bar Havana B2

Drinking

9 MP7 .... B1
Whisky Pub .... (see 14)

Entertainment

10 Divadlo Oskara Nedbala C2
11 Kino Svět D2

Sleeping

12 Hotel Dvořák A3
13 Hotel Nautilus B2
Pension Jana .... (see 6)
14 Penzión Alfa A2

Czech Republic. The entrance to Tábor's Underground Passages (p214) is also here.

UNDERGROUND PASSAGES UNDERGROUND

Map p214 (Podzemní Chodby; www.husitske muzeum.cz; Žižkovo náměstí; adult/concession 60/40Kč; ⏲8.30am-5pm daily Apr-Oct, Mon-Fri Nov-Mar) At the former Town Hall (now the Hussite Museum), you'll find the entrance to a fascinating 650m stretch of underground passageways, which you can visit by guided tour only. The passages, constructed in the 15th century as refuges during fires and times of war, were also used to store food and to mature beer.

CHURCH OF THE TRANSFIGURATION OF OUR LORD ON MT TÁBOR CHURCH, TOWER

Map p214 (kostel Proměnění Páně na hoře Tábor; Žižkovo náměstí; tower adult/concession 40/30Kč; ⏲tower 10am-5pm Apr-Aug, Sat & Sun only Sep & Oct) On the square's northern side is the Church of the Transfiguration of Our Lord on Mt Tábor, built between 1440 and 1512 and known for its stone vaulting and neo-Gothic altar. Its **tower** is open (weather dependent) for a sweeping view of Tábor.

KOTNOV TOWER TOWER

Map p214 (☎381 252 788; www.husitskemuzeum .cz; Klokotská; adult/concession 20/10Kč;

8.30am-5pm Apr-Sep) Kotnov castle, founded here in the 12th century, was destroyed by fire in 1532: in the 17th century the ruins were transformed into a brewery. The remnant 15th-century Kotnov Tower can be climbed from the Bechyně Gate for a broad view of Tábor and the Lužnice River.

HISTORICAL MUSEUM MUSEUM

Map p214 (381 252 788; www.husitskemuzeum.cz; Klokotská; adult/concession 40/20Kč; 8.30am-5pm May-Sep) Just next to Kotnov Tower, this small museum houses a permanent exhibition, 'Life & Work in Medieval Society', that's focused mainly on how the peasants lived. It's housed in the **Bechyně Gate**, the last of the town's original Gothic portals to remain standing.

EATING & DRINKING

GOLDIE CZECH €€

Map p214 (380 900 901; www.hotelnautilus.cz; Žižkovo náměstí 20; mains 250-360Kč;) The restaurant at the Hotel Nautilus (p216) is head and shoulders above anything else in town. It's a dressy affair, so get dolled up in your cleanest dirty shirt, and enjoy the classy French- and Italian-tinged menu and the very good wine list. There's a great terrace looking out over the main square.

DVOŘÁK CZECH €€

Map p214 (381 207 211; www.dvoraktabor.cz; Hradební 3037; mains 240-360Kč;) One of the better dining choices around town is the restaurant of the Hotel Dvořák (p216), which takes its food seriously indeed. The menu is filled with relatively rare treasures like venison, duck and rabbit, and each main course is paired with a wine recommendation.

CAFÉ PIZZERIE ITALIAN €

Map p214 (381 254 048; Kostnická 159; pizza 90-140Kč; 11am-10pm) Grab a spot on the tiny outside terrace and enjoy good pizza and Italian food. Inside there's a retro influence with lots of tin advertising signs.

KAFE & BAR HAVANA CZECH, MEXICAN €

Map p214 (381 253 383; Žižkovo náměstí 17; mains 80-250Kč) Is this place Czech-Mex or Czé Guevara? Either way the combination of Czech and Mexican food and good honest cocktails makes for main-square fun.

WHISKY PUB BAR

Map p214 (381 256 165; www.pensionalfa.cz; Klokotská 107;) This whisky-themed bar has occasional live gigs with a blues and country edge. Affiliated with the Penzión Alfa (p216).

MP7 BAR

Map p214 (606 856 994; www.facebook.com/cafemp7; Žižkovo náměstí 7; 2-10pm Mon-Thu, to midnight Fri & Sat;) Dance music, jazz, reggae and house all occasionally feature at this art gallery/garden cafe/cocktail bar. It's a good spot to ask about live gigs around town, too.

TÁBOR'S HERO: JAN ŽIŽKA

Hussite Count Jan Žižka, the legendary blind general, was born in Trocnov, just outside České Budějovice, in 1376. He spent his youth at King Wenceslas IV's court and fought as a mercenary in Poland, but returned to the Czech kingdom at the beginning of the Reformation and became the leader of the radical wing of the Hussite movement, the Taborites. His military genius was responsible for all of the Hussite victories, from the 1420 Battle of Žižkov onwards. After losing both eyes in two separate battles, Žižka eventually died of the plague in 1424.

Žižka's army was highly organised and was the first to use a system of wagons with mounted artillery – the earliest tanks in history. These vehicles allowed him to choose where to draw up position, taking the initiative away from the crusaders and making them fight where he wanted. The technique proved almost invincible.

The Hussites successfully saw off their enemies for a decade following Žižka's death, but were defeated by a combined army of the rival Hussite faction of the Utraquists and the Holy Roman Empire in 1434. Surprisingly, Žižka's invention was not incorporated into other armies until Sweden's King Gustavus II Adolphus adopted it two centuries later.

A LITTLE BACKGROUND ON THE HUSSITES

Tábor is often regarded as the spiritual home of the radical Hussite movement, but who exactly were the Hussites and what did they stand for?

The movement's history can be traced back to the 15th century and the decision by Catholic authorities to murder Czech religious reformer Jan Hus, who was famously burned at the stake in Constance, Germany, in 1415. The consequences of this act were far greater than the Catholic authorities could have foreseen. Hus's death caused a religious revolt among the Czechs, who had viewed his decision to preach in Czech language as a step toward religious and national self-determination.

Hus himself had not intended such a drastic revolution, focusing on a translation of the Latin rite, and the giving of bread and wine to all the congregation instead of to the clergy alone. But for many, the time was ripe for church reform.

Hus was born around 1372 in Husinec, in southern Bohemia. From a poor background, he managed to become a lecturer at Charles University in Prague and in 1402 was ordained a preacher. He dreamt of a return to the original doctrines of the church – tolerance, humility, simplicity – but such a message had political overtones for a church that treated forgiveness as an opportunity to make money.

Tried on a trumped-up charge of heresy at Constance, Hus's murder was doubly unjust in that he had been granted safe conduct by the Holy Roman Emperor Sigismund.

In Bohemia many nobles offered to guarantee protection to those who practised religion according to Hus's teachings, and Hussite committees became widespread. The movement split over its relationship with the secular authorities, with the moderate Utraquists siding in 1434 with the Catholic Sigismund.

The more radical Taborites, seeing themselves as God's warriors, fought the Catholics in every way. As the military base for the Hussites, Tábor – named after the biblical Mt Tabor – was successfully defended by a mainly peasant army under the brilliant Jan Žižka and Prokop Holý.

The movement also attracted supporters from other Protestant sects in Europe. Many converged on Tábor and the groups joined against the crusading armies of the Holy Roman Empire.

Hussite ideals were never fully extinguished in Bohemia. Although the Utraquists became the dominant force after defeating (with the help of Sigismund's Catholic forces) the Taborites at the Battle of Lipany in 1434, the resultant peace guaranteed religious freedom for the movement. It took almost 200 years before Protestantism was fully suppressed in the Czech lands by the Catholic Habsburg rulers following the Battle of White Mountain, near Prague, in 1620.

SLEEPING

TOP CHOICE **HOTEL NAUTILUS** BOUTIQUE HOTEL €€

Map p214 (☎380 900 900; www.hotelnautilus.cz; Žižkovo náměstí 20; s/d from 2250/2700Kč; P ⊖ ❄ ≋) From the effortlessly cool bar to the elegant rooms decorated with original art, Tábor's first and only boutique hotel is pure class, and surprisingly affordable for such international ambience right on the main square. Maybe it's time for a mini-splurge?

HOTEL DVOŘÁK HOTEL €€

Map p214 (☎381 207 211; www.dvoraktabor.cz; Hradební 3037; s/d 1400/2350Kč; P ⊖ @ ≋) The Dvořák occupies a renovated former brewery, near the Kotnov Tower and just a short walk from the town centre. The hotel boasts a spa and wellness centre (complete with special beer massages!) as well as clean, fashionable rooms and one of the city's best restaurants. Good value for money.

PENZIÓN ALFA PENSION €

Map p214 (☎381 256 165; www.pensionalfa.cz; Klokotská; s/d/tr 570/900/1300Kč; ≋) This popular spot occupies a cosy corner just metres from the main square. Upstairs the rooms are snug but not claustrophobic, and downstairs you can throw back a few quality shots at the **Whisky Pub** (p215). There's occasional live music in the bar, but gigs usually end around 11pm.

PENSION MILENA PENSION €
(☎381 254 755; www.pensionmilena.cz; Husovo náměstí 529; s/d from 600/700Kč; P) This welcoming hostel-style place can supply you with breakfast, or you can make your own mess in the Formica-encased shared kitchen.

PENSION DÁŠA PENSION €
(☎381 256 253; www.pensiondasa.cz; Bílkova 735; s/d incl breakfast 700/990Kč; P) Work off the *pivo* in the sauna and gym not far from this friendly and convenient pension, close to the bus and train stations. Rooms are tinged with '70s decor and there's a garden area complete with hammock.

PENSION JANA PENSION €
Map p214 (☎381 254 667; www.bedandbreakfast.euweb.cz; Kostnická 161; s/d/tr from 700/1100/1350Kč; P) Expect a warm welcome and spacious attic rooms at this friendly spot tucked down a quiet lane. Breakfast is served in a private flower-bedecked garden.

ENTERTAINMENT

DIVADLO OSKARA NEDBALA THEATRE, LIVE MUSIC
Map p214 (☎381 254 701; www.divadlotabor.cz; Divadelní 218) Everything from jazz and classical music to Czech theatre.

KINO SVĚT CINEMA
Map p214 (☎381 252 200; www.tzmt.cz; náměstí FR Křižíka 129) See Hollywood favourites, and chat about them afterwards at the cafe next door.

Plzeň

Explore

Plzeň, the regional capital of western Bohemia and the second-biggest city in Bohemia after Prague, is best known as the home of the Pilsner Urquell brewery, but it has a handful of other interesting sights and enough good restaurants and night-time pursuits to justify an overnight stay. Most of the sights are located near the central square, but the brewery itself is about a 15-minute walk beyond the centre. Try to arrive in the morning to tour the non-drinking attractions first, and save the brewery tour and inevitable post-tour beers for the late afternoon (...which makes for a more natural progression to dinner, continuing the pub crawl after dark).

The Best...

- **Sight** Pilsner Urquell Brewery (p217)
- **Place to Eat** Na Parkánu (p220)
- **Place to Drink** Na Spilce (p220)

Top Tip

If you're just coming for the brewery tour, it's possible to treat Plzeň as a day trip from Prague, but you'll have a better time if you plan to stay the night.

Getting There & Away

Train From Prague, eight trains daily leave from the main station, Hlavní nádraží (150Kč, 1½ hours).

Bus From Prague, the bus service to Plzeň (100Kč, one hour) is frequent (hourly), relatively fast and inexpensive.

Car The drive to Plzeň from Prague takes around one hour, depending on traffic, mostly along four-lane highway. It's a straight shot down the D5 motorway.

Need to Know

- **Location** 100km southwest of Prague.
- **City Information Centre** (Informační centrum města Plzně; ☎378 035 330; www.icpilsen.cz; náměstí Republiky 41; 9am-7pm Apr-Sep, to 6pm Oct-Mar) Arranges accommodation, organises guides, and sells maps and transport tickets.
- **American Center Plzeň** (☎377 237 722; www.americancenter.cz; Dominikánská 9; 9am-10pm) Has computers to surf the web (per 15 minutes 15Kč).

SIGHTS

PILSNER URQUELL BREWERY BREWERY
(Prazdroj; ☎377 062 888; www.prazdroj.cz; U Prazdroje 7; guided tour adult/child 150/80Kč; 8.30am-6pm Apr-Sep, to 5pm Oct-Mar; tours

Plzeň

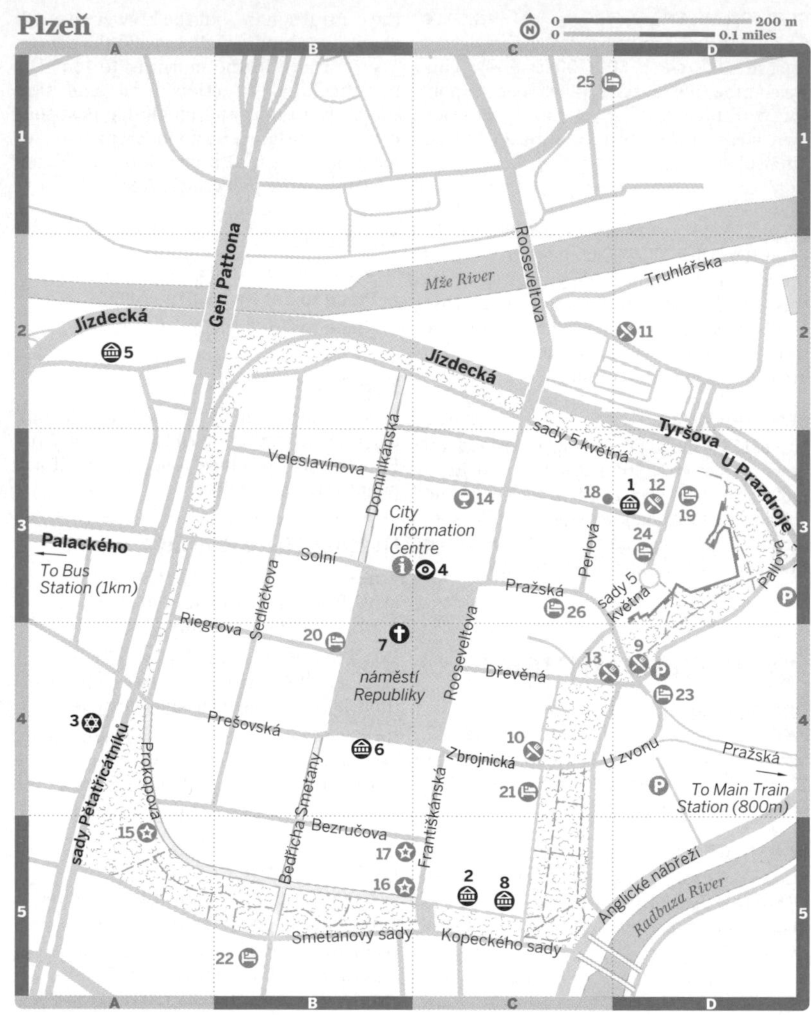

in English 12.45pm, 2.15pm & 4.15pm) Plzeň's most popular attraction is the tour of the Pisner Urquell Brewery, in operation since 1842 and arguably home to the world's best beer. Entry is by guided tour only, with three tours in English available daily. Tour highlights include a trip to the old cellars (dress warmly) and a glass of unpasteurised nectar at the end.

BREWERY MUSEUM MUSEUM

(☎377 235 574; www.prazdroj.cz; Veleslavínova 6; guided tour adult/child 120/90Kč, English text 90/60Kč; ⏰10am-6pm Apr-Dec, 10am-5pm Jan-Mar) The Brewery Museum offers an insight into how beer was made (and drunk) in the days before Prazdroj was founded. Highlights include a mock-up of a 19th-century pub, a huge wooden beer tankard from Siberia and a collection of beer mats. All have English captions and there's a good English written guide available.

UNDERGROUND PLZEŇ UNDERGROUND

(Plzeňské historické podzemí; ☎377 235 574; www.plzenskepodzemi.cz; Veleslavínova 6; adult/child 90/70Kč; ⏰10am-6pm Apr-Dec, 10am-5pm Feb-Mar, closed Jan; English tour 1pm daily) This extraordinary tour explores the passageways below the old city. The earliest were

Plzeň

Sights

1 Brewery Museum....D3
2 Diocese Museum....C5
3 Great Synagogue....A4
4 Old Town Hall....C3
5 Patton Memorial Pilsen....A2
6 Puppet Museum....B4
7 St Bartholomew Church....B4
8 West Bohemian Museum....C5

Eating

9 Aberdeen Angus Steakhouse....D4
10 El Cid....C4
11 Groll Pivovar....D2
12 Na Parkánu....D3
13 U Mansfelda....C4

Drinking

14 Galerie Azyl....C3

Entertainment

15 JK Tyla Theatre....A5
16 Konzervatoř....B5
17 Music Bar Anděl....B5

Sports & Activities

18 Underground Plzeň....C3

Sleeping

19 Courtyard By Marriott....D3
20 Hotel Central....B4
21 Hotel Continental....C4
22 Hotel Slovan....B5
23 Hotel U Zvonu....D4
24 Pension City....D3
25 Pension Stará Plzeň....C1
26 U Salzmannů....C3

probably dug in the 14th century, perhaps for beer production or defence; the latest date from the 19th century. Of an estimated 11km that have been excavated, some 500m of tunnels are open to the public. Bring extra clothes (it's a chilly 10°C underground).

ST BARTHOLOMEW CHURCH CHURCH
(kostel Sv Bartoloměje; ☎377 226 098; www.katedralaplzen.org; náměstí Republiky; adult/concession 20/10Kč, tower 35/25Kč; ⏰10am-6pm Wed-Sat Apr-Sep, Wed-Fri Oct-Dec) Gigantic Gothic St Bartholomew Church looms over the surrounding facades from the centre of náměstí Republiky. Ask at the City Information Centre (p217) about guided tours. Look inside at the delicate marble 'Pilsen Madonna' (dating from c 1390) on the main altar, or climb the 301 steps to the top of the tower (weather permitting) for serious views.

FREE **OLD TOWN HALL** TOWN HALL
(Staroměstská Radnice; www.pilsen.eu; náměstí Republiky 1; ⏰8am-6pm) The city's lovely Town Hall, which dates from the mid-16th century, was built in Italian Renaissance style, with signature sgraffito on the front facade. Inside you'll find a model of the old city centre. In front of the town hall stands a **plague column** that was built in 1681.

PUPPET MUSEUM MUSEUM
(muzeum Loutek; ☎378 370 801; www.muzeumloutek.cz; náměstí Republiky 23; adult/concession 60/30Kč; ⏰10am-6pm Tue-Sun) Since opening in 2011, this museum has been a hit with the younger set. The exhibitions are well done, and many are interactive, allowing visitors to indulge their inner puppeteers.

GREAT SYNAGOGUE SYNAGOGUE
(Velká Synagoga; ☎377 223 346; www.zoplzen.cz; sady Pětatřicátníků 11; adult/child 60/40Kč; ⏰10am-6pm Sun-Fri Apr-Oct) The Great Synagogue, west of the Old Town, is the third-largest in the world – only those in Jerusalem and Budapest are bigger. It was built in the Moorish style in 1892 by the 2000 Jews who lived in Plzeň at the time. The building is often used for concerts and art exhibitions.

PATTON MEMORIAL PILSEN MUSEUM
(☎378 037 954; www.patton-memorial.cz; Podřezni 10; adult/concession 60/40Kč; ⏰9am-1pm & 2-5pm Tue-Sun) The Patton Memorial Pilsen details the liberation of Plzeň in May 1945 by the American army, under General George S Patton. Especially poignant are the handwritten memories of former American soldiers who have returned to Plzeň over the years, and the museum's response to the communist-era revisionist fabrications that claimed Soviet troops, not Americans, were responsible for the city's liberation.

DIOCESE MUSEUM MUSEUM
(Diecésní muzeum; www.bip.cz; Františkánská 11; adult/concession 40/20Kč; ⏰10am-6pm Tue-Sun Apr-Sep) The Diocese Museum, in the former Franciscan monastery (klášter Františkánů), exhibits a fine collection of church statues. The real reason to visit is to see the little **St Barbara Chapel** (kaple sv Barbory) on the cloister's eastern side;

structurally unaltered since the 13th century, it bears the remains of decorative frescoes added in the 15th century.

WEST BOHEMIAN MUSEUM MUSEUM

(Západočeské muzeum; ☎377 329 380; www.zcm.cz; Kopeckého sady 2; per exhibit adult/concession 40/20Kč; ⏰9am-5pm Tue-Sun) This museum fills a magnificent agglomeration of buildings. In the basement the original **armoury** (zbrojnice) features a weapons collection. The ground floor has changing exhibits, while on the 2nd floor the superb art-nouveau **Jubilee Hall** (Jubilejní sál) houses an exhibit of glass and porcelain.

ZOO PLZEŇ ZOO

(☎378 038 325; www.zooplzen.cz; Pod Vinicemi 9; adult/concession 120/90Kč ; ⏰8am-7pm Apr-Oct, 9am-5pm Nov-Mar; 👪; 🚊1, 4) Plzeň's zoo is one of the best in the country, with a sizeable collection of exotic animals, including rhinos, hippos and giraffes. There are also camel and donkey rides for the kids. You can buy a combined-entry ticket for both the Zoo and DinoPark next door (adult/concession 190/130Kč).

DINOPARK THEME PARK

(☎377 223 575; www.dinopark.cz; Pod Vinicemi 9; adult/concession 90/60Kč ; ⏰8am-6pm Apr-Oct; 👪; 🚊1, 4) Adjacent to Zoo Plzeň is this dinosaur park, with life-sized replicas of some 30 dinosaurs, as well as films and playgrounds. You can buy a combined-entry ticket for both the DinoPark and the Zoo (adult/concession 190/130Kč).

EATING & DRINKING

Plzeň is good place to try a big pub meal, complete with excellent Pilsner Urquell beer. It's also a big student town, so there are plenty of good places to kick back afterwards with your beverage of choice.

NA PARKÁNU CZECH €

(☎377 324 485; www.naparkanu.com; Veleslavínova 4; mains 80-180Kč; 📶) Don't overlook this pleasant pub/restaurant, attached to the Brewery Museum. It may look a bit touristy, but the traditional Czech food is top rate, and the beer, naturally, could hardly be better. Try to snag a spot on the summer garden. Don't leave without trying the *nefiltrované pivo* (unfiltered beer).

U MANSFELDA CZECH, PUB €€

(☎377 333 844; www.umansfelda.cz; Dřevěná 9; mains 155-229Kč; 📶) Sure, it's a pub – remember you're in Plzeň now – but it's also more refined and has more interesting food than many other places. Try Czech cuisine like wild boar *gulaš* (spicy meat and potato soup). Downstairs from the beer-fuelled terrace is a more relaxed *vinárna* (wine bar).

ABERDEEN ANGUS STEAKHOUSE STEAKHOUSE €€

(☎725 555 631; www.angusfarm.cz; Pražská 23; mains 180-400Kč) For our money, this may be the best steakhouse in all of the Czech Republic. The meats hail from the nearby Angus Farm, where the livestock is raised organically. There are several cuts and sizes on offer; lunch options include a tantalizing cheeseburger. The downstairs dining room is cosy; there's also a creekside terrace. Book in advance.

GROLL PIVOVAR CZECH €€

(☎602 596 161; www.pivovargroll.cz; Truhlářska 10; mains 129-259Kč) If you've come to Plzeň on a beer pilgrimage, then another essential visit is for a beer-garden lunch at this spiffy microbrewery. Meals include well-priced steaks and salads. The highlight is the drinks menu: homemade 11° light and dark beers, complemented by an excellent (and still relatively rare) yeast beer.

EL CID SPANISH €€

(☎377 224 595; www.elcid.cz; Křižíkovy sady 1; mains 175-365Kč; 📶🌿) A highly regarded Spanish and tapas restaurant that manages to straddle the line between elegance and comfort. You'll find lots of excellent fish dishes on the menu, as well as an appetising array of tapas plates and paellas. Try to book a table on the terrace in nice weather.

NA SPILCE CZECH €

(☎377 062 755; www.naspilce.com; U Prazdroje 7; mains 80-230Kč; ⏰11am-10pm Sun–Thu, 11am-11pm Fri & Sat) This excellent pub and restaurant set within the confines of the Pilsner Urquell brewery feels like a factory canteen. The traditional Czech cooking is above average, and the beer is fresh from tanks next door.

SLUNEČNICE VEGETARIAN €

(☎377 236 093; www.slunecniceplzen.cz; Jungmanova 4; baguettes 60Kč; ⏰7.30am-6pm; 🌿) For fresh sandwiches, self-service salads and vegetarian dishes. Around 100Kč will buy a plateful.

GALERIE AZYL BAR

(☎377 235 507; www.galerieazyl.cz; Veleslavínova 17; ⏲8am-11pm Mon-Thu, 8am-1am Fri, 4pm-1am Sat, 4pm-10pm Sun; 📶) Locals kick-off the day with the excellent espresso here. Later in the day, Galerie Azyl morphs into Plzeň's classiest cocktail bar. Quirky artwork surrounds conversation-friendly booths.

SLEEPING

PENSION STARÁ PLZEŇ PENSION €

(☎377 259 901; www.pension-sp.cz; Na Roudné 12; s 600-1000Kč, d 800-1200Kč; P ⊖ @ 📶) The pension 'Old Pilsen' offers light-and-sunny rooms with skylights, wooden floors and comfy beds. The more expensive rooms offer antique-style beds, persian rugs and exposed wood-beam ceilings. To get here, walk north on Rooseveltova across the river, then turn right onto Na Roudné and continue for 300m.

COURTYARD BY MARRIOTT HOTEL €€

(☎373 370 100; www.marriott.com; sady 5 května 57; r 2000-2600Kč; P ⊖ ❄ @ 📶) This handsome branch of the Marriott has a good location, near the Brewery Museum (p218) and central sights. The rooms are relatively spacious, clean and bright, with all of the conveniences you'd expect. The reception desk is particularly helpful and can arrange brewery tours and sightseeing options. Expect sizable discounts on weekends.

HOTEL U ZVONU HOTEL €€

(☎731 506 705; www.hotel-uzvonu.cz; Pražská 27; s/d 1825/2750Kč ; P ⊖ ❄ @ 📶) This place is similar to the Marriott in that it is clean, modern and conveniently located, close to all of the main sights. The rooms are spacious and well-endowed: some are equipped with small kitchenettes, and one room is barrier-free for disabled access. There's ample parking out the front.

U SALZMANNŮ PENSION €

(☎377 235 476; www.usalzmannu.cz; Pražská 8; s & d 950-1350Kč, ste 1500Kč; ⊖ 📶) This pleasant pension, right in the heart of town, sits above a historic pub. The standard rooms are comfortable but basic; the more luxurious double 'suites' have antique beds and small sitting rooms, as well as kitchenettes. The pub location is convenient if you overdo it; to reach your bed, just climb the stairs.

PENSION CITY PENSION €

(☎377 326 069; www.pensioncityplzen.cz; sady 5 kvetna 52; s/d incl breakfast 1050/1450Kč; ⊖ 📶) On a quiet street near the river, Pension City has comfortable rooms and friendly, English-speaking staff armed with lots of local information.

HOTEL CENTRAL HOTEL €€

(☎378 011 855; www.central-hotel.cz; náměstí Republiky 33; s/d 1800/2700Kč; ⊖ @ 📶) This rather modern building across from St Bartholomew Church has an excellent location, right on the main square. The renovated rooms are clean and inviting, with the best rooms being those that face the square.

HOTEL CONTINENTAL HOTEL €€

(☎377 235 292; www.hotelcontinental.cz; Zbrojnická 8; s/d from 1090/1720Kč, ste s/d incl breakfast 2500/3200Kč; 📶) The Continental has survived being hit by an Allied bomb in WWII, and playing host at various times to Marlene Dietrich, General Patton and Ingrid Berman. The hotel's art-deco glory is being slowly resurrected, with newly renovated suites tinged with Asian design features.

HOTEL SLOVAN HOTEL €

(☎377 227 256; www.hotelslovan.pilsen.cz; Smetanovy sady 1; s 600-1100 Kč, d 900-1200Kč) The Slovan is one of a handful of unreconstructed, early 20th century, former luxury hotels in the Czech Republic that toggle somewhere between old-world charm and fleapit (minus the fleas). If you love flapper-era glamour but don't mind threadbare rooms and worn-out carpets, this place is for you. The central location is excellent.

ENTERTAINMENT

ZACH'S PUB LIVE MUSIC

(☎377 223 176; www.zachspub.cz; Palackého náměstí 2; ⏲1-9pm Mon-Thu, 1pm-2am Fri & Sat, to midnight Sun) Head to Zach's for live music and a suitably student atmosphere.

BUENA VISTA CLUB LIVE MUSIC

(☎377 921 291; www.buenavistaclub.cz; Kollárova 20; ⏲11am-3am Mon-Sat; 📶) This funky multipurpose space hosts everything from emerging Czech live acts to an eclectic range of DJs. English-language movies are occasionally screened.

MUSIC BAR ANDĚL LIVE MUSIC

(☎377 323 226; www.andelcafe.cz; Bezručova 7; ⏲10am-3am; 📶) By day a cool, hip cafe, the Anděl is transformed after dark into a rocking live-music venue featuring the best of touring Czech bands and occasional international acts. It also has a good vegetarian menu.

JK TYLA THEATRE THEATRE

(☎378 038 128; www.djkt-plzen.cz; Prokopova 14) Plzeň's main theatre stages regular Czech-language performances.

KONZERVATOŘ CLASSICAL MUSIC

(Conservatory; ☎377 226 325; www.konzervatorplzen.cz; Kopeckého sady 10) The majority of classical concerts in Plzeň are held here.

PLAZA CINEMA CITY PLZEŇ CINEMA

(☎255 742 021; www.cinemacity.cz/en/plzen; Radčická 2; 🚊2) A multiplex cinema in a shopping mall. Catch tram 2 and jump off two stops west from náměstí Republiky.

Karlovy Vary

Explore

Karlovy Vary is the closest the Czech Republic has to a glam resort, but it is still only glam with a small 'g'. While the resort was famous across Europe in the 19th century as a *kurort* (health spa), these days the town attracts mostly day-trippers, content to stroll the main colonnade area and sip on allegedly health-restoring sulphuric compounds from ceramic, spouted drinking cups. Despite the spa rep, Karlovy Vary is not entirely welcoming to walk-ins looking for high-end treatments like exotic massages and peelings; these services are available, but make advance bookings. Good bus services from Prague makes this an easy return day trip.

The Best...

- **Sight** Hot Spring Colonnade (p222)
- **Place to Eat** Hospoda U Švejka (p226)
- **Place to Drink** Café Elefant (p227)

Top Tip

The **Karlovy Vary International Film Festival** (www.kviff.com; ⏲Jul) in July is well worth attending. More than 200 films are shown, tickets are relatively easy to get, and there's a funky array of concurrent events (buskers, world-music concerts etc).

Getting There & Away

Bus Several companies offer bus services from Prague (155Kc, two hours), leaving at least hourly during the day. Check Student Agency (p199) or www.vlak-bus.cz for up-to-date timetables.

Train From Prague, the train takes a circuitous route that can take as long as seven hours: unless you've got nothing else to do, it's not recommended.

Car From Prague, Karlovy Vary is an easy two-hour drive due west, heading out of town on Hwy 6 (aka E48).

Need to Know

- **Location** 127km west of Prague.
- **Infocentrum Karlovy Vary** maintains branches at the lower bus station **Dolní nádrazi** (☎353 232 838; www.karlovyvary.cz; Západní 2a ; ⏲9am-6pm Mon-Fri, 10am-5pm Sat & Sun), Hotel Thermal and at the Hot Spring Colonnade in the main spa area. They all stocks maps, handle accommodation bookings and provide transport advice.
- **Česká Spořitelna** (☎956 748 000; www.csas.cz; TG Masaryka 14; ⏲8.30am-4pm Mon-Fri) Centrally located ATM and currency exchange.

SIGHTS

FREE **HOT SPRING COLONNADE** SPRING

(Vřídelní Kolonáda; www.karlovyvary.cz; Vřídelní Kolonáda; ⏲Pramen Vřídlo 6am-7pm) The Hot Spring Colonnade houses the most impressive of the town's geysers, **Pramen Vřídlo**. The building itself is an an incongruous, mid-'70s structure once dedicated to Soviet cosmonaut Yuri Gagarin. The geyser belches some 15m into the air; people lounge about inhaling the vapours or sampling the waters from a line of taps in the next room.

STROLLING THE COLONNADES

As you'll soon discover, there's not much to do in Karlovy Vary except to walk and gawk (and that's not such a bad thing). So make like a local and buy a little ceramic sipping cup (sold everywhere along the main colonnade) and enjoy a relaxing stroll. You can fill your cup for free at spa points along the way, but watch how much you sip, since too much 'health' has been known to cause to occasional gastric distress.

The spa proper begins at the northern end of the resort area, near the **Poštovní Bridge**, where late 19th- and early 20th-century mansions face-off with the rather blockish, communist-era (1976) **Hotel Thermal** sanatorium across the river.

The 13th spring is the most famous, but there are 15 springs housed in or near five colonnades *(kolonády)* along the Teplá. The first is the whitewashed and wrought-iron **Park Spring Colonnade** (Sadová kolonáda).

Further on is the biggest and most popular, the neo-Renaissance **Mill Colonnade** (Mlýnská kolonáda; 1881). Here you'll find five different springs, a small bandstand and even rooftop statues depicting the months of the year. Petra Restaurant, opposite, is the spot (but not the original building) where Peter the Great allegedly stayed in 1711.

Straight up Lázeňská is a gorgeous art-nouveau building called **dům Zawojski** (1901). It's been reopened as a classy boutique hotel. Nearby you can do some very upmarket window shopping along Lázeňská and Tržiště, including at the **Moser Glasswork Shop** (Tržiště 7), which features a range of tableware and gift items. The Moser company opened its first shop in Karlovy Vary in 1857, and by 1893 had established a glassworks in the town. Less than a decade later Moser became the official supplier to the Imperial Court of Franz Josef I, who obviously put in a good word to his English friend King Edward VII, as Moser also became the official supplier of glass to British royalty in 1907.

Across the road is the **Market Colonnade** (Tržní kolonáda; 1883) with its delicate white woodwork; one of its two springs, pramen Karla IV, is the spa's oldest. Behind this is the **Castle Colonnade** (Zámecká kolonáda) and a castle tower, the **Zámecká věž**, erected in place of Charles IV's hunting lodge after it was destroyed by fire in 1604.

The street Stará Louka continues south for more splendour. At the end of the stroll stands the magnificent **Grandhotel Pupp** (p228), the resort's choicest hotel and still housing well-heeled guests for the night.

CHURCH OF MARY MAGDALENE CHURCH

(kostel sv Maří Magdaléná; www.karlovyvary.cz; náměstí Svobody 2; ⊙open during mass times) Whatever your thoughts on the excesses of baroque architecture, it's hard not to fall for this confection by Kilian Ignatz Dientzenhofer, dating from the 1730s. You can arrange a tour through a branch of the Infocentrum to see the baroque **crypt** and the unique **funeral chapel**.

CHURCH OF STS PETER & PAUL CHURCH

(kostel Sv Petra a Pavla; Krále Jiřího; ⊙9am-6pm) The impressive Orthodox Church of Sts Peter & Paul, with five polished onion domes and art-nouveau exterior murals, was apparently modelled after a similar church near Moscow. One of the church's most prominent decorations is a relief depicting Tsar Peter the Great.

KARLOVY VARY MUSEUM MUSEUM

(Krajské muzeum Karlovy Vary; ☎353 226 252; www.kvmuz.cz; Nová Louka 23; adult/concession 60/30Kč; ⊙9am-noon & 1-5pm Wed-Sun) The Karlovy Vary Museum has extensive exhibits on the town's history as a spa resort, Czech glasswork and the area's natural history.

JAN BECHER MUSEUM MUSEUM

(☎359 578 142; www.becherovka.cz; TG Masaryka 57; adult/concession 100/50Kč; ⊙9am-5pm) The Jan Becher Museum deals with all things Becherovka, the town's famed herbal liqueur.

Karlovy Vary

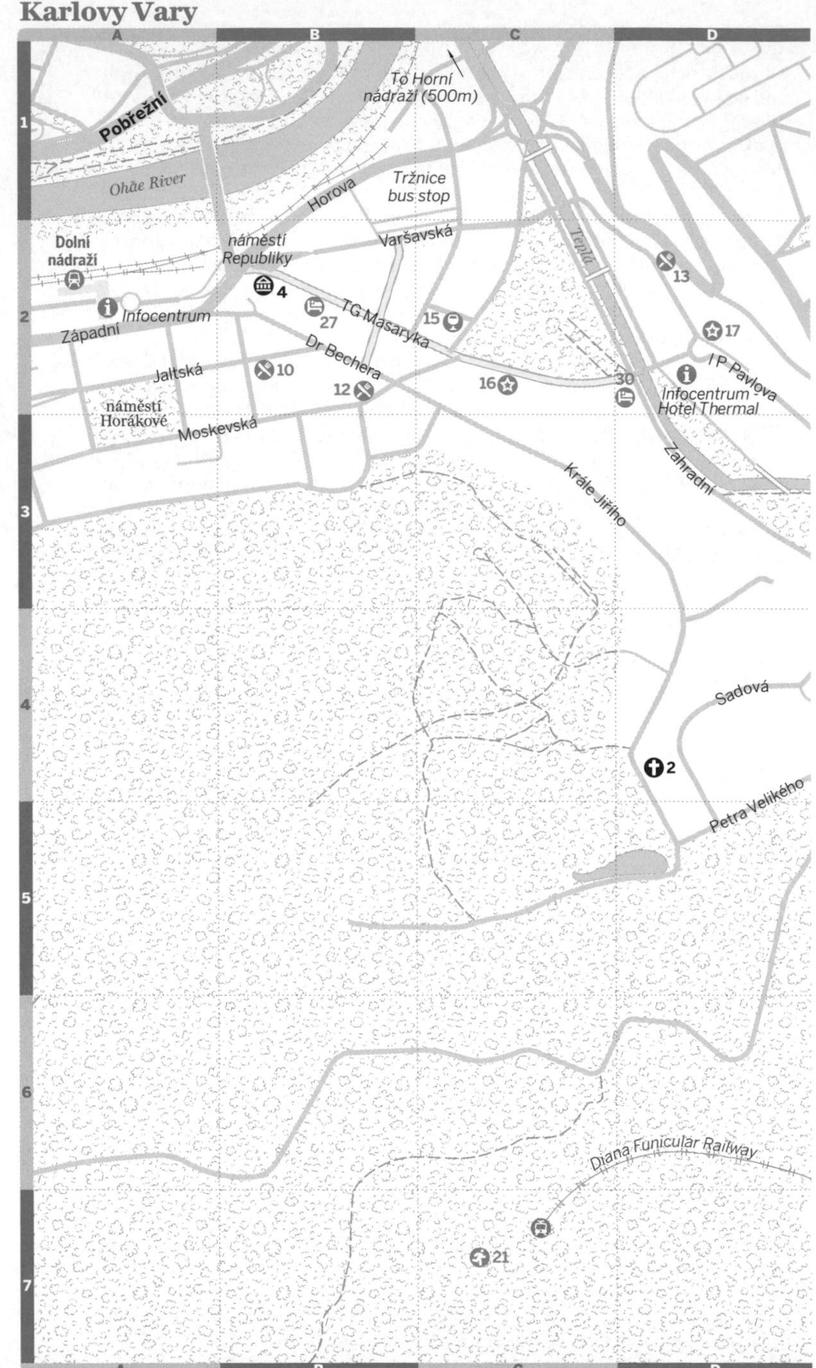

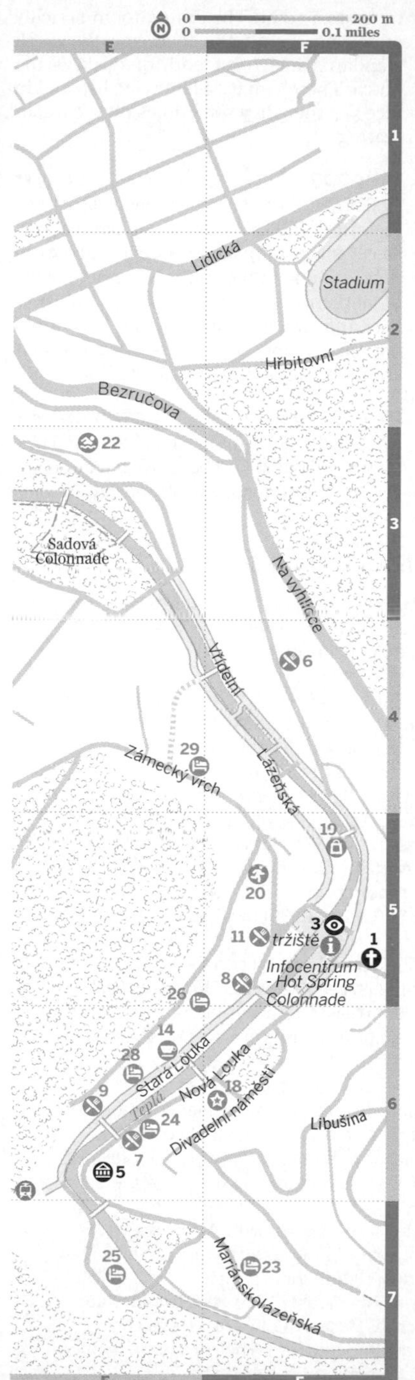

MOSER GLASS MUSEUM MUSEUM

(Sklářské muzeum Moser; ☎353 416 132; www.moser-glass.com; Kpt Jaroše 19; adult/child 80/50Kč, glassworks 120/70Kč, combined ticket 180/100Kč; ⏲9am-5pm, glassworks 9am-2.30pm; 🚌1) The Moser Glass Museum has more than 2000 items on display. Tours of the adjacent **glassworks** and combined tickets are also available. There is a shop here, too, but the prices are not anything special, and there's another shop in town. To get here catch bus 1 from the Tržnice bus station.

Karlovy Vary

Sights

1 Church of Mary Magdalene F5
2 Church of Sts Peter & Paul D4
3 Hot Spring Colonnade F5
4 Jan Becher Museum B2
5 Karlovy Vary Museum E6

Eating

6 Bornard F4
7 Embassy Restaurant E6
8 Hospoda U Švejka F5
9 Kafé Brejk E6
10 Kus Kus B2
11 Promenáda F5
12 Sklípek B2
13 Tandoor D2

Drinking

14 Café Elefant E6
15 Retro Cafe Bar C2

Entertainment

16 Čas Kino C2
17 Karlovy Vary Symphony Orchestra D2
18 Town Theatre F6

Shopping

19 Moser Glasswork Shop F5

Sports & Activities

20 Castle Spa F5
21 Diana Lookout Tower C7
22 Swimming Pool E3

Sleeping

23 Carlsbad Plaza F7
24 Embassy Hotel E6
25 Grandhotel Pupp E7
26 Hotel Boston E5
27 Hotel Kavalerie B2
28 Hotel Maltézsý Kříž E6
29 Hotel Ontario E4
30 Hotel Romania D2

EATING & DRINKING

Food prices, especially around the colonnades, will seem high unless you've arrived from Prague. And check your bill: 'mistakes' happen. You can buy *oplatky* (wafers; see boxed text) across town.

HOSPODA U ŠVEJKA — CZECH €€

(353 232 276; www.svejk-kv.cz; Stará Louka 10; mains 160–370Kč; 11am-11pm) A great choice for lunch or dinner, right in the heart of the spa centre. Though the presentation borders on extreme kitsch, the food is actually very good and the atmosphere not unlike a classic Czech pub.

EMBASSY RESTAURANT — CZECH €€€

(353 221 161; www.embassy.cz; Nová Louka 21; mains 200-500Kč) The in-house restaurant of the Embassy Hotel (p227) is a destination in its own right. The dining room is richly atmospheric and the food, mostly Czech standards like roast pork or duck, is top notch. There's an excellent wine list, and in nice weather they sometimes offer outdoor seating.

TANDOOR — INDIAN €€

(608 701 341; www.tandoor-kv.cz; IP Pavlova 25; mains 150-250Kč; noon-10pm Mon-Sat, noon-6pm Sun;) Located under a block of flats, Tandoor turns out a winning combo of authentic Indian flavours, Gambrinus beer and smooth, creamy lassis. Vegetarian options abound, or if you're after a serious chilli hit, order the chicken phall.

PROMENÁDA — INTERNATIONAL €€€

(353 225 648; www.hotel-promenada.cz; Tržiště 31; mains 250-650Kč) The house restaurant of the Hotel Promenáda has appeared in some

WORTH A DETOUR: THE 'ELBOW' OF LOKET NAD OHŘE

Surrounded by a wickedly serpentine loop in the Ohře River, the picturesque village of **Loket** may as well be on an island. According to the local tourist office, it was Goethe's favourite town and, after a lazily subdued stroll around the gorgeous main square and castle, it may be yours as well.

Loket's German name is **Elbogen** (meaning 'elbow', after the extreme bend in the river) – a name synonymous with the manufacturing of porcelain since 1815. Shops in town have a fine selection of the local craftsmanship. The neighbouring towns of Horní Slavkov (Schlackenwald) and Chodov (Chodan) also make porcelain.

Most people visit Loket as a day trip from Karlovy Vary, but it's also a sleepy place to ease off the travel accelerator for a few days, especially when the day-trippers have departed. Loket also makes a good base for visiting Karlovy Vary: the bus to/from Karlovy Vary stops across the bridge from the Old Town. Walk across the bridge to reach the castle, accommodation and **Infocentrum** (Loket Information Centre; 352 684 123; www.loket.cz; TG Masaryka 12; 10.30am-12.30pm & 1-5pm), which has internet access (per 15 minutes 10Kč).

The main site in town is the beautiful castle, **Hrad Loket** (Loket Castle ; 352 684 648; www.hradloket.cz; Hrad; with English guide adult/concession 110/90Kč, with English text 95/75Kč; 9am-4.30pm Apr-Oct, 9am-3.30pm Nov-Mar). It was built on the site of an earlier Romanesque fort, of which the only surviving bits are the tall, square tower and fragments of a rotunda and palace.

The castle was regarded as very defensively secure in earlier times, and was known as 'the key to Bohemia'. Its present late-Gothic look dates from the late 14th century. From 1788 to 1947 it was used as the town prison. Highlights of the tour include two rooms filled with the town's lustrous porcelain and views from the castle tower (96 steps). There's also a gleefully gruesome torture chamber, complete with stereophonic sound effects.

Ask at the Infocentrum about hiking possibilities in the surrounding forests, including a semi-ambitious day hike to Karlovy Vary (around four hours) along a 17km blue-marked trail. Karlovy Vary is also the destination for rafting trips.

There are several decent pensions in town. The nicest hotel is the **Hotel Císař Ferdinand** (352 327 130; www.hotel-loket.cz; TG Masaryka 136; s/d incl breakfast 1060/1850Kč; P), right across from the Infocentrum. This former post office has recently renovated rooms and the best little microbrewery in town.

OPLATKY: A WAFER WITH YOUR SULPHUR DRINK

To quote Monty Python, 'Do you get wafers with it?' The answer is a resounding 'yes' according to Karlovry Vary locals, who prescribe the following method of taking your spring water: have a sip from your *lázeňský pohárek* (spa cup), then dull the sulphurous taste with a big, round, sweet wafer called *oplatky*. *Oplatky* are sold for around 10Kč each at a few spa hotels and speciality shops, or you can pick them up at Kolonada Oplatky (cnr Nehrova and Masarykova). Steer clear of the fancy chocolate or hazelnut flavours, though; they're never as crunchily fresh and warm as the standard vanilla flavour.

'best of' lists for the Czech Republic and is a perennial favourite on online forums. The elegant dining area is conducive to a memorable evening, and the food is very good (though perhaps not always worth the steep prices).

SKLÍPEK CZECH €

(☎353 220 222; www.restaurantsklipek.com; Moskevská 2; meals 120-180Kč) Red-checked tablecloths and an emphasis on good steaks, fish and pasta give this place an honest, rustic ambience missing from the more chi chi spots in the spa district.

BERNARD CZECH €

(☎353 221 667; www.restaurace-bernard.cz; Ondřejská 120/14; mains 110-200Kč) This cosy pub with a backstreet location is a nice choice for well-prepared Czech specialties like pork knee (served in tradtional style with a side of mustard and several hunks of bread). The beer, from the small Bernard brewery, is a welcome change of pace from the larger national brands.

KUS KUS VEGETARIAN €

(☎774 409 910; www.kus-kus.cz; Bělehradská 8; snacks 50-70Kč; ⏰7am-5pm Mon-Fri; ✎) This cosy cafe-bakery serves salads, pasta and homemade desserts with an organic and vegetarian tinge.

KAFÉ BREJK SANDWICHES €

(☎353 229 638; Stará Louka 62; coffee 45Kč, baguettes 60Kč; ⏰9am-5pm) Trendy spot for takeaway coffees and design-your-own baguettes.

CAFÉ ELEFANT CAFE

(☎353 223 406; Stará Louka 30; coffee 50Kč) Classy old-school spot for coffee and cake. A tad touristy, but still elegant and refined.

RETRO CAFE BAR BAR

(☎353 100 710; www.retrocafebar.cz; TG Masaryka 18; ⏰10am-midnight Sun-Thu, to 3am Fri & Sat) A retro-themed bar, cafe and restaurant that defies easy categorisation. A nice place to chill for coffee or a cocktail, and the food is not bad either. There's music in the evenings and retro-themed nights.

SLEEPING

Accommodation prices in Karlovy Vary have risen steeply in recent years to be similar to those in Prague, especially in July during the film festival. Indeed, if you're planning a July arrival, make sure to book well in advance. Expect to pay an additional 'spa tax' (15Kč per bed per night). The Infocentrum can help out with hostel, pension and hotel bookings. Alternatively, consider staying in Loket and visiting Karlovy Vary as a day trip.

TOP CHOICE **HOTEL MALTÉZSÝ KŘÍŽ** HOTEL €€

(☎353 169 011; www.maltezskykriz.cz; Stará Louka 50; s/d 1650/2800Kč; @📶) Welcome to Karlovy Vary's best-value midrange hotel. Oriental rugs and wooden floors combine at this spiffy property, with cosy rooms and a more spacious double-storeyed apartment. The bathrooms are decked-out in warm, earthy tones.

CARLSBAD PLAZA HOTEL €€€

(☎353 225 501; www.carlsbadplaza.cz; Mariánskolázeňská 23; s/d 4000/6000Kč; P🚭❄@📶🏊) Seriously stylish, this relatively new hotel has raised the bar in spa town, with soothingly modern treatment facilities, classy rooms and a vegetarian-friendly Asian restaurant.

EMBASSY HOTEL HOTEL €€

(☎353 221 161; www.embassy.cz; Nová Luka 21; s/d incl breakfast from 2260/3130Kč; @📶) KV's not short of top-end hotels, but most lack the personal touch of the family-owned Embassy, with its riverside location and perfectly pitched heritage rooms. The hotel's pub and restaurant have seen visits from plenty of film-fest luminaries.

GRANDHOTEL PUPP HOTEL €€€
(353 109 631; www.pupp.cz; Mírové náměstí 2; r 4000-7000Kč;) No accounting of KV's hotels would be complete without mentioning the granddaddy, the Pupp, whose history dates back to the 18th century. Take a look at a few rooms, as layouts and furnishings differ from wing to wing. Even if you're not staying here, take a peek inside; the restaurants are very good, and the period-piece atmosphere is perfect.

HOTEL ROMANIA HOTEL €€
(353 222 822; www.romania.cz; Zahradni 49; s/d incl breakfast 1200/1950Kč;) Don't be put off by the ugly monolith of the Hotel Thermal dominating the views from this good-value, reader-recommended hotel (just squint a little). The spacious rooms are very tidy and the English-speaking staff very helpful.

HOTEL KAVALERIE HOTEL €
(353 229 613; www.kavalerie.cz; TG Masaryka 43; s/d incl breakfast from 850/1300Kč;) Friendly staff abound in this cosy spot above a cafe. It's close to the bus and train stations, and the nearby eateries can help you avoid the high prices at the spa district's restaurants. The rooms are starting to look a bit worn, but it's still OK value.

HOTEL BOSTON HOTEL €
(353 362 711; www.boston.cz; Luční vrch 9; s/d incl breakfast 1390/1570Kč;) Tucked away down a quiet lane, this family-owned hotel has relatively spacious rooms decorated in bright colours with updated bathrooms. The flash cafes of Stará Louka are just around the corner.

HOTEL ONTARIO HOTEL €€
(353 222 091; www.hotelontario.cz; Zámecký vrch 20; s/d incl breakfast 1875/2125Kč;) Look forward to great views from the Ontario, and just maybe Karlovy Vary's friendliest team on reception. They call the stylishly appointed lodgings 'rooms', but they're actually compact apartments. The hotel is a stiff five-minute walk uphill.

ENTERTAINMENT

TOWN THEATRE THEATRE
(Městské divadlo v Karlových Varech; 353 225 537; www.karlovarske-divadlo.cz; Divadelní náměstí 21) Drama, comedy and musicals all feature here. Tickets are available from the theatre or any of the Infocentrum offices.

KARLOVY VARY SYMPHONY ORCHESTRA CLASSICAL MUSIC
(353 228 707; www.kso.cz; IP Pavlova 14) The town's highly regarded orchestra stages a regular program of concerts; check the website for concerts during your visit. You

HIKING THE HILLS OF KARLOVY VARY

Once you've wearied of walking around town and taking the waters, a scenic network of trails lies in the hills waiting for exploration. One of the most popular trails ascends 1.5km from the Grandhotel Pupp to the hilltop **Diana Lookout Tower** (353 222 872; www.karlovy-vary.cz/en/diana-tower; 9am-7pm Jun-Sep, 9am-6pm Apr, May & Oct, 9am-5pm Feb, Mar, Nov & Dec). The woods on the way to the lookout are peppered with monuments, including one to that crusty old bourgeois, Karl Marx, who visited Karlsbad (Karlovy Vary) three times between 1874 and 1876.

Alternatively, you can ride a **funicular railway** (www.karlovy-vary.cz/en/diana-tower; one way/return 40/70Kc; 9am-7pm Jun-Sep, 9am-6pm Apr, May & Oct, 9am-5pm Feb, Mar, Nov & Dec) from behind Grandhotel Pupp. The trip to Diana takes five minutes. **Stag's Leap** (Jelení skok), the promontory from where legend has it that Charles IV, or rather his dogs, first discovered the town's healing waters, is 500m northeast from an intermediate stop on the funicular. Another lookout tower is on **Vyhlídka Karla IV**, south of Grandhotel Pupp.

If you're feeling energetic, it's a 17km hike on a blue-marked trail via the Diana lookout and along the Ohřě Rever to the romantic castle and village of **Loket nad Ohřě** (see boxed text p226).

can buy tickets at any of the Infocentrum offices.

ČAS KINO CINEMA
(353 223 272; www.kinocaskv.cz; TG Masaryka 3) Shows mainly Hollywood movies.

KINO PANASONIC CINEMA
(353 233 933; www.kinopanasonic.cz; Vitězná 50;) A compact art-house cinema with a good cafe and free wi-fi access.

SPORTS & ACTIVITIES

CASTLE SPA SPA
(Zámecké Lázně; 353 225 502; www.castle-spa.com; Zámecký vrch 1; prices vary with treatments; 7.30am-7.30pm Mon-Fri, from 8.30am Sat & Sun) Most KV accommodation offers some kind of a spa treatment for a fee, but if you're just a casual visitor or day-tripper, consider Castle Spa, a modernised spa centre complete with a subterranean thermal pool. Consult the website for a full menu of treatments and prices.

SWIMMING POOL SWIMMING
(359 001 111; www.thermal.cz; IP Pavlova 11; adult/child 100/80Kč; 8.30am-8pm) Hotel Thermal's 50m pool is open to the public year-round. The waters are heated by thermal springs. To find it, follow the 'Bazén' signs up the hill behind the hotel to the pool.

Mariánské Lázně

Explore

Mariánské Lázně (mari-*ahn*-skay *lahz*-nyeh; known internationally as Marienbad) is smaller, less urban and arguably prettier than Karlovy Vary, making it feel more like a classic spa destination (but also meaning there's even less to do in the evening). In the resort's heyday, Mariánské Lázně drew such luminaries as Goethe, Thomas Edison, Britain's King Edward VII and even American author Mark Twain. These days many visitors are day-trippers from Germany, hauled in by coach to stroll the gardens and colonnades before repairing to a cafe for the inevitable *apfelstrudel* then the ride back home. Beside the colonnades, the town is ringed by deep forests that make for great walks.

The Best...

- **Sight** Colonnade (p229)
- **Place to Eat** Medité (p232)
- **Place to Drink** Maui Lounge (p232)

Top Tip

If you're coming to Mariánské Lázně specifically for a spa treatment, book in advance: spas are ill-prepared for walk-ins. The website www.marienbad.cz has helpful lists of spas, treatments and prices.

Getting There & Away

Train Half-a-dozen fast trains per day run from Prague (250Kč, three hours) via Plzeň. Regular (slow) trains link Mariánské Lázně and Karlovy Vary (63Kč, 1¾ hours).

Bus Buses from Prague (190Kč, three hours) and Plzeň (120Kč, 1¼ hours) are less frequent (up to five per day) and take as long as the train.

Car From Prague, the drive takes about two hours. Head southwest out of the city along the D5 motorway past Plzeň, turning north on Hwy 21 at Bor.

Need to Know

- **Location** 173km due west of Prague.
- **Infocentrum** (ph 354 622 474; www.marianskelazne.cz; Hlavní třída 47; h 9am-6pm) Sells theatre tickets and maps, and books accommodation.
- **Internet Access** The Infocentrum has a computer on hand tocheck email (per minute 1Kč).

SIGHTS

FREE **COLONNADE** HISTORIC BUILDING
(Lázeňská kolonáda; Lázeňská kolonáda; Cross Spring 6am-6pm) The restored cast-iron Colonnade, east of the municipal park, is

Mariánské Lázně

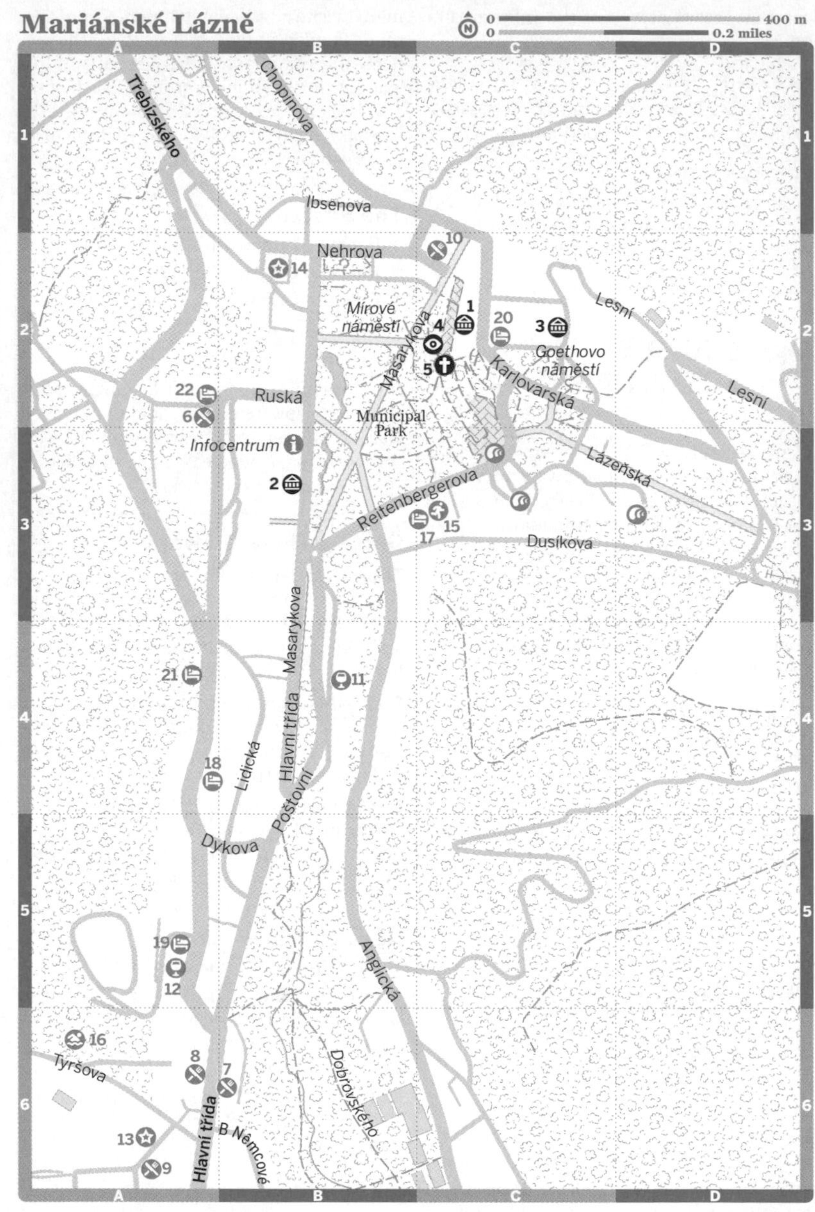

the spa's visual centrepiece. Classical and brass-band concerts are presented here two or three times a day in high season. Also here, in its own whitewashed pavilion, is the **Cross Spring** (Křížový pramen), the spa's first spring. Choose from a galaxy of souvenir porcelain mugs or bring along a plastic bottle.

FREE SINGING FOUNTAIN FOUNTAIN
(Zpívající fontána; www.marienbad.cz/en; Lázeňská kolonáda; ⏰May-Sep) Just in front

Mariánské Lázně

Sights
1 Colonnade........C2
2 Fryderyk Chopin Memorial Museum........B3
3 Municipal Museum........C2
4 Singing Fountain........C2
5 St Vladimír Church........C2

Eating
6 Maui Lounge........A2
7 Medité........B6
8 New York Barcaffe........A6
9 Piccolo........A6
10 U Zlaté Koule........C2

Drinking
11 Irish Pub........B4
12 Scottish Pub........A5

Entertainment
13 Kino Slavia........A6
14 Městské Divadlo........B2

Sports & Activities
15 Danubius Health Spa Resort Nové Lázně........C3
16 Public Pool........A6

Sleeping
17 Danubius Health Spa Resort Nové Lázně........C3
18 Falkensteiner Hotel Grand Spa........A4
19 Hostel Milano........A5
20 Hotel Paris........C2
21 Hotel Richard........A4
22 Olympia Hotel........A2
Pension Edinburgh........(see 12)

of the colonnade, the Singing Fountain sashays to recorded classical music every two hours from May to September. An information board details the musical schedule.

Goethovo Náměstí & Around

This manicured **square**, edged with extravagant late 19th- and early 20th-century buildings, probably looks much as it did when King Edward VII et al patronised the surrounding spas and hotels. The highlights here are the Municipal Museum and the nearby Church of the Assumption of the Virgin Mary, built in 1848 in neo-Byzantine style.

MUNICIPAL MUSEUM MUSEUM

(Městské muzeum; ☎354 622 740; www.muzeum-ml.cz; Goethovo náměstí 11; adult/concession 60/30Kč; ⌚9.30am-5.30pm Tue-Sun) The Municipal Museum stands on the site where Goethe stayed during his last visit to Mariánské Lázně. The exhibits present a good overview of the town's history (though only with Czech captions). Ask to see two English-language videos on the history and geology of the area. The **Church of the Assumption of the Virgin Mary** (kostel Nanebevzetí Panny Marie) is opposite the museum.

Hlavní Třída & Around

Hlavní třída, as the name implies (hlavní means 'main'), is the spa town's **central avenue**, lined on one side by big hotels, cafes and resorts, and on the other by a long, sloping park. The main attraction here, besides the cafes and the Infocentrum, is a small museum dedicated to Polish-French composer Frédéric Chopin, who visited the spa in 1836.

FRYDERYK CHOPIN MEMORIAL MUSEUM MUSEUM

(☎354 622 617; www.chopinfestival.cz; Hlavní třída 47; adult/concession 20/10Kč; ⌚2-5pm Tue, Thu & Sun Apr-Sep) This small museum displays personal effects and information on Chopin's life, and on his visit to the spa in 1836. Chopin's music is played in the background.

ST VLADIMÍR CHURCH CHURCH

(kostel Sv Vladimíra; Ruská 347-349; 20Kč; ⌚9am-noon & 1-5pm May-Oct, 9.30-11.30am & 2-4pm Nov-Apr) The 1901 red-and-yellow St Vladimír Church is a plush, Byzantine-style Orthodox church with an amazing porcelain iconostasis.

EATING & DRINKING

TOP CHOICE MEDITÉ SPANISH €€

(☎354 422 018; www.medite.cz; Hlavní třída 7/229; tapas 70-130Kč, mains 270-310Kč;) Mix and match relatively authentic tapas and good *paella* with German and Spanish wines (by the glass) at this modern spot with blonde-wood floors and a buzzy vibe. It's an energetic response to the languid spa-town atmosphere outside.

MAUI LOUNGE INTERNATIONAL €€

(☎607 879 813; www.maui.cz; Ruská 72; mains 225-428Kč; ⊙11am-1am;) This sleek and popular combo restaurant/cocktail bar features an inventive menu of salads, pastas, steaks and seafoods. They have a nice selection of tapas plates and special, mouth-watering five-course meals if you're really famished.

U ZLATÉ KOULE CZECH €€€

(☎354 624 455; www.uzlatekoule.com; Nehrova 26; mains 250-580Kč; ⊙noon-11pm) A stunning cocktail of five-star class and cosy informality, this swish eatery features creaking wooden beams, sparkling glassware and antiques. The game-rich menu effortlessly whips up the 'wow' factor. Order a day in advance for roast goose with apple stuffing and bread-and-bacon dumplings.

NEW YORK BARCAFFE INTERNATIONAL €

(☎776 007 921; www.newyorkml.cz; Hlavní třída 233; mains 60-160Kč; ⊙9am-2am;) Another one of those tough-to-pigeonhole places, this is a popular cafe most of the day, but transforms into a lively bar at night. We like it because they also do light international food items like salads and pastas – the kind of good (and quick) food that isn't easy to find in Mariánské Lázně.

PICCOLO ITALIAN €

(☎354 626 099; Nerudova 291; mains 90-140Kč;) The best pizza and pasta in town is at this rustic spot out of the spa district. It's local food at local prices. Catch a movie at **Kino Slavia** (p235) across the street when you're done.

IRISH PUB IRISH PUB

(☎608 303 838; www.irish-pub.cz; Poštovni 96; ⊙from 5pm) Old typewriters and vintage green bicycles create a suitably Irish ambience for the best craic in Mariánské Lázně. Lots of Irish whiskeys on hand, as well as light food items and pizza. Follow the signs that say 'Irish Pub'.

WORTH A DETOUR: 'BEER WELLNESS LAND'

In the village of **Planá**, 20 minutes by bus (25Kč) from Mariánské Lázně, the beer spa at the **Chodovar Brewery** (☎374 617 100; www.chodovar.cz; Pivovarská 107; treatments from 660Kc) is the perfect spot to simultaneously explore both of western Bohemia's claims to fame: world-class spas and beer.

'Beer spa' treatments at Chodovar's self-proclaimed 'Beer Welless Land' include a couple of glasses of the village's liquid gold. There are other tantalizing menu options, including massages, hot stones and even a 'beer bath for two'. Couples can book in for special Valentine's Day packages.

The beer spa experience goes something like this: after disrobing, you sink yourself into a hoppy bath of warm beer. Confetti-sized fragments of hops and yeast stud the water, and the overriding aroma features the grassy, zesty tones of world-renowned hops from nearby Žatec. The bath is heated to a comfy 34°C (93°F), and you're even allowed to sup on a glass of the Chodovar Brewery's fine golden lager for the duration.

After a relaxing soak of around 30 minutes, an attendant brings you your robe and leads you into some granite tunnels (used for 'lagering' beer as far back as the 12th century) for yet more rest and relaxation. According to the brewery's marketing spiel, the procedures will have 'curative effects on the complexion and hair, relieve muscle tension, warm-up joints and support the immune system of the organism'.

In the attached gift shop there's beer soap, shampoo and cosmetics. After all that hoppy goodness, visitors can even the score with tasty meat-heavy dishes and more brews in the subterranean restaurant and beer hall. Another above-ground restaurant features official beer sommeliers who can instruct in 10 different types of beer.

HIKING IN MARIÁNSKÉ LÁZNĚ

Mariánské Lázně is surrounded by dense forest, with more than a dozen trails winding through the woods and past pavilions and springs. The routes are shown on map boards at the south end of the Colonnade.

A popular trail climbs to Hotel Panoráma, round past an old stone **watchtower** (100 steps) and on to the ruin of Červená karkulka Café. Descend here to buses on Hlavní (total less than 4km) or keep going for a 7km round trip.

An easier loop trail heads north past Forest spring (Lesní pramen) to Lunapark, a pleasant cafe and spa hotel surrounded by forest.

Ask at Infocentrum for details of alternative hiking trails.

SCOTTISH PUB THEME BAR

(☎354 620 804; www.pensionedinburgh.com; Ruská 56; ⊙from 4pm) Lovers of all things Scottish should cross the Irish Sea to this pub for more Celtic shenanigans amid single-malt heaven and a memorial to William Wallace.

SLEEPING

While overnight stays are possible, most of the big hotels and resorts in town are geared for longer-term (one- to two-week) bookings, including full wellness packages. In practice that means reception desks are not always prepared to handle walk-in requests for a one- or two-night stay. You'll get better service (and often better prices) if you reserve a room in advance.

FALKENSTEINER HOTEL GRAND SPA HOTEL €€€

(☎354 929 396; www.falkensteiner.com; Ruská 123; r 3600-4800Kč; P🚭❄@📶🏊) This relatively recent opening towers over the spa resort in more ways than one. The hotel is in a senstively renovated 19th-century spa palace and offers every conceivable amenity. Staff will help arrange spa treatments; check the website for special deals and weekend packages.

DANUBIUS HEALTH SPA RESORT NOVÉ LÁZNĚ HOTEL €€€

(☎354 644 300; www.marienbad.cz; Reitenbergerova 53; d 3560-4560Kč, ste from 4700Kč; 🚭❄📶🏊) They say 'five star', but we reckon one of Mariánské Lázně's best hotels is a very good 'four star'. Either way you're guaranteed an elegant stay in this 19th-century confection that sits atop the 'new baths'. Exemplary spa services are virtually on tap as you're ushered into the gilded lobby. Check the website for spa packages.

PENSION EDINBURGH PENSION €

(☎354 620 804; www.pensionedinburgh.com; Ruská 56; s/d from 800/1000Kč, apt 1500Kč; @📶) This friendly, centrally located pension offers five refurbished rooms and one apartment, tucked away above the Scottish Pub (p233). In keeping with the Celtic theme, each room has a well-stocked minibar and dressing gowns. The owners offer transport around town and further afield.

PENSION ELBRS PENSION €

(☎354 623 619; www.pensionelbrs.sweb.cz; Palackého 316; per person incl breakfast 450Kč; 🚌3) Rooms here are handy upstairs/downstairs arrangements with huge beds, small lounge areas and compact kitchenettes. Breakfast is served in a pot-plant-trimmed conservatory. It's in a quiet residential neighbourhood a 15-minute walk from the centre. To get here catch bus 3 from the centre to the Lékárna stop.

HOSTEL MILANO HOSTEL €

(☎774 417 065; www.ubytovani.newyorkml.cz; Ruská 309; per person 250Kč; 📶) This hostel features Ikea-furnished dorms and modern art. There's a well-equipped shared kitchen if you're watching your budget.

HOTEL PARIS HOTEL €€

(☎354 628 897; www.hotelparis.cz; Goethovo náměstí 15/3; s/d incl breakfast 1450/2400Kč; 📶) High on the hill overlooking Goethovo náměstí, this is your chance to stay in the same ritzy area as King Edward VII, but at slightly less regal prices.

PENSION VILLA MARION PENSION €

(☎606 463 789; www.hotel-villa-marion-marianske-lazne.az-ubytovani.net; Palackého 360; s/d

WORTH A DETOUR: THE 'THIRD SPA' OF FRANTIŠKOVY LÁZNĚ

When people talk of western Bohemia's spas, it's usually only the two big ones that are mentioned: Karlovy Vary and Mariánské Lázně. There is, however, a third spa town, Františkovy Lázně (frantish-kovee *lahz*-nyeh), that's worth the relatively short hop from Mariánské Lázně if you're in the area and have an extra day to spend.

Indeed, with its buttery veneer of yellow paint, well-tended parklands with statues and springs, and spa patients and tourists walking around unbearably s...l...o...w... l...y, Františkovy Lázně may better fulfil your expectations of what a real spa town should look like.

Beethoven and Goethe were Františkovy Lázně's most famous guests, but with the spa best known for the treatment of female infertility, they were more likely drawn by a lively cafe society. Today, the sidewalk cafes are relaxingly soporific, and late-night action is sound asleep. So, make your visit here just for a sleepy day.

The **Town Information Centre** (Městské Informační Centrum; ☎354 543 162; www.frantiskolazensko.cz; Americká 2; ⏰8am-6pm Mon-Fri, 8am-2pm Sat & Sun) is a good place to start: pick up a free map and get your bearings. If you do decide to spend the night, the centre can advise on accommodations (and spa treatments).

Like its two big-brother spas, Františkovy Lázně is rather short on must-sees. The biggest attraction is simply to stroll the main drag, Národní, admiring the impossibly cute spa architecture and stopping for coffee or cake every couple of hours or so. The key sights are the **Church of the Ascension of the Cross** (kostel Povýšení sv Kříže) on Ruská, and the town's central spring, the **Františkův pramen**, at the southern end of Národní. To get a better understanding of the spa's history, drop by the **City Museum** (Městské muzeum; ☎354 544 307; www.frantiskolazensko.cz; Dlouhá 4; adult/child 30/10Kc ; ⏰10am-5pm Tue-Sun). You can also hire a boat at the small pond, the **Rybník Amerika**, about 2km from the city centre.

For a good meal, try **Restaurant Goethe** (☎354 500 146; www.franzensbad-casino.com; Národní 1; mains 150-300Kc; ⏰11.30am–2.30pm & 6pm–11pm, cafe 9am–7pm) for well-prepared international dishes served by waiters decked-out in period-piece garb.

There are plenty of hotels in town. One we like is **Hotel Kammený Dům** (☎354 541 037; www.kamennydum.cz; Ruská 6; s/d incl breakfast 1200/1500Kč). In a town where the cavalcade of yellow-painted heritage facades almost hurts your eyes, this place stands out with a more modern ambience, and spacious, contemporary rooms in a central location. Golf and spa packages can both be arranged.

You can get to Františkovy Lázně by bus or train from Plzeň or Mariánské Lázně. From the latter, the trip takes around an hour. Alternatively, the largish city of Cheb is just 30 minutes away by bus: from here you can catch regular trains back to Prague.

incl breakfast 600/900Kč, apt 1200-1800Kč) Just a few doors along from Pension Elbrs, this ivy-covered house has cosy rooms and apartments, and a garden restaurant. It's got a pretty good bar for a residential neighbourhood, too.

OLYMPIA HOTEL HOTEL €€

(☎354 931 810; www.olympiamarienbad.cz; Ruská 88/861; d incl breakfast from 2000Kč; ⊖❄📶🏊) With a slick but friendly edge, the modern Olympia offers decent midrange value with comfortable rooms, youthful staff, and a popular bar and restaurant in the lobby. See the website for a full array of spa services.

HOTEL RICHARD HOTEL €€

(☎354 696 111; www.hotelrichard.com; Ruská 487/28; s/d incl breakfast 1850/2890Kč; P❄📶🏊) It's named after composer Richard Wagner, but the stylish rooms and decor here are thankfully more low-key than his music. It's high on the hill, so expect good views.

ENTERTAINMENT

MĚSTSKÉ DIVADLO THEATRE

(Municipal Theatre; ☎354 622 036; www.marianskelazne.cz; Třebízského 106) Check the website for musical and theatrical performances.

KINO SLAVIA CINEMA

(☎354 622 347; www.kinoslavia.cz; Nerudova 437) This cinema shows mainly Hollywood films.

SPORTS & ACTIVITIES

DANUBIUS HEALTH SPA RESORT NOVÉ LÁZNĚ SPA

(☎354 644 111; www.marienbad.cz; Reitenbergerova 53; ⏲7am-7pm depending on treatment) Dozens of hotels and resorts offer various spa treatments for guests and occasianally walk-ins. There are Roman-style baths at the Hotel Nové Lázně as well as saunas and spa pools. See the website for a menu of one-off treatments available here and at other resorts.

ROYAL GOLF CLUB OF MARIÁNSKÉ LÁZNĚ GOLF

(☎354 624 300; www.golfml.cz; Mariánské Lázně 582; greens fees 1500-1700Kč; ⏲7am-9pm May-Sep) Mariánské Lázně is known around the country for its challenging and beautiful 6135-yard, par-72 golf course. The course has a long history, going back more than 100 years. You can hire clubs from the pro club; book in advance.

PUBLIC POOL SWIMMING

(Plavecký Stadión; ☎354 623 579; www.marianskelazne.cz; Tyršova 617; per 2hr adult/concession 100/40Kč; ⏲11am-9pm Mon-Sat) The public pool is southwest of the city centre.

Best of Moravia

Brno p237

Moravia's brawny capital boasts a spooky hilltop castle, mummies in a cellar, and a masterpiece of early modern architecture.

Telč p245

This small town's colourful Renaissance and baroque main square is so picture-perfect, it's a Unesco World Heritage Site.

Třebíč p248

This bustling city's tiny former Jewish Quarter, perched along a river, is unique in the Czech Republic.

Mikulov p249

Almost a piece of Italy in southern Moravia, complete with great wine and sparkling Renaissance architecture.

Valtice-Lednice p253

A Unesco-protected heritage landscape, with historic architecture amid lush, rolling hills.

Znojmo p255

Pleasant border town with atmospheric alleyways and a magnificent view out over the Dyje River valley.

Olomouc p257

Northern Moravian gem with a main square to rival Prague's, a lively student body and (at least two) great microbreweries.

Kroměříž p264

Another Unesco World Heritage site, this one with a magnificent 19th-century chateau.

EXPLORE MORAVIA

The Czech Republic's easternmost province, Moravia is yin to Bohemia's yang. If Bohemians love beer, Moravians love wine. If Bohemia is towns and cities, Moravia is rolling hills and pretty landscapes. Once you've seen the best of Bohemia, head east for a different side of the Czech Republic. The capital, Brno, has the museums, but the northern city of Olomouc has captivating architecture. The south is dominated by vineyards and, naturally, wine-drinking day-tipplers.

One Week in Moravia

Spend two days in Brno to experience the culture, modern architecture and nightlife. From there, head north to Olomouc for two days, with a day trip to Štramberk, or south to Mikulov, to enjoy the wine and nature.

Two Weeks in Moravia

In two weeks, you can see everything. Spend four days in Brno and at least a couple in Olomouc, before heading south to Znojmo and Mikulov. Rent a bike, pray for sun and spend the days on the trail and nights at a wine cellar.

Brno

Explore

Among Czechs, Moravia's capital has a dull rep; a likeable enough place where not much actually happens. There was even a hit movie a few years back called *Nuda v Brně* ('Boredom in Brno'). The reality,

Moravia

Brno

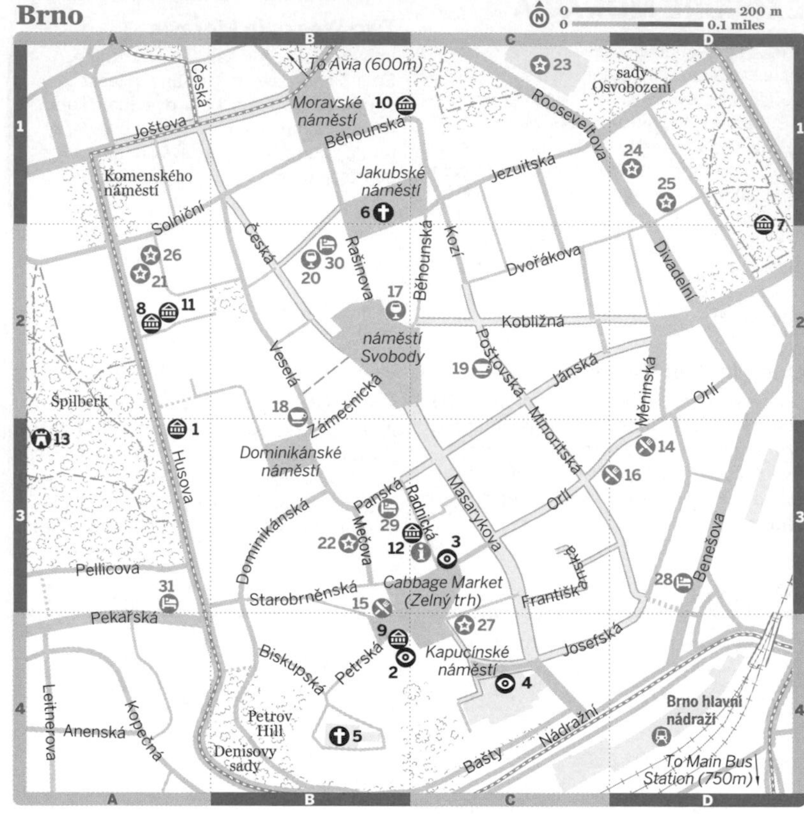

though, is very different. Tens of thousands of students ensure lively cafe and club scenes that easily rival Prague's. The museums are great too. If you add in two excellent microbreweries and one of the country's best restaurants, there's plenty to reward a stay of a couple days. Brno was one of the leading centres of experimental architecture in the early 20th century, and the Unesco-protected Vila Tugendhat (p241) is considered a masterwork of Functionalist design. The tourist information office has lots of material on the city's rich architectural heritage, including marked-out tours.

The Best...

- **Sight** Špilberk Castle (p239)
- **Place to Eat** Koishi (p242)
- **Place to Drink** U Richarda (p242)

Top Tip

Brno is a popular venue for trade fairs: hotels routinely raise rates by as much as 50% during large events. Check www.bvv.cz for event dates and plan your visit for an off-week.

Getting There & Away

Train Express trains to Brno depart Prague's Hlavní nádraží every couple of hours during the day (210Kč, 2½ hours). Brno is also a handy junction for onward train travel to Vienna (220Kč, two hours) and Bratislava (218Kč, 1½ hours).

Bus Buses depart Prague's Florenc bus station hourly for Brno (150Kč, 2½ hours). Buses to Prague leave from a small bus station opposite the Grandhotel (p243).

Car Brno is an easy two-hour drive from Prague, a straight shot down the D1

Brno

Sights

1 Applied Arts Museum....A3
2 Biskupský Yard Museum....B4
3 Brno Underground....C3
4 Capuchin Monastery....C4
5 Cathedral of Sts Peter & Paul....B4
6 Church of St James....B1
7 House of Arts....D1
8 Moravian Gallery....A2
9 Moravian Museum....B4
10 Museum of Art from the Gothic to the 19th Century....B1
11 Museum of Modern & Contemporary Art....A2
12 Old Town Hall....C3
13 Špilberk Castle....A3

Eating

14 Rebio....D3
15 Špaliček....B3
16 Spolek....D3

Drinking

17 Černohorský Sklep....B2
18 Kavárna Vladimíra Menšíka....B2
19 Minach....C2
20 Pivnice Pegas....B2

Entertainment

21 Brno State Philharmonic Orchestra....A2
22 Cinema City....B3
23 Janáček Theatre....C1
24 Klub Desert....D1
25 National Theatre Box Office....D1
26 Philharmonic Orchestra Box Office....A2
27 Reduta Theatre....C4

Sleeping

28 Grandhotel....D3
29 Hostel Mitte....B3
30 Hotel & Pivnice Pegas....B2
31 Hotel Pod Špilberkem....A3

highway. Bratislava is another hour to the east. The drive to Vienna takes 2 hours.

Need to Know

➡ **Location** 200km southeast of Prague.

➡ **Tourist Information Office** (☎542 211 090; www.ticbrno.cz; Radnická 8, Old Town Hall; ⏱8am-6pm Mon-Fri, 9am-5.30pm Sat & Sun Apr-Sep, to 5pm Sat, to 3pm Sun Oct-Mar) Lots of info in English, including free maps.

➡ **Cyber Café** (www.facebook.com/cybercafebrno; Mečova 2, Velký Spaliček shopping centre; per hr 60Kč; ⏱10am-10pm Mon-Sat; wi-fi) There's also free wi-fi in the Velký Spaliček shopping centre.

SIGHTS

ŠPILBERK CASTLE CASTLE

(☎542 123 611; www.spilberk.cz; combined entry ticket adult/concession 250/150Kč; ⏱10am-6pm Tue-Sun Jul-Sep, 9am-5pm Tue-Sun May & Jun, 10am-5pm Wed-Sun Apr & Oct) Brno's dramatic hilltop castle is considered the city's most important landmark, and is home to the **Brno City Museum** (muzeum města Brna; ☎542 123 611; www.spilberk.cz; Špilberk Castle; adult/concession 100/50Kč; ⏱9am-6pm Tue-Sun May-Sep, to 5pm Oct & Apr, 10am-5pm Wed-Sun Nov & Mar). You can also visit the **casements** (small rooms within the castle walls) and climb the lookout **tower**. Buy a combined entry ticket for all sights or purchase separate tickets; see the website for a full menu.

The two most popular exhibitions at the museum are **From Castle to Fortress**, about the castle's history, and **Prison of Nations**, on the role Špilberk played in the 18th and 19th centuries. Other exhibitions of the focus on the history, art and architecture of Brno. A combined ticket (adult/child 120/60Kč) gives access to all displays.

CATHEDRAL OF STS PETER & PAUL CHURCH, TOWER

Map p238 (katedrála sv Petra a Pavla; www.katedrala-petrov.cz; Petrov Hill; tower adult/concession 40/30Kč, crypts 20/10Kč; ⏱11am-6pm Mon-Sat, from 11.45am Sun) This 14th-century cathedral atop Petrov Hill was originally built on the site of a pagan temple to Venus, and has been reconstructed many times since. The highly decorated 11m-high main altar with figures of Sts Peter and Paul was carved by Viennese sculptor Josef Leimer in 1891. You can also climb the **tower** for dramatic views, or visit the **crypts**.

The Renaissance **Bishop's palace** (closed to the public) adjoins the cathedral. To the left is the pleasant **Denisovy sady**, a verdant park sweeping around Petrov Hill.

FREE **OLD TOWN HALL** HISTORIC BUILDING

Map p238 (Stará radnice; Radnická 8; tower adult/concession 30/15Kč; ⏱9am-5pm) Brno's

AHEAD OF THEIR TIME

The bells of the Cathedral of Sts Peter & Paul (p239) disconcertingly ring noon an hour early, at 11am. Legend has it that when the Swedish laid siege to the city in 1645, their commander, General Torstenson, who had been frustrated by Brno's defences for more than a week, decided to launch a final attack, with one caveat: if his troops could not prevail by noon, he would throw in his hand.

By 11am the Swedes were making headway, but the cathedral's tower-keeper had the inspired idea to ring noon early. The bells struck 12, the Swedes withdrew, and the city was saved.

atmospheric Old Town Hall dates from the early 13th century. The tourist office is here, plus oddities including a crocodile hanging from the ceiling (known affectionately as the Brno 'dragon') and a wooden wagon wheel with a unique story (see boxed text, p241). You can also climb the **tower**. Expected to reopen in 2013 after rennovations in 2012.

MORAVIAN GALLERY MUSEUM

Map p238 (☎532 169 111; www.moravska-galerie.cz; adult/concession 60/30Kč; ⏲10am-6pm Wed & Fri-Sun, to 7pm Thu) This gallery's extensive art holdings are displayed at three different branches: hours and admission prices are uniform for each. Adjoining the Church of St Thomas, the **Museum of Art from the Gothic to the 19th Century** (Map p238; ☎532 169 130; Moravské náměstí 1A, Místodržitelský Palace) presents six centuries of European art. The **Applied Arts Museum** (Uměleckoprůmyslové muzeum; Map p238; ☎532 169 130; Husova 14) focuses on arts and crafts from the Middle Ages to art nouveau. The third branch, the **Museum of Modern & Contemporary Art** (Map p238; ☎532 169 111; Husova 18, Pražákův Palace), focuses on Czech modernist and 20th-century art.

HOUSE OF ARTS GALLERY

Map p238 (Dům umění; ☎515 917 553; www.dum-umeni.cz; Malinovského náměstí 2; adult/concession 80/40Kč; ⏲10am-6pm Wed-Sun) Holds rotating contemporary art exhibitions. It is open only during shows.

Cabbage Market & Around

The **Cabbage Market** (Zelný trh) is the heart of the Old Town. Today it functions as a fruit-and-vegetable market, but at its centre is the curious baroque **Parnassus Fountain** (1695). The images here depict Hercules restraining the three-headed Cerberus, watchdog of the underworld. The three female figures represent the ancient empires of Babylon (crown), Persia (cornucopia) and Greece (quiver of arrows). The triumphant woman on top symbolises Europe.

CAPUCHIN MONASTERY CEMETERY

Map p238 (Kapucínský klášter; www.kapucini.cz; adult/concession 60/30Kč; ⏲9am-noon & 1pm-4.30pm May-Sep, closed Mon mid-Feb–Apr & Oct–mid-Dec, closed mid-Dec–mid-Feb) One of the city's leading attractions is this ghoulish cellar **crypt** that holds the mummified remains of several city noblemen from the 18th century. Apparently the dry, well-ventilated crypt has the natural ability to turn dead bodies into mummies. Up to 150 cadavers were deposited here prior to 1784, the desiccated corpses including monks, abbots and local notables.

BRNO UNDERGROUND UNDERGROUND

Map p238 (Brněnské podzemí; www.ticbrno.cz; Zelný trh 21; adult/concession 150/75Kč; ⏲9am-6pm Tue-Sun) In 2011, the city opened the first of what will be several opportunities to explore the underground passages of the medieval city. This tour takes around 40 minutes to explore several of the cellars situated six-to-eight metres below the Cabbage Market. The cellars were built for two purposes: to store goods and to hide in during wars.

MORAVIAN MUSEUM MUSEUM

Map p238 (Moravské zemské muzeum; ☎533 435 280; www.mzm.cz; Zelný trh 8; adult/concession 50/25Kč; ⏲9am-5pm Tue-Sat) Exhibits here straddle the intellectual gulf between extinct life and the medieval village. In a courtyard to the right of the museum is the **Biskupský Yard Museum** (Map p238; ☎542 321 205; Muzejní 1; adult/

concession 50/25Kč; ⌚9am-5pm Tue-Sat), with the largest freshwater aquarium in the country and plenty of information on Moravian wildlife.

Náměstí Svobody & Around

Spacious **náměstí Svobody** is the city's bustling central hub. It dates from the early 13th century, when it was called Dolní trh (lower market). The **plague column** here dates from 1680, and the **House of the Lords of Lipá** (Dům Pánů z Lipé) at No 17 is a Renaissance palace (1589–96) with a 19th-century sgraffito facade and an arcaded courtyard. On the eastern side of the square at No 10 is the **House of the Four Mamlases** (Dům U čtyř mamlasů). The facade here is supported by a quartet of well-muscled but clearly moronic 'Atlas' figures, each struggling to hold up the building and their loincloths at the same time.

CHURCH OF ST JAMES CHURCH

Map p238 (kostel sv Jakuba; ☎542 212 039; www.svatyjakubbrno.wz.cz; Jakubská 11; ⌚8am-6pm) This austere 15th-century church contains a baroque pulpit with reliefs of Christ dating from 1525. But the biggest drawcard is a small stone figure known as the 'Neհaňba' (The Shameless): above the 1st-floor window on the south side of the clock tower at church's west end is the figure of a man baring his buttocks towards the cathedral. Local legend claims this was a disgruntled mason's parting shot to his rivals working on Petrov Hill.

During our visit in 2012, the church was undergoing reconstruction to open up the cellars for visitors. Check with the tourist office for details.

Outside the Centre

TOP CHOICE **VILA TUGENDHAT** ARCHITECTURE

(Villa Tugendhat; ☎515 511 015; www.tugendhat.eu; Černopolni 45; adult/concession 300/180Kč; ⌚10am-6pm Tue-Sun; 🚋3, 5, 11) Brno had a reputation in the 1920s as a centre for modern architecture in the Functionalist and Bauhaus styles. Arguably the finest example is this family villa, designed by modern master Mies van der Rohe in 1930. Entry is by guided tour, booked in advance by phone or over the website.

If you can't book a tour, the front of the house is still worth a look for how sharply it contrasts with many of the other contemporaneous buildings in the neighbourhood. To find the villa, take tram 3, 5 or 11 from Moravské náměstí up Milady Horákové to Černopolní, then walk 300m north.

MENDEL MUSEUM MUSEUM

(Mendelianum; ☎543 424 043; www.mendel-museum.com; Mendlovo náměstí 1; adult/concession 60/30Kč; ⌚10am-6pm Tue-Sun Apr-Oct, to 5pm Nov-Mar) Gregor Mendel (1822–84), the Augustinian monk whose studies of peas and bees at Brno's Abbey of St Thomas established modern genetics, is commemorated here. In the garden are the

BRNO'S QUIRKY OLD TOWN HALL

No visit to Brno would be complete without a peek inside the city's medieval Old Town Hall (p239), parts of which date back to the 13th century. The oddities start right at the entrance on Radnická. Take a look at the Gothic portal made by Anton Pilgram in 1510 and notice the crooked middle turret. According to legend, this was intentional: Pilgram was not paid the agreed amount by the council so, in revenge, he left the turret slightly bent.

Take a stroll inside to see the corpse of the legendary Brno 'dragon' that supposedly once terrorised the city's waterways. The animal, in fact, is an Amazon River crocodile, donated by Archprince Matyáš in 1608. Near the dragon, you'll see a wooden wagon wheel hanging on the wall. It was apparently crafted by an enterprising cartwright from Lednice. In 1636 he bet a mate he could fell a tree, build a wheel and roll it 50km to Brno – all before dusk. He was successful and the hastily made and quickly rolled wheel has been on display ever since. Unfortunately, someone started the dodgy rumour that the cartwright had received assistance from the devil and he died penniless when his customers went elsewhere.

BRNO FOR KIDS

Brno will be a tough sell for kids. After the charms of the Brno 'dragon' and the wagon wheel in the Old Town Hall have worn off, you'll have to come up with some more inspired ideas. One possibility is the Brno **Planetarium** (541 321 287; www.hvezdarna.cz; Kraví hora 2; adult/concession 80/40Kč; 4). While most of the shows are in Czech, it's possible to arrange an English presentation if you contact the staff in advance. Brno's **City Zoological Garden** (Zoologická zahrada; 546 432 311; www.zoobrno.cz; Bystrc-Mniší hora; adult/concession 100/70Kč; 9am-6pm; 1, 3, 11) on the outskirts of town occupies a lovely setting and has a wide variety of animals. Brno's **Technical Museum** (Technické muzeum vs Brně; 541 421 411; www.technicalmuseum.cz; Purkyňova 105; adult/concession 80/40Kč; 9am-5pm Tue-Sun; 13) is worth a half-day of anyone's time. Don't miss the panoptikon on the 1st floor; this huge wooden stereoscope allows up to 20 viewers to look at 3D images from antique glass slides that are changed on a regular basis.

foundations of Mendel's original greenhouse.

MUSEUM OF ROMANY CULTURE MUSEUM

(muzeum romské kultury; 545 571 798; www.rommuz.cz; Bratislavská 67; adult/concession 40/20Kč; 10am-6pm Mon-Fri, to 5pm Sun, closed Sat) This excellent museum provides an overdue positive showcase of Romany culture. Highlights include a couple of music-packed videos, period photographs from across Europe, and regular special exhibitions.

EATING

KOISHI ASIAN €€€

(777 564 744; www.koishi.cz; Údolní 11; mains 395-490Kč; 11am-11pm Mon-Fri, 9am-11pm Sat & Sun;) Sushi master Tadayoshi Ebina and top seafood chef Petr Fučík have combined to bring award-winning cooking to Brno. Koishi has earned a reputation for excellent sushi, but it has since expanded its range to include more traditional European and Czech cooking, with an Asian touch. They have an excellent wine list as well. Reserve in advance.

SPOLEK CZECH €

Map p238 (774 814 230; www.spolek.net; Orli 22; mains 60-140Kč; 9am-10pm Mon-Fri, 10am-10pm Sun;) You'll get friendly, unpretentious service at this coolly 'bohemian' (yes, we're in Moravia) haven with interesting salads and soups, and a concise but diverse wine list. Photojournalism on the walls is complemented by a funky mezzanine bookshop. It has excellent coffee, too.

SABAIDY ASIAN €

(545 428 310; www.sabaidy.cz; trída kpt Jaroše 29; mains 150-230Kč; 5pm-11pm Mon-Fri;) With decor incorporating Buddhist statues and a talented Laotian chef delivering authentic flavours, Sabaidy delivers both 'om' and 'mmmm'. After lots of same-ish Czech food, this really is different. The easiest access is via the Hotel Amphone at trída kpt Jaroše 29.

ŠPALIČEK CZECH €€

Map p238 (542 215 526; Zelný trh 12; mains 160-310Kč) Brno's oldest (and maybe its 'meatiest') restaurant sits on the edge of the Cabbage Market. Ignore the irony and dig into huge Moravian meals, partnered with a local Starobrno beer or something from the decent local wine list.

REBIO VEGETARIAN €

Map p238 (542 211 110; www.rebio.cz; Orli 26; mains 80-100Kč; 8am-7pm Mon-Fri, 10am-3pm Sat;) Healthy risottos and veggie pies stand out in this self-service spot that changes its tasty menu every day. Organic beer and wine is available. There's another all-veggie branch on the 1st floor of the Velký Spaliček shopping centre.

DRINKING

U RICHARDA PUB

(775 027 918; www.uricharda2.cz; Údolní 7) This microbrewery is highly popular with

students, who come for the great house-brewed, unpasteurised yeast beers, including a rare cherry-flavoured lager, and good traditional Czech cooking (mains 109Kč to 149Kč). Book in advance.

PIVNICE PEGAS PUB

Map p238 (☎542 210 104; www.hotelpegas.cz; Jakubská 4) *Pivo* melts that old Moravian reserve as the locals become pleasantly noisy. Don't miss the 12° wheat beer with a slice of lemon. Try to book a table in advance, or grab a spot at one of Brno's longest bars. The food's pretty good too, but the interior can get smoky.

AVIA CAFE

(☎739 822 215; www.aviacafe.cz; Botanická 1; ⊙11am-10pm;) Popular student cafe/restaurant situated on the ground floor of the Jan Hus Congregational Church, a landmark Functionalist building from 1929. The architecture and location, close to the university, lend an intellectual atmosphere. When you've tired of talking Proust, you can shoot pool in the adjoining billiard room.

KAVÁRNA VLADIMÍRA MENŠÍKA CAFE

Map p238 (☎777 001 411; Veselá 3; coffee drinks 30-50Kč; ⊙9am-11pm Mon-Sat, 11.30am-10pm Sun;) One of our favourite places to hide away in Brno is this corner cafe dedicated to the late Czech film star Vladimír Menšík, a leading actor of the Czech New Wave. You'll find a relaxed space and good coffee, with pictures and film stills of Menšík all over the walls.

MINACH CAFE

Map p238 (www.cokoladovna.com; Poštovská 6; per chocolate 13Kč; ⊙9am-9pm Mon-Fri, 9am-7pm Sat, 2pm-7pm Sun) More than 50 kinds of handmade chocolates and bracing coffee make this an essential mid-morning or mid-afternoon detour.

ČERNOHORSKÝ SKLEP PUB

Map p238 (☎542 210 987; náměstí Svobody 5; ⊙closed Sun) Try the Black Hill aperitif beer or the honey-infused brew at the Black Mountain Brewery's Brno outpost. The waiters can be a bit surly downstairs, so grab an outside table on náměstí Svobody instead.

SLEEPING

TOP CHOICE **HOSTEL MITTE** HOSTEL €

Map p238 (☎734 622 340; www.hostelmitte.com; Panská 22; dm incl breakfast 490Kč, s/d incl breakfast 1000/1100Kč;) Set in the heart of the Old Town, this clean and stylish hostel opened in 2011 and still smells and looks brand new. The rooms are all named after famous Moravians (like Milan Kundera) or famous events (Austerlitz) and decorated accordingly. There's a cute cafe on the ground floor with free wi-fi.

HOTEL EUROPA HOTEL €€

(☎545 421 400; www.hotel-europa-brno.cz; třída kpt Jaroše 27; s/d incl breakfast 1375/1625Kč;) Set in a quiet neighbourhood a 10-minute walk from the centre, this self-proclaimed 'art' hotel (presumably for the wacky futuristic lobby furniture) offers clean and tastefully furnished modern rooms in a historic 19th-century building. The lobby has free wi-fi, while the rooms have cable (ethernet) connections. There is free street parking out the front.

HOTEL POD ŠPILBERKEM HOTEL €€

Map p238 (☎543 235 003; www.hotelpodspilberkem.cz; Pekařská 10; s/d/tr incl breakfast 1400/1600/2500Kč;) Tucked away near the castle are these quiet rooms, all clustered around a central courtyard. The secure car park is a good option for self-drive travellers.

HOTEL & PIVNICE PEGAS HOTEL €€

Map p238 (☎542 210 104; www.hotelpegas.cz; Jakubská 4; s/d 2000/2500Kč;) Centrally located, the Pegas has been refurbished to include huge beds, flat-screen TVs and updated bathrooms. Expect a friendly welcome at reception and the lure of the Pegas microbrewery and pub downstairs. The rooms are on the 4th floor, so there is no problem with noise from the bar.

GRANDHOTEL HOTEL €€

Map p238 (☎542 518 111; www.grandhotelbrno.cz; Benešova 18-20; r from 2500Kč;) Under Austrian ownership, Brno's oldest hotel has been refurbished to emerge as one of the city's most comfortable and characterful sleeping options. The building's heritage style now includes all mod cons, including a gym and sauna. Rooms are spacious and quiet, despite the location opposite the train station. Check online for good discounts.

PENZION NA STARÉM BRNĚ PENSION €
(☎543 247 872; www.pension-brno.com; Mendlovo náměstí 1a; s/d incl breakfast 990/1330Kč; P) An atmospheric Augustinian monastery conceals five compact rooms that come Lonely Planet reader-recommended. Just metres away there's a Moravian wine bar.

HOSTEL FLÉDA HOSTEL €
(☎533 433 638; www.hostelfleda.com; Štefánikova 24; dm/d from 300/800Kč; ; 1, 6) A quick tram ride from the centre, one of Brno's best music clubs offers funky and colourful rooms. A nonsmoking cafe and good bar reinforces the social vibe. Catch tram 1 or 6 to the Hrnčirská stop.

HOTEL OMEGA HOTEL €
(☎543 213 876; www.hotelomega.eu; Křídloviská 19B; s/d incl breakfast 1000/1500Kč; ; 1) In a quiet neighbourhood 1km from the centre (and recommended by the Tourist Information Office), Omega has spacious rooms with modern pine furniture. A couple of three- and four-bed rooms cater to travelling families, and breakfast comes complete with castle views. Catch tram 1 from the railway station to the Václavská stop.

ENTERTAINMENT

STARÁ PEKÁRNA CLUB, LIVE MUSIC
(☎541 210 040; www.starapekarna.cz; Štefánikova 8; 5pm-late Mon-Sat; 1, 6, 7) Old and new music with blues, world beats, DJs and rock. Catch the tram to Pionýrská. Gigs usually kick off at 8pm.

FLÉDA LIVE MUSIC
(☎533 433 559; www.fleda.cz; Štefánikova 24; to 2am; 1, 6) DJs, Brno's best up-and-coming bands and occasional touring performers all rock the stage at Brno's

WORTH A DETOUR

WORTH A DETOUR: CAVING IN MORAVIA

The area to the immediate north of Brno has some of the country's best caving in an area known as the **Moravian Karst** (Moravský kras). Carved with canyons and some 400 caves, the region is very pretty, with lots of woods and hills. See the excellent website www.cavemk.cz for information on the various caves in the area.

The karst formations here result from the seepage of faintly acidic rainwater through limestone, which over millions of years slowly dissolves it, creating hollows and fissures. In the caves themselves, the slow dripping of this water has produced extraordinary stalagmites and stalactites.

The organisational centre for any caving expedition is the town of **Blansko**, which has a good **tourist information office** (Blanenská Informační Kancelář; ☎516 410 470; www.blansko.cz; Rožmitálova 6, Blansko; 9am-6pm Mon-Fri, to noon Sat) that sells maps and advance tickets to two of the main caves: the Punkva and Kateřinská caves. The office can field transport questions and can help with accommodation. On weekends, particularly in July and August, cave-tour tickets sell out in advance, so try to book ahead with the tourist information office.

The most popular tour is through the **Punkva Cave** (Punkevní jeskyně; ☎516 418 602; www.smk.cz; adult/child 170/80Kč; 8.40am-2pm Tue-Sun Jan-Mar, 8.20am-4pm Tue-Sun Apr-Sep, 8.40am-2pm Tue-Sun Oct-Dec). It involves a 1 km walk through limestone caverns to the bottom of the Macocha Abyss, a 140m-deep sinkhole. Small, electric-powered boats then cruise along the underground river back to the entrance.

Another popular tour is to the **Kateřinská Cave** (Kateřinská jeskyně; ☎516 413 161; www.moravskykras.net; adult/child 80/60Kč; 8.20am-4pm daily May-Aug, 9am-4pm Tue-Sun Apr & Sep, 9am-2pm Tue-Sun Oct, 10am-2pm Tue-Fri Mar & Nov, closed Dec-Feb). It's usually a little less crowded than the Punkva option. The 30-minute tour here explores two massive chambers.

Though it's easiest to explore the cave region with your own wheels, it is possible to see the caves on a day trip from Brno with public transport. Trains make the 30-minute run to Blansko hourly most days (37Kč): ask at Brno's tourist information office (p239).

top music club. Catch tram 1 or 6 to the Hrnčirská stop.

KLUB DESERT LIVE MUSIC

Map p238 (☎608 079 226; www.dodesertu.com; Rooseveltova 24; ⌚5pm-3am Mon-Sat, 6pm-1am Sun) Part cool bar/cafe and part intimate performance venue, Klub Desert features Brno's most eclectic live late-night lineup. Gypsy bands, neofolk – anything goes.

BRNO STATE PHILHARMONIC ORCHESTRA CLASSICAL MUSIC

Map p238 (☎539 092 811; www.filharmonie-brno.cz; Komenského náměstí 8) City's main venue for classical music. Buy tickets at the **Philharmonic Orchestra Box Office** (Map p238; Besední ul; ⌚9am-2pm Mon & Wed, 1pm-6pm Tues, Thu & Fri).

JANÁČEK THEATRE OPERA, BALLET

Map p238 (Janáčkovo divadlo; Rooseveltova 1-7, sady Osvobození) Hosts high-quality opera and ballet. Buy tickets at the **National Theatre Box Office** (Národní Divadlo v Brně Prodej Vstupnek; Map p238; ☎542 158 120; www.ndbrno.cz; Dvořákova 11; ⌚8am-5.30pm Mon-Fri, to noon Sat).

REDUTA THEATRE CLASSICAL MUSIC, OPERA

Map p238 (Reduta divadlo; www.ndbrno.cz; Zelný trh 4) Opera and classical music with an emphasis on Mozart (he played there in 1767). Buy tickets at the National Theatre Box Office (p245).

KINO ART CINEMA

(☎541 213 542; www.kinoartbrno.cz; Cihlářská 19) Screens art-house films.

CINEMA CITY CINEMA

Map p238 (☎255 742 021; www.cinemacity.cz; Mečova 2) In the Velký Spaliček shopping centre, showing the latest from Hollywood.

Telč

Explore

The Unesco-protected town of Telč, perched on the border between Bohemia and Moravia, possesses one of the country's prettiest and best-preserved historic town squares. Actually, we can't think of another that comes close! The main attraction is the beauty of the square itself, lined by Renaissance and baroque burgers' houses, with their brightly coloured yellow, pink and green facades. Spend part of your visit simply ambling about, taking in the classic Renaissance chateau on the square's northwestern end and the parklands and ponds that surround the square on all sides. Telč empties out pretty quickly after the last tour bus leaves, so plan an overnight stay only if you're looking for some peace and quiet.

The Best...

➡ **Sight** Telč Chateau (p246)

➡ **Place to Eat** U Marušky (p247)

➡ **Place to Drink** Kavarná Antoniana (p247)

Top Tip

The best time to visit Telč is in late July and early August, when the town explodes into life during the Prázdniny v Telči music festival (www.prazdninyvtelci.ji.cz).

Getting There & Away

Train Passenger train services have been greatly scaled back and are not recommended.

Bus Around half-a-dozen buses make the run daily from Prague's Florenc bus station (170Kč, 2½ hours), with many connections requiring a change in Jihlava. Regional service is decent, with around five daily buses to and from Brno (100Kč, two hours). Check www.bus-vlak.cz for current times and prices.

Car From Prague, Telč is an easy two-hour drive, heading south toward Brno on the D1 motorway, and turning off at Jihlava. The trip takes about two hours.

Need to Know

➡ **Location** 160km southeast of Prague.

➡ **Tourist Information Office** (Informační Středisko; ☎567 112 407; www.telc.eu; náměstí Zachariáše z Hradce 10; ⌚8am-5pm Mon-Fri, 10am-4pm Sat & Sun May-Oct, 8am-5pm Mon-Fri Nov-Apr) Inside the Town Hall. Can book accommodation and has internet access (per minute 2Kč).

Telč

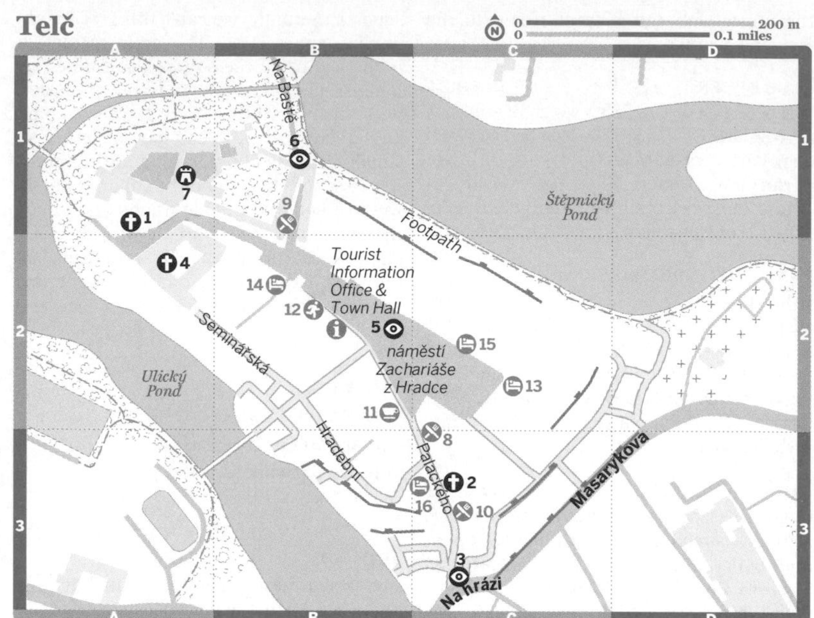

➡ **Miluše Spázalová** (Map p246; ☎567 243 562; náměstí Zachariáše z Hradce 8; per day from around 150Kč; ⊙8am-5pm Mon-Fri, 9am-noon Sat) Rents bikes.

SIGHTS

TELČ CHATEAU CASTLE

Map p246 (Zámek; www.zamek-telc.cz; náměstí Zachariáše z Hradce; Route A adult/concession 110/70Kč, Route B 90/60Kč; ⊙9-11.45am & 1-6pm Tue-Sun Apr-Oct) Telč's sumptuous Renaissance chateau, part of which is known as the Water Chateau, guards the north end of the Telč peninsula. Entry is by guided tour only: Route A takes one hour, passing through the Renaissance halls; Route B takes 45 minutes, exploring the castle's apartment rooms.

The chateau was rebuilt from the original Gothic structure by Antonio Vlach (between 1553 and 1556) and Baldassare Maggi (from 1566 to 1568). The surviving structure remains in remarkably fine fettle, with immaculately tended lawns and beautifully kept interiors. In the ornate Chapel of St George (kaple sv Jiří), opposite the ticket office, are the remains of the castle's founder Zachariáš z Hradce.

NÁMĚSTÍ ZACHARIÁŠE Z HRADCE SQUARE

Map p246 (Main Square; náměstí Zachariáše z Hradce) Telč's stunning town square is a tourist attraction in its own right. Most houses here were built in Renaissance style in the 16th century after a fire levelled the town in 1530. Some facades were given baroque facelifts in the 17th and 18th centuries, but the overall effect is harmoniously Renaissance.

Some famous houses on the square include **No 15**, which shows the characteristic Renaissance sgraffito. The house at **No 48** was given a baroque facade in the 18th century. **No 61** has a lively Renaissance facade rich in sgraffito. The **Marian column** in the middle of the square dates from 1717, and is a relatively late baroque addition.

HISTORIC CHURCHES CHURCHES

Dominating the town centre are the Gothic towers of the **Church of St James the Elderly** (kostel sv Jakuba Staršího; Map p246; adult/concession 20/15Kč; ⊙10-11.30am & 1-6pm Tue-Sun Jun-Aug, 1-5pm Sat & Sun May & Sep). Also watching over the square is the baroque **Holy Name of Jesus Church** (kostel Jména Ježíšova; Map p246; náměstí Zachariáše z Hradce 3; ⊙daily 8am-6pm), completed in 1667 as part of a Jesuit college.

Telč

Sights

1 Church of St James the Elderly A1
2 Church of the Holy Spirit C3
3 Great Gate C3
4 Holy Name of Jesus Church A2
5 Náměstí Zachariáše z Hradce B2
6 Small Gate B1
7 Telč Chateau A1

Eating

8 Pizzerie C3
9 Švejk B1
10 U Marušky C3

Drinking

11 Kavarná Antoniana B2

Sports & Activities

12 Miluše Spázalová B2

Sleeping

13 Hotel Celerin C2
14 Hotel Černý Orel B2
15 Pension Steidler C2
16 Penzin Kamenné Slunce C3

North of the square is a narrow lane leading to the old town's **Small Gate** (Malá brána; Map p246), through which is a large English-style park surrounding the **duck ponds** (once the town's defensive moat). South along Palackého, toward the **Great Gate** (Velká brána; Map p246), is the imposing Romanesque **Church of the Holy Spirit** (kostel sv Ducha; Map p246; Palackého; ⏲7am-6pm daily) from the early 13th century. Outside the Great Gate you can walk along parts of Telč's remaining bastions.

EATING & DRINKING

U MARUŠKY
CZECH €

Map p246 (☎602 432 904; Palackého 28; mains 90-170Kč) This simple pub caters more to locals than visitors, but offers decent home-cooked Czech meals with the added bonus of very good Ježek beer on tap. There's also a small beer garden open during summer. The daily lunch menu is a steal at 75Kč.

ŠVEJK
CZECH €

Map p246 (www.svejk-telc.cz; náměstí Zachariáše z Hradce 1; mains 105-165Kč; 📶) Classic Czech cooking in a pub-like setting next to the castle. The names of menu items, unsurprisingly, are taken from the classic WWI anti-war book, *The Good Soldier Švejk*. 'Cadet Biegler' chicken, for example, turns out to be a schnitzel that's stuffed with ham and cheese. The outdoor terrace is popular in nice weather.

PIZZERIE
ITALIAN €

Map p246 (☎567 223 246; náměstí Zachariáše z Hradce 32; pizza 80-130Kč) Right on the main square and right on the money for better-than-average pizza.

KAVARNÁ ANTONIANA
CAFE

Map p246 (☎603 519 903; náměstí Zachariáše z Hradce 23; coffee 24-30Kč, cake 35Kč; ⏲8am-2am) The best coffee on the square, plus beer and alcoholic drinks, and inspirational black-and-white photos of Telč plastered on the wall. There are only limited food options, but the late opening hours mean it's one of the few places in the centre where you can get a drink in the evening.

SLEEPING

PENSION STEIDLER
PENSION €

Map p246 (☎721 316 390; www.telc-accommodation.eu; náměstí Zachariáše z Hradce 52; s/d 500/800Kč, excluding breakfast) Rooms reconstructed with skylights and wooden floors combine with absolute town square location to deliver one of Telč's best-value places to stay. Some rooms have views of the lake. Breakfast costs 50Kč per person. Note there's a surcharge of 100Kč per room in summer (June to August) for stays of less than two nights.

HOTEL CELERIN
HOTEL €€

Map p246 (☎567 243 477; www.hotelcelerin.cz; náměstí Zachariáše z Hradce 43; s/d 980/1530Kč; 🚭❄📶) Variety is king in the Celerin's 12 comfortable rooms, with decor ranging from cosy wood to white-wedding chintz (take a look first). Rooms 4, 5, 9 and 10 have views out onto the square. The hotel sometimes closes in winter.

PENZIN KAMENNÉ SLUNCE
PENSION €

Map p246 (☎732 193 510; www.kamenne-slunce.cz; Palackého 2; s/d 450/900Kč; 🅿🚭📶) Lots of brick, exposed beams and warm wooden floors make this a very welcoming spot just off the main square. Hip bathrooms with colourful tiles add weight to claims that this is arguably Telč's coolest place to stay. Breakfast costs 70Kč.

PENZIÓN PETRA PENSION €

(☎567 213 059; www.penzionpetra.cz; Srázná 572; s 300-500Kč, d 600-1000Kč; P) This modern house just across the bridge from the town square has brightly coloured rooms, spotless bathrooms and a wading pool in the garden. The separate 'Garden House' (300-500Kč per person) sleeps up to five and has its own kitchen.

HOTEL ČERNÝ OREL HOTEL €€

Map p246 (☎567 243 222; www.cernyorel.cz; náměstí Zachariáše z Hradce 7; s/d 1200/1800Kč; P) Right on the main square, the 'Black Eagle' is just the ticket if you're into slightly faded, old-world ambience. While the rooms are comfortable, they don't rise to the level of the exquisite exterior. The ground floor restaurant is one of the town's more popular lunch venues.

Třebíč

Explore

Until a few years ago, the bustling, mid-sized Moravian city of Třebíč rarely made it onto travellers' itineraries. This changed in 2003, when Unesco placed the city's nearly perfectly preserved former Jewish Quarter on its list of protected World Heritage Sites. While the quarter is small, it's unique in the Czech Republic and worth searching out if you're coming this way. In addition, take in the impressive St Procopius's Basilica, another Unesco site. Třebíč is best approached as a day trip from Brno or Telč, though there are a couple of decent overnight options if you want to stay. Don't miss a meal at the curiously named Coqpit, one of the best restaurants in this part of the country.

The Best...

- **Sight** Jewish Quarter (p248)
- **Place to Eat** Coqpit (p249)
- **Place to Drink** Kavárna Vrátka (p249)

Top Tip

If you have a strong interest in Jewish heritage, be sure to book ahead with Jewish Quarter Tourist Information (p248) in the Rear Synagogue for a guided tour of the area.

Getting There & Away

Train From Brno, trains leave every hour or so for Třebíč (100 Kč, 1¼ hours). Train travel is less convenient from Prague (270Kč, 3¼ hours), with most connections requiring two changes.

Bus Buses run regularly to/from Brno (70Kč, 1¼ hours) and Telč (35Kč, 40 minutes). From Prague, there are around five direct buses per day (165Kč, 2½ hours).

Car Třebíč is an easy two-hour drive from Prague, down the D1 motorway in the direction of Brno, turning south at Velké Meziříčí and following the signs. From Brno, the one-hour drive heads northwest on the D1 toward Prague, turning south at Velké Meziříčí.

Need to Know

- **Location** 165km southeast of Prague.
- **Tourist Information** (informační a turistické centrum; ☎568 847 070; www.mkstrebic.cz; Karlovo náměstí 53; 9am-6pm Mon-Fri Apr-Oct, 9am-5pm Sat & Sun Jul-Aug, 9am-1pm Sat & Sun Apr-Jun & Sep-Oct) Books accommodation and has internet access (free for 15 minutes). Reduced hours November to March.
- **Jewish Quarter Tourist Information** (☎568 610 023; www.mkstrebic.cz; Subakova 1/44; 9am-5pm) This smaller branch of the main tourist office is better informed about the Jewish Quarter and leads guided tours of the area.

SIGHTS

JEWISH QUARTER NEIGHBOURHOOD

(ul Leopolda Pokorneho) Records of Třebíč's Jewish community go back until the 14th century, and the town's Jewish Quarter is the best-preserved ghetto in the Czech Republic. Most of Třebíč's Jews perished in WWII, but the buildings here, including two synagogues, survived and are being slowly refurbished. The highlight is the **Rear (New) Synagogue** (Zadní (Nová) synagóga; ☎568 823 005; Subakova 1/44; adult/concession 60/30Kč; ⊙10am-noon & 1-5pm), which has beautifully restored frescoes and a wonderful historical model of the ghetto.

JEWISH CEMETERY CEMETERY

(Židovský hřbitov; www.mkstrebic.cz; Hrádek; ⊙8am-8pm Sun-Fri May-Sep, 8am-6pm Mar, Apr & Oct, 9am-4pm Nov-Feb) The 17th-century burial ground on Hrádek, about 600m north of the Jewish Quarter, is the largest in the country, with more than 11,000 graves. The oldest dates back to 1641.

ST PROCOPIUS' BASILICA CHURCH

(Bazilika sv Prokopa; ☎568 610 022; www.mkstrebic.cz; adult/concession 60/30Kč; ⊙9am-5pm Mon-Fri, 12.30-6pm Sat & Sun Jun-Sep) The Unesco World Heritage–listed St Procopius' Basilica boasts an attractive chancel and carved north portal (portal Paradisi). The basilica is part of the Třebíč Chateau complex, which dates from the end of the 17th century. At the time of writing the chateau was closed for an extensive multi-year renovation. Reduced hours October to May.

EATING & DRINKING

TOP CHOICE **COQPIT** CZECH €€

(☎607 160 027; www.facebook.com/restaurantcoqpit; Havlíčkovo nábř 146/39; mains 125-245Kč; ⊙11am-10pm Mon-Sat, to 4pm Sun; 📶) One of the best restaurants in this part of Moravia stands on the edge of the Jewish Quarter. The bare-bones interior belies a highly skilled kitchen. On our visit, we went for braised pork tenderloin served with caramelised onion in red wine reduction, and the pumpkin soup as a starter. The homemade cheesecake for dessert was perfection.

RESTAURANT ČERNÝ DŮM CZECH €

(☎566 844 455; Karlovo náměstí 22/16; mains 90-170Kč) Choose from a breezy outdoor terrace or a cosy indoor space for excellent service, good-value grills and pasta, plus tasty beers from Moravia's Černá Hora (Black Mountain) brewery.

KAVÁRNA VRÁTKA CAFE

(☎737 565 011; www.kavarna-vratka.unas.cz; L Pokorného 29/42; coffee 30-50Kč; ⊙10am-6pm Mon-Thu, to 8pm Fri & Sat, noon-6pm Sun; 📶) This non-smoking, family-friendly coffeehouse has excellent coffee concoctions and homemade cakes, and is just steps away from the Rear (New) Synagogue.

SLEEPING

GRAND HOTEL HOTEL €€

(☎568 848 560; www.grand-hotel.cz; Karlovo náměstí 5; s/d incl breakfast 1380/1780Kč; P📶) The city's nicest hotel is a modern, four-star offering on the main square, an easy five-minute walk from the Jewish Quarter. There's a good restaurant in-house, plus extras like a music club and even a bowling alley!

TRAVELLERS HOSTEL HOSTEL €

(☎568 422 594; www.travellers.cz; Žerotínovo náměstí 17; dm 280-370Kč, s/d 600/800Kč, all incl breakfast; 📶) Right on the edge of the Jewish Quarter, these lovingly restored private rooms and dorms look down onto a private courtyard.

PENZIÓN U SYNAGOGY PENSION €

(☎775 707 506; www.mkstrebic.cz; Subakova 3; s/d incl breakfast 470/720Kč) Simple rooms in an atmospheric location near the Rear (New) Synagogue.

Mikulov

Explore

The 20th-century Czech poet Jan Skácel (1922–89) bequeathed Mikulov a tourist slogan for the ages when he penned that the town was a 'piece of Italy moved to Moravia by God's hand'. Mikulov is arguably the most attractive of the southern Moravian wine towns, surrounded by white, chalky hills and adorned with an amazing hilltop Renaissance chateau, visible for miles around. Mikulov was also once a thriving cultural centre for Moravia's Jewish community, and the former Jewish Quarter is slowly being rebuilt. Once you've tired of history, explore the surrounding countryside (on foot or bike) or relax with a glass of local wine.

DISCOVERING MORAVIAN WINE

Compared to the wine regions of France, California, Australia or New Zealand, the Moravian wine tourism experience is much more low-key and homespun. Rather than flash boutique hotels or Michelin-star restaurants, the wine scene here is more likely to involve energetic harvest festivals and leisurely cycle touring between family-owned vineyards.

South from Brno toward the borders with Austria and Slovakia, the Moravian wine region accounts for 96% of the total area under vine in the Czech Republic. Traditionally, robust red wines were part of the Moravian rural diet, but in recent years, late-ripening white wines have taken centre stage. With grape ripening occurring at a slower pace, the emphasis is on full-bodied, aromatic, and often spicy wines.

The Mikulov sub-region is characterised by the proximity of the Pavlovské hills, creating a local terrain rich in limestone and sand. Wines to look for during your visit include the mineral-rich white varietals of Rulandské šedé, Ryzlink vlašský (better known by its German name of Welschriesling) and Veltlínské zelené (Grüner Veltliner). Müller-Thurgau and Chardonnay grapes also do well.

Further west, the Znojmo sub-region is situated in the rain shadow of the Bohemian and Moravian highlands, and the soils are more likely to be studded with gravel and stones. Aromatic white wines including Sauvignon, Pálava and Ryzling rýnský (Riesling) are of notable quality, and red wines, especially Frankovka (Blaufränkisch), are also worth trying.

Keep an eye out for Czech Tourism's excellent *Through the Land of Wine* brochure or see www.wineofczechrepublic.cz for details of wine-touring routes and Moravia's growing profile in international wine competitions.

Top spots to try Moravian wines include Mikulov's Vinařské Centrum (p252) and the National Salon of Czech Republic Wines (p254) in Valtice.

The Best...

- **Sight** Mikulov Chateau (p250)
- **Place to Eat** Restaurace Templ (p252)
- **Place to Drink** Petit Café (p252)

Top Tip

Experience the countryside on a bike: the tourist office proffers advice, maps and the brochure *Viticulture and Viticulture Discovery Trails* (also available at pensions and hotels). Many pensions rent bikes.

Getting There & Away

Train There are several daily trains to and from Znojmo (66Kč, one hour) and Břeclav (39Kč, 30 minutes), an important junction for onward services to Brno, Bratislava and Vienna. See the online timetable at www.vlak-bus.cz.

Bus Mikulov is easily reached by bus from Brno (65Kč, 1½ hours), with coaches leaving hourly. From Prague, there are few direct buses; the best approach is to catch a bus for Brno and change. Regional bus services are good, with frequent buses to/from Znojmo, Valtice and Lednice.

Car Mikulov, situated between Prague and Vienna, is a three-hour drive from Prague. From Brno, the drive takes around an hour.

Need to Know

- **Location** 250km southeast of Prague.
- **Tourist Information Office** (☎519 510 855; www.mikulov.cz; náměstí 1; ⌚8am-6pm Mon-Fri, 9am-6pm Sat & Sun Jun-Sep, 8am-noon & 12.30-5pm Mon-Fri, 9am-4pm Sat & Sun Apr, May & Oct) Organises tours (including specialist outings for wine buffs) and accommodation. Reduced hours November to March.
- **Bike Hire** RentBike (p252) rents good-quality mountain bikes.

SIGHTS

MIKULOV CHATEAU CASTLE

Map p251 (Zámek; ☎519 309 019; www.rmm.cz; Zámek 1; adult/concession 100/50Kč; ⌚9am-5pm Tue-Sun May-Sep, to 4pm Apr & Oct) This chateau was the seat of the Dietrichstein family from 1575 to 1945, and played an important role in the 19th century, hosting on separate occasions French Emperor Napoleon, Russia's Tsar Alexander and Prussia's King Frederick. Much of the castle was destroyed by German forces in February 1945: the lavish interiors are the result of a painstaking reconstruction.

The castle is accessible by guided tour only. The full history tour takes two hours and visits significant castle rooms as well as exhibitions on viticulture and archaeology. Three more-specialised shorter tours are also available.

JEWISH QUARTER NEIGHBOURHOOD

Map p251 (Husova) Mikulov was a leading centre of Moravian Jewish culture for several centuries until WWII. The former **synagogue** (Synagóga; Map p251; ☎519 510 255; Husova 11; ⏰1-5pm Tue-Sun 15 May-30 Sep) has a small exhibition on the Jews of Mikulov. It was under reconstruction during our visit in 2012, but was expected to reopen in 2013. The evocative **Jewish Cemetery** (Židovský hřbitov; Map p251; Vinohrady; adult/concession 20/10Kč; ⏰9am-5pm Mon-Fri Jul-Aug) is a 10-minute walk from the tourist information office.

To find the cemetery, walk out Brněnská and look for a sign leading off to the right. Additionally, an 'instructive trail' runs through the Jewish Quarter, with information plaques in English. You can pick it up at the end of Husova near Alfonse Muchy.

GOAT HILL HILL, LOOKOUT

Map p251 (Kozí hrádek; Goat Hill; tower 20Kč; ⏰tower 9am-6pm May-Sep) Goat Hill is topped with an abandoned 15th-century **lookout tower** offerring stunning views over the Old Town. To find it, walk uphill from the Jewish Cemetery, following a red-marked trail. Note the tower keeps irregular hours: it's only open when the flag is flying. But even if the tower is closed, the views from the hilltop are spectacular.

HOLY HILL HILL, CHURCH

(Svatý kopeček; Gernerála Svobody) Another uphill venture is to scale the 1km path up this 363m peak, through a nature reserve and past grottos depicting the Stations of the Cross, to the compact **Church of St Sebastian**. The blue-marked trail begins at

Mikulov

Mikulov

Sights

1 Dietrichstein Burial Vault....B2
2 Goat Hill....B1
3 Jewish Cemetery....B1
4 Jewish Quarter....A2
5 Main Square....B2
6 Mikulov Chateau....A2
7 Synagogue....A2

Eating

8 Hospůdka Pod Zámkem....A2
9 Lahůdky V & V....B2
10 Restaurace Alfa....B2
Restaurace Templ....(see 17)

Drinking

11 Dobrý Ročník....B2
12 Petit Café....B2
13 U Obřího Soudku....B2
14 Vinařské Centrum....B2

Sports & Activities

15 RentBike....B2

Sleeping

16 Fajká Penzion....A3
17 Hotel Templ....A3
18 Pension Baltazar....A2
19 Pension Moravia....B1
20 Penzion Fontána Mikulov....A3
21 Penzión Husa....A2

the bottom of the main square on Svobody. The whitewashed church and the limestone on the hill give it a Mediterranean ambience.

DIETRICHSTEIN BURIAL VAULT MAUSOLEUM

Map p251 (Dietrichštejnská hrobka; náměstí 5; adult/concession 50/25Kč; ⌚10am-6pm daily Jun-Aug, 9am-5pm Tue-Sun Apr, May, Sep & Oct) The Dietrichstein family mausoleum occupies the former St Anne's Church. The front of the building features a remarkable baroque facade – the work of Austrian master Johann Bernhard Fischer von Erlach – dating from the early 18th century. Dating from 1617 to 1852, the tombs hold the remains of 45 family members.

MAIN SQUARE SQUARE

Map p251 (náměstí) Mikulov is filled with beautiful buildings, many still sporting impressive Renaissance and baroque facades. The main square, called simply 'náměstí' (square), has many houses of interest, including the **Town Hall** at No 1 and the sgraffitoed Restaurace Alfa (p252) at No 27.

MIKULOV WINE TRAIL HIKING, CYCLING

A pleasant way to visit smaller, local vineyards across the rolling countryside is by bicycle on the Mikulov Wine Trail. The tourist office can recommend a one-day ride that also takes in the nearby chateaux at Valtice and Lednice. Bicycles and additional cycle touring information are available from **RentBike** (Map p251; ☎737 750 105; www.rentbike.cz; Kostelní náměstí 1; rental per hour/day 110/330Kč).

EATING

RESTAURACE TEMPL CZECH €€

Map p251 (☎519 323 095; www.templ.cz; Husova 50; mains 165-280Kč; 📶) The best restaurant in town is matched by a fine wine list specialising in local varietals. The menu features an appetising mix of duck, pork and chicken dishes. Choose from either the formal restaurant or relaxed wine garden. There's also a small terrace out the back for dining alfresco on warm evenings.

HOSPŮDKA POD ZÁMKEM CZECH €

Map p251 (☎519 512 731; www.hospudkapodzamkem.cz; Husova 49; daily special 69Kč; 📶) This funky combination of old-school pub and coffee bar serves simple but very good Czech meals, usually limited to a few daily specials like soup plus roast pork or chicken drumsticks. It's also the unlikely home of Mikulov's best coffee and serves very good 11° Gambrinus beer to boot. Find it across the street from the Hotel Templ.

RESTAURACE ALFA CZECH €

Map p251 (☎519 510 877; náměstí 27; mains 130-200Kč) The Alfa's beautiful sgraffito building, just across the square from the tourist information office, hides what's basically an ordinary Czech pub on the inside. That said, the kitchen turns out well-done Czech cooking, and there are even a few game dishes on the menu.

LAHŮDKY V & V CZECH €

Map p251 (www.vyhodovy-lahudky.cz; náměstí 20; meals 60Kč; ⌚5.30am-5.30pm Mon-Fri, 7am-noon Sat) This self-serve cafeteria feels like a throwback to communist times, but has a couple things going for it: an unusually early opening time (a lifesaver when everything else is closed) and low prices for Czech staples like goulash and fried cheese. You can also pick up sandwiches to go.

DRINKING

PETIT CAFÉ CAFE

Map p251 (☎733 378 264; náměstí 27; crepes 40-70Kč; 📶) Tasty crepes and coffee are dished up in a hidden courtyard/herb-garden setting. Later at night, have a beer or a glass of wine.

VINAŘSKÉ CENTRUM WINE BAR

Map p251 (☎519 510 368; www.vinarskecentrum.com; náměstí 11; ⌚9am-9pm Mon-Sat, 10am-9pm Sun) This drinking room has an excellent range of local wines available in small tasting glasses (15Kč to 50Kč), or whole bottles when you've finally made up your mind.

DOBRÝ ROČNÍK WINE BAR

Map p251 (☎602 534 554; www.dobryrocnik.eu; náměstí 27; ⌚9am-9pm; 📶) A pleasant little wine and coffee bar, serving local wines by the glass or the bottle.

U OBŘÍHO SOUDKU CAFE

Map p251 (☎519 510 004; náměstí 24; cakes 30-50Kč; ⌚10am-6pm Sun-Thu, 10am-9pm Fri & Sat; 📶) This comfortable, conveniently central cafe has decent coffee, pastries and ice cream. Also serves good Czech food.

SLEEPING

Mikulov has some beautiful small hotels and pensions, and is a good town for an overnight stay. Most of the better properties are clustered along Husova in the former Jewish Quarter. Many properties offer sightseeing tours, wine tastings and have bikes to rent; ask when booking.

TOP CHOICE HOTEL TEMPL HOTEL €€

Map p251 (☎519 323 095; www.templ.cz; Husova 50; s/d incl breakfast from 1390/1650Kč; P ⊖ ᯤ) This beautifully reconstructed, family-run hotel comprises a main building and an annex, two doors down. The updated rooms are done out in cheerful tiles and stained glass. The baths are as stylish as the rooms. Some rooms, such as ours (No 11 in the annex), open onto a secluded patio with tables for relaxing in the evening.

PENSION BALTAZAR PENSION €€

Map p251 (☎519 324 327; www.pensionbaltazar.cz; Husova 44; d incl breakfast 1200-1800Kč; P ⊖ ᯤ) You'll find this place a few doors up from the Hotel Templ. Beautifully resurrected rooms effortlessly combine modern furniture with exposed-brick walls and wooden floors.

PENZIÓN HUSA PENSION €€

Map p251 (☎731 103 283; www.penzionhusa.cz; Husova 30; d incl breakfast 1590Kč; P ⊖ ᯤ) Yet another beautiful pension on Husova, the 'Goose' boasts furnishings with period flare, like canopy beds and big oriental rugs on top of hardwood floors. This place is popular, so try to book well in advance.

FAJKÁ PENZION PENSION €

Map p251 (☎732 833 147; www.fajka-mikulov.cz; Alfonse Muchy 18; s/d 400/800Kč; P ⊖) These bright, newly decorated rooms sit above a cosy wine bar. Out the back is a garden restaurant if you really, really like the local wine.

PENZION FONTÁNA MIKULOV PENSION €

Map p251 (☎519 510 241; www.fontana.euweb.cz; Piaristů 6; s/d/tr 500/650/950Kč) By day this friendly couple run the local stationery shop. After-hours the focus is on the clean and colourful rooms attached to their house. Buy a bottle of local wine and fire up the garden barbecue for dinner.

PENSION MORAVIA PENSION €

Map p251 (☎777 634 560; www.moravia.penzion.com; Poštovní 1; d/tr/q 900/1200/1500Kč) The location's a tad dull, but the bright exterior and spotless rooms here ensure a good night's sleep. Single travellers usually aren't accepted.

Valtice-Lednice

Explore

The Unesco-protected historic landscape of Valtice-Lednice is a popular weekend destination for Czechs, who tour the historic architecture, hike and bike, and sample the region's wines. The two towns are about 10km apart, connected by regular buses. Neither Valtice nor Lednice offer much in terms of nightlife, so they're best visited as a day trip from either Mikulov or Brno. But if you've got more time, either town makes a perfect base for exploring the rolling hills of the southern Moravian wine country: hundreds of miles of walking and cycling trails criss-cross a mostly unspoiled landscape. Tourist information offices in both towns have maps, and you can rent bikes from Cykloráj (p254) in Valtice.

The Best ...

- **Sight** Lednice Chateau (p254)
- **Place to Eat** Grand Moravia (p255)
- **Place to Drink** Vinotéka V Zámecké Bráně (p255)

Top Tip

Instead of the bus, hike the 10km trail between Valtice and Lednice. The path runs through some pretty hills and takes about two hours at a leisurely pace.

Getting There & Away

Train Valtice has regular train services throughout the day to/from Mikulov

(23Kč, 12 minutes) and Břeclav (25Kč, 15minutes), which has excellent onward connections to Brno, Bratislava and Vienna. From Mikulov some trains continue to Znojmo.

Bus Both Lednice and Valtice are easily reachable by bus from Brno or Mikulov. Regular buses shuttle the short distance between Lednice and Valtice (20Kč, 15 minutes).

Car From Brno, the drive to Valtice takes around an hour. Head south along the E65 highway, turning off at Podivín and following the signs.

Need to Know

➡ **Location** 263km southeast of Prague.

➡ **Tourist Information Offices Valtice** (Turistické Informační Centrum; ☎519 352 978; www.valtice.eu; náměstí Svobody 4, Valtice; ⏰9am-5pm daily Apr-Sep, 7am-3.30pm Mon-Fri Oct-Mar); **Lednice** (Lednice Informační Centrum; ☎519 340 986; www.lednice.cz; Zámecké náměstí 68, Lednice; ⏰9-11am & noon-3pm Mon-Fri, 10am-3pm Sat & Sun Apr-Oct)

➡ **Bike Hire Cykloráj** (☎605 983 978; www.cykloraj.com; Malá strana 781, Valtice ; rental per day 250Kč; ⏰9am-5pm Mon-Fri, 9am-noon Sat) Rents high-quality mountain and touring bikes and offers maps and advice on where to ride.

SIGHTS

Valtice

VALTICE CHATEAU CASTLE

(Zámek; ☎519 352 423; www.zamek-valtice.cz; Zámek 1, Valtice ; standard tour adult/concession 100/80Kč; ⏰9am-noon & 1-6pm Tue-Sun May-Aug, to 5pm Sep, to 4pm Apr & Oct) Valtice's 12th-century castle is one of the country's finest baroque structures, the work of JB Fischer von Erlach and Italian architect Domenico Martinelli. Entry is by guided tour only, with two different tours on offer (in Czech, with English text available). The grounds and gardens are free for you to explore during opening times.

The standard 45-minute 'Prince's Tour' (Knížecí okruh; adult/concession 100/80Kč) visits 15 castle rooms. The one-hour 'Emperor's Tour' (Císařský okruh; adult/concession 150/100Kč) includes 20 rooms (add wine tasting for 50Kč). Highlights include belongings left behind when the Liechtensteins fled the advancing Soviets in 1945. Notice the walls themselves, plastered with kilos of gold.

ASSUMPTION OF THE VIRGIN MARY CHURCH

(kostel Nanebevzetí Panny Marie; náměstí Svobody, Valtice; ⏰8am-5pm) Valtice's most significant church is this early baroque work, dating from the middle of the 17th century. Take a look inside to admire the rare baroque organ from the 18th century. Behind the main altar are two significant paintings: the larger is a copy of a Rubens, but the smaller one above it, depicting the Holy Trinity, is a Rubens original.

NATIONAL SALON OF CZECH REPUBLIC WINES WINE TASTING

(☎519 352 072; www.salonvin.cz; Zámek 1, Valtice; tastings 100-250Kč; ⏰9.30am-5pm Tue-Thu, 10.30am-6pm Fri, 10.30am-5pm Sat & Sun Jun-Sep) This handy wine salon, in the cellar of the chateau, is the place to try and buy local wines.

Lednice

TOP CHOICE **LEDNICE CHATEAU** CASTLE

(Zámek; ☎519 340 128; www.zamek-lednice.com; Zámek, Lednice; standard tour (tour 1) adult/child 150/100Kč; tour 2, 150/100Kč; ⏰9am-6pm Tue-Sun May-Aug, to 5pm Tue-Sun Sep, to 4pm Sat & Sun only Apr & Oct) Lednice's massive neo-Gothic chateau, owned by the Liechtenstein family from 1582 to 1945, is one of the country's most popular weekend destinations. The crowds come for the splendid interiors and extensive gardens, complete with an exotic-plant **greenhouse**, **lakes** with pleasure boats, and a mock Turkish **minaret** – architectural excess for the 19th-century nobility.

Entry is by guided tour only, with two main tours (45 minutes each) available. Tour 1 visits the chateau's major rooms, including the famous wooden spiral staircase. Tour 2 concentrates on the Liechtenstein apartments: the highlight is the lovely 19th-century Chinese salon.

EATING & DRINKING

GRAND MORAVIA CZECH €€

(☎519 340 130; www.grandmoravia.cz; ul 21. dubna 657, Lednice ; mains 130-240Kč; 📶) This restaurant, part of a hotel complex, is arguably Lednice's best (out of an admittedly meagre bunch). You'll find nicely done local specialties, including a couple of fish entrees like trout and pikeperch. Many of the menu items are given a special twist, like baked lamb with a hint of rosemary, served with leaf spinach. Call ahead to book a table on weekends.

RESTAURANT & ČAJOVNA AVALON CZECH €€

(☎739 368 595; www.avalonvaltice.cz; Příční 46, Valtice ; mains 130-320Kč; 🖉) An interesting selection of dishes some with a vegetarian slant – features in this nicely new-age spot just off the main square in Valtice.

VINOTÉKA V ZÁMECKÉ BRÁNĚ WINE BAR

(☎606 712 128; Zámek 1, Valtice; ⏲4pm-6pm Fri, 10am-6pm Sat & Sun, 10am-3pm Mon) Situated just to the right of the front of the chateau, this little wine shop and bar is a friendly place to sip the local varietals.

SLEEPING

TOP CHOICE **HOTEL MARIO** HOTEL €€

(☎731 607 210; www.hotelmario.cz; ul 21. dubna 55, Lednice; r incl breakfast 1400-1800Kč; P⊜@📶) The fully renovated Hotel Mario stands head and shoulders above any of the smaller hotels or pensions in the Valtice-Lednice area. The immaculate rooms are furnished in muted contemporary style, with thick cotton sheets on the beds and tastefully updated bathrooms. There's a small wine cellar in the basement and a few garden tables out the back for relaxing at.

HOTEL HUBERTUS HOTEL €€

(☎519 352 537; www.hotelhubertus.cz; Zámek 1, Valtice; s/d incl breakfast 1300/1600K; P@) Valtice's most unusual lodging option is to sleep in the chateau itself. While the facilities are not quite as bedazzling as the website might indicate, and there is a slight whiff of neglect about the place, the setting is amazing and the price affordable. The rooms are plainly furnished, in stark contrast to the opulence of the rest of chateau.

PENSION KLARET PENSION €

(☎733 348 305; www.pensionklaret.cz; Střelecká 106, Valtice; s/d incl breakfast 1040/1480Kč; P⊜📶) This pristine modern pension is set amid grassy lawns and has 12 rooms and two larger apartments. The cosy, brick-lined wine cellar is slightly less modern; it dates back to 1890.

Znojmo

Explore

The bustling border town of Znojmo is one of southern Moravia's most popular day trips, particularly for travellers from neighbouring Austria. People come for the wine and to stroll the town's village-like alleys, linking intimate plazas with bustling main squares. Znojmo lies midway between Prague and Vienna and could easily be covered in a few hours as a stopover en route. Alternatively, there are some very nice small hotels and pensions here, and Znojmo could easily serve as a base for exploring the entire southern Moravian wine region. The tourist information office has a wealth of brochures on hiking, biking and drinking possibilities. Time your visit for September to catch the town in full riot for the annual Znojmo Wine Festival.

The Best...

- **Sight** Znojmo Underground (p256)
- **Place to Eat** Veselá 13 (p256)
- **Place to Drink** Na Věčnosti (p256)

Top Tip

Don't miss the breathtaking view out over the Dyje River valley from behind the Church of St Nicholas (p256).

Getting There & Away

Train The bus is better for reaching Znojmo from Brno or Prague, but there is a regular train service to Mikulov (66Kč, one hour).

Bus Znojmo lies near the major north-south E59 highway and has hourly bus service most days from Brno (75Kč, 1¼ hours), plus a couple of direct buses per day from Prague (200Kč, three hours).

Car From Prague, Znojmo is an easy 2½-hour drive: head south on the D1 motorway then exit at route 38 (aka E59 highway) toward Jihlava and follow the signs. From Brno, head an hour south on Hwy E461.

Need to Know

- **Location** 210km southeast of Prague.
- **Znojmo Tourist Office** (☎515 222 552; www.znojmocity.cz; Obroková 10; ⌚8am-6pm Mon-Fri, 9am-5pm Sat, closed Sat afternoon Oct-April)
- **Internet Access** The tourist office maintains a computer for visitors to check email.

SIGHTS

ZNOJMO UNDERGROUND — UNDERGROUND

(Znojemské podzemí; ☎515 221 342; Slepičí trh 2; adult/concession 95/55Kč; ⌚9am-6pm Jul-Aug, to 4pm May, Jun & Sep, 10am-4pm Mon-Sat Apr, 10am-4pm Sat Oct) Znojmo's most popular attraction is this tour through the labyrinthine 14th-century tunnels and cellars below the old town. Dress warmly and expect lots of animated trolls and scary animatronic skeletons.

ROTUNDA OF OUR LADY & ST CATHERINE — CHURCH

(Rotunda Panny Marie a sv Kateřiny; ☎515 222 311; www.znojmuz.cz; Rotunda; 90Kč; ⌚9.15am-4pm Tue-Sun May-Sep, Sat & Sun only Apr) This 11th-century church is one of the republic's oldest Romanesque structures and contains a beautiful series of 12th-century frescoes depicting the life of Christ. Because of the sensitive nature of the frescoes, visitors are limited to groups of 10 or fewer, and are allowed in for 15 minutes at a time once per hour (at a quarter past the hour).

ZNOJMO CASTLE — CASTLE

(Znojemský hrad; ☎515 222 311; www.znojmuz.cz; Hrad; adult/concession 40/20Kč; ⌚9am-5pm Tue-Sun May-Sep, Sat & Sun only Apr) Znojmo has traditionally occupied a strategic position on the border between Austria and Moravia, and there's been a fortress here since the late 11th century. The castle has served as a residence for Moravian margraves (nobles), a garrison, and even housed a brewery in the 18th century. In 1335, King John of Luxembourg held a wedding ceremony here for his daughter Anne.

During our visit, the castle was undergoing renovation but was expected to reopen in 2013.

CHURCH OF ST NICHOLAS — CHURCH

(kostel sv Mikuláše; www.farnostznojmo.cz; náměstí Mikulášské; ⌚during services) This church was once Romanesque, but has been rebuilt in Gothic style. In a side chapel is the so-called 'Bread Madonna'. According to legend, during the Thirty Years' War a box beneath this image was always found to be full of food, no matter how much was removed. Beside the church is the small Orthodox **St Wenceslas Chapel** (kaple sv Václava).

TOWN HALL TOWER — TOWER, ARCHITECTURE

(Radniční věž; Obroková; adult/concession 40/20Kč; ⌚9am-5pm) The handsome and scalable 66m tower on Znojmo's town hall is one of Moravia's best examples of late Gothic architecture (c 1448).

EATING & DRINKING

VESELÁ 13 — CZECH €€

(☎515 220 323; www.lahofer.cz; Veselá 13; mains 185-400Kč; 📶) The in-house restaurant of the Hotel Lahofer is a real treat. The chef is talented at turning out great regional cooking with an international twist, and menu items are paired with wines from the Lahofer winery. Try to book a table in advance.

NA VĚČNOSTI — CZECH, PUB €

(☎776 856 650; www.navecnosti.cz; Velká Mikulášská 11; mains 70-120Kč; ⌚restaurant 10.30am-10pm, pub 6pm-1am; 📶🌿) Upstairs a tasty vegetarian restaurant; downstairs a pub-meets-club with occasional touring bands. Either way, you win.

KAFÉ OÁZA CAFE

(☎775 243 888; www.kafeoaza.cz; Kovářská 307; snacks 50-80Kč; ⌚9am-10pm Mon-Sat; 📶) Cane furniture and a veritable forest of potted plants provide the setting here for sweet and savoury crepes, local wines, coffee and cake. In summer, the place to be is the nicely secluded courtyard.

SLEEPING

TOP CHOICE HOTEL LAHOFER HOTEL €€

(☎515 220 323; www.lahofer.cz; Veselá 13; d/ste 1400/2100Kč; P⊖@📶) This relatively recent addition to the Znojmo hotel scene turns out to be easily one of the nicest small hotels in this part of the Czech Republic. The setting is a 13th-century house close to the main square. The rooms have been thoroughly modernised and outfitted in the best contemporary style, and the restaurant is the finest in the city.

TRAVELLERS HOSTEL HOSTEL €

(☎515 221 489; www.travellers.cz; Staré Město 22; dm 300-330Kč, s/d 380/760Kč; ⊖@📶) Could this hostel have one of the best locations in all the Czech Republic? While you're pondering the question – and the views – make yourself comfy in the sunny dorms and rooms, tucked into the river valley under St Wenceslas Chapel.

PENSION KAPLANKA PENSION €

(☎775 552 212; www.kaplanka.cz; U branky 6; s/d without bathroom 400/600Kč, d/tr with bathroom 900/1000Kč; ⊖@📶) This whitewashed heritage place has a variety of rooms ranging from so-so to respectable midrange (prices and bathroom facilities increase accordingly). Sample the local wine in the garden as you look across the Dyje River valley, and you could almost be in Tuscany.

REZIDENCE ZVON PENSION €

(☎775 611 128; www.rezidence-zvon.cz; Klácelova 61/11; s/d incl breakfast from 1100/1400Kč; @📶) Concealed in a restored 18th-century residence near the castle are six very comfortable rooms combining wooden floors, flat-screen TVs and modern furniture.

Olomouc

Explore

Olomouc is a sleeper. Practically unknown outside the Czech Republic and underappreciated even at home, the city is surprisingly majestic. The main square counts among the country's very nicest, surrounded by historic buildings and blessed with a Unesco-protected trinity column. The evocative central streets are dotted with beautiful churches, testifying to the city's long history as a bastion of the Catholic Church. Explore the foundations of ancient Olomouc Castle at the must-see Archdiocesan Museum (p259), then head for one of the city's many pubs or microbreweries. Don't forget to try the cheese, *Olomoucký sýr,* reputedly the smelliest in the Czech Republic.

The Best...

- **Sight** Holy Trinity Column (p258)
- **Place to Eat** Moritz (p261)
- **Place to Drink** Cafe 87 (p262)

Top Tip

Definitely plan for an overnight stay here; there's loads to see by day, and great restaurants and microbreweries to enjoy at night.

Getting There & Away

Train Olomouc is on a main rail line, with regular services from both Prague (240Kč, three hours) and Brno (100Kč, 1½ hours).

Bus There are around 15 buses daily to/from Brno (92Kč, 1¼ hours); see www.jizdnirady.idnes.cz.

Car From Prague, Olomouc is an easy three-hour drive along the main D1 motorway through Brno, then turning off on highway E462, following the signs. From Brno, the drive takes one hour along the same route.

Need to Know

- **Location** 280km southeast of Prague.
- **Tourist Information Office** (Olomoucká Informační Služba; ☎585 513 385; www.tourism.olomouc.eu; Horní náměstí; ⌚9am-7pm) Sells maps and books accommodation.

WORTH A DETOUR

WORTH A DETOUR: ZLÍN'S FUNKY FUNCTIONALISM

In the early 20th century, Moravia was a hotbed of ground-breaking modern architecture. Brno is recognized as the centre of the action, but the smaller industrial town of Zlín (pronounced 'zleen') was home to some radical and fascinating experimentation in Functionalist town planning, following the vision of philanthropist shoe millionaire Tomáš Baťa ('bah-tya').

Adhering to Bat'a's plan, the factories, offices, shopping centres and houses all use lookalike red bricks and a Functionalist template, to provide 'a total environment' to house, feed and entertain the workers at Baťa's massive shoe factory. Wide avenues and planned gardens produce a singular ambiance, giving Zlín an expansive and unnervingly modern appearance, in contrast with the saccharine historical centres of other towns.

The **Zlín Tourist Information Office** (Městské Informační a Turistické Středsiko; ☎577 630 270; www.zlin.eu; Náměstí Míru 12; ⏲8am-5.30pm Mon-Fri, to noon Sat) has lots of information on hand about the town's architectural heritage, including maps and walking tours (in English) of the most important buildings. One of the top sights is the surprisingly interesting **Zlín Shoe Museum** (Obuvnické muzeum; www.muzeum-zlin.cz; třída Tomaše Bati 1970; adult/concession with English text 50/30Kč; ⏲10am-noon & 1-5pm Tue-Sun Apr-Oct, Sat & Sun only Nov-Dec & Feb-Mar, closed Jan).

The most fascinating structure is the Baťa company's **Administration Building No 21**, also known as the Baťa Skyscraper. The 16-storey building is now home to the local regional government, but on the 8th floor is an interesting exhibition on the history of Baťa and Zlín. Also, don't miss the quirky **paternoster elevator** – two-person lifts that are continuously rotating: jump on...jump off...jump on again (don't blame us if you give it a second go). You'll find them in the side entrance to the regional government offices. In the same corner of the building is Tomáš Baťa's amazing **office**, which was also a self-contained lift that could travel up and down the building.

The best way to reach Zlín is by bus: there are regular links to Brno (100Kč, two hours) and Olomouc (80Kč, 1¾ hours).

➡ **Slam** (www.slam.cz; Slovenská 12; per min 1Kč; ⏲9am-9pm Mon-Fri, from 10am Sat & Sun; 📶) Internet access with wi-fi capability.

SIGHTS

Horní Náměstí & Around

Olomouc's main square, Horní (or 'upper') náměstí, will be your first port of call. This is where the tourist office is, as well the city's most important sight: a gargantuan **trinity column**. The square also contains two of the city's six baroque fountains. The **Hercules Fountain** (Herkulova kašna) dates from 1688 and features the muscular Greek hero standing astride a pit of writhing serpents, while the **Caesar Fountain** (Caeserova kašna), east of the town hall, was built in 1724 and is Olomouc's biggest.

HOLY TRINITY COLUMN MONUMENT

Map p260 (Sousoší Nejsvětější trojice; Horní náměstí) The town's pride and joy is this 35m-high (115ft) baroque sculpture that dominates the square and is a popular meeting spot for local residents. The trinity column was built between 1716 and 1754 and is allegedly the biggest single baroque sculpture in Central Europe. In 2000, the column was awarded an inscription on Unesco's World Heritage list.

The individual statues depict a bewildering array of Catholic religious motifs, including the Holy Trinity, the twelve apostles, the assumption of Mary, and some of the best-known saints. There's a small **chapel** at the base of the column that's sometimes open during the day for you to poke your nose in.

FREE **TOWN HALL** TOWER

Map p260 (Radnice; Horní náměstí; tower 15Kč) Olomouc's Town Hall dates from the 14th century and is home to one of the quirkier sights in town: an astronomical clock from the 1950s, with a face in Socialist Realist style. The original was damaged in WWII. At noon the figures put on a little performance. The tower is open twice daily to climb, at 11pm and 3pm.

ST MORITZ CATHEDRAL CHURCH

Map p260 (Chrám sv Mořice; www.moric-olomouc.cz; Opletalova 10; ⏲tower 9am-5pm Mon-Sat, noon-5pm Sun) This vast Gothic cathedral is Olomouc's original parish church, built between 1412 and 1540. The western tower is a remnant of its 13th-century predecessor. The cathedral's amazing sense of peace is shattered every September with an **International Organ Festival**; the cathedral's organ is Moravia's mightiest. The **tower** provides the best view in town.

Dolní Náměstí & Around

Dolní náměstí, or 'lower' square, runs south of Horní náměstí, and is lined by shops and restaurants. It sports its own **Marian Plague Column** (Mariánský morový sloup), and **baroque fountains** dedicated to Neptune and Jupiter. Also here, the 1661 **Church of Annunciation of St Mary** stands out with its beautifully sober interior.

ST MICHAEL CHURCH CHURCH

Map p260 (kostel sv Michala; www.svatymichal.cz; Žerotínovo náměstí 1; ⏲8am-6pm) This beautiful church on Žerotínovo náměstí sports a green dome and a robust baroque interior with a rare painting of a pregnant Virgin Mary. Wrapped around the entire block is an active Dominican seminary (Dominikánský klášter).

CHAPEL OF ST JAN SARKANDER CHURCH

Map p260 (kaple sv Jana Sarkandra; Žerotínovo náměstí; ⏲10am-noon & 1-5pm) This tiny, round chapel is named after a local priest who died under torture in 1620 for refusing to divulge false confessions. It's built on the site of the jail where he died, part of which is preserved in the cellar. Downstairs is an exhibition about his pious life.

Náměstí Republiky & Around

OLOMOUC MUSEUM OF ART MUSEUM

Map p260 (Olomoucký muzeum umění; ☎585 514 111; www.olmuart.cz; Denisova 47; adult/child 50/25Kč, free admission Wed & Sun; ⏲10am-6pm Tue-Sun) This popular museum houses an excellent collection of 20th-century Czech painting and sculpture. Admission includes entry to the Archdiocesan Museum (p259).

REGIONAL HISTORY MUSEUM MUSEUM

Map p260 (Vlastivědné muzeum; www.vmo.cz; náměstí Republiky 5; adult/child 40/20Kč; ⏲9am-6pm Tue-Sun Apr-Sep, 10am-5pm Wed-Sun Oct-Mar) In a former convent is the Regional History Museum, with historical, geographical and zoological displays.

ARCHBISHOP'S PALACE MUSEUM

(Arcibiskupský palác; ☎587 405 421; www.arcibiskupskypalac.ado.cz; Wurmova 9; adult/concession 60/30Kč; ⏲10am-5pm Tue-Sun May-Sep, 10am-5pm Sat & Sun Apr & Oct) This expansive former residence of the archbishop was built in 1685. Entry to see the lavish interiors is by guided tour only (free audioguide provided in English). It was here that Franz-Josef I was crowned Emperor of Austria in 1848 at the tender age of 18.

Václavské Náměstí & Around

It's hard to believe now, but this tiny square, northeast of the centre, was where Olomouc began. A thousand years ago, this was the site of Olomouc Castle. You can still see the castle foundations in the lower levels of the Archdiocesan Museum. The area still holds Olomouc's most venerable buildings and darkest secrets. Czech King Wenceslas III (Václav III) was murdered here in 1306 under circumstances that are still not clear to this day.

ARCHDIOCESAN MUSEUM MUSEUM

Map p260 (Arcidiecézni muzeum; ☎585 514 111; www.olmuart.cz; Václavské náměstí 3; adult/concession 50/25Kč, free Sun & Wed; ⏲10am-6pm Tue-Sun) The impressive holdings of the Archdiocesan Museum trace the history of Olomouc back 1000 years. The thoughtful layout, with helpful English signage, takes you through the original Romanesque foundations of Olomouc Castle, and

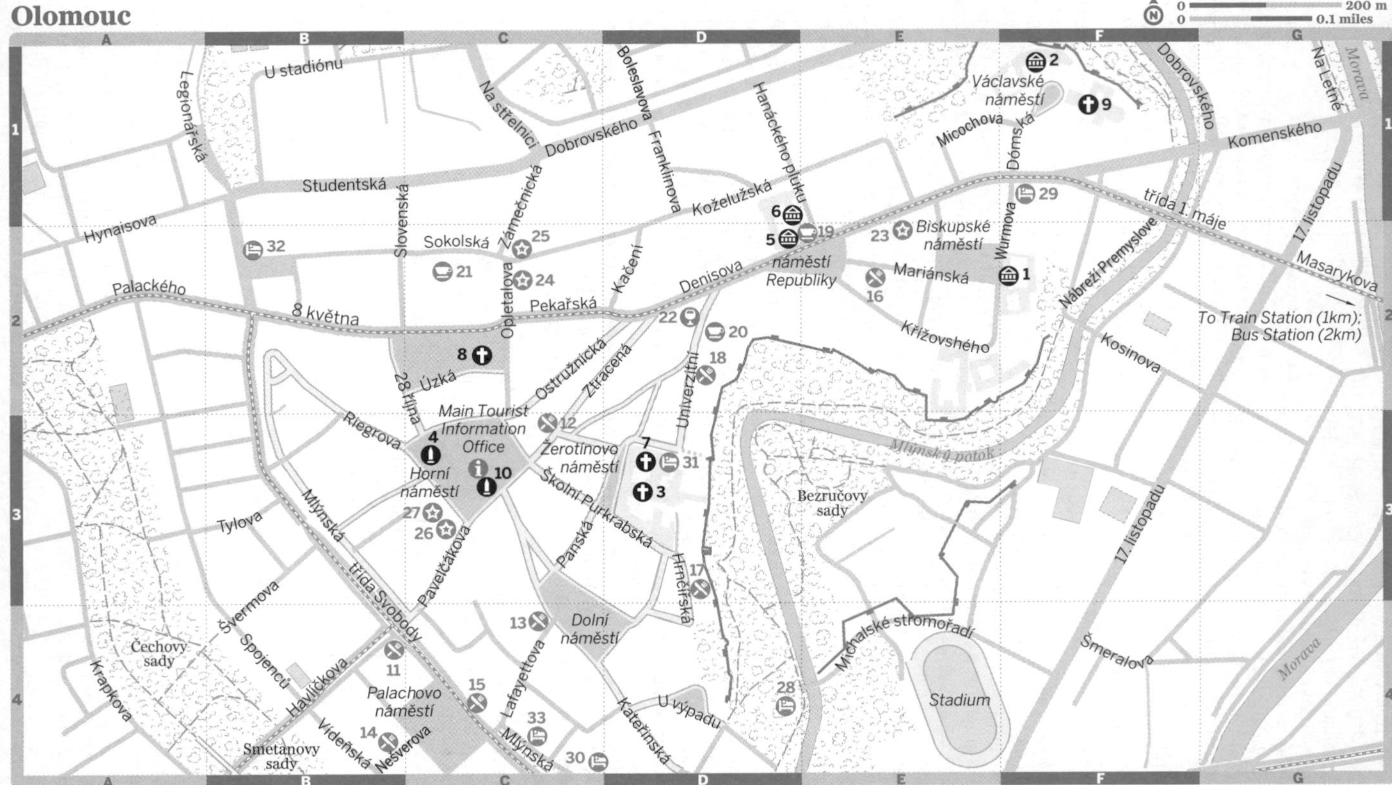
Olomouc
0 200 m
0 0.1 miles
U stadiónu
Legionářská
Na střelnici
Dobrovského
Boleslavova
Franklinova
Hanáckého pluku
Václavské náměstí
Micochova
Dómská
Na Letné
Morava
Komenského
Studentská
Koželužská
Hynaisova
Slovenská
Sokolská
Zámečnická
Kačení
Denisova
náměstí Republiky
Biskupské náměstí
Wurmova
třída 1. máje
17. listopadu
Nábřeží Přemyslovce
Masarykova
Mariánská
Křížovského
To Train Station (1km); Bus Station (2km)
Kosinova
Palackého
8 května
Opletalova
Pekařská
Úzká
28 října
Ostružnická
Ztracená
Univerzitní
Main Tourist Information Office
Riegrova
Horní náměstí
Žerotínovo náměstí
Školní
Purkrabská
Mlýnský potok
Bezručovy sady
Tylova
Mlýnská
třída Svobody
Pavelčákova
Panská
Hrnčířská
Dolní náměstí
Švermova
Spojenců
Čechovy sady
Krapkova
Havlíčkova
Palachovo náměstí
Lafayettova
Vídeňská
Nešverova
Smetanovy sady
Kateřinská
U výpadu
Michalské stromořadí
Stadium
Šmeralova

Olomouc

Sights

1 Archbishop's Palace F2
2 Archdiocesan Museum F1
3 Chapel of St Jan Sarkander D3
4 Holy Trinity Column C3
5 Olomouc Museum of Art D2
6 Regional History Museum D1
7 St Michael Church D3
8 St Moritz Cathedral C2
9 St Wenceslas Cathedral F1
10 Town Hall C3

Eating

11 Drápal B4
12 Green Bar C3
13 Hanácacká Hospoda C4
14 Moritz B4
15 Nepal C4
16 Svatováclavský Pivovar E2
17 U Anděla D3
18 Vila Primavesi D2

Drinking

19 Cafe 87 .... E2
20 Konvikt D2
21 Kratochvíle C2
22 Vertigo D2

Entertainment

23 Hospoda u Musea E2
24 Jazz Tibet Club C2
25 Kino Metropole C2
26 Moravská Filharmonie C3
27 Moravské Divadlo C3

Sleeping

28 Hotel Alley D4
29 Pension Angelus F1
30 Pension Křivá C4
31 Penzión Na Hradě D3
32 Poet's Corner B2
33 Ubytovna Marie C4

highlights the cultural and artistic development of the city during the Gothic and baroque periods.

Don't miss the magnificent Troyer Coach, definitely the stretch limo of the 18th century. Spring for the 20Kč English-language audioguide to get more out of the visit. Admission includes entry to the Olomouc Museum of Art (p259).

ST WENCESLAS CATHEDRAL — CHURCH

Map p260 (dóm sv Václava; Václavské náměstí; 8am-6pm) Adjacent to the museum, this cathedral, the seat of the Olomouc Archbishop, was originally a Romanesque basilica first consecrated way back in 1131. It was rebuilt several times before having a neo-Gothic makeover in the 1880s. There's a **crypt** inside that you can enter.

EATING

MORITZ — CZECH €€

Map p260 (585 205 560; www.hostinec-moritz.cz; Nešverova 2; mains 120-260Kč;) This microbrewery and restaurant is a firm local favourite. We reckon it's a combination of the terrific beers, good value food, and a praise-worthy 'no smoking' policy. In summer, the beer garden's the only place to be. Advance booking a must.

NEPAL — NEPALESE €

Map p260 (585 208 428; www.nepalska.cz; Mlýnská 4; mains 110-150Kč;) Located in a popular Irish pub, this Nepalese-Indian eatery is the place to go for something a little different. The 100Kč buffet lunch is the best deal, but loyal patrons say the quality of the food is better in the evening.

DRÁPAL — CZECH €

Map p260 (585 225 818; www.restauracedrapal.cz; Havlíčkova 1; mains 110-150Kč;) It's hard to go wrong with this big historic pub on a busy corner near the centre of town. The unpasteurised 12° Pilsner Urquell is arguably the best beer in Olomouc. The smallish menu is loaded with Czech classics, like the ever-popular *Španělský ptáček* (literally 'Spanish bird'), a beef roulade stuffed with smoked sausage, parsley and a hard-boiled egg.

SVATOVÁCLAVSKÝ PIVOVAR — CZECH €€

Map p260 (585 207 517; www.svatovaclavsky-pivovar.cz; Mariánská 4; mains 170-290Kč) Another microbrewery (what's in the water in Olomouc?), this is a bit bigger than Moritz and it's easier to find a walk-in table here. The microbrewery produces several excellent versions of unpasteurised yeast beer. The menu features mostly Czech standards done well, plus a few dishes that experiment with Olomouc's signature stinky cheese.

HANÁCACKÁ HOSPODA CZECH €

Map p260 (Dolní náměstí 38; mains 100-180Kč) The menu lists everything in the local Haná dialect at this popular pub/restaurant. It's worth persevering though because the huge Moravian meals are tasty and supreme value. Don't worry – they've got an English menu if you're still getting up-to-speed with Haná.

U ANDĚLA CZECH €€

Map p260 (☎585 228 755; www.uandela.cz; Hrnčířská 10; mains 170-380Kč) After you order, wander round and look at the fascinating memorabilia displayed in every nook and cranny here. Don't take too long though, because the service is prompt and the Moravian food very good. There's also a good (if pricey) international wine list.

VILA PRIMAVESI INTERNATIONAL €€€

Map p260 (☎777 749 288; Univerztiní 7; mains 300-450Kč; ⊙11am-11pm Mon-Sat, 11am-4pm Sun) In an art-nouveau villa that played host to Austrian artist Gustav Klimt in the early 20th century, the Vila Primavesi is one of Olomouc's most exclusive restaurants. On summer evenings enjoy meals like tuna steak and risotto in the lovely gardens. Lunch specials are better value than evening meals.

GREEN BAR VEGETARIAN €

Map p260 (☎777 749 274; www.greenbar.cz; Ztracená 3; meals 100Kč; ⊙10am-5pm Mon-Fri, 10am-2pm Sat; 🅥) Around 100Kč will get you a feast of salads, veggie lasagne and couscous at this self-service vegetarian cafe. It's popular with a cosmopolitan mix of overseas students.

DRINKING

TOP CHOICE CAFE 87 CAFE

Map p260 (☎585 202 593; Denisova 47; chocolate pie 35Kč, coffee 40Kč; ⊙7.30am-9pm Mon-Fri, 8am-9pm Sat & Sun; 📶) Locals come in droves to this funky cafe beside the Olo-

WORTH A DETOUR

WORTH A DETOUR: WHITE MOUNTAIN PARADISE OF ŠTRAMBERK

The village of Štramberk, nestled on the slopes of White Mountain (Bílá hora), is a pristine slice of northern Moravia that's easily reachable from Olomouc by bus or car, via the town of Nový Jičín.

The main attractions here are the undisturbed rural setting and a ruined clifftop castle you can hike to for views across the surrounding valleys. Oh, and there's a terrific microbrewery here too, so you'll have somewhere to recover after you've finished your walk.

The path up Bílá hora starts north of the main square and passes through a stone gate inscribed 'Cuius Regio – Eius Religio – 1111' ('Whose Place – His Place – 1111'). On the slopes are the remains of the Gothic castle walls; climb the 166 steps up the tower.

If you happen to catch a rainy day here, there are two museums on the square. The **Štramberk Museum** (☎556 852 284; www.muzeum.novy-jicin.cz; náměstí 31; adult/concession 50/20Kč; ⊙9am-noon & 1-5pm Tue-Sun) focuses on local archaeology, folk furniture and art. The **Museum Zdeňka Buriana** (☎556 852 240; www.stramberk.cz; náměstí 31; adult/concession 50/20Kč; ⊙9am-noon & 1-5pm Tue-Sun) exhibits the works of a locally born painter who chose Stone Age people as his subjects.

The **Štramberk Municipal Brewery** (Městský Pivovar; ☎556 813 710; www.relaxvpodhuri.cz; náměstí 5; mains 100-200Kč; ⊙11am-10pm Mon-Sat, to 8pm Sun; 📶) is the real centre of activity, offering its own light and dark beers as well as bar snacks and full meals. Be sure to try *Štramberské uši* (Štramberk ears), conical ginger biscuits with honey and spices, usually served with cream. According to legend, the ears originally belonged to unfortunate Tatar prisoners of war.

The **Štramberk Municipal Information Centre** (Městské informační centrum; ☎558 840 617; www.stramberk.cz; Zauličí 456) is situated near the square: they can help find and book accommodation.

Buses for Štramberk leave hourly most days from Nový Jičín (a stopover on most Olomouc–Ostrava buses). The ride takes about 20 minutes and costs about 25Kč.

mouc Museum of Art for coffee and their famous chocolate pie. Some people still apparently prefer the dark chocolate to the white chocolate. When will they learn? It's a top spot for breakfast and toasted sandwiches too.

KRATOCHVÍLE TEAHOUSE

Map p260 (☎603 564 120; www.kratochvile.com; Sokolská 36; ⏰11am-11pm Mon-Fri, from 3pm Sat & Sun) A global array of teas, interesting beer and wine, and a laid-back Zen ambiance make this a good spot to recharge. Stop by and see if there's any entertainment planned (Peter Gabriel played here once). The name means 'pastime' in Czech.

KONVIKT CAFE

Map p260 (☎585 631 190; www.konvikt-olomouc.webnode.cz; Univerzitní 5;) A family-friendly cafe and restaurant situated on a quiet street near the university. There's a small play area for children, and lots of mothers with strollers, enjoying coffee, cake and decent Czech food.

VERTIGO BAR

Map p260 (www.klubvertigo.cz; Univerzitní 6; ⏰1pm-midnight Mon-Thu, 4pm-2am Fri-Sun) A dark, dank student bar that reeks of spilled beer and stale smoke. In other words, a very popular drinking spot in a college town like Olomouc.

SLEEPING

PENZIÓN NA HRADĚ PENSION €€

Map p260 (☎585 203 231; www.penzionnahrade.cz; Michalská 4; s/d 1390/1890Kč;) Tucked away in the robust shadow of St Michael Church, this designer pension has sleek, cool rooms and professional service, creating a contemporary ambience in the heart of the Old Town.

POET'S CORNER HOSTEL €

Map p260 (☎777 570 730; www.hostelolomouc.com; Sokolská 1, 3rd fl; dm/tw/tr/q 350/900/1200/1600Kč;) The Australian-Czech couple who mind this friendly and exceptionally well-run hostel are a wealth of local information. Bicycles can be hired from 100Kč to 200Kč per day. In summer there's a two-night minimum stay, but Olomouc is definitely worth it, and there's plenty of day-trip information on offer.

PENSION ANGELUS PENSION €€

Map p260 (☎776 206 936; www.pensionangelus.cz; Wurmova 1; s/d 1250/1850Kč; ; 2, 4, 6) With antique furniture, crisp white duvets and Oriental rugs on wooden floors, the Angelus is a spacious and splurge-worthy romantic getaway. To get here catch bus 2 or 6 from the train station or bus 4 from the bus station, jumping off at the U Domů stop.

PENSION KŘIVÁ PENSION €€

Map p260 (☎585 209 204; www.pension-kriva.cz; Křivá 8; s/d/apt 1490/1950/2300Kč;) This modern pension gets a lot of things right: spacious rooms featuring cherry-wood furniture, flash bathrooms with even flasher toiletries, and a cosy cafe downstairs. The quiet laneway location doesn't hurt either.

HOTEL ALLEY HOTEL €€€

Map p260 (☎585 502 999; www.hotel-alley.com; Michalské stromořadí 1061; s/d 2600/3000Kč;) Hotel Alley combines solid four-star business cred with an in-house spa/massage centre. It's slightly characterless, but still the best digs in town. From Friday to Sunday there's a hefty 30% discount; check the website for the best deals.

UBYTOVNA MARIE GUESTHOUSE €

Map p260 (☎585 220 220; www.ubytovnamarie.cz; třída Svobody 41 5; per person 500Kč;) Spick and span (if spartan) double and triple rooms with shared bathrooms and kitchens make this spot popular with long-stay overseas students. Significant discounts kick in after two nights.

PENSION MORAVIA PENSION €

(☎603 748 188; www.pension-moravia.com; Dvořákova 37; s/d/tr 700/900/1400Kč; ; 19) A 10-minute walk from the town centre, this pension provides good value in a quiet residential street without the potential parking hassles of the Old Town. If you arrive by public transport, catch bus 19 from the railway station to the Dvořákova stop.

ENTERTAINMENT

JAZZ TIBET CLUB LIVE MUSIC

Map p260 (585 230 399; www.jazzclub.olomouc.com; Sokolská 48; admission free-250Kč) Blues, jazz and world music, including occasional international acts, feature at this popular spot, which also incorporates a good restaurant and wine bar.

HOSPODA U MUSEA CLUB, LIVE MUSIC

Map p260 (Ponorka; www.ponorka.com; třída 1 maje 8; 10am-midnight Mon-Fri, noon-midnight Sat, 4pm-midnight Sun) Usually known by its nickname 'Ponorka' (literally 'submarine'), this is possibly the loudest, smokiest and most crowded rock club/pub in the Czech Republic (and that's saying something). The scene is mostly aging rockers and punks still living in the good ol' days, but on occasional evenings there are legendary concerts.

KINO METROPOLE CINEMA

Map p260 (585 222 466; www.kinometropol.cz; Sokolská 25) For Hollywood hits and occasional art-house surprises.

MORAVSKÉ DIVADLO OPERA, BALLET

Map p260 (585 500 500; www.moravskedivadlo.cz; Horní náměstí 22) From opera to ballet, and all affordably priced.

MORAVSKÁ FILHARMONIE CLASSICAL MUSIC

Map p260 (585 206 520; www.mfo.cz; Horní náměstí 23) The local orchestra presents regular concerts and hosts Olomouc's International Organ Festival.

Kroměříž

Explore

Sleepy Kroměříž merits a detour if you happen to be in this part of the country. The main draw is the sumptuous early-baroque Archbishop's Palace, with its commanding tower, rococo interiors and even a certifiable masterpiece: Titian's *The Flaying of Marsyas*. The palace is a Unesco World Heritage Site – a great place to while away a few hours. Outside the palace, there are some attractive Renaissance and baroque buildings scattered about, and a lovely formal garden. While you only need a few hours to take in the sights, there's at least one compelling reason to spend the night: Kroměříž is home to an excellent microbrewery, an essential retreat once you've taken in the sights. Conveniently, the microbrewery also houses and very nice small hotel.

The Best...

- **Sight** Archbishop's Chateau (p264)
- **Place to Eat** Černý Orel (p265)
- **Place to Drink** Černý Orel (p265)

Top Tip

Addresses in Kroměříž are confusing. Each house bears two numbers: the street address and the city registry building number. We've used street addresses in our listings, but some places insist on using building numbers.

Getting There & Away

Train The train from Brno (110Kč, 1½ hours) usually requires a change in Kojetín. Trains from Olomouc (70Kč, one hour) often require a change in Kojetín or Hulín. See www.vlak-bus.cz for current details.

Bus There are regular buses to/from Brno (88Kč, 1¼ hours) and Olomouc (60Kč, 1¾ hours).

Car From Brno, it's a 45-minute drive northeast along the D1 motorway.

Need to Know

- **Location** 271km southeast of Prague.
- **Tourist Information Centre** (Informační Centrum; 573 221 473; www.mesto-kromeriz.cz; Velké náměstí 50; 8.30am-5pm Mon-Fri, 9am-1pm Sat & Sun) Organises accommodation and rents-out bikes (per day 200Kč).
- **Internet Access** The Tourist Information Centre has computers on hand for checking email.

SIGHTS

ARCHBISHOP'S CHATEAU CASTLE

(Arcibiskupský zámek; 573 502 011; www.zamek-kromeriz.cz; Zámek; adult/concession 200/120Kč, art gallery 90/80Kč, tower 50/40Kč;

9am-6pm Tue-Sun Jul-Aug, to 5pm Tue-Sun May, Jun & Sep, to 4pm Sat & Sun Apr & Oct) The Archbishop's Chateau dates from the late 17th century and is Kroměříž's big-ticket sight, with an 84m-high baroque **tower** visible for miles around. Main attractions include impressive interiors, boasting baroque and rococo murals, as well as the tower, **gardens**, and an impressive **art gallery** with works by the Venetian master Titian and other luminaries.

The palace was built by Charles II of Liechtenstein-Kastlekorn, a bishop, on the site of a previous Gothic and Renaissance castle levelled by the Swedes in the Thirty Years War. Entry is by guided tour only, but the art gallery and tower can be seen without a guide.

Velké Náměstí & Around

After visiting the Archbishop's Chateau, it's only a short walk to the main square, **Velké náměstí**. The 16th-century Renaissance **Town Hall** stands on the corner with Kovářská. At No 30 is the town's oldest **pharmacy**, U Zlatého lva, established in 1675. The cobblestone square also has a decorative **fountain** and **plague column**.

FLOWER GARDEN — GARDENS

(Květná zahrada; www.zamek-kromeriz.cz; ulice Gen Svobody; adult/concession 40/30Kč; 7am-7pm May-Sep, to 4pm Oct-Apr) This 17th-century baroque garden has a frequently photographed **rotunda** by Lucchese, and a **colonnade** by Tencalla. Enter from Gen Svobody, west of the city centre.

KROMĚŘÍŽ MUSEUM — MUSEUM

(muzeum Kroměřížska; 573 338 388; www.muzeum-km.cz; Velké náměstí 38; all exhibitions adult/concession 60/30Kč, Max Švabinský exhibition 40/20Kč; 9am-noon & 1-5pm Tue-Sun) The town's leading museum has a permanent collection of the works of Max Švabinský (born in Kroměříž in 1873), the designer of many of Czechoslovakia's early postage stamps. Also worth seeing are Švabinský's lunettes (arched paintings) on the walls of the Franciscan monastery that now houses the Hotel Octárna. (p265) The paintings were originally intended for Prague's National Theatre.

EATING & DRINKING

ČERNÝ OREL — CZECH €€

(www.pivovar-kromeriz.cz; Velké náměstí 24; mains 159-259Kč;) Some of the best food in this part of Moravia is served at this slick microbrewery on the main square. Choose from appetisers like duck cracklings and liver to a full range of duck, pork and venison mains. Pair your meal with one of the house brews, like the strong 17° dark beer with hints of caramel and coffee.

RADNIČNÍ SKLÍPEK — CZECH €

(Kovářská 20/2; mains 80-120Kč; 8am-10pm Mon-Fri, 9am-midnight Sat, 9am-6pm Sun) This cute-and-cosy subterranean space just off Velké náměstí offers good-value Czech dishes like chicken schnitzel served with potato salad. The homemade soups are brought to the table in big tureens for the whole family.

VEGETARIÁNSKÁ RESTAURACE — VEGETARIAN €

(Bio ; 573 342 711; www.vegjid.kvalitne.cz; Velké náměstí 40; mains 50-80Kč; 7am-2.30pm Mon-Fri;) This rather sterile but convenient courtyard cafe, just off the main square, has good daily specials. Look forward to one of Moravia's best apple crumbles (21Kč).

GREEN BAR — VEGETARIAN €

(724 176 926; www.greenbar.717.cz; Ztracená 68; mains 50-70Kč; 11.30am-4pm Mon-Thu, to 2.30pm Fri;) Salads and veggie main dishes, a nonsmoking environment and a kids' play area add up to a family-friendly joint. Also offers vegan entrees.

SLEEPING

TOP CHOICE HOTEL ČERNÝ OREL — HOTEL €€

(573 332 769; www.cerny-orel.eu; Velké náměstí 24; s 1200-1400Kč, d 1500-2000Kč;) The nicest hotel in town occupies prime real estate on the main square, right above the town's highly recommended restaurant/microbrewery. The rooms have a clean, modern look and are equipped with fancy baths and high-end amenities like flat-screen TVs and DVD players.

HOTEL OCTÁRNA — HOTEL €€

(573 505 655; www.octarna.cz; Tovačovského 318; s 1150-1400Kč, d 1500-2050Kč;) A restored Franciscan monastery is now a classy small hotel with a quiet courtyard

shaded by market umbrellas. Downstairs is a stylish candlelit wine cellar.

PENZIÓN EXCELLENT PENSION €

(☎573 333 023; www.excellent.tunker.com; Riegrovo náměstí 163/7; s/d 1090/1420Kč; @📶) 'Europe Standard' says its sign, and that's what you get – with a big buffet breakfast and brightly furnished rooms on a quiet square.

PENZIÓN DOMOV PENSION €

(☎573 344 744; www.penziondomov.cz; Riegrovo náměstí 157; r 1000-1300Kč; @📶) Another baroque-style building and another cosy pension, this time with recently restored rooms. Decor ranges from wedding-cake kitsch to crisp, modern timber (have a look at your room before you commit).

PENZIÓN MENŠÍK PENSION €

(☎602 569 863; www.penzionmensik.cz; Velké náměstí 107; r 750Kč) This budget place, with a main-square location and outside-the-centre prices, has simple (if slightly cramped) rooms.

HOTEL OSKOL HOTEL €

(☎573 341 240; www.hoteloskol.wz.cz; Oskol 3203; s/d 700/900Kč) Cheap sleeps in a multistorey building transplanted from pre-1989 Czechoslovakia.

Understand Prague & the Czech Republic

Prague & the Czech Republic Today

Prague remains one of Europe's leading tourist destinations. The capital heaves with more than four million foreign tourists a year, and most locals are accustomed to the throng. The crowds can make crossing the Charles Bridge trying on summer's day, but they bring vitality to the city and invigorate an already-booming culinary and cultural scene. The pace slows down markedly in the countryside, where unique aspects of Czech culture still flourish.

Best on Film

Amadeus (1985) Mozart's love affair with Prague gets brilliant treatment.
Kolya (1996) Velvet Revolution-era Prague never looked lovelier.
Loves of a Blonde (1965) Miloš Forman's 'New Wave' classic.
Mission Impossible (1996) Prague was the setting for the first instalment of Tom Cruise's blockbuster trilogy.
Alois Nebel (2011) Graphic novel adaptation set in WWII-era Moravia.

Best in Print

The Unbearable Lightness of Being (Milan Kundera; 1984) Prague before the 1968 Warsaw Pact invasion.
I Served the King of England (Bohumil Hrabal; 1990) The Hotel Paříž is the backdrop to this humorous classic.
The Castle (Franz Kafka; 1926) We wonder which castle Kafka was thinking about?
The Good Soldier Švejk (Jaroslav Hašek; 1923) Hašek's absurdist novel is set throughout the Czech Republic.
My Merry Mornings (Ivan Klima; 1986) The sweeter side of life in communist Prague.

The Passing of a Velvet Icon

The end of 2011 saw the death of Václav Havel, the country's first post-communist president and undisputed moral authority of the 1989 Velvet Revolution. Havel's death at 75 after a long bout with cancer wasn't unexpected, but seemed to catch the country by surprise. The outpouring of grief was uncharacteristically intense for normally stoic Czechs. News of the death brought tens of thousands onto Wenceslas Square to lay candles at the statue of St Wenceslas. Thousands more lined up days later to file past his coffin and pay their final respects.

Havel was broadly respected outside the country, but his legacy among Czechs was mixed. Many were grateful for his heroic 1989 stance that helped bring down communism, but his tenure as president (first of Czechoslovakia then the Czech Republic) was hit and miss. Ironically, many faulted Havel for being too soft on former communists. Havel's passing, however, appears temporarily to have healed the old divides and left a moral vacuum at the heart of Czech society that will be hard to fill. Czech writer Milan Kundera said it best: 'Havel's most important work was his own life.'

How 'not' to Govern a Country

Political scientists around the world will long have the Czech Republic to thank when studying dysfunctional political systems. Every year, it seems, brings a predictable number of government crises and threats of no-confidence votes that could bring down the whole edifice at any moment. A shaky right-leaning coalition, led by Prime Minister Petr Nečas of the Civic Democratic Party (ODS), remains under constant threat from the opposition Social Democrats (CSSD), and has been wracked by scandal.

But unstable governments are par-for-the-course here. In 2009 the government famously fell in a no-confidence vote, but new elections weren't held for more than a year. That escapade gave rise to the running joke at the time: 'What's the world's biggest nongovernmental organisation?' Answer: the Czech Republic.

Current President Václav Klaus, whose term runs to 2013, presides over this cacophony like a mother hen. The presidency is relatively weak on paper, but the controversial Klaus (a self-proclaimed Thatcherite and deeply hostile to the European Union) has used the divisions to consolidate his power. This may change in 2013, when the president for the first time will be chosen by direct popular (instead of parliamentary) vote.

Economic Crisis Averted?

After wallowing for years in the wake of the global recession, Prague and the Czech Republic appear to be slowly clawing their way back to prosperity. After suffering a decline in growth as recently as 2011, the Czech economy was poised to grow by 0.2% in 2012 and 1.6% in 2013. Much will depend on recovery in Germany, the Czechs' largest export market.

Visitors are not likely to notice any sign of a downturn in Prague, which remains partially buffered from the global economy due to tourist income. Indeed, a near 20-year boom in tourism has helped the Czech capital to become the seventh-richest region in the European Union. The effects are more pronounced in the countryside – particularly western Bohemia and northern Moravia – where much of the industry is located.

Construction & Corruption

Talk with a Czech for more than a few minutes and the twin topics of construction and corruption are bound to surface. The Czech capital is awash with unfinished major rebuilding projects, including the billion-euro 'Blanka' ring road and tunnel complex just north of the centre, that remain mired in mud and allegations of contractor bilking and missing funds.

The Blanka Tunnel is part of an even more ambitious scheme that proposes to re-route through-traffic around the city, and may even allow the city someday to abandon the unfortunate highway that drives straight through the centre just above Wenceslas Square (and cuts off the square from the National Museum and State Opera). Someday, if you believe the glossy catalogues, part of that highway may run underground and Wenceslas Square will once again be connected to residential Vinohrady.

if Prague were 100 people

91 would be Czech
3 would be Roma
2 would be Slovak
4 would be other

religion

(% of population)

population per sq km

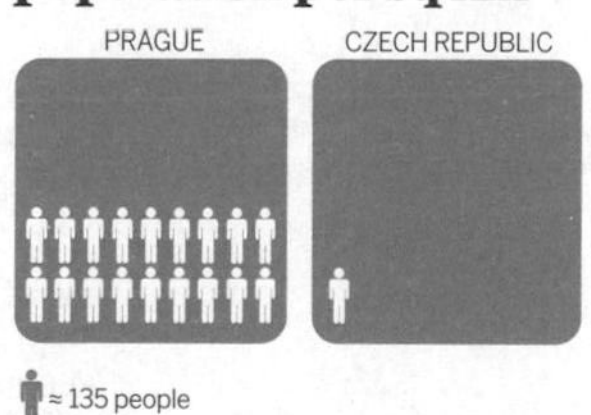

History

While modern-day visitors still tend to see the Czech Republic as part of 'Eastern Europe' or a former member of the Soviet bloc, for over a thousand years, the kingdoms of Bohemia and Moravia stood at the very heart of European affairs. Indeed, for much of the 14th century, under Emperor Charles IV, Prague was the seat of the Holy Roman Empire – in effect, the capital of Europe. Later, in the 16th century under Rudolf II, Prague served as the centre of the sprawling Habsburg empire, overseeing territories as far-flung as modern-day Italy and Poland.

THE EARLY YEARS WITH THE CELTS

There's been human habitation on the territory of the modern-day Czech Republic for some 600,000 years, with permanent communities since around 4000 BC, but it's the Celts, who came to the area around 500 BC, that arouse the most interest. The name 'Bohemia' for the western province of the Czech Republic derives from one of the most successful of these Celtic tribes, the Boii. Traces of Boii culture have been found as far away as southern Germany, leading some archaeologists to posit a relation between Celts here and those in France, and possibly even further afield to tribes in the British Isles.

IN COME THE SLAVS

It's unclear what prompted the great migration of peoples across Europe in the 6th and 7th centuries, but during this time large populations of Slavs began arriving in central Europe, driving out the Celts and pushing German tribes further to the west. The newcomers established several settlements along the Vltava, including one near the present site of Prague Castle and another upriver at Vyšehrad.

It was a highly unstable time, with the new arrivals themselves under threat from incoming peoples such as the Avars. A Frankish trader named Samo briefly succeeded in uniting the Slavs to repel the Avars, but the Slavs quickly resumed their squabbling.

TIMELINE	500 BC–AD 400	AD 500	Early 600s
	Celtic tribes thrive in the territory of the modern-day Czech Republic, building settlements whose remains will later be discovered in and around Prague.	Slavic tribes enter Central Europe during the Great Migration, forming settlements along the Vltava River. Excavations indicate the largest may have been near Roztoky, northwest of Prague.	Princess Libuše, the fabled founder of the Přemysl dynasty, looks out over the Vltava valley and predicts that a great city will emerge there someday.

THE MYTH OF LIBUŠE & THE FOUNDING OF PRAGUE

Fittingly for a city that embraces so much mystery, the origins of Prague are shrouded in a fairytale. Princess Libuše, the daughter of early ruler Krok, is said to have stood on a hill near the city's Vyšehrad castle one day around the 7th century and predicted a glorious city that would one day become Prague. According to the legend, Libuše needed to find a strong suitor who could yield sturdy heirs to the throne. Passing over a field of eligible bachelors, including some sickly-looking royals, she selected a simple ploughman, Přemysl. She chose well. The Přemysl dynasty would go on to rule for some 400 years.

In the 9th century, the Přemysl prince Bořivoj selected an outcropping in Hradčany to build Prague Castle, the dynasty's seat. Amazingly, the castle – the official seat of the Czech presidency – remains the centre of power to this day.

Christianity became the state religion under the rule of the pious Wenceslas (Václav in Czech), the Duke of Bohemia (r c 925–929) and now the chief patron saint of the Czech people (immortalised on

READING UP ON CZECH HISTORY

Prague and the Czech Republic are not lacking in well-written historical accounts in English. Some of the best of these include:

- *Prague, A Cultural History* (Richard Burton). A beautifully written cultural history by an English professor obviously in love with Prague and its myths. The first chapter, 'How to Read Prague', is especially helpful for visitors. The chapters are arranged around stories and characters – both real and fictional – that have shaped the city through the ages.
- *Under a Cruel Star, A Life in Prague 1941–1968* (Heda Margolius Kovály). One of the few books to forge a link between the Nazi and communist periods. The author, Jewish and born in Prague, had the double misfortune of being sent to Terezín and Auschwitz during WWII, only to survive the war and marry an up-and-coming communist who was executed in the show trials of the 1950s.
- *Prague in Danger* (Peter Demetz). Demetz's work is partly a classical history and partly a lively and moving chronicle of his own family – Demetz's mother was Jewish and died at Terezín. These personal remembrances are especially strong and give a first-hand feel for what life in Prague was like during the Nazi occupation.
- *The Magic Lantern: The Revolution of 1989 Witnessed in Warsaw, Budapest, Berlin, and Prague* (Timothy Garton Ash). Oxford professor Garton Ash had the professional and linguistic skills to interpret history as it was unfolding in 1989 – and the presence of mind to write it all down.

870s

Prince Bořivoj begins construction of Prague Castle in Hradčany to serve as the seat of his Přemysl dynasty – as it will for kings, emperors and presidents for centuries to come.

26 August 1278

King Otakar II is thrashed by the Habsburgs at the Battle of Marchfeld (*Moravské Pole* in Czech) at the height of the Přemysl dynasty's influence.

4 August 1306

The last Přemysl king, Wenceslas III, is murdered, leaving no male heir. The dynasty passes to John of Luxembourg, who will give Bohemia its greatest ruler, his son Charles IV.

26 August 1346

John of Luxembourg dies and Charles IV becomes Bohemian king. Later, he adds 'HolyRoman Emperor' to his list of titles. Prague booms as the seat of the empire.

horseback at the top of Wenceslas Square). Wenceslas was the 'Good King Wenceslas' of the well-known Christmas carol, written in 1853 by English clergyman John Mason Neale. Wenceslas's conversion to Christianity is said to have angered his mother and his brother, Boleslav, who ended up killing the young duke in a fit of jealousy.

Despite the dysfunctional family relations, the Přemysls proved to be highly effective rulers. During the 13th century, the Přemysl lands stretched from modern-day Silesia (near the Czech–Polish border) to the Mediterranean Sea.

Top Hussite Sights in Prague

- *Jan Hus Statue (Staré Město)*
- *Bethlehem Chapel (Staré Město)*
- *Týn Church (Staré Město)*

CHARLES IV & THE HOLY 'PRAGUE' EMPIRE

It's hard to imagine that Prague and the Czech Republic will ever exceed the position of power they held in the 14th century, when Prague for a time became the seat of the Holy Roman Empire under Emperor Charles IV (Karel IV, r 1346–78).

The path to glory began predictably enough with the murder of a Přemysl ruler, Wenceslas III, in 1306, leaving no male successor to the throne. Eventually, John of Luxembourg (Jan Lucemburský to the Czechs) assumed the Czech throne through his marriage to Wenceslas III's daughter Elyška in 1310.

Under the enlightened rule of John's son, Charles IV, Prague grew into one of the continent's largest and most prosperous cities. Charles commissioned both the bridge that now bears his name and St Vitus Cathedral, among other projects. He also established Charles University as the first university in central Europe.

Following Emperor Sigismund's death, George of Poděbrady (Jiří z Poděbrad) ruled as Bohemia's one and only Hussite king, from 1452 to 1471, with the backing of moderate Hussites, the Utraquists. By that time, however, the Hussite cause had been lost and once-prosperous Bohemia lay in ruin.

THE HUSSITE WARS & RELIGIOUS STRIFE

In contrast to the 14th century, the 15th century brought little but hardship and war to the Czechs. Much of the good of the preceding years was undone in an orgy of religion-inspired violence and intolerance. The period witnessed the rise of an impassioned Church-reform movement led by Jan Hus (see boxed text on opposite page). Hus's intentions to rid Rome's papal authorities of corruption were admirable, but his movement ended up dividing the country. In 1419, supporters of Hussite preacher Jan Želivský stormed Prague's New Town Hall and tossed several Catholic councillors out of the windows – thus introducing the word 'defenestration' (throwing someone from a window in order to do him or her bodily harm) into the political lexicon.

The Hussites (as the followers of Jan Hus were known) assumed control of Prague after the death of Holy Roman Emperor Wenceslas IV

6 July 1415

Religious reformer Jan Hus is burned at the stake at Konstanz, Germany, for refusing to recant his criticisms of the Catholic Church. His death enflames decades of religious strife.

Early 15th century

The Hussite Wars – pitting radical reformers against Catholics and, ultimately, different Hussite factions against each other – rage throughout Bohemia.

1583

Habsburg Emperor Rudolf II moves the dynasty's seat from Vienna to Prague, heralding a second golden age. It lasts for three decades, when Protestant/Catholic tensions boil over.

21 June 1621

Twenty-seven Czech noblemen are executed in Old Town Square for their part in instigating the anti-Habsburg revolt. Their severed heads are hung from the Old Town Tower on Charles Bridge.

in 1419. The move sparked the first anti-Hussite crusade, launched in 1420 by Emperor Sigismund, with the support of many pro-Catholic rulers around Europe. Hussite commander Jan Žižka successfully defended the city in the Battle of Vítkov Hill, but the religious strife spilled into the countryside. The Hussites themselves were torn into factions of those wanting to make peace with the emperor and others wanting to fight to the end. The more radical Hussites, the Taborites, were ultimately defeated in battle at Lipany, east of Prague, in 1434.

Best Books by Václav Havel

To the Castle and Back (2008)

Open Letters, Selected Writings (1992)

Disturbing the Peace (1991)

THE HABSBURGS TAKE OVER

The weakening of the Bohemian state left the region open to foreign intervention. Austria's Habsburg empire, ruled from Vienna, was able to take advantage and eventually came to dominate both Bohemia and Moravia. At first, in the mid-16th century, the Habsburgs were invited in by a weary Czech nobility weakened by constant warfare. Decades later, in 1620, the Austrians were able to cement their control over the region with a decisive victory over Czech forces at Bílá Hora, near Prague. The Austrians would continue to rule the Czechs for another 300 years, until the emergence of independent Czechoslovakia at the end of WWI.

RELIGIOUS REFORMER JAN HUS

Jan Hus was the Czech lands' foremost (and one of Europe's earliest) Christian reformers, preceding Martin Luther and the Lutheran reformation by more than a century.

Hus was born into a poor family in southern Bohemia in 1372. He studied at the Karolinum (Charles University) and eventually became dean of the philosophical faculty.

Like many of his colleagues, Hus was inspired by the English philosopher and radical reformist theologian John Wycliffe. The Roman Catholic clergy neatly meshed Wycliffe's ideas on reforming with growing Czech resentment at the wealth and corruption of the clergy.

In 1391, Prague reformers founded the Bethlehem Chapel, where sermons were given in Czech rather than Latin. Hus preached there for about 10 years, while continuing his duties at the university.

Hus's criticisms of the Catholic Church, particularly the practice of selling indulgences, endeared him to his followers but put him in the Pope's black book. In fact, the Pope had him excommunicated in 1410, but Hus continued to preach. In 1415, he was invited to the Council of Constance to recant his views. He refused and was burned at the stake on 6 July 1415.

29 October 1787

Wolfgang Amadeus Mozart, already more popular in Prague than in Vienna, conducts the premiere of his opera *Don Giovanni*, staged at the Estates Theatre near Old Town Square.

Estates Theatre (p103)

3 July 1883

German-Jewish writer Franz Kafka is born near Old Town Square. He'll lead a double life: mild-mannered insurance clerk by day, harried father of the modern novel by night.

Though the Austrians are generally knocked in Czech history books, it must be admitted that their leadership established some much-needed stability in the region. Indeed, the latter part of the 16th century under Habsburg Emperor Rudolf II (r 1576–1612) is considered a second 'golden age' in Czech history, comparable to Charles IV's rule in the 14th century. Eccentric Rudolf preferred Prague to his family's ancestral home in Vienna and moved the seat of the Habsburg empire to the Czech capital for the duration of his reign.

During the 17th and 18th centuries, Prague got a major baroque facelift, including the statues on the Charles Bridge and construction of St Nicholas Church in Malá Strana. This was mainly the work of the Austrians and the Jesuits, eager to mark their triumph.

Rudolf is typically viewed by historians as something of a kook. He had a soft spot for esoteric pursuits such as soothsaying and alchemy, and populated his court with wags and conjurers from around Europe. The English mathematician and occultist John Dee and his less-esteemed countryman Edward Kelly were just two of the noted mystics Rudolf kept at the castle in an eternal quest to turn base metals into gold. It's also true, though, that Rudolf's tutelage led to real advances in science, particularly astronomy.

For all his successes, though, Rudolf failed to heal the age-old rift between Protestants and Catholics, and the end of his reign in 1612 saw those tensions again rise to the forefront. The breaking point came in 1618 with the 'Second Defenestration of Prague', when a group of Protestant noblemen stormed into a chamber at Prague Castle and tossed two Catholic councillors and their secretary out the window. The men survived – legend has it they fell onto a dung heap – but the damage was done. The act sparked the Thirty Years' War – a precursor to WWI and WWII in the 20th century – that ultimately consumed the whole of Europe and left Bohemia again in ruins.

Prague joined in the 1848 democratic revolutions that swept Europe, and the city was first in line in the Austrian empire to rise in favour of reform. Yet, like most of the others, Prague's revolution was soon crushed.

REVIVAL OF THE CZECH NATION

Remarkably, Czech language and culture managed to endure through the years of Austrian occupation. As the Habsburgs eased their grip in the 19th century, Prague became the centre of the Czech National Revival. The revival found its initial expression not in politics – outright political activity was forbidden – but in Czech-language literature and drama. Important figures included linguists Josef Jungmann and Josef Dobrovský, and František Palacký, author of *Dějiny národu českého* (The History of the Czech Nation).

While many of the countries in post-Napoleonic Europe were swept up by similar nationalist sentiments, social and economic factors gave the Czech revival particular strength. Educational reforms by Empress Maria Theresa (r 1740–80) had given even the poorest Czechs access

28 October 1918

A newly independent Czechoslovakia is proclaimed at the Municipal House (Obecní dům) in the final days of WWI. Crowds throng Wenceslas Square in jubilation.

30 September 1938

European powers agree to Hitler's demand to annex Czechoslovakia's Sudetenland region. British PM Neville Chamberlain declares they have achieved 'peace in our time'.

15 March 1939

German soldiers cross the Czechoslovak frontier and occupy Bohemia and Moravia. Czechoslovak soldiers, ordered in advance not to resist, allow the Germans to enter without firing a shot.

27 May 1942

Czechoslovak patriots assassinate German Reichsprotektor Reinhard Heydrich, and are later found hiding in a Nové Město church. Trapped by Nazi soldiers, some suicide; others are killed.

THE JEWS OF PRAGUE

Prague was for centuries a traditional centre of Jewish life and scholarship. Jews first moved into a walled ghetto north of the Old Town Square in about the 13th century, in response to directives from Rome that Jews and Christians should live separately. Subsequent centuries of repression and pogroms culminated in a threat from Habsburg Emperor Ferdinand I (r 1526–64) that was never carried out – to throw all the Jews out of Bohemia.

Official attitudes changed under Emperor Rudolf II at the end of the 16th century. Rudolf bestowed honour on the Jews and encouraged a flowering of Jewish intellectual life. Mordechai Maisel, the mayor of the ghetto at the time, became Rudolf's finance minister and the city's wealthiest citizen. Another major figure was Judah Loew ben Bezalel (Rabbi Loew), a prominent theologian, chief rabbi, student of the mystical teachings of the Cabbala, and nowadays best known as the creator of the Golem (a kind of proto-robot made from the mud of the Vltava).

When they helped to repel the Swedes on Charles Bridge in 1648, the Jews won the favour of Ferdinand III to the extent he had the ghetto enlarged. But a century later they were driven out of the city, only to be welcomed back later when the residents missed their business.

In the 1780s, Habsburg Emperor Joseph II (r 1780–90) outlawed many forms of discrimination, and in the 19th century the Jews won the right to live wherever they wanted. Many chose to leave the ghetto for nicer areas of the city. At the end of the 19th century, municipal authorities decided to clear the ghetto, which had become a slum.

The ghetto, renamed Josefov in Joseph II's honour, remained the spiritual heart of Prague's Jewish community. That came to a brutal end with the Nazi occupation during WWII. Today the city is home to roughly 5000 Jews, a fraction of the community's former size.

to schooling, and a vocal middle class was emerging through the Industrial Revolution.

INDEPENDENCE AT LAST

For Czechs, the tragedy of WWI had one silver lining: the defeat of the Central powers, including Austria-Hungary, left the empire too weak to fight for its former holdings, paving the way for the creation of independent Czechoslovakia in 1918. Czech patriots Tomáš Masaryk and Edvard Beneš had spent the war years in the United States, where they lobbied ceaselessly with Czech and Slovak émigré communities to win

5 May 1945

Prague residents begin an armed uprising against the Germans, liberating the city after three days. The Germans are granted free exit in exchange for agreeing not to destroy the city.

9 May 1945

The Soviet Army formally liberates the city, though most German soldiers are already defeated or gone. Later, under the communists, this will be recognised as the official day of liberation.

25 February 1948

Communists stage a bloodless coup. Party leader Klement Gottwald proclaims the news and crowds cheer, but the coup ultimately leads to 40 years of oppressive communist rule.

20 November 1952

In a Soviet-style purge, communists accuse some of their own party functionaries, including General Secretary Rudolf Slánský, of treason. The prisoners are executed.

American backing for a joint Czech-Slovak state. The plea appealed especially to the idealistic American president, Woodrow Wilson, and his belief in the self-determination of peoples. The most workable solution appeared to be a single federal state of two equal republics, and this was spelled out in agreements signed in Cleveland, Ohio, in 1915 and Pittsburgh, Pennsylvania, in 1918 (both cities having large populations of Czechs and Slovaks).

As WWI drew to a close, Czechoslovakia declared its independence, with Allied support, on 28 October 1918. Prague became the capital and the popular Masaryk, a writer and political philosopher, the new republic's first president.

President Masaryk remains a beloved figure in Czech history and is regarded as the father of the country. But historians question his legacy, particularly pushing for the creation of independent, weak states in central Europe that left a power vacuum for the Germans and the Russians.

A TASTE OF FREEDOM, THEN NAZI DOMINATION

Czechoslovakia in the two decades between independence and the 1938 Munich agreement (that paved the way for the Nazi German invasion) was a remarkably successful state. Even now, Czechs consider the 'First Republic' another golden age of immense cultural and economic achievement.

Czechoslovakia's proximity to Nazi Germany – and its sizable German minority in the border area known as the Sudetenland – made the country a tempting a target for Adolf Hitler. Hitler correctly judged that neither Britain nor France had an appetite for war, and at a conference in Munich in 1938, the Nazi leader demanded that Germany be allowed to annex the Sudetenland. British Prime Minister Neville Chamberlain acquiesced, famously calling Germany's designs on Czechoslovakia a 'quarrel in a faraway country between people of whom we know nothing'.

On 15 March 1939 Germany occupied all of Bohemia and Moravia, declaring the region a 'protectorate', while Slovakia was permitted 'independence' as long as it remained a Nazi puppet state. During the war, Prague was spared significant physical damage, though the Germans destroyed the Czech resistance. Around two-thirds of Bohemia and Moravia's Jewish population of 120,000 perished in the war.

On 5 May 1945, with the war drawing to a close, the citizens of Prague staged an uprising against the Germans. The Red Army was advancing from the east and US troops had made it as far as Plzeň to the west, but were holding back from liberating the city in deference to their Soviet allies. Many people died in the uprising before the Germans pulled out on 8 May, having been granted free passage out in return for an agreement not to destroy more buildings.

20–21 August 1968

Soviet-led Warsaw Pact forces invade Czechoslovakia to end reforms called the 'Prague Spring'. Reforming communist leader Alexander Dubček is replaced by Gustáv Husák.

16 January 1969

Student Jan Palach immolates himself at Wenceslas Square to protest the Warsaw Pact invasion. Thousands come to the square to mark his memory and attend his funeral.

KRZYSZTOF DYDYNSKI / LPI ©

Palach memorial (p102) by Olbram Zoubek

1977

Life in Prague reaches a political nadir during 'normalisation'. Václav Havel signs Charter 77, calling on Czechoslovakia to meet its international human-rights obligations.

In 1945, Czechoslovakia was reconstituted as an independent state. One of its first acts was the expulsion of the remaining Sudeten Germans from the borderlands. By 1947, some 2½ million ethnic Germans had been stripped of their Czechoslovak citizenship and forcibly expelled to Germany and Austria.

Prague was the major objective in the 1968 Warsaw Pact invasion. Soviet special forces, with the help of the Czechoslovak secret police, secured Prague airport for Soviet transport planes. At the end of the first day of fighting, 58 people had died.

FROM HITLER'S ARMS INTO STALIN'S

Czechoslovak euphoria at the end of the war did not last long. The communists seized power just three years later, in 1948. While these days, the takeover is usually viewed as a naked power grab by Stalin's henchmen, the reality is more complicated. For many Czechs, WWII had tarnished the image of the Western democracies, and Stalin's Soviet Union commanded deep respect

By the 1950s, however, this initial enthusiasm faded as communist economic policies bankrupted the country and a wave of repression sent thousands to labour camps. In a series of Stalin-style purges staged by the KSČ (Communist Party of Czechoslovakia) in the early 1950s, many people, including top members of the party itself, were executed.

In the 1960s, Czechoslovakia enjoyed something of a renaissance, and under the leadership of reform communist Alexander Dubček, became a beacon for idealists wanting to chart a 'third way' between communism and capitalism. The reform movement was dubbed 'Socialism with a Human Face' and mixed elements of democracy with continued state control over the economy. This easing of hardline communism became known around the world as the 'Prague Spring'.

In a historical twist, Prague could have been liberated by US soldiers under General George S Patton, based in Plzeň, perhaps as early as May 6 1945. Despite Patton's pleas, US commanders called off the American advance to allow the Russians the 'honour' of liberating the capital.

In the end, though, it was the movement's success that eventually undid it. Soviet leaders were alarmed by the prospect of a partially democratic society within the Eastern bloc and any potential spillover it might have on Poland and Hungary. The Prague Spring was eventually crushed by a Soviet-led invasion of Eastern bloc states on the night of 20–21 August 1968. Much of the fighting took place near the top of Wenceslas Square – the front of the National Museum still bears the bullet marks.

In 1969 Dubček was replaced by hardliner Gustáv Husák and exiled to the Slovak forestry department. Thousands of people were expelled from the party and lost their jobs. Many left the country, while others were relegated to being manual labourers and street cleaners. The two decades of stagnation until 1989 are known today as the period of 'normalisation'.

17 November 1989

Police violently halt a student demonstration, sparking days of demonstrations culminating in the communists relinquishing power – the 'Velvet Revolution'.

1 January 1993

The Czech and Slovak republics agree peacefully to split into independent countries, formally bringing an end to Czechoslovakia. The split becomes known as the 'Velvet Divorce'.

22 February 1998

The Czech national ice hockey team defeats Russia 1-0 to win gold at the Nagano Winter Olympics. It was this hockey-crazed nation's first and only Olympic gold medal in the sport.

12 March 1999

The Czech Republic enters the NATO military alliance along with Poland and Hungary. The move initially angers Russia in spite of assurances from NATO that the alliance is purely defensive.

VELVET REVOLUTION & VELVET DIVORCE

The year 1989 was a momentous one throughout Eastern Europe as communist governments fell like dominoes in Hungary, Poland, East Germany, Bulgaria and Romania. But the revolution that toppled communism in Czechoslovakia was perhaps the greatest of them all. It remains the gold standard around the world for peaceful antigovernment protest.

In one of his most controversial acts as president, Václav Havel in 1990 offered a formal apology to the Sudeten Germans for the mass expulsions of ethnic Germans post-WWII.

Ironically, the Velvet Revolution actually had its start in a paroxysm of violence on the night of 17 November, when Czech riot police began attacking a group of peaceful student demonstrators. The protesters had organised an officially sanctioned demonstration in memory of students executed by the Nazis in 1939, but the marchers had always intended to make this demo a protest against the communist regime. What they didn't count on was the fierce resistance of the police, who confronted the crowd of about 50,000 on Prague's Národní třída and beat and arrested hundreds of protesters.

Czechs were electrified by this wanton police violence, and the following days saw nonstop demonstrations by students, artists, and finally most of the population, peaking at a rally on Prague's Letná hill that drew some 750,000 people. Leading dissidents, with Havel at the forefront, formed an anticommunist coalition, which negotiated the government's resignation on 3 December. A 'government of national understanding' was formed with the communists as a minority group. Havel was elected president by the Federal Assembly on 29 December.

In economic terms, Prague has prospered since the Velvet Revolution, becoming one of the biggest tourist draws on the continent. Unemployment is minimal, shops are full and the facades that were crumbling 20 years ago have been given facelifts.

Almost immediately after the revolution, problems arose between Czechs and Slovaks.The Slovaks had long harboured grievances against the dominant Czechs, and many Slovaks dreamed of having their own state. On 1 January 1993, amid much hand-wringing on both sides, especially from Havel, the Czechs and Slovaks peacefully divided into independent states.

THE CZECH REPUBLIC REJOINS 'EUROPE'

It would be impossible to summarize in just a few paragraphs the changes that have taken place in the more than 20 years since the Velvet Revolution. The big-picture view is largely positive. The Czech Republic achieved its two major long-term foreign-policy goals: joining NATO in 1999 and the European Union in 2004.

In terms of domestic politics, the country continues to ride a knife-edge. Neither major centrist party – the right-leaning Civic Democratic Party (ODS) or the left-leaning Social Democrats (ČSSD) – has been able

14 August 2002

Several city districts and the metro tunnels are inundated in the Vltava River's biggest modern-era flood. Damages cost several billion euros and spark redevelopment in hard-hit areas.

1 May 2004

The Czech Republic achieves its biggest foreign policy objective since the Velvet Revolution and joins the European Union, along with several other former communist countries.

15 February 2008

By a narrow margin, the Czech parliament re-elects conservative economist Václav Klaus to his second five-year term as President of the Czech Republic.

1 January 2009

Czech Republic assumes the rotating six-month EU presidency. The period is marked by gaffes and errors, and is hailed as the most chaotic EU presidency ever.

THE LATE PLAYWRIGHT-PRESIDENT VÁCLAV HAVEL

As Europeans lament the dearth of great men and women in modern times, one man whom everyone can look up to is the late Czech president and former dissident, Václav Havel. Havel, who died in 2011 at the age of 75, was the unshakeable moral authority behind the 1989 Velvet Revolution and the country's first post-communist president. He was also famously a playwright and communist-era essayist, whose underground letters simultaneously excoriated his collaborationist countrymen and held up a moral alternative to official communist pabulum based on universal concepts of dignity and human rights.

Havel was born into a wealthy family on October 5 1936. Had WWII and the subsequent communist coup not intervened, he might very well have lived out a successful life, minding his family's various businesses, but that trajectory changed forever with the communist takeover in 1948. His family was stripped of its property and the young Havel was denied access to higher education.

Havel's enthusiasm for the liberal reforms of the 'Prague Spring' of the 1960s and his avowed opposition to communist rule in the 1970s made him an enemy of the government. His plays – typically focusing on the absurdities and dehumanisation of totalitarian bureaucracy – were banned and his passport seized.

The massive demonstrations of November 1989 thrust Havel into the limelight as a leading organiser of the noncommunist Civic Forum movement, which ultimately negotiated a peaceful transfer of power. Havel was swept into office as president shortly after, propelled by a wave of thousands of cheering demonstrators, holding up signs saying *'Havel na hrad!'* (Havel to the castle!).

In 2003, after two terms in office as president, Havel was replaced by former prime minister Václav Klaus. After leaving office, Havel finished two sets of memoirs and even returned to the stage as the author of the highly acclaimed play *Odcházení* (Leaving). He died on 18 December 2011 at the age of 75 after battling cancer for many years.

cobble together a lasting consensus, so the country lurches from side to side with each election cycle.

Perhaps the biggest news since 1989 was the death of Havel himself on 18 December 2011. The former president and leader of the Velvet Revolution had served both as a symbol of the Czech Republic's commitment to Western ideals of democracy and human rights, and as a moral compass for a society still badly deformed by corrupt communist rule. As we go to press, that symbolic position had yet to be filled and may not be for years to come.

March 2009

Despite the fact the Czechs hold the EU presidency, the government collapses in a no-confidence vote. The unprecedented move throws the EU into disarray.

5 April 2009

US President Barack Obama addresses thousands of well-wishers at a speech near Prague Castle during which he promotes a policy of eventual nuclear disarmament.

28–29 May 2010

In landmark elections, Czechs vote in a new centre-right coalition, ending nearly a year without an elected government.

18 December 2011

Former president and leader of the Velvet Revolution, Václav Havel, dies after a long battle with cancer. The nation goes into prolonged mourning.

Czech Life

More than 20 years after the fall of communism, a welcome normality has descended on the Czech Republic. Seen from any measure – from what they value, how they work, what they study or how they relax – Czechs are well within the European mainstream. And that's not a bad thing. After a combined 50 years of war and communism, the over-riding social goal after 1989 was to create – or re-create – a prosperous, fully functioning democracy in the heart of Europe. In that, they've happily succeeded.

Guest Workers by Country

Ukraine (118,000 est)

Slovakia (84,000)

Vietnam (60,000)

Russia (38,000)

A NATION OF CZECHS ... & VIETNAMESE?

Compared with western European countries such as Germany, France and the Netherlands, the Czech Republic remains relatively homogenous. According to the 2011 census, nearly 95% of people living here identify themselves as either Czech or Moravian. (The figures mask the number of Roma in the country, estimated at somewhere between 200,000 and 300,000.) Of the rest, only about 2% are Slovaks, with smaller numbers of Poles, Germans and Hungarians.

It wasn't always this way. Until the start of WWII, the territory of the Czech Republic was home to around 3 million ethnic Germans (about 30% of the total population at the time). Many of those people were either killed in the war or forcibly expelled in the months after.

What the recent census numbers don't reflect, however, is the increasingly diverse mix of people coming to the Czech Republic to work, either

WHERE TOLERANCE ENDS: CZECHS & ROMA

Generally speaking, Czechs are a remarkably tolerant people, with relatively open attitudes when it comes to race, religion and sexual preference. That tolerance tends to fly out the window, however, when the subject of the country's Roma minority comes up.

The Roma, descendants of a tribe that migrated to Europe from India in the 10th century, have never been made to feel particularly welcome. Despite making up less than 3% of the population, they are a perpetual object of prejudice, harassment and occasional incidents of violence – such as a wave of Molotov cocktail attacks around the country in 2011 and 2012.

Part of the problem stems from communist-era housing policies that tended to group Roma populations together in run-down ghettos in city centres. Some Czechs living near Roma settlements feel that the areas tend to be unsightly, loud and dangerous.

There are no easy answers. Under increased pressure in recent years from international groups, Czech authorities have introduced more enlightened policies to try to educate and mainstream the Roma population. To date, these have had only mixed results.

The Budapest-based European Roma Rights Centre is a watchdog organisation that has kept a close eye on Czech authorities grappling with a rise in anti-Roma violence. The group maintains an informative website at www.errc.org.

RESTITUTION FOR CHURCHES

For the past 20 years, Czech courts have been busy adjudicating disputes between former property holders who saw their property seized by the communists in the late 1940s and '50s, and the current owners – often the state.

While the law is messy, in general if you lost property in the confiscations, you had a decent chance of getting it back. That is, unless you were a church. For years, both Catholic and Protestant groups had been lobbying the government to gain back their nationalised lands, churches and buildings. That effort finally bore fruit in early 2012, with a landmark government ruling to provide compensation to the churches, and in many cases to return their land and buildings.

While the details are yet to be worked out, the compensation – which could run to many billions of euros – will unfold over the next 30 years. The payouts are expected to be a big boost for the beleaguered church groups in their efforts to shore up their ranks.

permanently or temporarily. These include relatively large populations of Ukrainians and Russians, and, perhaps most curiously, Vietnamese. Partly because of close ties forged between the former communist government and the government of Vietnam, the Czech Republic has emerged as the destination of choice for Vietnamese people moving to Europe.

Hard numbers are difficult to come by, but it's thought that Vietnamese guest workers may total as many as 60,000. Indeed, the Vietnamese surname Nguyen is now reportedly the 9th most common family name in the country, according to a survey conducted by Czech website www.kdejsme.cz. Most of the Vietnamese live in Prague or the western Bohemian city of Cheb. Many make a living by running neighbourhood grocery shops, known in Czech as a *večerka.*

While the communists were in power, priesthood and church attendance were greatly discouraged. Priests were hounded by the secret service (StB) and people who attended services were also persecuted. Priests were ordained in secret and performed religious rites behind closed doors.

A MODERN-DAY LACK OF FAITH

Despite having an active and often violent religious history that stretches back several centuries, Czechs take a much more hands-off approach to the question of religion these days. While hard data is hard to come by, surveys indicate that more than half of all Czechs are either atheists or agnostics. Just 40% or so of the population professes a belief in God.

Among believers, the largest church is the Roman Catholic Church, which claims membership of around a third of the population (though some surveys put this number far lower). Compare this to neighbouring Poland, where 90% of the population say they are Catholic, and Slovakia, where the figure is around 70%. Protestant and other denominations make up another 5% or so.

It's hard to pinpoint exactly why Czechs, on balance, seem to shun religion, though going back as far as Jan Hus in the 15th century, one can trace a national scepticism towards organised faith. It was Hus, after all, who railed against the excesses of the Catholic Church in his day.

In addition, Catholicism has always been bound up to some degree with the Austrian conquest and overzealous efforts by the Jesuits in the 16th and 17th centuries to convert the local population. In more recent times, the former communist government went out of its way to discourage organised religion, going so far as to lock up priests and close down churches.

There are anecdotal signs of a modest rebirth in faith. More and more couples are choosing to be married in a church, and parents are

TENNIS, ANYONE?

In addition to ice hockey, Czechs over the years have excelled at international tennis, a source of no small measure of national pride and the reason why nearly every park or field of green in the country will have a tennis court nearby. Indeed, two of the sport's all-time greatest players, Ivan Lendl (b 1960) and Martina Navrátilová (b 1956), honed their craft here before moving to the big stage. Lendl dominated the men's circuit for much of the 1980s, winning a total of 11 Grand Slam tennis titles and participating in some 19 finals matches (a record only broken in recent years by Roger Federer).

Navrátilová's feats, if anything, are even more impressive. In the late 1970s and throughout the 1980s, she won some 18 Grand Slam singles titles, including a whopping nine victories at Wimbledon, the last coming in 1990. At one point she won six Grand Slam singles titles in a row.

Czechs continue to do well in the international game. The current darling is Petra Kvitová (b 1990), who won Wimbledon in 2011 and was ranked third in the world as this book went to press.

increasingly opting to baptise their children. Also, interest appears to be growing in more esoteric and spiritual beliefs.

WORLD BEATERS AT ICE HOCKEY

Czechs excel at many international sports, including tennis and speed skating, but they are truly masters of the universe when it comes to ice hockey. Since the debut of the annual World Hockey Championships in 1920, the Czech and Czechoslovak national teams have won gold no less than 12 times and taken home a total of 45 medals. Ice hockey plays such a role in the country's psyche that if you ask a Czech what the most significant year was in recent history, you might not hear 1989 or 1968, but rather 1998. That was the year the Czechs beat the Russians 1-0 for gold at the Nagano Winter Olympics, and the country erupted in joy.

It's not clear why Czechs are such hockey maniacs. Certainly, kids grow up playing the game on frozen ponds around the country during the winter, but that doesn't quite explain their world mastery. Part of the answer lies in the competitive nature of the junior leagues all the way up to the country's national hockey league, the Extraliga, where perennial powers HC Sparta Praha (www.hcsparta.cz) and HC Slavia Praha (www.hc-slavia.cz) battle for the top spot.

Czech players are a staple on the rosters of many teams in the North American National Hockey League. Past greats – and still household names – include Jaromír Jágr (b 1972), who won the Stanley Cup with Pittsburgh in 1991 and '92, and who still plays for the Philadelphia Flyers. Dominik Hašek (b 1965), the 'Dominator', was once regarded as the world's best goaltender after winning a Stanley Cup with the Detroit Red Wings in 2001.

Top English News Websites

Prague Post (www.praguepost.com)

Aktuálně.cz (http://aktualne.centrum.cz/czechnews)

Czech Happenings (www.ceskenoviny.cz/news)

Prague Daily Monitor (www.praguemonitor.com)

The Arts in Prague & the Czech Republic

Czechs have always been active contributors to the arts, and no trip to Prague would be complete without a stroll through the city's museums and galleries to admire the work of local painters, photographers and sculptors. In the evenings, you'll be spoiled for choice with offerings of classical music, jazz and rock. Two Czechs, Antonín Dvořák and Bedřich Smetana, are household names in classical music. Czechs are less well known for visual arts, but are still impressive in this field.

MUSIC

Classical

Classical music has a long, rich tradition in the Czech Republic, and Czechs have basked for centuries in the reputation that they know good music when they hear it. It was audiences in Prague, after all, who first 'discovered' the genius of Mozart long before the listening public in Mozart's home country of Austria warmed up to the composer.

Early classical music was heavily influenced by Austrian composers but began to develop distinctly Czech strains in the mid-19th century with the Czech National Revival. As part of this national awakening, Czech composers consciously drew on Czech folk music and historical legends for their compositions. The best-known composer to emerge from this period was Bedřich Smetana (1824–84). While Smetana wrote several operas and symphonies, his signature work remains his *Moldau* (Vlatva) symphony.

Antonín Dvořák (1841–1904) is the composer that most non-Czechs will have heard of. He too was heavily influenced by the Czech National Revival, which inspired his two *Slavonic Dances* (1878 and 1881), the operas *Rusalka* and *Čert a Kača* (The Devil and Kate), and his religious masterpiece, *Stabat Mater*. Dvořák spent four years in the USA, where he composed his famous *Symphony No 9, From the New World*.

Czech mastery of classical music continued into the 20th century, with the compositions of Moravian-born Leoš Janáček (1854–1928). Janáček's music is an acquired taste, though once you've got an ear for the haunting violin strains, it tends to stay with you. Janáček's better-known compositions include the operas *Cunning Little Vixen* and *Káťa Kabanová*, as well as the *Glagolská mše* (Glagolitic Mass).

Jazz

Jazz imported from the USA first burst onto the local scene in the 1930s, and has remained a fixture of the Prague music scene ever since (though it was frowned upon by the communist authorities as decadent Western art in the late 1940s and '50s).

Czech jazz came into its own in the 1960s, and one of the top bands of this period was SH Quartet, which played for three years at Reduta Jazz

Best Classical-Music Festivals

- *Prague Spring (www.festival.cz)*
- *Prague Proms (www.prague proms.cz)*
- *Dvořák Festival (www.dvorakova praha.cz)*
- *Český Krumlov Music Festival (www.ckrumlov .info)*
- *Janáčkovy Hukvaldy (www .janackovy hukvaldy.cz)*

Smetana's *Moldau* (Vlatva) is arguably the most beloved piece of classical music among Czechs and is traditionally played to start the annual Prague Spring music festival.

Club (p129), the city's first professional jazz club. The club is still going strong (though it's no longer quite the centre of the jazz scene). Another leading band from this period was Junior Trio, with Jan Hamr (1948–) and brothers Miroslav and Allan Vitouš, all of whom left for the USA after 1968. Hamr became prominent in American music circles in the 1970s and '80s as Jan Hammer.

Today, the scene feels no less relevant, and on any given night in Prague you can catch a number of decent shows. One of the most outstanding musicians is Jiří Stivín (1942–), who produced two excellent albums in the '70s with the band System Tandem and is regarded as one of the most innovative jazz musicians in Europe. Two others to watch for are Emil Viklický (1948–) and Milan Svoboda (1951–).

Mozart actively embraced Czech audiences and once even famously said of his adoring Prague public, 'My Praguers understand me', following the premiere of his opera *Don Giovanni* in Prague's Estates Theatre in 1787.

Rock & Pop

Rock has played an outsized role in modern Czech history, perhaps to an extent unique among European nations. It was rock (or more specifically the rock of the American band the Velvet Underground and clandestine Czech counterparts such as the Plastic People of the Universe) that nurtured and sustained the anti-communist movement in the 1970s and '80s. The late former president Václav Havel was a huge fan, and numbered among his closest friends the members of the Rolling Stones, Velvet Underground frontman Lou Reed, and even the late absurdist rocker Frank Zappa.

Rock music blossomed during the political thaw of the mid-1960s and home-grown rock acts began to emerge, showing the heavy influence of bands such as the Beatles, Beach Boys and Rolling Stones. The local 1967 hit single 'Želva' (Turtle) by the band Olympic bears the unmistakeable traces of mid-decade Beatles. One of the biggest stars of the time was pop singer Marta Kubišová (1942–). She was officially banned by the communists after the 1968 Warsaw Pact invasion, though she was rehabilitated after 1989 and still occasionally performs. Her voice and songs, to this day, capture something of that fated optimism of the 1960s, pre-invasion period.

The Warsaw Pact invasion silenced the rock revolution. Many bands were prohibited from openly performing or recording. In their place, the authorities encouraged more anodyne singers such as Helena Vondráčková (1947–) and Karel Gott (1939–). Many popular songs from those days, such as Gott's classic 'Je jaká je' (She is What She is), are simply Czech covers of the most innocuous Western music of the day.

Rock became heavily politicised in the 1980s in the run-up to the Velvet Revolution. Hard-core experimental bands such as the Plastic People of the Universe were forced underground and developed huge cult followings. Another banned performer, Karel Kryl (1944–94), became the unofficial bard of the people, singing from his West German exile. His album *Bratříčku, Zavírej Vrátka* (O' Brother, Shut the Door) came to symbolise the hopelessness of the Soviet-led invasion and the decades that followed.

Jan Hammer's theme song for the popular 1980s TV show *Miami Vice* remains one of the most popular jazz recordings of all time, selling some 4 million copies in the USA alone.

The Velvet Revolution opened the door to a flood of influences from around the world. Early-'90s Czech bands such as rockers Lucie and Žlutý pes soon gave way to a variety of sounds, from the Nina Hagen–like screeching of Lucie Bílá to the avant garde chirping of Iva Bittová, in addition to a flood of mainstream Czech acts. The best of these included Psí Vojáci, Buty, Laura a její tygři, Už jsme doma, and Support Lesbiens. Currently, the most popular acts include hard-rockers Kabát, pop balladeer Kryštof, and the softer folk band Čechomor.

VISUAL ARTS

Ask about Czech visual arts and many visitors will probably draw a blank. Some may be able to conjure up art nouveau images by Alfons Mucha, but that's about it. However, the country has much more to offer than Mucha's sultry maidens. Prague has both a long tradition of avant garde photography and a rich heritage of public sculpture, ranging from the baroque period to the present day.

Painting

The Czech Republic can look back on at least seven centuries of painting, starting with the luminously realistic 14th-century works of Magister Theodoricus (Master Theodorus). His paintings, which hang in the Chapel of the Holy Cross at Karlštejn Castle and in the Chapel of St Wenceslas in St Vitus Cathedral, influenced art throughout Central Europe. Another gem of Czech Gothic art is a late-14th-century altar panel by an artist known only as the Master of the Třeboň Altar; what remains of it is at the Convent of St Agnes in Prague's Old Town.

The Czech National Revival in the 19th century witnessed the revival of a Czech style of realism, in particular by Mikuláš Aleš and father and son Antonín and Josef Mánes. The National Revival sought, as well, to emphasise the natural beauty of the Czech countryside, and landscape painting from this time is soul-stirringly beautiful. You can see some of it at the Convent of St George at Prague Castle.

In the early 20th century, Prague became a centre of avant garde art, concentrated in a group called Osma (The Eight). Prague was also

Best Museums for Paintings

Convent of St Agnes (Staré Město)

Convent of St George (Hradčany)

Veletržní Palác (Holešovice)

Šternberg Palace (Hradčany)

TEN ICONIC CZECH TUNES

Czechs tend to be patriotic when it comes to their own music. Pop songs from the 1960s and '70s are beloved because they're sappy and inflected with nostalgia for simpler times. Tunes from the 1990s and 2000s tend to sound more authentic, with a harder edge. Together they form the perfect soundtrack when streaming from your iPod or MP3 player as you stroll around town. Here is our highly subjective list of favourites:

- **Želva** (Turtle; 1967) by Olympic – the Czech 'Beatles' in their day had the moves, the tunes and the hair.
- **Stín Katedrál** (1968) by Helena Vondráčková – one of the most beautiful pop songs to emerge from the 1960s.
- **Modlitba pro Martu** (Prayer for Marta; 1969) by Marta Kubišová – a sad song that still instantly recalls the 1968 Warsaw Pact invasion.
- **Bratříčku, Zavírej Vrátka** (O' Brother, Shut the Door; 1969) by Karel Kryl – the 'shut the door' part echoes the hopelessness many felt after the Warsaw Pact invasion.
- **Je jaká je** (She is What She is; 1974) by Karel Gott – the Czech crooner extraordinaire is still going strong today, well into his seventies.
- **Černí Andele** (Black Angels; 1991) by Lucie – critics' choice for the best rock band of the 1990s.
- **Láska je láska** (Love is Love; 1995) by Lucie Bílá – the ballad of mid-'90s Prague from a tough woman with a voice you won't soon forget.
- **Lolita** (2001) or **Srdce** (Heart; 2004) by Kryštof – this pop ensemble has had a string of instantly likeable, addictive hits going back to 2000.
- **Pohoda** (2005) by Kabát – abrasive tune from a band that attracts mostly hard-rocking guys holding beer bottles.
- **Proměny** (2006) by Čechomor – beautiful music from a band that almost single-handedly made folk music hip again.

Communist-era singers Helena Vondráčková and Karel Gott are still going strong today. Vondráčková turned 65 in 2012 and Gott is in his seventies.

a focus for cubist painters, including Josef Čapek (1887–1945) and the aptly named Bohumil Kubišta (1884–1918). The functionalist movement flourished between WWI and WWII in a group called Devětsíl, led by the adaptable Karel Teige (1900–51). Surrealists followed, including Zdeněk Rykr (1900–40) and Josef Šima (1891–1971). Many of the best works from this period hang in the National Gallery's Modern and Contemporary Art Exhibit at Veletržní Palác.

Visual arts were driven underground during the Nazi occupation, and in the early years of the communist period painters were forced to work in the official Socialist Realist style, usually depicting workers and peasants building the workers' state. Underground painters included Mikuláš Medek (1926–74), whose abstract, surrealist art was exhibited in out-of-the-way galleries, and Jiří Kolář (1914–2002), an outstanding graphic artist and poet whose name when pronounced sounds something like 'collage' – one of his favourite art forms.

Photography

Czech photographers have always been at the forefront of the medium. The earliest photographers, in the late 19th and early 20th centuries, worked in the pictorialist style, which viewed photography as an extension of painting.

It was after independence in 1918 and during the 1920s and '30s that early-modern styles captured the Czech imagination. Local photographers seized on trends such as cubism, functionalism, Dadaism and surrealism, turning out jarring abstracts that still look fresh today. Two of the best photographers from that time include František Drtikol (1883–1961) and Jaroslav Rössler (1902–90). Drtikol was a society portraitist who shot mainly nudes, poised against dramatic, angular backdrops. Rössler spent several years in Paris, refining a style of powerful abstract imagery that drew on constructivist trends.

During communism, photography was enlisted in the service of promoting the workers' state. Picture books from that time are comically filled with images of tractors, factories and housing projects. Serious photographers turned inward and intentionally chose subjects – such as landscapes and still lifes – that were, at least superficially, devoid of political content. Arguably, the best Czech photographer from this time was Josef Sudek (1896–1976). During a career that spanned five decades, Sudek turned his lens on the city of Prague to absolutely stunning effect.

For decades, Mucha's *Slav Epic* was on display in the town of Moravský Krumlov, about 200km southeast of Prague. In 2011, the panels were moved to Prague and as this book goes to press they are still awaiting a permanent display space.

Current Czech bad-boy photographer Jan Saudek (1935–) continues to delight his fans (or dismay his critics) with his dream-like, hand-tinted prints that evoke images of utopia or dystopia – usually involving a nude or semi-nude woman or child.

Sculpture

Public sculpture has always played a prominent role in Prague, from the baroque saints that line the parapets of Charles Bridge to the monumental statue of Stalin that once faced the Old Town from atop Letná Hill. More often than not, that role has been a political one.

In the baroque era, religious sculptures sprouted in public places; they included 'Marian columns' erected in gratitude to the Virgin Mary for protection against the plague or victory over anti-Catholic enemies. One such Marian column stood in the Old Town Square from 1650 until 1918. The placing of the statue of St John of Nepomuk on Charles Bridge in 1683 was a conscious act of propaganda designed to create a new – and Catholic – Czech national hero who would displace the Protestant reformer Jan Hus. As such, it was successful. John of Nepomuk was canonised in 1729 and the Nepomuk legend, invented by the Jesuits, has passed into the collective memory.

The period of the Czech National Revival saw Prague sculpture take a different tack – to raise public awareness of Czech traditions and culture. One of the most prolific sculptors of this period was Josef Václav Myslbek, whose famous statue of St Wenceslas, the Czech patron saint, dominates the upper end of Wenceslas Square.

The art nouveau sculptor Ladislav Šaloun was responsible for one of Prague's most iconic sculptures, the monument to Jan Hus that was unveiled in the Old Town Square in 1915 (to commemorate the 500th anniversary of Hus being burned at the stake).

Probably the most imposing and visible sculpture in Prague – reputedly the biggest equestrian statue in the world – is the huge, mounted figure of Hussite hero Jan Žižka that dominates the skyline above Žižkov (the city district named after him). Created by sculptor Bohumil Kafka (no relation to writer Franz) in 1950, it was originally intended to form part of the National Monument in memory of the Czechoslovak legions who had fought in WWI. It was instead hijacked by the communist government and made to serve as a political symbol of Czech workers and peasants.

The city's long tradition of politically charged sculpture continues today with the controversial and often wryly amusing works of contemporary artists Krištof Kintera (1973–) and David Černý.

Marionette plays have been popular since the 16th century, and puppet plays since before that. This form peaked in the 17th and early 18th centuries. A legendary figure was Matěj Kopecký (1775–1847), who performed original pieces.

THEATRE

Theatre remains a popular and vital art form in spite of rising competition from the internet, film and TV. Openings for key performances, such as Tom Stoppard's riveting *Rock 'n' Roll* at the National Theatre (p130) in 2007 or Václav Havel's acclaimed *Odcházení* (Leaving) at Archa Theatre (p130) in 2008, are often sold out months in advance and duly discussed in the papers and by the public for weeks after.

Unfortunately for non-Czech-speakers, much of the action remains inaccessible. Occasionally, big theatrical events will be subtitled in English, but the bread and butter of Czech drama is performed in Czech. Two theatres, Archa and the Švandovo Divadlo Na Smíchově (p172),

THE UNDERAPPRECIATED ALFONS MUCHA

Alfons Mucha (1860–1939) is probably the most famous visual artist to come out of the Czech lands, though because he attained his fame mostly in Paris, and not in Prague, his reputation remains more exalted abroad than at home.

Mucha is best known for his poster of French actress Sarah Bernhardt, promoting her new play at the time, *Giselda*. The poster, with its tall, narrow format, muted colours, rich decoration and sensual beauty, created a sensation. You can see the original lithograph at the Mucha Museum.

Although firmly associated with art nouveau, Mucha himself claimed he did not belong to any one artistic movement, and saw his work as part of a natural evolution of Czech art. His commitment to the culture and tradition of his native land was expressed in the second half of his career, when he worked on the decoration of the Lord Mayor's Hall in Prague's Municipal House, designed new stamps and banknotes, and created a superb stained-glass window for St Vitus Cathedral.

He devoted 18 years of his life (1910–1928) to creating his *Slovanské epopej* (Slav Epic),which he later donated to the Czech nation. The 20 monumental canvasses encompass a total area of around 0.5 sq km and depict events from Slavic history and myth. The massive work is now in storage awaiting a permanent home.

WEIRD ART OF DAVID ČERNÝ

David Černý's sculpture is often controversial, occasionally outrageous and always amusing. Following are six of his best-known works that are permanently on view in Prague:

➡ *Quo Vadis* (p86) (Where Are You Going; 1991) – in the garden of the German Embassy in Malá Strana. A Trabant (an East German car) on four human legs serves as a monument to the thousands of East Germans who fled the communist regime in 1989 prior to the fall of the Berlin Wall, and who camped out in the embassy garden seeking political asylum.

➡ *Viselec* (Hanging Out; 1997) – above Husova street in Staré Město. A bearded, bespectacled chap with a passing resemblance to Sigmund Freud, casually dangling by one hand from a pole way above the street.

➡ *Kun* (p121) (Horse; 1999) – in the Lucerna Palace shopping arcade, Nové Město. Amusing alternative version of the famous St Wenceslas Statue in Wenceslas Square, only this time the horse is dead.

➡ *Miminka* (p146) (Mummy; 2000) – on the TV Tower, Žižkov. Creepy, giant, slot-faced babies crawling all over a TV transmitter tower – something to do with consumerism and the media. We think.

➡ *Brownnosers* (p169) (2003) – in the Futura Gallery, Smíchov. Stick your head up a statue's backside and watch a video of the Czech president and the director of the National Gallery feeding each other baby food.

➡ *Proudy* (p84) (Streams; 2004) – in the courtyard of Hergetova Cíhelná, Malá Strana. Two guys pissing in a puddle (whose irregular outline, you'll notice, is actually the map outline of the Czech Republic) and spelling out famous quotations from Czech literature with their pee. (Yes, the sculpture moves! It's computer controlled.)

are committed to English-friendly performances and occasionally host English drama in the original language.

Theatre has always played a strong role in Czech national consciousness, both as a way of promoting linguistic development and defending the fledgling culture against the dominant Habsburg, German and later communist influences. Historical plays with a nationalist subtext flourished during the 19th century as part of the Czech National Revival.

Guns N' Roses frontman Axl Rose legendarily opened his May 1992 concert at Prague's Strahov stadium with the words: 'OK you ex-commie bastards, it's time to rock and roll!'

The decade-long construction of the National Theatre and its opening in 1881 was considered a watershed in Czech history. The theatre tragically burned down shortly after opening but was completely rebuilt, following a public outcry, just two years later.

Drama flourished in the early years of independent Czechoslovakia, but suffered under the Nazi occupation, when many Czech-language theatres were closed or converted into German theatres. Under communism, classical performances were of a high quality, but the modern scene was largely stifled. Many fine plays during this period, including those by Havel, were not performed locally because of their anti-government tone, but appeared in the West.

The centrality of theatre to Czech life was confirmed in 1989 during the Velvet Revolution, when Havel and his Civic Forum movement chose to base themselves at the Laterna Magika (p130) for their epic negotiations to push the communists from power.

Prague on Page & Screen

Reading a book or watching a film from a destination can facilitate a deeper understanding and add texture and depth. This is especially true for the Czech Republic, which has spawned many masterpieces. In literature, heavyweights such as Milan Kundera and Franz Kafka honed their craft here. The underrated, anti-war novel *The Good Soldier Švejk* is a stroke of comic genius that recalls something of *Catch-22*. In film, the Czech 'New Wave' of the 1960s took the world by storm with its bittersweet take on everyday life in a dysfunctional dictatorship.

The Czech language is highly inflected, giving writers ammo to build layers of meaning simply by playing with tenses and endings. The undisputed master was interwar writer Karel Čapek, author of several novels, including the science-fiction work *RUR*, from where the modern word 'robot' derives.

CZECHS IN PRINT

The communist period produced two Czech writers of world standing, both of whom hail originally from Brno: Milan Kundera (b 1929) and Bohumil Hrabal (1914–97). For visitors, Kundera remains the undisputed champ. His wryly told stories weave elements of humour and sex along with liberal doses of music theory, poetry and philosophy to appeal to both our low- and high-brow literary selves. His best known book, *The Unbearable Lightness of Being* (also made into a successful film in 1988), is set in Prague in the uncertain days ahead of the 1968 Warsaw Pact invasion. Look out too for Kundera's *The Joke* and *The Book of Laughter and Forgetting*.

Ask any Czech who their favourite author is and chances are they'll say Hrabal, and it's not hard to see why. Hrabal's writing captures what Czechs like best about themselves, including a keen wit, a sense of the absurd and a fondness for beer. Hrabal is also a great storyteller, and novels such as *I Served the King of England* and *The Little Town Where Time Stood Still* are both entertaining and insightful. Hrabal died in 1997 in classic Czech fashion: falling from a window.

The 2002 best seller *Prague* by American writer Arthur Phillips is not actually set in Prague, but in Budapest in the 1990s. Phillips apparently chose the title to reflect the envy his expat characters felt for their countrymen hanging out and partying at the time in the Czech capital.

Other major talents who came of age during the period from the Warsaw Pact invasion in 1968 to the 1989 Velvet Revolution include Ivan Klíma (b 1931) and Josef Škvorecký (1924–2012). Klíma, who survived the WWII Terezín concentration camp as a child and who still lives in Prague, is probably best known for his collections of bittersweet short stories of life in the 1970s and '80s, such as *My First Loves* and *My Merry Mornings*.

There's no shortage of new Czech literary talent. Names such as Jáchym Topol (b 1962), Petra Hůlová (b 1979), Michal Viewegh (b 1962), Michal Ajvaz (b 1949), Emil Hakl (b 1958), Miloš Urban (b 1967) and Petra Soukupová (1982) are taking their places among the country's leading authors. They are pushing out old-guard figures such as Kundera and Klíma, who are now seen as chroniclers of a very different age.

Until relatively recently, few books from these younger novelists had been translated into English. That's changing, though, and publishers such as Portobello Books and Peter Owen in the UK and Northwestern University Press in the USA have shown a recent willingness to take a chance on new Czech fiction. Let's hope the trend continues.

And Then There's Franz Kafka

No discussion of Czech literature would be complete without mentioning Franz Kafka (1883–1924), easily the best-known writer to have ever lived in Prague and the author of the modern classics *The Trial* and *The Castle*, among many others. Though Kafka was German-speaking and Jewish, he's as thoroughly connected to the city as any Czech writer could be. Kafka's birthplace is just a stone's throw from the Old Town Square and the author rarely strayed more than a couple of hundred metres in any direction during the course of his short life.

Czech poet Jaroslav Seifert (1901–86) won the Nobel Prize for Literature in 1984, though Seifert is not universally considered by Czechs to be their best poet. That distinction often belongs to poet-scientist Miroslav Holub (1923–98).

Kafka's Czech contemporary, and polar opposite, was the pub scribe Jaroslav Hašek (1883–1923), author of *The Good Soldier Švejk,* a book that is loved and reviled in equal doses. For those who get the jokes, it is a comic masterpiece of a bumbling, likeable Czech named Švejk and his (intentional or not) efforts to avoid military service for Austria-Hungary during WWI. Czechs tend to bridle at the assertion that an idiot like Švejk could somehow embody any national characteristic.

CZECHS ON FILM

Though films have been made on the territory of the Czech Republic since the dawn of motion pictures in the early 20th century, it wasn't until the 1960s and the Czech New Wave that Czechoslovak film first caught the attention of international audiences.

The 1960s was a decade of relative artistic freedom, and talented young directors such as Miloš Forman and Jiří Menzel crafted bittersweet films that charmed moviegoers with their grit and wit, while at the same time poking critical fun at their communist overlords. During that decade, Czechoslovak films twice won the Oscar for Best Foreign Language Film, for the *Little Shop on Main Street* in 1965 and *Closely Watched Trains* in 1967. Forman eventually left the country and went on to win Best Picture Oscars for *One Flew Over the Cuckoo's Nest* and *Amadeus*.

Czech film-maker Jan Švankmajer is celebrated for his bizarre, surrealist animation work and stop-motion feature films, including his 1988 version of *Alice in Wonderland (Něco z Alenky)* and his 1994 classic, *Faust (Lekce Faust)*.

Since the Velvet Revolution, Czech directors have struggled to make meaningful films, given the tiny budgets and a constant flood of Hollywood blockbusters. At the same time, they've had to endure non-stop critical scrutiny that their output meet the high standards for Czech films set during the New Wave.

Given these high expectations, the newer Czech directors have largely succeeded, settling for smaller, ensemble-driven films that focus on

BEST POST-'89 CZECH LITERATURE

More and more books by younger Czech writers are finding English-language publishers. Here's a short list of some of our favourites:

- **The Seven Churches** (Miloš Urban, 1997) A brilliant modern-day Gothic murder story set among the seven major churches of Prague's Nové Město by one of the rising stars of Czech literature.
- **All This Belongs to Me** (Petra Hůlová, 2009) Hůlová's debut novel chronicles the lives of three generations of women living in Mongolia. It was a local sensation on its first Czech printing in 2002.
- **Bringing Up Girls in Bohemia** (Michal Viewegh, 1996) Humorously captures the early years of newly capitalist Prague.
- **City Sister Silver** (Jáchym Topol, 1994) Translator Alex Zucker modestly describes this rambling, words-on-speed novel as 'the story of a young man trying to find his way in the messy landscape of post-communist Czechoslovakia'.

BEST NEW-WAVE FILMS

Many of the great Czech films from the 1960s are available on DVD or through download services such as Netflix. Some of the best:

➡ **Closely Watched Trains** (1966) Jiří Menzel's adaptation of Bohumil Hrabal's comic WWII classic set in a small railway town won an Oscar in 1967 and put the Czech New Wave on the international radar. Watch for the scene where young Miloš gently broaches the subject of premature ejaculation with an older woman while she lovingly strokes the neck of a goose.

➡ **Loves of a Blonde** (1965) Miloš Forman's poignant love story between a naïve girl from a small factory town and her more sophisticated Prague beau. Arguably Forman's finest film, effortlessly capturing both the innocence and the hopelessness of those grey days of the mid-1960s.

➡ **Black Peter** (1963) On its debut, this early Forman effort wowed New York critics with its cinematic illusions to the French New Wave and its slow but mesmerising teenage-boy-comes-of-age storyline.

the hardships and moral ambiguities of life in a society rapidly transiting from communism to capitalism. If the Czech New Wave was mostly about making light of a bad situation, it wouldn't be a stretch to say that today's films strive to make bad out of a comparatively light situation.

Films such as David Ondříček's *Loners* (2000), Jan Hřebejk's *Up and Down* (2004), Sasha Gedeon's *Return of the Idiot* (1999), Bohdan Sláma's *Something Like Happiness* (2005) and Petr Zelenka's *Wrong Side Up* (2005) are all different, yet each explores the same familiar dark terrain of money, marital problems and shifting moral sands.

In recent years, historical films have made a comeback, particularly films that explore WWII and the Nazi occupation. The best include director Adam Dvořák's *Lidice* (2011), Hřebejk's *Kawasaki Rose* (2009) and Tomáš Lunák's *Alois Nebel* (2010). The latter is an inventive interpretation of a graphic novel concerning a murder committed in the final days of the war and the subsequent expulsion of Czech Germans.

Running against the grain has been director Jan Svěrák, who continues to make big-budget films that have attracted international attention. In 1996 he took home the country's first Oscar since the 1960s – for the film *Kolja*.

Hollywood Comes to Prague

In addition to Czech films, the Czech Republic has managed to position itself as a lower-cost production centre for Hollywood films. Part of the pitch has been the excellent production facilities at the Barrandov studios, south of the centre in Smíchov. The effort has paid off and dozens of big-budget films, including the first instalment of Tom Cruise's epic *Mission Impossible* (1996), have been filmed here.

Hollywood Films Shot in Prague

Amadeus (1980)

Mission Impossible (1996)

Hostel (2005)

Casino Royale (2006)

The Chronicles of Narnia: Prince Caspian (2008)

A Nation of Beer Lovers

No matter how many times you tell yourself, 'today is an alcohol-free day', Czech beer (*pivo*) will be your undoing. Light, clear, refreshing and cheaper than water, Czech beer is recognised as one of the world's best – the Czechs claim it's so pure it's impossible to get a hangover from drinking it (scientific tests conducted by Lonely Planet authors have found this to be not entirely true). Brewing traditions go back nearly 1000 years, and the beer has only gotten better since then.

According to a 2003 British study, drinking beer does not give you a beer gut.

TYPES OF CZECH BEERS

Nearly all Czech beers are bottom-fermented lagers, naturally brewed using Moravian malt and hand-picked hops from Žatec in northwestern Bohemia. The brewing and fermentation process normally uses only natural ingredients – water, hops, yeast and barley – though some brewers these days use a chemically modified hops extract that, regrettably, probably wouldn't pass German purity laws.

While both light – *světlé* – and dark – *tmavé* or *černé* – beers are readily available, the overwhelming favourite among Czech drinkers remains the classic golden lager, or pilsner, developed in the city of Plzeň in the mid-19th century. These light lagers are marked by a tart flavour and crisp finish. It's worth pointing out that the word 'light' here is not to be confused with the light, low-calorie beers sold in the USA and other countries.

Dark beers are slowly gaining in popularity but run a distant second to light beers at most pubs, and among old-school beer drinkers dark beers still retain a faint wisp of not being entirely a man's drink. It's perfectly acceptable, even common, in pubs to order half and half, a Czech 'black and tan', known locally as *řezané pivo* (literally 'cut' beer). This is an agreeable compromise that reduces the tartness of the pilsner without adding the traditional heaviness of a dark beer.

Argentinean expat Max Bahnson has established himself as a local beer expert, and his blog, *Pivní Filosof* (the Beer Philosopher), is a great place to catch up on local trends and beer lore. Find it at www.pivnifilosof.com or at the *Prague Post* (www.praguepost.com).

Czech beer drinkers are conservative, and more exotic brews such as wheat beer *(pšeničné pivo)* and yeast beer *(kvasnicové pivo)* have only begun to gain traction in recent years. You'll almost never find these at traditional pubs, but they're often a staple at the growing number of brew pubs and at more modern, multi-tap places that specialise in a wider variety of beers.

DRINKING BY DEGREES

By tradition, Czech beers are usually labelled either *dvanáctka* (12°) or *desítka* (10°), a designation that can lead to confusion among visitors. This measure does not refer directly to the percentage of alcohol; instead, it's an indicator of specific gravity known as the 'Balling' rating (invented by Czech scientist Karl Josef Balling in the 19th century).

In technical speak, 1° Balling represents 1% by weight of malt-derived sugar in the brewing liquid before fermentation. In practice, a 12° brew, such as Pilsner Urquell, tends to be richer in flavour (as well as being slightly stronger in alcohol) than a 10° label, such as Gambrinus, which will be slightly sweeter and less bitter.

Czech beers are also rated according to the alcohol-by-volume (ABV) content, and the law recognises a handful of categories: *'výčepní pivo'* (less than 4.5% ABV), *'ležák'* (4.5% to 5.5% ABV) and 'special' (more than 5.5% ABV).

Brewery Tours

Pilsner Urquell Brewery (www.prazdrojvisit.cz).

Budweiser Budvar Brewery (www.visitbudvar.cz).

Velké Popovice Brewery (www.kozel.cz).

LAND OF THE GIANTS

Though there are more than 100 breweries, large and small, around the country, the local market is dominated by a handful of giants. The largest and most important remains the Pilsner Urquell brewery in Plzeň, now a subsidiary of global mega-brewer SABMiller. Pilsner Urquell produces not only its signature 12° brew, but also the 10° Gambrinus (often shortened to 'Gambáč' and inexplicably the country's most popular beer) and Velkopopovický Kozel. Pilsner Urquell pubs around the country will normally carry the first two beers, and usually the dark version of Kozel.

The country's number-two brewer is Prague-based Staropramen, owned by the Central European brewing group Starbev, which in turn is owned by American giant Molson Coors. The company's brands include the flagship Staropramen lager and Velvet bitter, as well as international names such as Stella Artois and Hoegaarden, which are produced under license. Staropramen pubs usually carry the brewer's light lagers (including an increasingly popular unfiltered variety), as well as Stella, Hoegaarden and occasionally Leffe. While it was once viewed as nothing short of blasphemy to order a Stella in a Czech pub, we've – gasp – even seen Czechs do it, so if you're in the mood for a Stella, why not?

Czechs drink more beer per capita than anywhere else in the world (around 160L per head per year, easily beating both Germany and Australia), and the local *hospoda* or *pivnice* (pub or small beer hall) remains the social hub of the neighbourhood.

Beers made by Budvar (Budweiser) of České Budějovice (South Bohemia), the country's third-biggest brewer, are a little harder to find in Prague but are common throughout southern Bohemia and much of the rest of the country. The brewery's 12° premium lager is worth seeking out, as well as its highly regarded premium dark, which it first launched on the local market in 2004. The Budvar Brewery is partly state-owned and, despite a long-running battle with the far-larger US-based Budweiser (see the boxed text), owned by the InBev group, and persistent rumours of an imminent privatisation, it remains the only major brewery in the country that's still 100% Czech-owned.

MICROBREWERS & MULTI-TAP PUBS

The takeover of the Czech Republic's breweries by multinational companies has been accompanied by a welcome resurgence of interest in traditional beer-making and a growing appreciation for smaller and regional breweries.

The microbrew trend is most pronounced in Prague, which boasts around a dozen brew pubs where DIY brewers proffer their own concoctions, usually accompanied by decent-to-very-good traditional Czech cooking. Because of the discerning beer-drinking public, standards are remarkably high. Additionally, these pubs are often freer to experiment with more exotic variations, such as wheat- and yeast-based beers or fruit-infusions, that bigger breweries seem loathe to take on.

Alongside this brew-your-own trend, there's been a similar increase in the number of taverns that offer beers produced by the country's smaller but highly regarded regional breweries. This represents a

Best Smaller Breweries

Primátor (www.primator.cz)

Klášter (www.pivovarklaster.cz)

Svijany (www.pivovarsvijany.cz)

Bernard (www.bernard.cz)

THE KING OF BEERS VS THE BEER OF KINGS

In this big wide world, who could have imagined that two major brewers located thousands of miles apart on different continents would each want to sell beer by the name 'Budweiser'? As remarkable as it seems, that's the case, and for more than 100 years now, US-based Anheuser-Busch, owned by the InBev group, and the Czech Budvar Budweiser brewery have been locked in a trademark dispute to determine where each brewer can sell their beer and what they can call it.

The dispute arose innocently enough in the 1870s, after the co-founder of the American brewery, Adolphus Busch, returned home from a tour of Bohemia. Busch wanted to create a light lager based on his experience abroad and dubbed his new concoction 'Budweiser' to lend an air of authenticity. Ironically, the American claim may actually pre-date the Czech one. Though beer has been brewed in the town of České Budějovice for some 800 years, the Czech 'Budweiser' name was apparently only registered in the 1890s.

By the early 20th century, the two brewers, eyeing eventual overseas markets, were already locked in battle. In 1907, they agreed that the American company could use the Budweiser name in North America, while the Czechs could keep it in Europe. That fragile compromise held up remarkably well for decades, though there are signs it's now fraying around the edges.

InBev sells what many consider its inferior Budweiser brand throughout Europe under the 'Bud' label. In some markets, including in the UK, the courts have ruled that neither company can claim the name, allowing both to use Budweiser. The American Budweiser is not sold in the Czech Republic. In the USA, Czech Budweiser is sold under the somewhat awkward name of 'Czechvar'.

Meantime, rumours abound in the Czech Republic about the eventual privatisation of the state-controlled Czech brewer and its possible sale someday to the far-larger InBev group. Such a move wouldn't shock many people, though true beer lovers would likely shed a few tears into their beer mugs.

change in how pubs normally operate. Traditionally, the big national brewers have forced exclusivity deals on pubs whereby the pubs agree to sell only that brewer's beer in exchange for publicity material, discounts, and mountains of swag such as beer mats and ashtrays. Increasingly, however, more and more pubs are setting aside a 'fourth tap' – *čtvrtá pípa* in Czech – for dispensing independently sourced smaller brews of invariably excellent quality.

The Czech language is filled with proverbs about beer. Our favourite is: *'Kde se pivo vaří, tam se dobře daří'*, which translates loosely as 'Life is good wherever beer is brewed'.

The big brewers are not taking the trends lying down. To compete with the microbrews and the growing demand for higher-quality craft beers, the larger breweries have come up with no end of innovations, including offering unfiltered *(nefiltrované)* beer (cloudier and arguably more authentic than its filtered cousin) and hauling beer directly to pubs in supersized tanks (called, unsurprisingly, *tankové pivo*). Tank beer is said to be fresher than beer transported in traditional kegs. Who are we to argue with that?

Survival Guide

Transport

GETTING TO PRAGUE

Prague sits at the heart of Europe and is well served by air, road and rail. The city has an excellent integrated public-transport system with frequent tram, metro and bus services, though the historic central neighbourhoods are small enough to cover easily on foot.

Air

Prague Airport (Letiště Praha; ☎220 111 888; www.prg.aero), 17km west of the city centre, is the main international gateway to the Czech Republic and the hub for the national carrier **Czech Airlines** (ČSA; ☎239 007 007; www.csa.cz; V Celnici 5), which operates direct flights to Prague from many European cities, and also from New York. Note: as this book was going to press, the Czech government had passed a measure to change the airport's official name to 'Václav Havel Airport Prague', after the late former president. The move was scheduled to go into effect at the end of 2012.

Prague Airport has two international terminals. Terminal 1 is for flights to/from non–Schengen Zone countries (including the UK, Ireland and countries outside Europe), and Terminal 2 is for flights to/from Schengen Zone countries (most EU nations plus Switzerland, Iceland and Norway).

In both terminals the arrival and departure halls are next to each other on the same level. The arrival halls have exchange counters, ATMs, accommodation and car-hire agencies, public-transport information desks, taxi services and 24-hour **left-luggage counters** (per piece per day 120Kč). The departure halls have restaurants and bars, information offices, airline offices, an exchange counter and travel agencies. Once you're through security, there are shops, restaurants, bars, internet access and wi-fi.

There's a post office in the corridor that connects Terminals 1 and 2.

Train

Prague is well integrated into European rail networks and if you're arriving from somewhere in Europe, chances are you're coming by train. The Czech rail network is operated by **České dráhy** (☎840 112 113; www.cd.cz). Timetable information is available online at www.vlak-bus.cz. Most trains arrive at Praha hlavní nádraží. Some trains, particularly from Berlin, Vienna and Budapest, also stop at **Praha-Holešovice** (☎840 112 113; www.cd.cz; Vrbenského, Holešovice; Ⓜ Nádraží Holešovice), north of the city centre. Both stations have their own stops on the metro line C (red).

CLIMATE CHANGE & TRAVEL

Every form of transport that relies on carbon-based fuel generates CO_2, the main cause of human-induced climate change. Modern travel is dependent on aeroplanes, which might use less fuel per kilometre per person than most cars but travel much greater distances. The altitude at which aircraft emit gases (including CO_2) and particles also contributes to their climate change impact. Many websites offer 'carbon calculators' that allow people to estimate the carbon emissions generated by their journey and, for those who wish to do so, to offset the impact of the greenhouse gases emitted with contributions to portfolios of climate-friendly initiatives throughout the world. Lonely Planet offsets the carbon footprint of all staff and author travel.

Negotiating the Main Station

Prague's main station, **Praha hlavní nádraží** (Main Train Station; ☎840 112 113; www.cd.cz; Wilsonova 8, Nové Město), is a cacophonous space that's in the midst of a long-overdue, multi-year renovation. On arrival, take the underpass from the platforms to the busy main concourse, where you'll find shops, restaurants and ATMs, as well as a branch of the tourist information office, **Prague Welcome** (☎221 714 444; www.praguewelcome.cz; Wilsonova 8 , Nové Město; ⏰10am-6pm Mon-Sat; Ⓜ Hlavní Nádraží), a 24-hour **left-luggage office** (úschovna; per bag per day 15Kč or 30Kč) and **luggage lockers** (60Kč) that accept 5Kč, 10Kč and 20Kč coins.

Wenceslas Square is a 10-minute walk south of the station; alternatively take metro line C one stop (direction Háje) to Muzeum. Public-transport tickets are available at ticketing ma chines (have coins ready) or at newspaper kiosks in the station.There are taxi ranks at either end of the concourse. To find the nearest tram stop (for trams 5, 9 and 26), exit the main concourse and turn right; the stop is at the far end of the park.

Try not to arrive in the middle of the night – the station closes from 12.40am to 3.40am, and the surrounding area is a magnet for pickpockets and drunks.

Leaving Prague by Train

Buy international train tickets in advance from **ČD Travel** (☎972 241 861; www.cdtravel.cz; Wilsonova 8) agency, which has a large ticketing office on the lower level of the main station and another **office** (☎972 233 930; V Celnici 6) in the city centre not far from náměstí Republiky. Sales counters are divided into those selling domestic tickets (*vnitrostátní jízdenky*) and international tickets (*mezínárodní jizdenky*), so make sure you're in the right line. The windows also sell seat reservations. Credit cards are accepted.

In addition to ticket windows, there are two information counters and a smaller office on the left side that specialises in working out complicated international connections. You can also buy tickets online through the České dráhy main website (www.cd.cz). There are interactive electronic timetables here, and timetable information is available online at www.vlak.cz.

The big electronic display board on the main concourse lists departures with columns marked *vlak* (type of train – EC for international, IC for domestic etc), *číslo* (train number), *doprav* (carrier), *cilová stanice* (final destination), *směr jízdy* (via), *odjezd* (departure time), *našt* (platform number) and *zpoz'vdení* (delay).

Bus

Long-haul bus service is not what it was before the advent of budget air travel. That said, several bus companies do offer services to Prague from around Europe. Nearly all international buses (and most domestic services) use the renovated and user-friendly **Florenc bus station** (ÚAN Praha Florenc; ☎900 144 444; www.florenc.cz; Křižíkova 4; ⏰4am-midnight, information counter 6am-9.30pm; Ⓜ Florenc).

In addition to the main station, there are several smaller bus stations that service mostly regional

GETTING INTO TOWN

To get into town from the airport, buy a full-price public transport ticket (32Kč) from the **Prague Public Transport Authority** desk in the arrivals hall and take bus 119 (20 minutes; every 10 minutes, 4am to midnight) to the end of metro line A (Dejvická), then continue by metro into the city centre (another 10 to 15 minutes; no new ticket needed). Note you'll also need a half-fare (16Kč) ticket for your bag or suitcase (per piece) if it's larger than 25cm x 45cm x 70cm.

If you're heading to the southwestern part of the city, take bus 100, which goes to the Zličín metro station (line B). There's also an Airport Express bus (50Kč, 35 minutes, every 30 minutes, 5am to 10pm) which runs to Praha hlavní nádraží (main train station), where you can connect to metro line C (buy ticket from driver, luggage goes free).

Alternatively, take a **Cedaz** (☎220 116 758; www.cedaz.cz; ⏰7.30am-7pm) minibus from outside either arrival terminal to the Czech Airlines office near náměstí Republiky (130Kč, 20 minutes, every 30 minutes, 7.30am to 7pm); buy a ticket from the driver. The minibus service also runs in the opposite direction for returning to the airport.

AAA Radio Taxi (☎222 333 222, 14014; www.aaataxi.cz) operates a 24-hour taxi service, charging around 500Kč to 650Kč to get to the centre of Prague. You'll find taxi stands outside both arrivals terminals. Drivers usually speak some English and accept credit cards.

YOU'RE GOING WHERE?

Although most staff at the international ticket counters in Prague's main train station speak at least some English, those selling domestic tickets may not. In order to speed up the process of buying a ticket, and to avoid misunderstandings, it's often easier to write down what you want on a piece of paper and hand it to the clerk (this works for bus tickets, too).
Write it down like this:

➡ **z** departure station, eg PRAHA

➡ **do** destination station, eg KARLŠTEJN

➡ **čas** departure time, using 24-hour clock

➡ **datum** date, eg for 2.30pm on 20 May, write '14.30h. 20/05'. Or just *dnes* (today)

➡ **osoby** number of passengers

➡ **jednosměrný** (one way) or **zpáteční** (return)

If you're making a reservation on an EC (international) or IC (domestic) train, you may also want to specify *1. třídá* or *2. třídá* (1st or 2nd class), and whether you want an *okno* (window) or *chodba* (aisle) seat.

destinations and lie along outlying metro stations. Buses to the northeastern Czech Republic (including Mělník) depart from **Holešovice bus station** (ÚAN Praha Holešovice; Vrbenského, Holešovice; MNádraží Holešovice). Other buses leave from a small stop at the Černý Most station (line B, yellow) or Roztyly station (line C, red). Check the online timetable at www.vlak-bus.cz to make sure you have the right station. On these services, buy your ticket from the driver as you board.

International bus operators include **Eurolines** (☎245 005 245; www.elines.cz) and the excellent **Student Agency** (☎800 100 300; www.studentagency.cz); both have offices at Florenc bus station, or you can buy tickets online.

Car & Motorcycle

Prague lies at the nexus of several European four-lane highways and is a relatively easy drive from major regional cities.

DRIVING RULES

The minimum driving age is 18. Traffic moves on the right. The use of seat belts is compulsory for front- and rear-seat passengers.

➡ Children under 12 or shorter than 1.5m (4ft 9in) are prohibited from sitting in the front seat and must use a child-safety seat.

➡ Headlights must be always on, even in bright daylight.

➡ The legal blood alcohol limit is zero; if the police pull you over for any reason, they are required to administer a breathalyser.

➡ For highway driving, motorists are required to display on their windscreen a special prepaid sticker (*dálniční známka*), purchased on the border or at petrol stations. A sticker valid for 10 days costs 310Kč, for 30 days 440Kč, and for a year 1500Kč.

➡ Trams have the right of way when making any signalled turn across your path. Drivers may overtake a tram only on the right, and only if it's in motion. You must stop behind any tram taking on or letting off passengers where there's no passenger island.

➡ In case of an accident, contact the police immediately if repairs are likely to exceed 20,000Kč or if there is an injury. Even if damage is slight, it's a good idea to report the accident to obtain a police statement for insurance purposes.

➡ For emergency breakdowns, the **ÚAMK** (ÚAMK; ☎1230) (Central Automobile & Motorcycle Club) provides nationwide assistance 24 hours a day.

PARKING

Parking in Prague is tight and in several districts, including the centre, mostly off limits to non-residents. In areas with restricted parking, a blue marking on the street indicates that only residents may park there. A white line allows for metered, paid parking. Meter fees run from 20Kč to 40Kč per hour, depending on the area. Parking is limited to six hours (some places just two hours). In outlying areas, you're generally allowed to park where you want, but finding an available space is tough.

Both the InterContinental Hotel and **Kotva** (Map p332; www.od-kotva.cz; Revoluční 1; ⌚9am-8pm Mon-Fri, 9am-6pm Sat, 10am-6pm Sun; MNáměstí Republiky) department store have centrally located parking garages, where paid parking is allowed, though at

DRIVING TIMES FROM MAJOR CITIES

* **Munich** 4 hours
* **Berlin** 4 hours
* **Nuremberg** 3 hours
* **Vienna** 4 hours
* **Bratislava** 3 hours

100Kč per hour rates can add up. Try arranging parking in advance through your hotel. Most offer some form of parking for an additional fee (per night 200Kč to 300Kč).

A cheaper alternative is to use the 'Park & Ride' (P&R) spaces near metro stations on the outskirts. The best of these include Skalka (metro line A); Zličín, Nové Butovice, Palmovka, Rajská Zahrada and Černý Most (line B); and Nádraží Holešovice, Ladví and Opatov (line C).

The fine for illegal parking is normally a clamp on the car wheel or (worse) having the car towed to a police parking compound. Figure on a couple of hours of bureaucracy and fines and fees of about 1500Kč.

GETTING AROUND PRAGUE

The centre of Prague is compact and walking is usually the best option. For longer distances, look no further than the city's excellent public transportation system of metros, trams and buses. The system is integrated, meaning that tickets bought for one mode of transport are transferable to another. For late-night transit, there is a special line of night trams that operate past midnight, or simply grab a taxi.

Public Transport

Prague's excellent public-transport system combines tram, metro and bus services. It's operated by the **Prague Public Transport Authority** (DPP; ☎800 191 817; www.dpp.cz), DPP, which has information desks at Prague Airport (7am to 10pm) and in several metro stations, including Muzeum, Můstek, Anděl and Nádraží Holešovice. The metro operates daily from 5am to midnight.

The metro has three lines: line A (shown on transport maps in green) runs from the northwestern side of the city at Dejvická to the east at Depo Hostivař; line B (yellow) runs from the southwest at Zličín to the northeast at Černý Most; and line C (red) runs from the north at Letňany to the southeast at Háje. Convenient stops for visitors include Staroměstská (closest to Old Town Square), Malostranská (Malá Strana), Můstek (Wenceslas Square), Muzeum (National Museum), and Hlavní nádraží (main train station).

After the metro closes, night trams (51 to 58) rumble across the city about every 40 minutes through the night (only full-price 32Kč tickets are valid on these services). If you're planning a late evening, find out if one of these lines passes near where you are staying.

Tickets

You need to buy a ticket before boarding a tram or bus or descending into the metro. Tickets are sold from machines at metro stations and some tram stops (coins only), as well as at DPP information offices and many newsstands and kiosks. Tickets are valid on all metros, trams and buses, as well as the **Petřín funicular** (Lanová draha na Petřín; Map p328; ☎800 19 18 17; www.dpp.cz; Újezd; adult/child 24/12Kč; ⏲9am-11.30pm Apr-Oct, 9am-11.20pm Nov-Mar; 🚋12, 20, 22).

Tickets can be purchased individually or as discounted day passes valid for one or three days. A full-price individual ticket costs 32/16Kč per adult/child aged six to 15 years and seniors aged 65 to 70 (kids under six ride free) and is valid for 90 minutes of unlimited travel, including transfers. For shorter journeys, buy short-term tickets that are valid for 30 minutes of unlimited travel. These cost 24/12Kč per adult/child and senior. You'll also need a 16Kč ticket for each large suitcase or backpack. Bikes and prams travel free.

If you're planning on staying more than a few hours, it makes sense to buy either a one- or three-day pass. These not only save money but are more convenient. One-day passes cost 110/55Kč per adult/child and senior; 3-day passes cost 310Kč (no discounts available for children or seniors). There are also heavily discounted 30-day, quarterly and yearly passes aimed primarily at residents. Ask at DPP information centres for more information.

Note that you must validate (punch) your ticket before descending into the

DON'T BLAME US...

...when it comes to sorting out Prague's ever-changing tram and bus schedules. As we go to press, the **Prague Public Transport Authority** has announced a number of changes that will affect the transport information in this guidebook. The most important of these is the closing of the Národní třída metro station (on line B) for two years (until at least mid-2014). In addition, work continues near the Hradčanská metro station in Prague 6 on the Blanka motorway tunnel, making frequent changes to tram routes in that area just another part of life. While we've tried to provide the most up-to-date transport information possible in this guidebook, if you do find yourself on a tram (or metro) that zigs when it should have zagged, just settle in and enjoy the ride.

metro or on entering a tram or bus (day passes must be stamped the first time you use them). For the metro, you'll see stamping machines at the top of the escalators. In trams and buses there will be a stamping machine by the door. While ticket inspections are infrequent, getting caught without a validated ticket can be expensive. The fine if paid on the spot is 800Kč, or 1000Kč if paid later at a police station. Controllers are required to show a valid red and gold badge. A few may demand a higher fine from foreigners and pocket the difference, so insist on a receipt (*doklad*) before paying.

Car & Motorcycle

If you've brought your own car, don't even think of trying to use it for getting around the city. Car travel in the centre is often restricted, and the warren of one-way streets takes years of driving to get to know well. The only exception might be to destinations outside the centre or to cross town, but even then you'll have to contend with soul-crushing traffic jams. Instead, find a decent place to leave your vehicle for the duration and use public transport.

Bicycle

Biking is gaining in popularity and several parts of the city now have marked bike lanes (look for yellow bike-path signage). Still, with its tram tracks, cobblestones and multitudes of pedestrians, Prague has a long way to go to catch up with far bike-friendlier cities like Vienna or Amsterdam.

For more on cycling, see Prague By Bike, p28.

CZECH SPEED LIMITS

- **50kph** (30 mph) in towns and cities
- **90kph** (56 mph) on the open road
- **130kph** (78 mph) on expressways

- Nearly everyone wears a helmet, and this is always a good idea.
- The black market for stolen bikes is thriving, so don't leave bikes unattended for longer than a few minutes and always use the sturdiest lock money can buy.
- Cycling is prohibited in pedestrian zones such as on Charles Bridge. Technically you could be fined up to 1000Kč, but more often than not, the police will simply tell you to dismount.
- Bikes are transported free of charge on the metro, but cyclists are required to obey certain rules. Bikes can only ride near the last door of the rear carriage, and only two bikes are allowed per train. Bikes are not permitted if the carriage is full, or if there's already a pram in the carriage.

Several companies rent bikes. Two centrally located outfits include:

City Bike (☎776 180 284; www.citybike-prague.com; Králodvorská 5, Staré Město; rental per day 500Kč, tours per person 550-800Kč; ⌚9am-7pm Apr-Oct; Ⓜ Náměstí Republiky) Rental includes helmet, padlock and map; good-quality Trek mountain bikes are available for 750Kč per 24 hours.

Praha Bike (☎732 388 880; www.prahabike.cz; Dlouhá 24; rental per day 500Kč, tours per person 490Kč; ⌚9am-8pm; Ⓜ Náměstí Republiky) Hires out good, new bikes with lock, helmet and map, plus offers free luggage storage. It also offers student discounts and group bike tours.

Taxi

Taxis are frequent and relatively expensive. The official rate for licensed cabs is 40Kč flag fall plus 28Kč per kilometre and 6Kč per minute while waiting. On this basis, any trip within the city centre – say, from Wenceslas Square to Malá Strana – should cost about 170Kč. A trip to the suburbs, depending on the distance, should be around 200Kč to 400Kč, and to the airport between 500Kč and 700Kč.

While the number of dishonest drivers has fallen in recent years, taxi rip-offs are still an occasional problem, especially among drivers who congregate in popular tourist areas like Old Town Square and Wenceslas Square. The usual tactic is to quote an inflated fare in advance and then refuse to budge when you complain that it seems high. Avoid unmarked cabs, ie those that aren't obviously part of a reputable firm.

Instead of hailing cabs off the street, call a radio taxi, as they're better regulated and more responsible. From our experience the following companies have honest drivers and offer 24-hour service and English-speaking operators:

AAA Radio Taxi (☎222 333 222, 14014; www.aaataxi.cz)

City Taxi (☎257 257 257; www.citytaxi.cz)

ProfiTaxi (☎14015; www.profitaxi.cz)

Directory A–Z

Business Hours

Most places adhere roughly to the hours listed below. Shopping centres and malls have longer hours and are open daily from at least 10am to 8pm. Museums are usually closed on Mondays, and have shorter hours outside of high season. In this guidebook's reviews and listings, we've removed business hours for restaurants and attractions that adhere to standard opening hours.

Bars and Clubs 11am–1am Tue–Sat, normally shorter hours Sunday and Monday.

Banks 9am–4pm Mon–Fri, with some banks offering limited hours on Saturday from 9am to 1pm.

Offices 8am–5pm Mon–Fri, 9am–1pm Sat (varies).

Museums 9am–5pm Tue–Sun; some attractions are closed or have shorter hours from October to April.

Post Offices 7am–8pm Mon–Fri, 8am–1pm Sat (cities).

Restaurants 11am–11pm daily; many kitchens close by 10pm.

Shops 9am–6pm Mon-Fri, 9am–1pm Sat (varies). Shops that cater mainly to tourists in the city centre have longer opening hours and are normally open on weekends.

Customs Regulations

Customs formalities have been greatly simplified. On arrival at Prague Airport, if you have nothing to declare, simply walk through the green (customs free) line. Bags are rarely checked. Formal customs regulations are as follows:

- On travel between the Czech Republic and other EU countries, you can import/export 800 cigarettes, 400 cigarillos, 200 cigars, 1kg of smoking tobacco, 10L of spirits, 20L of fortified wine, 90L of wine and 110L of beer, provided the goods are for personal use only (each country sets its own guide levels; these figures are minimums).
- Travellers from outside the EU can import or export duty-free a maximum of 200 cigarettes or 100 cigarillos or 50 cigars or 250g of tobacco; 2L of still table wine; 1L of spirits or 2L of fortified wine, sparkling wine or liqueurs; 60mL of perfume; 250mL of eau de toilette; and €175 worth of all other goods (including gifts and souvenirs).

Discount Cards

If you intend to visit several museums during your stay, you might consider purchasing a **Prague Card**, which offers free or discounted entry to around 50 sights. Included are Prague Castle, the Old Town Hall, the National Gallery museums, the Petřín Lookout Tower and Vyšehrad. Note that the pass does not include the Prague Jewish Museum.

The pass is available for two to four days, starting at 880/580Kč per adult/child for two days. Cards can be purchased at **Prague Welcome** (☎221 714 444; www.praguewelcome.cz; Old Town Hall, Staroměstské náměstí 5; ⏰9am-7pm; Ⓜ Staroměstská) offices as well as some hotels. You can buy the card online at www.praguecitycard.com. Passes purchased online have the option to buy unlimited public transport, though prices are about the same as you would pay normally.

Electricity

Electricity in Prague is 230V, 50Hz AC. Outlets have the standard European socket with two small round holes and a protruding earth (ground) pin. If you have a different plug, bring an adapter. North American 110V appliances will also need a transformer if they don't have built-in voltage adjustment.

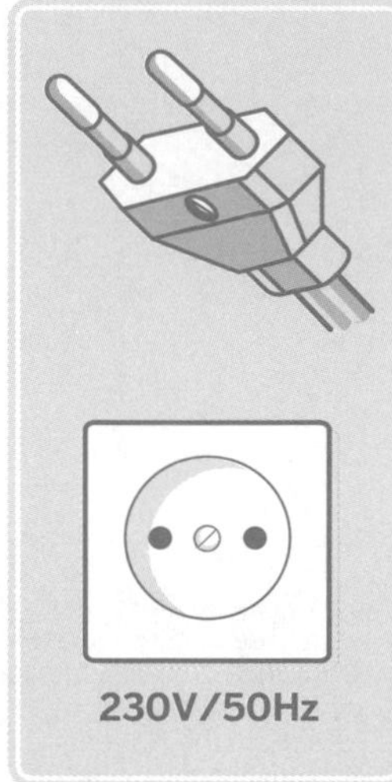

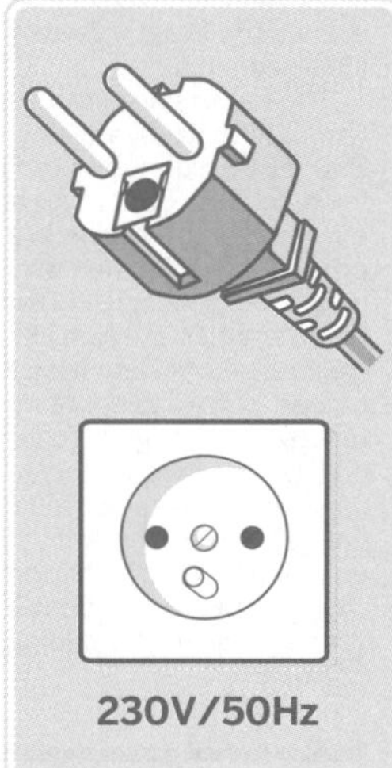

Embassies & Consulates

Australia (☎221 729 260; www.dfat.gov.au/missions/countries/cz.html; 6th fl, Klimentská 10, Nové Město; 🚋5, 8, 14, 26) Honorary consulate for emergency assistance only (eg a stolen passport); the nearest Australian embassy is in Vienna.

Canada (☎272 101 800; www.canadainternational.gc.ca; Muchova 6, Bubeneč; Ⓜ Hradčanská)

France (☎251 171 711; www.france.cz; Velkopřevorské náměstí 2, Malá Strana; 🚋12, 20, 22)

Germany (☎257 113 111; www.deutschland.cz; Vlašská 19, Malá Strana); 🚋12, 20, 22)

Ireland (☎257 530 061; www.embassyofireland.cz; Tržiště 13, Malá Strana; 🚋12, 20, 22)

Netherlands (☎233 015 200; www.netherlandsembassy.cz; Gotthardská 6/27, Bubeneč; 🚋1, 8, 15, 25, 26 plus walk)

New Zealand (☎222 514 672; egermayer@nzconsul.cz; Dykova 19, Vinohrady; Ⓜ Jiřího z Poděbrad) Honorary consulate providing emergency assistance only (eg stolen passport); the nearest NZ embassy is in Berlin.

Russia (☎233 375 650; www.czech.mid.ru; Korunovační 34, Bubeneč; 🚋1, 8, 15, 25, 26)

Slovakia (☎233 113 051; www.mzv.sk/praha; Pelléova 12, Bubeneč; Ⓜ Hradčanská)

UK (☎257 402 111; http://ukinczechrepublic.fco.gov.uk; Thunovská 14, Malá Strana; 🚋12, 20, 22)

USA (☎257 022 000; http://czech.prague.usembassy.gov; Tržiště 15, Malá Strana; 🚋12, 20, 22)

Emergency

Ambulance (☎155)

Breakdown Assistance for Motorists (ÚAMK; ☎1230)

EU-Wide Emergency Hotline (☎112) English- and German-speaking operators are available.

Fire (☎150)

Municipal Police (☎156)

State Police (☎158)

Gay & Lesbian Travellers

Prague and the Czech Republic are tolerant destinations for gay and lesbian travellers. Homosexuality is legal in the Czech Republic and since 2006, the country has allowed gay couples to form registered partnerships.

➡ Prague has a lively gay scene and in 2011 was home to the country's first 'gay pride' march. Attitudes are less accepting outside of the capital, but even here homosexual couples are not likely to suffer overt discrimination.

➡ Most gay bars and clubs are located in Vinohrady.

➡ Useful websites include the Gay Guide Prague (http://prague.gayguide.net) and Prague Saints (www.praguesaints.cz).

Internet Access

Prague and the Czech Republic are well wired. Wi-fi (pronounced *vee-fee* in Czech) is ubiquitous. Most hotels, including pensions and youth hostels, offer it free of charge to guests; though occasionally more expensive properties charge (or only offer free wi-fi in the lobby). Additionally, a growing number of bars, cafes and restaurants offer free wi-fi (usually marked on the door with the international wi-fi sign).

➡ Often the most convenient and reliable places to get wi-fi access in a pinch are McDonald's and KFC restaurants, which offer free wi-fi around the country.

➡ Many hotels, regrettably, are dropping the practice of making a computer terminal available for guests, though some still do, including many hostels. Larger hotels will sometimes have a business centre for guests to use (often for a fee).

➡ In this guide, we've used the wi-fi icon to identify hotels, restaurants, cafes and bars that have wi-fi access for guests and customers. We've used the @ icon to indicate hotels that have computers available for guests.

➡ For those without a laptop, Prague has dozens of internet cafes. Conveniently located ones include the following:

Bohemia Bagel (☎224 812 560; www.bohemiabagel.cz; Masná 2; per min 1.50Kč; ⏲8am-9pm; wi-fi; Ⓜ Náměstí Republiky)

Globe Bookstore & Café (☎224 934 203; www.globebookstore.cz; Pštrossova 6; per min 1Kč; ⏲9.30am-midnight; wi-fi; Ⓜ Karlovo Náměstí) No minimum. Also has ethernet ports so you can connect your own laptop (same price; cables provided, 50Kč deposit), and free wifi.

Relax Café-Bar (☎224 211 521; www.relaxcafebar.cz; Dlážděná 4; per 15min 20Kč; ⏲8am-10pm Mon-Fri, 2-10pm Sat; wi-fi; Ⓜ Náměstí Republiky) A conveniently located internet cafe. Wi-fi is free.

PRACTICALITIES

➡ **Current Events** The English-language weekly newspaper *The Prague Post* (www.praguepost.com) is the best source of local news available in English. Find it on news stands or often for free on flights or at reception desks of upscale hotels. Read it for free online. Foreign newspapers can be found at larger newsagents, bookshops and news stands.

➡ **Radio** The BBC World Service broadcasts part of the day in English on FM101.1. The state-run Czech Radio (www.rozhlas.cz) is the main Czech broadcaster, operating on FM around the country; all programmes in Czech.

➡ **Smoking** It is prohibited to smoke at most indoor public places, including schools, government offices, hospitals, libraries, railway stations and public transport. Smoking is permitted in some restaurants and bars, provided the smoking section is physically separated from the non-smoking section. In practice, most upscale restaurants are non-smoking, while most pubs and bars allow smoking. Most hotels are non smoking.

➡ **Television** Most hotels offer satellite television with some English-language channels, including usually at a minimum CNN International, Eurosport and BBC World. Czech Television (www.ceskatelevize.cz) operates two state-controlled broadcast channels; additionally, there are several private channels. All broadcasts are in Czech.

➡ **Tipping** In restaurants, tip 10% of the bill to reward good service. Leave the tip on the tray that the bill is delivered in or hand the money directly to the waiter. Taxi drivers won't expect a tip, but it's fine to round the fare up to the nearest 10Kč increment to reward special service.

➡ **Weights & Measures** The Czech Republic uses the metric system.

Legal Matters

Foreigners in the Czech Republic, as elsewhere, are subject to the laws of the host country. While your embassy or consulate is the best stop in any emergency, bear in mind that there are some things it can't do for you, like getting local laws or regulations waived, investigating a crime, providing legal advice or representation, getting you out of jail and lending you money.

A consul can, however, issue emergency passports, contact relatives and friends, advise on how to transfer funds, provide lists of reliable local doctors, lawyers and interpreters, and visit you if you've been arrested or jailed.

Medical Services

The quality of medical care in Prague and the Czech Republic is high. Rest assured, if you do suffer a medical emergency you will receive proper care. Citizens of EU countries can obtain a European Health Insurance Card (EHIC); this entitles you to free state-provided medical treatment in the Czech Republic (see www.cmu.cz – click on the UK flag – for information on using the card in the Czech Republic).

Non-EU citizens must pay for treatment, and at least some of the fee must usually be paid upfront. Bring cash or credit cards.

If you do need to seek emergency medical treatment, be sure to bring along your passport and any insurance information you have with you. Save all bills and receipts for later reimbursement with your insurance company.

Clinics

American Dental Associates (☎733 737 337; www.americandental.cz; Hvězdova 33, Pankrác; ⏱9am-7pm Mon-Fri; Ⓜ Pankrác) Standard, English-speaking dental practice.

Canadian Medical Care (☎724 300 301, 235 360 133; www.cmcpraha.cz; Veleslavínská 1, Veleslavín; ⏱8am-6pm Mon-Fri, to 8pm Tue & Thu; 🚌20, 26) A pricey but professional private clinic with English-speaking doctors; an initial consultation will cost from 1500Kč to 2500Kč.

Polyclinic at Národní (Poliklinika na Národní; ☎222 075 120, 24hr emergencies 777 942 270; www.poliklinika.narodni.cz; Národní třída 9, Nové Město; ⏱8.30am-5pm Mon-Fri; Ⓜ Národní Třída) A central clinic with staff who speak English, German, French and Russian. Expect to pay around 800Kč to 1500Kč for an initial consultation.

Emergency Rooms

Na Homolce Hospital (☎257 271 111; www.homolka.cz; 5th fl, Foreign Pavilion, Roentgenova 2, Motol; 🚌167, Ⓜ Anděl) The best hospital in Prague, equipped and staffed to Western standards, with staff who speak English, French, German and Spanish.

Pharmacies

You'll see plenty of pharmacies (*lékárna* or *apteka*) throughout Prague and the Czech Republic. These are identified by a big green cross on the outside.

In addition to dispensing prescription medications, pharmacies are the only places that can sell common over-the-counter drugs like aspirin, cough syrup, cold medications, and the like.

Most pharmacies keep normal business hours, but each district has at least one late-hour dispensary for emergencies. To find the pharmacy in your district, go to any pharmacy. Information is usually posted on the door.

Money

The Czech crown (*Koruna česká*, or Kč) is divided into 100 hellers or *haléřů*. Bank notes come in denominations of 100Kč, 200Kč, 500Kč, 1000Kč, 2000Kč and 5000Kč; coins are of 1Kč, 2Kč, 5Kč, 10Kč, 20Kč and 50Kč. Hellers do not circulate, but prices are sometimes denominated in fractions of crowns. In these instances, the total will be rounded to the nearest whole crown.

Keep small change handy for use at public toilets and tram-ticket machines, and try to keep some small-denomination notes for shops, cafes and bars – getting change for the 2000Kč notes that ATMs often spit out can be a problem.

ATMs

You'll find ATMs all around Prague and in the central areas of towns and cities around the country. There are ATMs in the concourse of Prague's main train station as well as at both arrivals terminals at Prague Airport. Most ATMs accept any valid credit or debit card, provided you have a four-digit PIN code.

Black Market

Changing money on the black market is illegal and dangerous. Rates are no better than at the banks or ATMs and the chance of getting ripped off is infinitely greater. Firmly decline any offers you may hear to 'change money?'. If you are foolish enough to change money on the street, make sure you receive valid Czech notes in exchange. The black market is flooded with outdated Polish zlotys and other worthless bills.

Changing Money

The main banks – including Komerční banka, Česká spořitelna and UniCredit Bank – are the best places to exchange cash. They normally charge around a 2% commission with a 50Kč minimum (but always check, as commissions vary). They will also provide a cash advance on Visa or MasterCard without commission.

The easiest and cheapest way to carry money is in the form of a credit or debit card from your bank, which you can use to withdraw cash either from an ATM or over the counter in a bank. Using an ATM will result in your home bank charging a fee (usually 1.5% to 2.5%), but you'll get a decent exchange rate, and provided you make withdrawals of at least a couple of thousand crowns at a time, you'll pay less than the assorted commissions on travellers cheques, etc. Check with your bank about transaction fees and withdrawal limits.

Avoid private exchange booths (*směnárna*) in the main tourist areas. They lure you in with attractive-looking exchange rates that turn out to be 'sell' (*prodej*) rates; if you want to change foreign currency into Czech crowns, the 'buy' (*nákup*) rate applies. Moreover, the best rates are usually only for very large transactions, above €500. Check the rates carefully, and ask exactly how much you will get before parting with any money. Similarly, hotel reception desks sometimes exchange money for guests but seldom offer an attractive rate.

Credit Cards

Visa and MasterCard are widely accepted for goods and services. The only places you may experience a problem are at small establishments or for small transactions (under 250Kč). American Express cards are typically accepted at larger hotels and restaurants, though they are not as widely recognised as other cards.

Travellers Cheques

Travellers cheques are not much use, as they are not accepted by shops and restaurants and can be exchanged only at banks and currency-exchange counters.

Post

The Czech postal service (Česká Pošta; www.cpost.cz) is efficient, though post offices can be tricky to negotiate since signage is only in Czech. For mailing letters and postcards, be sure to get into the proper line, identified as '*listovní zásilky*' (correspondence). Anything you can't afford to lose should go by registered mail (*doporučený dopis*) or by Express Mail Service (EMS).

A standard postcard or letter up to 20g costs 20Kč to other European countries and 21Kč for destinations outside Europe. Buy stamps at post offices or have the letter weighed to ensure proper postage.

Prague's main post office in Nové Město uses an automated queuing system. Take a ticket from one of the machines in the entrance corridors – press button No 1 for stamps, letters and parcels, or No 4 for EMS. Then watch the display boards in the main hall – when your ticket number appears (flashing), go to the desk number shown.

Main Post Office (☎221 131 111; www.cpost.cz; Jindřišská 14 , Nové Město; ⏰2am-midnight; Ⓜ Můstek) Prague's main post office is centrally located not far from Wenceslas Square and keeps longer hours than other post offices. It can be a life-saver if you've got something that needs to be sent quickly. In addition, there are copy and fax services here, and you can use the telephone booths to dial international numbers.

Public Holidays

Banks, offices, department stores and some shops are closed on public holidays. Restaurants, museums and tourist attractions tend to stay open, though many may close on the first working day after a holiday.

New Year's Day 1 January

Easter Monday March/April

Labour Day 1 May

Liberation Day 8 May

Sts Cyril & Methodius Day 5 July

Jan Hus Day 6 July

Czech Statehood Day 28 September

Republic Day 28 October

Struggle for Freedom & Democracy Day 17 November

Christmas Eve (Generous Day) 24 December

Christmas Day 25 December

St Stephen's Day 26 December

Taxes & Refunds

Czech prices, including at shops, restaurants and hotels, normally include the value added tax (VAT), so the price you see is the price you pay. Only rarely will this not be the case and it will be clearly marked or stated in advance.

Non-EU residents can qualify for a tax refund on large purchases (over 2000Kč), subject to certain conditions. Look for retailers displaying a 'Tax Free Shopping' sign and then inform the clerk you intend to get a refund. You'll need to save the sales receipt and ensure the goods are not used. Normally you collect the tax at the airport on departure or by mail once you return home. For details, see the Global Blue website (www.global-blue.com).

Telephone

Most Czech telephone numbers, both landline and mobile (cellphone) numbers, have nine digits. There are no city or area codes in the Czech Republic, so to call any Czech number, simply dial the nine-digit number. To call abroad from the Czech Republic, dial the international access code (☎00), then the country code, then the area code (minus any initial zero) and the number. To dial the Czech Republic from abroad, dial your country's international access code, then 420 (the Czech Republic country code) and then the unique nine-digit local number.

Mobile Phones

The Czech Republic uses the GSM 900/1800 system, the same system in use around Europe, as well as in Australia and New Zealand. It's not compatible with most mobile phones in North America or Japan (though many mobiles have multiband GSM 1900/900 phones that will work in the Czech Republic). If you have a GSM phone, check with your service provider about using it in the Czech Republic, and beware of calls being routed internationally (very expensive for a 'local' call).

➡ If your mobile phone is unlocked, a cheaper and often better option is to buy a prepaid SIM card, available from any mobile-phone shop for around 450Kč (including 300Kč of calling credit). Prepaid SIMs allow you to make local calls at cheaper local rates. In this case, of course, you can't use your existing mobile number.

- The situation is more complicated if you plan on using a 'smartphone' like an iPhone, Android or Blackberry that may not be easily unlocked to accommodate a local SIM card. With these phones, it's best to contact your home provider to consider short-term international calling and data plans appropriate to what you might need.
- Smartphones can still be used as handy wi-fi devices, even without a special plan. Be sure to switch your phone to 'airplane' mode on arrival, which blocks out calls and text messages, but still allows wi-fi. Also remember to turn off your phone's 'data roaming' setting on arrival to avoid unwanted roaming fees.

Phonecards

Local prepaid cards include Smartcall (www.smartcall.cz) and Karta X Plus – you can buy them from hotels, newspaper kiosks and tourist information offices for 300Kč to 1000Kč. To use one, follow the instructions on the card – dial the access number, then the PIN code beneath the scratch-away panel, then the number you want to call (including any international code). Rates from Prague to the UK, USA and Australia with Smartcall are around 6.6Kč to 10Kč a minute; the more expensive the card, the better the rate.

Time

The Czech Republic lies within the same time zone, GMT/UTC+1, as most of continental Europe. Czech local time is one hour ahead of London and six hours ahead of New York. The Czech Republic observes Daylight Saving Time (DST), and puts the clock forward one hour at 2am on the last Sunday in March, and back again at 3am on the last Sunday in October. The 24-hour clock is used for official purposes, including all transport schedules. In everyday conversation people commonly use the 12-hour clock.

Toilets

Public toilets are free in state-run museums, galleries and concert halls. Elsewhere, such as in train, bus and metro stations, public toilets are staffed by attendants who charge 5Kč to 10Kč. Men's are marked *muži* or *páni*, and women's *ženy* or *dámy*. In the main tourist areas, there are public toilets in Prague Castle; opposite the tram stop on Malostranské náměstí; next to the Goltz-Kinský Palace on Old Town Square; on Templova, just off Celetná close to the Powder Gate; on Uhelný trh in the Old Town; and next to the Laterna Magika on Národní třída.

Tourist Information

In Prague, Prague Welcome is the official provider of tourist information. It has good maps and detailed brochures, with most of the material available for free. There are several Prague Welcome offices around town, including:

Prague Welcome (☎221 714 444; www.praguewelcome.cz; Old Town Hall, Staroměstské náměstí 5; ⏰9am-7pm; Ⓜ Staroměstská) Has maps and detailed brochures (including accommodation options and historical monuments), all free. Also sells public transport tickets and provides information on guided tours.

Prague Welcome (☎221 714 444; www.praguewelcome.cz; Malá Strana Bridge Tower, Mostecká ; ⏰10am-6pm Apr-Oct; 🚋12, 20, 22)

Prague Welcome (☎221 714 444; www.praguewelcome.cz; Rytírská 31, Staré Město; ⏰10am-7pm Mon-Sat; Ⓜ Můstek)

Overseas Offices

The official travel promotion bureau for the Czech Republic is Czech Tourism (www.czechtourism.com), which maintains offices in several major countries. Check the website for contact information.

Travellers With Disabilities

Prague and the Czech Republic are generally behind the curve when it comes to catering to the needs of the disabled. Cobblestones and high curbs present challenging mobility issues, and many older buildings, including hotels and museums, are not wheelchair accessible.

The situation is better with newer buildings, which are required by law to make doorways and lavatories accessible. Many McDonald's and KFC restaurants are wheelchair-friendly.

In terms of public transport, Prague is slowly making progress on accessibility. Some buses and trams are low riders and, in theory, should accommodate a wheelchair. These services are marked on timetables with a wheelchair symbol. A handful of metro stations, including newer stations, are equipped with lifts.

In the USA, travellers with disabilities may like to contact the Society for Accessible Travel & Hospitality (www.sath.org). In the UK a useful contact is the Royal Association for Disability & Rehabilitation (www.radar.org.uk).

Some helpful local groups include the following:

Prague Wheelchair Users Organisation (Pražská organizace vozíčkářů; ☎224 827 210; www.pov.cz;

Benediktská 6, Staré Město) This is a watchdog organisation for the disabled. While it's mostly geared toward local residents, it can help to organise a guide and transportation at about half the cost of a taxi, and has information on barrier-free Prague in Czech, English and German.

Czech Blind United (Sjednocená Organizace Nevidomých a Slabozrakých v ČR; ☎221 462 146; www.braillnet.cz; Krakovská 21) Represents the vision-impaired; provides information but no services.

Visas

Citizens of EU countries do not need a visa to visit the Czech Republic and can stay indefinitely.

Citizens of the USA, Canada, Australia, New Zealand, Israel, Japan and many other countries can stay in the Czech Republic for up to 90 days without a visa. Other nationalities should check current visa requirements with the Czech embassy in their home country. There's more information on the Czech Ministry of Foreign Affairs (www.mzv.cz) website.

The Czech Republic is a member of the EU's common border and customs area, the Schengen Zone, which imposes its own 90-day visa-free travel limit on many visitors from outside the European Union. In practice, this means your time in the Czech Republic counts against your stay within the entire Schengen Zone – so plan your travel accordingly.

Women Travellers

Solo women travellers are not likely to experience any special difficulties in Prague or the Czech Republic. Walking alone on the street is generally as safe – or as dangerous – as in most large European cities.

In Prague, a couple areas for women to avoid at night would be the park in front of the main train station, which attracts a lot of vagrants, and the upper part of Wenceslas Square, which becomes effectively a red-light district at night.

Language

Czech (*Čeština chesh*·tyi·nuh) belongs to the western branch of the Slavic language family, with Slovak and Polish as its closest relatives. It has approximately 12 million speakers.

Most of the sounds in Czech are also found in English. If you read our coloured pronunciation guides as if they were English, you shouldn't have problems being understood. Note that ai is pronounced as in 'aisle', air as in 'hair' (without the 'r'), aw as in 'law', oh as the 'o' in 'note', ow as in 'how' and uh as the 'a' in 'ago'. An accent mark over a vowel in written Czech indicates it's pronounced as a long sound.

For the consonants, note that kh is pronounced like the *ch* in the Scottish *loch* (a throaty sound), zh is pronounced as the 's' in 'pleasure' and r is rolled. The apostrophe (') indicates a slight y sound. The sounds r, s and l can be used as quasi-vowels – this explains why some written Czech words or syllables appear to have no vowels, eg *krk* krk (neck), *osm o*·sm (eight), *vlk* vlk (wolf). If you find these clusters of consonants difficult, just try putting a tiny uh sound between them. Stress is always on the first syllable of a word – this is indicated with italics in our pronunciation guides. Masculine and feminine forms are indicated with (m/f) where needed.

BASICS

Hello.	*Ahoj.*	*uh*·hoy
Goodbye.	*Na shledanou.*	*nuh*·skhle·duh·noh
Excuse me.	*Promiňte.*	*pro*·min'·te
Sorry.	*Promiňte.*	*pro*·min'·te
Please.	*Prosím.*	*pro*·seem
Thank you.	*Děkuji.*	*dye*·ku·yi
You're welcome.	*Prosím.*	*pro*·seem
Yes./No.	*Ano./Ne.*	*uh*·no/ne

WANT MORE?

For in-depth language information and handy phrases, check out Lonely Planet's *Czech Phrasebook*. You'll find it at **shop.lonelyplanet.com**, or you can buy Lonely Planet's iPhone phrasebooks at the Apple App Store.

How are you?
Jak se máte? — yuhk se *ma*·te

Fine. And you?
Dobře. A vy? — *dob*·rzhe a vi

What's your name?
Jak se jmenujete? — yuhk se *yme*·nu·ye·te

My name is ...
Jmenuji se ... — *yme*·nu·yi se ...

Do you speak English?
Mluvíte anglicky? — *mlu*·vee·te *uhn*·glits·ki

I don't understand.
Nerozumím. — *ne*·ro·zu·meem

One moment, please.
Počkejte chvíli. — *poch*·key·te *khvee*·li

ACCOMMODATION

Do you have a double room?
Máte pokoj s manželskou postelí? — *ma*·te *po*·koy s *muhn*·zhels·koh *pos*·te·lee

Do you have a single/twin room?
Máte jednolůžkový/dvoulůžkový pokoj? — *ma*·te *yed*·no·loozh·ko·vee/*dvoh*·loozh·ko·vee *po*·koy

How much is it per ...?	*Kolik to stojí ...?*	*ko*·lik to *sto*·yee ...
night	*na noc*	nuh nots
person	*za osobu*	zuh *o*·so·bu
week	*na týden*	nuh *tee*·den

campsite	*tábořiště*	*ta*·bo·rzhish·tye
guesthouse	*penzion*	*pen*·zi·on
hotel	*hotel*	*ho*·tel
youth hostel	*mládežnická ubytovna*	*mla*·dezh·nyits·ka *u*·bi·tov·nuh

DIRECTIONS

Where's the (market)?
Kde je (trh)? — gde ye (trh)

What's the address?
Jaká je adresa? — *yuh*·ka ye *uh*·dre·suh

Can you show me (on the map)?
Můžete mi to ukázat (na mapě)? — *moo*·zhe·te mi to *u*·ka·zuht (nuh *muh*·pye)

It's ...	*Je to ...*	ye to ...
behind ...	*za ...*	zuh ...
in front of ...	*před ...*	przhed ...
near	*blízko*	*bleez*·ko
next to ...	*vedle ...*	*ved*·le ...
on the corner	*na rohu*	nuh *ro*·hu
opposite ...	*naproti ...*	*nuh*·pro·tyi ...
straight ahead	*přímo*	*przhee*·mo

Turn ...	*Odbočte ...*	*od*·boch·te ...
at the corner	*za roh*	zuh rawh
at the traffic lights	*u semaforu*	u *se*·muh·fo·ru
left	*do leva*	do *le*·vuh
right	*do prava*	do *pruh*·vuh

EATING & DRINKING

What would you recommend?
Co byste doporučil/doporučila? (m/f) — tso *bis*·te *do*·po·ru·chil/*do*·po·ru·chi·luh

What's the local speciality?
Co je místní specialita? — tso ye *meest*·nyee *spe*·tsi·uh·li·tuh

Do you have vegetarian food?
Máte vegetariánská jídla? — *ma*·te *ve*·ge·tuh·ri·ans·ka *yeed*·luh

That was delicious!
To bylo lahodné! — to *bi*·lo *luh*·hod·nair

I'll have ...	*Dám si ...*	dam si ...
Cheers!	*Na zdraví!*	nuh *zdruh*·vee

I'd like the ..., please.	*Chtěl/Chtěla bych ..., prosím.* (m/f)	khtyel/*khtye*·luh bikh ... *pro*·seem
bill	*účet*	*oo*·chet
menu	*jídelníček*	*yee*·del·nyee·chek

Key Words

bar	*bar*	buhr
bottle	*láhev*	*la*·hef
bowl	*miska*	*mis*·kuh
breakfast	*snídaně*	*snee*·duh·nye
cafe	*kavárna*	*kuh*·var·nuh
children's menu	*dětský jídelníček*	*dyets*·kee *yee*·del·nyee·chek
cold	*chladný*	*khluhd*·nee
delicatessen	*lahůdky*	*luh*·hood·ki
dinner	*večeře*	*ve*·che·rzhe
dish	*pokrm*	*po*·krm
drink list	*nápojový lístek*	*na*·po·yo·vee *lees*·tek
food	*jídlo*	*yeed*·lo
fork	*vidlička*	*vid*·lich·kuh
glass	*sklenička*	*skle*·nyich·kuh
grocery store	*konzum*	*kon*·zum
highchair	*dětská stolička*	*dyet*·ska *sto*·lich·kuh
hot (warm)	*teplý*	*tep*·lee
knife	*nůž*	noozh

KEY PATTERNS

To get by in Czech, mix and match these simple patterns with words of your choice:

When's (the next bus)?
V kolik jede (příští autobus)? — f *ko*·lik *ye*·de (*przhee*·shtyee *ow*·to·bus)

Where's (the station)?
Kde je (nádraží)? — gde ye (*na*·dra·zhee)

Where can I (buy a ticket)?
Kde (koupím jízdenku)? — gde (*koh*·peem *yeez*·den·ku)

How much is (a room)?
Kolik stojí (pokoj)? — *ko*·lik *sto*·yee (*po*·koy)

Is there (a toilet)?
Je tam (toaleta)? — ye tuhm (*to*·uh·le·tuh)

Do you have (a map)?
Máte (mapu)? — *ma*·te (*muh*·pu)

I'd like (to hire a car).
Chtěl/Chtěla bych (si půjčit auto). (m/f) — khtyel/*khtye*·luh bikh (si *pooy*·chit *ow*·to)

I need (a can opener).
Potřebuji (otvírák na konzervy). — *po*·trzhe·bu·yi (*ot*·vee·rak nuh *kon*·zer·vi)

Can I (camp here)?
Mohu (zde stanovat)? — *mo*·hu (zde *stuh*·no·vuht)

Could you please (help me)?
Můžete prosím (pomoci)? — *moo*·zhe·te *pro*·seem (*po*·mo·tsi)

lunch	*oběd*	*o*·byed
market	*trh*	trh
plate	*talíř*	*tuh*·leerzh
restaurant	*restaurace*	*res*·tow·ruh·tse
spoon	*lžíce*	*lzhee*·tse
with	*s*	s
without	*bez*	bez

Meat & Fish

bacon	*slanina*	*sluh*·nyi·nuh
beef	*hovězí*	*ho*·vye·zee
chicken	*kuře*	*ku*·rzhe
duck	*kachna*	*kuhkh*·nuh
fish	*ryba*	*ri*·buh
ham	*šunka*	*shun*·kuh
herring	*sleď*	sled'
lamb	*jehněčí*	*yeh*·nye·chee
meat	*maso*	*muh*·so
mussel	*slávka jedlá*	*slaf*·kuh *yed*·la
pork	*vepřové*	*vep*·rzho·vair
pork sausage	*vuřt*	vurzht
prawn	*kreveta*	*kre*·ve·tuh
salami	*salám*	*suh*·lam
salmon	*losos*	*lo*·sos
steak (beef)	*biftek*	*bif*·tek
tuna	*tuňák*	*tu*·nyak
turkey	*krůta*	*kroo*·tuh
veal	*telecí*	*te*·le·tsee
oyster	*ústřice*	*oost*·rzhi·tse

Fruit & Vegetables

apple	*jablko*	*yuh*·bl·ko
apricot	*meruňka*	*me*·run'·kuh
banana	*banán*	*buh*·nan
bean	*fazole*	*fuh*·zo·le
broccoli	*brokolice*	*bro*·ko·li·tse
cabbage	*kapusta*	*kuh*·pus·tuh
capsicum	*paprika*	*puh*·pri·kuh
carrot	*mrkev*	*mr*·kef
cauliflower	*květák*	*kvye*·tak
cherry	*třešeň*	*trzhe*·shen'
corn	*kukuřice*	*ku*·ku·rzhi·tse
cucumber	*okurka*	*o*·kur·kuh
date	*datle*	*duht*·le
eggplant	*lilek*	*li*·lek
garlic	*česnek*	*ches*·nek
grapes	*hrozny*	*hroz*·ni
legume	*luštěnina*	*lush*·tye·nyi·nuh
lemon	*citron*	*tsi*·tron
lentil	*čočka*	*choch*·ka
lettuce	*hlávkový salát*	*hlaf*·ko·vee *suh*·lat
mushroom	*houba*	*hoh*·buh
nut	*ořech*	*o*·rzhekh
olive	*oliva*	*o*·li·vuh
onion	*cibule*	*tsi*·bu·le
orange	*pomeranč*	*po*·me·ruhnch
pea	*hrách*	hrakh
peach	*broskev*	*bros*·kef
pear	*hruška*	*hrush*·kuh
pepper (bell)	*paprika*	*puh*·pri·kuh
pineapple	*ananas*	*uh*·nuh·nuhs
plum	*švestka*	*shvest*·kuh
potato	*brambor*	*bruhm*·bor
pumpkin	*dýně*	*dee*·nye
radish	*ředkvička*	*rzhed*·kvich·kuh
raisin	*hrozinka*	*hro*·zin·kuh
raspberry	*malina*	*muh*·li·nuh
spinach	*špenát*	*shpe*·nat
strawberry	*jahoda*	*yuh*·ho·duh
tomato	*rajské jablko*	*rais*·kair *yuh*·bl·ko
zucchini	*cuketa*	*tsu*·ke·tuh

Other

bread	*chléb*	khlairb
butter	*máslo*	*mas*·lo
cheese	*sýr*	seer
chilli	*feferon*	*pfe*·fe·ron
egg	*vajíčko*	*vuh*·yeech·ko
honey	*med*	med
ice cream	*zmrzlina*	*zmrz*·li·nuh
jam	*džem*	dzhem

Signs

Vjezd	Entrance
Východ	Exit
Otevřeno	Open
Zavřeno	Closed
Zákazáno	Prohibited
Toalety/WC	Toilets
Páni/Muži	Men
Dámy/Ženy	Women

noodles	*nudle*	*nud*·le
pasta	*těstovina*	*tyes*·to·vi·nuh
pepper	*pepř*	*pe*·przh
rice	*rýže*	*ree*·zhe
salad	*salát*	*suh*·lat
salt	*sůl*	sool
sauce	*omáčka*	*o*·mach·kuh
soup	*polévka*	*po*·lairf·kuh
sugar	*cukr*	*tsu*·kr
vinegar	*ocet*	*o*·tset

Drinks

beer	*pivo*	*pi*·vo
coffee	*káva*	*ka*·vuh
lemonade	*limonáda*	*li*·mo·na·duh
milk	*mléko*	*mlair*·ko
orange juice	*pomerančový džus*	*po*·me·ruhn·cho·vee dzhus
red wine	*červeného víno*	*cher*·ve·nair·ho *vee*·no
[illegible]	[illegible] *nápoj*	[illegible] lits·kee *na*·poy
tea	*čaj*	chai
(mineral) water	*(minerální) voda*	(*mi*·ne·ral·nyee) *vo*·duh
white wine	*bílého víno*	*bee*·lair·ho *vee*·no

EMERGENCIES

Help!	*Pomoc!*	*po*·mots
Go away!	*Běžte pryč!*	*byezh*·te prich

Call ...!	*Zavolejte ...!*	*zuh*·vo·ley·te ...
a doctor	*lékaře*	*lair*·kuh·rzhe
the police	*policii*	*po*·li·tsi·yi

I'm lost.
Zabloudil/ Zabloudila jsem. (m/f) — *zuh*·bloh·dyil/ *zuh*·bloh·dyi·luh ysem

Question Words

How?	*Jak?*	yuhk
What?	*Co?*	tso
When?	*Kdy?*	gdi
Where?	*Kde?*	gde
Who?	*Kdo?*	gdo
Why?	*Proč?*	proch

I'm ill.
Jsem nemocný/ nemocná. (m/f) — ysem *ne*·mots·nee/ *ne*·mots·na

Where are the toilets?
Kde jsou toalety? — gde ysoh *to*·uh·le·ti

SHOPPING & SERVICES

I'd like to buy ...
Chtěl/Chtěla bych koupit ... (m/f) — khtyel/*khtye*·la bikh *koh*·pit ...

I'm just looking.
Jenom se dívám. — *ye*·nom se *dyee*·vam

Do you have any others?
Máte ještě jiné? — *ma*·te *yesh*·tye *yi*·nair

Can I look at it?
Mohu se na to podívat? — *mo*·hu se nuh to *po*·dyee·vuht

How much is it?
Kolik to stojí? — *ko*·lik to *sto*·yee

That's too expensive.
To je moc drahé. — to ye mots *druh*·hair

Can you lower the price?
Můžete mi snížit cenu? — *moo*·zhe·te mi *snyee*·zhit *tse*·nu

ATM	*bankomat*	*uhn*·ko·muht
internet cafe	*internetová kavárna*	*in*·ter·ne·to·va *kuh*·var·nuh
mobile phone	*mobil*	*mo*·bil
post office	*pošta*	*posh*·tuh
tourist office	*turistická informační kancelář*	*tu*·ris·tits·ka *in*·for·muhch·nyee *kuhn*·tse·larzh

TIME & DATES

What time is it?
Kolik je hodin? — *ko*·lik ye *ho*·dyin

It's (10) o'clock.
Je (deset) hodin. — ye (*de*·set) *ho*·dyin

Half past 10.
Půl jedenácté. (lit: half eleven) — pool *ye*·de·nats·tair

am (midnight–8am)
ráno — *ra*·no

am (8am–noon)
dopoledne — *do*·po·led·ne

pm (noon–7pm)
odpoledne — *ot*·po·led·ne

pm (7pm–midnight)
večer — *ve*·cher

yesterday	*včera*	*fche*·ruh
today	*dnes*	dnes
tomorrow	*zítra*	*zee*·truh

Numbers

1	*jeden*	*ye*·den
2	*dva*	dvuh
3	*tři*	trzhi
4	*čtyři*	*chti*·rzhi
5	*pět*	pyet
6	*šest*	shest
7	*sedm*	*se*·dm
8	*osm*	*o*·sm
9	*devět*	*de*·vyet
10	*deset*	*de*·set
20	*dvacet*	*dvuh*·tset
30	*třicet*	*trzhi*·tset
40	*čtyřicet*	*chti*·rzhi·tset
50	*padesát*	*puh*·de·sat
60	*šedesát*	*she*·de·sat
70	*sedmdesát*	*se*·dm·de·sat
80	*osmdesát*	*o*·sm·de·sat
90	*devadesát*	*de*·vuh·de·sat
100	*sto*	sto
1000	*tisíc*	*tyi*·seets

Monday	*pondělí*	*pon*·dye·lee
Tuesday	*úterý*	*oo*·te·ree
Wednesday	*středa*	*strzhe*·duh
Thursday	*čtvrtek*	*chtvr*·tek
Friday	*pátek*	*pa*·tek
Saturday	*sobota*	*so*·bo·tuh
Sunday	*neděle*	*ne*·dye·le

January	*leden*	*le*·den
February	*únor*	*oo*·nor
March	*březen*	*brzhe*·zen
April	*duben*	*du*·ben
May	*květen*	*kvye*·ten
June	*červen*	*cher*·ven
July	*červenec*	*cher*·ve·nets
August	*srpen*	*sr*·pen
September	*září*	*za*·rzhee
October	*říjen*	*rzhee*·yen
November	*listopad*	*li*·sto·puht
December	*prosinec*	*pro*·si·nets

TRANSPORT

What time does the bus/train leave?
V kolik hodin odjíždí autobus/vlak? — f *ko*·lik *ho*·dyin *od*·yeezh·dyee *ow*·to·bus/vluhk

Please tell me when we get to ...
Prosím vás řekněte mi kdy budeme v ... — *pro*·seem vas *rzhek*·nye·te mi kdi *bu*·de·me f ...

Does it stop at ...?
Staví v ...? — *sta*·vee v ...

What's the next stop?
Která je příští zastávka? — *kte*·ra ye *przheesh*·tyee *zuhs*·taf·kuh

Please stop here.
Prosím vás zastavte. — *pro*·seem vas *zuhs*·tuhf·te

Please take me to (this address).
Prosím odvezte mě na (tuto adresu). — *pro*·seem *od*·ves·te mye na (*tu*·to *uh*·dre·su)

One ... ticket to (Telč), please.	*... jízdenku do (Telče), prosím.*	... *yeez*·den·ku do (*tel*·che) *pro*·seem
one-way	*Jedno-směrnou*	*yed*·no·smyer·noh
return	*Zpátečni*	*zpa*·tech·nyee

first	*první*	*prv*·nyee
last	*poslední*	*po*·sled·nyee
next	*příští*	*przhee*·shtyee

bus	*autobus*	*ow*·to·bus
plane	*letadlo*	*le*·tuhd·lo
train	*vlak*	vluhk
tram	*tramvaj*	*truhm*·vai

I'd like to hire a ...	*Chtěl/Chtěla bych si půjčit ...* (m/f)	khtyel/*khtye*·luh bikh si *pooy*·chit ...
bicycle	*kolo*	*ko*·lo
car	*auto*	*ow*·to
motorbike	*motorku*	*mo*·tor·ku

Is this the road to ...?
Vede tato silnice do ...? — *ve*·de *tuh*·to *sil*·ni·tse do ...

Can I park here?
Mohu zde parkovat? — *mo*·hu zde *puhr*·ko·vuht

Where's a petrol station?
Kde je benzinová pumpa? — gde ye *ben*·zi·no·va *pum*·puh

I need a mechanic.
Potřebuji mechanika. — *pot*·rzhe·bu·yi *me*·khuh·ni·kuh

Do I need a helmet?
Potřebuji helmu? — *pot*·rzhe·bu·yi *hel*·mu

The car/motorbike won't start.
Auto/Motorka nechce nastartovat. — *ow*·to/*mo*·tor·kuh *nekh*·tse *nuhs*·tuhr·to·vuht

I have a puncture.
Mám defekt. — mam *de*·fekt

GLOSSARY

You may encounter these terms and abbreviations while in Prague.

Becherovka – potent herb liqueur
čajovná – teahouse
ČD – Czech Railways
chrám/dóm – cathedral
ČSSD – Social Democratic Party
cukrárna – cake shop
dámy – sign on women's toilet
divadlo – theatre
doklad – receipt or document
dům – house or building
dům umění – house of art, for exhibitions and workshops
galérie – gallery, arcade
hlavní nádraží (hl nád) main train station
hora – hill, mountain
hospoda or **hostinec** – pub
hrad – castle
hřbitov (Czech) – cemetery
kaple – chapel
katedralá – cathedral
kavárna – café or coffee shop
Kč – koruna česká; Czech crown
kino – cinema
kostel – church
lékárna – pharmacy
město – town
most – bridge
muzeum – museum
muži – sign on men's toilet
nábřeží – embankment
nádraží – station
náměstí (nám) – square
národní – national
ostrov – island
palác – palace
páni – sign on men's toilet
pasáž – passage, shopping arcade
pekárna – bakery
penzión – guest house
pivnice – small beer hall
pivo – beer
pivovar – brewery
potok – stream
Praha – Prague
radnice – town hall
restaurace – restaurant
Roma – a tribe of people who migrated from India to Europe in the 10th century
rybník – fish pond
sady – garden, park, orchard
sgraffito – mural technique whereby the top layer of plaster is scraped away or incised to reveal the layer beneath
stanice – train stop or station
svatý – saint
tramvaj– tram
třída – avenue
ubytovna – dorm accommodation
ulice (ul) – street
ulička (ul) – lane
Velvet Divorce – separation of Czechoslovakia into fully independent Czech and Slovak republics in 1993
Velvet Revolution – bloodless overthrow of Czechoslovakia's communist regime in 1989
vinárna – wine bar/restaurant
vlak – train
záchod – toilet
zahrada – gardens, park
zámek – chateau
ženy – sign on women's toilet
Zimmer frei – room free (for rent)

Behind the Scenes

SEND US YOUR FEEDBACK

We love to hear from travellers – your comments keep us on our toes and help make our books better. Our well-travelled team reads every word on what you loved or loathed about this book. Although we cannot reply individually to postal submissions, we always guarantee that your feedback goes straight to the appropriate authors, in time for the next edition. Each person who sends us information is thanked in the next edition – the most useful submissions are rewarded with a selection of digital PDF chapters.

Visit **lonelyplanet.com/contact** to submit your updates and suggestions or to ask for help. Our award-winning website also features inspirational travel stories, news and discussions.

Note: We may edit, reproduce and incorporate your comments in Lonely Planet products such as guidebooks, websites and digital products, so let us know if you don't want your comments reproduced or your name acknowledged. For a copy of our privacy policy visit lonelyplanet.com/privacy.

OUR READERS

Many thanks to the travellers who used the last edition and wrote to us with helpful hints, useful advice and interesting anecdotes:

R Hemingway, Anita Martin, Mauricio Matsumoto, John, Diane & Natalia Quick, Clare Staines, Stan Vicich

AUTHOR THANKS

Neil Wilson

Many thanks to the usual gang, especially Carol Downie and Brendan Bolland, and also to all the bartenders, bookshop owners, baristas and bellhops who helped out with my endless questions about the best places to eat, drink etc. Plus a big thank you to co-author Mark for making the book so much fun to research, and to Joe and Angela at Lonely Planet for behind-the-scenes support.

Mark Baker

I would like to thank my good friends in the Czech Republic, both Czechs and expats, who have helped me to learn about the country and to feel at home here. Thanks too to my co-author, Neil Wilson, for making this edition a pleasure to research and a relatively smooth ride.

ACKNOWLEDGMENTS

Cover photograph: Prague Castle, Prague
Christer Fredriksson/Lonely Planet Images

THIS BOOK

This 10th edition of Lonely Planet's *Prague & the Czech Republic* guidebook was researched and written by Neil Wilson and Mark Baker. The previous two editions were also written by Neil Wilson and Mark Baker. This guidebook was commissioned in Lonely Planet's London office, and produced by the following:

Commissioning Editor Joe Bindloss
Coordinating Editor Luna Soo
Coordinating Cartographer Andrew Smith
Coordinating Layout Designer Yvonne Bischofberger
Managing Editor Angela Tinson
Managing Cartographers Alison Lyall, Amanda Sierp
Managing Layout Designer Jane Hart
Assisting Editors Carolyn Boicos, Kate Evans, Carly Hall, Pat Kinsella, Charles Rawlings-Way, Saralinda Turner
Assisting Cartographers Valentina Kremenchutskaya, Alex Leung
Assisting Layout Designers Adrian Blackburn, Nicholas Colicchia, Carol Jackson
Cover Research Naomi Parker
Internal Image Research Aude Vauconsant
Language Content Branislava Vladisavljevic
Thanks to Dan Austin, Anita Banh, Imogen Bannister, David Carroll, Laura Crawford, Ryan Evans, Tobias Gattineau, Chris Girdler, Mark Griffiths, Jouve India, Asha Ioculari, Andrea McGinniss, Annelies Mertens, Anna Metcalfe, Trent Paton, Anthony Phelan, Martine Power, Averil Robertson, Wibowo Rusli, Fiona Siseman, Carlos Solarte, Gerard Walker, Amanda Williamson

See also separate subindexes for:

- EATING P320
- DRINKING & NIGHTLIFE P321
- ENTERTAINMENT P322
- SHOPPING P323
- SLEEPING P323
- SPORTS & ACTIVITIES P324

Index

EATING

DRINKING & NIGHTLIFE

ENTERTAINMENT

SHOPPING

SLEEPING

SPORTS & ACTIVITIES

Prague Maps

Map Legend

Sights
- Beach
- Buddhist
- Castle
- Christian
- Hindu
- Islamic
- Jewish
- Monument
- Museum/Gallery
- Ruin
- Winery/Vineyard
- Zoo
- Other Sight

Eating
- Eating

Drinking & Nightlife
- Drinking & Nightlife
- Cafe

Entertainment
- Entertainment

Shopping
- Shopping

Sleeping
- Sleeping
- Camping

Sports & Activities
- Diving/Snorkelling
- Canoeing/Kayaking
- Skiing
- Surfing
- Swimming/Pool
- Walking
- Windsurfing
- Other Sports & Activities

Information
- Post Office
- Tourist Information

Transport
- Airport
- Border Crossing
- Bus
- Cable Car/ Funicular
- Cycling
- Ferry
- Metro
- Monorail
- Parking
- S-Bahn
- Taxi
- Train/Railway
- Tram
- Tube Station
- U-Bahn
- Other Transport

Routes
- Tollway
- Freeway
- Primary
- Secondary
- Tertiary
- Lane
- Unsealed Road
- Plaza/Mall
- Steps
- Tunnel
- Pedestrian Overpass
- Walking Tour
- Walking Tour Detour
- Path

Boundaries
- International
- State/Province
- Disputed
- Regional/Suburb
- Marine Park
- Cliff
- Wall

Geographic
- Hut/Shelter
- Lighthouse
- Lookout
- Mountain/Volcano
- Oasis
- Park
- Pass
- Picnic Area
- Waterfall

Hydrography
- River/Creek
- Intermittent River
- Swamp/Mangrove
- Reef
- Canal
- Water
- Dry/Salt/ Intermittent Lake
- Glacier

Areas
- Beach/Desert
- Cemetery (Christian)
- Cemetery (Other)
- Park/Forest
- Sportsground
- Sight (Building)
- Top Sight (Building)

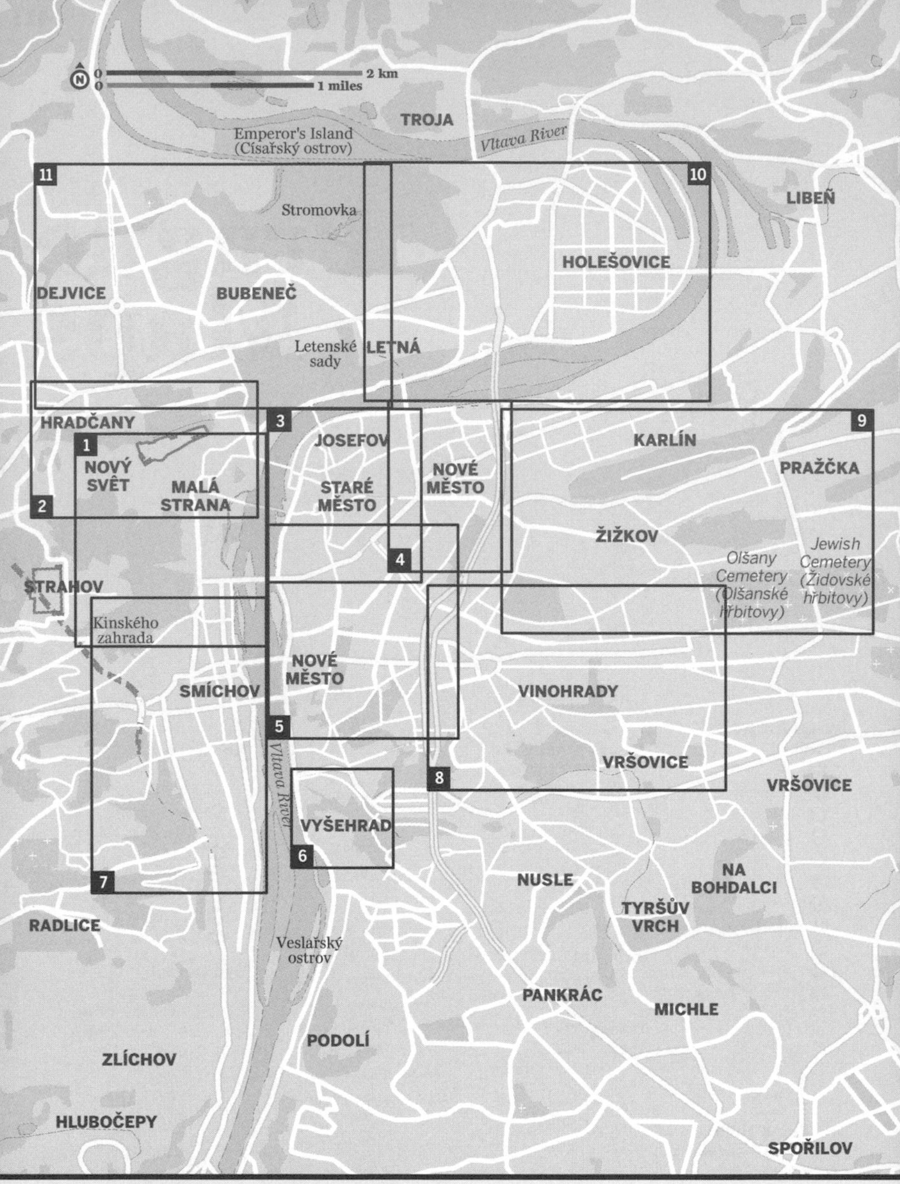
0 2 km
0 1 miles
TROJA
Emperor's Island
(Císařský ostrov)
Vltava River
11
10
LIBEŇ
Stromovka
HOLEŠOVICE
DEJVICE
BUBENEČ
Letenské
sady
LETNÁ
HRADČANY
3
9
1
JOSEFOV
KARLÍN
NOVÝ
SVĚT
MALÁ
STRANA
NOVÉ
MĚSTO
STARÉ
MĚSTO
PRAŽČKA
2
ŽIŽKOV
4
Jewish
Cemetery
(Židovské
hřbitovy)
Olšany
Cemetery
(Olšanské
hřbitovy)
STRAHOV
Kinského
zahrada
NOVÉ
MĚSTO
SMÍCHOV
VINOHRADY
5
Vltava River
VRŠOVICE
8
VRŠOVICE
VYŠEHRAD
6
7
NUSLE
NA
BOHDALCI
TYRŠŮV
VRCH
RADLICE
Veslařský
ostrov
PANKRÁC
MICHLE
PODOLÍ
ZLÍCHOV
HLUBOČEPY
SPOŘILOV

MAP INDEX

MALÁ STRANA *Map on p328*

Top Sights (p79)

Charles Bridge G3
John Lennon Wall F3
Museum of the Infant Jesus of Prague E4
St Nicholas Church E3

Sights (p82)

1 Bell Tower E3
2 Bretfeld Palace C2
3 Children's Island G7
4 Church of Our Lady of Unceasing Succour D2
5 Czech Museum of Music E4
6 Franz Kafka Museum G3
7 House at the Three Fiddles D2
8 House of the Golden Horseshoe C2
9 House of the Two Suns C2
10 Kampa F4
11 Kampa Museum F5
12 KGB Museum C3
13 Malá Strana Bridge Tower F3
14 Malostranské náměstí E2
15 Maltese Square E4
16 Memorial to the Victims of Communism E6
17 Mirror Maze B5
18 Musaion C8
19 Museum Montanelli D2
20 Nerudova C2
21 Petřín C5
22 Petřín Funicular Railway E5
23 Petřín Lookout Tower B5
24 Proudy (David Černý Sculpture) G3
25 Quo Vadis (David Černý Sculpture) C3
26 Smiřický Palace E2
27 St John of Nepomuk House D2
28 Vojan Gardens F2
29 Vrtbov Garden E3
30 Wallenstein Garden F2
31 Wallenstein Palace E1
32 Wallenstein Riding School F1

Eating (p87)

33 Bangkok E3
34 Café de Paris E4
35 Café Lounge E6
36 Café Savoy F6
37 Cukrkávalimonáda E3
38 Hergetova Cihelna G3
39 Lichfield F2
40 Noi E5
41 U Malé Velryby E4
42 U Modré Kachničky E4

Drinking & Nightlife (p89)

43 Blue Light E3
44 Hostinec U Kocoura D2
45 Kafíčko F3
46 Klub Újezd E6
47 Malostranská beseda E2
48 Mlýnská Kavárna F5
49 U Malého Glena E3
50 U Zeleného Čaje D2

Shopping (p90)

51 Pavla & Olga C3
52 Shakespeare & Sons F3
53 Vetešnictvi E6

Sports & Activities (p30)

54 Prague on Segway D3
55 Prague Segway Tours E3

Sleeping (p188)

56 Design Hotel Sax C3
57 Dům u velké boty C3
58 Golden Well Hotel E1
59 Hotel Aria E3
60 Hotel Neruda C2
Hunger Wall Residence (see 35)
61 Lokál Inn F3
62 Pension Dientzenhofer F4

MALÁ STRANA

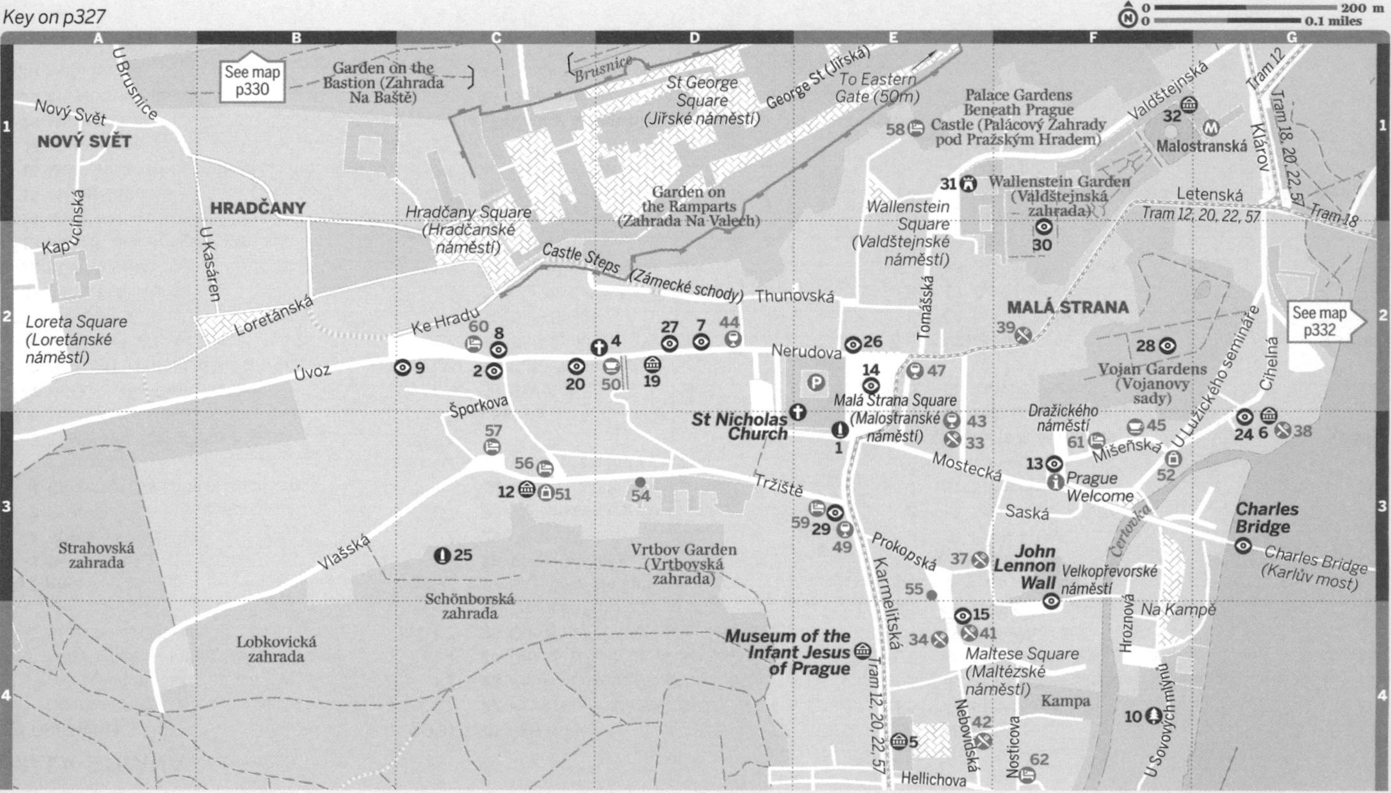

Key on p327
200 m
0.1 miles
See map p330
See map p332
Garden on the Bastion (Zahrada Na Baště)
Brusnice
St George Square (Jiřské náměstí)
George St (Jiřská)
To Eastern Gate (50m)
Palace Gardens Beneath Prague Castle (Palácový Zahrady pod Pražským Hradem)
Valdštejnská
Malostranská
Tram 12
Tram 18, 20, 22, 57
Klárov
Nový Svět
U Brusnice
NOVÝ SVĚT
HRADČANY
Kapucínská
U Kasáren
Hradčany Square (Hradčanské náměstí)
Garden on the Ramparts (Zahrada Na Valech)
Castle Steps (Zámecké schody)
Wallenstein Garden (Valdštejnská zahrada)
Wallenstein Square (Valdštejnské náměstí)
Letenská
Tram 12, 20, 22, 57
Tram 18
Thunovská
Tomášská
MALÁ STRANA
Loreta Square (Loretánské náměstí)
Loretánská
Ke Hradu
Úvoz
Nerudova
Vojan Gardens (Vojanovy sady)
U Lužického semináře
Cihelná
Šporkova
Malá Strana Square (Malostranské náměstí)
St Nicholas Church
Dražického náměstí
Mišeňská
Mostecká
Prague Welcome
Tržiště
Saská
Čertovka
Charles Bridge
Charles Bridge (Karlův most)
Strahovská zahrada
Vlašská
Vrtbov Garden (Vrtbovská zahrada)
Schönborská zahrada
Prokopská
Karmelitská
John Lennon Wall
Velkopřevorské náměstí
Na Kampě
Hroznová
Lobkovická zahrada
Museum of the Infant Jesus of Prague
Maltese Square (Maltézské náměstí)
Kampa
U Sovových mlýnů
Tram 12, 20, 22, 57
Nebovidská
Nosticova
Hellichova

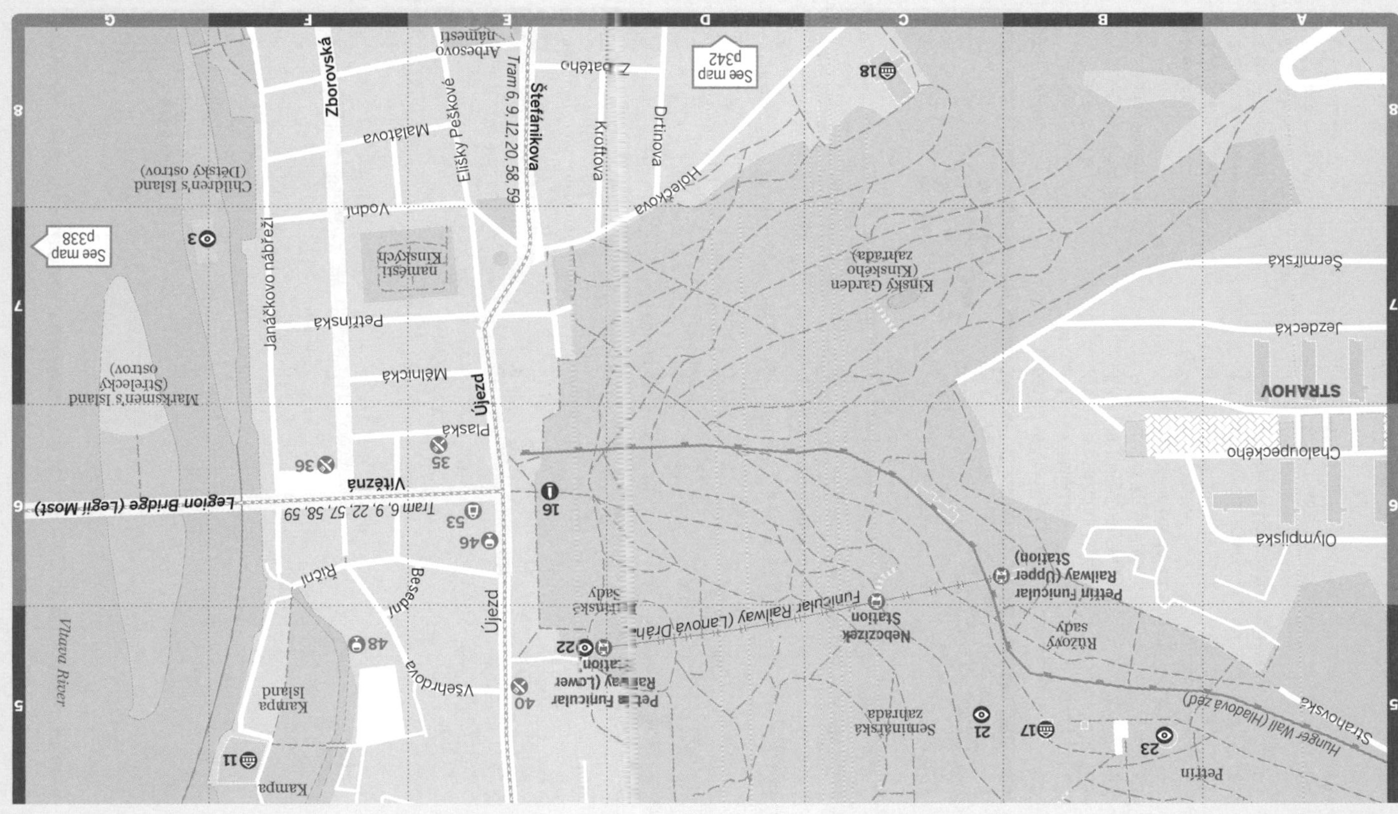
Vltava River
Legion Bridge (Legií Most)
Marksmen's Island (Střelecký ostrov)
Children's Island (Dětský ostrov)
See map p338
See map p342
Kampa
Kampa Island
Říční
Všehrdova
Besední
Újezd
Tram 6, 9, 22, 57, 58, 59
Vítězná
Janáčkovo nábřeží
Zborovská
Plaská
Mělnická
Petřínská
náměstí Kinských
Vodní
Malátova
Elišky Peškové
Arbesovo náměstí
Tram 6, 9, 12, 20, 58, 59
Štefánikova
Kroftova
Zubatého
Drtinova
Holečkova
Petřín Funicular Railway (Lower Station)
Funicular Railway (Lanová Dráha)
Nebozízek Station
Petřín Funicular Railway (Upper Station)
Seminářská zahrada
Růžový sady
Kinský Garden (Kinského zahrada)
Petřín
Hunger Wall (Hladová zeď)
Strahovská
Olympijská
Chaloupeckého
STRAHOV
Jezdecká
Šermířská
11
48
46
53
35
36
40
22
16
3
21
17
23
18
A
B
C
D
E
F
G
5
6
7
8

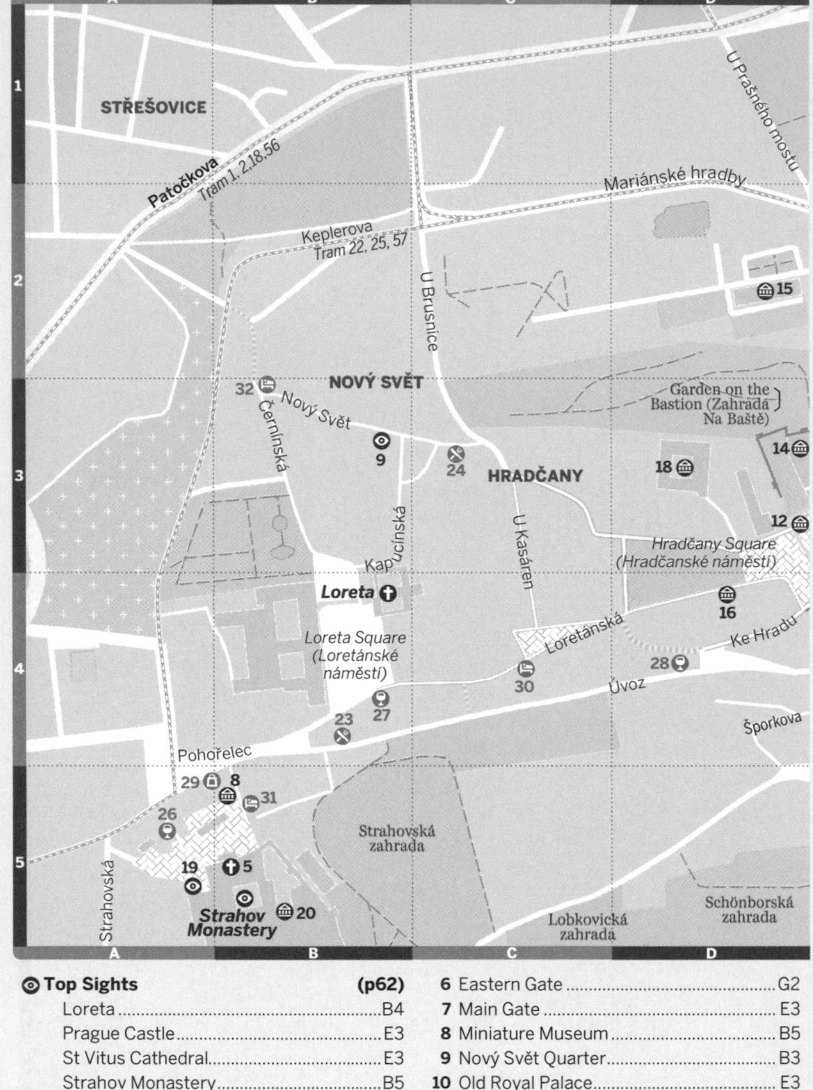

Top Sights **(p62)**

Loreta	B4
Prague Castle	E3
St Vitus Cathedral	E3
Strahov Monastery	B5

Sights **(p74)**

1	All Saints' Chapel	F3
2	Ball-Game House	E2
3	Basilica of St George	F3
4	Bílek Villa	H1
5	Church of the Assumption of Our Lady	B5
6	Eastern Gate	G2
7	Main Gate	E3
8	Miniature Museum	B5
9	Nový Svět Quarter	B3
10	Old Royal Palace	E3
11	Palace Gardens Beneath Prague Castle	G3
12	Plečnik Hall	D3
13	Powder Tower	E3
14	Prague Castle Picture Gallery	D3
15	Riding School	D2
16	Schwarzenberg Palace	D4
17	St Vitus Treasury	E3

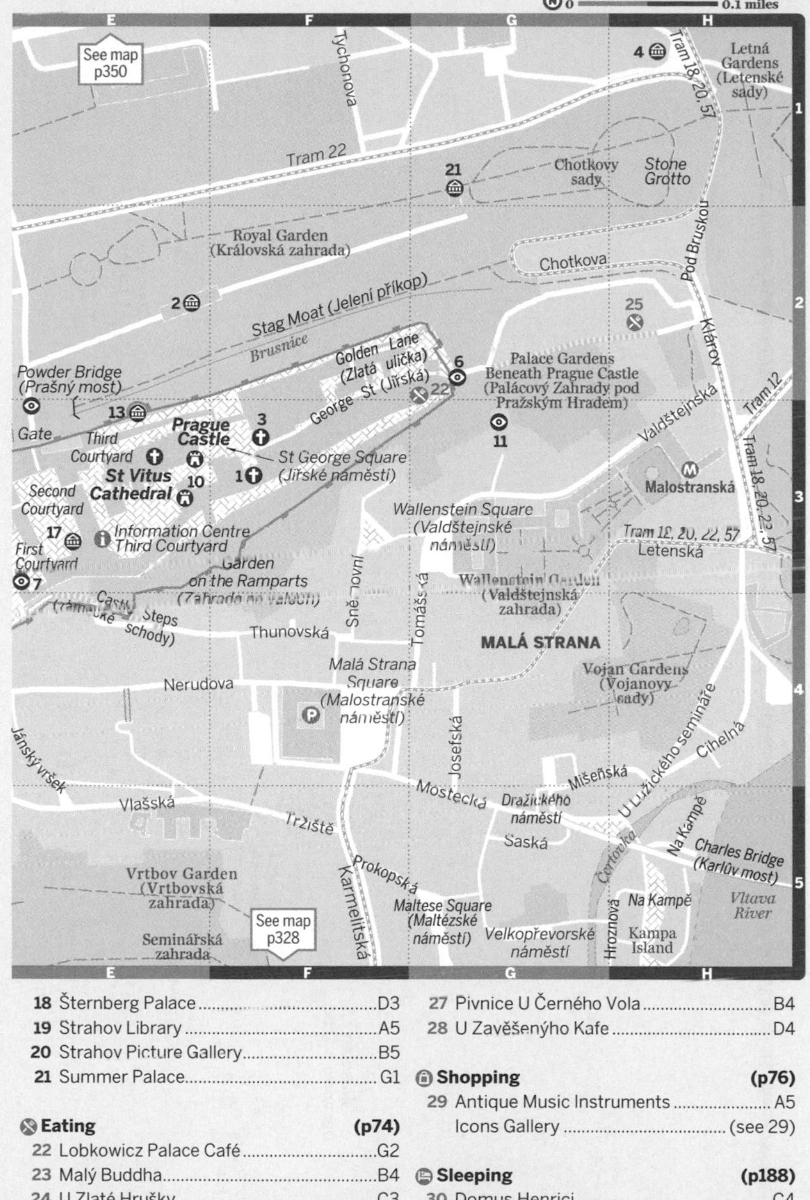

18 Šternberg Palace D3
19 Strahov Library A5
20 Strahov Picture Gallery B5
21 Summer Palace G1

Eating (p74)
22 Lobkowicz Palace Café G2
23 Malý Buddha B4
24 U Zlaté Hrušky C3
25 Villa Richter H2

Drinking & Nightlife (p76)
26 Klášterní pivovar Strahov A5
27 Pivnice U Černého Vola B4
28 U Zavěšenýho Kafe D4

Shopping (p76)
29 Antique Music Instruments A5
Icons Gallery (see 29)

Sleeping (p188)
30 Domus Henrici C4
31 Hotel Monastery B5
32 Romantik Hotel U Raka B3

STARÉ MĚSTO

Key on p334

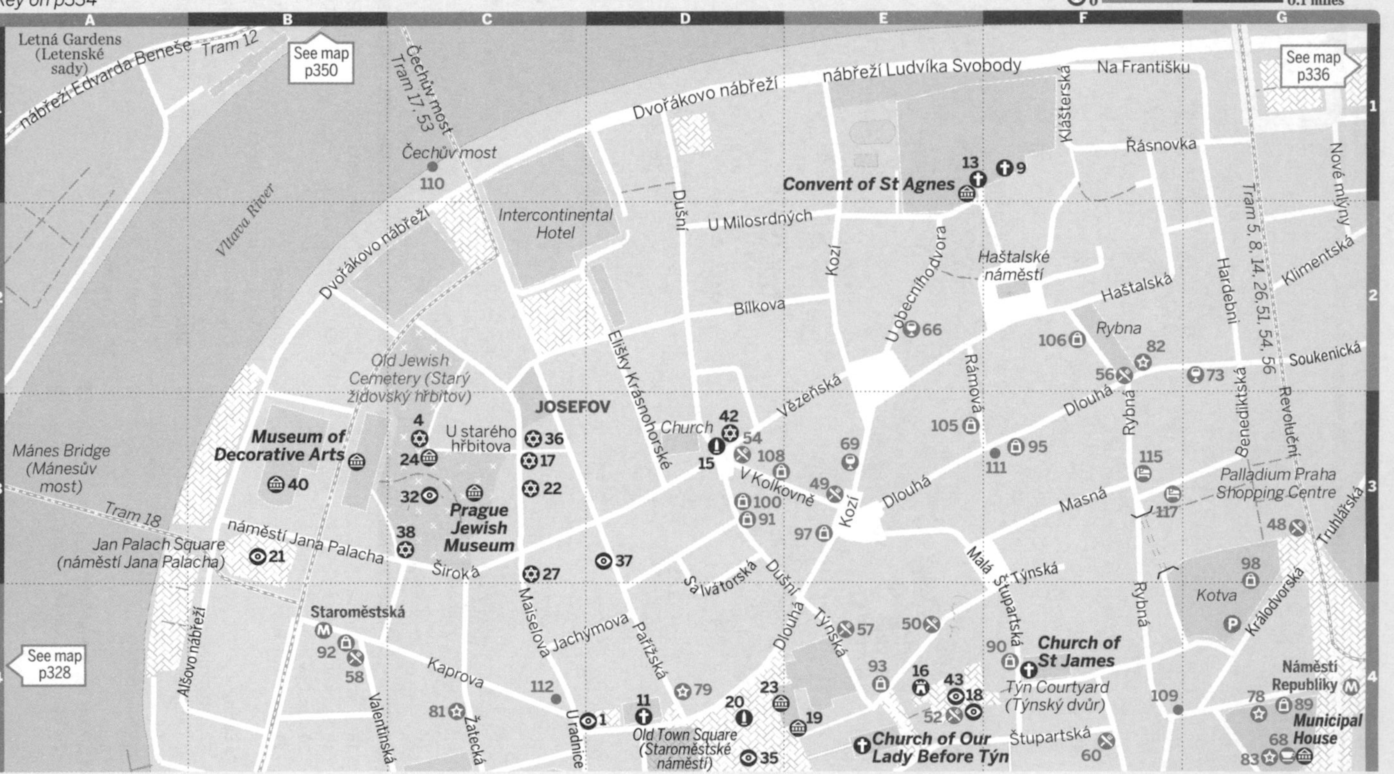

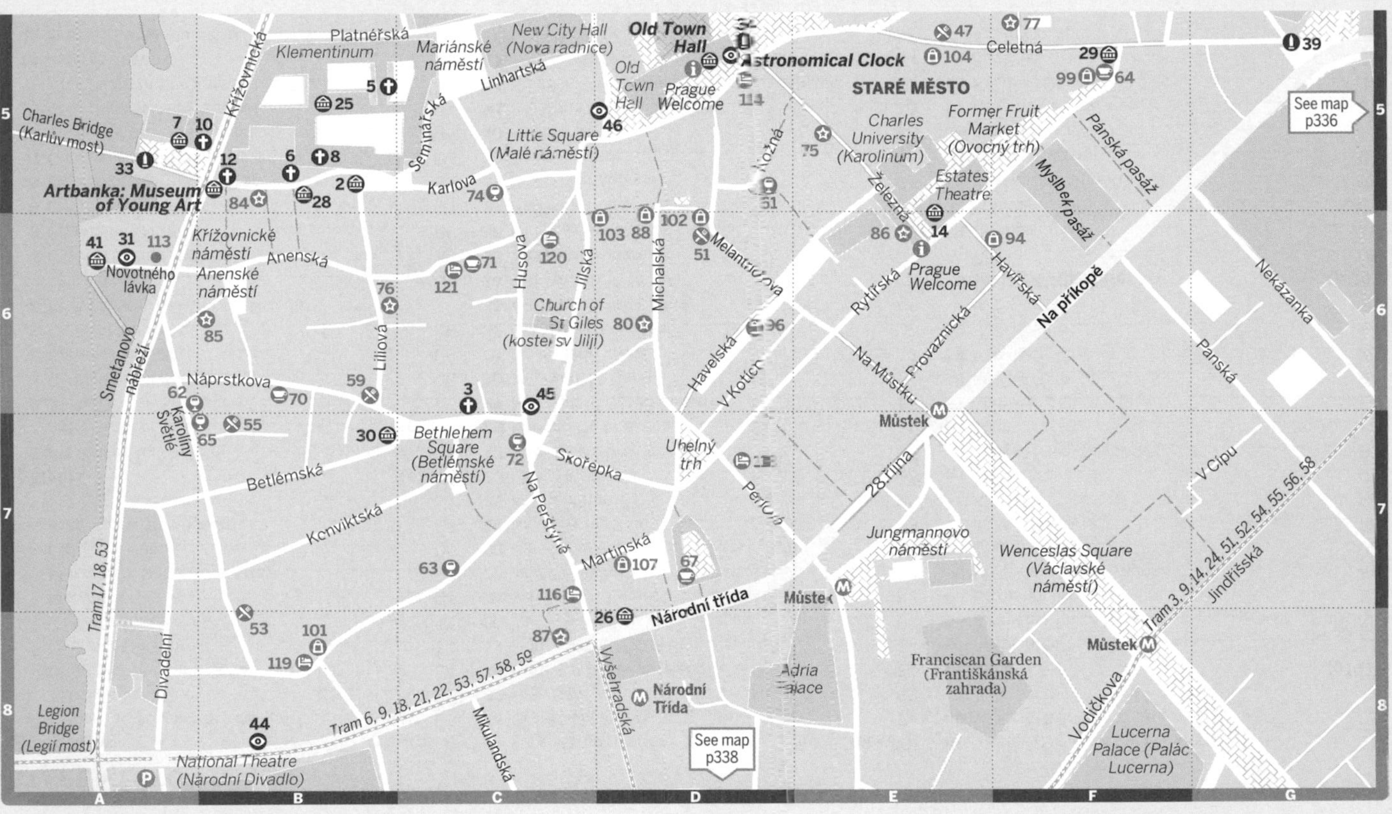
Charles Bridge (Karlův most)
Artbanka: Museum of Young Art
Křižovnická
Platnéřská
Klementinum
Mariánské náměstí
New City Hall (Nova radnice)
Linhartská
Old Town Hall
Old Town Hall
Astronomical Clock
Prague Welcome
STARÉ MĚSTO
Celetná
Little Square (Malé náměstí)
Seminářská
Karlova
Charles University (Karolinum)
Former Fruit Market (Ovocný trh)
Estates Theatre
Pánská pasáž
Myslbek pasáž
Železná
Křižovnické náměstí
Anenská
Anenské náměstí
Novotného lávka
Husova
Jilská
Michalská
Church of St Giles (kostel sv Jiljí)
Rytířská
Prague Welcome
Havířská
Na příkopě
Nekázanka
Panská
Havelská
Provaznická
Na Můstku
Můstek
Smetanovo nábřeží
Náprstkova
Liliová
Karolíny Světlé
Bethlehem Square (Betlémské náměstí)
Skořepka
Uhelný trh
28.října
V Cípu
Betlémská
Konviktská
Na Perštýně
Martinská
Jungmannovo náměstí
Wenceslas Square (Václavské náměstí)
Tram 3, 9, 14, 24, 51, 52, 54, 55, 56, 58
Jindřišská
Tram 17, 18, 53
Národní třída
Můstek
Divadelní
Tram 6, 9, 18, 21, 22, 53, 57, 58, 59
Vyšehradská
Národní Třída
Franciscan Garden (Františkánská zahrada)
Vodičkova
Legion Bridge (Legií most)
National Theatre (Národní Divadlo)
Mikulandská
See map p338
See map p336
Lucerna Palace (Palác Lucerna)
A
B
C
D
E
F
G
5
6
7
8
2
3
5
6
7
8
10
12
14
25
26
28
29
30
31
33
39
41
44
45
46
47
51
53
55
59
62
63
64
65
67
70
71
72
74
75
76
77
80
84
85
86
87
88
94
99
101
102
103
104
107
113
114
116
119
120
121

STARÉ MĚSTO *Map on p332*

Top Sights **(p93)**

- Artbanka: Museum of Young Art ... B5
- Astronomical Clock ... D5
- Church of Our Lady Before Týn ... E4
- Church of St James ... F4
- Convent of St Agnes ... E1
- Municipal House ... G4
- Museum of Decorative Arts ... B3
- Old Town Hall ... D5
- Prague Jewish Museum ... C3

Sights **(p100)**

- **1** Art Gallery for Children ... D4
- Astronomical Tower ... (see 25)
- **2** At the Golden Snake ... B5
- **3** Bethlehem Chapel ... C6
- **4** Ceremonial Hall ... C3
- **5** Chapel of Mirrors ... B5
- **6** Chapel of the Assumption of the Virgin Mary ... B5
- **7** Charles Bridge Museum ... A5
- **8** Church of St Clement ... B5
- **9** Church of St Francis ... F1
- **10** Church of St Francis Seraphinus ... B5
- **11** Church of St Nicholas ... D4
- **12** Church of the Holy Saviour ... B5
- **13** Church of the Holy Saviour (Convent of St Agnes) ... E1
- **14** Estates Theatre ... E6
- **15** Franz Kafka Monument ... D3
- Galerie Rudolfinum ... (see 40)
- **16** Granovsky Palace ... E4
- **17** High Synagogue ... C3
- **18** House at the Black Bear ... E4
- **19** House at the Stone Bell ... E4
- **20** Jan Hus Statue ... D4
- **21** Jan Palach Square ... B3
- **22** Jewish Town Hall ... C3
- **23** Kinský Palace ... D4
- **24** Klaus Synagogue ... C3
- **25** Klementinum ... B5
- **26** Lego Museum ... D8
- **27** Maisel Synagogue ... C3
- **28** Marionette Museum ... B5
- **29** Museum of Czech Cubism ... F5
- **30** Náprstek Museum ... B7
- **31** Novotného lávka ... A6
- **32** Old Jewish Cemetery ... C3
- **33** Old Town Bridge Tower ... A5
- **34** Old Town Hall Tower ... D5
- **35** Old Town Square ... D4
- **36** Old-New Synagogue ... C3
- **37** Pařížská ... D3
- **38** Pinkas Synagogue ... C3
- **39** Powder Gate ... G5
- **40** Rudolfinum ... B3
- **41** Smetana Museum ... A6
- **42** Spanish Synagogue ... D3
- **43** Týn Courtyard ... E4
- **44** Viola Building ... B8
- **45** Viselec (David Černý Sculpture) ... C6
- **46** VJ Rott Building ... D5

Eating **(p107)**

- **47** Ambiente Pasta Fresca ... E5
- **48** Ambiente Pizza Nuova ... G3
- **49** Bakeshop Praha ... E3
- **50** Beas Vegetarian Dhaba ... E4
- **51** Country Life ... D6
- **52** Indian Jewel ... E4
- **53** Kabul ... B8
- **54** Kolkovna ... D3
- **55** Lehká Hlava ... B7
- **56** Lokál ... F2
- **57** Maitrea ... E4
- **58** Mistral Café ... B4
- **59** V zátiší ... B6
- **60** Vino di Vino ... F4

Drinking & Nightlife **(p110)**

- **61** Čili Bar ... D5
- **62** Duende ... A6
- **63** Friends ... C7
- **64** Grand Cafe Orient ... F5
- **65** Hemingway Bar ... B7
- **66** James Joyce ... E2
- **67** Káva Káva Káva ... D7
- **68** Kavárna Obecní dům ... G4
- **69** Kozička ... E3
- **70** Krásný ztráty ... B6

71 Literární Kavárna Řetězová ... C6
72 Monarch Vinný Sklep ... C7
73 Prague Beer Museum ... G2
U Medvídků ... (see 116)
74 U Zlatého Tygra ... C5

Entertainment (p112)

75 AghaRTA Jazz Centrum ... E5
76 Blues Sklep ... B6
77 Celetná Theatre ... F5
Chapel of Mirrors ... (see 5)
Dvořák Hall ... (see 40)
Estates Theatre ... (see 14)
78 FOK Box Office ... G4
79 Image Theatre ... D4
80 Jazz Club U Staré Paní ... D6
81 National Marionette Theatre ... C4
Prague Spring Box Office ... (see 40)
82 Roxy ... F2
83 Smetana Hall ... G4
84 Ta Fantastika ... B5
85 Theatre on the Balustrade ... B6
86 Ticketcentrum ... E6
87 Vagon ... C8

Shopping (p113)

88 Art Deco Galerie ... D6
89 Art Décoratif ... G4
90 Big Ben ... F4
91 Bohème ... D3
92 Bořek Šípek ... B4
93 Bric A Brac ... E4
94 Frey Wille ... F6
95 Granát Turnov ... F3
96 Havelská Market ... D6
97 Klara Nademlýnská ... E3
98 Kotva ... G3
99 Kubista ... F5
100 Le Patio Lifestyle ... D3
101 Leeda ... B8
102 Manufaktura ... D6
103 Maximum Underground ... D6
104 Modernista ... E5
105 Qubus ... E3
106 Talacko ... F2
107 TEG ... D7
108 TEG ... D3

Sports & Activities (p29, 300)

109 City Bike ... F4
110 Evropská Vodní Doprava ... C1
111 Praha Bike ... F3
112 Precious Legacy Tours ... C4
113 Wittmann Tours ... A6

Sleeping (p189)

114 Grand Hotel Praha ... D5
115 Hotel Josef ... F3
116 Hotel U Medvídků ... C7
117 Old Prague Hostel ... F3
118 Perla Hotel ... D7
119 Residence Karolina ... B8
120 Savic Hotel ... C5
121 U Zeleného Věnce ... C6

NORTH NOVÉ MĚSTO

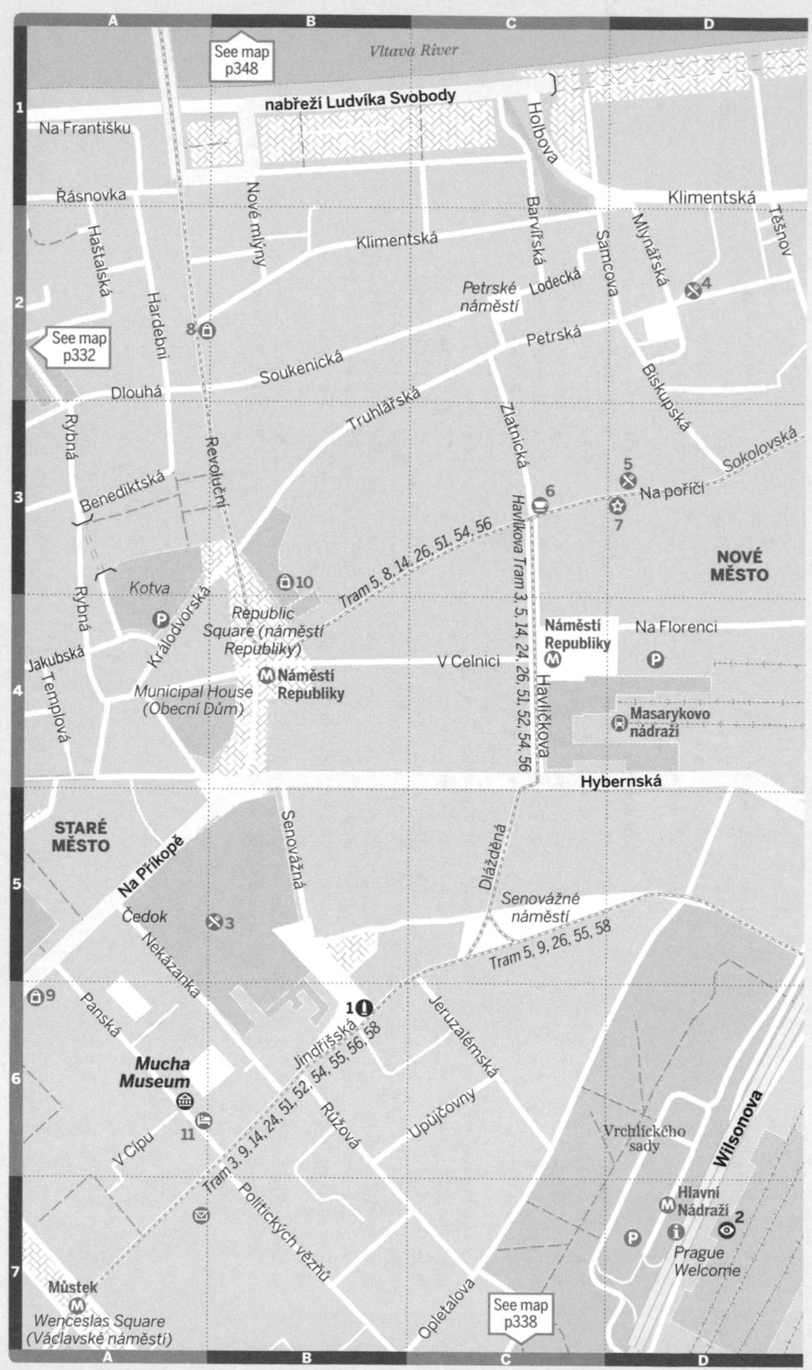

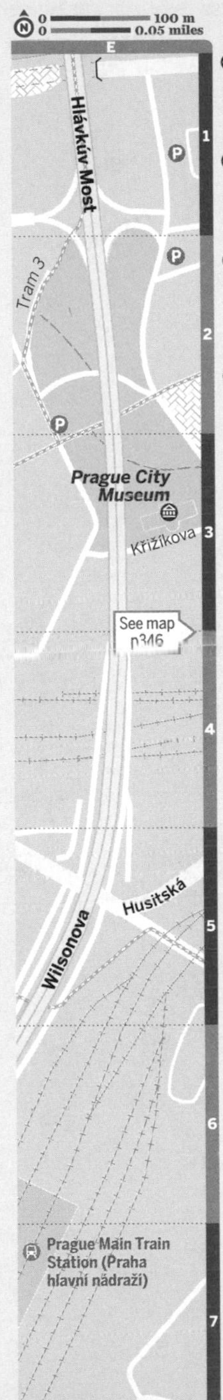
0 100 m
0 0.05 miles
E
Hlávkův Most
Tram 3
Prague City Museum
Křižíkova
See map p346
Husitská
Wilsonova
Prague Main Train Station (Praha hlavní nádraží)
E

SOUTH NOVÉ MĚSTO

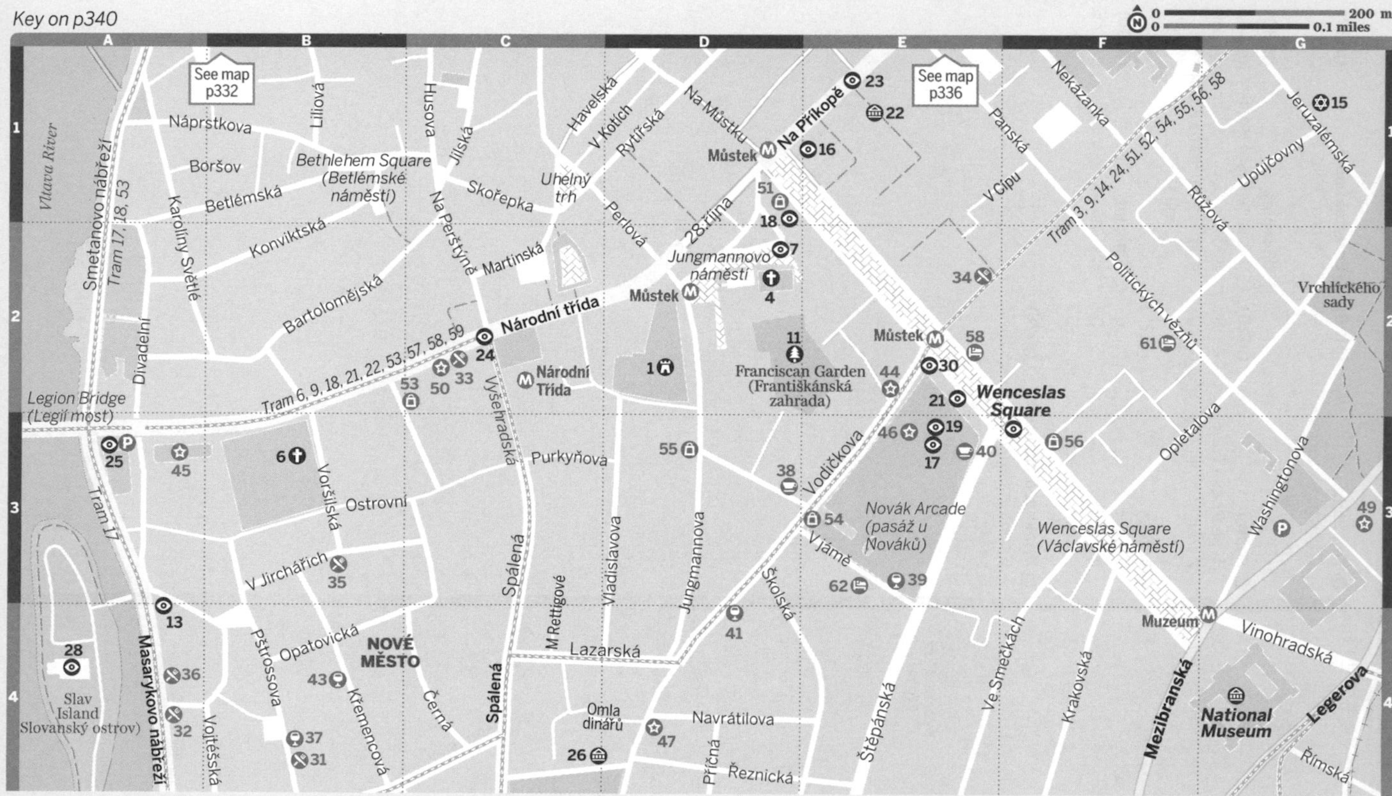

SOUTH NOVÉ MĚSTO

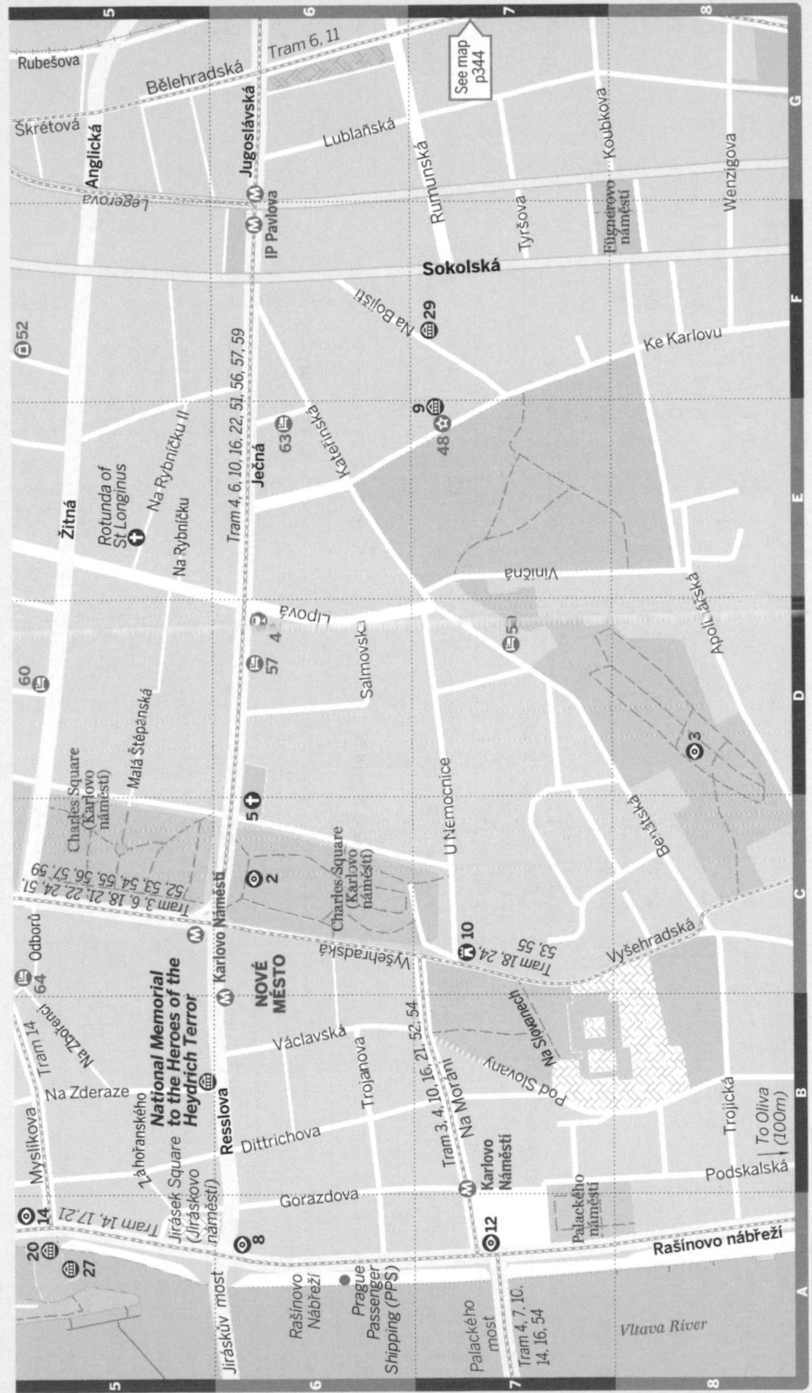

SOUTH NOVÉ MĚSTO *Map on p338*

Top Sights **(p118)**
- National Memorial to the Heroes of the Heydrich Terror ... B5
- National Museum ... G4
- Wenceslas Square ... F3

Sights **(p121)**
- 1 Adria Palace ... D2
- 2 Charles Square ... C6
- 3 Charles University Botanical Garden ... D8
- 4 Church of Our Lady of the Snows ... D2
- 5 Church of St Ignatius ... C6
- 6 Convent of St Ursula ... B3
- 7 Cubist Lamp Post ... D2
- 8 Dancing Building ... A6
- 9 Dvořák Museum ... E7
- 10 Faust House ... C7
- 11 Franciscan Garden ... D2
- 12 František Palacký Memorial ... A7
- 13 Goethe Institute ... A4
- 14 House of the Hlahol Choir ... A5
- 15 Jubilee Synagogue ... G1
- 16 Koruna Palace ... E1
- 17 Kun (David Černý Sculpture) ... E3
- 18 Lindt Building ... D1
- 19 Lucerna Palace ... E3
- 20 Mánes Gallery ... A5
- 21 Melantrich Building ... E2
- 22 Museum of Communism ... E1
- 23 Na Příkopě ... E1
- 24 Národní Třída ... C2
- 25 National Theatre ... A3
- 26 New Town Hall ... C4
- 27 Šitovská věž ... A5
- 28 Slav Island ... A4
- 29 U Kalicha ... F7
- 30 Wiehl House ... E2

Eating **(p125)**
- 31 Globe Bookstore & Café ... B4
- 32 Karavanseráj ... A4
- 33 Le Patio ... C2
- 34 Modrý Zub ... E2
- 35 Pizzeria Kmotra ... B3
- 36 Suterén ... A4

Drinking & Nightlife **(p128)**
- 37 Bokovka ... B4
- 38 Friends Coffee House ... D3
- 39 Jáma ... E3
- Kavárna Evropa ... (see 58)
- Kavárna Lucerna ... (see 19)
- 40 Kávovarna ... E3
- 41 Novoměstský pivovar ... D4
- 42 Pivovarský Dům ... D6
- 43 U Fleků ... B4

Entertainment **(p129)**
- 44 Kino Světozor ... E2
- 45 Laterna Magika ... A3
- 46 Lucerna Music Bar ... E3
- 47 Minor Theatre ... D4
- National Theatre ... (see 25)
- 48 Original Music Theatre of Prague ... E7
- 49 Prague State Opera ... G3
- 50 Reduta Jazz Club ... C2
- Rock Café ... (see 50)

Shopping **(p130)**
- 51 Bat'a ... D1
- 52 Bazar ... F5
- 53 Belda Jewellery ... C2
- Bontonland ... (see 16)
- Globe Bookstore & Café ... (see 31)
- 54 Jan Pazdera ... E3
- 55 Kiwi ... D3
- 56 Palác Knih Neo Luxor ... F3

Sleeping **(p190)**
- 57 ArtHarmony ... D6
- 58 Grand Hotel Evropa ... E2
- 59 Hotel 16 U Sv Kateřiny ... D7
- 60 Hotel Suite Home ... D5
- 61 Hotel Yasmin ... F2
- 62 Icon Hotel ... E3
- 63 Miss Sophie's ... E6
- 64 Mosaic House ... C5

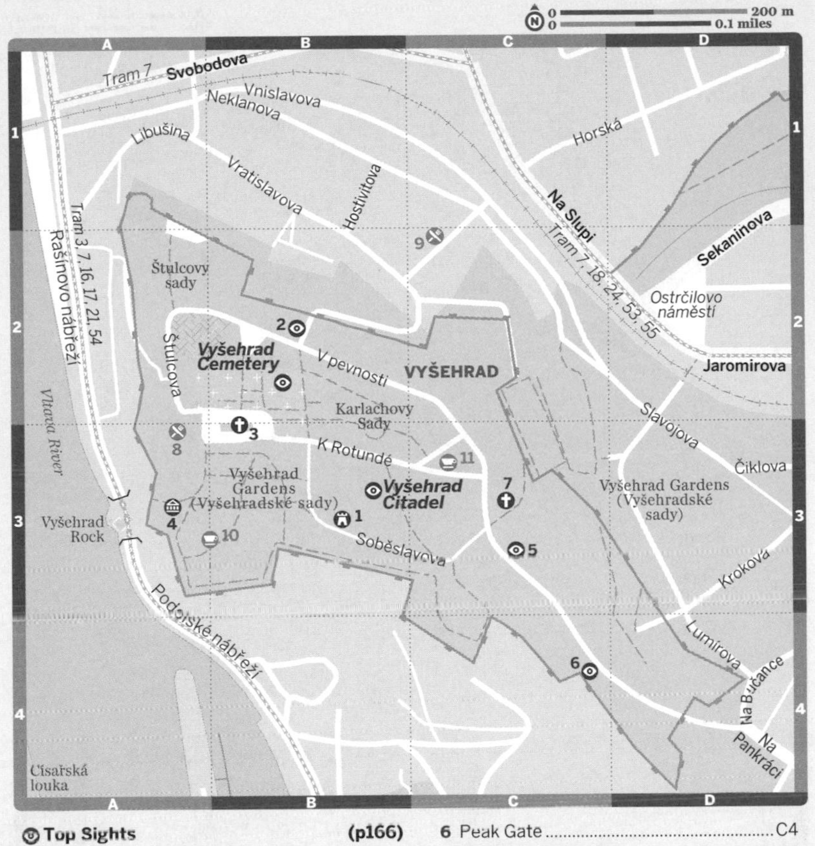

Top Sights (p166)
Vyšehrad Cemetery ... B2
Vyšehrad Citadel ... B3

Sights (p167)
1 Basilica of St Lawrence ... B3
2 Brick Gate & Casements ... B2
3 Church of Sts Peter & Paul ... B3
4 Gothic Cellar ... A3
5 Leopold Gate ... C3
6 Peak Gate ... C4
7 Rotunda of St Martin ... C3

Eating (p170)
8 Rio's Vyšehrad ... A3
9 U Neklana ... C2

Drinking & Nightlife (p172)
10 Cafe Citadela ... B3
11 V Cafe ... C3

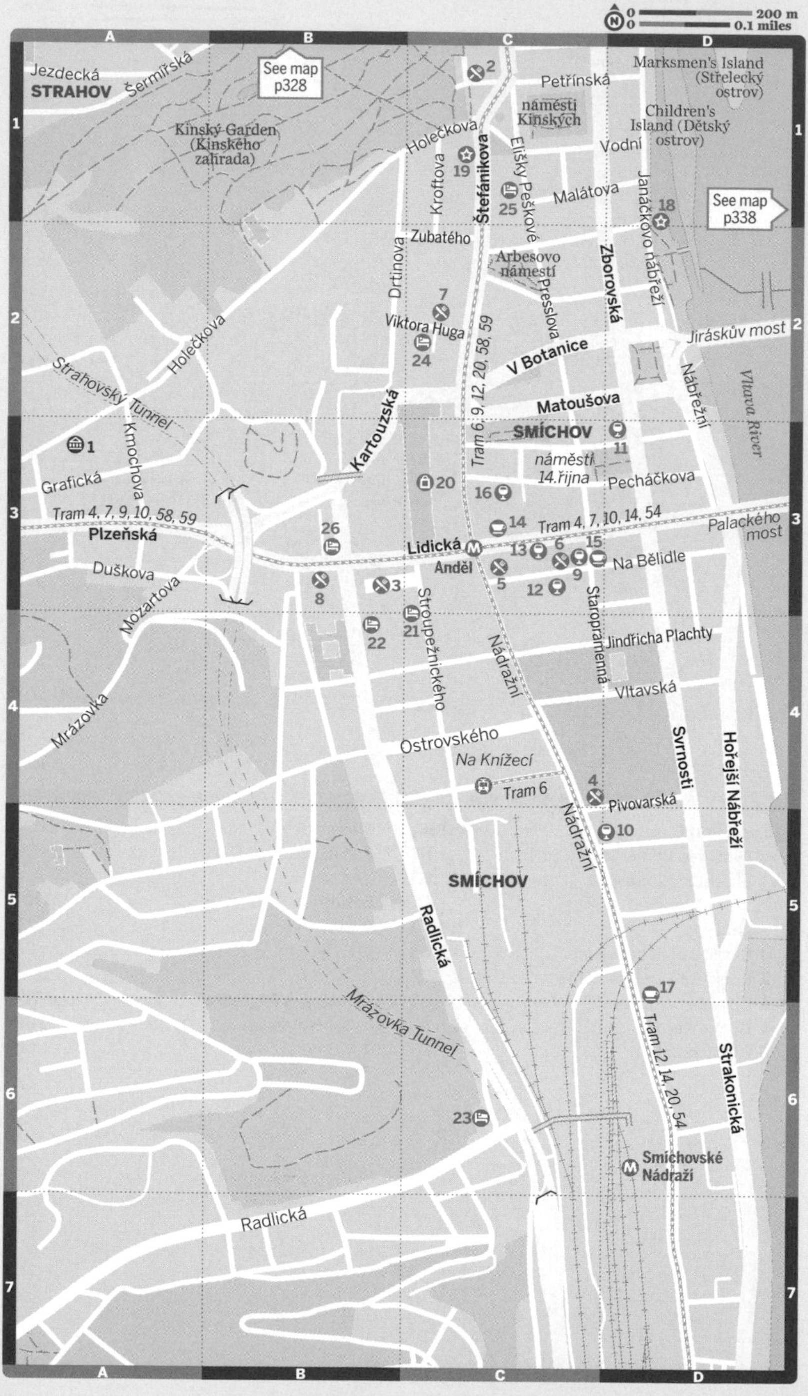

SMÍCHOV

0 — 200 m
0 — 0.1 miles

See map p328
See map p338

Jezdecká
STRAHOV
Šermířská
Kinský Garden (Kinského zahrada)
Petřínská
náměstí Kinských
Marksmen's Island (Střelecký ostrov)
Children's Island (Dětský ostrov)
Vodní
Holečkova
Kroftova
Štefánikova
Elišky Peškové
Malátova
Janáčkovo nábřeží
Zubatého
Drtinova
Arbesovo náměstí
Zborovská
Presslova
Viktora Huga
Jiráskův most
V Botanice
Nábřežní
Vltava River
Strahovský Tunnel
Kartouzská
Matoušova
Tram 6, 9, 12, 20, 58, 59
SMÍCHOV
Kmochova
náměstí 14.října
Pecháčkova
Grafická
Tram 4, 7, 9, 10, 58, 59
Plzeňská
Tram 4, 7, 10, 14, 54
Palackého most
Lidická
Anděl
Na Bělidle
Duškova
Mozartova
Stroupežnického
Staropramenná
Nádražní
Jindřicha Plachty
Vltavská
Mrázovka
Ostrovského
Na Knížecí
Tram 6
Pivovarská
Svornosti
Hořejší Nábřeží
SMÍCHOV
Radlická
Mrázovka Tunnel
Tram 12, 14, 20, 54
Strakonická
Smíchovské Nádraží
Radlická

SMÍCHOV

Sights (p169)
Brownnosers (David Černý Sculpture) (see 1)
1 Futura Gallery A3

Eating (p169)
2 Artisan C1
3 Babička Restaurace B3
4 Na Verandách C4
5 Pizzeria Corleone C3
6 U Bílého lva C3
7 U Míkuláše Dačíckého C2
8 Zlatý klas B3

Drinking & Nightlife (p171)
9 Back Doors C3
10 Dog's Bollocks D5
11 Futurum D3
12 Hells Bells C3
13 Hlubina C3
14 Káva Káva Káva C3
15 Kavárna Jarda Mayer C3
16 Lokal Blok C3
17 Wash Café D5

Entertainment (p172)
18 JazzDock D1
19 Švandovo Divadlo Na Smíchově C1

Shopping (p173)
Mapis (see 19)
20 Nový Smíchov C3

Sleeping (p195)
21 Anděl's Hotel Prague C4
22 Angelo Hotel B4
23 Arpacay Hostel C6
24 Hotel Arbes-Mepro C2
25 Hotel Julian C1
26 Ibis Praha Malá Strana B3

VINOHRADY & VRŠOVICE

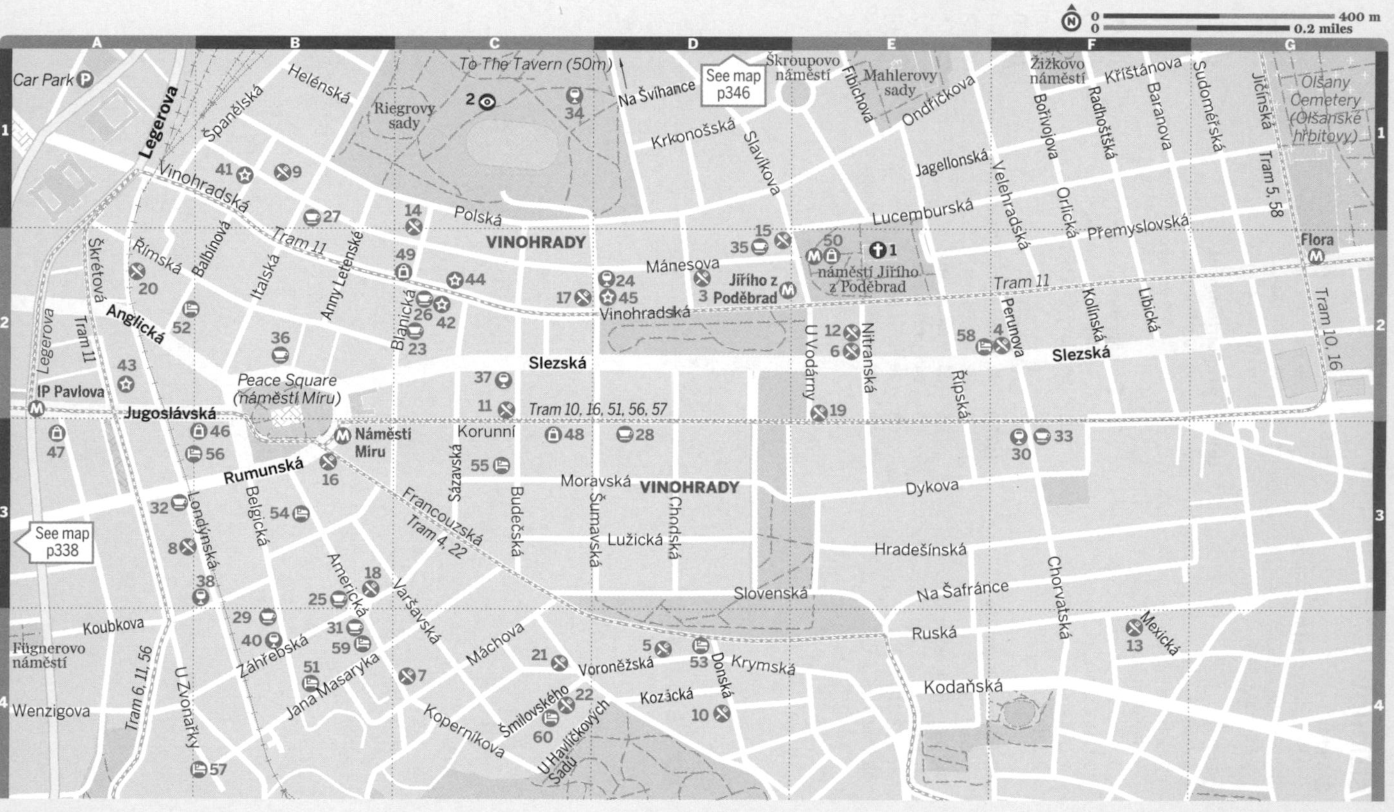

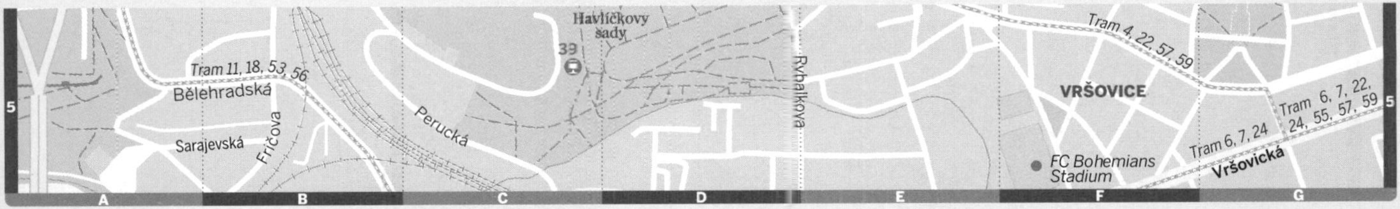

Tram 11, 18, 53, 56
Bělehradská
Sarajevská
Fričova
Perucká
39
Havlíčkovy sady
Rybalkova
Tram 4, 22, 57, 59
VRŠOVICE
FC Bohemians Stadium
Tram 6, 7, 24
Vršovická
Tram 6, 7, 22, 24, 55, 57, 59
A B C D E F G
5

Sights (p134)

1 Church of the Most Sacred Heart of Our Lord E2
2 Riegrovy sady C1

Eating (p134)

3 Aromi D2
Café FX ..... (see 43)
4 Ha Noi F2
5 Hamtam D4
6 Kofein E2
7 Las Adelitas C4
8 Loving Hut A3
9 Masala B1
10 Massimo D4
11 Mirellie C2
12 Mozaika E2
13 Osteria Da Clara F4
14 Pastička C1
15 Pho Vietnam D2
16 Pizzeria Grosseto B3
17 Restaurace Chudoba C2
18 Ristorante Sapori B3
19 The Pind E2
20 U Bílé Krávy A2
21 U Dědka C4
22 Zelená Zahrada C4

Drinking & Nightlife (p137)

23 Al Cafetero C2
24 Bar & Books Mánesova D2
25 Blatouch B3
26 Café Celebrity C2
27 Café Kaaba B1
28 Dobrá Trafika D3
29 Galerie Kavárna Róza K B4
30 Hospůdka Obyčejný Svět F3
31 Kavárna Zanzibar B4
32 Mama Coffee A3
33 Motor Cafe F3
34 Riegrovy Sady Beer Garden C1
35 Ryba Na Ruby D2
36 Sahara Café B2
37 Sokolovna C2
38 Vinárna Vínečko B3
39 Viniční Altán C5
40 Žlutá Pumpa B4

Entertainment (p140)

41 Le Clan B1
42 ON Club C2
43 Radost FX A2
44 Techtle Mechtle C2
45 Termix D2

Shopping (p140)

46 Dům Porcelánu B3
47 Karel Vávra A3
48 Obchod S Uměním C3
49 Stockist C2
50 Vinohrady Farmers Market E2

Sleeping (p191)

51 Ametyst B4
52 Arkada A2
53 Czech Inn D4
54 Holiday Home B3
55 Hotel Anna C3
56 Hotel Luník B3
57 Le Palais Hotel B4
58 Louren Hotel E2
59 Orion B4
60 Pension Královský Vinohrad C4

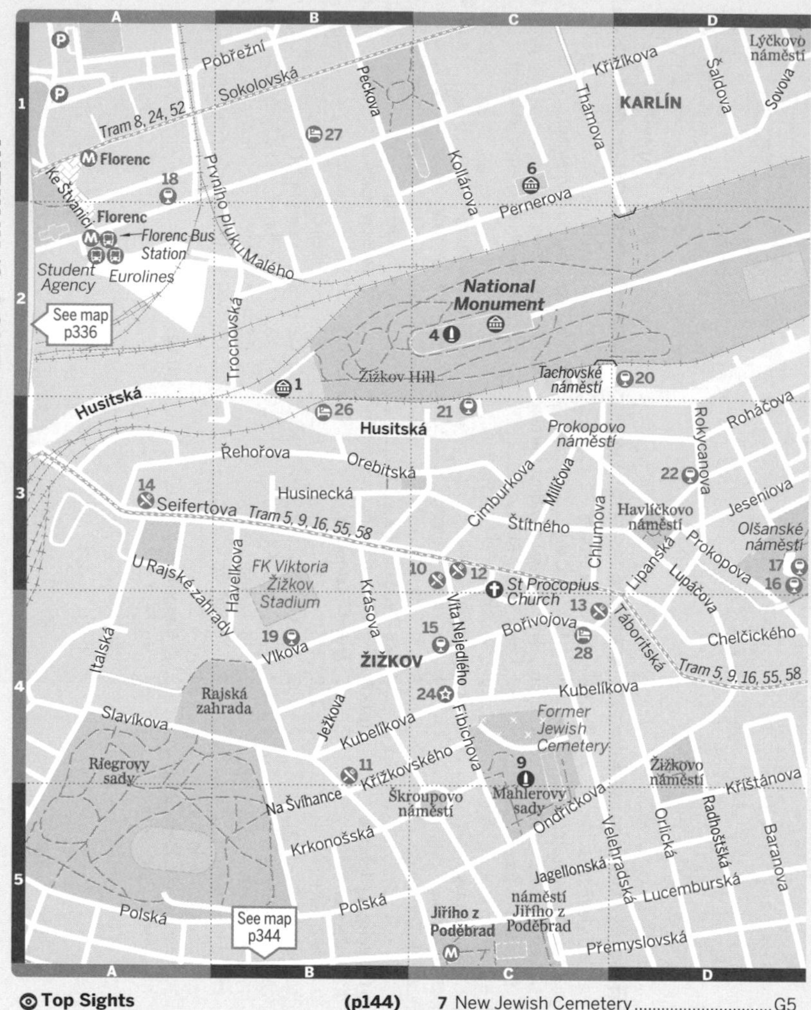

Top Sights (p144)

National Monument ... C2

Sights (p146)

1 Army Museum ... B2
2 Chapel of St Roch ... E4
3 Jan Palach's grave ... F5
4 Jan Žižka statue ... C2
5 Kafka's grave ... H5
6 Karlín Studios ... C1
Miminka (David Černý Sculpture) ... (see 9)
7 New Jewish Cemetery ... G5
8 Olšany Cemetery ... F5
9 TV Tower ... C4

Eating (p146)

10 Café Pavlač ... C3
11 Hanil ... B4
12 Kuře V Hodinkách ... C3
13 Mailsi ... C4
14 Manni ... A3
Restaurace Akropolis ... (see 24)

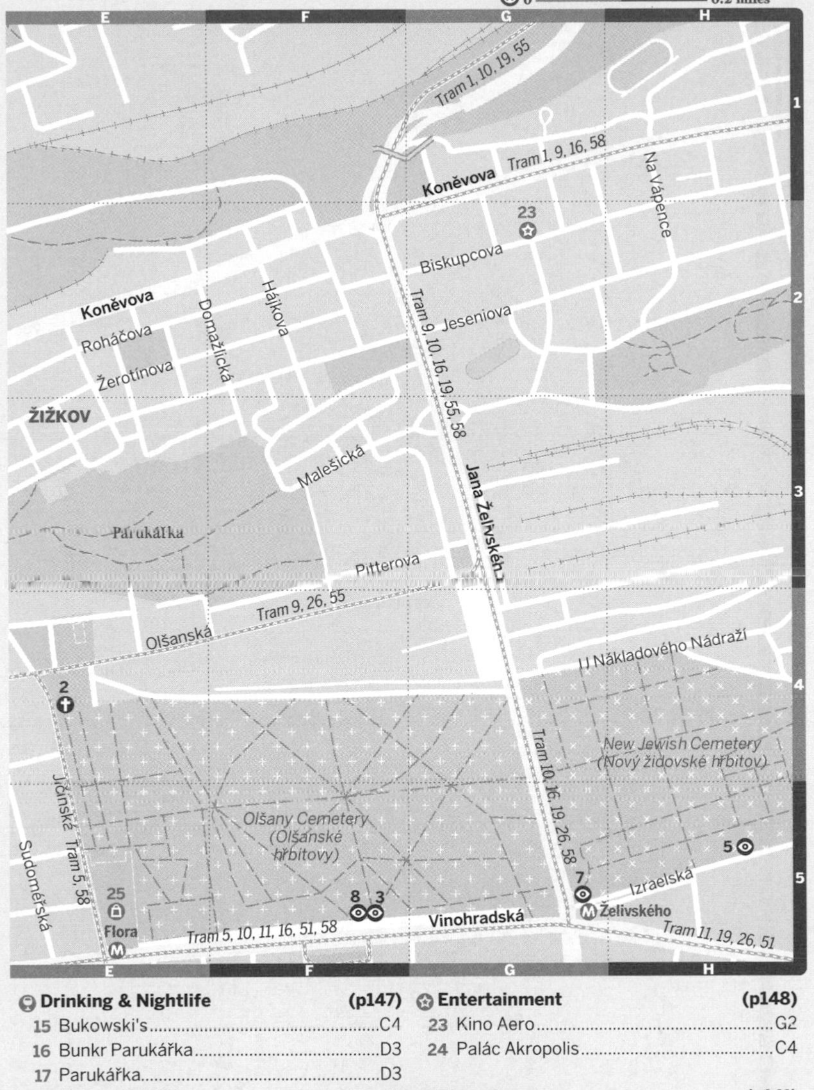

Drinking & Nightlife (p147)

15 Bukowski's C4
16 Bunkr Parukářka D3
17 Parukářka D3
18 Pivovarský Klub A1
19 Sedm Vlků B4
20 U Slovanské Lípy D2
21 U Vystřeleného oka C3
22 XT3 .... D3

Entertainment (p148)

23 Kino Aero G2
24 Palác Akropolis C4

Shopping (p141)

25 Atrium Flóra E5

Sleeping (p193)

26 Hostel Elf B3
27 Hotel Alwyn B1
28 Hotel Theatrino C4

HOLEŠOVICE

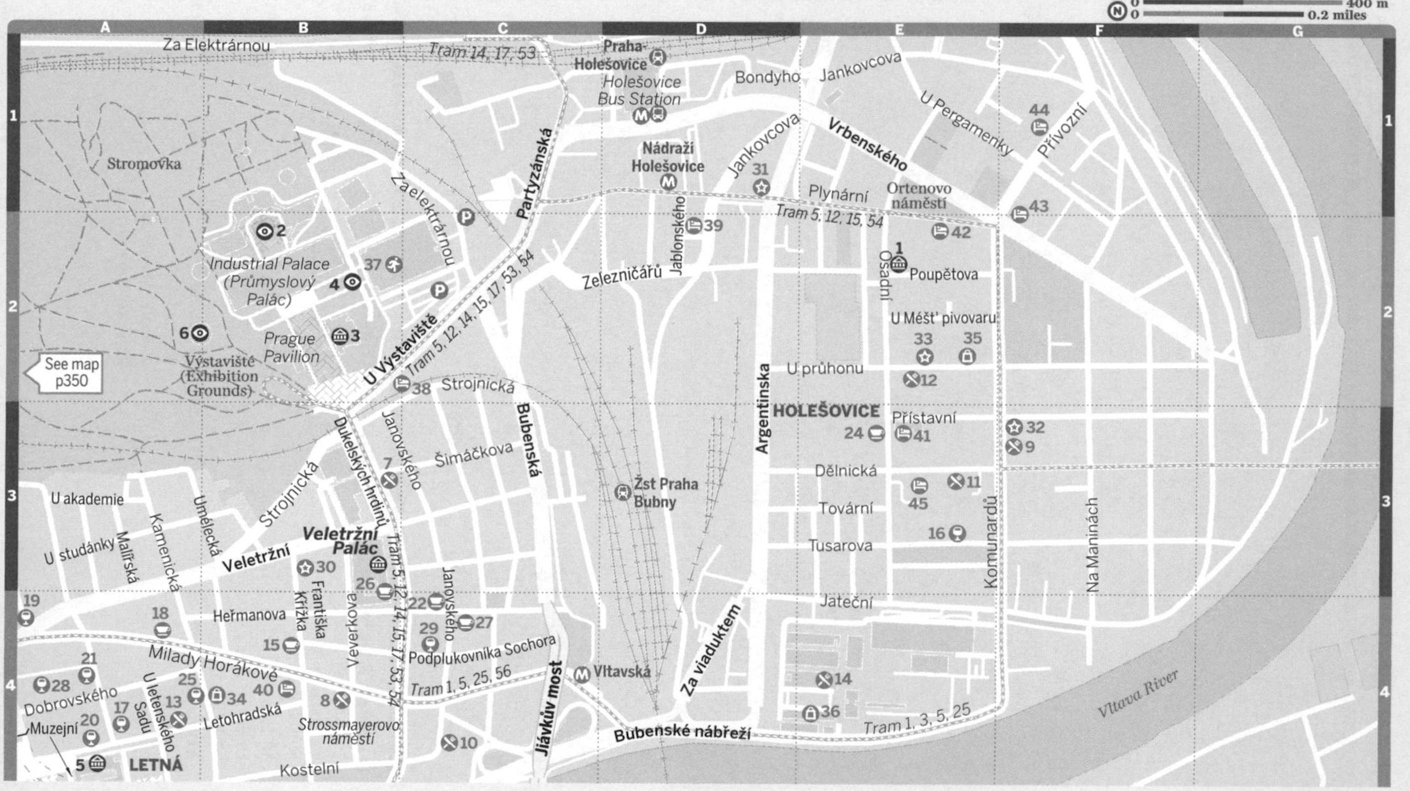

0 400 m
0 0.2 miles
Za Elektrárnou
Tram 14, 17, 53
Praha-Holešovice
Holešovice Bus Station
Bondyho
Jankovcova
U Pergamenky
Přívozní
Stromovka
Nádraží Holešovice
Vrbenského
Partyzánská
Zaelektrárnou
Plynární
Ortenovo náměstí
Tram 5, 12, 15, 54
Jablonského
Industrial Palace (Průmyslový Palác)
Železničářů
Osadní
Poupětova
U Měšť pivovaru
Prague Pavilion
Tram 5, 12, 14, 15, 17, 53, 54
U Výstaviště
See map p350
Výstaviště (Exhibition Grounds)
Strojnická
U průhonu
Argentinska
HOLEŠOVICE
Přístavní
Bubenská
Janovského
Šimáčkova
Dukelských hrdinů
Dělnická
Žst Praha Bubny
U akademie
Tovární
Veletržní Palác
Umělecká
Kamenická
Malířská
U studánky
Veletržní
Tusarova
Komunardů
Na Maninách
Heřmanova
Františka Křížka
Veverkova
Jateční
Milady Horákové
Podplukovníka Sochora
Tram 1, 5, 25, 56
Vltavská
Za viaduktem
Dobrovského
U letenského Sadu
Letohradská
Strossmayerovo náměstí
Jiávkův most
Bubenské nábřeží
Tram 1, 3, 5, 25
Vltava River
Muzejní
LETNÁ
Kostelní

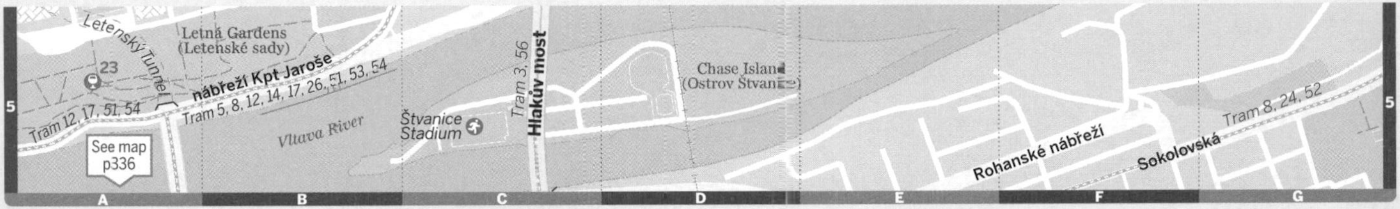

Letenský Tunnel
Letná Gardens (Letenské sady)
nábřeží Kpt Jaroše
Tram 12, 17, 51, 54
Tram 5, 8, 12, 14, 17, 26, 51, 53, 54
Vltava River
Štvanice Stadium
Tram 3, 56
Hlaků̇v most
Chase Island (Ostrov Štvanice)
Rohanské nábřeží
Sokolovská
Tram 8, 24, 52
See map p336

Top Sights (p151)
Veletržní Palác B3

Sights (p152)
1 Dox Centre for Contemporary Art E2
2 Křižík's Fountain B2
3 Lapidárium B2
4 Mořský Svět B2
5 National Technical Museum A4
6 Prague Planetarium A2

Eating (p154)
7 Bohemia Bagel B3
8 Capua B4
9 Korbel F3
10 La Crêperie C4
11 Lucky Luciano E3
12 Molo 22 E2
13 Peperoncino A4
14 Sasazu E4

Drinking & Nightlife (p158)
15 Bio Oko B4
16 Bondy Bar E3
17 Club Club A4
18 Erhartova Cukrárna A4
19 Fraktal A4
20 Hells Bells A4
21 Klášterní Pivnice A4
22 Kumbal C4
23 Letná Beer Garden A5
24 Long Tale Café E3
25 Na Staré Kovárně A4
26 Nová Syntéza B3
27 Ouky Douky C4
28 Svijanský Rytíř A4
29 U Sv Antoníčka C4

Entertainment (p161)
30 Alfred Ve Dvoře B3
Bio Oko (see 15)
31 Cross Club D1
32 La Fabrika F3
33 Mecca E2
Sasazu (see 14)

Shopping (p162)
34 Hunt-Kastner Artworks B4
35 Pivní Galerie E2
36 Pražská Tržnice E4

Sports & Activities (p163)
37 Tipsport Aréna B2

Sleeping (p193)
38 A&O Hostel C2
39 Absolutum Hotel D2
40 Hotel Belvedere B4
41 Hotel Extol Inn E3
42 Hotel Leon E2
43 Plaza Alta Hotel F1
44 Plus Prague Hostel F1
45 Sir Toby's Hostel E3

BUBENEČ & DEJVICE

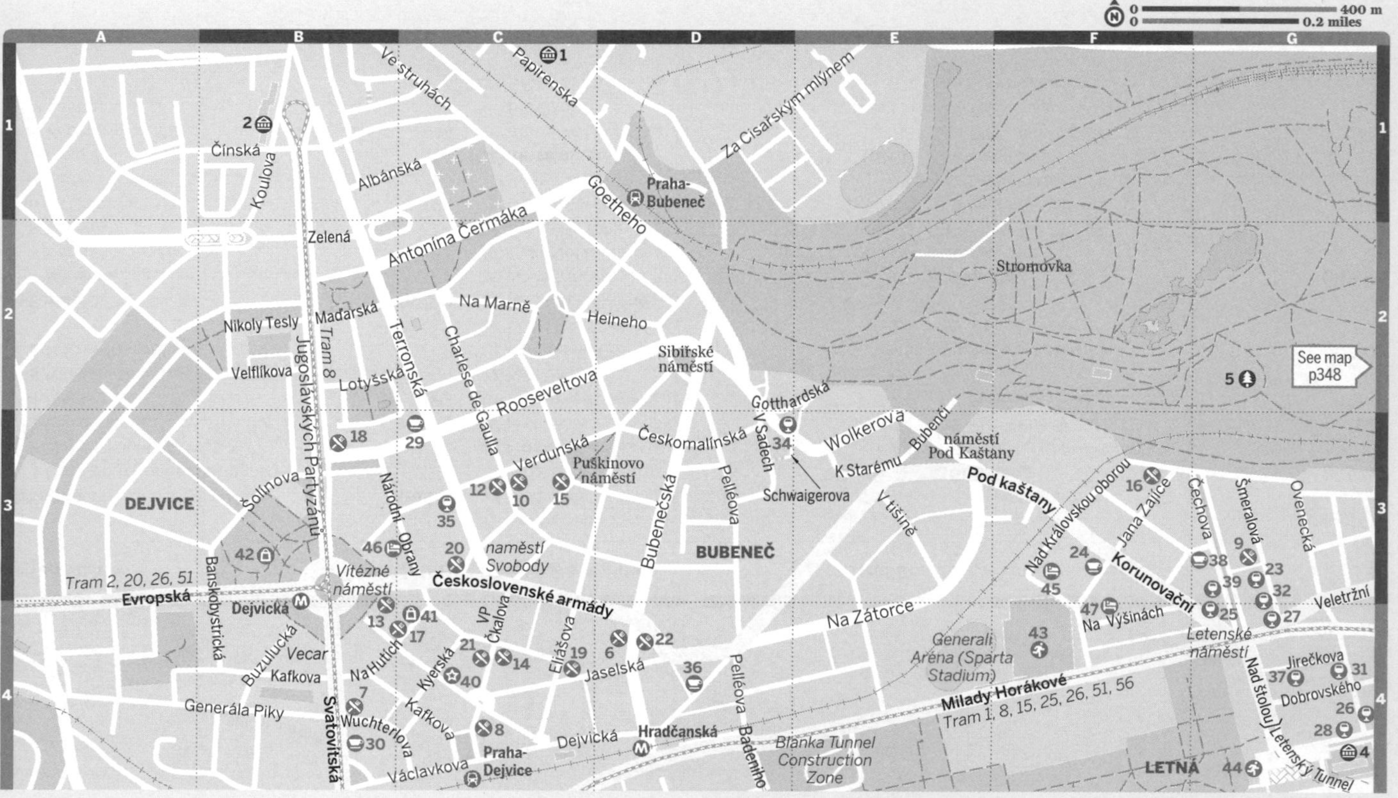

Sights (p153)

1 Ecotechnical Museum C1
2 Hotel Crowne Plaza B1
3 Letná Gardens F5
4 National Technical Museum G4
5 Stromovka G2

Eating (p156)

6 Argument D4
7 Budvarká B4
8 Cafe Calma C4
9 Čínská Zahrada G3
10 Da Emanuel C3
11 Hanavský Pavilón E5
12 Kavala C3
13 Kulat'ák B4
14 Mirellie C4
15 Na Urale C3
16 Nad Královskou Oborou F3
17 Perpetuum C4
18 Pizzeria Grosseto B3
19 Restaurace U Veverky C4
20 Sakura C3
21 Staročeská Krčma C4
22 U Viléma D4

Drinking & Nightlife (p159)

23 Akádemie G3
24 Alchymista F3
25 Andaluský Pes G4
26 Club Club G4
27 Frakta G4
28 Hells Bells G4
29 Kabinet C3
30 Kavárna Alibi B4
31 Klášterní Pivnice G4
32 La Bodega Flamenca G3
33 Letná Beer Garden G5
34 Na Slamníku D3
35 Potrefená Husa C3
36 Potrvá D4
37 Svijanský Rytíř G4
38 Těsně Vedle Burundi G3
39 Ztracený Ráj G3

Entertainment (p162)

40 Spejbl & Hurvínek Theatre C4

Shopping (p162)

41 Antikvita C4
42 Dejvice Farmers Market B3

Sports & Activities (p163)

43 Generali Aréna F4
44 Půjčovna Bruslí Miami G4

Sleeping (p194)

45 Art Hotel F3
Hotel Crowne Plaza (see 2)
46 Hotel Denisa B3
47 Hotel Letná F4

Our Story

A beat-up old car, a few dollars in the pocket and a sense of adventure. In 1972 that's all Tony and Maureen Wheeler needed for the trip of a lifetime – across Europe and Asia overland to Australia. It took several months, and at the end – broke but inspired – they sat at their kitchen table writing and stapling together their first travel guide, *Across Asia on the Cheap*. Within a week they'd sold 1500 copies. Lonely Planet was born.

Today, Lonely Planet has offices in Melbourne, London and Oakland, with more than 600 staff and writers. We share Tony's belief that 'a great guidebook should do three things: inform, educate and amuse'.

OUR WRITERS

Neil Wilson

Co-ordinating Author, Prague Castle & Hradčany, Malá Strana, Staré Město, Nové Město, Žižkov & Karlín Neil first succumbed to the pleasures of Prague back in 1995, beguiled, like everyone else, by its ethereal beauty, but also drawn to the darker side of its hidden history. He has returned regularly to enjoy the world's finest beers, the city's quirky sense of humour, and the chance to track down yet another obscure monument, having worked on seven consecutive editions of Lonely Planet's *Prague* guide. A full-time freelance writer since 1988, Neil has travelled in five continents and written more than 50 travel and walking guides for various publishers; he is based in Edinburgh, Scotland. For more information see www.neil-wilson.com. Neil also wrote the Planning and Day Trips chapters and half of the Sleeping chapter.

Read more about Neil at:
lonelyplanet.com/members/neilwilson

Mark Baker

Vinohrady & Vršovice, Holešovice, Bubeneč & Dejvice, Smíchov & Vyšehrad Mark first visited Prague in the 1980s as a journalist for the Economist Group. Those were the dark days of the dying communist regime, yet even then he was hooked by the city's beauty, mysticism and roast pork. He moved to Prague permanently in the early '90s. He was a co-founder-owner of the Globe Bookstore & Coffeehouse and journalist for Radio Free Europe/Radio Liberty. Now he works as a freelance travel writer. In addition to this book, Mark is co-author of the Lonely Planet guides to Romania and Poland. Mark also wrote the Architecture, Best of Bohemia and Best of Moravia chapters, the Understand and Survival chapters, and half of the Sleeping chapter.

Read more about Mark at:
lonelyplanet.com/members/markbaker

Published by Lonely Planet Publications Pty Ltd
ABN 36 005 607 983
10th edition – November 2012
ISBN 978 1 74220 139 9

10 9 8 7 6 5 4 3 2 1
Printed in China